Greek Grammar

William Watson Goodwin

A GREEK GRAMMAR

BY

WILLIAM W. GOODWIN, Hon. LL.D. and D.C.L.

ELIOT PROFESSOR OF GREEK LITERATURE IN
HARVARD UNIVERSITY

REVISED AND ENLARGED

BOSTON
PUBLISHED BY GINN & COMPANY
1898

Typography by J. S. Cushing & Co., Boston.

Presswork by Ginn & Co., Boston.

PREFACE.

The present work is a revised and enlarged edition of the Greek Grammar published in 1879, which was itself a revised and enlarged edition of the Elementary Greek Grammar of only 235 pages published in 1870. I trust that no one will infer from this repeated increase in the size of the book that I attribute ever increasing importance to the study of formal grammar in school. On the contrary, the growth of the book has come from a more decided opinion that the amount of grammar which should be learned by rote is exceedingly small compared with that which every real student of the Classics must learn in a very different way. When it was thought that a pupil must first learn his Latin and Greek Grammars and then learn to read Latin and Greek, it was essential to reduce a school grammar to its least possible dimensions. Now when a more sensible system leaves most of the details of grammar to be learned by the study of special points which arise in reading or writing, the case is entirely different; and few good teachers or good students are any longer grateful for a small grammar, which must soon be discarded as the horizon widens and new questions press for an answer. The forms of a language and the essential principles of its construction must be learned in the old-fashioned way, when the memory is vigorous and retentive; but, these once mastered, the true time to teach each principle of grammar is the moment when the pupil meets with it in his studies, and no grammar which is not thus practically illustrated ever becomes a living reality to the student. But it is not enough for a learner merely to meet each construction or form in isolated instances; for he may do this repeatedly, and yet know little of the general principle which the single example partially illustrates. Men saw apples fall and the moon and planets roll ages before the principle of gravitation was thought of. It is necessary, therefore, not merely to bring the pupil face to face with the facts of a language by means of examples carefully selected to exhibit them, but also to refer him to a statement of the general principles which show the full meaning of the facts and their relation to other principles.[1] In other words, systematic practice in reading and writing must be supplemented from the beginning by equally systematic reference to the grammar. Mechanics are not learned by merely observing the working of levers and pulleys, nor is chemistry by watching experiments on gases; although no one would undertake to teach either without such practical illustrations. It must always be remembered that grammatical study of this kind is an essential part of classical study; and no one must be deluded by the idea that if grammar is not learned by rote it is not to be learned at all. It cannot be too strongly emphasized, that there has been no change of opinion among classical scholars about the importance of grammar as a basis of all sound classical scholarship; the only change concerns the time and manner of studying grammar and the importance to be given to different parts of the subject.

What has been said about teaching by reference and by example applies especially to syntax, the chief principles of which have always seemed to me more profitable for a pupil in the earlier years of his classical studies than the details of vowel-changes and exceptional forms which are often thought more seasonable. The study of Greek syntax, properly pursued, gives the pupil an insight into the processes of thought and the manner of expression of a highly cultivated people; and while it stimulates his own powers of thought, it teaches him habits of more careful expression by making him familiar with many forms of statement more precise than those to which he is accustomed in his own language. The Greek syntax, as it was developed and refined by the Athenians, is a most important chapter in the history of thought, and even those whose classical studies are limited to the rudiments cannot afford to neglect it entirely. For these reasons the chief increase in the present work has been made in the department of Syntax.

[1] These objects seem to me to be admirably attained in the *First Lessons in Greek*, prepared by my colleague, Professor John W. White, to be used in connection with this Grammar. A new edition of this work is now in press.

The additions made in Part I. are designed chiefly to make the principles of inflection and formation in Parts II. and III. intelligible. Beyond this it seems inexpedient for a general grammar to go. In Part II. the chief changes are in the sections on the Verb, a great part of which have been remodelled and rewritten. The paradigms and synopses of the verb are given in a new form. The nine tense systems are clearly distinguished in each synopsis, and also in the paradigms so far as is consistent with a proper distinction of the three voices. The verbs in μι are now inflected in close connection with those in ω, and both conjugations are included in the subsequent treatment. The now established Attic forms of the pluperfect active are given in the paradigms. The old makeshift known as the "connecting-vowel" has been discarded, and with no misgivings. Thirteen years ago I wrote that I did not venture "to make the first attempt at a popular statement of the tense stems with the variable vowel attachment"; and I was confirmed in this opinion by the appearance of the *Schulgrammatik* of G. Curtius the year previous with the "Bindevocal" in its old position. Professor F. D. Allen has since shown us that the forms of the verb can be made perfectly intelligible without this time-honored fiction. I have now adopted the familiar term "thematic vowel," in place of "variable vowel" which I used in 1879, to designate the ο or ε added to the verb stem to form the present stem of verbs in ω. I have attempted to make the whole subject of tense stems and their inflection more clear to beginners, and at the same time to lay the venerable shade of the connecting-vowel, by the distinction of "simple and complex tense stems," which correspond generally to the two forms of inflection, the "simple" form (the μι-form) and the "common" form (that of verbs in ω). See 557–565. I use the term "verb stem" for the stem from which the chief tenses are formed, *i.e.* the single stem in the first class, the "strong" stem in the second class, and the simple stem in the other classes (except the anomalous eighth). Part III. is little changed, except by additions. In the Syntax I have attempted to introduce greater simplicity with greater detail into the treatment of the Article, the Adjectives, the Cases, and the Prepositions. In the Syntax of the Verb, the changes made in my new edition of the *Greek Moods and Tenses* have been adopted, so far as is possible in a school-book. The independent uses of the moods are given before the dependent constructions, except in the case of wishes, where the independent optative can hardly be treated apart from the other constructions. The Potential Optative and Indicative are made more prominent as original constructions, instead of being treated merely as elliptical apodoses. The independent use of μή in Homer to express fear with a desire to avert the object feared is recognized, and also the independent use of μή and μὴ οὐ in cautious assertions and negations with both subjunctive and indicative, which is common in Plato. The treatment of ὥστε is entirely new; and the distinction between the infinitive with ὥστε μή and the indicative with ὥστε οὐ is explained. The use of πρίν with the infinitive and the finite moods is more accurately stated. The distinction between the Infinitive with the Article and its simple constructions without the Article is more clearly drawn, and the whole treatment of the Infinitive is improved. In the chapter on the Participle, the three classes are carefully marked, and the two uses of the Supplementary Participle in and out of *oratio obliqua* are distinguished. In Part V. the principal additions are the sections on dactylo-epitritic rhythms, with greater detail about other lyric verses, and the use of two complete strophes of Pindar to illustrate that poet's two most common metres. The Catalogue of Verbs has been carefully revised, and somewhat enlarged, especially in the Homeric forms.

The quantity of long α, ι, and υ is marked in Parts I., II., and III., and wherever it is important in Part V., but not in the Syntax. The examples in the Syntax and in Part V. have been referred to their sources. One of the most radical changes is the use of 1691 new sections in place of the former 302. References can now be made to most paragraphs by a single number; and although special divisions are sometimes introduced to make the connection of paragraphs clearer, these will not interfere with references to the simple sections. The evil of a want of distinction between the main paragraphs and notes has been obviated by prefixing N. to sections which would ordinarily be marked as notes. I feel that a most humble apology is due to all teachers and students who have submitted to the unpardonable confusion of paragraphs, with their divisions, subdivisions, notes, and remarks, often with (*a*), (*b*), etc., in the old edition. This arrangement was thoughtlessly adopted to preserve the numbering of sections in the Syntax of the previous edition, to which many references had already been made; but this object was gained at far too great a cost. I regret that I can make no better amends than this to those who have suffered such an infliction. A complete table of Parallel References is given in pp. xxvi.–xxxv., to make references to the former edition available for the new sections.

I have introduced into the text a section (28) on the probable ancient pronunciation of Greek. While the sounds of most of the letters are well established, on many important points our knowledge is still very unsatisfactory. With our doubts about the sounds of *θ*, *φ*, *χ*, and *ζ*, of the double *ει* and *ου*, not to speak of *ξ* and *ψ*, and with our helplessness in expressing anything like the ancient force of the three accents or the full distinction of quantity, it is safe to say that no one could now pronounce a sentence of Greek so that it would have been intelligible to Demosthenes or Plato. I therefore look upon the question of Greek Pronunciation chiefly as it concerns the means of communication between modern scholars and between teachers and pupils. I see no prospect of uniformity here, unless at some future time scholars agree to unite on the modern Greek pronunciation, with all its objectionable features. As Athens becomes more and more a centre of civilization and art, her claim to decide the question of the pronunciation of her ancient language may sometime be too strong to resist. In the meantime, I see no reason for changing the system of pronunciation[1] which I have followed and advocated more than thirty years, which adopts what is tolerably certain and practicable in the ancient pronunciation and leaves the rest to modern usage or to individual judgment. This has brought scholars in the United States nearer to uniformity than any other system without external authority is likely to bring them. In England the retention of the English

[1] By this the consonants are sounded as in 28, 3, except that *ζ* has the sound of *z*; *ξ* and *ψ* have the sounds of *x* (*ks*) and *ps*; *θ*, *φ*, and *χ* those of *th* in *thin*, *ph* in *Philip*, and hard German *ch* in *machen*. The vowels are sounded as in 28, 1, *υ* being pronounced like French *u* or German *ü*. The diphthongs follow 28, 2; but *ου* always has the sound of *ou* in *youth*, and *ει* that of *ei* in *height*. I hold to this sound of *ει* to avoid another change from English, German, and American usage. If any change is desired, I should much prefer to adopt the sound of ī (our *i* in *machine*), which *ει* has held more than 1900 years, rather than to attempt to catch any one of the sounds through which either genuine or spurious *ει* must have passed on its way to this (see 28, 2).

pronunciation of Greek with Latin accents has at least the advantage of local uniformity.

Since the last edition was published, Allen's new edition of Hadley's Grammar has appeared and put all scholars under new obligations to both author and editor. The new edition of Monro's Homeric Grammar is of the greatest value to all students of Homer. Blass's new edition of the first quarter of Kühner is really a new work, abounding in valuable suggestions. From the German grammars of Koch and Kaegi I have gained many practical hints. I am also greatly indebted to many letters from teachers containing criticisms of the last edition and suggestions for making it more useful in schools, too many indeed to be acknowledged singly by name. Among them is one from which I have derived special help in the revision, a careful criticism of many parts of the book by Professor G. F. Nicolassen of Clarksville, Tennessee. Another of great value came to me without signature or address, so that I have been unable even to acknowledge it by letter. I must ask all who have thus favored me to accept this general expression of my thanks. Professor Herbert Weir Smyth of Bryn Mawr has done me the great service of reading the proofs of Parts I. and II. and aiding me by his valuable suggestions. His special knowledge of Greek morphology has been of the greatest use to me in a department in which without his aid I should often have been sorely perplexed amid conflicting views. All scholars are looking for the appearance of Professor Smyth's elaborate work on the Greek Dialects, now printing at the Clarendon Press, with great interest and hope.

WILLIAM W. GOODWIN.

HARVARD UNIVERSITY,
CAMBRIDGE, MASS., June 30, 1892.

CONTENTS.

PART I.

LETTERS, SYLLABLES, AND ACCENTS.

PART II.

INFLECTION.

ADJECTIVES.

COMPARISON OF ADJECTIVES.

ADVERBS AND THEIR COMPARISON.

NUMERALS.

THE ARTICLE.

PRONOUNS.

VERBS.

CONJUGATION OF VERBS IN Ω.

CONJUGATION OF VERBS IN μι.

AUGMENT AND REDUPLICATION.

ENDINGS.

TENSE STEMS AND FORMS OF INFLECTION.

FORMATION AND INFLECTION OF TENSE SYSTEMS.

FORMATION OF DEPENDENT MOODS AND PARTICIPLE.

DIALECTS.

ENUMERATION AND CLASSIFICATION OF MI-FORMS.

PART III.

FORMATION OF WORDS.

SIMPLE WORDS.

FORMATION OF NOUNS.

THE CASES.

NOMINATIVE AND VOCATIVE.

ACCUSATIVE.

GENITIVE.

DATIVE.

II. TENSES OF THE DEPENDENT MOODS.

A. NOT IN INDIRECT DISCOURSE.

B. IN INDIRECT DISCOURSE.

III. TENSES OF THE PARTICIPLE.

IV. GNOMIC AND ITERATIVE TENSES.

THE PARTICLE Ἄν.

THE MOODS.

GENERAL STATEMENT AND CLASSIFICATION.

THE PARTICIPLE.

ATTRIBUTIVE PARTICIPLE.

CIRCUMSTANTIAL PARTICIPLE.

SUPPLEMENTARY PARTICIPLE.

NOT IN INDIRECT DISCOURSE.

IN INDIRECT DISCOURSE.

VERBAL ADJECTIVES IN -τέος AND -τέον.

INTERROGATIVE SENTENCES.

NEGATIVES.

PART V.

VERSIFICATION.

APPENDIX.

PARALLEL REFERENCES

FROM THE EDITION OF 1879 TO THE PRESENT EDITION.

OLD	NEW
1	1
Note 1	2
N. 2	3
2	5
Note	6
3	7
Note	10
4, 1	11
N. 1	12
N. 2	13
2	15
5, 1	16
2	18
6	19
1	20
2	21; 22
Note	23; 24
7	25
Note	26
8	34
9	35; 36
1	37
2	38, 2
Note	39, 1
3	38, 1
Note	39, 1 & 2
4	38, 4
N. 1	39, 3
N. 2	39, 4 & 5
5	40, 1
Remark	40, 2
10	47
11, 1	42
(a)	43, 1
(b)	43, 2
2	44
N. 1	45
N. 2	46
N. 3	47, 2
11, 2, N. 4	55
N. 5	42
12, 1	48
2	54
N. 1	51
N. 2	50
N. 3	53
N. 4	52
13, 1	56
N. 1	57; 59
N. 2	60
2	62; 63
3	63
14, 1	64
2	65
N. 1	66
N. 2	67
15, 1	68, 1
2	69
16	70
1	71
N. 1	72
N. 2	73
2	74
3	75
Note	76; 77
4, Note	88
5	78, 1
6	78, 2 & 3
N. 1	79
N. 2	80
N. 3	81
N. 4	83
7	84
(a)	84, 1
(b)	84, 3
(c)	84, 4
(d)	84, 5 & 6
17, 1	92; 93
17, 1, Note	94
2	95, 1
Note	95, 3 & 5
3	95, 2
18, 1, 2	96
2, Note	97
19, 1	98
2	99
3	100
N. 1	101
N. 2	102
20	103
1, 2, 3	104
21, 1	106
Rem.	107, 2
N. 1	108
N. 2	109
2	110, 1–3
3	110, 4
22, 1	111
2	112
N. 1	113
N. 2	114
23, 1	115, 1
Note	115, 2
2	116
24, 1	117
Note	118
2	119
3	120
25, 1	121
Note	122
2	123; 124
Note	125
3	127
N. 1	128
N. 2	129
26	130
N. 1	132; 133, 1

OLD		NEW
26	N. 2	134
	N. 3 (1)	131, 4; 133, 2
	(2)	131, 5; 131, 2
	(3)	131, 1; 133, 3
	N. 4	135
27		140
1		141, 1
2		141, 2
3		141, 3
4		141, 4
28, 1–3		142; 143
	N. 1	144
	N. 2	145
	N. 3	146
29		136; 137
	N. 1	138
	N. 2	139
30, 1		147
2		148
3		149
31		150
32, 1		151
2		152
	Note	153; 154
33, 1		155
2		156
	N. 1	157
	N. 2	158
	N. 3	159
3		160; 161
	N. 1	162
	N. 2	163
34		164; 165
	Note	166
35		168
36		169
	Note	170
37, 1		171; 179
2		173–175
	N. 1	182
	N. 2	177
	N. 3, 4	178
38		183; 184
	N. 1	186
	N. 2	187
39		188

OLD		NEW
40		189
41		190
	Note	191
42, 1		192; 193
	Note	195
2		196; 197
	N. 1	199
	N. 2	200
43		201
	Note	203
44		204
45, 1		205
	Note	206
2		207
	Note	167; 208
46		209
1		209, 4
2		209, 1
3		209, 2
4		209, 3
	N. 1	212,1; 210,1&3
	N. 2	212, 2
	N. 3	213
47, 1		214, 1; 214, 2 & 3; 216
	N. 1	217
	N. 2	218
48, 1		219
2		220–222
3		223
49		224
50		225
51, 1		226
2		208, 3
	Note	88, 1; 90, 3
52, 1		227
	Note	85; 88, 1
2		228; 234
	N. 1	228; 230; 235
	N. 2	39, 2
	N. 3	231
	N. 4	232
53		249; 256
1		249; 250
	N. 1	254
	N. 2	251
	N. 3	255
2		257
	N. 1	261

OLD		NEW
53, 2, N. 2		319
3		263
	N. 1	265
	N. 2	266
	N. 3	267
	N. 4	264
54		268
	Note	269; 270
55		242; 245
	N. 1	238–241; 243; 244
	N. 2	248
	N. 3	246; 247
56, 1		228
2 & Note		237, 1
57		273
1		274, 1
	N. 1	274; 275
	N. 2	276; 279
2		277, 1; 278
3		277, 2; 278
58		280
1–3		281–285
59		286
60, 1		287
2		288
3		289
4		290
5		291
61		292–294
	N. 1	295
	N. 2	296
	N. 3	297
62, 1, 2		298
3		299–301
	Note	302
63		304; 306
	Note	307
64		305; 306
65		310
66		312; 313
	N. 1	333
	N. 2	344
	N. 3	316
	N. 4	343; 345
67, 1, 2		318–320; 324; 325; 328; 329
	N. 1	322; 74
	N. 2	332
	N. 3	325–327

OLD		NEW
68		334; 335; 338
	Note	336; 337
69		340; 341
	Note	342
70		346
	N. 1	347
	N. 2	348
71		350
	N. 1	351
	N. 2	352
	N. 3	353
	N. 4	354
	N. 5	355
72, 1		357
2		358
	N. 1	359
	N. 2	360
73, 1		361
	Note	362
2		363
3		364
74, 1		365
	Note	366
2		367
	Note	368
75		369
	N. 1	370
	N. 2	371
76		372; 373
	Note	374
77, 1		375
	N. 1	376; 377
	N. 2	378
	N. 3	379
2		380
	N. 1	381; 382, 2
	N. 2 (a)	382, 1
	(b)	382, 3
	N. 3	383
	N. 4	384
	N. 5	385
78		386
	N. 1	387
	N. 2	388
79, 1		389
	N. 1	391; 392
	N. 2	393
	N. 3	394
	N. 4	395

OLD		NEW
79, 1, N. 5		396
	N. 6	397
	N. 7	398
2		399; 989, 2
	Note	400
80		401
	Note	402; 403
81		404
82		406
	N. 1	407
	N. 2	408
83		409
	N. 1	411
	N. 2	412
	N. 3	413
84, 1		415
2		416
	N. 1	417
	N. 2	418
3		419
85		420
86		421; 425
	N. 1	426
	N. 2	424; 428
87, 1		429; 430
	Note	434
2		436
	Note	438
88, 1		441
	Note	442
2		443
	Note	444
89		445
	Note	446
90, 1		447
2		448
	N. 1	449
	N. 2	450
	N. 3	451
91		452; 453
	Note	454
92, 1, 2 & Note		458; 459; 567
3		460
	Note	461
4		459
	I–VII	455–457
5		462
6		463

OLD		NEW
93, 1		464
2 (a)–(c)		465; 466
3		467
	Note	468
94		456; 458; 561
95, 1		469; 470
	I	474
	II	476
	III	478
	Note	472
2, I		474; 475
	II	477
	III	479
	Note	473
96, I		480
	II	481
	III	482
	N. 1	483
	N. 2	484
	N. 3	485
97, 1 & 2		486, 1 & 2
3		487, 1
4		487, 2
	N. 1	488
	N. 2	489
	N. 3	490
98		492
	Rem.	493
	N. 1	495
	N. 2	496
	N. 3	497
	N. 4	498
	N. 5	499
	N. 6	737
99, 1		510; 520
2 (a)		511, 1
(b)		511, 2
(c)		521
	Rem.	512; 520
100, 1		513
2		515
	N. 1	516
	N. 2	517
	N. 3	534
	N. 4	535
	N. 5	514
101, 1		521
	Note	522
2		523

OLD	NEW
101, 2, N. 1	524
N. 2	525
3	526
4	527
102	529–531
N. 1	532
N. 2	533
103	518
Note	519
104	537
N. 1	538
N. 2	539
105, 1	540
N. 1	541
N. 2	543
N. 3	544
2	545, 1
Note	545, 2
3	546
106, 1	547; 548
Note	550
2	549
107	567
108	568
I	569
Note	571
II, 1	572
2	574
Note	575; 642
III	576–578
IV	579
1 (*a*)	580
Note	582; 583
(*b*)	585; 588
N. 1	590
N. 2	591
2	592
(*c*)	593
(*d*)	594; 596
N. 1	598
N. 2	599
N. 3	600
3 (*e*)	601
Note	602
V, 1	603
2	605
3	607
4	608
N. 1 (*a*)	610

OLD	NEW
108, V, N. 1 (*b*)	611
N. 2	612
VI	613
N. 1	615
N. 2	616
N. 3	617
N. 4	618
VII	653; 654
Note	656
VIII	621
Note	622
Rem.	634
109, 1	635; 636
N. 1	471; 638
N. 2	639
2	640; 641
3	643; 644
N. 1	693; 689
N. 2	See 692
4	645
N. 1	646
N. 2	711
5	672
6	647
Note	648
7 (*a*)	649
(*b*)	650
(*c*)	651; 652
8	653; 657
(*a*)	658, 1
(*b*)	658, 2
Note	659
Rem.	661
110, I	660
II, 1	662
2	663
N. 1 (*a*)	665, 1
(*b*)	665, 2
(*c*)	665, 3
(*d*)	665, 4
N. 2	666
N. 3	667
N. 4	668
III, 1	669
N. 1	670
N. 2	671
2	672
N. 1	673
N. 2	674

OLD	NEW
110, IV, (*a*)	698
(1)–(5)	699–702
(*b*)	682; 683
(1)–(5)	684
Note	686; 694
(*c*)	703
N. 1	704
N. 2	705
(*d*)	687; 692
N. 1	690
N. 2	See 693
N. 3	691; 773
N. 4	774
V	675
N. 1	676
N. 2	677
N. 3	678
VI	707; 710
N. 1	708
N. 2, 3	709
VII	712; 715
N. 1	716
N. 2	713
N. 3	714
111	717
112, 1	551
2	552
Note	556
3, 4	557–561
113, 1	See 561, 1; 623
2, N. 1	565, 6; 624
N. 2	625
N. 3	556, 2
N. 5	556, 3
114	718
(end)	721
N. 1	723; 725
N. 2	724; 727
115	730
1	731
2	740
3	739
4	737
N. 1	735
N. 2	732
116, 1	553
2	746; 747
3	757

OLD	NEW
117, 1	554; 759; 765
1 (end)	766–769
2	770; 772; 775
Note	337
3	776, 1
N. 1	776, 2
N. 2	776, 3
118, 1	721; 733
Note	734
2	720; 733
Note	751; 748
3	706
5	486, 2; 701
Note	701
6	1254
119, 1–9	777, 1–9
10	778
11	779
12 (*a*)	780, 1
(*b*)	780, 2
(*c*)	780, 3
(*d*)	780, 4
13	781
14	782
15	783
120, 1 (*a*)	784, 1
(*b*)	784, 2
(*c*)	784, 3
(*d*)	784, 4
(*e*)	784, 5
2 (*a*)	785, 1
(*b*)	785, 2
(*c*)	785, 3
(*d*)	785, 4
3 (*a*)	786, 1
(*b*)	786, 2
Rem. before 121	468; 500; 501
121, 1	557; 558; 627
N. 1	801; 802, 1
N. 2	629
2 (*a*)–(*f*)	564, 1–6
3	794, 2
122	509; 793
1	794
2	797
N. 1	630; 741
N. 2	729; 742
N. 3	632
122, 2, N. 4	724
N. 5	728; 631
N. 6	803, 1
123, 1	504; 505
2	506
3	509
124, 1	507; 508
2	804
125, 1, 2	794, 1, 2
N. 1	795
N. 2	796
3	798; 799
N. 1	801
N. 2	802; 803, 2
4	804
5	797
126, 1–5	787, 1–5
6	800, 2
7 (*a*)	788, 1
(*b*)	788, 2
(*c*)	788, 3
8	789
9	791
10	792
127	805
I	806, 1
N. 1, 2	806, 2, 3; 807
II	808, 1
N. 1–3	808, 2; 809
III	810, 1
N. 1, 2	810, 2; 811
IV	812
N. 1, 2	813
V	814–816
Note	817
VI	818
Note	819
VII	820
Note	821
128, 1	822
2 (*a*)	823
(*b*)	824
Note	825
3	826
N. 1	827
N. 2	828
N. 3	829
N. 4	830
N. 5	831
129, 1	832
2 (*a*)	833, 1; 841
Note	841
(*b*)	833, 1, 2; 841
Note	833, 3
3	834
N. 1	835
N. 2	836
4	837
Note	837 (end)
5	838
Note	839
6	843
7	842 (837)
Note	842
8	844
Note	845
9	846
(*a*)–(*c*)	846, 1–3
Note	847
10	848, 1
Note	848, 2
11	849, 1
12	850
13	851
14	852
Note	853
15	854
16	849, 4
17	855
18	859; 860
130, 1–8	861, 1–8
N. 1	868
N. 2	866
N. 3	867
131	869
Rem.	870
1	871
Note	872
2	873
(*a*)	873, 1
(*b*)	873, 2
3	874
4 (*a*)–(*d*)	875, 1–4
N. 1	876
N. 2	877
5	878
6	879; 881
Note	880

OLD		NEW
131, 7		882
132		883
	1	884
	Note	885
	2	886
	Note	887
	3	888
	Rem.	889
133, 1		890
	N. 1	891
	2	892
	Note	893
134, 1		894
	2	895, 1
	3	895, 2 & 3
	N. 1	896
	N. 1 (*a*)–(*e*)	897, 1–5
	N. 2	898
135, 1		899, 1
	2	899, 2
	3	900
	N. 1	901
	N. 2	902
	N. 3	903
	N. 4	904
	N. 5	905
136		907
	Rem.	908
	N. 1	909
	N. 2	910
	N. 3 (*a*)	927; 928
	(*b*)	931
	N. 4	930
137		911
	N. 1	913
	N. 2	914
	N. 3	915
	N. 4	916
138		918
	Rem.	919
	N. 1 (*a*)	923
	N. 2 (*a*)	924, *a*
	(*b*)	924, *b*
	(*c*)	925
	N. 3	920
	N. 4	921
	N. 5	388; 410
	N. 6	922
138,	N. 7	926
	N. 8	927; 928
139, 1		932, 1
	Note	932, 2
	2	933
	Note	934
140		935
	N. 1	936
	N. 2 (*a*)–(*d*)	937, 1–4
	N. 3	938
	N. 4	939
	N. 5	940
141		941
	N. 1	942
	(*a*)	943
	(*b*)	944
	(*c*)	945; 946
	(*d*)	947
	N. 2	949
	N. 3	952
	N. 4	953
	N. 5	954
	N. 6	955, 1
	N. 7	955, 2
	N. 8	956
142, 1		959, 1; 962
	Note	960
	2	959, 2
	Rem.	963
	N. 1	964
	N. 2	965
	N. 3 (*a*)	966
	(*b*)	967
	N. 4	968
	N. 5	969
	N. 6	970
	3	971; 972; 973
	4	974
	N. 1	975
	N. 2	976
	N. 3 (*a*)	977, 1
	(*b*)	977, 2
	N. 4	978
	N. 5	979
	N. 6	980
143, 1		981
	N. 1	982
	N. 2	983
143, 2		984
144, 1		985
	Note	986
	2 (*a*)	987
	(*b*)	988
145, 1		989, 1
	Note	990
	2	989, 3
	Note	992
146		993
	N. 1	994
	N. 2	995
	N. 3	996
147		998
	N. 1	999
	N. 2	1000
	N. 3	1002
	N. 4	1003
148		1004
	N. 1	1005
	N. 2	1006
	N. 3	1007
	N. 4	1010
149, 1		1011
	2	1012
	(last part)	1013
	Note	1014
150		1015
	Note	1017
151		1019
	N. 1	1020
	N. 2 (*a*)	1021, *a*, *b*
	(*b*)	1021, *c*
	N. 3	1023
	N. 4	1024
152		1026; 1027
	N. 1	1028
	N. 2	1029
	N. 3	1030
153		1031
	N. 1	1032
	N. 2	1033
	N. 3	1034
	N. 4	1035
	N. 5	1036
154		1037
	Note	1038
155		1039
156		1040

OLD	NEW
156, Note	1041
Rem. before 157	1042
157, 1	1043
2	1044
Note	1045
Rem. before 158	1046
158	1047
N. 1	1048
N. 2	1049
N. 3	1050
159	1051
Rem.	1052
N. 1	1053
N. 2	1054
N. 3	1055
N. 4	1076
N. 5	1057
160, 1	1058
Note	1059
2	1060
Note	1061
161	1062
Note	1063; 1064
162	1065
163	1066; 1067
N. 1	1067
N. 2	1068
164	1069
N. 1	1070
N. 2	1071
N. 3	1072
165	1073
N. 1	1074
N. 1 (last pt.)	1241
N. 2	1075
166	1077
N. 1	1078
N. 2	1080
N. 3	1081
N. 4	1078
Rem. before 167	1083
167	1084
1–5	1085, 1–5
6	1085, 7
Note	1086
168	1088
N. 1	1090
N. 2	1091
N. 3	1092

OLD	NEW
169, 1	1094, 1 & 7
2	1095
Note	1096
3	1094
170, 1	1097, 1
2	1097, 2
Note	1098
171, 1	1099
Note	1100
2	1102
N. 1	1103
N. 2	1105
N. 3	1106
Rem.	1107; 1108
3	1109; 1110
Note	1164
172, 1	1112
2	1113
N. 1	1114
N. 2 (a)	1115
(b)	1116
173, 1	1126
N. 1	1127
N. 2	1128
2	1121
Note	1123; 1124
3	1129
174	1117
175, 1	1153
N. 1	1154
N. 2	1156
2	1120
176, 1	1130
2	1131
177	1132
178	1133
Note	1135
179, 1	1136
2	1137
180	1139
1	1140
N. 1	1140
N. 2	1141
2	1142
181	1143
Note	1146
182, 1	1147
2	1148–1150
Note	1151

OLD	NEW
183	1152
Rem. before 184	1157
184, 1	1158
2	1159; 1160
N. 1 (a)	1161
(b)	1162
N. 2	1163
3	1165
N. 1	1166
N. 2	1167
N. 3	1168; 1169
N. 4	1170
N. 5	1584
N. 6	1171
4	1173
5	1172
185	1174
186	1175
N. 1	1177
N. 2	1178
187	1179; 1180
188, 1	1181
N. 1	1182
N. 2	1183
2	1184; 1185
3	1186; 1187
4	1188
5	1189; 1190
Note	1191
189	1192
N. 1	1193
N. 2	1194
190	1196
N. 1	1197
N. 2	1198
191	1199; 1200; 1220
I–VI	1201–1219 (w. prepositions alphabetically)
N. 1	1221
N. 2	1222, 1
N. 3	1222, 2
N. 4	1223
N. 5	1224
N. 6	1225
193	1227
194	1228
195	1230

OLD	NEW	OLD	NEW	OLD	NEW
195, N. 1	1231	205, 2	1292	218, N. 1	1379
N. 2	1232	N. 1	1293	N. 2	1350
196	1233	N. 2	1294	N. 3	1380
197, 1	1234; 1236	3	1295	219, 1	1381
N. 1	1237	206	1296	2	1382
N. 2	1239	Rem.	1297	3	1383, 1
2	1238	Note	1298	Note	1383, 2
198	1240	207	1299	220	1384; 1385–1387
199, 1–3	1242, 1–3	1	1299, 1	Rem. 1	1388
Rem.	1243	2	1299, 2; 1300	Rem. 2	1389
N. 1	1244	Rem.	1301	221	1390
N. 2	1245	208, 1	1302	Note	1391
N. 3	1246; 1247	2	1303	222	1397
N. 4	1248	3	1304	N. 1	1402
200	1250; 1251	209, 1	1305, 1	N. 2	1400
N. 1	1252	2	1305, 2	N. 3	1398; 1399
N. 2	1255	210	1306	223	1403
N. 3 (a)	1256	Note	1307	Rem.	1404
(b)	1257	211	1308	N. 1	1405
N. 4	1258	Note	1309	N. 2	1406; 1305, 2
N. 5 (a)	1259, 1	212, 1	1310	224	1408
(b)	1260	2	1312	N. 1	1332; 1333
(c)	1259, 2	3	1313	N. 2	1412
N. 6	1263	4	1314	225	1393, 1, 2
N. 7	1264	Note	1316	Rem.	1394
N. 8	1265	213, 1	1317; 1318	N. 1	1395
N. 9	1266	Rem.	1319	N. 2	1396
201	1267	2	1320	226, 1	1413
Rem.	1268	Rem.	1321	2 (a)	1329; 1340
N. 1	1269	3	1322	(b)	1327; 1328;
N. 2	1270	Rem.	1323		1335; 1336
202	1271	4	1324	N. 1	1330; 1328
1	1272	5	1325	N. 2	1337
2	1273	214	1326	3	1418
N. 1	1274	215	1362	4	1419
N. 2	1275	Rem.	1363	N. 1	1420
3 (a)	1276	N. 1	1364	N. 2	1416
(b)	1277	N. 2	1362; 1368	227, 1	1421, 1
Note	1278	216, 1	1365	Note	1421, 2
4	1287	N. 1	1366	2	1422
Rem. before 203	1279	N. 2	1367	228	1423
203	1280; 1281	2	1369; 1370	Note	1424
N. 1	1285	3	1371	Rem. before 229	1425
N. 2	1286	217	1372	229	1426
N. 3	1287	N. 1	1374; 1375	230	1427
204	1288	N. 2	1373	231	1428, 1
N. 1	1289	N. 3	1377	Note	1428, 2
N. 2	1290	N. 4	1352–1354	232	1429
205, 1	1291	218	1378	1	1430

OLD		NEW
232, 2		**1433**
3		1434
	Note	1435
4		**1436**
233		1431
	N. 1	1432
	N. 2	1438
234		**1437**
235, 1		1439
2		1440
	Note	**1441**
236		1442
	N. 1	**1443**
	N. 2	1460
	N. 3	1444
237		1449
	Rem.	**1450**
	Note	1445
238		1461
239, 1		1464
2		**1465**
	N. 1	**1466**; 1473
	N. 2	1467
240, 1		1469; 1471, 2
2		1470
	Note	1474
241, 1		1475
2		1476
	Note	1477
3		1479
	Note	1480
242, 1		1481
	Note	1482
2		1483
3		1484
	Note	1485
4		**1486**; 1496
243		**1487**
	N. 1	1488
	N. 2	1489
244		**1490**
	N. 1	1492
	N. 2	1491
245		**1493**
246		**1494**
	Note	**1495**
247		1497
	N. 1	**1498**
	N. 2	1499

OLD		NEW
247,	N. 3	**1500**
	N. 4	1501
248, 1–4		**1502**, 1–4
	Note	1503
249, 1		1478, 1
2		1478, 2
250		1505
	Note	**1506**
251, 1		1507
	N. 1	1508
	N. 2	1509
	N. 3	**1510**
2		1511
	N. 1	1512
	N. 2	**1513**
252		1342
	Note	**1343**
253		1344
	Note	**1345**
254		1346
	Note	**1347**
255		1355
	Note	1356
256		1358; 1359
257		1360
	Note	**1361**
258		1516
259		1517
	Note	1542
260		1518
1		1519
	N. 1	1520
	N. 2	1543; 1544
2		**1522**
	N. 1	**1523**
	N. 2	1524
261, 1		1526
	N. 1	**1527**; 1521
	N. 2	**1545**
2		1528
	Rem.	1529
	Note	1530
262, 1		1546
2		**1547**
263, 1		1549
	Note	1550
2		1551
	Note	1552
264		**1555**

OLD		NEW
265		**1532**
	Note	1533
266, 1		**1449**
2		**1453**
	N. 1	1456
	N. 2	1449
	N. 3	1455
	N. 4 (*a*)	**1458**
	(*b*)	**1531**
	N. 5	1457
267		1460
268		1534
269		1536
	Note	**1535**; 1537
270		**1537**
	Note	1538
271		1540
272		1554
273		1525
274		1470; 1471, 1
	Note	1474
275		1557
276, 1		1559
2		1560
277		1563
1		1563, 1
2		**1563**, 2 & 3
3		1563, 4
4		1563, 5
5		1563, 6
6		1563, 7
	N. 1 (*a*)	**1572**
	(*b*)	1573
	N. 2 (*a*)	1574
	(*b*)	1575
	N. 3	**1576**; 1577
278, 1		1568
	Note	1568
2		1569
	Note	1570
279		1578
1		**1580**
	N. 1	1581
	N. 2	1262
2		1582
	Note	**1583**
3		1585
4		1586
	Note	**1587**

OLD	NEW
280	1588
N. 1	1589
N. 2	1590
N. 3	1591; 1592
N. 4	1593
281	1594
1	1595; 1596
2	1597–1599
282, 1	1600
2	1603
3	1604
4	1605
5	1606
283	1607
1	1608
Note	1609
2	1610
3	1611
4	1612
5	1613
6	1615
7	1616
Note	1617
8	1618
9	1619
284, 1	1620
2	1621
3	1622
284, 3, Note	1623–1625
285, 1	1626
2	1627
Note	1628
3	1629
N. 1	1630
4	1635
286, 1	1631
2	1626, 2; 1632
3	1633
4	1634
5	1636
287, 1	1637
2	1638
3	1639
4	1640
288, 1	1642
2	1643
Note	1644
289, 1	1645
2	1646; 1647
3	1648
4	1649
290	1650
291, 1	1653, 3 & 4
2	1651
3	1653, 1
292	1657
293, 1	1665, 1
2	1665, 3
3	1664
4	1658–1662
294	1668
295, 1	1674, 1
2	1674, 2
3	1674, 3
4	1669
5	1670; 1671
Note	1672; 1673
296	1675
Note	1675
297, 1	1676, 1
2	1676, 2
3	1676, 3
4	1676, 4
298	1677
Note	1654; 1666
299, 1	1679
2	1680; 1681
300, 1–7	1682, 1–7
Note	1687, 2
301, 1	1687
2	1688
3	1689
4	1690
302	1691
Catalogue of Verbs	1692

CITATIONS OF GREEK AUTHORS

In Parts IV. and V.

- Aeschines . . . Aesch.
- Aeschylus . . . A.
  - Agamemnon . . . *Ag.*
  - Choëphori . . . *Ch.*
  - Eumenides . . . *Eu.*
  - Persians . . . *Pe.*
  - Prometheus . . . *Pr.*
  - Septem . . . *Se.*
  - Supplices . . . *Sp.*
- Alcaeus . . . Alcae.
- Andocides . . . And.
- Antiphon . . . Ant.
- Aristophanes . . . Ar.
  - Acharnenses . . . *Ach.*
  - Aves . . . *Av.*
  - Ecclesiazusae . . . *Eccl.*
  - Equites . . . *Eq.*
  - Lysistrata . . . *Ly.*
  - Nubes . . . *N.*
  - Pax . . . *Pa.*
  - Plutus . . . *Pl.*
  - Ranae . . . *R.*
  - Thesmophoriazusae . . . *Th.*
  - Vespae . . . *V.*
- Demosthenes . . . D.
- Euripides . . . E.
  - Alcestis . . . *Al.*
  - Andromache . . . *And.*
  - Bacchae . . . *Ba.*
  - Cyclops . . . *Cyc.*
  - Electra . . . *El.*
  - Hecuba . . . *Hec.*
  - Helena . . . *Hel.*
  - Heraclidae . . . *Her.*
  - Hercules Furens . . . *H. F.*
  - Hippolytus . . . *Hip.*
  - Medea . . . *Me.*
  - Orestes . . . *Or.*
  - Phoenissae . . . *Ph.*
  - Rhesus . . . *Rh.*
  - Troades . . . *Tro.*
- Hesiod . . . Hes.
  - Theogonia . . . *Th.*
- Herodotus . . . Hd.
- Herondas . . . Herond.
- Hipponax . . . Hipp.
- Homer: —
  - Iliad . . . *Il.*
  - Odyssey . . . *Od.*
- Isaeus . . . Isae.
- Isocrates . . . I.
- Lysias . . . L.
- Mimnermus . . . Mimn.
- Menander . . . Men.
  - Monostichi . . . *Mon.*
- Pindar . . . Pind.
  - Olympian Odes . . . *Ol.*
  - Pythian Odes . . . *Py.*
- Plato . . . P.
  - Alcibiades i. . . . *Alc.* i.
  - Apology . . . *Ap.*
  - Charmides . . . *Ch.*
  - Crito . . . *Cr.*
  - Cratylus . . . *Crat.*
  - Critias . . . *Critias.*
  - Euthydemus . . . *Eu.*
  - Euthyphro . . . *Euthyph.*
  - Gorgias . . . *G.*
  - Hippias Major . . . *H. M.*
  - Laches . . . *Lach.*
  - Leges . . . *Lg.*
  - Lysis . . . *Lys.*
  - Meno . . . *Men.*
  - Menexenus . . . *Menex.*
  - Phaedo . . . *Ph.*
  - Phaedrus . . . *Phdr.*
  - Philebus . . . *Phil.*
  - Politicus . . . *Pol.*
  - Protagoras . . . *Pr.*
  - Republic . . . *Rp.*
  - Sophist . . . *So.*
  - Symposium . . . *Sy.*
  - Theaetetus . . . *Th.*
  - Timaeus . . . *Ti.*
- Sappho . . . Sapph.
- Sophocles . . . S.
  - Ajax . . . *Aj.*
  - Antigone . . . *An.*
  - Electra . . . *El.*
  - Oedipus at Colonus . . . *O. C.*
  - Oedipus Tyrannus . . . *O. T.*
  - Philoctetes . . . *Ph.*
  - Trachiniae . . . *Tr.*
- Stobaeus . . . Stob.
- Theocritus . . . Theoc.
- Theognis . . . Theog.
- Thucydides . . . T.
- Xenophon . . . X.
  - Agesilaus . . . *Ag.*
  - Anabasis . . . *A.*
  - Cyropaedia . . . *C.*
  - De re Equestri . . . *Eq.*
  - Hellenica . . . *H.*
  - Hipparchicus . . . *Hip.*
  - Memorabilia . . . *M.*
  - Oeconomicus . . . *Oe.*
  - De Republica Atheniensi . . . *Rp. A.*
  - Symposium . . . *Sy.*

The dramatists are cited by Dindorf's lines, except the tragic fragments (frag.), which follow Nauck's numbers. The orators are cited by the numbers of the orations and the German sections.

INTRODUCTION.

THE GREEK LANGUAGE AND DIALECTS.

THE Greek language is the language spoken by the Greek race. In the historic period, the people of this race called themselves by the name *Hellenes*, and their language *Hellenic*. We call them *Greeks*, from the Roman name *Graeci*. They were divided into Aeolians, Dorians, and Ionians. The Aeolians inhabited Aeolis (in Asia), Lesbos, Boeotia, and Thessaly; the Dorians inhabited Peloponnesus, Doris, Crete, some cities of Caria (in Asia), with the neighboring islands, many settlements in Southern Italy, which was known as *Magna Graecia*, and a large part of the coast of Sicily; the Ionians inhabited Ionia (in Asia), Attica, many islands in the Aegean Sea, a few towns in Sicily, and some other places.

In the early times of which the Homeric poems are a record (before 850 B.C.), there was no such division of the whole Greek race into Aeolians, Dorians, and Ionians as that which was recognized in historic times; nor was there any common name of the whole race, like the later name of Hellenes. The Homeric Hellenes were a small tribe in South-eastern Thessaly, of which Achilles was king; and the Greeks in general were called by Homer Achaeans, Argives, or Danaans.

The dialects of the Aeolians and the Dorians are known as the *Aeolic* and *Doric* dialects. These two dialects are much more closely allied to each other than either is to the Ionic. In the language of the Ionians we must distinguish the *Old Ionic,* the *New Ionic,* and the *Attic* dialects. The Old Ionic or Epic is the language of the Homeric poems, the oldest Greek literature. The New Ionic was the language of Ionia in the fifth century B.C., as it appears in Herodotus and Hippocrates. The Attic was the language of Athens during her period of literary eminence (from about 500 to 300 B.C.).[1] In it were written the tragedies of Aeschylus, Sophocles, and Euripides, the comedies of Aristophanes, the histories of Thucydides and Xenophon, the orations of Demosthenes and the other orators of Athens, and the philosophical works of Plato.

The Attic dialect is the most cultivated and refined form of the Greek language. It is therefore made the basis of Greek Grammar, and the other dialects are usually treated, for convenience, as if their forms were merely variations of the Attic. This is a position, however, to which the Attic has no claim on the ground of age or primitive forms, in respect to which it holds a rank below the other dialects.

The literary and political importance of Athens caused her dialect gradually to supplant the others wherever Greek was spoken; but, in this very extension to regions widely separated, the Attic dialect itself was not a little modified by various local influences, and lost some of its

[1] The name *Ionic* includes both the Old and the New Ionic, but not the Attic. When the Old and the New Ionic are to be distinguished in the present work, Ep. (for Epic) or Hom. (for Homeric) is used for the former, and Hdt. or Hd. (Herodotus) for the latter.

early purity. The universal Greek language which thus arose is called the *Common Dialect.* This begins with the Alexandrian period, the time of the literary eminence of Alexandria in Egypt, which dates from the accession of Ptolemy II. in 285 B.C. The Greek of the philosopher Aristotle lies on the border line between this and the purer Attic. The name *Hellenistic* is given to that form of the Common Dialect which was used by the Jews of Alexandria who made the Septuagint version of the Old Testament (283–135 B.C.) and by the writers of the New Testament, all of whom were *Hellenists* (*i.e.* foreigners who spoke Greek). Towards the end of the twelfth century A.D., the popular Greek then spoken in the Byzantine Roman Empire began to appear in literature by the side of the scholastic ancient Greek, which had ceased to be intelligible to the common people. This popular language, the earliest form of *Modern Greek,* was called *Romaic* (Ῥωμαϊκή), as the people called themselves Ῥωμαῖοι. The name *Romaic* is now little used; and the present language of the Greeks is called simply Ἑλληνική, while the kingdom of Greece is Ἑλλάς and the people are Ἕλληνες. The literary Greek has been greatly purified during the last half-century by the expulsion of foreign words and the restoration of classic forms; and the same process has affected the spoken language, especially that of cultivated society in Athens, but to a far less extent. It is not too much to say, that the Greek of most of the books and newspapers now published in Athens could have been understood without difficulty by Demosthenes or Plato. The Greek language has thus an unbroken literary history, from Homer to the present day, of at least twenty-seven centuries.

The Greek is descended from the same original language with the Indian (*i.e.* Sanskrit), Persian, German, Slavonic, Celtic, and Italian languages, which together form the Indo-European (sometimes called the Aryan) family of languages. Greek is most closely connected with the Italian languages (including Latin), to which it bears a relation similar to the still closer relation between French and Spanish or Italian. This relation accounts for the striking analogies between Greek and Latin, which appear in both roots and terminations; and also for the less obvious analogies between Greek and the German element in English, which are seen in a few words like *me*, *is*, *know*, etc.

PART I.

LETTERS, SYLLABLES, AND ACCENTS.

THE ALPHABET.

1. The Greek alphabet has twenty-four letters: —

Form.		Equivalent.	Name.	
Α	α	a	ἄλφα	*Alpha*
Β	β	b	βῆτα	*Beta*
Γ	γ	g	γάμμα	*Gamma*
Δ	δ	d	δέλτα	*Delta*
Ε	ε	e (*short*)	εἶ, ἒ ψιλόν	*Epsilon*
Ζ	ζ	z	ζῆτα	*Zeta*
Η	η	e (*long*)	ἦτα	*Eta*
Θ	θ ϑ	th	θῆτα	*Theta*
Ι	ι	i	ἰῶτα	*Iota*
Κ	κ	k *or hard* c	κάππα	*Kappa*
Λ	λ	l	λά(μ)βδα	*Lambda*
Μ	μ	m	μῦ	*Mu*
Ν	ν	n	νῦ	*Nu*
Ξ	ξ	x	ξεῖ, ξῖ	*Xi*
Ο	ο	o (*short*)	οὖ, ὂ μῖκρόν	*Omicron*
Π	π	p	πεῖ, πῖ	*Pi*
Ρ	ρ	r	ῥῶ	*Rho*
Σ	σ ς	s	σίγμα	*Sigma*
Τ	τ	t	ταῦ	*Tau*
Υ	υ	(u) y	ὖ, ὒ ψιλόν	*Upsilon*
Φ	φ	ph	φεῖ, φῖ	*Phi*
Χ	χ	kh	χεῖ, χῖ	*Chi*
Ψ	ψ	ps	ψεῖ, ψῖ	*Psi*
Ω	ω	o (*long*)	ὦ, ὦ μέγα	*Omĕga*

2. N. At the end of a word the form ς is used, elsewhere the form σ; thus, σύστασις.

3. N. Three letters belonging to the primitive Greek alphabet, *Vau* or *Digamma* (ϝ), equivalent to V or W, *Koppa* (ϙ), equivalent to Q, and *Sampi* (ϡ), a form of *Sigma*, are not in the ordinary written alphabet. They were used as numerals (384), *Vau* here having the form ϛ, which is used also as an abbreviation of στ. *Vau* had not entirely disappeared in pronunciation when the Homeric poems were composed, and the metre of many verses in these is explained only by admitting its presence. Many forms also which seem irregular are explained only on the supposition that ϝ has been omitted (see 269).

4. N. The Athenians of the best period used the names εἶ for *epsilon*, οὖ for *omicron*, ὖ for *upsilon*, and ὦ for *omega;* the present names for these letters being late. Some Greek grammarians used ἒ ψῑλόν (*plain* ε) and ὒ ψῑλόν (*plain* υ) to distinguish ε and υ from αι and οι, which in their time had similar sounds.

VOWELS AND DIPHTHONGS.

5. The vowels are α, ε, η, ι, ο, ω, and υ. Of these, ε and ο are always short; η and ω are always long; α, ι, and υ are long in some syllables and short in others, whence they are called *doubtful* vowels.

6. N. Α, ε, η, ο, and ω from their pronunciation are called *open* vowels (α being the most open); ι and υ are called *close* vowels.

7 The diphthongs (*δί-φθογγοι, double-sounding*) are αι, αυ, ει, ευ, οι, ου, ηυ, υι, ᾳ, ῃ, ῳ. These (except υι) are formed by the union of an open vowel with a close one. The long vowels (ᾱ, η, ω) with ι form the (so called) *improper* diphthongs ᾳ, ῃ, ῳ. The Ionic dialect has also ωυ.

8. N. Besides the genuine ει (= ε + ι) and ου (= ο + υ) there are the so-called *spurious* diphthongs ει and ου, which arise from contraction (ει from εε, and ου from εο, οε, or οο) or from compensative lengthening (30); as in ἐποίει (for ἐποίεε), λέγειν (for λεγεεν, 565, 4), χρῡσοῦς (for χρύσεος), θείς (for θεντς, 79), τοῦ and τούς (190). In the fourth century B.C. these came to be written like genuine ει and ου; but in earlier times they were written E and O, even in inscriptions which used H and Ω for ē and ō. (See 27.)

9. N. The mark of *diaeresis* (*διαίρεσις, separation*), a double dot, written over a vowel, shows that this does not form a diphthong with the preceding vowel; as in προϊέναι (προ-ιέναι), *to go forward,* Ἀτρεΐδης, *son of Atreus* (in Homer).

10. N. In ᾳ, ῃ, ῳ, the ι is now written and printed below the first vowel, and is called *iota subscript.* But with capitals it is written in the line; as in ΤΗΙ ΚΩΜΩΙΔΙΑΙ, τῇ κωμῳδίᾳ, and in Ὠιχετο, ᾤχετο. This ι was written as an ordinary letter as long as it was pronounced, that is, until the first century B.C., after which it was sometimes written (always in the line) and sometimes omitted. Our *iota subscript* is not older than the twelfth century A.D.

BREATHINGS.

11. Every vowel or diphthong at the beginning of a word has either the *rough* breathing (ʽ) or the *smooth* breathing (ʼ). The rough breathing shows that the vowel is *aspirated*, i.e. that it is preceded by the sound *h;* the smooth breathing shows that the vowel is not aspirated. Thus ὁρῶν, *seeing*, is pronounced *hŏrōn;* but ὀρῶν, *of mountains*, is pronounced *ŏrōn.*

12. N. A diphthong takes the breathing, like the accent (109), upon its *second* vowel. But ᾳ, ῃ, and ῳ (10) have both breathing and accent on the first vowel, even when the ι is written in the line. Thus οἴχεται, εὐφραίνω, Αἴμων; but ᾤχετο or Ὤιχετο, ᾄδω or Ἄιδω, ᾔδειν or Ἤιδειν. On the other hand, the writing of ἀΐδιος (Ἀΐδιος) shows that α and ι do not form a diphthong.

13. N. The rough breathing was once denoted by H. When this was taken to denote ē (which once was not distinguished from ĕ), half of it Ⱶ was used for the rough breathing; and afterwards the other half ⊣ was used for the smooth breathing. From these fragments came the later signs ʽ and ʼ.

14. N. In Attic words, initial υ is always aspirated.

15. At the beginning of a word ρ is written ῥ; as in ῥήτωρ (Latin *rhetor*), *orator.* In the middle of a word ρρ is sometimes written ῤῥ; as ἄῤῥητος, *unspeakable;* Πύῤῥος, *Pyrrhus* (ῤῥ = *rrh*).

CONSONANTS.

16. The simple consonants are divided into

labials, π, β, φ, μ,
palatals, κ, γ, χ,
linguals, τ, δ, θ, σ, λ, ν, ρ.

17. Before κ, γ, χ, or ξ, *gamma* (γ) had a *nasal* sound, like that of *n* in *anger* or *ink*, and was represented by *n* in Latin; as ἄγγελος, (Latin *angelus*), *messenger;* ἄγκῡρα, (*ancora*), *anchor;* σφίγξ, *sphinx.*

18. The *double* consonants are ξ, ψ, ζ. Ξ is composed of κ and σ; ψ, of π and σ. Ζ arises from a combination of δ with a soft *s* sound; hence it has the effect of two consonants in lengthening a preceding vowel (99).

19. By another classification, the consonants are divided into *semivowels* and *mutes*.

20. The semivowels are λ, μ, ν, ρ, and σ, with nasal γ (17). Of these

λ, μ, ν, and ρ are *liquids;*
μ, ν, and nasal γ (17) are *nasals;*
σ is a *spirant* (or *sibilant*);
ϝ of the older alphabet (3) is also a spirant.

21. The mutes are of three *orders:* —

smooth mutes π κ τ
middle mutes β γ δ
rough mutes φ χ θ

22. These mutes again correspond in the following *classes:* —

labial mutes (π-mutes) π β φ
palatal mutes (κ-mutes) κ γ χ
lingual mutes (τ-mutes) τ δ θ

23. N. Mutes of the same *order* are called *co-ordinate;* those of the same *class* are called *cognate.*

24. N. The smooth and rough mutes, with σ, ξ, and ψ, are called surd (*hushed* sounds); the other consonants and the vowels are called sonant (*sounding*).

25. The only consonants which can end a Greek word are ν, ρ, and ς. If others are left at the end in forming words, they are dropped.

26. N. The only exceptions are ἐκ and οὐκ (or οὐχ), which have other forms, ἐξ and οὐ. Final ξ and ψ (κσ and πσ) are no exceptions.

---

27. The Greek alphabet above described is the *Ionic*, used by the Asiatic Ionians from a very early period, but first introduced officially at Athens in 403 B.C. The Athenians had previously used an alphabet which had no separate signs for *ē*, *ō*, *ks*, or *ps*. In this E was used for *ĕ* and *ē* and also for the spurious ει (8); O for *ŏ* and *ō* and for spurious ου (8); H was still an aspirate (*h*); ΧΣ stood for Ξ, and ΦΣ for Ψ. Thus the Athenians of the time of Pericles wrote ΕΔΟΧΣΕΝ ΤΕΙ ΒΟϜΕΙ ΚΑΙ ΤΟΙ ΔΕΜΟΙ for ἔδοξεν τῇ βουλῇ καὶ τῷ δήμῳ, — ΤΟ ΦΣΕΦΙΣΜΑ ΤΟ ΔΕΜΟ for τὸ ψήφισμα τοῦ δήμου, — ΗΕΣ for ἧς, —

HEI for ᾖ, — ΠΕΜΠΕΝ for πέμπειν, — ΧΡΥΣΟΣ for χρυσοῦς, — ΤΟΥΤΟ for both τοῦτο and τούτου, — ΤΟΣ ΠΡΥΤΑΝΕΣ for τοὺς πρυτάνεις, — ΑΡΧΟΣΙ for ἄρχουσι, — ΔΕΟΣΟΝ for δεουσῶν, — ΗΟΠΟΣ for ὅπως, — ΠΟΙΕΝ for ποιεῖν, — ΤΡΕΣ for τρεῖς, — ΑΠΟ ΤΟ ΦΟΡΟ for ἀπὸ τοῦ φόρου, — ΧΣΕΝΟΣ for ξένος or ξένους.

Ancient Pronunciation.[1]

28. 1. (*Vowels.*) The long vowels ᾱ, η, ῑ, and ω were pronounced at the best period much like *a* in *father*, *e* in *fête* (French ê or è), *i* in *machine*, and *o* in *tone*. Originally υ had the sound of Latin *u* (our *u* in *prune*), but before the fourth century B.C. it had come to that of French *u* or German *ü*. The short vowels had the same sounds as the long vowels, but shortened or less prolonged: this is hard to express in English, as our short *a*, *e*, *i*, and *o*, in *pan*, *pen*, *pit*, and *pot*, have sounds of a different nature from those of *ā*, *ē*, *ī*, and *ō*, given above. We have an approach to ᾰ, ε̆, ῐ, and ŏ in the second *a* in *grand-father*, French *é* in *réal*, *i* in *verity*, and *o* in *monastic*, *renovate*.

2. (*Diphthongs.*) We may assume that the diphthongs originally had the sounds of their two vowels, pronounced as one syllable. Our *ai* in *aisle*, *eu* in *feud*, *oi* in *oil*, *ui* in *quit*, will give some idea of αι, ευ, οι, and υι; and *ou* in *house* of αυ. Likewise the genuine ει must have been pronounced originally as ε + ι, somewhat like *ei* in *rein* (cf. Hom. Ἀτρεΐδης, Attic Ἀτρείδης); and ου was a compound of ο and υ. But in the majority of cases ει and ου are written for simple sounds, represented by the Athenians of the best period by E and O (see 8 and 27). We do not know how these sounds were related to ordinary ε and ο on one side and to ει and ου on the other; but after the beginning of the fourth century B.C. they appear to have agreed substantially with ει and ου, since EI and OY are written for both alike. In ει the sound of ι appears to have prevailed more and more, so that by the first century B.C. it had the sound of ῑ. On the other hand, ου became (and still remains) a simple sound, like *ou* in *youth*.

The diphthongs ᾳ, ῃ, and ῳ were probably always pronounced with the chief force on the first vowel, so that the ι gradually disappeared (see 10). The rare ηυ and ωυ probably had the sounds of η and ω with an additional sound of υ.

3. (*Consonants.*) Probably β, δ, κ, λ, μ, ν, π, and ρ were sounded as *b*, *d*, *k*, *l*, *m*, *n*, *p*, and *r* in English. Ordinary γ was always hard, like *g* in *go*; for nasal γ, see 17. Τ was always like *t* in *tin* or *to*; σ was generally (perhaps always) like *s* in *so*. Ζ is called a compound of δ and σ; but opinions differ whether it was δσ or σδ, but the ancient testimony seems to point to σδ. In late Greek, ζ came to the sound of English *z*, which it still keeps. Ξ represents κσ, and ψ represents πσ, although the older Athenians felt an aspirate in both, as they wrote χσ for ξ and φσ for ψ. The rough consonants θ, χ, and φ in the best period were τ, κ, and π followed by *h*, so that ἔνθα was ἐν-τά, ἀφίημι was ἀ-πίημι, ἔχω was ἐ-κώ, etc. We cannot represent these rough mutes in English; our nearest approach is in words like ho*th*ouse, bloc*k*head, and u*p*hill, but here the *h* is not in the same syllable with the mute. In later Greek θ and φ came to the modern pronunciation of *th* (in *thin*) and *f*, and χ to that resembling German *ch* in *machen*.

[1] For practical remarks on pronunciation, see the Preface.

CHANGES OF VOWELS.

29. (*Lengthening.*) Short vowels are often lengthened in the formation and the inflection of words. Here the following changes generally take place: —

ᾰ	becomes	η (ᾱ after ε, ι, or ρ)			
ε	"	η,	ῐ	becomes	ῑ,
ο	"	ω,	ῠ	"	ῡ.

Thus τῑμάω (stem τῑμα-), fut. τῑμή-σω; ἐά-ω, fut. ἐᾱ́-σω; τί-θη-μι (stem θε-); δί-δω-μι (stem δο-); ἱκετεύω, aor. ῑ̔κέτευσα; πέ-φῡ-κα, perf. of φύω, from root φῠ- (see φύσις).

30. (*Compensative Lengthening.*) 1. When one or more consonants are dropped for euphony (especially before σ), a preceding short vowel is very often lengthened to make up for the omission. Here

ᾰ	becomes	ᾱ,	ῐ	becomes	ῑ,
ε	"	ει,	ῠ	"	ῡ.
ο	"	ου,			

Thus μέλᾱς for μελανς (78), ἱστᾱ́ς for ἱσταντς (79), θείς for θεντς (79), δούς for δοντς, λῡ́ουσι for λῡοντσι, ἔκρῑνα for ἐκρινσα, δεικνῡ́ς for δεικνυντς (79). Here ει and ου are the spurious diphthongs (8).

2. In the first aorist of liquid verbs (672), ᾰ is lengthened to η (or ᾱ) when σ is dropped; as ἔφηνα for ἐφαν-σα, from φαίνω (φαν-), cf. ἐστελ-σα, ἔστειλα, from στέλλω (στελ-).

31. (*Strong and Weak Forms.*) In some formations and inflections there is an interchange in the root of ει, οι, and ῐ, — of ευ, (sometimes ου,) and ῠ, — and of η, (rarely ω,) and ᾰ. The long vowels and diphthongs in such cases are called *strong* forms, and the short vowels *weak* forms.

Thus λείπ-ω, λέ-λοιπ-α, ἔ-λιπ-ον; φεύγ-ω, πέ-φευγ-α, ἔ-φυγ-ον; τήκ-ω, τέ-τηκ-α, ἐ-τάκ-ην; ῥήγ-νῡμι, ἔρ-ρωγ-α, ἐρ-ράγ-ην; ἐλεύ-σομαι (74), ἐλ-ήλουθ-α, ἤλυθ-ον (see ἔρχομαι); so σπεύδ-ω, *hasten*, and σπουδ-ή, *haste*; ἀρήγω, *help*, and ἀρωγός, *helping*. Compare English *smite, smote, smit* (*smitten*). (See 572.)

32. An interchange of the short vowels ᾰ, ε, and ο takes place in certain forms; as in the tenses of τρέπ-ω, τέτροφ-α, ἐ-τράπ-ην, and in the noun τρόπ-ος, from stem τρεπ-. (See 643, 645, and 831.)

33. (*Exchange of Quantity.*) An exchange of quantity sometimes takes place between a long vowel and a succeeding short one; as in epic *νᾱός*, *temple*, and Attic *νεώς*; epic *βασιλῆος*, *βασιλῆα*, *king*, Attic *βασιλέως*, *βασιλέᾱ*; epic *μετήορος*, *in the air*, Attic *μετέωρος*; *Μενέλᾱος*, Attic *Μενέλεως* (200).

EUPHONY OF VOWELS.

Collision of Vowels. — Hiatus.

34. A succession of two vowel sounds, not forming a diphthong, was generally displeasing to the Athenians. In the middle of a word this could be avoided by *contraction* (35–41). Between two words, where it is called *hiatus*, it could be avoided by *crasis* (42–46), by *elision* (48–54) or *aphaeresis* (55), or by adding a *movable consonant* (56–63) to the former word.

Contraction of Vowels.

35. Two successive vowels, or a vowel and a diphthong, may be united by *contraction* in a single long vowel or a diphthong; *φιλέω*, *φιλῶ*; *φίλεε*, *φίλει*; *τίμαε*, *τίμᾱ*. It seldom takes place unless the former vowel is *open* (6).

36. The regular use of contraction is one of the characteristics of the Attic dialect. It follows these general principles: —

37. I. Two vowels which can form a diphthong (7) simply unite in one syllable; as *τείχεϊ*, *τείχει*; *γέραϊ*, *γέραι*; *ῥάϊστος*, *ῥᾷστος*.

38. II. When the two vowels cannot form a diphthong, —

1. Two *like* vowels (i.e. two *a*-sounds, two *e*-sounds, or two *o*-sounds, without regard to quantity) unite to form the common long (ᾱ, η, or ω). But εε gives ει (8), and οο gives ου (8). *E.g.*

Μνάᾱ, *μνᾶ* (184); *φιλέητε*, *φιλῆτε*; *δηλόω*, *δηλῶ*; — but *ἐφίλεε*, *ἐφίλει*; *πλόος*, *πλοῦς*.

2. When an *o*-sound precedes or follows an *a*- or an *e*-sound, the two become ω. But οε and εο give ου (8). *E.g.*

Δηλόητε, δηλῶτε; φιλέωσι, φιλῶσι; τῑμάομεν, τῑμῶμεν; τῑμάωμεν, τῑμῶμεν; — but νόε, νοῦ; γένεος, γένους.

3. When an *a*-sound precedes or follows an *e*-sound, the first (in order) prevails, and we have ᾱ or η. *E.g.*

Ἐτίμαε, ἐτίμᾱ; τῑμάητε, τῑμᾶτε; τείχεα, τείχη; Ἑρμέᾱς, Ἑρμῆς.

4. A vowel disappears by absorption before a diphthong beginning with the *same* vowel, and ε is always absorbed before οι. In other cases, a simple vowel followed by a diphthong is contracted with the *first vowel* of the diphthong; and a following ι remains as *iota subscript*, but a following υ disappears. *E.g.*

Μνάαι, μναῖ; μνάᾳ, μνᾷ; φιλέει, φιλεῖ; φιλέῃ, φιλῇ; δηλόοι, δηλοῖ; νόῳ, νῷ; δηλόου, δηλοῦ; φιλέοι, φιλοῖ; χρύσεοι, χρῡσοῖ; τῑμάει, τῑμᾷ; τῑμάῃ, τῑμᾷ; τῑμάοι, τῑμῷ; τῑμάου, τῑμῶ; φιλέου, φιλοῦ; λύεαι, λύῃ (39, 3); λύηαι, λύῃ; μεμνήοιο, μεμνῷο.

39. *Exceptions.* 1. In contracts of the first and second declensions, every short vowel before α, or before a long vowel or a diphthong, is absorbed. But in the *singular* of the first declension εᾱ is contracted regularly to η (after a vowel or ρ, to ᾱ). (See 184.)

2. In the third declension εα becomes ᾱ after ε, and ᾱ or η after ι or υ. (See 229, 267, and 315.)

3. In the second person singular of the passive and middle, εαι (for εσαι) gives the common Attic form in ει as well as the regular contract form in ῃ; as λύεαι, λύῃ or λύει. (See 565, 6.)

4. In verbs in οω, οει gives οι, as δηλόεις, δηλοῖς; οι is found also in the subjunctive for οῃ, as δηλόῃ, δηλοῖ.

5. The spurious diphthong ει is contracted like simple ε; as πλακόεις, πλακοῦς, *cake*. Thus infinitives in αειν and οειν lose ι in the contracted forms; as τιμάειν, τιμᾶν; δηλόειν, δηλοῦν. (See 761.)

40. 1. The close vowel ι is contracted with a following ι in the Ionic dative singular of nouns in ις (see 255); and υ is contracted with ι or ε in a few forms of nouns in υς (see 257 and 258).

2. In some classes of nouns and adjectives of the third declension, contraction is confined to certain cases; see 226–263. For exceptions in the contraction of verbs, see 496 and 497. See dialectic forms of verbs in αω, εω, and οω, in 784–786.

41. *Table of Contractions.*

α + α = ᾱ	γέραα, γέρᾱ
α + αι = αι	μνάαι, μναῖ
α + ᾳ = ᾳ	μνάᾳ, μνᾷ
α + ε = ᾱ	ἐτίμαε, ἐτίμᾱ
α + ει = ᾳ	τῑμάει, τῑμᾷ; τῑμάειν,
or ᾱ	τῑμᾶν (39, 5)
α + η = ᾱ	τῑμάητε, τῑμᾶτε
α + ῃ = ᾳ	τῑμάῃ, τῑμᾷ
ᾰ + ι = αι	γέραϊ, γέραι
ᾱ + ι = ᾳ	γρᾱ-ίδιον, γρᾴδιον
α + ο = ω	τῑμάομεν, τῑμῶμεν
α + οι = ῳ	τῑμάοιμι, τῑμῷμι
α + ου = ω	τῑμάου, τῑμῶ
α + ω = ω	τῑμάω, τῑμῶ
ε + α = η	γένεα, γένη; Ἑρμέας,
or ᾱ	Ἑρμῆς; ὀστέα, ὀστᾶ (39, 1)
ε + αι = ῃ	λύεαι, λύῃ; χρύσεαι,
or αι	χρυσαῖ (39, 1 and 3)
ε + ε = ει	ἐφίλεε, ἐφίλει
ε + ει = ει	φιλέει, φιλεῖ
ε + η = η	φιλέητε, φιλῆτε
ε + ῃ = ῃ	φιλέῃ, φιλῇ
ε + ι = ει	τείχεϊ, τείχει
ε + ο = ου	γένεος, γένους
ε + οι = οι	φιλέοι, φιλοῖ
ε + ου = ου	φιλέου, φιλοῦ
ε + υ = ευ	ἐύ, εὖ
ε + ω = ω	φιλέω, φιλῶ

ε + ῳ = ῳ	ὀστέῳ, ὀστῷ
η + αι = ῃ	λύηαι, λύῃ
η + ε = η	τῑμήεντι, τῑμῆντι
η + ει = ῃ	τῑμήεις, τιμῆς (39, 5)
η + ι = ῃ	κλῄ-ιθρον, κλῇθρον
η + οι = ῳ	μεμνηοίμην, μεμνῴμην
ι + ι = ῑ	Χίιος, Χῖος
ο + α = ω	αἰδόα, αἰδῶ; ἁπλόα,
or ᾱ	ἁπλᾶ (39, 1)
ο + αι = αι	ἁπλόαι, ἁπλαῖ
ο + ε = ου	νόε, νοῦ
ο + ει = οι	δηλόει, δηλοῖ (39, 4);
or ου	δηλόειν, δηλοῦν (39, 5)
ο + η = ω	δηλόητε, δηλῶτε
ο + ῃ = ῳ	διδόῃς, διδῷς; ἁπλόῃ,
or ῃ	ἁπλῇ (39, 1)
ο + ι = οι	πειθόι, πειθοῖ
ο + ο = ου	νόος, νοῦς
ο + οι = οι	δηλόοι, δηλοῖ
ο + ου = ου	δηλόου, δηλοῦ
ο + ω = ω	δηλόω, δηλῶ
ο + ῳ = ῳ	ἁπλόῳ, ἁπλῷ
Rarely the following: —	
ω + α = ω	ἥρωα, ἥρω
ω + ε = ω	ἥρωες, ἥρως
ω + ι = ῳ	ἥρωι, ἥρῳ
ω + ο = ω	σῶος, σῶς

Crasis.

42. A vowel or diphthong at the end of a word may be contracted with one at the beginning of the following word. This occurs especially in poetry, and is called *crasis* (κρᾶσις, *mixture*). The *corōnis* (') is placed over the contracted syllable. The first of the two words is generally an article, a relative (ὅ or ἅ), καί, πρό, or ὦ.

43. Crasis generally follows the laws of contraction, with these modifications: —

1. A diphthong at the end of the first word drops its last vowel before crasis takes place.

2. The article loses its final vowel or diphthong in crasis before α; the particle τοί drops οι before α; and καί drops αι before all vowels and diphthongs except ε and ει. But we have κεἰ and κεἰς for καὶ εἰ and καὶ εἰς.

44. The following are examples of crasis: —

Τὸ ὄνομα, τοὔνομα; τὰ ἀγαθά, τἀγαθά; τὸ ἐναντίον, τοὐναντίον; ὁ ἐκ, οὑκ; ὁ ἐπί, οὑπί; τὸ ἱμάτιον, θοἰμάτιον (93); ἃ ἄν, ἅν; καὶ ἄν, κἄν; καὶ εἶτα, κᾆτα; — ὁ ἀνήρ, ἁνήρ; οἱ ἀδελφοί, ἁδελφοί; τῷ ἀνδρί, τἀνδρί; τὸ αὐτό, ταὐτό; τοῦ αὐτοῦ, ταὐτοῦ; — τοι ἄν, τἄν (μέντοι ἄν, μεντἄν); τοι ἄρα, τἆρα; — καὶ αὐτός, καὐτός; καὶ αὕτη, χαὔτη (93); καὶ ἔστι, κἄστι; καὶ εἰ, κεἰ; καὶ οὐ, κοὐ; καὶ οἱ, χοἰ; καὶ αἱ, χαἰ. So ἐγὼ οἶδα, ἐγᾧδα; ὦ ἄνθρωπε, ὤνθρωπε; τῇ ἐπαρῇ, τήπαρῇ. Likewise we have προὔργου, *helpful*, for πρὸ ἔργου, *ahead in work;* cf. φροῦδος for πρὸ ὁδοῦ (93).

45. N. If the first word is an article or relative with the rough breathing, this breathing is retained on the contracted syllable, taking the place of the *coronis;* as in ἅν, ἁνήρ.

46. N. In crasis, ἕτερος, *other*, takes the form ἅτερος, — whence ἅτερος (for ὁ ἕτερος), θἀτέρου (for τοῦ ἑτέρου), θἀτέρῳ, etc. (43, 2; 93).

Synizesis.

47. 1. In poetry, two successive vowels, not forming a diphthong, are sometimes united in pronunciation for the sake of the metre, although no contraction appears in writing. This is called *synizēsis* (συνίζησις, *settling together*). Thus, θεοί may make one syllable in poetry; στήθεα or χρῡσέῳ may make two.

2. Synizesis may also take the place of crasis (42), when the first word ends in a long vowel or a diphthong, especially with ἐπεί, *since*, μή, *not*, ἤ, *or*, ἦ (interrog.), and ἐγώ, *I*. Thus, ἐπεὶ οὐ may make two syllables, μὴ εἰδέναι may make three; μὴ οὐ always makes one syllable in poetry.

Elision.

48. A short final vowel may be dropped when the next word begins with a vowel. This is called *elision*. An *apostrophe* (') marks the omission. *E.g.*

Δι' ἐμοῦ for διὰ ἐμοῦ; ἀντ' ἐκείνης for ἀντὶ ἐκείνης; λέγοιμ' ἂν for λέγοιμι ἄν; ἀλλ' εὐθύς for ἀλλὰ εὐθύς; ἐπ' ἀνθρώπῳ for ἐπὶ ἀνθρώπῳ. So ἐφ' ἑτέρῳ; νύχθ' ὅλην for νύκτα ὅλην (92).

49. Elision is especially frequent in ordinary prepositions, conjunctions, and adverbs; but it may also be used with short vowels at the end of nouns, adjectives, pronouns, and verbs.

50. Elision never occurs in

(*a*) the prepositions περί and πρό, except περί in Aeolic (rarely before ι in Attic),

(*b*) the conjunction ὅτι,

(*c*) monosyllables, except those ending in ε,

(*d*) the dative singular in ι of the third declension and the dative plural in σι, except in epic poetry,

(*e*) words ending in υ.

51. N. The epic and comic poets sometimes elide αι in the verbal endings μαι, σαι, ται, and σθαι (θαι). So οι in οἴμοι, and rarely in μοι.

52. N. Elision is often neglected in prose, especially by certain writers (as Thucydides). Others (as Isocrates) are more strict in its use.

53. (*Apocope.*) The poets sometimes cut off a short vowel before a consonant. Thus in Homer we find ἄν, κάτ, and πάρ, for ἀνά, κατά, and παρά. Both in composition and alone, κάτ assimilates its τ to a following consonant and drops it before two consonants, and ν in ἄν is subject to the changes of 78; as κάββαλε and κάκτανε, for κατέβαλε and κατέκτανε, — but κατθανεῖν for καταθανεῖν (68, 1), κὰκ κορυφήν, κὰγ γόνυ, κὰπ πεδίον; ἀμ-βάλλω, ἀλ-λέξαι, ἂμ πεδίον, ἂμ φόνον. So ὑβ-βάλλειν (once) for ὑπο-βάλλειν.

54. A short final vowel is generally elided also when it comes before a vowel in forming a compound word. Here no apostrophe is used. *E.g.*

Ἀπ-αιτέω (ἀπό and αἰτέω), δι-έβαλον (διά and ἔβαλον). So ἀφ-αιρέω (ἀπό and αἱρέω, 92); δεχ-ήμερος (δέκα and ἡμέρα).

Aphaeresis.

55. In poetry, a short vowel at the beginning of a word is sometimes dropped after a long vowel or a diphthong, especially after μή, *not*, and ἤ, *or*. This is called *aphaeresis* (ἀφαίρεσις, *taking off*). Thus, μὴ 'γώ for μὴ ἐγώ; ποῦ 'στιν for ποῦ ἔστιν; ἐγὼ 'φάνην for ἐγὼ ἐφάνην; ἢ 'μοῦ for ἢ ἐμοῦ.

Movable Consonants.

56. Most words ending in -σι (including -ξι and -ψι), and all verbs of the third person ending in ε, generally add ν when the next word begins with a vowel. This is called *ν movable*. *E.g.*

Πᾶσι δίδωσι ταῦτα; but πᾶσιν ἔδωκεν ἐκεῖνα. So δίδωσί μοι; but δίδωσιν ἐμοί.

57. N. Ἐστί takes ν movable, like third persons in σι.

58. N. The third person singular of the pluperfect active in -ει has ν movable; as ᾔδει(ν), *he knew*. But contracted imperfects in -ει (for -εε), as ἐφίλει, never take ν in Attic.

59. N. The epic κέ (for ἄν) is generally κέν before a vowel, and the poetic νύν (enclitic) has an epic form νύ. Many adverbs in -θεν (as πρόσθεν) have poetic forms in -θε.

60. N. N movable may be added at the end of a sentence or of a line of poetry. It may be added even before a consonant in poetry, to make position (99).

61. N. Words which may have ν movable are not elided in prose, except ἐστί.

62. Οὐ, *not*, becomes οὐκ before a smooth vowel, and οὐχ before a rough vowel; as οὐ θέλω, οὐκ αὐτός, οὐχ οὗτος. Μή inserts κ in μηκ-έτι, *no longer*, by the analogy of οὐκ-έτι.

63. Οὕτως, *thus*, ἐξ (ἐκς), *from*, and some other words may drop ς before a consonant; as οὕτως ἔχει, οὕτω δοκεῖ, ἐξ ἄστεως, ἐκ πόλεως.

METATHESIS AND SYNCOPE.

64. 1. *Metathesis* is the transposition of a short vowel and a liquid in a word; as in κράτος and κάρτος, *strength;* θάρσος and θράσος, *courage*.

2. The vowel is often lengthened; as in βέ-βλη-κα (from stem βᾰλ-), τέ-τμη-κα (from stem τεμ-), θρῴ-σκω (from stem θορ-). (See 649.)

65. *Syncope* is the dropping of a short vowel between two consonants; as in πατέρος, πατρός (274); πτήσομαι for πετήσομαι (650).

66. N. (*a*) When μ is brought before ρ or λ by syncope or metathesis, it is strengthened by inserting β; as μεσημβρίᾱ, *midday*, for μεσημ(ε)ριᾱ (μέσος and ἡμέρᾱ); μέμβλωκα, epic perfect of βλώσκω, *go*, from stem μολ-, μλο-, μλω- (636), με-μλω-κα, μέ-μβλω-κα. Thus the vulgar *chimley* (for *chimney*) generally becomes *chimbley*.

(*b*) At the beginning of a word such a μ is dropped before β;

as in βροτός, *mortal*, from stem μορ-, μρο- (cf. Lat. *morior*, *die*), μβρο-τος, βροτός (but the μ appears in composition, as in ἄ-μβροτος, *immortal*). So βλίττω, *take honey*, from stem μελιτ- of μέλι, *honey* (cf. Latin *mel*), by syncope μλιτ-, μβλιτ-, βλιτ-, βλίττω (582).

67. N. So δ is inserted after ν in the oblique cases of ἀνήρ, *man* (277), when the ν is brought by syncope before ρ; as ἀνέρος (ἀν-ρος), ἀνδρός.

CHANGES OF CONSONANTS.

Doubling of Consonants.

68. 1. A rough mute (21) is never doubled; but πφ, κχ, and τθ are always written for φφ, χχ, and θθ. Thus Σαπφώ, Βάκχος, κατθανεῖν, not Σαφφώ, Βάχχος, καθθανεῖν (53). So in Latin, *Sappho*, *Bacchus*.

2. A middle mute is never doubled in Attic Greek. In γγ the first γ is always nasal (17).

3. The later Attic has ττ for the earlier σσ in certain forms; as πράττω for πράσσω, ἐλάττων for ἐλάσσων; θάλαττα for θάλασσα. Also ττ (not for σσ) and even τθ occur in a few other words; as Ἀττικός, Ἀτθίς, *Attic*. See also 72.

69. Initial ρ is doubled when a vowel precedes it in forming a compound word; as in ἀναρρίπτω (ἀνά and ῥίπτω). So after the syllabic augment; as in ἔρρῖπτον (imperfect of ῥίπτω). But after a diphthong it remains single; as in εὔροος, εὔρους.

Euphonic Changes of Consonants.

70. The following rules (71–95) apply chiefly to changes made in the final consonant of a stem in adding the endings, especially in forming and inflecting the tenses of verbs and cases of nouns, and to those made in forming compounds: —

71. (*Mutes before other Mutes.*) Before a τ-mute (22), a π-mute or a κ-mute is made coördinate (23), and another τ-mute becomes σ. *E.g.*

Τέτρῖπται (for τετρῖβ-ται), δέδεκται (for δεδεχ-ται), πλεχθῆναι (for πλεκ-θηναι), ἐλείφθην (for ἐλειπ-θην), γράβδην (for γραφ-δην). Πέπεισται (πεπειθ-ται), ἐπείσθην (ἐπειθ-θην), ᾗσται (ᾐδ-ται), ἴστε (ἰδ-τε), χαριέστερος (χαριετ-τερος).

72. N. Ἐκ, *from*, in composition retains κ unchanged; as in ἐκ-κρίνω, ἐκ-δρομή, ἔκ-θεσις. For ττ and τθ, see 68, 3.

73. N. No combinations of different mutes, except those included in 68 and in 71 (those in which the second is τ, δ, or θ), are allowed in Greek. When any such arise, the first mute is dropped; as in πέπεικα (for πεπειθ-κα). When γ stands before κ, γ, or χ, as in συγ-χέω (σύν and χέω), it is not a mute but a nasal (20).

74. (*Mutes before* Σ.) No mute can stand before σ except π and κ. A π-mute with σ forms ψ, a κ-mute forms ξ, and a τ-mute is dropped. *E.g.*

Τρίψω (for τρῑβ-σω), γράψω (for γραφ-σω), λέξω (for λεγ-σω), πείσω (for πειθ-σω), ᾄσω (for ᾀδ-σω), σώμασι (for σωματ-σι), ἐλπίσι (for ἐλπιδ-σι). So φλέψ (for φλεβ-ς), ἐλπίς (for ἐλπιδ-ς), νύξ (for νυκτ-ς). So χαρίεσι (for χαριετ-σι, 331). See examples under 209, 1.

75. (*Mutes before* M.) Before μ, a π-mute becomes μ, and a κ-mute becomes γ. *E.g.*

Λέλειμμαι (for λελειπ-μαι), τέτρῖμμαι (for τετρῑβ-μαι), γέγραμμαι (for γεγραφ-μαι), πέπλεγμαι (for πεπλεκ-μαι), τέτευγμαι (for τετευχ-μαι).

76. N. But κμ can stand when they come together by metathesis (64); as in κέ-κμη-κα (κάμ-νω). Both κ and χ may stand before μ in the formation of nouns; as in ἀκμή, *edge*, ἄκμων, *anvil*, αἰχμή, *spear-point*, δραχμή, *drachma*.

Ἐκ here also remains unchanged, as in ἐκ-μανθάνω (cf. 72).

77. N. When γγμ or μμμ would thus arise, they are shortened to γμ or μμ; as ἐλέγχω, ἐλήλεγ-μαι (for ἐληλεγχ-μαι, ἐληλεγγ-μαι); κάμπτω, κέκαμμαι (for κεκαμπ-μαι, κεκαμμ-μαι); πέμπω, πέπεμμαι (for πεπεμπ-μαι, πεπεμμ-μαι. (See 489, 3.)

78. (N *before other Consonants.*) 1. Before a π-mute ν becomes μ; before a κ-mute it becomes nasal γ (17); before a τ-mute it is unchanged. *E.g.*

Ἐμπίπτω (for ἐν-πιπτω), συμβαίνω (for συν-βαινω), ἐμφανής (for ἐν-φανης); συγχέω (for συν-χεω), συγγενής (for συν-γενης); ἐν-τρέπω.

2. Before another liquid ν is changed to that liquid. *E.g.*

Ἐλλείπω (for ἐν-λειπω), ἐμμένω (for ἐν-μενω), συρρέω (for συν-ρεω), σύλλογος (for συν-λογος).

3. N before σ is generally dropped and the preceding vowel is lengthened (30), α to ᾱ, ε to ει, ο to ου. *E.g.*

Μέλᾱς (for μελαν-ς), εἷς (for ἑν-ς), λύουσι (for λῡο-νσι): see 210, 2; 556, 5. So λύουσα (for λῡοντ-ια, λῡον-σα), λυθεῖσα (for λυθεντ-ια, λυθεν-σα), πᾶσα (for παντ-ια, πάν-σα): see 84, 2.

79. The combinations ντ, νδ, νθ, when they occur before

σ in inflections, are always dropped, and the preceding vowel is lengthened, as above (78, 3). *E.g.*

Πᾶσι (for παντ-σι), γίγᾱς (for γιγαντς), δεικνύς (for δεικνυντς), λέουσι (for λεοντ-σι), τιθεῖσι (for τιθεντ-σι), τιθείς (for τιθεντ-ς), δούς (for δοντ-ς), σπείσω (for σπενδ-σω), πείσομαι (for πενθ-σομαι).

For nominatives in ων (for οντ-), see 209, 3 (cf. 212, 1).

80. N. N standing *alone* before σι of the dative plural is dropped without lengthening the vowel; as δαίμοσι (for δαιμον-σι).

81. N. The preposition ἐν is not changed before ρ or σ; as ἐνράπτω, ἔνσπονδος, ἐνστρέφω.

Σύν becomes συσ- before σ and a *vowel*, but συ- before σ and a *consonant* or before ζ; as σύσ-σιτος, σύ-στημα, σύ-ζυγος.

82. N. Πᾶν and πάλιν may retain ν in composition before σ or change it to σ; as πάν-σοφος or πάσσοφος, παλίν-σκιος, παλίσσυτος.

83. Most verbs in νω have σ for ν before μαι in the perfect middle (648); as φαίνω, πέφασ-μαι (for πεφαν-μαι); and the ν reappears before τ and θ, as in πέφαν-ται, πέφαν-θε. (See 489, 2; 700.)

84. (*Changes before ι.*) The following changes occur when ι (representing an original *j*) follows the final consonant of a stem.

1. Palatals (κ, γ, χ) and sometimes τ and θ with such an ι become σσ (later Attic ττ); as φυλάσσ-ω (stem φυλακ-) for φυλακ-ι-ω; ἥσσων, *worse*, for ἡκ-ι-ων (361, 2); τάσσ-ω (ταγ-), for ταγ-ι-ω (580); ταράσσ-ω (ταραχ-), for ταραχ-ι-ω; κορύσσ-ω (κορυθ-), for κορυθ-ι-ω; Κρῆσσα, for Κρητ-ια.

Thus is formed the feminine in εσσα of adjectives in εις, from a stem in ετ-, ετ-ια becoming εσσα (331, 2).

2. Ντ with this ι becomes νσ in the feminine of participles and adjectives (331, 2; 337, 1), in which ν is regularly dropped with lengthening of the preceding vowel (78, 3); as παντ-, παντ-ια, πάνσα (Thessalian and Cretan), πᾶσα; λῡοντ-, λῡοντ-ια, λυον-σα, λύουσα.

3. Δ (sometimes γ or γγ) with ι forms ζ; as φράζ-ω (φραδ-), for φραδ-ι-ω (585); κομίζ-ω (κομιδ-), for κομιδ-ι-ω; κράζ-ω (κραγ-), for κραγ-ι-ω (589); μέζων (Ion.) or μείζων (comp. of μέγας, *great*), for μεγ-ι-ων (361, 4).

4. Λ with ι forms λλ; as στέλλ-ω (στελ-), for στελ-ι-ω; ἅλλο-μαι (ἀλ-), *leap*, for ἀλ-ι-ομαι (cf. Lat. *salio*); ἄλλος, *other*, for ἀλ-ι-ος (cf. Lat. *alius*). (See 593.)

5. After αν or αρ the ι is transposed, and is then contracted with α to αι; as φαίν-ω (φαν-), for φαν-ι-ω; χαίρ-ω (χαρ-), for χαρ-ι-ω; μέλαινα (μελαν-), fem. of μέλας (326), for μελαν-ι-α.

6. After εν, ερ, ιν, ιρ, υν, or υρ, the ι disappears, and the preceding ε, ι, or υ is lengthened (ε to ει); as τείν-ω (τεν-), for τεν-ι-ω; χείρων (stem χερ-), *worse*, for χερ-ι-ων; κείρ-ω (κερ-), for κερ-ι-ω; κρίνω (κριν-), for κριν-ι-ω; οἰκτίρω (οἰκτιρ-), for οἰκτιρ-ι-ω; ἀμύνω (ἀμυν-), for ἀμυν-ι-ω; σύρω, for συρ-ι-ω. So σώτειρα (fem. of σωτήρ, *saving, saviour*, stem σωτερ-), for σωτερ-ι-α. (See 594 and 596.)

85. (*Omission of* Σ *and* ϝ.) Many forms are explained by the omission of an original spirant (*s* or ϝ), which is seen sometimes in earlier forms in Greek and sometimes in kindred languages.

86. (Σ.) At the beginning of a word, an original *s* sometimes appears as the rough breathing. *E.g.*

Ἵστημι, *place*, for σιστημι, Lat. *sisto*; ἥμισυς, *half*, cf. Lat. *semi-*; ἕζομαι, *sit* (from root ἑδ- σεδ-), Lat. *sed-eo*; ἑπτά, *seven*, Lat. *septem*.

87. N. In some words both σ and ϝ have disappeared; as ὅς, *his*, for σϝος, *suus*; ἡδύς, *sweet* (from root ἁδ- for σϝαδ-), Lat. *suavis*.

88. In some inflections, σ is dropped between two vowels.

1. Thus, in stems of nouns, εσ- and ασ- drop σ before a vowel of the ending; as γένος, *race* (stem γενεσ-), gen. γένε-ος for γενεσ-ος. (See 226.)

2. The middle endings σαι and σο often drop σ (565, 6); as λύε-σαι, λύε-αι, λύῃ or λύει (39, 3); ἐ-λύε-σο, ἐλύεο, ἐλύου; but σ is retained in such μι- forms as ἵστα-σαι and ἵστα-σο. (See also 664.)

89. In the first aorist active and middle of liquid verbs, σ is generally dropped before α or αμην; as φαίνω (φαν-), aor. ἔφην-α for ἐφανσ-α, ἐφην-άμην for ἐφανσ-αμην. So ὀκέλλω (ὀκελ-), aor. ὤκειλ-α for ὠκελσ-α; but poetic κέλλω has ἔκελσ-α. (See 672.)

90. (ϝ.) Some of the cases in which the omission of *vau* (or *digamma*) appears in inflections are these: —

1. In the augment of certain verbs; as 2 aor. εἶδον, *saw*, from root ϝιδ- (Lat. *vid-eo*), for ἐ-ϝιδον, ἐ-ιδον, εἶδον: see also the examples in 539.

2. In verbs in εω of the Second Class (574), where ευ became εϝ and finally ε; as ῥέ-ω, *flow* (stem ῥευ-, ῥεϝ-), fut. ῥεύ-σο-μαι. See also 601.

3. In certain nouns of the third declension, where final υ of the stem becomes ϝ, which is dropped; as ναῦς (ναυ-), gen. νᾱ-ός for νᾱυ-ος, νᾱϝ-ος (269); see βασιλεύς (265). See also 256.

91. The Aeolic and Doric retained ϝ long after it disappeared in Ionic and Attic. The following are a few of the many words in which its former presence is known: —

βοῦς, *ox* (Lat. *bov-is*), ἔαρ, *spring* (Lat. *ver*), δῖος, *divine* (*divus*), ἔργον, *work* (Germ. *werk*), ἐσθής, *garment* (Lat. *vestis*), ἕσπερος, *evening* (*vesper*), ἴς, *strength* (*vis*), κλῄς (Dor. κλᾱΐς), *key* (*clavis*), οἶς, *sheep* (*ovis*), οἶκος *house* (*vicus*), οἶνος, *wine* (*vinum*), σκαιός, *left* (*scaevus*).

92. (*Changes in Aspirates.*) When a smooth mute (π, κ, τ) is brought before a rough vowel (either by elision or in forming a compound), it is itself made rough. *E.g.*

Ἀφίημι (for ἀπ-ἵημι), καθαιρέω (for κατ-αἱρεω), ἀφ᾽ ὧν (for ἀπὸ ὧν), νύχθ᾽ ὅλην (for νύκτα ὅλην, 48; 71).

93. N. So in crasis (see examples in 44). Here the rough breathing may affect even a consonant not immediately preceding it; as in φροῦδος, *gone*, from πρὸ ὁδοῦ; φρουρός, *watchman* (προ-ὁρος).

94. N. The Ionic generally does not observe this principle in writing, but has (for example) ἀπ᾽ οὗ, ἀπίημι (from ἀπό and ἵημι).

95. The Greeks generally avoided two rough consonants in successive syllables. Thus

1. In reduplications (521) an initial rough mute is always made smooth. *E.g.*

Πέφῡκα (for φεφῡκα), perfect of φύω; κέχηνα (for χεχηνα), perf. of χάσκω; τέθηλα (for θεθηλα), perf. of θάλλω. So in τί-θημι (for θι-θημι), 794, 2.

2. The ending θι of the first aorist imperative passive becomes τι after θη- of the tense stem (757, 1). *E.g.*

Λύθητι (for λυθη-θι), φάνθητι (for φανθη-θι); but 2 aor. φάνη-θι (757, 2).

3. In the aorist passive ἐτέθην from τίθημι (θε-), and in ἐτύθην from θύω (θυ-) θε and θυ become τε and τυ before θην.

4. A similar change occurs in ἀμπ-έχω (for ἀμφ-εχω) and ἀμπ-ίσχω (for ἀμφ-ισχω), *clothe*, and in ἐκε-χειρίᾱ (ἔχω and χείρ), *truce*. So an initial aspirate is lost in ἔχω (stem ἐχ- for σεχ-, 539), but reappears in fut. ἕξω.

5. There is a transfer of the aspirate in a few verbs which are supposed to have had originally two rough consonants in the stem; as τρέφω (stem τρεφ- for θρεφ-), *nourish*, fut. θρέψω (662); τρέχω (τρεχ- for θρεχ-), *run*, fut. θρέξομαι; ἐτάφην, from θάπτω (ταφ- for θαφ-), *bury*; see also θρύπτω, τύφω, and stem θαπ-, in the Catalogue of Verbs. So in θρίξ (225), *hair*, gen. τριχός (stem τριχ- for θριχ-); and in ταχύς, *swift*, comparative θάσσων for θαχ-ιων (84, 1). Here

the first aspirate reappears whenever the second is lost by any euphonic change.

In some forms of these verbs both rough consonants appear; as ἐ-θρέφ-θην, θρεφ-θῆναι, τε-θράφ-θαι, τε-θάφ-θαι, ἐ-θρύφ-θην. (See 709.)

SYLLABLES.

96. A Greek word has as many syllables as it has separate vowels or diphthongs. The syllable next to the last is called the *penult* (paen-ultima, *almost last*); the one before the penult is called the *antepenult*.

97. The following rules, based on ancient tradition, are now generally observed in dividing syllables at the end of a line: —

1. Single consonants, combinations of consonants which can begin a word (which may be seen from the Lexicon), and mutes followed by μ or ν, are placed at the beginning of a syllable. Other combinations of consonants are divided. Thus, ἔ-χω, ἐ-γώ, ἐ-σπέ-ρα, νέ-κταρ, ἀ-κμή, δε-σμός, μι-κρόν, πρᾶ-γμα-τος, πρᾶσ-σω, ἐλ-πίς, ἔν-δον, ἅρ-μα-τα.

2. Compound words are divided into their original parts; but when the final vowel of a preposition has been elided in composition, the compound is sometimes divided like a simple word: thus προσ-ά-γω (from πρός and ἄγω); but πα-ρά-γω or παρ-άγω (from παρά and ἄγω).

Quantity of Syllables.

98. A syllable is long by *nature* (φύσει) when it has a long vowel or a diphthong; as in τῑμή, κτείνω.

99. 1. A syllable is long by *position* (θέσει) when its vowel is followed by two consonants or a double consonant; as in ἵσταντες, τράπεζα, ὄρτυξ.

2. The length of the *vowel* itself is not affected by position. Thus α was sounded as long in πρᾱ́σσω, πρᾶγμα, and πρᾶξις, but as short in τάσσω, τάγμα, and τάξις.

3. One or both of the consonants which make position may be in the next word; thus the second syllable in οὗτός φησιν and in κατὰ στόμα is long by position.

100. When a vowel *short by nature* is followed by a mute and a liquid, the syllable is *common* (*i.e.* it may be either long or short); as in τέκνον, ὕπνος, ὕβρις. But in Attic poetry such a syllable is generally short; in other poetry it is generally long.

101. N. A *middle* mute (β, γ, δ) before μ or ν, and generally before λ, lengthens a preceding vowel; as in ἁγνώς, βιβλίον, δόγμα.

102. N. To allow a preceding vowel to be short, the mute and the liquid must be in the same word, or in the same part of a compound. Thus ε in ἐκ is long when a liquid follows, either in composition or in the next word; as ἐκλέγω, ἐκ νεῶν (both — ◡ —).

103. The quantity of most syllables can be seen at once. Thus η and ω and all diphthongs are long by nature; ε and ο are short by nature. (See 5.)

104. When α, ι, and υ are not long by position, their quantity must generally be learned by observing the usage of poets or from the Lexicon. But it is to be remembered that

1. Every vowel arising from contraction or crasis is long; as α in γέρᾱ (for γέραα), ᾱ̈κων (for ἀέκων), and κᾱ̈ν (for καὶ ἄν).

2. The endings ας and υς are long when ν or ντ has been dropped before σ (79).

3. The accent often shows the quantity of its own vowel, or of vowels in following syllables.

Thus the circumflex on κνῖσα, *savor*, shows that ι is long and α is short; the acute on χώρᾱ, *land*, shows that α is long; on τίνες; *who?* that ι is short; the acute on βασιλείᾱ, *kingdom*, shows that the final α is long, on βασίλεια, *queen*, that final α is short. (See 106, 3; 111; 112.)

105. The quantity of the terminations of nouns and verbs will be stated below in the proper places.

ACCENT.

General Principles.

106. 1. There are three accents,

the acute (´), as λόγος, αὐτός,
the grave (`), as αὐτὸς ἔφη (115, 1),
the circumflex (῀ or ῀), as τοῦτο, τῑμῶν.

2. The acute can stand only on one of the last three syllables of a word, the circumflex only on one of the last two, and the grave only on the last.

3. The circumflex can stand only on a syllable long by *nature*.

107. 1. The Greek accent was not simply a *stress* accent (like ours), but it raised the musical *pitch* or *tone* (τόνος) of the syllable on which it fell. This appears in the terms τόνος and προσῳδία, which designated the accent, and also in ὀξύς, *sharp*, and βαρύς, *grave, flat*, which described it. (See 110, 1 and 3.) As the language declined, the musical accent gradually changed to a stress accent, which is now its only representative in Greek as in other languages.

2. The marks of accent were invented by Aristophanes of Byzantium, an Alexandrian scholar, about 200 B.C., in order to teach foreigners the correct accent in pronouncing Greek. By the ancient theory every syllable not having either the acute or the circumflex was said to have the grave accent; and the circumflex, originally formed thus ´`, was said to result from the union of an acute and a following grave.

108. N. The grave accent is written only in place of the acute in the case mentioned in 115, 1, and occasionally on the indefinite pronoun τὶς, τὶ (418).

109. N. The accent (like the breathing) stands on the second vowel of a diphthong (12); as in αἴρω, μοῦσα, τοὺς αὐτούς. But in the improper diphthongs (ᾳ, ῃ, ῳ) it stands on the first vowel even when the ι is written in the line; as in τιμῇ, ἁπλῷ, Ὠι (ᾧ), Ὠιξα (ᾦξα).

110. 1. A word is called *oxytone* (ὀξύ-τονος, *sharp-toned*) when it has the acute on the last syllable, as βασιλεύς; *paroxytone*, when it has the acute on the penult, as βασιλέως; *proparoxytone*, when it has the acute on the antepenult, as βασιλεύοντος.

2. A word is called *perispomenon* (περισπώμενον) when it has the circumflex on the last syllable, as ἐλθεῖν; *properispomenon*, when it has the circumflex on the penult, as μοῦσα.

3. A word is called *barytone* (βαρύ-τονος, *grave* or *flat-toned*) when its last syllable has no accent (107, 2). Of course, all paroxytones, proparoxytones, and properispomena are at the same time barytones.

4. When a word throws its accent as far back as possible (111), it is said to have *recessive* accent. This is especially the case with verbs (130). (See 122.).

111. The antepenult, if accented, takes the acute. But it can have no accent if the last syllable is long by nature or ends in ξ or ψ; as πέλεκυς, ἄνθρωπος, προφύλαξ.

112. An accented penult is circumflexed when it is long by nature while the last syllable is short by nature;

as μῆλον, νῆσος, ἧλιξ. Otherwise it takes the acute; as λόγος, τούτων.

113. N. Final αι and οι are counted as short in determining the accent; as ἄνθρωποι, νῆσοι: except in the optative, and in οἴκοι, *at home;* as τιμήσαι, ποιήσοι (not τίμησαι or ποίησοι).

114. N. Genitives in εως and εων from nouns in ις and υς of the third declension (251), all cases of nouns and adjectives in ως and ων of the *Attic* second declension (198), and the Ionic genitive in εω of the first (188, 3), allow the acute on the antepenult; as εὔγεως, πόλεως, Τήρεω (Τήρης). So some compound adjectives in ως; as ὑψί-κερως, *high-horned.* For the acute of ὥσπερ, οἴδε, etc., see 146.

115. 1. An oxytone changes its acute to the grave before other words in the same sentence; as τοὺς πονηροὺς ἀνθρώπους (for τούς πονηρούς ἀνθρώπους).

2. This change is not made before *enclitics* (143) nor before an elided syllable (48), nor in the interrogative τίς, τί (418). It is not made before a colon: before a comma modern usage differs, and the tradition is uncertain.

116. (*Anastrophe.*) Dissyllabic prepositions (regularly oxytone) throw the accent back on the penult in two cases. This is called *anastrophe* (ἀναστροφή, *turning back*). It occurs

1. When such a preposition follows its case; as in τούτων πέρι (for περὶ τούτων), *about these.*

This occurs in prose only with περί, but in the poets with all the dissyllabic prepositions except ἀνά, διά, ἀμφί, and ἀντί. In Homer it occurs also when a preposition follows a verb from which it is separated by *tmesis;* as ὀλέσας ἄπο, *having destroyed.*

2. When a preposition stands for itself compounded with ἐστίν; as πάρα for πάρεστιν, ἔνι for ἔνεστιν (ἐνί being poetic for ἐν). Here the poets have ἄνα (for ἀνά-στηθι), *up!*

Accent of Contracted Syllables and Elided Words.

117. A contracted syllable is accented if either of the original syllables had an accent. A contracted penult or antepenult is accented regularly (111; 112). A contracted final syllable is circumflexed; but if the original word was oxytone, the acute is retained. *E.g.*

Τιμώμενος from τῑμαόμενος, φιλεῖτε from φιλέετε, φιλοῖμεν from φιλέοιμεν, φιλούντων from φιλεόντων, τῑμῶ from τῑμάω; but βεβώς from βεβαώς.

This proceeds from the ancient principle that the circumflex comes from ´+` (107, 2), never from `+´; so that τιμάὼ gives τιμῶ, but βεβὰώς gives βεβώς.

118. N. If neither of the original syllables had an accent, the contracted form is accented without regard to the contraction; as τίμᾱ for τίμαε, εὖνοι for εὔνοοι.

Some exceptions to the rule of 117 will be noticed under the declensions. (See 203; 311.)

119. In crasis, the accent of the first word is lost and that of the second remains; as τἀγαθά for τὰ ἀγαθά, ἐγᾦδα for ἐγὼ οἶδα, κᾆτα for καὶ εἶτα; τἆλλα for τὰ ἄλλα; τἄρα for τοι ἄρα.

120. In elision, oxytone prepositions and conjunctions lose their accent with the elided vowel; other oxytones throw the accent back to the penult, but without changing the acute to the grave (115, 1). *E.g.*

Ἐπ' αὐτῷ for ἐπὶ αὐτῷ, ἀλλ' εἶπεν for ἀλλὰ εἶπεν, φήμ' ἐγώ for φημὶ ἐγώ, κάκ' ἔπη for κακὰ ἔπη.

ACCENT OF NOUNS AND ADJECTIVES.

121. 1. The place of the accent in the nominative singular of a noun (and the nominative singular *masculine* of an adjective) must generally be learned by observation. The other forms accent *the same syllable* as this nominative, if the last syllable permits (111); otherwise the following syllable. *E.g.*

Θάλασσα, θαλάσσης, θάλασσαν, θάλασσαι, θαλάσσαις; κόραξ, κόρακος, κόρακες, κοράκων; πρᾶγμα, πρᾶγματος, πρᾱγμάτων; ὀδούς, ὀδόντος, ὀδοῦσιν. So χαρίεις, χαρίεσσα, χαρίεν, gen. χαρίεντος, etc.; ἄξιος, ἀξίᾱ, ἄξιον, ἄξιοι, ἄξιαι, ἄξια.

2. The *kind* of accent is determined as usual (111; 112); as νῆσος, νήσου, νῆσον, νῆσοι, νήσοις. (See also 123; 124.)

122. N. The following nouns and adjectives have *recessive* accent (110, 4): —

(*a*) Contracted compound adjectives in οος (203, 2):

(*b*) The neuter singular and vocative singular of adjectives in ων, ον (except those in φρων, compounds of φρήν), and the neuter of comparatives in ων; as εὐδαίμων, εὔδαιμον (313); βελτίων, βέλτῑον (358); but δαΐφρων, δαΐφρον:

(*c*) Many barytone compounds in ης in all forms; as αὐτάρκης, αὔταρκες, gen. pl. αὐτάρκων; φιλαλήθης, φιλάληθες (but ἀληθής, ἀληθές); this includes vocatives like Σώκρατες, Δημόσθενες (228); so some other adjectives of the third declension (see 314):

(*d*) The vocative of syncopated nouns in ηρ (273), of compound proper names in ων, as Ἀγάμεμνον, Αὐτόμεδον (except Λακεδαῖμον), and of Ἀπόλλων, Ποσειδῶν (Hom. Ποσειδάων), σωτήρ, *saviour*, and (Hom.) δαήρ, *brother-in-law*, — voc. Ἄπολλον, Πόσειδον (Hom. Ποσείδαον), σῶτερ, δᾶερ (see 221, 2).

123. The last syllable of the genitive and dative of oxytones of the first and second declensions is circumflexed. *E.g.*

Τιμῆς, τιμῇ, τιμαῖν, τιμῶν, τιμαῖς; θεοῦ, θεῷ, θεῶν, θεοῖς.

124. In the *first* declension, ων of the genitive plural (for έων) is circumflexed (170). But the feminine of adjectives and participles in ος is spelt and accented like the masculine and neuter. *E.g.*

Δικῶν, δοξῶν (from δίκη, δόξα), πολιτῶν (from πολίτης); but ἀξίων, λεγομένων (fem. gen. plur. of ἄξιος, λεγόμενος, 302). For the genitive plural of other adjectives and participles, see 318.

125. N. The genitive and dative of the Attic second declension (198) are exceptions; as νεώς, gen. νεώ, dat. νεῴ.

126. N. Three nouns of the first declension are paroxytone in the genitive plural: ἀφύη, *anchovy*, ἀφύων; χρήστης, *usurer*, χρήστων; ἐτησίαι, *Etesian winds*, ἐτησίων.

127. Most monosyllables of the third declension accent the last syllable in the genitive and dative of all numbers: here ων and οιν are circumflexed. *E.g.*

Θής, *servant*, θητός, θητί, θητοῖν, θητῶν, θησί.

128. N. Δᾴς, *torch*, δμώς, *slave*, οὖς, *ear*, παῖς, *child*, Τρώς, *Trojan*, φῶς, *light*, and a few others, violate the last rule in the genitive dual and plural; so πᾶς, *all*, in both genitive and dative plural: as παῖς, παιδός, παιδί, παισί, but παίδων; πᾶς, παντός, παντί, πάντων, πᾶσι.

129. N. The interrogative τίς, τίνος, τίνι, etc., always accents the first syllable. So do all monosyllabic participles; as ὤν, ὄντος, ὄντι, ὄντων, οὖσι; βάς, βάντος.

ACCENT OF VERBS.

130. Verbs generally have recessive accent (110, 4); as βουλεύω, βουλεύομεν, βουλεύουσιν; παρέχω, πάρεχε; ἀποδίδωμι, ἀπόδοτε; βουλεύονται, βουλεύσαι (aor. opt. act.), but βούλευσαι (aor. imper. mid.). See 113.

131. The chief exceptions to this principle are these: —

1. The second aorist active infinitive in ειν and the second aorist middle imperative in ου are perispomena: as λαβεῖν, ἐλθεῖν, λιπεῖν, λιποῦ, λαβοῦ. For compounds like *κατά-θου*, see 133, 3.

2. These second aorist imperatives active are oxytone: εἰπέ, ἐλθέ, εὑρέ, λαβέ. So ἰδέ in the sense *behold!* But their compounds are regular; as ἄπ-ειπε.

3. Many *contracted* optatives of the *μι*-inflection regularly circumflex the penult; as ἱσταῖτο, διδοῖσθε (740).

4. The following forms accent the penult: the first aorist active infinitive, the second aorist middle infinitive (except πρίασθαι and ὄνασθαι, 798), the perfect middle and passive infinitive and participle, and all infinitives in ναι or μεν (except those in μεναι). Thus, βουλεῦσαι, γενέσθαι, λελύσθαι, λελυμένος, ἱστάναι, διδόναι, λελυκέναι, δόμεν and δόμεναι (both epic for δοῦναι).

5. The following participles are oxytone: the second aorist active; and all of the third declension in -ς, except the first aorist active. Thus, λιπών, λυθείς, διδούς, δεικνύς, λελυκώς, ἱστάς (pres.); but λύσας and στήσας (aor.).

So ἰών, present participle of εἶμι, *go*.

132. Compound verbs have recessive accent like simple verbs; as σύνειμι (from σύν and εἰμί), σύνοιδα (σύν and οἶδα), ἔξειμι (ἐξ and εἶμι), πάρ-εστε.

133. But there are these exceptions to 132:—

1. The accent cannot go further back than the augment or reduplication; as παρ-εῖχον (not πάρειχον), *I provided*, παρ-ῆν (not πάρην), *he was present*, ἀφ-ῖκται (not ἄφικται), *he has arrived*.

So when the augment falls on a long vowel or a diphthong which is not changed by it; as ὑπ-εῖκε (imperfect), *he was yielding*; but ὕπ-εικε (imperative), *yield!*

2. Compounds of δός, ἕς, θές, and σχές are paroxytone; as ἀπόδος, παράσχες (not ἄποδος, etc.).

3. Monosyllabic second aorist middle imperatives in -ου have recessive accent when compounded with a *dissyllabic* preposition; as κατά-θου, *put down*, ἀπό-δου, *sell:* otherwise they circumflex the ου (131, 1); as ἐν-θοῦ, *put in*.

134. N. Participles in their *inflection* are accented as adjectives (121), not as verbs. Thus, βουλεύων has in the neuter βουλεῦον (not βούλευον); φιλέων, φιλῶν has φιλέον (not φίλεον), φιλοῦν. (See 335.)

135. For the accent of optatives in αι and οι, see 113. Some other exceptions to 130 occur, especially in poetic forms.

PROCLITICS.

136. Some monosyllables have no accent and are closely attached to the following word. These are called proclitics (from προκλίνω, *lean forward*).

137. The proclitics are the articles ὁ, ἡ, οἱ, αἱ; the prepositions εἰς (ἐς), ἐξ (ἐκ), ἐν; the conjunctions εἰ and ὡς (so ὡς used as a preposition); and the negative οὐ (οὐκ, οὐχ).

138. *Exceptions.* 1. Οὔ takes the acute at the end of a sentence; as πῶς γὰρ οὔ; *for why not?* So when it stands alone as Οὔ, *No.*

2. Ὥς and sometimes ἐξ and εἰς take the acute when (in poetry) they follow their noun; as κακῶν ἔξ, *from evils;* θεὸς ὥς, *as a God.*

3. Ὥς is accented also when it means *thus;* as ὣς εἶπεν, *thus he spoke.* This use of ὥς is chiefly poetic; but καὶ ὥς, *even thus,* and οὐδ᾽ ὥς or μηδ᾽ ὥς, *not even thus,* sometimes occur in Attic prose.

For a proclitic before an enclitic, see 143, 4.

139. N. When ὁ is used for the relative ὅς, it is accented (as in *Od.* 2, 262); and many editors accent all articles when they are demonstrative, as *Il.* 1, 9, ὃ γὰρ βασιλῆι χολωθείς, and write ὃ μὲν . . . ὃ δέ, and οἳ μὲν . . . οἳ δέ, even in Attic Greek.

ENCLITICS.

140. An enclitic (ἐγκλίνω, *lean upon*) is a word which loses its own accent, and is pronounced as if it were part of the preceding word; as ἄνθρωποί τε (like *hóminésque* in Latin).

141. The enclitics are:—

1. The personal pronouns μοῦ, μοί, μέ; σοῦ, σοί, σέ; οὗ, οἷ, ἕ, and (in poetry) σφίσι.

To these are added the dialectic and poetic forms, μεῦ, σέο, σεῦ, τοί, τύ (accus. for σέ), ἕο, εὗ, ἕθεν, μίν, νίν, σφί, σφίν, σφέ, σφωέ, σφωΐν, σφέων, σφέας, σφάς, σφέα.

2. The indefinite pronoun τὶς, τὶ, in all its forms (except ἄττα); also the indefinite adverbs πού, ποθί, πῄ, ποί, ποθέν, ποτέ, πώ, πώς. These must be distinguished from the interrogatives τίς, ποῦ, πόθι, πῇ, ποῖ, πόθεν, πότε, πῶ, πῶς.

3. The present indicative of εἰμί, *be,* and of φημί, *say,* except the forms εἶ and φῄς. But epic ἐσσί and Ionic εἷς are enclitic.

4. The particles γέ, τέ, τοί, πέρ: the inseparable -δε in ὅδε, τούσδε, etc. (not δέ, *but*); and -θε and -χι in εἴθε and ναίχι (146). So also the poetic νύν (not νῦν), and the epic κέ (κέν), θήν, and ῥά.

142. The enclitic always loses its accent, except a dissyllabic enclitic after a paroxytone (143, 2). See examples in 143.

143. The word before the enclitic always retains its own accent, and it never changes a final acute to the grave (115, 2).

1. If this word is proparoxytone or properispomenon, it receives from the enclitic an acute on the last syllable as a second accent. Thus ἄνθρωπός τις, ἄνθρωποί τινες, δεῖξόν μοι, παῖδές τινες, οὗτός ἐστιν.

2. If it is paroxytone, it receives no additional accent (to avoid two acutes on successive syllables). Here a dissyllabic enclitic keeps its accent (to avoid three successive unaccented syllables). Thus, λόγος τις (not λόγός τις), λόγοι τινές (not λόγοι τινες), λόγων τινῶν, οὕτω φησίν (but οὗτός φησιν by 1).

3. If its last syllable is accented, it remains unchanged; as τῑμαί τε (115, 2), τῑμῶν γε, σοφός τις, σοφοί τινες, σοφῶν τινες.

4. A proclitic before an enclitic receives an acute; as εἴ τις, εἴ φησιν οὗτος.

144. Enclitics retain their accent whenever special emphasis falls upon them: this occurs

1. When they begin a sentence or clause; or when pronouns express antithesis, as οὐ τἄρα Τρωσὶν ἀλλὰ σοὶ μαχούμεθα, *we shall fight then not with Trojans but with you*, S. *Ph.* 1253.

2. When the preceding syllable is elided; as in πόλλ' ἐστίν (120) for πολλά ἐστιν.

3. The personal pronouns generally retain their accent after an *accented* preposition; here ἐμοῦ, ἐμοί, and ἐμέ are used (except in πρός με).

4. The personal pronouns of the third person are not enclitic when they are direct reflexives (988); σφίσι never in Attic prose.

5. Ἐστί at the beginning of a sentence, and when it signifies *existence* or *possibility*, becomes ἔστι; so after οὐκ, μή, εἰ, the adverb ὡς, καί, ἀλλ' or ἀλλά, and τοῦτ' or τοῦτο.

145. When several enclitics occur in succession, each takes an acute from the following, the last remaining without accent; as εἴ τίς τί σοί φησιν, *if any one is saying anything to you.*

146. When an enclitic forms the last part of a compound word, the compound is accented as if the enclitic were a separate word. Thus, οὗτινος, ᾧτινι, ὧντινων, ὥσπερ, ὥστε, οἶδε, τούσδε, εἴτε, οὔτε, μήτε, are only apparent exceptions to 106; 111; 112.

DIALECTIC CHANGES.

147. The Ionic dialect is marked by the use of η where the Attic has ᾱ; and the Doric and Aeolic by the use of ᾱ where the Attic has η.

Thus, Ionic γενεή for γενεά, ἰήσομαι for ἰάσομαι (from ἰάομαι, 635); Doric τιμᾱσῶ for τιμήσω (from τιμάω); Aeolic and Doric λᾱ́θᾱ for λήθη. But an Attic ᾱ caused by contraction (as in τίμᾱ from τίμαε), or an Attic η lengthened from ε (as in φιλήσω from φιλέω, 635), is never thus changed.

148. The Ionic often has ει, ου, for Attic ε, ο; and ηϊ for Attic ει in nouns and adjectives in ειος, ειον; as ξεῖνος for ξένος, μοῦνος for μόνος; βασιλήϊος for βασίλειος.

149. The Ionic does not avoid successive vowels to the same extent as the Attic; and it therefore very often omits contraction (36). It contracts εο and εου into ευ (especially in Herodotus); as ποιεῦμεν, ποιεῦσι (from ποιέομεν, ποιέουσι), for Attic ποιοῦμεν, ποιοῦσι. Herodotus does not use ν *movable* (56). See also 94 and 785, 1.

PUNCTUATION MARKS.

150. 1. The Greek uses the *comma* (,) and the *period* (.) like the English. It has also a *colon*, a point above the line (·), which is equivalent to the English colon and semicolon; as οὐκ ἔσθ᾽ ὅ γ᾽ εἶπον· οὐ γὰρ ὧδ᾽ ἄφρων ἔφυν, *it is not what I said; for I am not so foolish.*

2. The mark of interrogation (;) is the same as the English semicolon; as πότε ἦλθεν; *when did he come?*

PART II.

INFLECTION.

151. INFLECTION is a change in the form of a word, made to express its relation to other words. It includes the *declension* of nouns, adjectives, and pronouns, and the *conjugation* of verbs.

152. Every inflected word has a fundamental part, which is called the *stem*. To this are appended various letters or syllables, to form cases, tenses, persons, numbers, etc.

153. Most words contain a still more primitive element than the stem, which is called the *root*. Thus, the stem of the verb *τῑμάω*, *honor*, is *τῑμα-*, and that of the noun *τῑμή*, is *τῑμᾱ-*, that of *τίσις*, *payment*, is *τισι-*, that of *τίμιος*, *held in honor*, is *τῑμιο-*, that of *τίμημα* (*τῑμήματος*), *valuation*, is *τῑμηματ-*; but all these stems are developed from one root, *τι-*, which is seen pure in the verb *τί-ω*, *honor*. In *τίω*, therefore, the verb stem and the root are the same.

154. The stem itself may be modified and assume various forms in different parts of a noun or verb. Thus the same verb stem may in different tense stems appear as *λιπ-*, *λειπ-*, and *λοιπ-* (see 459). So the same noun stem may appear as *τῑμᾱ-*, *τῑμᾰ-*, and *τῑμη-* (168).

155. There are three *numbers;* the singular, the dual, and the plural. The singular denotes one object, the plural more than one. The dual is sometimes used to denote two objects, but even here the plural is more common.

156. There are three *genders*; the masculine, the feminine, and the neuter.

157. N. The *grammatical* gender in Greek is very often different from the *natural* gender. Especially many names of things are masculine or feminine. A Greek noun is called masculine, feminine, or neuter, when it requires an adjective or article to take the form adapted to either of these genders, and the adjective or article is then said to have the gender of the corresponding noun; thus ὁ εὐρὺς ποταμός, *the broad river* (masc.), ἡ καλὴ οἰκίᾱ, *the beautiful house* (fem.), τοῦτο τὸ πρᾶγμα, *this thing* (neut.).

The gender of a noun is often indicated by prefixing the article (386); as (ὁ) ἀνήρ, *man*; (ἡ) γυνή, *woman*; (τὸ) πρᾶγμα, *thing*.

158. Nouns which may be either masculine or feminine are said to be of the *common* gender: as (ὁ, ἡ) θεός, *God* or *Goddess*. Names of animals which include both sexes, but have only one grammatical gender, are called *epicene* (ἐπίκοινος); as ὁ ἀετός, *the eagle*; ἡ ἀλώπηξ, *the fox*; both including males and females.

159. The gender must often be learned by observation. But

(1) Names of males are generally masculine, and names of females feminine.

(2) Most names of *rivers*, *winds*, and *months* are masculine; and most names of *countries*, *towns*, *trees*, and *islands* are feminine.

(3) Most nouns denoting *qualities* or *conditions* are feminine; as ἀρετή, *virtue*, ἐλπίς, *hope*.

(4) Diminutive nouns are neuter; as παιδίον, *child*; γύναιον, *old woman* (literally, *little woman*).

Other rules are given under the declensions (see 168; 189; 281–284).

160. There are five *cases*; the nominative, genitive, dative, accusative, and vocative.

161. 1. The nominative and vocative plural are always alike.

2. In neuters, the nominative, accusative, and vocative are alike in all numbers; in the plural these end in ᾰ.

3. The nominative, accusative, and vocative dual are always alike; and the genitive and dative dual are always alike.

162. The cases of nouns have in general the same meaning as the corresponding cases in Latin; as Nom. *a man* (as subject),

Gen. *of a man*, Dat. *to* or *for a man*, Accus. *a man* (as object), Voc. *O man*. The chief functions of the Latin ablative are divided between the Greek genitive and dative. (See 1042.)

163. All the cases except the nominative and vocative are called *oblique* cases.

NOUNS.

164. There are three declensions of nouns, in which also all adjectives and participles are included.

165. These correspond in general to the first three declensions in Latin. The first is sometimes called the *A declension* (with stems in ᾱ), and the second the *O declension* (with stems in ο). These two together are sometimes called the *Vowel declension*, as opposed to the third or *Consonant declension* (206).

The principles which are common to adjectives, participles, and substantives are given under the three declensions of nouns.

166. N. The name *noun* (ὄνομα), according to ancient usage, includes both substantives and adjectives. But by modern custom *noun* is generally used in grammatical language as synonymous with *substantive*, and it is so used in the present work.

167. CASE-ENDINGS OF NOUNS.

	Vowel Declension.		Consonant Declension.	
SING.	*Masc. and Fem.*	*Neuter.*	*Masc. and Fem.*	*Neuter.*
Nom.	ς or none	ν	ς or none	none
Gen.	ς or ιο		ος	
Dat.	ι		ι	
Acc.	ν		ν or ᾰ	none
Voc.	none	ν	none or like Nom.	none
DUAL.				
N. A. V.	none		ε	
G. D.	ιν		οιν	
PLUR.				
N. V.	ι	ᾰ	ες	ᾰ
Gen.	ων		ων	
Dat.	ισι (ις)		σι, σσι, εσσι	
Acc.	νς (ᾱς)	ᾰ	νς, ᾰς	ᾰ

The relations of some of these endings to the terminations actually in use will be explained under the different declensions. The agreement of the two classes in many points is striking.

FIRST DECLENSION.

168. Stems of the first declension end originally in ᾱ. This is often modified into η in the singular, and it becomes ᾰ in the plural. The nominative singular of feminines ends in α or η; that of masculines ends in ᾱς or ης. There are no neuters.

169. The following table shows how the final α or η of the stem unites with the case endings (167), when any are added, to form the actual terminations:—

	SINGULAR.				PLURAL.
	Feminine.		*Masculine.*		*Masc. and Fem.*
Nom.	ᾱ or ᾰ	η	ᾱ-ς	η-ς	α-ι
Gen.	ᾱ-ς or η-ς	η-ς		α-ιο (Hom. ᾱ-ο)	ῶν (for έ-ων)
Dat.	ᾱ-ι or η-ι	η-ι	ᾱ-ι	η-ι	α-ισι or α-ις
Acc.	ᾱ-ν or ᾰ-ν	η-ν	ᾱ-ν	η-ν	ᾱς (for α-νς)
Voc.	ᾱ or ᾰ	η	ᾱ	ᾰ or η	α-ι

DUAL.

	Masc. and Fem.
N. A. V.	ᾱ
G. D.	αιν

170. N. In the genitive singular of masculines Homeric ᾱο comes from α-ιο (169); but Attic ου probably follows the analogy of ου for οο in the second declension (191). Circumflexed ῶν in the genitive plural is contracted from Ionic έων (188, 5). The stem in ᾱ (or ᾰ) may thus be seen in all cases of *οἰκίᾱ* and *χώρᾱ*, and (with the change of ᾱ to η in the singular) also in the other paradigms (except in ου of the genitive). The forms ending in α and η have no case-endings.

FEMININES.

171. The nouns (ἡ) *χώρᾱ, land,* (ἡ) *τῑμή, honor,* (ἡ) *οἰκίᾱ, house,* (ἡ) Μοῦσα, *Muse,* are thus declined:—

Stem.	(χωρᾱ-)		(τῑμᾱ-)	(οἰκιᾱ-)	(μουσᾱ-)
		SINGULAR.			
Nom.	χώρᾱ	*a land*	τῑμή	οἰκίᾱ	Μοῦσα
Gen.	χώρᾱς	*of a land*	τῑμῆς	οἰκίᾱς	Μούσης
Dat.	χώρᾳ	*to a land*	τῑμῇ	οἰκίᾳ	Μούσῃ
Acc.	χώρᾱν	*a land*	τῑμήν	οἰκίᾱν	Μοῦσαν
Voc.	χώρᾱ	*O land*	τῑμή	οἰκίᾱ	Μοῦσα

		DUAL.			
N. A. V.	χώρᾱ	*two lands*	τῑμά	οἰκίᾱ	Μούσᾱ
G. D.	χώραιν	*of* or *to two lands*	τῑμαῖν	οἰκίαιν	Μούσαιν
		PLURAL.			
Nom.	χῶραι	*lands*	τῑμαί	οἰκίαι	Μοῦσαι
Gen.	χωρῶν	*of lands*	τῑμῶν	οἰκιῶν	Μουσῶν
Dat.	χώραις	*to lands*	τῑμαῖς	οἰκίαις	Μούσαις
Acc.	χώρᾱς	*lands*	τῑμάς	οἰκίᾱς	Μούσᾱς
Voc.	χῶραι	*O lands*	τῑμαί	οἰκίαι	Μοῦσαι

172. The following show varieties of quantity and accent: —

θάλασσα, sea, θαλάσσης, θαλάσσῃ, θάλασσαν; Pl. *θάλασσαι, θαλασσῶν, θαλάσσαις, θαλάσσᾱς*.

γέφῡρα, bridge, γεφῡ́ρᾱς, γεφῡ́ρᾳ, γέφῡραν; Pl. *γέφῡραι*, etc.

σκιά, shadow, σκιᾶς, σκιᾷ, σκιάν; Pl. *σκιαί, σκιῶν, σκιαῖς*, etc.

γνώμη, opinion, γνώμης, γνώμῃ, γνώμην; Pl. *γνῶμαι, γνωμῶν*, etc.

πεῖρα, attempt, πείρᾱς, πείρᾳ, πεῖραν; Pl. *πεῖραι, πειρῶν*, etc.

173. The stem generally retains ᾱ through the singular after ε, ι, or ρ, but changes ᾱ to η after other letters. See *οἰκίᾱ, χώρᾱ*, and *τῑμή* in 171.

174. But nouns having σ, λλ, or a double consonant (18) before final α of the stem, and some others, have ᾰ in the nominative, accusative, and vocative singular, and η in the genitive and dative, like Μοῦσα.

Thus *ἅμαξα, wagon; δίψα, thirst; ῥίζα, root; ἅμιλλα, contest; θάλασσα* (with later Attic *θάλαττα*), *sea*. So *μέριμνα, care; δέσποινα, mistress; λέαινα, lioness; τρίαινα, trident;* also *τόλμα, daring; δίαιτα, living; ἄκανθα, thorn; εὔθῡνα, scrutiny.*

175. The following have ᾰ in the nominative, accusative, and vocative, and ᾱ in the genitive and dative, singular (after ε, ι, or ρ): —

(*a*) Most ending in ρα preceded by a diphthong or by ῡ; as *μοῖρα, γέφῡρα*.

(*b*) Most abstract nouns formed from adjectives in ης or οος; as *ἀλήθεια, truth* (*ἀληθής, true*), *εὔνοια, kindness* (*εὔνοος, kind*). (But the Attic poets sometimes have *ἀληθείᾱ, εὐνοίᾱ*, etc.)

(*c*) Nouns in εια and τρια designating females; as *βασίλεια, queen, ψάλτρια, female harper* (but *βασιλείᾱ, kingdom*). So *μυῖα, fly*, gen. *μυίᾱς*.

For feminine adjectives in ᾰ, see 318.

176. (*Exceptions.*) Δέρη, *neck*, and κόρη, *girl* (originally δέρϝη, κόρϝη), have η after ρ (173). Ἕρση, *dew*, and κόρση (new Attic κόρρη), *temple*, have η after σ (174). Some proper names have ᾰ irregularly; as Λήδᾱ, *Leda*, gen. Λήδᾱς. Both οᾱ and οη are allowed; as βοή, *cry*, στοᾱ́, *porch*.

177. N. It will be seen that α of the nominative singular is always short when the genitive has ης, and generally long when the genitive has ᾱς.

178. N. Αν of the accusative singular and α of the vocative singular agree in quantity with α of the nominative. The quantity of all other vowels of the terminations may be seen from the table in 169.

Most nouns in ᾰ have *recessive* accent (110, 4).

MASCULINES.

179. The nouns (ὁ) ταμίᾱς, *steward*, (ὁ) πολίτης, *citizen*, and (ὁ) κριτής, *judge*, are thus declined: —

Stem.	(ταμιᾱ-)	(πολῑτᾱ-)	(κριτᾱ-)
		SINGULAR.	
Nom.	ταμίᾱς	πολίτης	κριτής
Gen.	ταμίου	πολίτου	κριτοῦ
Dat.	ταμίᾳ	πολίτῃ	κριτῇ
Acc.	ταμίᾱν	πολίτην	κριτήν
Voc.	ταμίᾱ	πολῖτα	κριτά
		DUAL.	
N.A.V.	ταμίᾱ	πολίτᾱ	κριτά
G.D.	ταμίαιν	πολίταιν	κριταῖν
		PLURAL.	
Nom.	ταμίαι	πολῖται	κριταί
Gen.	ταμιῶν	πολῑτῶν	κριτῶν
Dat.	ταμίαις	πολίταις	κριταῖς
Acc.	ταμίᾱς	πολίτᾱς	κριτάς
Voc.	ταμίαι	πολῖται	κριταί

180. Thus may be declined νεᾱνίᾱς, *youth*, στρατιώτης, *soldier*, ποιητής, *poet*.

181. The ᾱ of the stem is here retained in the singular after ε, ι, or ρ; otherwise it is changed to η: see the paradigms. For irregular ου in the genitive singular, see 170.

182. The following nouns in ης have ᾰ in the vocative singular (like πολίτης): those in της; national names, like Πέρσης, *Persian*, voc. Πέρσᾰ; and compounds in ης, like γεω-μέτρης, *geometer*, voc. γεωμέτρᾰ. Δεσπότης, *master*, has voc. δέσποτᾰ. Other nouns in ης of this declension have the vocative in η; as Κρονίδης, *son of Cronos*, Κρονίδη.

CONTRACTS OF THE FIRST DECLENSION.

183. Most nouns in αᾱ, εᾱ, and εᾱς are contracted (35) in all their cases.

184. Μνάᾱ, μνᾶ, *mina*, σῡκέᾱ, σῡκῆ, *fig-tree*, and Ἑρμέᾱς, Ἑρμῆς, *Hermes*, are thus declined: —

Stem.	(μνᾱ- for μναᾱ-)		(σῡκᾱ- for συκεᾱ-)		(Ἑρμᾱ- for Ἑρμεᾱ-)	
			SINGULAR.			
Nom.	(μνάᾱ)	**μνᾶ**	(σῡκέᾱ)	**σῡκῆ**	(Ἑρμέᾱς)	**Ἑρμῆς**
Gen.	(μνάᾱς)	**μνᾶς**	(σῡκέᾱς)	**σῡκῆς**	(Ἑρμέου)	**Ἑρμοῦ**
Dat.	(μνάᾳ)	**μνᾷ**	(σῡκέᾳ)	**σῡκῇ**	(Ἑρμέᾳ)	**Ἑρμῇ**
Acc.	(μνάᾱν)	**μνᾶν**	(σῡκέᾱν)	**σῡκῆν**	(Ἑρμέᾱν)	**Ἑρμῆν**
Voc.	(μνάᾱ)	**μνᾶ**	(σῡκέᾱ)	**σῡκῆ**	(Ἑρμέᾱ)	**Ἑρμῆ**
			DUAL.			
N. A. V.	(μνάᾱ)	**μνᾶ**	(σῡκέᾱ)	**σῡκᾶ**	(Ἑρμέᾱ)	**Ἑρμᾶ**
G. D.	(μνάαιν)	**μναῖν**	(σῡκέαιν)	**σῡκαῖν**	(Ἑρμέαιν)	**Ἑρμαῖν**
			PLURAL.			
N. V.	(μνάαι)	**μναῖ**	(σῡκέαι)	**σῡκαῖ**	(Ἑρμέαι)	**Ἑρμαῖ**
Gen.	(μναῶν)	**μνῶν**	(σῡκεῶν)	**σῡκῶν**	(Ἑρμεῶν)	**Ἑρμῶν**
Dat.	(μνάαις)	**μναῖς**	(σῡκέαις)	**σῡκαῖς**	(Ἑρμέαις)	**Ἑρμαῖς**
Acc.	(μνάᾱς)	**μνᾶς**	(σῡκέᾱς)	**σῡκᾶς**	(Ἑρμέᾱς)	**Ἑρμᾶς**

185. So γῆ, *earth* (from an uncontracted form γε-ᾱ or γα-ᾱ), in the singular: γῆ, γῆς, γῇ, γῆν, γῆ (Doric γᾶ, γᾶς, etc.).

186. N. Βορέᾱς, *North wind*, which appears uncontracted in Attic, has also a contracted form Βορρᾶς (with irregular ρρ), gen. Βορρᾶ (of Doric form), dat. Βορρᾷ, acc. Βορρᾶν, voc. Βορρᾶ.

187. N. For εα contracted to ᾱ in the dual and the accusative plural, see 39, 1. For contract adjectives (feminines) of this class, see 310.

DIALECTS OF THE FIRST DECLENSION.

188. 1. The Ionic has η for ᾱ throughout the singular, even after ε, ι, or ρ; as γενέη, χώρη, ταμίης. But Homer has θεά, *God-*

dess. The Doric and Aeolic have ᾱ unchanged in the singular. The Ionic generally uses uncontracted forms of contract nouns and adjectives.

2. *Nom. Sing.* Hom. sometimes ᾰ for ης; as ἱππότα for ἱππότης, *horseman*, sometimes with recessive accent, as μητίετα, *counsellor*. (Compare Latin *poeta* = ποιητής.)

3. *Gen. Sing.* For ου Homer has the original form ᾱο, as Ἀτρεΐδᾱο; sometimes ω (for εο) after vowels, as Βορέω (from Βορέας). Hom. and Hdt. have Ionic εω (always one syllable in Hom.), as Ἀτρεΐδεω (114), Τήρεω (gen. of Τήρης); and εω occurs in proper names in older Attic. The Doric has ᾱ for ᾱο, as Ἀτρεΐδᾱ.

4. *Acc. Sing.* Hdt. sometimes forms an acc. in εα (for ην) from nouns in -ης, as in the third declension, as δεσπότεα (for δεσπότην) from δεσπότης, *master* (179): so Ξέρξης, acc. Ξέρξεα or Ξέρξην.

5. *Gen. Pl.* Hom. ά́ων, the original form, as κλισιάων, *of tents;* sometimes ῶν (170). Hom. and Hdt. have Ionic έων (one syllable in Hom.), as πυλέων, *of gates*. Doric ᾶν for ά́ων, also in dramatic chorus.

6. *Dat. Pl.* Poetic αισι (also Aeolic and old Attic form); Ionic ῃσι (Hom., Hdt., even oldest Attic), Hom. also ῃς (rarely αις).

7. *Acc. Pl.* Lesbian Aeolic αις for ᾱς.

SECOND DECLENSION.

189. Stems of the second declension end in ο, which is sometimes modified to ω. The nominative singular regularly ends in ος or ον (gen. ου). Nouns in ος are masculine, rarely feminine; those in ον are neuter.

190. The following table shows how the terminations of nouns in ος and ον are formed by the final ο of the stem (with its modifications) and the case-endings:—

SINGULAR.			DUAL.		PLURAL.		
	Masc. & Fem.	*Neuter.*	*Masc., Fem., & Neuter.*			*Masc. & Fem.*	*Neuter.*
N.	ο-ς	ο-ν			N.	ο-ι	ᾰ
G.	ου (for ο-ο)		N. A. V.	ω (for ο)	G.	ων	
D.	ῳ (for ο-ι)		G. D.	ο-ιν	D.	ο-ισι or ο-ις	
A.	ο-ν				A.	ους (for ο-νς)	ᾰ
V.	ε	ο-ν			V.	ο-ι	ᾰ

191. N. In the genitive singular the Homeric ο-ιο becomes ο-ο and then ου. In the dative singular and the nominative etc. dual, ο becomes ω. Ε takes the place of ο in the vocative singular of nouns in ος, and ᾰ takes the place of ο in the nominative etc. of neuters. There being no genitive plural in **οων**, **ων** is not accented as a contracted syllable (**λόγων**, not **λογῶν**).

192. The nouns (ὁ) λόγος, *word*, (ἡ) νῆσος, *island*, (ὁ, ἡ) ἄνθρωπος, *man* or *human being*, (ἡ) ὁδός, *road*, (τὸ) δῶρον, *gift*, are thus declined: —

Stem.	(λογο-)		(νησο-)	(ἀνθρωπο-)	(ὁδο-)	(δωρο-)
			SINGULAR.			
Nom.	**λόγος**	*a word*	**νῆσος**	**ἄνθρωπος**	**ὁδός**	**δῶρον**
Gen.	**λόγου**	*of a word*	**νήσου**	**ἀνθρώπου**	**ὁδοῦ**	**δώρου**
Dat.	**λόγῳ**	*to a word*	**νήσῳ**	**ἀνθρώπῳ**	**ὁδῷ**	**δώρῳ**
Acc.	**λόγον**	*a word*	**νῆσον**	**ἄνθρωπον**	**ὁδόν**	**δῶρον**
Voc.	**λόγε**	*O word*	**νῆσε**	**ἄνθρωπε**	**ὁδέ**	**δῶρον**
			DUAL.			
N. A. V	**λόγω**	*two words*	**νήσω**	**ἀνθρώπω**	**ὁδώ**	**δώρω**
G. D.	**λόγοιν**	*of* or *to two words*	**νήσοιν**	**ἀνθρώποιν**	**ὁδοῖν**	**δώροιν**
			PLURAL.			
Nom.	**λόγοι**	*words*	**νῆσοι**	**ἄνθρωποι**	**ὁδοί**	**δῶρα**
Gen.	**λόγων**	*of words*	**νήσων**	**ἀνθρώπων**	**ὁδῶν**	**δώρων**
Dat.	**λόγοις**	*to words*	**νήσοις**	**ἀνθρώποις**	**ὁδοῖς**	**δώροις**
Acc.	**λόγους**	*words*	**νήσους**	**ἀνθρώπους**	**ὁδούς**	**δῶρα**
Voc.	**λόγοι**	*O words*	**νῆσοι**	**ἄνθρωποι**	**ὁδοί**	**δῶρα**

193. Thus may be declined **νόμος**, *law*, **κίνδῡνος**, *danger*, **ποταμός**, *river*, **βίος**, *life*, **θάνατος**, *death*, **ταῦρος**, *bull*, **σῦκον**, *fig*, **ἱμάτιον**, *outer garment*.

194. The chief feminine nouns of the second declension are the following: —

1. *βάσανος*, *touch-stone*, *βίβλος*, *book*, *γέρανος*, *crane*, *γνάθος*, *jaw*, *δοκός*, *beam*, *δρόσος*, *dew*, *κάμῑνος*, *oven*, *κάρδοπος*, *kneading-trough*, *κιβωτός*, *chest*, *νόσος*, *disease*, *πλίνθος*, *brick*, *ῥάβδος*, *rod*, *σορός*, *coffin*, *σποδός*, *ashes*, *τάφρος*, *ditch*, *ψάμμος*, *sand*, *ψῆφος*, *pebble;* with **ὁδός** and **κέλευθος**, *way*, **ἁμαξιτός**, *carriage-road*, **ἀτραπός**, *path*.

2. Names of *countries*, *towns*, *trees*, and *islands*, which are regularly feminine (159, 2): so **ἤπειρος**, *mainland*, and **νῆσος**, *island*.

195. The nominative in **ος** is sometimes used for the vocative in **ε**; as **ὦ φίλος**. **Θεός**, *God*, has always **θεός** as vocative.

ATTIC SECOND DECLENSION.

196. A few masculine and feminine nouns of this declension have stems in **ω**, which appears in all the cases. This is called the *Attic declension*, though it is not confined to Attic Greek. The noun (ὁ) νεώς, *temple*, is thus declined:—

SINGULAR.		DUAL.		PLURAL.	
Nom.	νεώς			Nom.	νεῴ
Gen.	νεώ	N. A. V.	νεώ	Gen.	νεών
Dat.	νεῴ	G. D.	νεῴν	Dat.	νεῴς
Acc.	νεών			Acc.	νεώς
Voc.	νεώς			Voc.	νεῴ

197. N. There are no neuter nouns of the Attic declension in good use. But the corresponding adjectives, as ἵλεως, *propitious*, εὔγεως, *fertile*, have neuters in ων, as ἵλεων, εὔγεων. (See 305.)

198. N. The accent of these nouns is irregular, and that of the genitive and dative is doubtful. (See 114; 125.)

199. N. Some nouns of this class may have ω in the accusative singular; as λαγώς, accus. λαγών or λαγώ. So Ἄθως, τὸν Ἄθων or Ἄθω; Κῶς, τὴν Κῶν or Κῶ; and Κέως, Τέως, Μίνως. Ἕως, *dawn*, has regularly τὴν Ἕω.

200. N. Most nouns of the Attic declension have older forms in ᾱος or ηος, from which they are probably derived by exchange of quantity (33); as Hom. λᾱός, *people*, Att. λεώς; Dor. νᾱός, Ion. νηός, Att. νεώς; Hom. Μενέλᾱος, Att. Μενέλεως. But some come by contraction; as λαγώς, *hare*, from λαγωός. In words like Μενέλεως, the original accent is retained (114).

CONTRACT NOUNS OF THE SECOND DECLENSION.

201. 1. From stems in οο- and εο- are formed contract nouns in οος and εον.

For contract adjectives in εος, εᾱ, εον, and οος, οᾱ, οον, see 310.

2. Νόος, νοῦς, *mind*, and ὀστέον, ὀστοῦν, *bone*, are thus declined:—

SINGULAR.			DUAL.			PLURAL.		
Nom.	(νόος)	νοῦς				Nom.	(νόοι)	νοῖ
Gen.	(νόου)	νοῦ	N. A. V.	(νόω)	νώ	Gen.	(νόων)	νῶν
Dat.	(νόῳ)	νῷ	G. D.	(νόοιν)	νοῖν	Dat.	(νόοις)	νοῖς
Acc.	(νόον)	νοῦν				Acc.	(νόους)	νοῦς
Voc.	(νόε)	νοῦ				Voc.	(νόοι)	νοῖ
N. A. V.	(ὀστέον)	ὀστοῦν	N. A. V.	(ὀστέω)	ὀστώ	N. A. V.	(ὀστέα)	ὀστᾶ
Gen.	(ὀστέου)	ὀστοῦ	G. D.	(ὀστέοιν)	ὀστοῖν	Gen.	(ὀστέων)	ὀστῶν
Dat.	(ὀστέῳ)	ὀστῷ				Dat.	(ὀστέοις)	ὀστοῖς

202. So may be declined (πλόος) πλοῦς, *voyage*, (ῥόος) ῥοῦς, *stream*, (κάνεον) κανοῦν, *basket* (accented like adjectives in εος, 311).

203. The accent of some of these forms is irregular: —

1. The dual contracts έω and όω into ώ (not ῶ).

2. Compounds in οος accent all forms like the *contracted* nominative singular; as περίπλοος, περίπλους, *sailing round*, gen. περιπλόου, περίπλου, etc.

3. For εα contracted to ᾱ in the plural, see 39, 1.

DIALECTS OF THE SECOND DECLENSION.

204. 1. *Gen. Sing.* Hom. οιο and ου, Aeolic and Doric ω (for οο); as θεοῖο, μεγάλω.

2. *Gen. and Dat. Dual.* Hom. οιιν for οιν; as ἵπποιιν.

3. *Dat. Plur.* Ionic and poetic οισι; as ἵπποισι; also Aeolic and old Attic, found occasionally even in prose.

4. *Acc. Plur.* Doric ως or ος for ους; as νόμως, τὼς λύκος; Lesbian Aeolic οις.

5. The Ionic generally omits contraction.

THIRD DECLENSION.

205. This declension includes all nouns not belonging to either the first or the second. Its genitive singular ends in ος (sometimes ως).

206. N. This is often called the *Consonant Declension* (165), because the stem here generally ends in a consonant. Some stems, however, end in a close vowel (ι or υ), some in a diphthong, and a few in ο or ω.

207. The stem of a noun of the third declension cannot always be determined by the nominative singular; but it is generally found by dropping ος of the genitive. The cases are formed by adding the case-endings (167) to the stem.

208. 1. For final ως in the genitive singular of nouns in ις, υς, υ, ευς, and of ναῦς, *ship*, see 249; 265; 269.

2. For ᾱ and ᾱς in the accusative singular and plural of nouns in ευς, see 265.

3. The contracted accusative plural generally has εις for εάς irregularly, to conform to the contracted nominative in εις for εες. (See 313.) So ους in the accusative plural of comparatives in ίων (358).

4. The original νς of the accusative plural is seen in ἰχθῦς (for ἰχθυ-νς) from ἰχθύς (259), and the Ionic πολῖς (for πολι-νς) from πόλις (255).

FORMATION OF CASES.

Nominative Singular.

209. The numerous forms of the nominative singular of this declension must be learned partly by practice. The following are the general principles on which the nominative is formed from the stem.

1. Masculine and feminine stems, except those in ν, ρ, σ, and οντ (2 and 3), add ς, and make the needful euphonic changes. *E.g.*

Φύλαξ, *guard*, **φύλακ-ος**; **γύψ**, *vulture*, **γῡπ-ός**; **φλέψ**, *vein*, **φλεβ-ός** (74); **ἐλπίς** (for **ἐλπιδς**), *hope*, **ἐλπίδ-ος**; **χάρις**, *grace*, **χάριτ-ος**; **ὄρνῑς**, *bird*, **ὄρνῑθ-ος**; **νύξ**, *night*, **νυκτ-ός**; **μάστιξ**, *scourge*, **μάστῑγ-ος**; **σάλπιγξ**, *trumpet*, **σάλπιγγ-ος**. So **Αἴᾱς**, *Ajax*, **Αἴαντ-ος** (79); **λύσᾱς**, **λύσαντ-ος**; **πᾶς**, **παντ-ός**; **τιθείς**, **τιθέντ-ος**; **χαρίεις**, **χαρίεντ-ος**; **δεικνύς**, **δεικνύντ-ος**. (The *neuters* of the last five words, **λῦσαν**, **πᾶν**, **τιθέν**, **χαρίεν**, and **δεικνύν**, are given under 4, below.)

2. Masculine and feminine stems in ν, ρ, and σ merely lengthen the last vowel, if it is short. *E.g.*

Αἰών, *age*, **αἰῶν-ος**; **δαίμων**, *divinity*, **δαίμον-ος**; **λιμήν**, *harbor*, **λιμέν-ος**; **θήρ**, *beast*, **θηρ-ός**; **ἀήρ**, *air*, **ἀέρ-ος**; **Σωκράτης** (**Σωκρατεσ-**), *Socrates*.

3. Masculine stems in οντ drop τ, and lengthen ο to ω. *E.g.*

Λέων, *lion*, **λέοντ-ος**; **λέγων**, *speaking*, **λέγοντ-ος**; **ὤν**, *being*, **ὄντ-ος**.

4. In neuters, the nominative singular is generally the same as the stem. Final τ of the stem is dropped (25). *E.g.*

Σῶμα, *body*, **σώματ-ος**; **μέλᾰν** (neuter of **μέλᾱς**), *black*, **μέλᾰν-ος**; **λῦσαν** (neuter of **λύσᾱς**), *having loosed*, **λύσαντ-ος**; **πᾶν**, *all*, **παντ-ός**; **τιθέν**, *placing*, **τιθέντ-ος**; **χαρίεν**, *graceful*, **χαρίεντ-ος**; **διδόν**, *giving*, **διδόντος**; **λέγον**, *saying*, **λέγοντ-ος**; **δεικνύν**, *showing*, **δεικνύντ-ος**. (For the *masculine* nominatives of these adjectives and participles, see 1, above.)

210. (*Exceptions* to 209, 1–3.) 1. In **πούς**, *foot*, **ποδ-ός**, οδς becomes ους. **Δάμαρ**, *wife*, **δάμαρτ-ος**, does not add ς. Change in quantity occurs in **ἀλώπηξ**, *fox*, **ἀλώπεκ-ος**, **κῆρυξ**, *herald*, **κήρῡκ-ος**, and **Φοῖνιξ**, **Φοίνῑκ-ος**.

2. Stems in ῑν- add ς and have ῑς (78, 3) in the nominative; as **ῥίς**, *nose*, **ῥῑν-ός**. These also add ς: **κτείς**, *comb*, **κτεν-ός** (78, 3); **εἷς**, *one*, **ἑν-ός**; and the adjectives **μέλᾱς**, *black*, **μέλαν-ος**, and **τάλᾱς**, *wretched*, **τάλαν-ος**.

3. Ὀδούς (Ionic ὀδών), *tooth*, gen. ὀδόντ-ος, forms its nominative like participles in ους: for these see 212, 1.

211. (*Exceptions to* 209, 4.) Some neuter stems in ατ- have αρ in the nominative; as ἧπαρ, *liver*, gen. ἥπατ-ος (225), as if from a stem in αρτ-. For nouns in ας with double stems in ατ- (or ᾱτ-) and ασ-, as κρέας, πέρας (225), and τέρας, see 237. Φῶς (for φάος), *light*, has gen. φωτ-ός; but Homer has φάος (stem φαεσ-). For πῦρ, *fire*, gen. πυρ-ός, see 291.

212. (*Participles.*) 1. Masculine participles from verbs in ωμι add ς to οντ- and have nominatives in ους (79); as διδούς, *giving*, διδόντ-ος. Neuters in οντ- are regular (209, 4).

Other participles from stems in οντ- have nominatives in ων, like nouns (209, 3).

2. The perfect active participle, with stem in οτ-, forms its nominative in ως (masc.) and ος (neut.); as λελυκώς, *having loosed*, neut. λελυκός, gen. λελυκότ-ος. (See 335.)

213. N. For nominatives in ης and ος, gen. εος, from stems in εσ-, see 227. For peculiar formations from stems in ο (nom. ώ), see 242.

Accusative Singular.

214. 1. Most masculines and feminines with consonant stems add α to the stem in the accusative singular; as φύλαξ (φυλακ-), φύλακα; λέων (λεοντ-), *lion*, λέοντα.

2. Those with vowel stems add ν; as πόλις, *state*, πόλιν; ἰχθύς, *fish*, ἰχθύν; ναῦς, *ship*, ναῦν; βοῦς, *ox*, βοῦν.

3. *Barytones* in ις and υς with lingual (τ, δ, θ) stems generally drop the lingual and add ν; as ἔρις (ἐριδ-), *strife*, ἔριν; χάρις (χαριτ-), *grace*, χάριν; ὄρνῑς (ὀρνῑθ-), *bird*, ὄρνῑν; εὔελπις (εὐελπιδ-), *hopeful*, εὔελπιν (but the oxytone ἐλπίς, *hope*, has ἐλπίδα).

215. N. κλείς (κλειδ-), *key*, has κλεῖν (rarely κλεῖδα).

216. N. Homer, Herodotus, and the Attic poets make accusatives in α of the nouns of 214, 3; as ἔριδα (Hom.) χάριτα (Hdt.), ὄρνῑθα (Aristoph.).

217. N. Ἀπόλλων and Ποσειδῶν (Ποσειδάων) have accusatives Ἀπόλλω and Ποσειδῶ, besides the forms in ωνα.

For ω in the accusative of comparatives in ῑων, see 359.

218. N. For accusatives in εα from nominatives in ης, in εᾶ from those in ευς, and in ω (for ωα or οα) from those in ως or ω, see 228; 265; 243.

Vocative Singular.

219. The vocative singular of masculines and feminines is sometimes the same as the nominative, and sometimes the same as the stem.

220. It is the same as the nominative

1. In nouns with mute stems; as nom. and voc. φύλαξ (φυλακ-), *watchman*. (See the paradigms in 225.)

2. In *oxytones* with liquid stems; as nom. and voc. ποιμήν (ποιμεν-), *shepherd*, λιμήν (λιμεν-), *harbor*.

But barytones have the vocative like the stem; as δαίμων (δαιμον-), voc. δαῖμον. (See the paradigms in 225.)

221. (*Exceptions.*) 1. Those with stems in ιδ-, and *barytones* with stems in ντ- (except participles), have the vocative like the stem; as ἐλπίς (ἐλπιδ-), *hope*, voc. ἐλπί (cf. 25): see λέων and γίγᾱς, declined in 225. So Αἴᾱς (Αἰαντ-), *Ajax*, voc. Αἶαν (Hom.), but Αἴᾱς in Attic.

2. Σωτήρ (σωτηρ-), *preserver*, Ἀπόλλων (Ἀπολλων-), and Ποσειδῶν (Ποσειδων- for Ποσειδᾱον-) shorten η and ω in the vocative. Thus voc. σῶτερ, Ἄπολλον, Πόσειδον (Hom. Ποσείδᾱον). For the recessive accent here and in similar forms, see 122 (*d*).

222. All others have the vocative the same as the stem. See the paradigms.

223. There are a few vocatives in οῖ from nouns in ώ and ών, gen. οῦς: see 245; 248.

For the vocative of syncopated nouns, see 273.

Dative Plural.

224. The dative plural is formed by adding σι to the stem, with the needful euphonic changes. *E.g.*

Φύλαξ (φυλακ-), φύλαξι; ῥήτωρ (ῥητορ-), ῥήτορσι; ἐλπίς (ἐλπιδ-), ἐλπίσι (74); πούς (ποδ-), ποσί; λέων (λεοντ-), λέουσι (79); δαίμων (δαιμον-), δαίμοσι (80); τιθείς (τιθεντ-), τιθεῖσι; χαρίεις (χαριεντ-), χαρίεσι (74); ἱστάς (ἱσταντ-), ἱστᾶσι; δεικνύς (δεικνυντ-), δεικνῦσι; βασιλεύς (βασιλευ-), βασιλεῦσι; βοῦς (βου-), βουσί; γραῦς (γραυ-), γραυσί.

For a change in syncopated nouns, see 273.

NOUNS WITH MUTE OR LIQUID STEMS.

225. The following are examples of the most common forms of nouns of the third declension with mute or liquid stems.

For the formation of the cases, see 209–224. For euphonic changes in nearly all, see 74 and 79. For special changes in θρίξ, see 95, 5.

MUTE STEMS.

I. *Masculines and Feminines.*

	(ὁ) φύλαξ *watchman*	(ἡ) φλέψ *vein*	(ὁ) σάλπιγξ *trumpet*	(ἡ) θρίξ *hair*	(ὁ) λέων *lion*
Stem.	(φυλακ-)	(φλεβ-)	(σαλπιγγ-)	(τριχ-)	(λεοντ-)
			SINGULAR.		
Nom.	φύλαξ	φλέψ	σάλπιγξ	θρίξ	λέων
Gen.	φύλακος	φλεβός	σάλπιγγος	τριχός	λέοντος
Dat.	φύλακι	φλεβί	σάλπιγγι	τριχί	λέοντι
Acc.	φύλακα	φλέβα	σάλπιγγα	τρίχα	λέοντα
Voc.	φύλαξ	φλέψ	σάλπιγξ	θρίξ	λέον
			DUAL.		
N. A. V.	φύλακε	φλέβε	σάλπιγγε	τρίχε	λέοντε
G. D.	φυλάκοιν	φλεβοῖν	σαλπίγγοιν	τριχοῖν	λεόντοιν
			PLURAL.		
N. V.	φύλακες	φλέβες	σάλπιγγες	τρίχες	λέοντες
Gen.	φυλάκων	φλεβῶν	σαλπίγγων	τριχῶν	λεόντων
Dat.	φύλαξι	φλεψί	σάλπιγξι	θριξί	λέουσι
Acc.	φύλακας	φλέβας	σάλπιγγας	τρίχας	λέοντας

	(ὁ) γίγᾱς *giant*	(ὁ) θής *hired man*	(ἡ) λαμπάς *torch*	(ὁ ἡ) ὄρνῑς *bird*	(ἡ) ἐλπίς *hope*
Stem.	(γιγαντ-)	(θητ-)	(λαμπαδ-)	(ὀρνῑθ-)	(ἐλπιδ-)
			SINGULAR.		
Nom.	γίγᾱς	θής	λαμπάς	ὄρνῑς	ἐλπίς
Gen.	γίγαντος	θητός	λαμπάδος	ὄρνῑθος	ἐλπίδος
Dat.	γίγαντι	θητί	λαμπάδι	ὄρνῑθι	ἐλπίδι
Acc.	γίγαντα	θῆτα	λαμπάδα	ὄρνῑν	ἐλπίδα
Voc.	γίγαν	θής	λαμπάς	ὄρνῑς	ἐλπί
			DUAL.		
N. A. V.	γίγαντε	θῆτε	λαμπάδε	ὄρνῑθε	ἐλπίδε
G. D.	γιγάντοιν	θητοῖν	λαμπάδοιν	ὀρνίθοιν	ἐλπίδοιν
			PLURAL.		
N. V.	γίγαντες	θῆτες	λαμπάδες	ὄρνῑθες	ἐλπίδες
Gen.	γιγάντων	θητῶν	λαμπάδων	ὀρνίθων	ἐλπίδων
Dat.	γίγᾱσι	θησί	λαμπάσι	ὄρνῑσι	ἐλπίσι
Acc.	γίγαντας	θῆτας	λαμπάδας	ὄρνῑθας	ἐλπίδας

II. *Neuters.*

	(τὸ) σῶμα *body*	(τὸ) τέρας *end*	(τὸ) ἧπαρ *liver*
Stem.	(σωματ-)	(τερατ-)	(ἡπατ-)
	SINGULAR.		
N. A. V.	σῶμα	τέρας (237)	ἧπαρ
Gen.	σώματος	τέρατος	ἥπατος
Dat.	σώματι	τέρατι	ἥπατι
	DUAL.		
N. A. V.	σώματε	τέρατε	ἥπατε
G. D.	σωμάτοιν	τεράτοιν	ἡπάτοιν
	PLURAL.		
N. A. V.	σώματα	τέρατα	ἥπατα
Gen.	σωμάτων	τεράτων	ἡπάτων
Dat.	σώμασι	τέρασι	ἥπασι

Liquid Stems.

	(ὁ) ποιμήν *shepherd*	(ὁ) αἰών *age*	(ὁ) ἡγεμών *leader*	(ὁ) δαίμων *divinity*	(ὁ) σωτήρ *preserver*
Stem.	(ποιμεν-)	(αἰων-)	(ἡγεμον-)	(δαιμον-)	(σωτερ-)
			SINGULAR.		
Nom.	ποιμήν	αἰών	ἡγεμών	δαίμων	σωτήρ
Gen.	ποιμένος	αἰῶνος	ἡγεμόνος	δαίμονος	σωτῆρος
Dat.	ποιμένι	αἰῶνι	ἡγεμόνι	δαίμονι	σωτῆρι
Acc.	ποιμένα	αἰῶνα	ἡγεμόνα	δαίμονα	σωτῆρα
Voc.	ποιμήν	αἰών	ἡγεμών	δαῖμον	σῶτερ (122)
			DUAL.		
N. A. V.	ποιμένε	αἰῶνε	ἡγεμόνε	δαίμονε	σωτῆρε
G. D.	ποιμένοιν	αἰώνοιν	ἡγεμόνοιν	δαιμόνοιν	σωτήροιν
			PLURAL.		
N. V.	ποιμένες	αἰῶνες	ἡγεμόνες	δαίμονες	σωτῆρες
Gen.	ποιμένων	αἰώνων	ἡγεμόνων	δαιμόνων	σωτήρων
Dat.	ποιμέσι	αἰῶσι	ἡγεμόσι	δαίμοσι	σωτῆρσι
Acc.	ποιμένας	αἰῶνας	ἡγεμόνας	δαίμονας	σωτῆρας

	(ὁ) ῥήτωρ *orator*	(ὁ) ἅλς *salt*	(ὁ) θήρ *beast*	(ἡ) ῥίς *nose*	(ἡ) φρήν *mind*
Stem.	(ῥητορ-)	(ἁλ-)	(θηρ-)	(ῥῑν-)	(φρεν-)
			SINGULAR.		
Nom.	ῥήτωρ	ἅλς	θήρ	ῥίς	φρήν
Gen.	ῥήτορος	ἁλός	θηρός	ῥῑνός	φρενός
Dat.	ῥήτορι	ἁλί	θηρί	ῥῑνί	φρενί
Acc.	ῥήτορα	ἅλα	θῆρα	ῥῖνα	φρένα
Voc.	ῥῆτορ	ἅλς	θήρ	ῥίς	φρήν
			DUAL.		
N. A. V.	ῥήτορε	ἅλε	θῆρε	ῥῖνε	φρένε
G. D.	ῥητόροιν	ἁλοῖν	θηροῖν	ῥῑνοῖν	φρενοῖν
			PLURAL.		
N. V.	ῥήτορες	ἅλες	θῆρες	ῥῖνες	φρένες
Gen.	ῥητόρων	ἁλῶν	θηρῶν	ῥῑνῶν	φρενῶν
Dat.	ῥήτορσι	ἁλσί	θηρσί	ῥῑσί	φρεσί
Acc.	ῥήτορας	ἅλας	θῆρας	ῥῖνας	φρένας

STEMS ENDING IN Σ.

226. The final σ of the stem appears only where there is no case-ending, as in the nominative singular, being elsewhere dropped. (See 88, 1.) Two vowels brought together by this omission of σ are generally contracted.

227. The proper substantive stems in εσ- are chiefly neuters, which change εσ- to ος in the nominative singular. Some masculine proper names change εσ- regularly to ης (209, 2). Stems in ασ- form nominatives in ας, all neuters (228).

228. Σωκράτης (Σωκρατεσ-), *Socrates*, (τὸ) γένος (γενεσ-), *race*, and (τὸ) γέρας (γερασ-), *prize*, are thus declined:—

	SINGULAR.			
Nom.	Σωκράτης	N. A. V.	γένος	γέρας
Gen.	(Σωκράτεος) Σωκράτους	Gen.	(γένεος) γένους	(γέραος) γέρως
Dat.	(Σωκράτεϊ) Σωκράτει	Dat.	(γένεϊ) γένει	(γέραϊ) γέραι
Acc.	(Σωκράτεα) Σωκράτη		DUAL.	
Voc.	Σώκρατες	N. A. V.	(γένεε) γένει	(γέραε) γέρᾱ
		G. D.	(γενέοιν) γενοῖν	(γεράοιν) γερῷν
			PLURAL.	
		N. A. V.	(γένεα) γένη	(γέραα) γέρᾱ
		Gen.	(γενέων) γενῶν	(γεράων) γερῶν
		Dat.	γένεσι	γέρασι

229. In the genitive plural εων is sometimes uncontracted, even in prose; as τειχέων from τεῖχος. For εεα contracted εᾶ, see 39, 2.

230. Proper names in ης, gen. εος, besides the accusative in η, have a form in ην of the first declension; as Σωκράτην, Δημοσθένην, Πολυνείκην.

For the recessive accent in the vocative of these nouns, see 122.

231. Proper names in κλεης, compounds of κλέος, *glory*, are doubly contracted in the dative, sometimes in the accusative. Περικλέης, Περικλῆς, *Pericles*, is thus declined:—

Nom.	(Περικλέης)	Περικλῆς		
Gen.	(Περικλέεος)	Περικλέους		
Dat.	(Περικλέεϊ)	(Περικλέει)	Περικλεῖ	
Acc.	(Περικλέεα)	Περικλέᾶ	(poet. Περικλῆ)	
Voc.	(Περίκλεες)	Περίκλεις		

232. N. In proper names in κλεης, Homer has ῆος, ῆι, ῆα, Herodotus έος (for έεος), έϊ, έα. In adjectives in εης Homer sometimes contracts εε to ει: as, εὐκλεής, acc. plur. εὐκλεῖας for εὐκλέεας.

233. Adjective stems in εσ- change εσ- to ης in the masculine and feminine of the nominative singular, but leave ες in the neuter. For the declension of these, see 312.

234. The adjective τριήρης, *triply fitted*, is used as a feminine noun, (ἡ) τριήρης (sc. ναῦς), *trireme*, and is thus declined:—

SINGULAR.			DUAL.		PLURAL.		
Nom.	τριήρης		N. A. V.	(τριήρεε) τριήρει	N. V.	(τριήρεες)	τριήρεις
Gen.	(τριήρεος)	τριήρους			Gen.	(τριηρέων)	τριήρων
Dat.	(τριήρεϊ)	τριήρει	G. D.	(τριηρέοιν) τριήροιν	Dat.	τριήρεσι	
Acc.	(τριήρεα)	τριήρη			Acc.	τριήρεις	
Voc.	τριῆρες						

235. N. Τριήρης has recessive accent in the genitive dual and plural: for this in other adjectives in ης, see 122.

For the accusative plural in εις, see 208, 3.

236. N. Some poetic nominatives in ας have ε for α in the other cases; as οὖδας, *ground*, gen. οὔδεος, dat. οὔδεϊ, οὔδει (Homer). So βρέτας, *image*, gen. βρέτεος, plur. βρέτη, βρετέων, in Attic poetry.

237. 1. Some nouns in ας have two stems,—one in ατ- or ᾱτ- with gen. ατος (like πέρας, 225), and another in ασ- with gen.

α(σ-)ος, αος, contracted ως (like γέρας, 228). Thus κέρας (κερᾱτ-, κερασ-), *horn*, is doubly declined.

SINGULAR.		
N. A. V.	κέρας	
Gen.	κέρᾱτος,	(κεραος) κέρως
Dat.	κέρᾱτι,	(κεραϊ) κέρᾳ

DUAL.		
N. A. V.	κέρᾱτε,	(κεραε) κέρᾱ
G. D.	κεράτοιν,	(κεραοιν) κερῷν

PLURAL.		
N. A. V.	κέρᾰτα,	(κεραα) κέρᾱ
Gen.	κεράτων,	(κεραων) κερῶν
Dat.	κέρᾱσι	

2. So τέρας, *prodigy*, τέρατ-ος, which has also Homeric forms from the stem in ασ-, as τέραα, τεράων, τεράεσσι. Πέρας, *end* (225), has only πέρατ-ος, etc.

238. There is one Attic noun stem in οσ-, αἰδοσ-, with nominative (ἡ) αἰδώς, *shame*, which is thus declined:—

SINGULAR.		
Nom.		αἰδώς
Gen.	(αἰδοος)	αἰδοῦς
Dat.	(αἰδοϊ)	αἰδοῖ
Acc.	(αἰδοα)	αἰδῶ
Voc.		αἰδώς

DUAL AND PLURAL wanting.

239. Αἰδώς has the declension of nouns in ώ (242), but the accusative in ῶ has the regular accent. (See also 359.)

240. The Ionic (ἡ) ἠώς, *dawn*, has stem ἠοσ-, and is declined like αἰδώς:—gen. ἠοῦς, dat. ἠοῖ, acc. ἠῶ. The Attic ἕως is declined like νεώς (196): but see 199.

STEMS IN Ω OR O.

241. A few stems in ω- form masculine nouns in ως, gen. ω-ος, which are often contracted in the dative and accusative singular and in the nominative and accusative plural.

242. A few in ο- form feminines in ώ, gen. οῦς (for ο-ος), which are always contracted in the genitive, dative, and accusative singular. The original form of the stems of these nouns is uncertain. (See 239.)

243. The nouns (ὁ) ἥρως, *hero*, and (ἡ) πειθώ, *persuasion*, are thus declined:—

SINGULAR.	Nom.	**ἥρως**	**πειθώ**
	Gen.	**ἥρωος**	(πειθόος) **πειθοῦς**
	Dat.	**ἥρωι** or **ἥρῳ**	(πειθόϊ) **πειθοῖ**
	Acc.	**ἥρωα** or **ἥρω**	(πειθόα) **πειθώ**
	Voc.	**ἥρως**	**πειθοῖ**
DUAL.	N. A. V.	**ἥρωε**	
	G. D.	**ἡρώοιν**	
PLURAL.	N. V.	**ἥρωες** or **ἥρως**	
	Gen.	**ἡρώων**	
	Dat.	**ἥρωσι**	
	Acc.	**ἥρωας** or **ἥρως**	

244. These nouns in ως sometimes have forms of the Attic second declension; as gen. ἥρω (like νεώ), accus. ἥρων. Like ἥρως are declined Τρώς, *Trojan* (128), and μήτρως, *mother's brother*.

245. N. The feminines in ώ are chiefly proper names. Like πειθώ may be declined Σαπφώ (Aeolic Ψάπφω), *Sappho*, gen. Σαπφοῦς, dat. Σαπφοῖ, acc. Σαπφώ, voc. Σαπφοῖ. So Λητώ, Καλυψώ, and ἠχώ, *echo*. No dual or plural forms of these nouns are found in the third declension; but a few occur of the second, as acc. plur. γοργούς from γοργώ, *Gorgon*. No uncontracted forms of nouns in ώ occur.

246. N. The vocative in οῖ seems to belong to a form of the stem in οι-; and there was a nominative form in ῳ, as Λητῴ, Σαπφῴ.

247. N. Herodotus has an accusative singular in οῦν; as Ἰοῦν (for Ἰώ) from Ἰώ, *Io*, gen. Ἰοῦς.

248. A few feminines in ων (with regular stems in ον-) have occasional forms like those of nouns in ώ; as ἀηδών, *nightingale*, gen. ἀηδοῦς, voc. ἀηδοῖ; εἰκών, *image*, gen. εἰκοῦς, acc. εἰκώ; χελῑδών, *swallow*, voc. χελῑδοῖ.

STEMS IN I AND Υ.

249. Most stems in ι (with nominatives in ις) and a few in υ (with nominatives in υς and υ) have ε in place of their final ι or υ in all cases except the nominative, accusative, and vocative singular, and have ως for ος in the genitive singular. The dative singular and the nominative plural are contracted.

250. The nouns (ἡ) πόλις (πολι-), *state*, (ὁ) πῆχυς (πηχυ-), *cubit*, and (τὸ) ἄστυ (ἀστυ-), *city*, are thus declined: —

	SINGULAR.		
Nom.	πόλις	πῆχυς	ἄστυ
Gen.	πόλεως	πήχεως	ἄστεως
Dat.	(πόλεϊ) πόλει	(πήχεϊ) πήχει	(ἄστεϊ) ἄστει
Acc.	πόλιν	πῆχυν	ἄστυ
Voc.	πόλι	πῆχυ	ἄστυ
	DUAL.		
N. A. V.	(πόλεε) πόλει	(πήχεε) πήχει	(ἄστεε) ἄστει
G. D.	πολέοιν	πηχέοιν	ἀστέοιν
	PLURAL.		
N. V.	(πόλεες) πόλεις	(πήχεες) πήχεις	(ἄστεα) ἄστη
Gen.	πόλεων	πήχεων	ἄστεων
Dat.	πόλεσι	πήχεσι	ἄστεσι
Acc.	πόλεις	πήχεις	(ἄστεα) ἄστη

251. For the accent of genitives in εως and εων, see 114. For accusatives like πόλεις and πήχεις, see 208, 3.

252. N. The dual in εε is rarely left uncontracted.

253. N. Ἄστυ is the principal noun in υ, gen. εως. Its genitive plural is found only in the poetic form ἀστέων, but analogy leads to Attic ἄστεων.

254. No nouns in ι, gen. εως, were in common Attic use. See κόμμι and πέπερι in the Lexicon.

255. N. The original ι of the stem of nouns in ις (Attic gen. εως) is retained in Ionic. Thus, πόλις, πόλιος, (πόλῑ) πόλῑ, πόλιν; plur. πόλιες, πολίων; Hom. πολίεσσι (Hdt. πόλισι), πόλιας (Hdt. also πόλῑς for πολι-νς, see 208, 4). Homer has also πόλει (with πτόλεϊ) and πόλεσι in the dative. There are also epic forms πόληος, πόληϊ, πόληες, πόληας. The Attic poets have a genitive in εος.

The Ionic has a genitive in εος in nouns in υς of this class.

256. N. Stems in υ with gen. εως have also forms in ευ, in which ευ becomes εϝ, and drops ϝ, leaving ε: thus πηχυ-, πηχευ-, πηχεϝ-, πηχε-. (See 90, 3.)

257. Most nouns in υς retain υ; as (ὁ) ἰχθῦς (ἰχθυ-), *fish*, which is thus declined: —

SINGULAR.		DUAL.		PLURAL.	
Nom.	ἰχθῦς			Nom.	ἰχθύες
Gen.	ἰχθύος	N. A. V.	ἰχθύε	Gen.	ἰχθύων
Dat.	ἰχθύϊ (Hom. ἰχθυῖ)	G. D.	ἰχθύοιν	Dat.	ἰχθύσι
Acc.	ἰχθύν			Acc.	ἰχθῦς
Voc.	ἰχθύ				

258. N. The nominative plural and dual rarely have ῦς and ῦ; as ἰχθῦς (like accus.) and ἰχθῦ (for ἰχθύε) in comedy.

259. N. Homer and Herodotus have both ἰχθύας and ἰχθῦς in the accusative plural. Ἰχθῦς here is for ἰχθυ-νς (208, 4).

260. Oxytones and monosyllables have ῡ in the nominative, accusative, and vocative singular: see ἰχθύς. Monosyllables are circumflexed in these cases; as μῦς (μυ-), *mouse*, μυός, μυΐ, μῦν, μῦ; plur. μύες, μυῶν, μυσί, μύας.

261. N. Ἔγχελυς, *eel*, is declined like ἰχθύς in the singular, and like πῆχυς in the plural, with gen. sing. ἐγχέλυ-ος and nom. plur. ἐγχέλεις.

262. N. For adjectives in υς, εια, υ, see 319.

STEMS ENDING IN A DIPHTHONG.

263. 1. In nouns in ευς, ευ of the stem is retained in the nominative and vocative singular and dative plural, but loses υ before a vowel; as (ὁ) βασιλεύς (βασιλευ-), *king*, which is thus declined: —

SINGULAR.		DUAL.		PLURAL.	
Nom.	**βασιλεύς**			N. V.	(βασιλέες) **βασιλεῖς**
Gen.	**βασιλέως**	N. A. V.	**βασιλέε**	Gen.	**βασιλέων**
Dat.	(βασιλέϊ) **βασιλεῖ**	G. D.	**βασιλέοιν**	Dat.	**βασιλεῦσι**
Acc.	**βασιλέᾱ**			Acc.	**βασιλέᾱς**
Voc.	**βασιλεῦ**				

2. So γονεύς (γονευ-), *parent*, ἱερεύς (ἱερευ-), *priest*, Ἀχιλλεύς (Ἀχιλλευ-), *Achilles*, Ὀδυσσεύς (Ὀδυσσευ-), *Ulysses*.

264. Homer has ευ in three cases, βασιλεύς, βασιλεῦ, and βασιλεῦσι; but in the other cases βασιλῆος, βασιλῆι, βασιλῆα, βασιλῆες, βασιλῆας, also dat. plur. ἀριστή-εσσι (from ἀριστεύς); in proper names he has εος, εϊ, etc., as Πηλέος, Πηλέϊ (rarely contracted, as Ἀχιλλεῖ). Herodotus has gen. εος.

265. Nouns in ευς originally had stems in ηυ, before vowels ηϝ. From forms in ηϝος, ηϝι, ηϝα, etc., came the Homeric ηος, ηι, ηᾰ, etc. The Attic εως, εᾱ, εᾱς came, by exchange of quantity (33), from ηος, ηᾰ, ηᾰς.

266. The older Attic writers (as Thucydides) with Plato have ῆς (contracted from ῆες) in the nominative plural; as ἱππῆς, βασιλῆς, for later ἱππεῖς, βασιλεῖς. In the accusative plural, εᾱς usually remains unchanged, but there is a late form in εις.

267. When a vowel precedes, έως of the genitive singular may be contracted into ῶς, and έᾱ of the accusative singular into ᾶ; rarely έᾱς of the accusative plural into ᾶς, and έων of the genitive plural into ῶν. Thus, Πειραιεύς, *Peiraeus*, has gen. Πειραιέως, Πειραιῶς, dat. Πειραιέϊ, Πειραιεῖ, acc. Πειραιέᾱ, Πειραιᾶ; Δωριεύς, *Dorian*, has gen. plur. Δωριέων, Δωριῶν, acc. Δωριέᾱς, Δωριᾶς.

268. The nouns (ὁ, ἡ) βοῦς (βου-), *ox* or *cow*, (ἡ) γραῦς (γραυ-), *old woman*, (ἡ) ναῦς (ναυ-), *ship*, and οἶς (οἰ-), *sheep*, are thus declined:—

		SINGULAR.		
Nom.	βοῦς	γραῦς	ναῦς	οἶς
Gen.	βοός	γρᾱός	νεώς	οἰός
Dat.	βοΐ	γρᾱΐ	νηΐ	οἰΐ
Acc.	βοῦν	γραῦν	ναῦν	οἶν
Voc.	βοῦ	γραῦ	ναῦ	οἶ
		DUAL.		
N. A. V.	βόε	γρᾶε	νῆε	οἶε
G. D.	βοοῖν	γρᾱοῖν	νεοῖν	οἰοῖν
		PLURAL.		
N. V.	βόες	γρᾶες	νῆες	οἶες
Gen.	βοῶν	γρᾱῶν	νεῶν	οἰῶν
Dat.	βουσί	γραυσί	ναυσί	οἰσί
Acc.	βοῦς	γραῦς	ναῦς	οἶς

269. N. The stems of βοῦς, γραῦς, and ναῦς became βοϝ-, γρᾱϝ-, and νᾱϝ- before a vowel of the ending (compare Latin *bŏv-is* and *nāv-is*). The stem of οἶς, the only stem in οι-, was ὀϝι- (compare Latin *ŏvis*). Afterwards ϝ was dropped (90, 3), leaving βο-, γρᾱ-, νᾱ-, and οἰ-. Attic νεώς is for νηός (33).

270. In Doric and Ionic ναῦς is much more regular than in Attic:—

	SINGULAR.			PLURAL.		
	Doric.	Homer.	Herod.	Doric.	Homer.	Herod.
Nom.	ναῦς	νηῦς	νηῦς	νᾶες	νῆες, νέες	νέες
Gen.	νᾱός	νηός, νεός	νεός	νᾱῶν	νηῶν, νεῶν	νεῶν
Dat.	νᾱΐ	νηΐ	νηΐ	ναυσί, νάεσσι	νηυσί, νήεσσι, νέεσσι	νηυσί
Acc.	ναῦν	νῆα, νέα	νέα	νᾶας	νῆας, νέας	νέας

271. Homer has γρηῦς (γρηυ-) and γρηΰς (γρηϋ-) for γραῦς. He has βόας and βοῦς in the accusative plural of βοῦς.

272. Χοῦς, *three-quart measure*, is declined like βοῦς, except in the accusatives χόᾱ and χόας. (See χοῦς in 291.)

SYNCOPATED NOUNS.

273. Four nouns in ηρ (with stems in ερ-) are syncopated (65) in the genitive and dative singular by dropping ε. The syncopated genitive and dative are oxytone; and the vocative singular has recessive accent (122), and ends in ερ as a barytone (220, 2). In the other cases ε is retained and is always accented. But in the dative plural ερ- is changed to ρα-.

274. These are (ὁ) πατήρ (πατερ-), *father*, (ἡ) μήτηρ (μητερ-), *mother*, (ἡ) θυγάτηρ (θυγατερ-), *daughter*, and (ἡ) γαστήρ (γαστερ-) *belly*.

1. The first three are thus declined: —

		SINGULAR.	
Nom.	**πατήρ**	**μήτηρ**	**θυγάτηρ**
Gen.	(πατέρος) **πατρός**	(μητέρος) **μητρός**	(θυγατέρος) **θυγατρός**
Dat.	(πατέρι) **πατρί**	(μητέρι) **μητρί**	(θυγατέρι) **θυγατρί**
Acc.	**πατέρα**	**μητέρα**	**θυγατέρα**
Voc.	**πάτερ**	**μῆτερ**	**θύγατερ**
		DUAL.	
N. A. V.	**πατέρε**	**μητέρε**	**θυγατέρε**
G. D.	**πατέροιν**	**μητέροιν**	**θυγατέροιν**
		PLURAL.	
N. V.	**πατέρες**	**μητέρες**	**θυγατέρες**
Gen.	**πατέρων**	**μητέρων**	**θυγατέρων**
Dat.	**πατράσι**	**μητράσι**	**θυγατράσι**
Acc.	**πατέρας**	**μητέρας**	**θυγατέρας**

2. Γαστήρ is declined and accented like πατήρ.

275. Ἀστήρ (ὁ), *star*, has ἀστράσι, like a syncopated noun, in the dative plural, but is otherwise regular (without syncope).

276. N. The unsyncopated forms of all these nouns are often used by the poets, who also syncopate other cases of θυγάτηρ; as θύγατρα, θύγατρες, θυγατρῶν. Homer has dat. plur. θυγατέρεσσι, and πατρῶν for πατέρων.

277. 1. Ἀνήρ (ὁ), *man*, drops ε whenever a vowel follows ερ, and inserts δ in its place (67). It has ἀνδροῖν and ἀνδρῶν. In other respects it follows the declension of πατήρ.

2. Δημήτηρ, *Demeter* (*Ceres*), syncopates all the oblique cases, and then accents them on the *first* syllable.

278. Ἀνήρ and Δημήτηρ are thus declined:—

SINGULAR.	Nom.	ἀνήρ	Δημήτηρ
	Gen.	(ἀνέρος) ἀνδρός	(Δημήτερος) Δήμητρος
	Dat.	(ἀνέρι) ἀνδρί	(Δημήτερι) Δήμητρι
	Acc.	(ἀνέρα) ἄνδρα	(Δημήτερα) Δήμητρα
	Voc.	ἄνερ	Δήμητερ
DUAL.	N. A. V.	(ἀνέρε) ἄνδρε	
	G. D.	(ἀνέροιν) ἀνδροῖν	
PLURAL.	N. V.	(ἀνέρες) ἄνδρες	
	Gen.	(ἀνέρων) ἀνδρῶν	
	Dat.	ἀνδράσι	
	Acc.	(ἀνέρας) ἄνδρας	

279. The poets often use the unsyncopated forms. Homer has ἄνδρεσσι as well as ἀνδράσι in the dative plural.

GENDER OF THE THIRD DECLENSION.

280. The gender in this declension must often be learned by observation. But some general rules may be given.

281. 1. MASCULINE are stems in

ευ-; as βασιλεύς (βασιλευ-), *king.*

ρ- (except those in ἄρ-); as κρᾱτήρ (κρᾱτηρ-), *mixing-bowl,* ψάρ (ψᾱρ-), *starling.*

ν- (except those in ῑν-, γον-, δον-); as κανών (κανον-), *rule.*

ντ-; as ὀδούς (ὀδοντ-), *tooth.*

ητ- (except those in τητ-); as λέβης (λεβητ-), *kettle.*

ωτ-; as ἔρως (ἐρωτ-), *love.*

2. *Exceptions.* Feminine are γαστήρ, *belly,* κήρ, *fate,* χείρ, *hand,* φρήν, *mind,* ἀλκύων, *halcyon,* εἰκών, *image,* ἠιών, *shore,* χθών, *earth,* χιών, *snow,* μήκων, *poppy,* ἐσθής (ἐσθητ-), *dress.*

Neuter are πῦρ, *fire,* φῶς (φωτ-), *light.*

282. 1. FEMININE are stems in

ι- and υ-, with nomin. in ις and υς; as πόλις (πολι-), *city,* ἰσχύς (ἰσχυ-), *strength.*

αυ-; as ναῦς (ναυ-).

δ-, θ-, τητ-; as ἐρίς (ἐριδ-), *strife,* ταχυτής (ταχυτητ-), *speed.*

ῑν-, γον-, δον-; as ἀκτίς (ἀκτῑν-), *ray,* σταγών (σταγον-), *drop,* χελῑδών (χελῑδον-), *swallow.*

2. *Exceptions.* Masculine are ἔχι-ς, *viper,* ὄφι-ς, *serpent,* βότρυ-ς, *cluster of grapes,* θρῆνυ-ς, *footstool,* ἰχθύ-ς, *fish,* μῦ-ς, *mouse,* νέκυ-ς,

corpse, στάχυ-ς, *ear of grain*, πέλεκυ-ς, *axe*, πῆχυ-ς, *cubit*, πούς (ποδ-), *foot*, δελφίς (δελφῖν-), *dolphin*.

283. Neuter are stems in
ι and υ with nomin. in ι and υ; as πέπερι, *pepper*, ἄστυ, *city*.
ας-; as γέρας, *prize* (see 227).
ες-, with nomin. in ος; as γένος (γενεσ-), *race* (see 227).
ᾰρ-; as νέκταρ, *nectar*.
ατ-; as σῶμα (σωματ-), *body*.

284. Labial and palatal stems are always either masculine or feminine. (See 225.)

285. Variations in gender sometimes occur in poetry: see, for example, αἰθήρ, *sky*, and θίς, *heap*, in the Lexicon. See also 288.

Dialects.

286. 1. *Gen. and Dat. Dual.* Homeric οιιν for οιν.

2. *Dat. Plur.* Homeric εσσι, rarely εσι, and σσι (after vowels); also σι.

3. Most of the uncontracted forms enclosed in ( ) in the paradigms, which are not used in Attic prose, are found in Homer or Herodotus; and some of them occur in the Attic poets.

4. For special dialectic forms of some nouns of the third declension, see 232, 236, 237, 240, 247, 255, 259, 264, 270, 271, 276, 279.

IRREGULAR NOUNS.

287. 1. Some nouns belong to more than one declension. Thus σκότος, *darkness*, is usually declined like λόγος (192), but sometimes like γένος (228). So Οἰδίπους, *Oedipus*, has genitive Οἰδίποδος or Οἰδίπου, dative Οἰδίποδι, accusative Οἰδίποδα or Οἰδίπουν.

See also γέλως, ἔρως, ἱδρώς, and others, in 291.

2. For the double accusatives in η and ην of Σωκράτης, Δημοσθένης, etc., see 230.

288. Nouns which are of different genders in different numbers are called *heterogeneous*; as (ὁ) σῖτος, *corn*, plur. (τὰ) σῖτα, (ὁ) δεσμός, *chain*, (οἱ) δεσμοί and (τὰ) δεσμά.

289. *Defective* nouns have only certain cases; as ὄναρ, *dream*, ὄφελος, *use* (only nom. and accus.); (τὴν) νίφα, *snow* (only accus.). Some, generally from their meaning, have only one number; as πειθώ, *persuasion*, τὰ Ὀλύμπια, *the Olympic games*.

290. *Indeclinable* nouns have one form for all cases. These are chiefly foreign words, as Ἀδάμ, Ἰσραήλ; and names of letters, Ἄλφα, Βῆτα, etc.

291. The following are the most important irregular nouns:—

1. Ἅιδης, *Hades*, gen. ου, etc., regular. Hom. Ἀΐδης, gen. αο or εω, dat. ῃ, acc. ην; also Ἄϊδος, Ἄϊδι (from stem Ἀϊδ-).

2. ἄναξ (ὁ), *king*, ἄνακτος, etc., voc. ἄναξ (poet. ἄνα, in addressing Gods).

3. Ἄρης, *Ares*, Ἄρεως (poet. Ἄρεος), (Ἄρεϊ) Ἄρει, (Ἄρεα) Ἄρη or Ἄρην, Ἄρες (Hom. also Ἆρες). Hom. also Ἄρηος, Ἄρηι, Ἄρηα.

4. Stem (ἀρν-), gen. (τοῦ or τῆς) ἀρνός, *lamb*, ἀρνί, ἄρνα; pl. ἄρνες, ἀρνῶν, ἀρνάσι, ἄρνας. In the nom. sing. ἀμνός (2d decl.) is used.

5. γάλα (τό), *milk*, γάλακτος, γάλακτι, etc.

6. γέλως (ὁ), *laughter*, γέλωτος, etc., regular: in Attic poets acc. γέλωτα or γέλων. In Hom. generally of second declension, dat. γέλῳ, acc. γέλω, γέλων (γέλον?). (See 287, 1.)

7. γόνυ (τό), *knee*, γόνατος, γόνατι, etc. (from stem γονατ-); Ion. and poet. γούνατος, γούνατι, etc.; Hom. also gen. γουνός, dat. γουνί, pl. γοῦνα, γούνων, γούνεσσι.

8. γυνή (ἡ) *wife*, γυναικός, γυναικί, γυναῖκα, γύναι; dual γυναῖκε, γυναικοῖν; pl. γυναῖκες, γυναικῶν, γυναιξί, γυναῖκας.

9. δένδρον (τό), *tree*, δένδρου, regular (Ion. δένδρεον); dat. sing. δένδρει; dat. pl. δένδρεσι.

10. δέος (τό), *fear*, δέους, δέει, etc. Hom. gen. δείους.

11. δόρυ (τό), *spear* (cf. γόνυ); (from stem δορατ-) δόρατος, δόρατι; pl. δόρατα, etc. Ion. and poet. δούρατος, etc.; Epic also gen. δουρός, dat. δουρί; dual δοῦρε; pl. δοῦρα, δούρων, δούρεσσι. Poetic gen. δορός, dat. δορί and δόρει.

12. ἔρως (ὁ), *love*, ἔρωτος, etc. In poetry also ἔρος, ἔρῳ, ἔρον.

13. Ζεύς (Aeol. Δεύς), *Zeus*, Διός, Διί, Δία, Ζεῦ. Ion. and poet. Ζηνός, Ζηνί, Ζῆνα. Pindar has Δί for Διί.

14. Θέμις (ἡ), *justice* (also as proper name, *Themis*), gen. Θέμιδος, etc., reg. like ἔρις. Hom. θέμιστος, etc. Pind. θέμιτος, etc. Hdt. gen. θέμιος. In Attic prose, indeclinable in θέμις ἐστί, *fas est*; as θέμις εἶναι.

15. ἱδρώς (ὁ), *sweat*, ἱδρῶτος, etc. Hom. has dat. ἱδρῷ, acc. ἱδρῶ (243).

16. κάρᾱ (τό), *head*, poetic; in Attic only nom., accus., and voc. sing., with dat. κάρᾳ (tragic). Hom. κάρη, gen. κάρητος, καρήατος, κράατος, κρᾱτός; dat. κάρητι, καρήατι, κράατι, κρᾱτί; acc. (τὸν) κρᾶτα, (τὸ) κάρη or κάρ; plur. nom. κάρᾱ, καρήατα, κράατα; gen.

κρᾱ́των; dat. κρᾱσί; acc. κάρᾱ with (τοὺς) κρᾶτας; nom. and acc. pl. also κάρηνα, gen. καρήνων. Soph. (τὸ) κρᾶτα.

17. κρίνον (τό), *lily*, κρίνου, etc. In plural also κρίνεα (Hdt.) and κρίνεσι (poetic). (See 287, 1.)

18. κύων (ὁ, ἡ), *dog*, voc. κύον: the rest from stem κυν-, κυνός, κυνί, κύνα; pl. κύνες, κυνῶν, κυσί, κύνας.

19. λᾶς (ὁ), *stone*, Hom. λᾶας, poetic; gen. λᾶος (or λάου), dat. λᾶϊ, acc. λᾶαν, λᾶν; dual λᾶε; plur. λᾱῶν, λάεσσι, or λάεσι.

20. λίπα (Hom. λίπ', generally with ἐλαίῳ, *oil*), *fat*, *oil*; probably λίπα is neut. accus., and λίπ' is dat. for λιπί. See Lexicon.

21. μάρτυς (ὁ, ἡ), *witness*, gen. μάρτυρος, etc., dat. pl. μάρτυσι. Hom. nom. μάρτυρος (2d decl.).

22. μάστιξ (ἡ), *whip*, gen. μάστῑγος, etc., Hom. dat. μάστῑ, acc. μάστιν.

23. οἶς (ἡ), *sheep*, for Attic declension see 268. Hom. ὄϊς, ὄϊος, ὄϊν, ὄϊες, ὀΐων, ὀΐεσσι (οἴεσι, ὄεσσι), ὄϊς. Aristoph. has dat. ὀΐ.

24. ὄνειρος (ὁ), ὄνειρον (τό), *dream*, gen. ου; also ὄναρ (τό), gen. ὀνείρατος, dat. ὀνείρατι; plur. ὀνείρατα, ὀνειράτων, ὀνείρασι.

25. ὄσσε (τώ), dual, *eyes*, poetic; plur. gen. ὄσσων, dat. ὄσσοις or ὄσσοισι.

26. ὄρνῑς (ὁ, ἡ), *bird*, see 225. Also poetic forms from stem ὀρνῐ-, nom. and acc. sing. ὄρνῐς, ὄρνῐν; pl. ὄρνεις, ὀρνέων, acc. ὄρνεις or ὄρνῑς. Hdt. acc. ὄρνῑθα. Doric gen. ὄρνῑχος, etc.

27. οὖς (τό), *ear*, ὠτός, ὠτί; pl. ὦτα, ὤτων (128), ὠσί. Hom. gen. οὔατος; pl. οὔατα, οὔασι, and ὦσί. Doric ὦς.

28. Πνύξ (ἡ), *Pnyx*, Πυκνός, Πυκνί, Πύκνα (also Πνυκ-ός, etc.).

29. πρέσβυς (ὁ), *old man*, *elder* (properly adj.), poetic, acc. πρέσβυν (as adj.), voc. πρέσβυ; pl. πρέσβεις (Ep. πρέσβηες), *chiefs*, *elders*: the common word in this sense is πρεσβύτης, distinct from πρεσβευτής. Πρέσβυς = *ambassador*, w. gen. πρέσβεως, is rare and poetic in sing.; but common in prose in plur., πρέσβεις, πρέσβεων, πρέσβεσι, πρέσβεις (like πῆχυς). Πρεσβευτής, *ambassador*, is common in sing., but rare in plural.

30. πῦρ (τό), *fire* (stem πῡρ-), πυρός, πυρί; pl. (τὰ) πυρά, *watch-fires*, dat. πυροῖς.

31. σπέος or σπεῖος (τό), *cave*, Epic; σπείους, σπῆι, σπείων, σπήεσσι or σπέεσσι.

32. ταώς or ταῶς, Attic ταὧς (ὁ), *peacock*, like νεώς (196): also dat. ταῶνι, ταῶσι, chiefly poetic.

33. τῡφῶς (ὁ), *whirlwind*; declined like νεώς (196). Also proper name Τῡφῶς, in poetry generally Τῡφῶνος, Τῡφῶνι, Τῡφῶνα. (See 287, 1.)

34. ὕδωρ (τό), *water*, ὕδατος, ὕδατι, etc.; dat. plur. ὕδασι.

35. υἱός (ὁ), *son*, υἱοῦ, etc., reg.; also (from stem υἱυ-) υἱέος, (υἱέϊ) υἱεῖ, (υἱέα), υἱέε, υἱέοιν; (υἱέες) υἱεῖς, υἱέων, υἱέσι, (υἱέας) υἱεῖς: also with υ for υι; as ὑός, ὑοῦ, ὑέος, etc. Hom. also (from stem υἱ-) gen. υἷος, dat. υἷι, acc. υἷα; dual υἷε; pl. υἷες, υἷας, also dat. υἱάσι.

36. χείρ (ἡ), *hand*, χειρός, χειρί, etc.; but χεροῖν (poet. χειροῖν) and χερσί (poet. χείρεσσι or χείρεσι): poet. also χερός, χερί, etc.

37. (χόος) χοῦς (ὁ), *mound*, χοός, χοΐ, χοῦν (like βοῦς, 268).

38. χοῦς (ὁ), *three-quart measure:* see 272. Ionic and late nom. χοεύς, with gen. χοέως, χοῶς, etc., regularly like Πειραιεύς and Δωριεύς (267).

39. χρώς (ὁ), *skin*, χρωτός, χρωτί, χρῶτα; poet. also χροός, χροΐ, χρόα; dat. χρῷ (only in ἐν χρῷ, *near*).

Local Endings.

292. The endings -θι and -θεν may be added to the stem of a noun or pronoun to denote place: —

1. -θι, denoting *where;* as ἄλλο-θι, *elsewhere;* οὐρανό-θι, *in heaven.*

2. -θεν denoting *whence;* as οἴκο-θεν, *from home;* αὐτό-θεν, *from the very spot.*

293. The enclitic -δε (141, 4) added to the accusative denotes *whither;* as Μέγαράδε, *to Megara,* Ἐλευσῖνάδε, *to Eleusis.* After σ, -δε becomes ζε (see 18; 28, 3); as Ἀθήνᾱζε (for Ἀθήνᾱς-δε), *to Athens,* Θήβᾱζε (for Θήβᾱς-δε), *to Thebes,* θύρᾱζε, *out of doors.*

294. The ending -σε is sometimes added to the stem, denoting *whither;* as ἄλλοσε, *in another direction,* πάντοσε, *in every direction.*

295. N. In Homer, the forms in -θι and -θεν may be governed by a preposition as genitives; as Ἰλιόθι πρό, *before Ilium;* ἐξ ἁλόθεν, *from the sea.*

296. N. Sometimes a relic of an original *locative* case is found with the ending ι in the singular and σι in the plural; as Ἰσθμοῖ, *at the Isthmus;* οἴκοι (οἰκο-ι), *at home;* Πυθοῖ, *at Pytho;* Ἀθήνησι, *at Athens;* Πλαταιᾶσι, *at Plataea;* Ὀλυμπίᾱσι, *at Olympia;* θύρᾱσι, *at the gates.* These forms (and also those of 292) are often classed among adverbs; but inscriptions show that forms in ᾱσι and in ησι were both used as datives in the early Attic.

297. N. The Epic ending φι or φιν forms a genitive or dative in both singular and plural. It is sometimes locative, as κλισίηφι, *in the tent;* and sometimes it has other meanings of the genitive or dative, as βίηφι, *with violence.* These forms may follow prepositions; as παρὰ ναῦφι, *by the ships.*

ADJECTIVES.

FIRST AND SECOND DECLENSIONS (Vowel Declension).

298. 1. Most adjectives in *ος* have three endings, *ος*, *η*, *ον*. The masculine and neuter are of the second declension, and the feminine is of the first; as *σοφός*, *σοφή*, *σοφόν*, *wise*.

2. If a vowel or *ρ* precedes *ος*, the feminine ends in *ᾱ*; as *ἄξιος*, *ἀξίᾱ*, *ἄξιον*, *worthy*. But adjectives in *οος* have *οη* in the feminine, except those in *ροος*; as *ἁπλόος*, *ἁπλόη*, *ἁπλόον*, *simple; ἀθρόος*, *ἀθρόᾱ*, *ἀθρόον*, *crowded*.

299. Σοφός, *wise*, and *ἄξιος*, *worthy*, are thus declined:—

			SINGULAR.			
Nom.	**σοφός**	**σοφή**	**σοφόν**	**ἄξιος**	**ἀξίᾱ**	**ἄξιον**
Gen.	**σοφοῦ**	**σοφῆς**	**σοφοῦ**	**ἀξίου**	**ἀξίᾱς**	**ἀξίου**
Dat.	**σοφῷ**	**σοφῇ**	**σοφῷ**	**ἀξίῳ**	**ἀξίᾳ**	**ἀξίῳ**
Acc.	**σοφόν**	**σοφήν**	**σοφόν**	**ἄξιον**	**ἀξίᾱν**	**ἄξιον**
Voc.	**σοφέ**	**σοφή**	**σοφόν**	**ἄξιε**	**ἀξίᾱ**	**ἄξιον**
			DUAL.			
N.A.V.	**σοφώ**	**σοφά**	**σοφώ**	**ἀξίω**	**ἀξίᾱ**	**ἀξίω**
G. D.	**σοφοῖν**	**σοφαῖν**	**σοφοῖν**	**ἀξίοιν**	**ἀξίαιν**	**ἀξίοιν**
			PLURAL.			
N. V.	**σοφοί**	**σοφαί**	**σοφά**	**ἄξιοι**	**ἄξιαι**	**ἄξια**
Gen.	**σοφῶν**	**σοφῶν**	**σοφῶν**	**ἀξίων**	**ἀξίων**	**ἀξίων**
Dat.	**σοφοῖς**	**σοφαῖς**	**σοφοῖς**	**ἀξίοις**	**ἀξίαις**	**ἀξίοις**
Acc.	**σοφούς**	**σοφάς**	**σοφά**	**ἀξίους**	**ἀξίᾱς**	**ἄξια**

300. So *μακρός*, *μακρά*, *μακρόν*, *long;* gen. *μακροῦ*, *μακρᾶς*, *μακροῦ*; dat. *μακρῷ*, *μακρᾷ*, *μακρῷ*; acc. *μακρόν*, *μακράν*, *μακρόν*, etc., like *ἄξιος* (except in accent).

301. This is by far the largest class of adjectives. All participles in *ος* and all superlatives (350) are declined like *σοφός*, and all comparatives in *τερος* (350) are declined like *μακρός* (except in accent).

302. The nominative and genitive plural of adjectives in *ος* accent the feminine like the masculine: thus *ἄξιος* has *ἄξιαι, ἀξίων* (*not ἀξίαι, ἀξιῶν*, as if from *ἀξία*; see 124).

For feminines in ᾰ of the third and first declensions combined, see 318.

303. The masculine dual forms in *ω* and *οιν* in all adjectives and participles may be used for the feminine forms in ᾱ and *αιν*.

304. Some adjectives in *ος*, chiefly compounds, have only two endings, *ος* and *ον*, the feminine being the same as the masculine. They are declined like *σοφός*, omitting the feminine.

305. There are a few adjectives of the Attic second declension ending in *ως* and *ων*.

306. Ἄλογος, *irrational* (304), and ἵλεως, *gracious* (305), are thus declined:—

	SINGULAR.	
Nom.	ἄλογος ἄλογον	ἵλεως ἵλεων
Gen.	ἀλόγου	ἵλεω
Dat.	ἀλόγῳ	ἵλεῳ
Acc.	ἄλογον	ἵλεων
Voc.	ἄλογε ἄλογον	ἵλεως ἵλεων
	DUAL.	
N. A. V.	ἀλόγω	ἵλεω
G. D.	ἀλόγοιν	ἵλεῳν
	PLURAL.	
N. V.	ἄλογοι ἄλογα	ἵλεῳ ἵλεα
Gen.	ἀλόγων	ἵλεων
Dat.	ἀλόγοις	ἵλεῳς
Acc.	ἀλόγους ἄλογα	ἵλεως ἵλεα

307. Some adjectives in *ος* may be declined with either two or three endings, especially in poetry.

308. Adjectives in *ως*, *ων*, commonly have *α* in the neuter plural. But *ἔκπλεω* from *ἔκπλεως* occurs.

309. Πλέως, *full*, has a feminine in *α*: *πλέως, πλέᾱ, πλέων*. The defective *σῶς* (from *σα-ος*), *safe*, has nom. *σῶς, σῶν* (also fem. *σᾶ*), acc. *σῶν*, neut. pl. *σᾶ*, acc. pl. *σῶς*. The Attic has *σῶοι, σῶαι, σῶα* in nom. pl. Homer has *σόος*.

310. Many adjectives in **εος** and **οος** are contracted. **Χρῡ́σεος**, *golden*, **ἀργύρεος**, *of silver*, and **ἁπλόος**, *simple*, are thus declined:—

SINGULAR.

Nom.	(χρῡ́σεος)	**χρῡσοῦς**	(χρῡσέα)	**χρῡσῆ**	(χρῡ́σεον)	**χρῡσοῦν**
Gen.	(χρῡσέου)	**χρῡσοῦ**	(χρῡσέας)	**χρῡσῆς**	(χρῡσέου)	**χρῡσοῦ**
Dat.	(χρῡσέῳ)	**χρῡσῷ**	(χρῡσέᾳ)	**χρῡσῇ**	(χρῡσέῳ)	**χρῡσῷ**
Acc.	(χρῡ́σεον)	**χρῡσοῦν**	(χρῡσέαν)	**χρῡσῆν**	(χρῡ́σεον)	**χρῡσοῦν**

DUAL.

N. A.	(χρῡσέω)	**χρῡσώ**	(χρυσέα)	**χρῡσᾶ**	(χρυσέω)	**χρῡσώ**
G. D.	(χρῡσέοιν)	**χρῡσοῖν**	(χρυσέαιν)	**χρῡσαῖν**	(χρυσέοιν)	**χρῡσοῖν**

PLURAL.

Nom.	(χρῡ́σεοι)	**χρῡσοῖ**	(χρῡ́σεαι)	**χρῡσαῖ**	(χρῡ́σεα)	**χρῡσᾶ**
Gen.	(χρῡσέων)	**χρῡσῶν**	(χρυσέων)	**χρῡσῶν**	(χρῡσέων)	**χρῡσῶν**
Dat.	(χρῡσέοις)	**χρῡσοῖς**	(χρυσέαις)	**χρῡσαῖς**	(χρῡσέοις)	**χρῡσοῖς**
Acc.	(χρῡσέους)	**χρῡσοῦς**	(χρυσέας)	**χρῡσᾶς**	(χρῡ́σεα)	**χρῡσᾶ**

SINGULAR.

Nom.	(ἀργύρεος)	**ἀργυροῦς**	(ἀργυρέα)	**ἀργυρᾶ**	(ἀργύρεον)	**ἀργυροῦν**
Gen.	(ἀργυρέου)	**ἀργυροῦ**	(ἀργυρέας)	**ἀργυρᾶς**	(ἀργυρέου)	**ἀργυροῦ**
Dat.	(ἀργυρέῳ)	**ἀργυρῷ**	(ἀργυρέᾳ)	**ἀργυρᾷ**	(ἀργυρέῳ)	**ἀργυρῷ**
Acc.	(ἀργύρεον)	**ἀργυροῦν**	(ἀργυρέαν)	**ἀργυρᾶν**	(ἀργύρεον)	**ἀργυροῦν**

DUAL.

N. A.	(ἀργυρέω)	**ἀργυρώ**	(ἀργυρέα)	**ἀργυρᾶ**	(ἀργυρέω)	**ἀργυρώ**
G. D.	(ἀργυρέοιν)	**ἀργυροῖν**	(ἀργυρέαιν)	**ἀργυραῖν**	(ἀργυρέοιν)	**ἀργυροῖν**

PLURAL.

Nom.	(ἀργύρεοι)	**ἀργυροῖ**	(ἀργύρεαι)	**ἀργυραῖ**	(ἀργύρεα)	**ἀργυρᾶ**
Gen.	(ἀργυρέων)	**ἀργυρῶν**	(ἀργυρέων)	**ἀργυρῶν**	(ἀργυρέων)	**ἀργυρῶν**
Dat.	(ἀργυρέοις)	**ἀργυροῖς**	(ἀργυρέαις)	**ἀργυραῖς**	(ἀργυρέοις)	**ἀργυροῖς**
Acc.	(ἀργυρέους)	**ἀργυροῦς**	(ἀργυρέας)	**ἀργυρᾶς**	(ἀργύρεα)	**ἀργυρᾶ**

SINGULAR.

Nom.	(ἁπλόος)	**ἁπλοῦς**	(ἁπλόη)	**ἁπλῆ**	(ἁπλόον)	**ἁπλοῦν**
Gen.	(ἁπλόου)	**ἁπλοῦ**	(ἁπλόης)	**ἁπλῆς**	(ἁπλόου)	**ἁπλοῦ**
Dat.	(ἁπλόῳ)	**ἁπλῷ**	(ἁπλόῃ)	**ἁπλῇ**	(ἁπλόῳ)	**ἁπλῷ**
Acc.	(ἁπλόον)	**ἁπλοῦν**	(ἁπλόην)	**ἁπλῆν**	(ἁπλόον)	**ἁπλοῦν**

DUAL.

N. A.	(ἁπλόω)	**ἁπλώ**	(ἁπλόα)	**ἁπλᾶ**	(ἁπλόω)	**ἁπλώ**
G. D.	(ἁπλόοιν)	**ἁπλοῖν**	(ἁπλόαιν)	**ἁπλαῖν**	(ἁπλόοιν)	**ἁπλοῖν**

PLURAL.

Nom.	(ἁπλόοι)	**ἁπλοῖ**	(ἁπλόαι)	**ἁπλαῖ**	(ἁπλόα)	**ἁπλᾶ**
Gen.	(ἁπλόων)	**ἁπλῶν**	(ἁπλόων)	**ἁπλῶν**	(ἁπλόων)	**ἁπλῶν**
Dat.	(ἁπλόοις)	**ἁπλοῖς**	(ἁπλόαις)	**ἁπλαῖς**	(ἁπλόοις)	**ἁπλοῖς**
Acc.	(ἁπλόους)	**ἁπλοῦς**	(ἁπλόας)	**ἁπλᾶς**	(ἁπλόα)	**ἁπλᾶ**

311. All contract forms of these adjectives are *perispomena;* except ώ for έω and όω in the dual (see 203, 1). See also 203, 2 and 39, 1. Compounds in οος leave οα in the neuter plural uncontracted. No distinct vocative forms occur.

THIRD (OR CONSONANT) DECLENSION.

312. Adjectives belonging only to the third declension have two endings, the feminine being the same as the masculine. Most of these end in ης and ες (stems in εσ-), or in ων and ον (stems in ον-). See 233.

313. Ἀληθής, *true*, and εὐδαίμων, *happy*, are thus declined: —

	M. F.	*N.*	*M. F.*	*N.*
		SINGULAR.		
Nom.	**ἀληθής**	**ἀληθές**	**εὐδαίμων**	**εὔδαιμον**
Gen.	(ἀληθέος) **ἀληθοῦς**		**εὐδαίμονος**	
Dat.	(ἀληθέϊ) **ἀληθεῖ**		**εὐδαίμονι**	
Acc.	(ἀληθέα) **ἀληθῆ**	**ἀληθές**	**εὐδαίμονα**	**εὔδαιμον**
Voc.	**ἀληθές**		**εὔδαιμον**	
		DUAL.		
N. A. V.	(ἀληθέε) **ἀληθεῖ**		**εὐδαίμονε**	
G. D.	(ἀληθέοιν) **ἀληθοῖν**		**εὐδαιμόνοιν**	
		PLURAL.		
N. V.	(ἀληθέες) **ἀληθεῖς**	(ἀληθέα) **ἀληθῆ**	**εὐδαίμονες**	**εὐδαίμονα**
Gen.	(ἀληθέων) **ἀληθῶν**		**εὐδαιμόνων**	
Dat.	**ἀληθέσι**		**εὐδαίμοσι**	
Acc.	**ἀληθεῖς**	(ἀληθέα) **ἀληθῆ**	**εὐδαίμονας**	**εὐδαίμονα**

314. For the recessive accent of neuters like εὔδαιμον and of many barytone compounds in ης (as αὐτάρκης, αὔταρκες), see 122. Ἄληθες, *indeed!* is proparoxytone.

315. In adjectives in ης, εα is contracted to ᾱ after ε, and to ᾱ or η after ι or υ; as εὐκλεής, *glorious*, acc. (εὐκλεέα) εὐκλεᾶ; ὑγιής, *healthy*, (ὑγιέα) ὑγιᾶ and ὑγιῆ; εὐφυής, *comely*, (εὐφυέα) εὐφυᾶ and εὐφυῆ. (See 39, 2.)

For εις in the accusative plural, see 208, 3.

316. N. Adjectives compounded of nouns and a prefix are generally declined like those nouns; as εὔελπις, εὔελπι, *hopeful*, gen. εὐέλπιδος, acc. εὔελπιν (214, 3), εὔελπι; εὔχαρις, εὔχαρι, *graceful*, gen. εὐχάριτος, acc. εὔχαριν, εὔχαρι. But compounds of πατήρ and μήτηρ end in ωρ (gen. ορος), and those of πόλις in ις (gen. ιδος); as ἀπάτωρ, ἄπατορ, gen. ἀπάτορος, *fatherless*; ἄπολις, ἄπολι, *without a country*, gen. ἀπόλιδος.

317. For the peculiar declension of comparatives in ων (stem in ον-), see 358.

FIRST AND THIRD DECLENSIONS COMBINED.

318. Adjectives of this class have the masculine and neuter of the third declension and the feminine of the first. The feminine always has ᾰ in the nominative and accusative singular (175); in the genitive and dative singular it has ᾱ after a vowel or diphthong, otherwise η.

Ων of the feminine genitive plural is circumflexed regularly (124). Compare 302.

For feminine dual forms, see 303.

319. (*Stems in υ.*) Stems in υ form adjectives in υς, εια, υ. The masculine and neuter are declined like πῆχυς and ἄστυ (250), except that the genitive singular ends in ος (not ως) and the neuter plural in εα is not contracted.

320. Γλυκύς, *sweet*, is thus declined: —

		SINGULAR.	
Nom.	γλυκύς	γλυκεῖα	γλυκύ
Gen.	γλυκέος	γλυκείας	γλυκέος
Dat.	(γλυκέϊ) γλυκεῖ	γλυκείᾳ	(γλυκέϊ) γλυκεῖ
Acc.	γλυκύν	γλυκεῖαν	γλυκύ
Voc.	γλυκύ	γλυκεῖα	γλυκύ
		DUAL.	
N. A. V.	(γλυκέε) γλυκεῖ	γλυκείᾱ	(γλυκέε) γλυκεῖ
G. D.	γλυκέοιν	γλυκείαιν	γλυκέοιν

PLURAL.

N. V.	(γλυκέες) γλυκεῖς	γλυκεῖαι	γλυκέα
Gen.	γλυκέων	γλυκειῶν	γλυκέων
Dat.	γλυκέσι	γλυκείαις	γλυκέσι
Acc.	γλυκεῖς	γλυκείᾱς	γλυκέα

321. The feminine stem in *εια*- comes from the stem in *εν*- (*εϝ*-) by adding *ια*: thus γλυκευ-, γλυκε- (256), γλυκε-ια, γλυκεῖα. (See 90, 3.)

322. N. The Ionic feminine of adjectives in *υς* has *εα*. Homer has εὐρέα (for εὐρύν) as accusative of εὐρύς, *wide*.

323. N. Adjectives in *υς* are oxytone, except θῆλυς, *female, fresh*, and ἥμισυς, *half*. Θῆλυς sometimes has only two terminations in poetry.

324. 1. (*Stems in αν and εν.*) Two adjectives have stems in *αν*, μέλᾱς (μελαν-), μέλαινα, μέλαν, *black*, and τάλᾱς (ταλαν-), τάλαινα, τάλαν, *wretched*.

2. One has a stem in *εν*, τέρην (τερεν-), τέρεινα, τέρεν, *tender* (Latin *tener*).

325. Μέλᾱς and τέρην are thus declined: —

SINGULAR.

Nom.	μέλᾱς	μέλαινα	μέλαν	τέρην	τέρεινα	τέρεν
Gen.	μέλανος	μελαίνης	μέλανος	τέρενος	τερείνης	τέρενος
Dat.	μέλανι	μελαίνῃ	μέλανι	τέρενι	τερείνῃ	τέρενι
Acc.	μέλανα	μέλαιναν	μέλαν	τέρενα	τέρειναν	τέρεν
Voc.	μέλαν	μέλαινα	μέλαν	τέρεν	τέρεινα	τέρεν

DUAL.

N. A. V.	μέλανε	μελαίνᾱ	μέλανε	τέρενε	τερείνᾱ	τέρενε
G. D.	μελάνοιν	μελαίναιν	μελάνοιν	τερένοιν	τερείναιν	τερένοιν

PLURAL.

N. V.	μέλανες	μέλαιναι	μέλανα	τέρενες	τέρειναι	τέρενα
Gen.	μελάνων	μελαινῶν	μελάνων	τερένων	τερεινῶν	τερένων
Dat.	μέλασι	μελαίναις	μέλασι	τέρεσι	τερείναις	τέρεσι
Acc.	μέλανας	μελαίνᾱς	μέλανα	τέρενας	τερείνᾱς	τέρενα

326. The feminine stems *μελαινα*- and *τερεινα*- come from *μελαν-ια*- and *τερεν-ια*- (84, 5).

327. Like the masculine and neuter of τέρην is declined ἄρρην, ἄρρεν (older ἄρσην, ἄρσεν), *male*.

328. (*Stems in ντ.*) Adjectives from stems in *εντ* end in *εις*, *εσσα*, *εν*. From a stem in *αντ* comes *πᾶς*, *πᾶσα*, *πᾶν*, *all*.

329. *χαρίεις*, *graceful*, and *πᾶς* are thus declined: —

			SINGULAR.			
Nom.	χαρίεις	χαρίεσσα	χαρίεν	πᾶς	πᾶσα	πᾶν
Gen.	χαρίεντος	χαριέσσης	χαρίεντος	παντός	πάσης	παντός
Dat.	χαρίεντι	χαριέσσῃ	χαρίεντι	παντί	πάσῃ	παντί
Acc.	χαρίεντα	χαρίεσσαν	χαρίεν	πάντα	πᾶσαν	πᾶν
Voc.	χαρίεν	χαρίεσσα	χαρίεν			
			DUAL.			
N. A. V.	χαρίεντε	χαριέσσᾱ	χαρίεντε			
G. D.	χαριέντοιν	χαριέσσαιν	χαριέντοιν			
			PLURAL.			
N. V.	χαρίεντες	χαρίεσσαι	χαρίεντα	πάντες	πᾶσαι	πάντα
Gen.	χαριέντων	χαριεσσῶν	χαριέντων	πάντων	πᾱσῶν	πάντων
Dat.	χαρίεσι	χαριέσσαις	χαρίεσι	πᾶσι	πάσαις	πᾶσι
Acc.	χαρίεντας	χαριέσσᾱς	χαρίεντα	πάντας	πάσᾱς	πάντα

330. Most adjective stems in *εντ*, all in *αντ* except *παντ-* (*πᾶς*), and all in *οντ* except *ἑκοντ-* and *ἀκοντ-* (*ἑκών* and *ἄκων*, 333), belong to participles. (See 334.)

331. 1. The nominatives *χαρίεις* and *χαρίεν* are for *χαριεντ-ς* and *χαριεντ-*, and *πᾶς* and *πᾶν* for *παντ-ς* and *παντ-* (79). The ᾱ in *πᾶν* is irregular; but Homer has *ἅπᾰν* and *πρόπᾰν*. For the accent of *πάντων* and *πᾶσι*, see 128. Πᾱσῶν is regular (318).

2. For the feminine *χαρίεσσα* (for *χαριετ-ια* from a stem in *ετ-*), see 84, 1; and for dat. plur. *χαρίεσι* (for *χαριετ-σι*), see 74. Πᾶσα is for *παντ-ια* (84, 2).

332. Homer occasionally contracts adjectives in *ήεις*, as *τιμῆς* (for *τιμήεις*), *τιμῆντα* (for *τιμήεντα*), *valuable*. The Attic poets sometimes contract those in *όεις*; as *πλακοῦς*, *πλακοῦντος* (for *πλακόεις*, *πλακόεντος*), *flat* (*cake*), *πτεροῦντα* (for *πτερόεντα*), *winged*, *αἰθαλοῦσσα* (for *αἰθαλόεσσα*), *flaming*, *πτεροῦσσα* (for *πτερόεσσα*), *μελιτοῦττα* (for *μελιτόεσσα*, 68, 3), *honied* (*cake*). So names of places (properly adjectives); as Ἐλαιοῦς, Ἐλαιοῦντος, *Elaeus*, Ἐλαιοῦσσα (an island), from forms in *-οεις*, *-οεσσα*. So Ῥαμνοῦς, Ῥαμνοῦντος, *Rhamnus* (from *-όεις*). (See 39, 5.)

333. One adjective in *ων*, *ἑκών*, *ἑκοῦσα*, *ἑκόν*, *willing*, gen. *ἑκόντος*, etc., has three endings, and is declined like participles in *ων* (330). So its compound, *ἄκων* (*ἀέκων*), *unwilling*, *ἄκουσα*, *ἆκον*, gen. *ἄκοντος*.

PARTICIPLES IN ων, ους, ᾱς, εις, ῡς, AND ως.

334. All participles, except those in ος, belong to the first and third declensions combined.

335. Λύων (λῡοντ-), *loosing*, διδούς (διδοντ-), *giving*, τιθείς (τιθεντ-), *placing*, δεικνύς (δεικνυντ-), *showing*, ἱστάς (ἱσταντ-), *erecting*, ὤν (ὀντ-), *being*, (present active participles of λύω, δίδωμι, τίθημι, δείκνῡμι, ἵστημι, and εἰμί), λύσᾱς (λῡσαντ-), *having loosed*, and λελυκώς (λελυκοτ-), *having loosed* (first aorist and perfect participles of λύω), are thus declined:—

SINGULAR.

Nom.	λύων	λύουσα	λῦον	διδούς	διδοῦσα	διδόν
Gen.	λύοντος	λῡούσης	λύοντος	διδόντος	διδούσης	διδόντος
Dat.	λύοντι	λῡούσῃ	λύοντι	διδόντι	διδούσῃ	διδόντι
Acc.	λύοντα	λύουσαν	λῦον	διδόντα	διδοῦσαν	διδόν
Voc.	λύων	λύουσα	λῦον	διδούς	διδοῦσα	διδόν

DUAL.

N. A. V.	λύοντε	λῡούσᾱ	λύοντε	διδόντε	διδούσᾱ	διδόντε
G. D.	λῡόντοιν	λῡούσαιν	λῡόντοιν	διδόντοιν	διδούσαιν	διδόντοιν

PLURAL.

N. V.	λύοντες	λύουσαι	λύοντα	διδόντες	διδοῦσαι	διδόντα
Gen.	λῡόντων	λῡουσῶν	λῡόντων	διδόντων	διδουσῶν	διδόντων
Dat.	λύουσι	λῡούσαις	λύουσι	διδοῦσι	διδούσαις	διδοῦσι
Acc.	λύοντας	λῡούσᾱς	λύοντα	διδόντας	διδούσᾱς	διδόντα

SINGULAR.

Nom.	τιθείς	τιθεῖσα	τιθέν	δεικνύς	δεικνῦσα	δεικνύν
Gen.	τιθέντος	τιθείσης	τιθέντος	δεικνύντος	δεικνύσης	δεικνύντος
Dat.	τιθέντι	τιθείσῃ	τιθέντι	δεικνύντι	δεικνύσῃ	δεικνύντι
Acc.	τιθέντα	τιθεῖσαν	τιθέν	δεικνύντα	δεικνῦσαν	δεικνύν
Voc.	τιθείς	τιθεῖσα	τιθέν	δεικνύς	δεικνῦσα	δεικνύν

DUAL.

N. A. V.	τιθέντε	τιθείσᾱ	τιθέντε	δεικνύντε	δεικνύσᾱ	δεικνύντε
G. D.	τιθέντοιν	τιθείσαιν	τιθέντοιν	δεικνύντοιν	δεικνύσαιν	δεικνύντοιν

PLURAL.

N. V.	τιθέντες	τιθεῖσαι	τιθέντα	δεικνύντες	δεικνῦσαι	δεικνύντα
Gen.	τιθέντων	τιθεισῶν	τιθέντων	δεικνύντων	δεικνῡσῶν	δεικνύντων
Dat.	τιθεῖσι	τιθείσαις	τιθεῖσι	δεικνῦσι	δεικνύσαις	δεικνῦσι
Acc.	τιθέντας	τιθείσᾱς	τιθέντα	δεικνύντας	δεικνύσᾱς	δεικνύντα

SINGULAR.

Nom.	ἱστάς	ἱστᾶσα	ἱστάν	λύσᾱς	λύσᾱσα	λῦσαν
Gen.	ἱστάντος	ἱστάσης	ἱστάντος	λύσαντος	λῡσάσης	λύσαντος
Dat.	ἱστάντι	ἱστάσῃ	ἱστάντι	λύσαντι	λῡσάσῃ	λύσαντι
Acc.	ἱστάντα	ἱστᾶσαν	ἱστάν	λύσαντα	λύσᾱσαν	λῦσαν
Voc.	ἱστάς	ἱστᾶσα	ἱστάν	λύσᾱς	λύσᾱσα	λῦσαν

DUAL.

N. A. V.	ἱστάντε	ἱστάσᾱ	ἱστάντε	λύσαντε	λῡσάσᾱ	λύσαντε
G. D.	ἱστάντοιν	ἱστάσαιν	ἱστάντοιν	λῡσάντοιν	λῡσάσαιν	λῡσάντοιν

PLURAL.

N. V.	ἱστάντες	ἱστᾶσαι	ἱστάντα	λύσαντες	λύσᾱσαι	λύσαντα
Gen.	ἱστάντων	ἱστᾱσῶν	ἱστάντων	λῡσάντων	λῡσᾱσῶν	λῡσάντων
Dat.	ἱστᾶσι	ἱστάσαις	ἱστᾶσι	λύσᾱσι	λῡσάσαις	λύσᾱσι
Acc.	ἱστάντας	ἱστάσᾱς	ἱστάντα	λύσαντας	λῡσάσᾱς	λύσαντα

SINGULAR.

Nom.	ὤν	οὖσα	ὄν	λελυκώς	λελυκυῖα	λελυκός
Gen.	ὄντος	οὔσης	ὄντος	λελυκότος	λελυκυίας	λελυκότος
Dat.	ὄντι	οὔσῃ	ὄντι	λελυκότι	λελυκυίᾳ	λελυκότι
Acc.	ὄντα	οὖσαν	ὄν	λελυκότα	λελυκυῖαν	λελυκός
Voc.	ὤν	οὖσα	ὄν	λελυκώς	λελυκυῖα	λελυκός

DUAL.

N. A. V.	ὄντε	οὔσᾱ	ὄντε	λελυκότε	λελυκυίᾱ	λελυκότε
G. D.	ὄντοιν	οὔσαιν	ὄντοιν	λελυκότοιν	λελυκυίαιν	λελυκότοιν

PLURAL.

N. V.	ὄντες	οὖσαι	ὄντα	λελυκότες	λελυκυῖαι	λελυκότα
Gen.	ὄντων	οὐσῶν	ὄντων	λελυκότων	λελυκυιῶν	λελυκότων
Dat.	οὖσι	οὔσαις	οὖσι	λελυκόσι	λελυκυίαις	λελυκόσι
Acc.	ὄντας	οὔσᾱς	ὄντα	λελυκότας	λελυκυίᾱς	λελυκότα

336. All participles in ων are declined like λύων (those in ών being accented like ὤν); all in ους, ῡς, and ως are declined like διδούς, δεικνύς, and λελυκώς; all in εις (aorist passive as well as active) are declined like τιθείς; present and second aorist active participles in άς (from verbs in μι) are declined like ἱστάς, and first aorists in ᾱς like λύσᾱς.

337. 1. For feminines in ουσα, εισα, ῡσα, and ᾱσα (for οντ-ια, εντ-ια, υντ-ια, αντ-ια), formed by adding ια to the stem, see 84, 2.

2. Perfects in ως (with stems in οτ-) have an irregular feminine in υια.

338. The full accent of polysyllabic barytone participles appears in *βουλεύων*, *βουλεύουσα*, *βουλεῦον*, and *βουλεύσᾱς*, *βουλεύσᾱσα*, *βουλεῦσαν*. (See 134.)

339. For the accent of the genitive and dative of monosyllabic participles, see 129 and the inflection of *ὤν* above. Thus *θείς* has gen. *θέντος*, *θέντων*, etc.

340. Participles in *άων*, *έων*, and *όων* are contracted. Τῑμάων, *τῑμῶν*, *honoring*, and *φιλέων*, *φιλῶν*, *loving*, are declined as follows: —

SINGULAR.

N.	(τῑμάων)	**τῑμῶν**	(τῑμάουσα)	**τῑμῶσα**	(τῑμάον)	**τῑμῶν**
G.	(τῑμάοντος)	**τῑμῶντος**	(τῑμαούσης)	**τῑμώσης**	(τῑμάοντος)	**τῑμῶντος**
D.	(τῑμάοντι)	**τῑμῶντι**	(τῑμαούσῃ)	**τῑμώσῃ**	(τῑμάοντι)	**τῑμῶντι**
A.	(τῑμάοντα)	**τῑμῶντα**	(τῑμάουσαν)	**τῑμῶσαν**	(τῑμάον)	**τῑμῶν**
V.	(τῑμάων)	**τῑμῶν**	(τῑμάουσα)	**τῑμῶσα**	(τῑμάον)	**τῑμῶν**

DUAL.

N.	(τῑμάοντε)	**τῑμῶντε**	(τῑμαούσᾱ)	**τῑμώσᾱ**	(τῑμάοντε)	**τῑμῶντε**
G.	(τῑμαόντοιν)	**τῑμώντοιν**	(τῑμαούσαιν)	**τῑμώσαιν**	(τιμαόντοιν)	**τῑμώντοιν**

PLURAL.

N.	(τῑμάοντες)	**τῑμῶντες**	(τῑμάουσαι)	**τῑμῶσαι**	(τῑμάοντα)	**τῑμῶντα**
G.	(τῑμαόντων)	**τῑμώντων**	(τῑμαουσῶν)	**τῑμωσῶν**	(τῑμαόντων)	**τῑμώντων**
D.	(τῑμάουσι)	**τῑμῶσι**	(τῑμαούσαις)	**τῑμώσαις**	(τῑμάουσι)	**τῑμῶσι**
A.	(τῑμάοντας)	**τῑμῶντας**	(τῑμαούσᾱς)	**τῑμώσᾱς**	(τῑμάοντα)	**τῑμῶντα**
V.	(τῑμάοντες)	**τῑμῶντες**	(τῑμάουσαι)	**τῑμῶσαι**	(τῑμάοντα)	**τῑμῶντα**

SINGULAR.

N.	(φιλέων)	**φιλῶν**	(φιλέουσα)	**φιλοῦσα**	(φιλέον)	**φιλοῦν**
G.	(φιλέοντος)	**φιλοῦντος**	(φιλεούσης)	**φιλούσης**	(φιλέοντος)	**φιλοῦντος**
D.	(φιλέοντι)	**φιλοῦντι**	(φιλεούσῃ)	**φιλούσῃ**	(φιλέοντι)	**φιλοῦντι**
A.	(φιλέοντα)	**φιλοῦντα**	(φιλέουσαν)	**φιλοῦσαν**	(φιλέον)	**φιλοῦν**
V.	(φιλέων)	**φιλῶν**	(φιλέουσα)	**φιλοῦσα**	(φιλέον)	**φιλοῦν**

DUAL.

N.	(φιλέοντε)	**φιλοῦντε**	(φιλεούσᾱ)	**φιλούσᾱ**	(φιλέοντε)	**φιλοῦντε**
G.	(φιλεόντοιν)	**φιλούντοιν**	(φιλεούσαιν)	**φιλούσαιν**	(φιλεόντοιν)	**φιλούντοιν**

PLURAL.

N.	(φιλέοντες)	**φιλοῦντες**	(φιλέουσαι)	**φιλοῦσαι**	(φιλέοντα)	**φιλοῦντα**
G.	(φιλεόντων)	**φιλούντων**	(φιλεουσῶν)	**φιλουσῶν**	(φιλεόντων)	**φιλούντων**
D.	(φιλέουσι)	**φιλοῦσι**	(φιλεούσαις)	**φιλούσαις**	(φιλέουσι)	**φιλοῦσι**
A.	(φιλέοντας)	**φιλοῦντας**	(φιλεούσᾱς)	**φιλούσᾱς**	(φιλέοντα)	**φιλοῦντα**
V.	(φιλέοντες)	**φιλοῦντες**	(φιλέουσαι)	**φιλοῦσαι**	(φιλέοντα)	**φιλοῦντα**

341. Present participles of verbs in όω (contracted ῶ) are declined like φιλῶν. Thus δηλῶν, δηλοῦσα, δηλοῦν, *manifesting*; gen. δηλοῦντος, δηλούσης; dat. δηλοῦντι, δηλούσῃ, etc. No uncontracted forms of verbs in όω are used (493).

342. A few second perfect participles in αώς of the μι- form have ῶσα in the feminine, and retain ω in the oblique cases. They are contracted in Attic; as Hom. ἑσταώς, ἑσταῶσα, ἑσταός, Attic ἑστώς, ἑστῶσα, ἑστός or ἑστώς, *standing*, gen. ἑστῶτος, ἑστώσης, ἑστῶτος, etc.; pl. ἑστῶτες, ἑστῶσαι, ἑστῶτα, gen. ἑστώτων, ἑστωσῶν, ἑστώτων, etc. (See 508.)

ADJECTIVES WITH ONE ENDING.

343. Some adjectives of the third declension have only one ending, which is both masculine and feminine; as φυγάς, φυγάδος, *fugitive*; ἄπαις, ἄπαιδος, *childless*; ἀγνώς, ἀγνῶτος, *unknown*; ἄναλκις, ἀνάλκιδος, *weak*. The oblique cases occasionally occur as neuter.

344. The poetic ἴδρις, *knowing*, has acc. ἴδριν, voc. ἴδρι, nom. pl. ἴδριες.

345. A very few adjectives of one termination are of the first declension, ending in ας or ης; as γεννάδας, *noble*, gen. γεννάδου.

IRREGULAR ADJECTIVES.

346. The irregular adjectives, μέγας (μεγα-, μεγαλο-), *great*, πολύς (πολυ-, πολλο-), *much*, and πρᾶος (πρᾳο-, πρᾱϋ-), or πρᾶος, *mild*, are thus declined:—

			SINGULAR.			
Nom.	μέγας	μεγάλη	μέγα	πολύς	πολλή	πολύ
Gen.	μεγάλου	μεγάλης	μεγάλου	πολλοῦ	πολλῆς	πολλοῦ
Dat.	μεγάλῳ	μεγάλῃ	μεγάλῳ	πολλῷ	πολλῇ	πολλῷ
Acc.	μέγαν	μεγάλην	μέγα	πολύν	πολλήν	πολύ
Voc.	μεγάλε	μεγάλη	μέγα			
			DUAL.			
N. A. V.	μεγάλω	μεγάλᾱ	μεγάλω			
G. D.	μεγάλοιν	μεγάλαιν	μεγάλοιν			
			PLURAL.			
N. V.	μεγάλοι	μεγάλαι	μεγάλα	πολλοί	πολλαί	πολλά
Gen.	μεγάλων	μεγάλων	μεγάλων	πολλῶν	πολλῶν	πολλῶν
Dat.	μεγάλοις	μεγάλαις	μεγάλοις	πολλοῖς	πολλαῖς	πολλοῖς
Acc.	μεγάλους	μεγάλᾱς	μεγάλα	πολλούς	πολλάς	πολλά

		SINGULAR.	
Nom.	πρᾶος	πραεῖα	πρᾶον
Gen.	πρᾴου	πρᾱείᾱς	πρᾴου
Dat.	πρᾴῳ	πρᾱείᾳ	πρᾴῳ
Acc.	πρᾶον	πρᾱεῖαν	πρᾶον
		DUAL.	
N. V.	πρᾴω	πρᾱείᾱ	πρᾴω
G. D.	πρᾴοιν	πρᾱείαιν	πρᾴοιν
		PLURAL.	
N. A.	πρᾶοι or πρᾱεῖς	πρᾱεῖαι	πρᾶα or πρᾱέα
Gen.	πρᾱέων	πρᾱειῶν	πρᾱέων
Dat.	πρᾴοις or πρᾱέσι	πρᾱείαις	πρᾴοις or πρᾱέσι
Acc.	πρᾴους	πρᾱείᾱς	πρᾶα or πρᾱέα

347. N. Πολλός, ή, όν, is found in Homer and Herodotus, declined regularly throughout. Homer has forms πολέος, πολέες, πολέων, πολέσι, etc., not to be confounded with epic forms of πόλις (255): also πουλύς, πουλύ.

348. N. Πρᾶος has two stems, one πρᾳο-, from which the masculine and neutėr are generally formed; and one πρᾱῠ-, from which the feminine and some other forms come. There is an epic form πρηΰς (lyric πρᾱΰς) coming from the latter stem. The forms belonging to the two stems differ in accent.

349. N. Some compounds of πούς (ποδ-), *foot*, have ουν in the nominative neuter and the accusative masculine; as τρίπους, τρίπουν, *three-footed.*

COMPARISON OF ADJECTIVES.

I. Comparison by -τερος, -τατος.

350. Most adjectives add τερος (stem τερο-) to the *stem* to form the comparative, and τατος (stem τατο-) to form the superlative. Stems in ο with a short penult lengthen ο to ω before τερος and τατος. For the declension, see 301. *E.g.*

Κοῦφος (κουφο-), *light*, κουφότερος (-ᾱ, -ον), *lighter*, κουφότατος (-η, -ον), *lightest.*

Σοφός (σοφο-), *wise*, σοφώτερος, *wiser*, σοφώτατος, *wisest.*

Ἄξιος (ἀξιο-), *worthy*, ἀξιώτερος, ἀξιώτατος.

΄- (σεμνο-), *august*, σεμνότερος, σεμνότατος.

N. (φιλέοντες) ψκρο-), *bitter*, πικρότερος, πικρότατος.

G. (φιλεόντων) φιλ*sharp*, ὀξύτερος, ὀξύτατος.

D. (φιλέουσι) φιλο *black*, μελάντερος, μελάντατος.

A. (φιλέοντας) φιλοῦντ), *true*, ἀληθέστερος, ἀληθέστατος (312).

V. (φιλέοντες) φιλοῦντ

351. Stems in ο do not lengthen ο to ω if the penultimate vowel is followed by a mute and a liquid (100). See *πικρός* above.

352. Μέσος, *middle*, and a few others, drop ο of the stem and add *αίτερος* and *αίτατος*; as *μέσος* (*μεσο-*), *μεσαίτερος*, *μεσαίτατος*.

353. Adjectives in *οος* drop final *ο* of the stem and add *έστερος* and *έστατος*, which are contracted with ο to *ούστερος* and *ούστατος*; as (*εὔνοος*) *εὔνους* (*εὐνοο-*), *well-disposed*, *εὐνούστερος*, *εὐνούστατος*.

354. Adjectives in *ων* add *έστερος* and *έστατος* to the stem; as *σώφρων* (*σωφρον-*), *prudent*, *σωφρονέστερος*, *σωφρονέστατος*.

355. Adjectives in *εις* add *τερος* and *τατος* to the stem in *ετ-* (331, 2); as *χαρίεις*, *graceful*, fem. *χαρίεσσα* (*χαριετ-*), *χαριέστερος*, *χαριέστατος* for *χαριετ-τερος*, *χαριετ-τατος* (71).

356. Adjectives may be compared by prefixing *μᾶλλον*, *more*, and *μάλιστα*, *most*; as *μᾶλλον σοφός*, *more wise*, *μάλιστα κακός*, *most bad*.

II. Comparison by -ῑων, -ιστος.

357. 1. Some adjectives, chiefly in *υς* and *ρος*, are compared by changing *these endings* to *ῑων* and *ιστος*. *E.g.*

Ἡδύς, *sweet*, ἡδίων, ἥδιστος.

Ταχύς, *swift*, ταχίων (rare), commonly θάσσων (95, 5), τάχιστος.

Αἰσχρός, *base*, αἰσχίων, αἴσχιστος.

Ἐχθρός, *hostile*, ἐχθίων, ἔχθιστος.

Κυδρός (poet.), *glorious*, κυδίων κύδιστος.

2. The terminations *ῑων* and *ιστος* are thus added to the *root* of the word (153), not to the adjective stem.

358. Comparatives in *ῑων*, neuter *ῑον*, are thus declined: —

	SINGULAR.			PLURAL.	
Nom.	ἡδίων	ἥδῑον	N. V.	ἡδίονες ἡδίους	ἡδίονα ἡδίω
Gen.	ἡδίονος		Gen.	ἡδῑόνων	
Dat.	ἡδίονι		Dat.	ἡδίοσι	
Acc.	ἡδίονα ἡδίω	ἥδῑον	Acc.	ἡδίονας ἡδίους	ἡδίονα ἡδίω

	DUAL.
N. A. V.	ἡδίονε
G. D.	ἡδῑόνοιν

359. N. (*a*) The shortened forms come from a stem in *οσ-* (cf. 238), *ω* and *ους* being contracted from *ο-α* and *ο-ες*. The accusative plural in *ους* follows the form of the nominative (208, 3).

(*b*) Homer sometimes has comparatives in *ἴων*.

(*c*) The vocative singular of these comparatives seems not to occur.

(*d*) For the recessive accent in the neuter singular, see 122.

360. The irregular comparatives in ων (361) are declined like ἡδίων.

III. Irregular Comparison.

361. The following are the most important cases of irregular comparison: —

1. **ἀγαθός**, *good*,	**ἀμείνων**,	
	(ἀρείων),	**ἄριστος**,
	βελτίων,	**βέλτιστος**,
	(βέλτερος),	(βέλτατος),
	κρείσσων or **κρείττων** (κρέσσων),	**κράτιστος**,
	(φέρτερος),	(κάρτιστος),
		(φέρτατος, φέριστος),
	λῴων (λωίων, λωίτερος),	**λῷστος**.
2. **κακός**, *bad*,	**κακίων** (κακώτερος),	**κάκιστος**,
	χείρων (χερείων),	**χείριστος**,
	(χειρότερος, χερειότερος),	
	ἥσσων (for ἡκ-ι-ων, 84,1) or **ἥττων** (ἕσσων),	(ἥκιστος, rare); adv. **ἥκιστα**, *least*.
3. **καλός**, *beautiful*,	**καλλίων**,	**κάλλιστος**.
4. **μέγας**, *great*,	**μείζων** (μέζων for μεγ-ι-ων, 84, 3),	**μέγιστος**.
5. **μικρός**, *small*,	**μικρότερος**,	**μικρότατος**,
(Hom. **ἐλάχεια**, fem. of **ἐλαχύς**),	**ἐλάσσων** or **ἐλάττων** (84, 1), **μείων**	**ἐλάχιστος**, (μεῖστος, rare).
6. **ὀλίγος**, *little*,	(ὑπ-ολίζων, *rather less*),	**ὀλίγιστος**.
7. **πένης** (πενητ-), *poor*,	**πενέστερος**,	**πενέστατος**.
8. **πολύς**, *much*,	**πλείων** or **πλέων** (neut. sometimes πλεῖν),	**πλεῖστος**.
9. **ῥᾴδιος**, *easy*,	**ῥᾴων**,	**ῥᾷστος**,
(Ion. ῥηΐδιος),	(ῥηΐτερος),	(ῥηΐτατος, ῥήϊστος).
10. **φίλος**, *dear*,	**φίλτερος** (poetic),	**φίλτατος**,
	φιλαίτερος (rare),	**φιλαίτατος** (rare).
	(φιλίων, twice in Hom.)	

Ionic or poetic forms are in ( ).

362. Irregularities in the comparison of the following words will be found in the Lexicon: —

αἰσχρός, ἀλγεινός, ἅρπαξ, ἄφθονος, ἄχαρις, βαθύς, βλάξ, βραδύς, γεραιός, γλυκύς, ἐπιλήσμων, ἐπίχαρις, ἥσυχος, ἴδιος, ἴσος, λάλος, μάκαρ, μακρός, νέος, παλαιός, παχύς, πέπων, πίων, πλησίος, πρέσβυς, προὔργου, πρώιος, σπουδαῖος, σχολαῖος, ψευδής, ὠκύς.

363. Some comparatives and superlatives have no positive, but their stem generally appears in an adverb or preposition. *E.g.*

Ἀνώτερος, *upper*, ἀνώτατος, *uppermost*, from ἄνω, *up*; πρότερος, *former*, πρῶτος or πρώτιστος, *first*, from πρό, *before*; κατώτερος, *lower*, κατώτατος, *lowest*, from κάτω, *downward*.

See in the Lexicon ἀγχότερος, ἀφάρτερος, κερδίων, ὁπλότερος, προσώτερος, ῥίγιον (neuter), ὑπέρτερος, ὕστερος, ὑψίων, φαάντερος, with their regular superlatives; also ἔσχατος, ὕπατος, and κήδιστος.

364. Comparatives and superlatives may be formed from nouns, and even from pronouns. *E.g.*

Βασιλεύς, *king*, βασιλεύτερος, *a greater king*, βασιλεύτατος, *the greatest king*; κλέπτης, *thief*, κλεπτίστερος, κλεπτίστατος; κύων, *dog*, κύντερος, *more impudent*, κύντατος, *most impudent*. So αὐτός, *self*, αὐτότατος, *his very self*, ipsissimus.

ADVERBS AND THEIR COMPARISON.

365. Adverbs are regularly formed from adjectives. Their form (including the accent) may be found by changing ν of the genitive plural masculine to ς. *E.g.*

Φίλως, *dearly*, from φίλος; δικαίως, *justly* (δίκαιος); σοφῶς, *wisely* (σοφός); ἡδέως, *sweetly* (ἡδύς, gen. plur. ἡδέων), ἀληθῶς, *truly* (ἀληθής, gen. plur. ἀληθέων, ἀληθῶν); σαφῶς (Ionic σαφέως), *plainly* (σαφής, gen. plur. σαφέων, σαφῶν); πάντως, *wholly* (πᾶς, gen. plur. πάντων).

366. Adverbs are occasionally formed in the same way from participles; as διαφερόντως, *differently*, from διαφέρων (διαφερόντων); τεταγμένως, *regularly*, from τεταγμένος (τάσσω, *order*).

367. The neuter accusative of an adjective (either singular or plural) may be used as an adverb. *E.g.*

Πολύ and πολλά, *much* (πολύς); μέγα or μεγάλα, *greatly* (μέγας); also μεγάλως (365), μόνον, *only* (μόνος, *alone*).

368. Other forms of adverbs occur with various terminations; as *μάλα*, *very*, *τάχα*, *quickly*, *ἄνω*, *above*, *ἐγγύς*, *near*.

369. The neuter accusative *singular* of the comparative of an adjective forms the comparative of the corresponding adverb, and the neuter accusative *plural* of the superlative forms the superlative of the adverb. *E.g.*

Σοφῶς (σοφός), *wisely*; σοφώτερον, *more wisely*; σοφώτατα, *most wisely*. Ἀληθῶς (ἀληθής), *truly*; ἀληθέστερον, ἀληθέστατα. Ἡδέως (ἡδύς), *sweetly*, ἥδιον, ἥδιστα. Χαριέντως (χαρίεις), *gracefully*; χαριέστερον, χαριέστατα. Σωφρόνως (σώφρων), *prudently*; σωφρονέστερον, σωφρονέστατα.

370. 1. Adverbs in ω generally form a comparative in τέρω, and a superlative in τάτω; as ἄνω, *above*, ἀνωτέρω, ἀνωτάτω.

2. A few comparatives derived from adjectives end in τέρως; as βεβαιοτέρως, *more firmly*, for βεβαιότερον, from βεβαίως.

371. N. Μάλα, *much*, *very*, has comparative μᾶλλον (for μαλ-ι-ον, 84, 4), *more*, *rather*; superlative μάλιστα, *most*, *especially*.

NUMERALS.

372. The *cardinal* and *ordinal* numeral adjectives, and the numeral adverbs which occur, are as follows: —

Sign.		*Cardinal.*	*Ordinal.*	*Adverb.*
1	α′	εἷς, μία, ἕν, *one*	πρῶτος, *first*	ἅπαξ, *once*
2	β′	δύο, *two*	δεύτερος, *second*	δίς, *twice*
3	γ′	τρεῖς, τρία	τρίτος	τρίς
4	δ′	τέσσαρες, τέσσαρα (τέτταρες, τέτταρα)	τέταρτος	τετράκις
5	ε′	πέντε	πέμπτος	πεντάκις
6	ϛ′	ἕξ	ἕκτος	ἑξάκις
7	ζ′	ἑπτά	ἕβδομος	ἑπτάκις
8	η′	ὀκτώ	ὄγδοος	ὀκτάκις
9	θ′	ἐννέα	ἔνατος	ἐνάκις
10	ι′	δέκα	δέκατος	δεκάκις
11	ια′	ἕνδεκα	ἑνδέκατος	ἑνδεκάκις
12	ιβ′	δώδεκα	δωδέκατος	δωδεκάκις
13	ιγ′	τρεῖς καὶ δέκα (or τρεισκαίδεκα)	τρίτος καὶ δέκατος	

Sign.		*Cardinal.*	*Ordinal.*	*Adverb.*
14	ιδ'	τέσσαρες καὶ δέκα (or τεσσαρεσκαίδεκα)	τέταρτος καὶ δέκατος	
15	ιε'	πεντεκαίδεκα	πέμπτος καὶ δέκατος	
16	ιϛ'	ἑκκαίδεκα	ἕκτος καὶ δέκατος	
17	ιζ'	ἑπτακαίδεκα	ἕβδομος καὶ δέκατος	
18	ιη'	ὀκτωκαίδεκα	ὄγδοος καὶ δέκατος	
19	ιθ'	ἐννεακαίδεκα	ἔνατος καὶ δέκατος	
20	κ'	εἴκοσι(ν)	εἰκοστός	εἰκοσάκις
21	κα'	εἷς καὶ εἴκοσι(ν) or εἴκοσι (καὶ) εἷς	πρῶτος καὶ εἰκοστός	
30	λ'	τριάκοντα	τριᾱκοστός	τριᾱκοντάκις
40	μ'	τεσσαράκοντα	τεσσαρακοστός	τεσσαρακοντάκις
50	ν'	πεντήκοντα	πεντηκοστός	πεντηκοντάκις
60	ξ'	ἑξήκοντα	ἑξηκοστός	ἑξηκοντάκις
70	ο'	ἑβδομήκοντα	ἑβδομηκοστός	ἑβδομηκοντάκις
80	π'	ὀγδοήκοντα	ὀγδοηκοστός	ὀγδοηκοντάκις
90	ϙ'	ἐνενήκοντα	ἐνενηκοστός	ἐνενηκοντάκις
100	ρ'	ἑκατόν	ἑκατοστός	ἑκατοντάκις
200	σ'	διᾱκόσιοι, αι, α	διᾱκοσιοστός	διᾱκοσιάκις
300	τ'	τριᾱκόσιοι, αι, α	τριᾱκοσιοστός	
400	υ'	τετρακόσιοι, αι, α	τετρακοσιοστός	
500	φ'	πεντακόσιοι, αι, α	πεντακοσιοστός	
600	χ'	ἑξακόσιοι, αι, α	ἑξακοσιοστός	
700	ψ'	ἑπτακόσιοι, αι, α	ἑπτακοσιοστός	
800	ω'	ὀκτακόσιοι, αι, α	ὀκτακοσιοστός	
900	ϡ'	ἐνακόσιοι, αι, α	ἐνακοσιοστός	
1000	͵α	χίλιοι, αι, α	χῑλιοστός	χῑλιάκις
2000	͵β	δισχίλιοι, αι, α	δισχῑλιοστός	
3000	͵γ	τρισχίλιοι, αι, α	τρισχῑλιοστός	
10000	͵ι	μύριοι, αι, α	μῡριοστός	μῡριάκις
20000	͵κ	δισμύριοι		
100000	͵ρ	δεκακισμύριοι		

373. Above 10,000, δύο μῡριάδες, 20,000, τρεῖς μῡριάδες, 30,000, etc., may be used.

374. The dialects have the following peculiar forms:—

1—4. See 377.

5. Aeolic πέμπε for πέντε.

9. Herod. εἴνατος for ἔνατος; also εἰνάκις, etc.

12. Doric and Ionic δυώδεκα; Poetic δυοκαίδεκα.

20. Epic ἐείκοσι; Doric εἴκατι.

30, 80, 90, 200, 300. Ionic τριήκοντα, ὀγδώκοντα, ἐννήκοντα (Hom.), διηκόσιοι, τριηκόσιοι.

40. Herod. τεσσεράκοντα.

Homer has τρίτατος, τέτρατος, ἑβδόματος, ὀγδόατος, εἴνατος, δυωδέκατος, ἐεικοστός, and also the Attic form of each.

375. The cardinal numbers *εἷς*, *one*, *δύο*, *two*, *τρεῖς*, *three*, and *τέσσαρες* (or *τέτταρες*), *four*, are thus declined: —

Nom.	εἷς	μία	ἕν		
Gen.	ἑνός	μιᾶς	ἑνός	N. A.	δύο
Dat.	ἑνί	μιᾷ	ἑνί	G. D.	δυοῖν
Acc.	ἕνα	μίαν	ἕν		

Nom.	τρεῖς	τρία	τέσσαρες	τέσσαρα
Gen.	τριῶν		τεσσάρων	
Dat.	τρισί		τέσσαρσι	
Acc.	τρεῖς	τρία	τέσσαρας	τέσσαρα

376. N. Δύο, *two*, with a plural noun, is sometimes indeclinable.

377. N. Homer has fem. ἴα, ἰῆς, ἰῇ, ἴαν, for μία; and ἰῷ for ἑνί. Homer has δύο and δύω, both indeclinable; and δοιώ and δοιοί, declined regularly. Herodotus has δυῶν, δυοῖσι, and other forms: see the Lexicon. Homer sometimes has πίσυρες for τέσσαρες. Herodotus has τέσσερες, and the poets have τέτρασι.

378. The compounds οὐδείς and μηδείς, *no one, none*, are declined like εἷς. Thus, οὐδείς, οὐδεμία, οὐδέν; gen. οὐδενός, οὐδεμιᾶς; dat. οὐδενί, οὐδεμιᾷ; acc. οὐδένα, οὐδεμίαν, οὐδέν, etc. Plural forms sometimes occur; as οὐδένες, οὐδένων, οὐδέσι, οὐδένας, μηδένες, etc. When οὐδέ or μηδέ is written separately or is separated from εἷς (as by a preposition or by ἄν), the negative is more emphatic; as ἐξ οὐδενός, *from no one*; οὐδ' ἐξ ἑνός, *from not even one*; οὐδὲ εἷς, *not a man*.

379. *Both* is expressed by ἄμφω, *ambo*, ἀμφοῖν; and by ἀμφότερος, generally plural, ἀμφότεροι, αι, α.

380. The cardinal numbers from 5 to 100 are indeclinable. The higher numbers in ιοι and all the ordinals are declined regularly, like other adjectives in ος.

381. In τρεῖς (τρία) καὶ δέκα and τέσσαρες (τέσσαρα) καὶ δέκα for 13 and 14, the first part is declined. In ordinals (13th to 19th) the forms τρεισκαιδέκατος etc. are Ionic, and are rarely found in the best Attic.

382. 1. In compound expressions like 21, 22, etc., 31, 32, etc., the numbers can be connected by καί in either order; but if καί is omitted, the larger precedes. Thus, εἷς καὶ εἴκοσι, *one and twenty*, or εἴκοσι καὶ εἷς, *twenty and one;* but (without καί) only εἴκοσιν εἷς, *twenty-one*.

2. In ordinals we have πρῶτος καὶ εἰκοστός, *twenty-first*, and also εἰκοστὸς καὶ πρῶτος, etc.; and for 21 εἷς καὶ εἰκοστός.

3. The numbers 18 and 19, 28 and 29, 38 and 39, etc., are often expressed by ἑνὸς (or δυοῖν) δέοντες εἴκοσι (τριάκοντα, τεσσαράκοντα, etc.); as ἔτη ἑνὸς δέοντα τριάκοντα, *29 years*.

383. 1. With collective nouns in the singular, especially ἡ ἵππος, *cavalry*, the numerals in ιοι sometimes appear in the singular; as τὴν διᾱκοσίαν ἵππον, *the (troop of)* 200 *cavalry* (200 *horse*); ἀσπὶς μῡρία καὶ τετρακοσία (X. *An.* i, 7[10]), 10,400 *shields* (i.e. *men with shields*).

2. Μῡ́ριοι means *ten thousand; μῡρίοι, innumerable*. Μῡρίος sometimes has the latter sense; as μῡρίος χρόνος, *countless time;* μῡρίᾱ πενίᾱ, *incalculable poverty*.

384. N. The Greeks often expressed numbers by letters; the two obsolete letters *Vau* (in the form ϛ) and *Koppa*, and the character *San*, denoting 6, 90, and 900. (See 3.) The last letter in a numerical expression has an accent above. Thousands begin anew with ͵α, with a stroke below. Thus, ͵αωξη', 1868; ͵βχκε', 2625; ͵δκε', 4025; ͵βγ', 2003; φμ', 540; ρδ', 104. (See 372.)

385. N. The letters of the ordinary Greek alphabet are often used to number the books of the Iliad and Odyssey, each poem having twenty-four books. Α, Β, Γ, etc. are generally used for the Iliad, and α, β, γ, etc. for the Odyssey.

THE ARTICLE.

386. The definite article ὁ (stem το-), *the*, is thus declined:—

SINGULAR.				DUAL.				PLURAL.			
Nom.	ὁ	ἡ	τό					Nom.	οἱ	αἱ	τά
Gen.	τοῦ	τῆς	τοῦ	N. A.	τώ	τώ	τώ	Gen.		τῶν	
Dat.	τῷ	τῇ	τῷ	G. D.	τοῖν	τοῖν	τοῖν	Dat.	τοῖς	ταῖς	τοῖς
Acc.	τόν	τήν	τό					Acc.	τούς	τάς	τά

387. N. The Greek has no indefinite article; but often the indefinite τὶς (415, 2) may be translated by *a* or *an;* as ἄνθρωπός τις, *a certain man*, often simply *a man*.

388. N. The regular feminine dual forms τᾱ́ and ταῖν (especially τά) are very rare, and τώ and τοῖν are generally used for all genders (303). The regular plural nominatives τοί and ταί are epic and Doric; and the article has the usual dialectic forms of the first and second declensions, as τοῖο, τοῦιν, τάων, τοῖσι, τῇσι, τῇς. Homer has rarely τοῖσδεσσι or τοῖσδεσι in the dative plural.

PRONOUNS.

PERSONAL AND INTENSIVE PRONOUNS.

389. The *personal* pronouns are ἐγώ, *I*, σύ, *thou*, and οὗ (genitive), *of him*, *of her*, *of it*. Αὐτός, *himself*, is used as a personal pronoun for *him*, *her*, *it*, etc. in the oblique cases, but never in the nominative.

They are thus declined: —

			SINGULAR.			
Nom.	ἐγώ, *I*	σύ, *thou*	—	αὐτός	αὐτή	αὐτό
Gen.	ἐμοῦ, μοῦ	σοῦ	οὗ	αὐτοῦ	αὐτῆς	αὐτοῦ
Dat.	ἐμοί, μοί	σοί	οἷ	αὐτῷ	αὐτῇ	αὐτῷ
Acc.	ἐμέ, μέ	σέ	ἕ	αὐτόν	αὐτήν	αὐτό
			DUAL.			
N. A.	νώ	σφώ		αὐτώ	αὐτά	αὐτώ
G. D.	νῷν	σφῷν		αὐτοῖν	αὐταῖν	αὐτοῖν
			PLURAL.			
Nom.	ἡμεῖς, *we*	ὑμεῖς, *you*	σφεῖς, *they*	αὐτοί	αὐταί	αὐτά
Gen.	ἡμῶν	ὑμῶν	σφῶν	αὐτῶν	αὐτῶν	αὐτῶν
Dat.	ἡμῖν	ὑμῖν	σφίσι	αὐτοῖς	αὐταῖς	αὐτοῖς
Acc.	ἡμᾶς	ὑμᾶς	σφᾶς	αὐτούς	αὐτάς	αὐτά

390. N. The stems of the personal pronouns in the first person are ἐμε- (cf. Latin *me*), νω- (cf. *nos*), and ἡμε-, ἐγώ being of distinct formation; in the second person, σε- (cf. *te*), σφω-, ὑμε-, with σύ distinct; in the third person, ἑ- (cf. *se*) and σφε-.

391. Αὐτός in all cases may be an intensive adjective pronoun, like *ipse*, *self* (989, 1).

392. For the uses of οὗ, οἷ, etc., see 987; 988. In Attic prose, οἷ, σφεῖς, σφῶν, σφίσι, σφᾶς, are the only common forms; οὗ and ἕ never occur in ordinary language. The orators seldom use this pronoun at all. The tragedians use chiefly σφίν (not σφί) and σφέ (394).

393. 1. The following is the Homeric declension of ἐγώ, σύ, and οὗ. The forms not in ( ) are used also by Herodotus. Those with αμμ- and υμμ- are Aeolic.

		SINGULAR.	
Nom.	ἐγώ (ἐγών)	σύ (τύνη)	——
Gen.	ἐμέο, ἐμεῦ, μεῦ (ἐμεῖο, ἐμέθεν)	σέο, σεῦ (σεῖο, σέθεν)	(ἕο) εὗ εἷο (ἕθεν)
Dat.	ἐμοί, μοί	σοί, τοί (τεΐν)	οἷ (ἑοῖ)
Acc.	ἐμέ, μέ	σέ	(ἕ) (ἑέ) μίν
		DUAL.	
N. A.	(νῶϊ, νώ)	(σφῶϊ, σφώ)	(σφωέ)
G. D.	(νῶϊν)	(σφῶϊν, σφῷν)	(σφωΐν)
		PLURAL.	
Nom.	ἡμεῖς (ἄμμες)	ὑμεῖς (ὕμμες)	σφεῖς (not in Hom.)
Gen.	ἡμέων (ἡμείων)	ὑμέων (ὑμείων)	σφέων (σφείων)
Dat.	ἡμῖν (ἄμμι)	ὑμῖν (ὕμμι)	σφίσι, σφί(ν)
Acc.	ἡμέας (ἄμμε)	ὑμέας (ὕμμε)	σφέας, σφέ

2. Herodotus has also *σφέα* in the neuter plural of the third person, which is not found in Homer.

394. The tragedians use *σφέ* and *σφίν* as personal pronouns, both masculine and feminine. They sometimes use *σφέ* and rarely *σφίν* as singular.

395. 1. The tragedians use the Doric accusative *νίν* as a personal pronoun in all genders, and in both singular and plural.

2. The Ionic *μίν* is used in all genders, but only in the singular.

396. N. The penult of *ἡμῶν, ἡμῖν, ἡμᾶς, ὑμῶν, ὑμῖν,* and *ὑμᾶς* is sometimes accented in poetry, when they are not emphatic, and *ῑν* and *ᾱς* are shortened. Thus *ἥμων, ἧμιν, ἧμας, ὕμων, ὗμιν, ὗμας*. If they are emphatic, they are sometimes written *ἡμίν, ἡμάς, ὑμίν, ὑμάς*. So *σφάς* is written for *σφᾶς*.

397. N. Herodotus has *αὐτέων* in the *feminine* for *αὐτῶν* (188, 5). The Ionic contracts *ὁ αὐτός* into *ωὑτός* or *ωὑτός*, and *τὸ αὐτό* into *τωὐτό* (7).

398. N. The Doric has *ἐγών*; *ἐμέος, ἐμοῦς, ἐμεῦς* (for *ἐμοῦ*); *ἐμίν* for *ἐμοί*; *ἁμές, ἁμέων, ἁμίν, ἁμέ* (for *ἡμεῖς, ἡμῶν, ἡμῖν, ἡμᾶς*); *τύ* for *σύ*; *τεῦ* (for *τέο*), *τέος, τεοῦ, τεοῦς, τεῦς* (for *σοῦ*); *τοί, τίν* (for *σοί*); *τέ, τύ* (enclitic) for *σέ*; *ὑμές* and *ὑμέ* (for *ὑμεῖς* and *ὑμᾶς*); *ἵν* for *οἷ*; *ψέ* for *σφέ*. Pindar has only *ἐγών, τύ, τοί, τίν*.

399. Αὐτός preceded by the article means *the same* (*idem*); as ὁ αὐτὸς ἀνήρ, *the same man.* (See 989, 2.)

400. *Αὐτός* is often united by crasis (44) with the article; as *ταὐτοῦ* for *τοῦ αὐτοῦ*; *ταὐτῷ* for *τῷ αὐτῷ*; *ταὐτῇ* for *τῇ αὐτῇ* (not to be confounded with *ταύτῃ* from *οὗτος*). In the contracted form the neuter singular has *ταὐτό* or *ταὐτόν*.

REFLEXIVE PRONOUNS.

401. The *reflexive* pronouns are ἐμαυτοῦ, ἐμαυτῆς, *of myself;* σεαυτοῦ, σεαυτῆς, *of thyself;* and ἑαυτοῦ, ἑαυτῆς, *of himself, herself, itself.* They are thus declined: —

SINGULAR.

	Masc.	Fem.	Masc.	Fem.		Masc.	Fem.
Gen.	ἐμαυτοῦ	ἐμαυτῆς	σεαυτοῦ	σεαυτῆς		σαυτοῦ	σαυτῆς
Dat.	ἐμαυτῷ	ἐμαυτῇ	σεαυτῷ	σεαυτῇ	or	σαυτῷ	σαυτῇ
Acc.	ἐμαυτόν	ἐμαυτήν	σεαυτόν	σεαυτήν		σαυτόν	σαυτήν

PLURAL.

	Masc.	Fem.	Masc.	Fem.
Gen.	ἡμῶν αὐτῶν		ὑμῶν αὐτῶν	
Dat.	ἡμῖν αὐτοῖς	ἡμῖν αὐταῖς	ὑμῖν αὐτοῖς	ὑμῖν αὐταῖς
Acc.	ἡμᾶς αὐτούς	ἡμᾶς αὐτάς	ὑμᾶς αὐτούς	ὑμᾶς αὐτάς

SINGULAR.

	Masc.	Fem.	Neut.		Masc.	Fem.	Neut.
Gen.	ἑαυτοῦ	ἑαυτῆς	ἑαυτοῦ		αὑτοῦ	αὑτῆς	αὑτοῦ
Dat.	ἑαυτῷ	ἑαυτῇ	ἑαυτῷ	or	αὑτῷ	αὑτῇ	αὑτῷ
Acc.	ἑαυτόν	ἑαυτήν	ἑαυτό		αὑτόν	αὑτήν	αὑτό

PLURAL.

Gen.	ἑαυτῶν	ἑαυτῶν	ἑαυτῶν		αὑτῶν	αὑτῶν	αὑτῶν
Dat.	ἑαυτοῖς	ἑαυταῖς	ἑαυτοῖς	or	αὑτοῖς	αὑταῖς	αὑτοῖς
Acc.	ἑαυτούς	ἑαυτάς	ἑαυτά		αὑτούς	αὑτάς	αὑτά

also

Gen.	σφῶν αὐτῶν	
Dat.	σφίσιν αὐτοῖς	σφίσιν αὐταῖς
Acc.	σφᾶς αὐτούς	σφᾶς αὐτάς

402. The reflexives are compounded of the stems of the personal pronouns (390) and αὐτός. But in the plural the two pronouns are declined separately in the first and second persons, and often in the third.

403. N. In Homer the two pronouns are always separated in all persons and numbers; as σοὶ αὐτῷ, οἷ αὐτῷ, ἓ αὐτήν. Herodotus has ἐμεωυτοῦ, σεωυτοῦ, ἑωυτοῦ.

RECIPROCAL PRONOUN.

404. The reciprocal pronoun is ἀλλήλων, *of one another*, used only in the oblique cases of the dual and plural. It is thus declined: —

	DUAL.			PLURAL.		
Gen.	ἀλλήλοιν	ἀλλήλαιν	ἀλλήλοιν	ἀλλήλων	ἀλλήλων	ἀλλήλων
Dat.	ἀλλήλοιν	ἀλλήλαιν	ἀλλήλοιν	ἀλλήλοις	ἀλλήλαις	ἀλλήλοις
Acc.	ἀλλήλω	ἀλλήλᾱ	ἀλλήλω	ἀλλήλους	ἀλλήλᾱς	ἄλληλα

405. The stem is ἀλληλο- (for ἀλλ-αλλο-).

POSSESSIVE PRONOUNS.

406. The *possessive* pronouns ἐμός, *my*, σός, *thy*, ἡμέτερος, *our*, ὑμέτερος, *your*, σφέτερος, *their*, and the poetic ὅς, *his*, are declined like adjectives in ος (298).

407. Homer has dual possessives νωΐτερος, *of us two*, σφωΐτερος, *of you two;* also τεός (Doric and Aeolic, = *tuus*) for σός, ἑός for ὅς, ἁμός for ἡμέτερος, ὑμός for ὑμέτερος, σφός for σφέτερος. The Attic poets sometimes have ἁμός or ἀμός for ἐμός (often as *our* for *my*).

408. Ὅς not being used in Attic prose, *his* is there expressed by the genitive of αὐτός, as ὁ πατὴρ αὐτοῦ, *his father*.

DEMONSTRATIVE PRONOUNS.

409. The *demonstrative* pronouns are οὗτος and ὅδε, *this*, and ἐκεῖνος, *that*. They are thus declined: —

	SINGULAR.			PLURAL.		
Nom.	οὗτος	αὕτη	τοῦτο	οὗτοι	αὗται	ταῦτα
Gen.	τούτου	ταύτης	τούτου	τούτων	τούτων	τούτων
Dat.	τούτῳ	ταύτῃ	τούτῳ	τούτοις	ταύταις	τούτοις
Acc.	τοῦτον	ταύτην	τοῦτο	τούτους	ταύτᾱς	ταῦτα

DUAL.

N. A.	τούτω	τούτω	τούτω
G. D.	τούτοιν	τούτοιν	τούτοιν

			SINGULAR.			
Nom.	ὅδε	ἥδε	τόδε	ἐκεῖνος	ἐκείνη	ἐκεῖνο
Gen.	τοῦδε	τῆσδε	τοῦδε	ἐκείνου	ἐκείνης	ἐκείνου
Dat.	τῷδε	τῇδε	τῷδε	ἐκείνῳ	ἐκείνῃ	ἐκείνῳ
Acc.	τόνδε	τήνδε	τόδε	ἐκεῖνον	ἐκείνην	ἐκεῖνο
			DUAL.			
N. A.	τώδε	τώδε	τώδε	ἐκείνω	ἐκείνω	ἐκείνω
G. D.	τοῖνδε	τοῖνδε	τοῖνδε	ἐκείνοιν	ἐκείνοιν	ἐκείνοιν
			PLURAL.			
Nom.	οἵδε	αἵδε	τάδε	ἐκεῖνοι	ἐκεῖναι	ἐκεῖνα
Gen.	τῶνδε	τῶνδε	τῶνδε	ἐκείνων	ἐκείνων	ἐκείνων
Dat.	τοῖσδε	ταῖσδε	τοῖσδε	ἐκείνοις	ἐκείναις	ἐκείνοις
Acc.	τούσδε	τάσδε	τάδε	ἐκείνους	ἐκείνᾱς	ἐκεῖνα

410. Feminine dual forms in ᾱ and αιν are very rare (303).

411. Ἐκεῖνος is regular except in the neuter ἐκεῖνο. Κεῖνος is Ionic and poetic. Ὅδε is formed of the article ὁ and -δε (141, 4). For its accent, see 146.

412. N. The demonstratives, including some adverbs (436), may be emphasized by adding ί, before which a short vowel is dropped. Thus οὑτοσί, αὑτηί, τουτί; ὁδί, ἡδί, τοδί; τουτουί, ταυτί, τουτωνί. So τοσουτοσί (429), ὡδί, οὑτωσί. In comedy γέ (rarely δέ) may precede this ί, making γί or δί; as τουτογί, τουτοδί.

413. N. Herodotus has τουτέων in the *feminine* for τούτων (cf. 397). Homer has τοῖσδεσσι or τοῖσδεσι for τοῖσδε.

414. N. Other demonstratives will be found among the pronominal adjectives (429).

INTERROGATIVE AND INDEFINITE PRONOUNS.

415. 1. The *interrogative* pronoun τίς, τί, *who? which? what?* always takes the acute on the first syllable.

2. The *indefinite* pronoun τὶς, τὶ, *any one*, *some one*, is enclitic, and its proper accent belongs on the last syllable.

416. 1. These pronouns are thus declined: —

	Interrogative.		*Indefinite.*	
		SINGULAR.		
Nom.	τίς	τί	τὶς	τὶ
Gen.	τίνος, τοῦ		τινός, του	
Dat.	τίνι, τῷ		τινί, τῳ	
Acc.	τίνα	τί	τινά	τὶ
		DUAL.		
N. A.	τίνε		τινέ	
G. D.	τίνοιν		τινοῖν	
		PLURAL.		
Nom.	τίνες	τίνα	τινές	τινά
Gen.	τίνων		τινῶν	
Dat.	τίσι		τισί	
Acc.	τίνας	τίνα	τινάς	τινά

2. For the indefinite plural τινά there is a form ἄττα (Ionic ἄσσα).

417. Οὔτις and μήτις, poetic for οὐδείς and μηδείς, *no one*, are declined like τὶς.

418. 1. The acute accent of τίς is never changed to the grave (115, 2). The forms τὶς and τὶ of the indefinite pronoun very rarely occur with the grave accent, as they are enclitic (141, 2).

2. The Ionic has τέο and τεῦ for τοῦ, τέῳ for τῷ, τέων for τίνων, and τέοισι for τίσι; also these same forms as enclitics, for του, τῳ, etc.

419. Ἄλλος, *other*, is declined like αὐτός (389), having ἄλλο in the neuter singular.

420. 1. The indefinite δεῖνα, *such a one*, is sometimes indeclinable, and is sometimes declined as follows: —

	SINGULAR. (*All Genders*).	PLURAL. (*Masculine*).
Nom.	δεῖνα	δεῖνες
Gen.	δεῖνος	δείνων
Dat.	δεῖνι	——
Acc.	δεῖνα	δεῖνας

2. Δεῖνα in all its forms always has the article.

RELATIVE PRONOUNS.

421. The *relative* pronoun ὅς, ἥ, ὅ, *who*, is thus declined: —

SINGULAR.				DUAL.				PLURAL.			
Nom.	ὅς	ἥ	ὅ					Nom.	οἵ	αἵ	ἅ
Gen.	οὗ	ἧς	οὗ	N. A.	ὥ	ὥ	ὥ	Gen.	ὧν	ὧν	ὧν
Dat.	ᾧ	ᾗ	ᾧ	G. D.	οἷν	οἷν	οἷν	Dat.	οἷς	αἷς	οἷς
Acc.	ὅν	ἥν	ὅ					Acc.	οὕς	ἅς	ἅ

422. Feminine dual forms ἅ and αἷν are very rare and doubtful (303).

423. N. For ὅς used as a demonstrative, especially in Homer, see 1023. For the article (τ- forms) as a relative in Homer and Herodotus, see 935 and 939.

424. N. Homer has ὅου (ὅο) and ἕης for οὗ and ἧς.

425. The indefinite relative ὅστις, ἥτις, ὅ τι, *whoever, whatever*, is thus declined:—

		SINGULAR.	
Nom.	ὅστις	ἥτις	ὅ τι
Gen.	οὗτινος, ὅτου	ἧστινος	οὗτινος, ὅτου
Dat.	ᾧτινι, ὅτῳ	ᾗτινι	ᾧτινι, ὅτῳ
Acc.	ὅντινα	ἥντινα	ὅ τι
		DUAL.	
N. A.	ὥτινε	ὥτινε	ὥτινε
G. D.	οἷντινοιν	οἷντινοιν	οἷντινοιν
		PLURAL.	
Nom.	οἵτινες	αἵτινες	ἅτινα, ἅττα
Gen.	ὧντινων, ὅτων	ὧντινων	ὧντινων, ὅτων
Dat.	οἷστισι, ὅτοις	αἷστισι	οἷστισι, ὅτοις
Acc.	οὕστινας	ἅστινας	ἅτινα, ἅττα

426. N. Ὅστις is compounded of the relative ὅς and the indefinite τὶς, each part being declined separately. For the accent, see 146. The plural ἅττα (Ionic ἅσσα) for ἅτινα must not be confounded with ἄττα (416, 2). Ὅ τι is thus written (sometimes ὅ, τι) to distinguish it from ὅτι, *that*.

427. N. The shorter forms ὅτου, ὅτῳ, ὅτων, and ὅτοις, which are genuine old Attic forms, are used by the tragedians to the exclusion of οὗτινος, etc.

428. 1. The following are the peculiar Homeric forms of ὅστις:—

	SINGULAR.		PLURAL.	
Nom.	ὅτις	ὅ ττι		ἅσσα
Gen.	ὅτευ, ὅττεο, ὅττευ		ὅτεων	
Dat.	ὅτεῳ		ὀτέοισι	
Acc.	ὅτινα	ὅ ττι	ὅτινας	ἅσσα

2. Herodotus has ὅτευ, ὅτεῳ, ὅτεων, ὁτέοισι, and ἅσσα (426).

PRONOMINAL ADJECTIVES AND ADVERBS.

429. There are many *pronominal adjectives* which correspond to each other in form and meaning. The following are the most important:—

INTERROGATIVE.	INDEFINITE.	DEMONSTRATIVE.	RELATIVE.
πόσος; *how much? how many?* quantus?	ποσός, *of some quantity.*	(τόσος), τοσόσδε, τοσοῦτος, *so much,* tantus, *so many.*	ὅσος, ὁπόσος, (*as much, as many*) *as,* quantus.
ποῖος; *of what kind?* qualis?	ποιός, *of some kind.*	(τοῖος), τοιόσδε, τοιοῦτος, *such,* talis.	οἷος, ὁποῖος, *of which kind,* (*such*) *as,* qualis.
πηλίκος; *how old? how large?*		(τηλίκος), τηλικόσδε, τηλικοῦτος, *so old* or *so large.*	ἡλίκος, ὁπηλίκος, *of which age* or *size,* (*as old*) *as,* (*as large*) *as.*
πότερος; *which of the two?*	πότερος (or ποτερός), *one of two* (rare).	ἕτερος, *the one* or *the other* (*of two*).	ὁπότερος, *whichever of the two.*

430. The pronouns τίς, τὶς, etc. form a corresponding series: —

τίς; *who?*	τὶς, *any one.*	ὅδε, οὗτος, *this, this one.*	ὅς, ὅστις, *who, which.*

431. Τὶς may be added to οἷος, ὅσος, ὁπόσος, ὁποῖος, and ὁπότερος, to make them more indefinite; as ὁποῖός τις, *of what kind soever.*

432. 1. Οὖν added to indefinite relatives gives them a purely indefinite force; as ὁστισοῦν, ὁτιοῦν, *any one, anything, soever,* with no relative character. So sometimes δή; as ὅτου δή.

2. N. Rarely ὁπότερος (without οὖν) has the same meaning, *either of the two.*

433. N. Homer doubles π in many of these relative words; as ὁππότερος, ὁππoῖος. So in ὅππως, ὁππότε, etc. (436). Herodotus has ὁκότερος, ὁκόσος, ὅκου, ὁκόθεν, ὁκότε, etc., for ὁπότερος, etc.

434. N. Τόσος and τοῖος seldom occur in Attic prose, τηλίκος never. Τοσόσδε, τοιόσδε, and τηλικόσδε are declined like τόσος and τοῖος; as τοσόσδε, τοσήδε, τοσόνδε, etc., — τοιόσδε, τοιάδε, τοιόνδε. Τοσοῦτος, τοιοῦτος, and τηλικοῦτος are declined like οὗτος (omitting the first τ in τούτου, τοῦτο, etc.), except that the neuter singular has ο or ον; as τοιοῦτος, τοιαύτη, τοιοῦτο or τοιοῦτον; gen. τοιούτου, τοιαύτης, etc.

435. There are also negative pronominal adjectives; as οὔτις, μήτις (poetic for οὐδείς, μηδείς), οὐδέτερος, μηδέτερος, *neither of two.* (For adverbs, see 440.)

436. Certain *pronominal adverbs* correspond to each other, like the adjectives given above. Such are the following: —

INTERROGATIVE.	INDEFINITE.	DEMONSTRATIVE.	RELATIVE.
ποῦ; where?	*πού, somewhere.*	(ἔνθα), ἐνθάδε, ἐνταῦθα, ἐκεῖ, *there.*	οὗ, ὅπου, *where.*
πῇ; which way? how?	*πῄ, some way, somehow.*	(τῇ), τῇδε, ταύτῃ, *this way, thus.*	ᾗ, ὅπῃ, *which way, as.*
ποῖ; whither?	*ποί, to some place.*	ἐκεῖσε, *thither.*	οἷ, ὅποι, *whither.*
πόθεν; whence?	*ποθέν, from some place.*	(ἔνθεν), ἐνθένδε, ἐντεῦθεν, ἐκεῖθεν, *thence.*	ὅθεν, ὁπόθεν, *whence.*
πῶς; how?	*πώς, in some way, somehow.*	(τώς), (ὥς), ὧδε, οὕτως, *thus.*	ὡς, ὅπως, *in which way, as.*
πότε; when?	*ποτέ, at some time.*	τότε, *then.*	ὅτε, ὁπότε, *when.*
πηνίκα; at what time?		(τηνίκα), τηνικάδε, τηνικαῦτα, *at that time.*	ἡνίκα, ὁπηνίκα, *at which time, when.*

437. The indefinite adverbs are all enclitic (141, 2).

438. Forms which seldom or never occur in Attic prose are in ( ). Ἔνθα and ἔνθεν are relatives in prose, *where, whence;* as demonstratives they appear chiefly in a few expressions like **ἔνθα καὶ ἔνθα**, *here and there*, **ἔνθεν καὶ ἔνθεν**, *on both sides.* For **ὥς**, *thus*, in Attic prose, see 138, 3. Τώς (from το-), like **οὕτως** (from **οὗτος**), *thus*, is poetic.

439. 1. The poets have **κεῖθι, κεῖθεν, κεῖσε** for **ἐκεῖ, ἐκεῖθεν**, and **ἐκεῖσε**, like **κεῖνος** for **ἐκεῖνος** (411).

2. Herodotus has **ἐνθαῦτα, ἐνθεῦτεν** for **ἐνταῦθα, ἐντεῦθεν**.

3. There are various poetic adverbs; as **πόθι, ποθί, ὅθι** (for **ποῦ, πού, οὗ**), **τόθι**, *there*, **τόθεν**, *thence.*

440. There are negative adverbs of *place, manner*, etc.; as **οὐδαμοῦ, μηδαμοῦ**, *nowhere*, **οὐδαμῇ, μηδαμῇ**, *in no way*, **οὐδαμῶς, μηδαμῶς**, *in no manner.* (See 435.)

VERBS.

441. The Greek verb has three *voices*, the active, middle, and passive.

442. 1. The middle voice generally signifies that the subject performs an action *upon himself* or *for his own benefit* (1242), but sometimes it is not distinguished from the active voice in meaning.

2. The passive differs from the middle *in form* in only two tenses, the future and the aorist.

443. Deponent verbs are those which have no active voice, but are used in the middle (or the middle and passive) forms with an active sense.

444. N. Deponents generally have the aorist and future of the middle form. A few, which have an aorist (sometimes a future) of the passive form, are called *passive* deponents; while the others are called *middle* deponents.

445. There are four *moods* (properly so called), the indicative, subjunctive, optative, and imperative. To these are added, in the conjugation of the verb, the infinitive, and participles of the chief tenses. The verbal adjectives in τος and τεος have many points of likeness to participles (see 776).

446. The four proper moods, as opposed to the *infinitive*, are called *finite* moods. The subjunctive, optative, imperative, and infinitive, as opposed to the *indicative*, are called *dependent* moods.

447. There are seven *tenses*, the present, imperfect, future, aorist, perfect, pluperfect, and future perfect. The imperfect and pluperfect are found only in the indicative. The future and future perfect are wanting in the subjunctive and imperative. The future perfect belongs regularly to the passive voice, but sometimes has the meaning of the active or middle.

448. The present, perfect, future, and future perfect indicative are called *primary* (or *principal*) tenses; the imperfect, pluperfect, and aorist indicative are called *secondary* (or *historical*) tenses.

449. Many verbs have tenses known as the *second* aorist (in all voices), the *second* perfect and pluperfect (active), and the *second* future (passive). These tenses are generally of more simple formation than the *first* (or ordinary) aorist, perfect, etc. Few verbs have both forms in any tense; when this occurs, the two forms generally differ in meaning (for example, by the first being transitive, the second intransitive), but not always.

450. The aorist corresponds generally to the *indefinite* or *his-*

torical perfect in Latin, and the perfect to the English perfect or the *definite* perfect in Latin.

451. N. No Greek verb is in use in all these tenses, and the full paradigm of the regular verb must include parts of three different verbs. See 470.

452. There are three *numbers*, as in nouns, the singular, dual, and plural.

453. In each tense of the indicative, subjunctive, and optative, there are three *persons* in each number, the first, second, and third; in each tense of the imperative there are two, the second and third.

454. N. The first person dual is the same as the first person plural, except in a very few poetic forms (556, 2). This person is therefore omitted in the paradigms.

TENSE SYSTEMS AND TENSE STEMS.

455. The tenses are divided into nine classes or *tense systems*, each with its own *tense stem*.

456. The tense systems are the following: —

	SYSTEMS.		TENSES.
I.	*Present,*	including	*present* and *imperfect.*
II.	*Future,*	"	*future active* and *middle.*
III.	*First-aorist,*	"	*first aorist active* and *middle.*
IV.	*Second-aorist,*	"	*second aorist active* and *middle.*
V.	*First-perfect,*	"	*first perfect* and *pluperfect active.*
VI.	*Second-perfect,*	"	*second perfect* and *pluperfect active.*
VII.	*Perfect-middle,*	"	*perfect* and *pluperfect middle* and *future perfect.*
VIII.	*First-passive,*	"	*first aorist* and *future passive.*
IX.	*Second-passive,*	"	*second aorist* and *future passive.*

457. 1. The last five tense stems are further modified to form special stems for the two pluperfects, the future perfect, and the two passive futures.

2. As few verbs have both the first and the second forms of any tense (449), most verbs have only six tense stems, and many have even less.

458. The various tense stems are almost always formed from one fundamental stem, called the verb stem. These formations will be explained in 568–622.

459. Before learning the paradigms, it is important to distinguish between verbs in which the verb stem appears without change in all the tense systems, and those in which it is modified more or less in different systems (154).

Thus in λέγω, *speak*, the verb stem λεγ- is found in λέξω (λεγ-σω), ἔλεξα, λέ-λεγ-μαι, ἐ-λέχ-θην (71), and all other forms. But in φαίνω, *show*, the verb stem φαν- is seen pure in the second aorist ἐ-φάν-ην and kindred tenses, and in the futures φανῶ and φανοῦμαι; while elsewhere it appears modified, as in present φαίν-ω, first aorist ἔφην-α, second perfect πέφην-α. In λείπ-ω the stem λειπ- appears in all forms except in the second-aorist system (ἔ-λιπ-ον, ἐ-λιπ-όμην) and the second-perfect system (λέ-λοιπ-α).

460. Verb stems are called *vowel* stems or *consonant* stems, and the latter are called *mute* stems (including *labial*, *palatal*, and *lingual* stems) or *liquid* stems, according to their final letter. Thus we may name the stems of φιλέω (φιλε-), λείπω (λειπ-, λιπ-), τρίβω (τριβ-), γράφω (γραφ-), πλέκω (πλεκ-), φεύγω (φευγ-, φυγ-), πείθω (πειθ-, πιθ-), φαίνω (φαν-), στέλλω (στελ-).

461. A verb which has a vowel verb stem is called a *pure* verb; and one which has a mute stem or a liquid stem is called a *mute* or a *liquid* verb.

462. 1. The *principal parts* of a Greek verb are the first person singular of the present, future, first aorist, and (first or second) perfect, indicative active; the perfect middle, and the (first or second) aorist passive; with the second aorist (active or middle) when it occurs. These generally represent all the tense systems which the verb uses. *E.g.*

Λύω, λύσω, ἔλῡσα, λέλυκα, λέλυμαι, ἐλύθην (471).

Λείπω (λειπ-, λιπ-), λείψω, λέλοιπα, λέλειμμαι, ἐλείφθην, ἔλιπον.

Φαίνω (φαν-), φανῶ, ἔφηνα, πέφαγκα (2 pf. πέφηνα), πέφασμαι, ἐφάνθην (and ἐφάνην).

Πράσσω (πρᾱγ-), *do*, πρᾱ́ξω, ἔπρᾱξα, 2 perf. πέπρᾱχα and πέπρᾱγα, πέπρᾱγμαι, ἐπρᾱ́χθην.

Στέλλω (στελ-), *send*, στελῶ, ἔστειλα, ἔσταλκα, ἔσταλμαι, ἐστάλην.

2. If a verb has no future active, the future middle may be given among the principal parts; as σκώπτω, *jeer*, σκώψομαι, ἔσκωψα, ἐσκώφθην.

463. In deponent verbs the principal parts are the present, future, perfect, and aorist (or aorists) indicative. *E.g.*

(Ἡγέομαι) ἡγοῦμαι, *lead*, ἡγήσομαι, ἡγησάμην, ἥγημαι, ἡγήθην (in compos.).

Βούλομαι, *wish*, βουλήσομαι, βεβούλημαι, ἐβουλήθην.

Γίγνομαι (γεν-), *become*, γενήσομαι, γεγένημαι, ἐγενόμην.

(Αἰδέομαι) αἰδοῦμαι, *respect*, αἰδέσομαι, ᾔδεσμαι, ᾐδέσθην.

Ἐργάζομαι, *work*, ἐργάσομαι, εἰργασάμην, εἴργασμαι, εἰργάσθην.

CONJUGATION.

464. To *conjugate* a verb is to give all its voices, moods, tenses, numbers, and persons in their proper order.

465. These parts of the verb are formed as follows: —

1. By modifying the verb stem itself to form the different tense stems. (See 568–622; 660–717.)

2. By affixing certain syllables called *endings* to the tense stem; as in λέγο-μεν, λέγε-τε, λέγε-ται, λεγό-μεθα, λέγο-νται, λέξε-ται, λέξε-σθε. (See 551–554.)

3. In the secondary tenses of the indicative, by also prefixing ε to the tense stem (if this begins with a consonant), or lengthening its initial vowel (if it begins with a short vowel); as in ἔ-λεγο-ν, ἔ-λεξε, ἐ-φήνα-το; and in ἤκουο-ν and ἤκουσα, imperfect and aorist of ἀκούω, *hear*. This prefix or lengthening is confined to the indicative.

4. A prefix, seen in λε- of λέλυκα and λέλειμμαι, in πε- of πέφασμαι, and ε of ἔσταλμαι (487, 1), for which a lengthening of the initial vowel is found in ἤλλαγμαι (ἀλλαγ-) from ἀλλάσσω (487, 2), belongs to the perfect *tense stem*, and remains in all the moods and in the participle.

466. These prefixes and lengthenings, called *augment* (3) and *reduplication* (4), are explained in 510–550.

467. There are two principal forms of conjugation of Greek verbs, that of verbs in ω and that of verbs in μι.

468. Verbs in μι form a small class, compared with those in ω, and are distinguished in their inflection almost exclusively in the present and second-aorist systems, generally agreeing with verbs in ω in the other systems.

CONJUGATION OF VERBS IN Ω.

469. The following synopses (474–478) include —

I. All the tenses of λύω (λῡ-), *loose*, representing tense systems I., II., III., V., VII., VIII.

II. All the tenses of λείπω (**λειπ-**, λιπ-), *leave;* the second perfect and pluperfect active and the second aorist active and middle, representing tense systems IV. and VI., being in heavy-faced type.

III. All the tenses of φαίνω (φαν-), *show;* the future and aorist active and middle (liquid form) and the second aorist and second future passive, representing tense systems II., III., and IX., being in heavy-faced type.

470. The full synopsis of λύω, with the forms in heavier type in the synopses of λείπω and φαίνω, will thus show the full conjugation of the verb in ω, with the nine tense systems; and all these forms are inflected in 480–482. For the peculiar inflection of the perfect and pluperfect middle and passive of verbs with consonant stems, see 486 and 487.

471. N. Λύω in the present and imperfect generally has ῡ in Attic poetry and ῠ in Homer; in other tenses, it has ῡ in the future and aorist active and middle and the future perfect, elsewhere ῠ.

472. The paradigms include the perfect imperative active, although it is hardly possible that this tense can actually have been formed in any of these verbs. As it occurs, however, in a few verbs (748), it is given here to complete the illustration of the forms. For the rare perfect subjunctive and optative active, see 720 and 731.

473. Each tense of λύω is translated in the synopsis of 474, except rare untranslatable forms like the future perfect infinitive and participle, and the tenses of the subjunctive and optative. The meaning of these last cannot be fully understood until the constructions are explained in the Syntax. But the following examples will make them clearer than any possible translation of the forms, some of which (*e.g.* the future optative) cannot be used in independent sentences.

Λύωμεν (or λύσωμεν) αὐτόν, *let us loose him;* μὴ λύσῃς αὐτόν, *do not loose him.* Ἐὰν λύω (or λύσω) αὐτὸν, χαιρήσει, *if I (shall) loose him, he will rejoice.* Ἔρχομαι, ἵνα αὐτὸν λύω (or λύσω), *I am coming that I may loose him.* Εἴθε λύοιμι (or λύσαιμι) αὐτόν, *O that I may loose him.* Εἰ λύοιμι (or λύσαιμι) αὐτὸν, χαίροι ἄν, *if I should loose him, he would rejoice.* Ἦλθον ἵνα αὐτὸν λύοιμι (or λύσαιμι), *I came that I might loose him.* Εἶπον ὅτι αὐτὸν λύοιμι, *I said that I was loosing him;* εἶπον ὅτι αὐτὸν λύσαιμι, *I said that I had loosed him;* εἶπον ὅτι αὐτὸν λύσοιμι, *I said that I would loose him.* For the difference between the present and aorist in these moods, see 1272, 1; for the perfect, see 1273.

474. SYNOPSIS OF

	I. *PRESENT SYSTEM.*	II. *FUTURE SYSTEM.*	III. *FIRST-AORIST SYSTEM.*
ACTIVE VOICE.	*Present & Imperfect Active.*	*Future Active.*	1 *Aorist Active.*
Indic.	**λύω** *I loose* or *am loosing*	**λύσω** *I shall loose*	
	ἔλῡον *I was loosing*		**ἔλῡσα** *I loosed*
Subj.	**λύω**		**λύσω**
Opt.	**λύοιμι**	**λύσοιμι**	**λύσαιμι**
Imper.	**λῦε** *loose*		**λῦσον** *loose*
Infin.	**λύειν** *to loose*	**λύσειν** *to be about to loose*	**λῦσαι** *to loose* or *to have loosed.*
Part.	**λύων** *loosing*	**λύσων** *about to loose*	**λύσᾱς** *having loosed*
MIDDLE VOICE.	*Present & Imperfect Middle.*	*Future Middle.*	1 *Aorist Middle.*
Indic.	**λύομαι** *I loose (for myself)*	**λύσομαι** *I shall loose (for myself)*	
	ἐλῡόμην *I was loosing (for myself)*		**ἐλῡσάμην** *I loosed (for myself).*
Subj.	**λύωμαι**		**λύσωμαι**
Opt.	**λῡοίμην**	**λῡσοίμην**	**λῡσαίμην**
Imper.	**λύου** *loose (for thyself)*		**λῦσαι** *loose (for thyself)*
Infin.	**λύεσθαι** *to loose (for one's self)*	**λύσεσθαι** *to be about to loose (for one's self)*	**λύσασθαι** *to loose* or *to have loosed (for one's self)*
Part.	**λῡόμενος** *loosing (for one's self)*	**λῡσόμενος** *about to loose (for one's self)*	**λῡσάμενος** *having loosed (for one's self)*
		VIII. *FIRST-PASSIVE SYSTEM.*	
PASSIVE VOICE.	*Pres. & Imperf. Passive.*	1 *Future Passive.*	1 *Aorist Passive.*
Indic.	**λύομαι** *I am* / **ἐλῡόμην** *I was* } *(being) loosed*	**λυθήσομαι** *I shall be loosed*	**ἐλύθην** *I was loosed*
Subj.			**λυθῶ** (for *λυθέω*)
Opt.	etc.	**λυθησοίμην**	**λυθείην**
Imper.	with same		**λύθητι** *be loosed*
Infin.	forms as the	**λυθήσεσθαι** *to be about to be loosed*	**λυθῆναι** *to be loosed* or *to have been loosed*
Part.	Middle	**λυθησόμενος** *about to be loosed*	**λυθείς** *having been loosed*

VERBAL ADJECTIVES: { **λυτός** *that may be loosed* / **λυτέος** *that must be loosed* } λύω (λῡ̆-), *loose.*

V. *FIRST-PERFECT SYSTEM.*	VII. *PERFECT-MIDDLE SYSTEM.*	
1 *Perfect & Pluperfect Active.* λέλυκα *I have loosed* ἐλελύκη *I had loosed* λελύκω or λελυκὼς ὦ λελύκοιμι or λελυκὼς εἴην [λέλυκε] (472) λελυκέναι *to have loosed* λελυκώς *having loosed*		
	Perfect & Pluperfect Middle. λέλυμαι *I have loosed (for myself)* ἐλελύμην *I had loosed (for myself)* λελυμένος ὦ λελυμένος εἴην λέλυσο (750) λελύσθαι *to have loosed (for one's self)* λελυμένος *having loosed (for one's self)*	
	Perf. & Pluperf. Passive. λέλυμαι *I have* { *been* ἐλελύμην *I had* { *loosed* etc. with same forms as the Middle	*Future Perfect Passive.* λελύσομαι *I shall have been loosed* λελῡσοίμην λελύσεσθαι (1283) λελῡσόμενος (1284)

475. The middle of λύω commonly means *to release for one's self*, or *to release some one belonging to one's self*, hence *to ransom* (a captive) or *to deliver* (one's friends from danger). See 1242, 3.

476. SYNOPSIS OF λείπω (λειπ-, λιπ-), *leave*.

TENSE SYSTEM:	I.	II.	IV.	VI.
ACTIVE VOICE.	*Pres. & Impf. Active.*	*Future Active.*	*2 Aorist Active.*	*2 Perf. & Plup. Active.*
Indic.	λείπω ἔλειπον	λείψω	ἔλιπον	λέλοιπα ἐλελοίπη
Subj.	λείπω		λίπω	λελοίπω or λελοιπὼς ὦ
Opt.	λείποιμι	λείψοιμι	λίποιμι	λελοίποιμι or λελοιπὼς εἴην
Imper.	λεῖπε		λίπε	[λέλοιπε]
Infin.	λείπειν	λείψειν	λιπεῖν	λελοιπέναι
Part.	λείπων	λείψων	λιπών	λελοιπώς
				VII.
MIDDLE VOICE.	*Pres. & Impf. Middle.*	*Future Middle.*	*2 Aorist Middle.*	*Perf. & Plup. Mid.*
Indic.	λείπομαι ἐλειπόμην	λείψομαι	ἐλιπόμην	λέλειμμαι ἐλελείμμην
Subj.	λείπωμαι		λίπωμαι	λελειμμένος ὦ
Opt.	λειποίμην	λειψοίμην	λιποίμην	λελειμμένος εἴην
Imper.	λείπου		λιποῦ	λέλειψο
Infin.	λείπεσθαι	λείψεσθαι	λιπέσθαι	λελεῖφθαι
Part.	λειπόμενος	λειψόμενος	λιπόμενος	λελειμμένος
		VIII.		
PASSIVE VOICE.	*Pres. & Impf. Passive.*	*1 Fut. Pass.*	*1 Aor. Pass.*	*Perf. & Plup. Passive* same as the Middle. *Future Perfect.*
Indic.		λειφθήσομαι	ἐλείφθην	λελείψομαι
Subj.	same forms		λειφθῶ (for λειφθέω)	
Opt.	as the	λειφθησοίμην	λειφθείην	λελειψοίμην
Imper.	Middle		λείφθητι	
Infin.		λειφθήσεσθαι	λειφθῆναι	λελείψεσθαι
Part.		λειφθησόμενος	λειφθείς	λελειψόμενος

VERBAL ADJECTIVES: λειπτός, λειπτέος

477. 1. The active of λείπω in the various tenses means *I leave* (or *am leaving*), *I left* (or *was leaving*), *I shall leave*, etc. The second perfect means *I have left*, or *I have failed* or *am wanting*. The first aorist ἔλειψα is not in good use.

2. The middle of λείπω means properly *to remain* (*leave one's self*), in which sense it differs little (or not at all) from the passive. But the second aorist ἐλιπόμην often means *I left for myself* (*e.g.* a memorial or monument): so the present and future middle in composition. Ἐλιπόμην in Homer sometimes means *I was left behind* or *was inferior*, like the passive.

3. The passive of λείπω is used in all tenses, with the meanings *I am left, I was left, I have been left, I had been left, I shall have been left, I was left, I shall be left.* It also means *I am inferior* (*left behind*).

478. SYNOPSIS OF φαίνω (φαν-), *show.*

TENSE-SYSTEM:	I.	II.	III.	V.	VI.
ACTIVE VOICE.	*Pres. & Impf. Active.*	*Future Active.*	*1 Aorist Active.*	*1 Perf. & Plup. Active.*	*2 Perf. & Plup. Active.*
Indic.	φαίνω / ἔφαινον	(φανέω) φανῶ	ἔφηνα	πέφαγκα / ἐπεφάγκη	πέφηνα / ἐπεφήνη
Subj.	φαίνω		φήνω	πεφάγκω or πεφαγκὼς ὦ	πεφήνω or πεφηνὼς ὦ
Opt.	φαίνοιμι	(φανέοιμι) φανοῖμι or (φανεοίην) φανοίην	φήναιμι	πεφάγκοιμι or πεφαγκὼς εἴην	πεφήνοιμι or πεφηνὼς εἴην
Imper.	φαῖνε		φῆνον	[πέφαγκε]	[πέφηνε]
Infin.	φαίνειν	(φανέειν) φανεῖν	φῆναι	πεφαγκέναι	πεφηνέναι
Part.	φαίνων	(φανέων) φανῶν	φήνας	πεφαγκώς	πεφηνώς
MIDDLE VOICE.	*Pres. & Impf. Middle.*	*Future Middle.*	*1 Aorist Middle.*	VII. *Perf. & Plup. Middle.*	
Indic.	φαίνομαι / ἐφαινόμην	(φανέομαι) φανοῦμαι	ἐφηνάμην	πέφασμαι / ἐπεφάσμην	
Subj.	φαίνωμαι		φήνωμαι	πεφασμένος ὦ	
Opt.	φαινοίμην	(φανεοίμην) φανοίμην	φηναίμην	πεφασμένος εἴην	
Imper.	φαίνου		φῆναι	[πέφανσο]	
Infin.	φαίνεσθαι	(φανέεσθαι) φανεῖσθαι	φήνασθαι	πεφάνθαι	
Part.	φαινόμενος	(φανεόμενος) φανούμενος	φηνάμενος	πεφασμένος	
PASSIVE VOICE.	*Pres. & Impf. Passive.*	IX. *2 Future Passive.*	*2 Aorist Passive.*	VIII. *1 Aorist Passive.*	*1 Future Passive* wanting
Indic.	same forms as the Middle	φανήσομαι	ἐφάνην	ἐφάνθην	
Subj.			φανῶ (for φανέω)	φανθῶ (for φανθέω)	
Opt.		φανησοίμην	φανείην	φανθείην	
Imper.			φάνηθι	φάνθητι	
Infin.		φανήσεσθαι	φανῆναι	φανθῆναι	
Part.		φανησόμενος	φανείς	φανθείς	

VERBAL ADJECTIVE: φαντός (ἄ-φαντος)

479. 1. The first perfect πέφαγκα means *I have shown;* the second perfect πέφηνα means *I have appeared.*

2. The passive of φαίνω means properly *to be shown* or *made evident;* the middle, *to appear* (*show one's self*). The second future passive φανήσομαι, *I shall appear* or *be shown,* does not differ in sense from φανοῦμαι; but ἐφάνθην is generally passive, *I was shown,* while ἐφάνην is *I appeared.* The aorist middle ἐφηνάμην means *I showed;* the simple form is rare and poetic; but ἀπ-εφηνάμην, *I declared,* is common.

480. 1. ACTIVE VOICE OF λύω.

			Present.	*Imperfect.*	*Future.*
INDICATIVE.	S.	1.	λύω	ἔλῡον	λύσω
		2.	λύεις	ἔλῡες	λύσεις
		3.	λύει	ἔλῡε	λύσει
	D.	2.	λύετον	ἐλύετον	λύσετον
		3.	λύετον	ἐλῡέτην	λύσετον
	P.	1.	λύομεν	ἐλύομεν	λύσομεν
		2.	λύετε	ἐλύετε	λύσετε
		3.	λύουσι	ἔλῡον	λύσουσι
SUBJUNCTIVE.	S.	1.	λύω		
		2.	λύῃς		
		3.	λύῃ		
	D.	2.	λύητον		
		3.	λύητον		
	P.	1.	λύωμεν		
		2.	λύητε		
		3.	λύωσι		
OPTATIVE.	S.	1.	λύοιμι		λύσοιμι
		2.	λύοις		λύσοις
		3.	λύοι		λύσοι
	D.	2.	λύοιτον		λύσοιτον
		3.	λῡοίτην		λῡσοίτην
	P.	1.	λύοιμεν		λύσοιμεν
		2.	λύοιτε		λύσοιτε
		3.	λύοιεν		λύσοιεν
IMPERATIVE.	S.	2.	λῦε		
		3.	λῡέτω		
	D.	2.	λύετον		
		3.	λῡέτων		
	P.	2.	λύετε		
		3.	λῡόντων or λῡέτωσαν		
INFINITIVE.			λύειν		λύσειν
PARTICIPLE.			λύων, λύουσα, λῦον (335)		λύσων, λύσουσα, λῦσον (335)

			1 *Aorist.*	1 *Perfect.*	1 *Pluperfect.*
INDICATIVE.	S.	1.	ἔλῡσα	λέλυκα	ἐλελύκη
		2.	ἔλῡσας	λέλυκας	ἐλελύκης
		3.	ἔλῡσε	λέλυκε	ἐλελύκει
	D.	2.	ἐλύσατον	λελύκατον	ἐλελύκετον
		3.	ἐλῡσάτην	λελύκατον	ἐλελυκέτην
	P.	1.	ἐλύσαμεν	λελύκαμεν	ἐλελύκεμεν
		2.	ἐλύσατε	λελύκατε	ἐλελύκετε
		3.	ἔλῡσαν	λελύκᾱσι	ἐλελύκεσαν
					(See 683, 2)
SUBJUNCTIVE.	S.	1.	λύσω	λελύκω (720)	
		2.	λύσῃς	λελύκῃς	
		3.	λύσῃ	λελύκῃ	
	D.	2.	λύσητον	λελύκητον	
		3.	λύσητον	λελύκητον	
	P.	1.	λύσωμεν	λελύκωμεν	
		2.	λύσητε	λελύκητε	
		3.	λύσωσι	λελύκωσι	
OPTATIVE.	S.	1.	λύσαιμι	λελύκοιμι (733)	
		2.	λύσαις, λύσειας	λελύκοις	
		3.	λύσαι, λύσειε	λελύκοι	
	D.	2.	λύσαιτον	λελύκοιτον	
		3.	λῡσαίτην	λελυκοίτην	
	P.	1.	λύσαιμεν	λελύκοιμεν	
		2.	λύσαιτε	λελύκοιτε	
		3.	λύσαιεν, λύσειαν	λελύκοιεν	
IMPERATIVE.	S.	2.	λῦσον	[λέλυκε (472)	
		3.	λῡσάτω	λελυκέτω	
	D.	2.	λύσατον	λελύκετον	
		3.	λῡσάτων	λελυκέτων	
	P.	2.	λύσατε	λελύκετε	
		3.	λῡσάντων or λῡσάτωσαν	λελυκέτωσαν]	
INFINITIVE.			λῦσαι	λελυκέναι	
PARTICIPLE.			λύσᾱς, λύσᾱσα, λῦσαν (335)	λελυκώς, λελυκυῖα, λελυκός (335)	

2. Middle Voice of λύω.

			Present.	*Imperfect.*	*Future.*
Indicative.	S.	1.	λύομαι	ἐλῡόμην	λύσομαι
		2.	λύει, λύῃ	ἐλύου	λύσει, λύσῃ
		3.	λύεται	ἐλύετο	λύσεται
	D.	2.	λύεσθον	ἐλύεσθον	λύσεσθον
		3.	λύεσθον	ἐλῡέσθην	λύσεσθον
	P.	1.	λῡόμεθα	ἐλῡόμεθα	λῡσόμεθα
		2.	λύεσθε	ἐλύεσθε	λύσεσθε
		3.	λύονται	ἐλύοντο	λύσονται
Subjunctive.	S.	1.	λύωμαι		
		2.	λύῃ		
		3.	λύηται		
	D.	2.	λύησθον		
		3.	λύησθον		
	P.	1.	λῡώμεθα		
		2.	λύησθε		
		3.	λύωνται		
Optative.	S.	1.	λῡοίμην		λῡσοίμην
		2.	λύοιο		λύσοιο
		3.	λύοιτο		λύσοιτο
	D.	2.	λύοισθον		λύσοισθον
		3.	λῡοίσθην		λῡσοίσθην
	P.	1.	λῡοίμεθα		λῡσοίμεθα
		2.	λύοισθε		λύσοισθε
		3.	λύοιντο		λύσοιντο
Imperative.	S.	2.	λύου		
		3.	λῡέσθω		
	D.	2.	λύεσθον		
		3.	λῡέσθων		
	P.	2.	λύεσθε		
		3.	λῡέσθων or λῡέσθωσαν		
Infinitive.			λύεσθαι		λύσεσθαι
Participle.			λῡόμενος, λῡομένη, λῡόμενον (301)		λῡσόμενος, -η, -ον (301)

			1 *Aorist.*	*Perfect.*	*Pluperfect.*
INDICATIVE.	S.	1.	ἐλῡσάμην	λέλυμαι	ἐλελύμην
		2.	ἐλύσω	λέλυσαι	ἐλέλυσο
		3.	ἐλύσατο	λέλυται	ἐλέλυτο
	D.	2.	ἐλύσασθον	λέλυσθον	ἐλέλυσθον
		3.	ἐλῡσάσθην	λέλυσθον	ἐλελύσθην
	P.	1.	ἐλῡσάμεθα	λελύμεθα	ἐλελύμεθα
		2.	ἐλύσασθε	λέλυσθε	ἐλέλυσθε
		3.	ἐλύσαντο	λέλυνται	ἐλέλυντο
SUBJUNCTIVE.	S.	1.	λύσωμαι	λελυμένος ὦ	
		2.	λύσῃ	λελυμένος ᾖς	
		3.	λύσηται	λελυμένος ᾖ	
	D.	2.	λύσησθον	λελυμένω ἦτον	
		3.	λύσησθον	λελυμένω ἦτον	
	P.	1.	λῡσώμεθα	λελυμένοι ὦμεν	
		2.	λύσησθε	λελυμένοι ἦτε	
		3.	λύσωνται	λελυμένοι ὦσι	
OPTATIVE.	S.	1.	λῡσαίμην	λελυμένος εἴην	
		2.	λύσαιο	λελυμένος εἴης	
		3.	λύσαιτο	λελυμένος εἴη	
	D.	2.	λύσαισθον	λελυμένω εἶτον or εἴητον	
		3.	λῡσαίσθην	λελυμένω εἴτην or εἰήτην	
	P.	1.	λῡσαίμεθα	λελυμένοι εἶμεν or εἴημεν	
		2.	λύσαισθε	λελυμένοι εἶτε or εἴητε	
		3.	λύσαιντο	λελυμένοι εἶεν or εἴησαν	
IMPERATIVE.	S.	2.	λῦσαι	λέλυσο (750)	
		3.	λῡσάσθω	λελύσθω (749)	
	D.	2.	λύσασθον	λέλυσθον	
		3.	λῡσάσθων	λελύσθων	
	P.	2.	λύσασθε	λέλυσθε	
		3.	λῡσάσθων or λῡσάσθωσαν	λελύσθων or λελύσθωσαν	
INFINITIVE.			λύσασθαι	λελύσθαι	
PARTICIPLE.			λῡσάμενος, -η, -ον (301)	λελυμένος, -η, -ον (301)	

3. Passive Voice of λύω.

			Future Perfect.	1 *Aorist.*	1 *Future.*
Indicative.	S.	1.	λελύσομαι	ἐλύθην	λυθήσομαι
		2.	λελύσει, λελύσῃ	ἐλύθης	λυθήσει, λυθήσῃ
		3.	λελύσεται	ἐλύθη	λυθήσεται
	D.	2.	λελύσεσθον	ἐλύθητον	λυθήσεσθον
		3.	λελύσεσθον	ἐλυθήτην	λυθήσεσθον
	P.	1.	λελῡσόμεθα	ἐλύθημεν	λυθησόμεθα
		2.	λελύσεσθε	ἐλύθητε	λυθήσεσθε
		3.	λελύσονται	ἐλύθησαν	λυθήσονται
Subjunctive.	S.	1.		λυθῶ	
		2.		λυθῇς	
		3.		λυθῇ	
	D.	2.		λυθῆτον	
		3.		λυθῆτον	
	P.	1.		λυθῶμεν	
		2.		λυθῆτε	
		3.		λυθῶσι	
Optative.	S.	1.	λελῡσοίμην	λυθείην	λυθησοίμην
		2.	λελύσοιο	λυθείης	λυθήσοιο
		3.	λελύσοιτο	λυθείη	λυθήσοιτο
	D.	2.	λελύσοισθον	λυθεῖτον or λυθείητον	λυθήσοισθον
		3.	λελῡσοίσθην	λυθείτην or λυθειήτην	λυθησοίσθην
	P.	1.	λελῡσοίμεθα	λυθεῖμεν or λυθείημεν	λυθησοίμεθα
		2.	λελύσοισθε	λυθεῖτε or λυθείητε	λυθήσοισθε
		3.	λελύσοιντο	λυθεῖεν or λυθείησαν	λυθήσοιντο
Imperative.	S.	2.		λύθητι	
		3.		λυθήτω	
	D.	2.		λύθητον	
		3.		λυθήτων	
	P.	2.		λύθητε	
		3.		λυθέντων or λυθήτωσαν	
Infinitive.			λελύσεσθαι	λυθῆναι	λυθήσεσθαι
Participle.			λελῡσόμενος, -η, -ον (301)	λυθείς, λυθεῖσα, λυθέν (335)	λυθησόμενος, -η, -ον (301)

481. Second Aorist (Active and Middle) and Second Perfect and Pluperfect of λείπω.

			2 *Aorist Active.*	2 *Aorist Middle.*	2 *Perfect.*	2 *Pluperfect.*
Indicative.	S.	1.	ἔλιπον	ἐλιπόμην	λέλοιπα	ἐλελοίπη
		2.	ἔλιπες	ἐλίπου	λέλοιπας	ἐλελοίπης
		3.	ἔλιπε	ἐλίπετο	λέλοιπε	ἐλελοίπει
	D.	2.	ἐλίπετον	ἐλίπεσθον	λελοίπατον	ἐλελοίπετον
		3.	ἐλιπέτην	ἐλιπέσθην	λελοίπατον	ἐλελοιπέτην
	P.	1.	ἐλίπομεν	ἐλιπόμεθα	λελοίπαμεν	ἐλελοίπεμεν
		2.	ἐλίπετε	ἐλίπεσθε	λελοίπατε	ἐλελοίπετε
		3.	ἔλιπον	ἐλίποντο	λελοίπᾱσι	ἐλελοίπεσαν
Subjunctive.	S.	1.	λίπω	λίπωμαι	λελοίπω	(See 683, 2)
		2.	λίπῃς	λίπῃ	λελοίπῃς	
		3.	λίπῃ	λίπηται	λελοίπῃ	
	D.	2.	λίπητον	λίπησθον	λελοίπητον	
		3.	λίπητον	λίπησθον	λελοίπητον	
	P.	1.	λίπωμεν	λιπώμεθα	λελοίπωμεν	
		2.	λίπητε	λίπησθε	λελοίπητε	
		3.	λίπωσι	λίπωνται	λελοίπωσι	
Optative.	S.	1.	λίποιμι	λιποίμην	λελοίποιμι	
		2.	λίποις	λίποιο	λελοίποις	
		3.	λίποι	λίποιτο	λελοίποι	
	D.	2.	λίποιτον	λίποισθον	λελοίποιτον	
		3.	λιποίτην	λιποίσθην	λελοιποίτην	
	P.	1.	λίποιμεν	λιποίμεθα	λελοίποιμεν	
		2.	λίποιτε	λίποισθε	λελοίποιτε	
		3.	λίποιεν	λίποιντο	λελοίποιεν	
Imperative.	S.	2.	λίπε	λιποῦ	λέλοιπε	
		3.	λιπέτω	λιπέσθω	λελοιπέτω	
	D.	2.	λίπετον	λίπεσθον	λελοίπετον	
		3.	λιπέτων	λιπέσθων	λελοιπέτων	
	P.	2.	λίπετε	λίπεσθε	λελοίπετε	
		3.	λιπόντων or λιπέτωσαν	λιπέσθων or λιπέσθωσαν	λελοιπέτων	
Infinitive.			λιπεῖν	λιπέσθαι	λελοιπέναι	
Participle.			λιπών, λιποῦσα, λιπόν (335)	λιπόμενος, -η, -ον (301)	λελοιπώς, λελοιπυῖα, λελοιπός (335)	

482. Future and First Aorist Active and Middle (Liquid Forms) and Second Aorist and Second Future Passive of **φαίνω**.

			Future Active.[1]	*Future Middle.*[1]	*1 Aorist Active.*
Indicative.	S.	1.	φανῶ	φανοῦμαι	ἔφηνα
		2.	φανεῖς	φανεῖ, φανῇ	ἔφηνας
		3.	φανεῖ	φανεῖται	ἔφηνε
	D.	2.	φανεῖτον	φανεῖσθον	ἐφήνατον
		3.	φανεῖτον	φανεῖσθον	ἐφηνάτην
	P.	1.	φανοῦμεν	φανούμεθα	ἐφήναμεν
		2.	φανεῖτε	φανεῖσθε	ἐφήνατε
		3.	φανοῦσι	φανοῦνται	ἔφηναν
Subjunctive.	S.	1.			φήνω
		2.			φήνῃς
		3.			φήνῃ
	D.	2.			φήνητον
		3.			φήνητον
	P.	1.			φήνωμεν
		2.			φήνητε
		3.			φήνωσι
Optative.	S.	1.	φανοίην or φανοῖμι	φανοίμην	φήναιμι
		2.	φανοίης or φανοῖς	φανοῖο	φήναις or φήνειας
		3.	φανοίη or φανοῖ	φανοῖτο	φήναι or φήνειε
	D.	2.	φανοῖτον	φανοῖσθον	φήναιτον
		3.	φανοίτην	φανοίσθην	φηναίτην
	P.	1.	φανοῖμεν	φανοίμεθα	φήναιμεν
		2.	φανοῖτε	φανοῖσθε	φήναιτε
		3.	φανοῖεν	φανοῖντο	φήναιεν or φήνειαν
Imperative.	S.	2.			φῆνον
		3.			φηνάτω
	D.	2.			φήνατον
		3.			φηνάτων
	P.	2.			φήνατε
		3.			φηνάντων or φηνάτωσαν
Infinitive.			φανεῖν	φανεῖσθαι	φῆναι
Participle.			φανῶν, φανοῦσα, φανοῦν (340)	φανούμενος, -η, -ον (301)	φήνᾱς, φήνᾱσα, φῆναν (335)

[1] The uncontracted futures, *φανέω* and *φανέομαι* (478; 483), are inflected like *φιλέω* and *φιλέομαι* (492).

			1 *Aor. Mid.*	2 *Aor. Pass.*	2 *Fut. Pass.*
INDICATIVE.	S.	1.	ἐφηνάμην	ἐφάνην	φανήσομαι
		2.	ἐφήνω	ἐφάνης	φανήσει, φανήσῃ
		3.	ἐφήνατο	ἐφάνη	φανήσεται
	D.	2.	ἐφήνασθον	ἐφάνητον	φανήσεσθον
		3.	ἐφηνάσθην	ἐφανήτην	φανήσεσθον
	P.	1.	ἐφηνάμεθα	ἐφάνημεν	φανησόμεθα
		2.	ἐφήνασθε	ἐφάνητε	φανήσεσθε
		3.	ἐφήναντο	ἐφάνησαν	φανήσονται
SUBJUNCTIVE.	S.	1.	φήνωμαι	φανῶ	
		2.	φήνῃ	φανῇς	
		3.	φήνηται	φανῇ	
	D.	2.	φήνησθον	φανῆτον	
		3.	φήνησθον	φανῆτον	
	P.	1.	φηνώμεθα	φανῶμεν	
		2.	φήνησθε	φανῆτε	
		3.	φήνωνται	φανῶσι	
OPTATIVE.	S.	1.	φηναίμην	φανείην	φανησοίμην
		2.	φήναιο	φανείης	φανήσοιο
		3.	φήναιτο	φανείη	φανήσοιτο
	D.	2.	φήναισθον	φανεῖτον or φανείητον	φανήσοισθον
		3.	φηναίσθην	φανείτην or φανειήτην	φανησοίσθην
	P.	1.	φηναίμεθα	φανεῖμεν or φανείημεν	φανησοίμεθα
		2.	φήναισθε	φανεῖτε or φανείητε	φανήσοισθε
		3.	φήναιντο	φανεῖεν or φανείησαν	φανήσοιντο
IMPERATIVE.	S.	2.	φῆναι	φάνηθι	
		3.	φηνάσθω	φανήτω	
	D.	2.	φήνασθον	φάνητον	
		3.	φηνάσθων	φανήτων	
	P.	2.	φήνασθε	φάνητε	
		3.	φηνάσθων or φηνάσθωσαν	φανέντων or φανήτωσαν	
INFINITIVE.			φήνασθαι	φανῆναι	φανήσεσθαι
PARTICIPLE.			φηνάμενος, -η, -ον (301)	φανείς, φανεῖσα, φανέν (335)	φανησόμενος, -η, -ον (301)

483. The uncontracted forms of the future active and middle of *φαίνω* (478) and of other liquid futures are not Attic, but are found in Homer and Herodotus. So with some of the uncontracted forms of the aorist subjunctive passive in *εω* (474).

484. The tenses of *λείπω* and *φαίνω* which are not inflected above follow the corresponding tenses of *λύω*; except the perfect and pluperfect middle, for which see 486. *Λέλειμ-μαι* is inflected like *τέτριμ-μαι* (487, 1), and *πέφασ-μαι* is inflected in 487, 2.

485. Some of the dissyllabic forms of *λύω* do not show the accent so well as polysyllabic forms, *e.g.* these of *κωλύω*, *hinder*:—

Pres. Imper. Act. κώλυε, κωλυέτω, κωλύετε. *Aor. Opt. Act.* κωλῦσαιμι, κωλῦσειας (or κωλῦσαις), κωλῦσειε (or κωλῦσαι). *Aor. Imper. Act.* κώλῡσον, κωλῡσάτω. *Aor. Inf. Act.* κωλῦσαι. *Aor. Imper. Mid.* κώλῡσαι, κωλῡσάσθω.

The three forms κωλῦσαι, κωλῦσαι, κώλῡσαι (cf. λῦσαι, λῦσαι, λῦσαι) are distinguished only by accent. See 130; 113; 131, 4.

PERFECT AND PLUPERFECT MIDDLE AND PASSIVE OF VERBS WITH CONSONANT STEMS.

486. 1. In the perfect and pluperfect middle, many euphonic changes (489) occur when a consonant of the tense-stem comes before *μ*, *τ*, *σ*, or *θ* of the ending.

2. When the stem ends in a consonant, the third person plural of these tenses is formed by the perfect middle participle with *εἰσί*, *are*, and *ἦσαν*, *were* (806).

487. 1. These tenses of *τρίβω*, *rub*, *πλέκω*, *weave*, *πείθω* *persuade*, and *στέλλω* (*σταλ-*), *send*, are thus inflected:—

Perfect Indicative.

S.	1.	τέτρῑμμαι	πέπλεγμαι	πέπεισμαι	ἔσταλμαι
	2.	τέτρῑψαι	πέπλεξαι	πέπεισαι	ἔσταλσαι
	3.	τέτρῑπται	πέπλεκται	πέπεισται	ἔσταλται
D.	2.	τέτρῑφθον	πέπλεχθον	πέπεισθον	ἔσταλθον
	3.	τέτρῑφθον	πέπλεχθον	πέπεισθον	ἔσταλθον
P.	1.	τετρίμμεθα	πεπλέγμεθα	πεπείσμεθα	ἐστάλμεθα
	2.	τέτρῑφθε	πέπλεχθε	πέπεισθε	ἔσταλθε
	3.	τετρῑμμένοι εἰσί	πεπλεγμένοι εἰσί	πεπεισμένοι εἰσί	ἐσταλμένοι εἰσί

Perfect Subjunctive and Optative.

Subj.	τετρῑμμένος ὦ	πεπλεγμένος ὦ	πεπεισμένος ὦ	ἐσταλμένος ὦ
Opt.	" εἴην	" εἴην	" εἴην	" εἴην

Perfect Imperative.

S.	2.	τέτρῑψο	πέπλεξο	πέπεισο	ἔσταλσο
	3.	τετρίφθω	πεπλέχθω	πεπείσθω	ἐστάλθω
D.	2.	τέτρῑφθον	πέπλεχθον	πέπεισθον	ἔσταλθον
	3.	τετρίφθων	πεπλέχθων	πεπείσθων	ἐστάλθων
P.	2.	τέτρῑφθε	πέπλεχθε	πέπεισθε	ἔσταλθε
	3.	τετρίφθων or	πεπλέχθων or	πεπείσθων or	ἐστάλθων or
		τετρίφθωσαν	πεπλέχθωσαν	πεπείσθωσαν	ἐστάλθωσαν

Perfect Infinitive and Participle.

Inf.	τετρῖφθαι	πεπλέχθαι	πεπεῖσθαι	ἐστάλθαι
Part.	τετρῑμμένος	πεπλεγμένος	πεπεισμένος	ἐσταλμένος

Pluperfect Indicative.

S.	1.	ἐτετρίμμην	ἐπεπλέγμην	ἐπεπείσμην	ἐστάλμην
	2.	ἐτέτρῑψο	ἐπέπλεξο	ἐπέπεισο	ἔσταλσο
	3.	ἐτέτρῑπτο	ἐπέπλεκτο	ἐπέπειστο	ἔσταλτο
D.	2.	ἐτέτρῑφθον	ἐπέπλεχθον	ἐπέπεισθον	ἔσταλθον
	3.	ἐτετρίφθην	ἐπεπλέχθην	ἐπεπείσθην	ἐστάλθην
P.	1.	ἐτετρίμμεθα	ἐπεπλέγμεθα	ἐπεπείσμεθα	ἐστάλμεθα
	2.	ἐτέτρῑφθε	ἐπέπλεχθε	ἐπέπεισθε	ἔσταλθε
	3.	τετρῑμμένοι	πεπλεγμένοι	πεπεισμένοι	ἐσταλμένοι
		ἦσαν	ἦσαν	ἦσαν	ἦσαν

2. The same tenses of (τελέω) τελῶ (stem τελε-), *finish*, φαίνω (φαν-), *show*, ἀλλάσσω (ἀλλαγ-), *exchange*, and ἐλέγχω (ἐλεγχ-), *convict*, are thus inflected: —

Perfect Indicative.

S.	1.	τετέλεσμαι	πέφασμαι	ἤλλαγμαι	ἐλήλεγμαι
	2.	τετέλεσαι	[πέφανσαι, 700]	ἤλλαξαι	ἐλήλεγξαι
	3.	τετέλεσται	πέφανται	ἤλλακται	ἐλήλεγκται
D.	2.	τετέλεσθον	πέφανθον	ἤλλαχθον	ἐλήλεγχθον
	3.	τετέλεσθον	πέφανθον	ἤλλαχθον	ἐλήλεγχθον
P.	1.	τετελέσμεθα	πεφάσμεθα	ἠλλάγμεθα	ἐληλέγμεθα
	2.	τετέλεσθε	πέφανθε	ἤλλαχθε	ἐλήλεγχθε
	3.	τετελεσμένοι	πεφασμένοι	ἠλλαγμένοι	ἐληλεγμένοι
		εἰσί	εἰσί	εἰσί	εἰσί

Perfect Subjunctive and Optative.

Subj.	τετελεσμένος ὦ	πεφασμένος ὦ	ἠλλαγμένος ὦ	ἐληλεγμένος ὦ
Opt.	" εἴην	" εἴην	" εἴην	" εἴην

Perfect Imperative.

S.	2.	τετέλεσο	[πέφανσο]	ἤλλαξο	ἐλήλεγξο
	3.	τετελέσθω	πεφάνθω	ἠλλάχθω	ἐληλέγχθω
D.	2.	τετέλεσθον	πέφανθον	ἤλλαχθον	ἐλήλεγχθον
	3.	τετελέσθων	πεφάνθων	ἠλλάχθων	ἐληλέγχθων
P.	2.	τετέλεσθε	πέφανθε	ἤλλαχθε	ἐλήλεγχθε
	3.	τετελέσθων or	πεφάνθων or	ἠλλάχθων or	ἐληλέγχθων or
		τετελέσθωσαν	πεφάνθωσαν	ἠλλάχθωσαν	ἐληλέγχθωσαν

Perfect Infinitive and Participle.

Inf.	τετελέσθαι	πεφάνθαι	ἠλλάχθαι	ἐληλέγχθαι
Part.	τετελεσμένος	πεφασμένος	ἠλλαγμένος	ἐληλεγμένος

Pluperfect Indicative.

S.	1.	ἐτετελέσμην	ἐπεφάσμην	ἠλλάγμην	ἐληλέγμην
	2.	ἐτετέλεσο	[ἐπέφανσο]	ἤλλαξο	ἐλήλεγξο
	3.	ἐτετέλεστο	ἐπέφαντο	ἤλλακτο	ἐλήλεγκτο
D.	2.	ἐτετέλεσθον	ἐπέφανθον	ἤλλαχθον	ἐλήλεγχθον
	3.	ἐτετελέσθην	ἐπεφάνθην	ἠλλάχθην	ἐληλέγχθην
P.	1.	ἐτετελέσμεθα	ἐπεφάσμεθα	ἠλλάγμεθα	ἐληλέγμεθα
	2.	ἐτετέλεσθε	ἐπέφανθε	ἤλλαχθε	ἐλήλεγχθε
	3.	τετελεσμένοι	πεφασμένοι	ἠλλαγμένοι	ἐληλεγμένοι
		ἦσαν	ἦσαν	ἦσαν	ἦσαν

488. N. The regular third person plural here (*τετριβ-νται, ἐπεπλεκ-ντο*, etc., formed like *λέλυ-νται, ἐλέλυ-ντο*) could not be pronounced. The periphrastic form is necessary also when *σ* is added to a vowel stem (640), as in *τετέλεσ-μαι*. But when final *ν* of a stem is dropped (647), the regular forms in *νται* and *ντο* are used; as *κλίνω, κέκλι-μαι, κέκλινται* (not *κεκλιμένοι εἰσί*).

489. For the euphonic changes here, see 71–77 and 83.

1. Thus *τέτρῑμ-μαι* is for *τετριβ-μαι* (75); *τέτρῑψαι* for *τετριβ-σαι* (74); *τέτρῑπ-ται* for *τετριβ-ται, τέτρῖφ-θον* for *τετριβ-θον* (71). So *πέπλεγ-μαι* is for *πεπλεκ-μαι* (75); *πέπλεχ-θον* for *πεπλεκ-θον* (71). *Πέπεισ-ται* is for *πεπειθ-ται*, and *πέπεισ-θον* is for *πεπειθ-θον* (71); and *πέπεισμαι* (for *πεπειθ-μαι*) probably follows their analogy; *πέπει-σαι* is for *πεπειθ-σαι* (74).

2. In *τετέλε-σ-μαι*, *σ* is added to the stem before *μ* and *τ* (640), the stem remaining pure before *σ*. *Τετέλεσμαι* and *πέπεισμαι*, therefore, inflect these tenses alike, though on different principles. On the other hand, the *σ* before *μ* in *πέφασμαι* (487, 2) is a sub-

stitute for ν of the stem (83), which ν reappears before other letters (700). In the following comparison the distinction is shown by the hyphens:—

τετέλε-σ-μαι	**πέπεισ-μαι**	**πέφασ-μαι**
τετέλε-σαι	**πέπει-σαι**	[**πέφαν-σαι**]
τετέλε-σ-ται	**πέπεισ-ται**	**πέφαν-ται**
τετέλε-σθε	**πέπεισ-θε**	**πέφαν-θε**

3. Under *ἤλλαγ-μαι*, *ἤλλαξαι* is for *ἤλλαγ-σαι*, *ἤλλακ-ται* for *ἤλλαγ-ται*, *ἤλλαχ-θον* for *ἤλλαγ-θον* (74; 71). Under *ἐλήλεγ-μαι*, *γγμ* (for *γχμ*) drops one *γ* (77); *ἐλήλεγξαι* and *ἐλήλεγκ-ται* are for *ἐληλεγχ-σαι* and *ἐληλεγχ-ται* (74; 71). See also 529.

490. 1. All perfect-middle stems ending in a labial inflect these tenses like *τέτρῑμ-μαι*; as *λείπω*, *λέλειμ-μαι*; *γράφω* (*γραφ-*), *write*, *γέγραμ-μαι* (75); *ῥίπτω* (*ῥῑφ-*, *ῥῐφ-*), *throw*, *ἔρρῑμ-μαι*. But when final *μπ* of the stem loses *π* before *μ* (77), the *π* recurs before other consonants; as *κάμπτω* (*καμπ-*), *bend*, *κέκαμ-μαι*, *κέκαμψαι*, *κέκαμπ-ται*, *κέκαμφ-θε*; *πέμπω* (*πεμπ-*), *send*, *πέπεμ-μαι*, *πέπεμψαι*, *πέπεμπ-ται*, *πέπεμφ-θε*: compare *πέπεμ-μαι* from *πέσσω* (*πεπ-*), *cook*, inflected *πέπεψαι*, *πέπεπ-ται*, *πέπεφ-θε*, etc.

2. All ending in a palatal inflect these tenses like *πέπλεγ-μαι* and *ἤλλαγ-μαι*; as *πρᾱ́σσω* (*πρᾱγ-*), *do*, *πέπρᾱγ-μαι*; *ταράσσω* (*ταραχ-*), *confuse*, *τετάραγ-μαι*; *φυλάσσω* (*φυλακ-*), *πεφύλαγ-μαι*. But when *γ* before *μ* represents *γγ*, as in *ἐλήλεγ-μαι* from *ἐλέγχ-ω* (489, 3), the second palatal of the stem recurs before other consonants (see 487, 2).

3. All ending in a lingual mute inflect these tenses like *πέπεισ-μαι*, etc.; as *φράζω* (*φραδ-*), *tell*, *πέφρασ-μαι*, *πέφρα-σαι*, *πέφρασ-ται*; *ἐθίζω* (*ἐθιδ-*), *accustom*, *εἴθισ-μαι*, *εἴθι-σαι*, *εἴθισ-ται*, *εἴθισ-θε*; pluf. *εἰθίσ-μην*, *εἴθι-σο*, *εἴθισ-το*; *σπένδω* (*σπενδ-*), *pour*, *ἔσπεισ-μαι* (like *πέπεισ-μαι*, 489, 1) for *ἐσπενδ-μαι*, *ἔσπει-σαι*, *ἔσπεισ-ται*, *ἔσπεισ-θε*.

4. Most ending in *ν* (those in *αν-* and *υν-* of verbs in *αινω* or *ῡνω*) are inflected like *πέφασ-μαι* (see 489, 2).

5. When final *ν* of a stem is dropped (647), as in *κλίνω*, *bend*, *κέκλι-μαι*, the tense is inflected like *λέλυ-μαι* (with a vowel stem).

6. Those ending in *λ* or *ρ* are inflected like *ἔσταλ-μαι*; as *ἀγγέλλω* (*ἀγγελ-*), *announce*, *ἤγγελ-μαι*; *αἴρω* (*ἀρ-*), *raise*, *ἦρ-μαι*; *ἐγείρω* (*ἐγερ-*), *rouse*, *ἐγήγερ-μαι*; *πείρω* (*περ-*), *pierce*, *πέπαρ-μαι* (645).

491. For the full forms of these verbs, see the Catalogue. For **φαίνω**, see also 478.

CONTRACT VERBS.

492. Verbs in *αω*, *εω*, and *οω* are contracted in the present and imperfect. These tenses of *τῑμάω* (*τῑμα-*), *honor*, *φιλέω* (*φιλε-*), *love*, and *δηλόω* (*δηλο-*), *manifest*, are thus inflected:—

ACTIVE.

Present Indicative.

1.	(τῑμάω)	**τῑμῶ**	(φιλέω)	**φιλῶ**	(δηλόω)	**δηλῶ**
2.	(τῑμάεις)	**τῑμᾷς**	(φιλέεις)	**φιλεῖς**	(δηλόεις)	**δηλοῖς**
3.	(τῑμάει)	**τῑμᾷ**	(φιλέει)	**φιλεῖ**	(δηλόει)	**δηλοῖ**
2.	(τῑμάετον)	**τῑμᾶτον**	(φιλέετον)	**φιλεῖτον**	(δηλόετον)	**δηλοῦτον**
3.	(τῑμάετον)	**τῑμᾶτον**	(φιλέετον)	**φιλεῖτον**	(δηλόετον)	**δηλοῦτον**
1.	(τῑμάομεν)	**τῑμῶμεν**	(φιλέομεν)	**φιλοῦμεν**	(δηλόομεν)	**δηλοῦμεν**
2.	(τῑμάετε)	**τῑμᾶτε**	(φιλέετε)	**φιλεῖτε**	(δηλόετε)	**δηλοῦτε**
3.	(τῑμάουσι)	**τῑμῶσι**	(φιλέουσι)	**φιλοῦσι**	(δηλόουσι)	**δηλοῦσι**

Present Subjunctive.

1.	(τῑμάω)	**τῑμῶ**	(φιλέω)	**φιλῶ**	(δηλόω)	**δηλῶ**
2.	(τῑμάῃς)	**τῑμᾷς**	(φιλέῃς)	**φιλῇς**	(δηλόῃς)	**δηλοῖς**
3.	(τῑμάῃ)	**τῑμᾷ**	(φιλέῃ)	**φιλῇ**	(δηλόῃ)	**δηλοῖ**
2.	(τῑμάητον)	**τῑμᾶτον**	(φιλέητον)	**φιλῆτον**	(δηλόητον)	**δηλῶτον**
3.	(τῑμάητον)	**τῑμᾶτον**	(φιλέητον)	**φιλῆτον**	(δηλόητον)	**δηλῶτον**
1.	(τῑμάωμεν)	**τῑμῶμεν**	(φιλέωμεν)	**φιλῶμεν**	(δηλόωμεν)	**δηλῶμεν**
2.	(τῑμάητε)	**τῑμᾶτε**	(φιλέητε)	**φιλῆτε**	(δηλόητε)	**δηλῶτε**
3.	(τῑμάωσι)	**τῑμῶσι**	(φιλέωσι)	**φιλῶσι**	(δηλόωσι)	**δηλῶσι**

Present Optative (see 737).

1.	(τῑμάοιμι)	**[τῑμῷμι**	(φιλέοιμι)	**[φιλοῖμι**	(δηλόοιμι)	**[δηλοῖμι**
2.	(τῑμάοις)	**τῑμῷς**	(φιλέοις)	**φιλοῖς**	(δηλόοις)	**δηλοῖς**
3.	(τῑμάοι)	**τῑμῷ]**	(φιλέοι)	**φιλοῖ]**	(δηλόοι)	**δηλοῖ]**
2.	(τῑμάοιτον)	**τῑμῷτον**	(φιλέοιτον)	**φιλοῖτον**	(δηλόοιτον)	**δηλοῖτον**
3.	(τῑμαοίτην)	**τῑμῴτην**	(φιλεοίτην)	**φιλοίτην**	(δηλοοίτην)	**δηλοίτην**
1.	(τῑμάοιμεν)	**τῑμῷμεν**	(φιλέοιμεν)	**φιλοῖμεν**	(δηλόοιμεν)	**δηλοῖμεν**
2.	(τῑμάοιτε)	**τῑμῷτε**	(φιλέοιτε)	**φιλοῖτε**	(δηλόοιτε)	**δηλοῖτε**
3.	(τῑμάοιεν)	**τῑμῷεν**	(φιλέοιεν)	**φιλοῖεν**	(δηλόοιεν)	**δηλοῖεν**
	or	or	or	or	or	or
1.	(τῑμαοίην)	**τῑμῴην**	(φιλεοίην)	**φιλοίην**	(δηλοοίην)	**δηλοίην**
2.	(τῑμαοίης)	**τῑμῴης**	(φιλεοίης)	**φιλοίης**	(δηλοοίης)	**δηλοίης**
3.	(τῑμαοίη)	**τῑμῴη**	(φιλεοίη)	**φιλοίη**	(δηλοοίη)	**δηλοίη**
2.	(τῑμαοίητον)	**[τῑμῴητον**	(φιλεοίητον)	**[φιλοίητον**	(δηλοοίητον)	**[δηλοίητον**
3.	(τῑμαοιήτην)	**τῑμῳήτην]**	(φιλεοιήτην)	**φιλοιήτην]**	(δηλοοιήτην)	**δηλοιήτην]**
1.	(τῑμαοίημεν)	**[τῑμῴημεν**	(φιλεοίημεν)	**[φιλοίημεν**	(δηλοοίημεν)	**[δηλοίημεν**
2.	(τῑμαοίητε)	**τῑμῴητε**	(φιλεοίητε)	**φιλοίητε**	(δηλοοίητε)	**δηλοίητε**
3.	(τῑμαοίησαν)	**τῑμῴησαν]**	(φιλεοίησαν)	**φιλοίησαν]**	(δηλοοίησαν)	**δηλοίησαν]**

Present Imperative.

S.	2.	(τίμαε)	**τίμᾱ**	(φίλεε)	**φίλει**	(δήλοε)	**δήλου**
	3.	(τῑμαέτω)	**τῑμάτω**	(φιλεέτω)	**φιλείτω**	(δηλοέτω)	**δηλούτω**
D.	2.	(τῑμάετον)	**τῑμᾶτον**	(φιλέετον)	**φιλεῖτον**	(δηλόετον)	**δηλοῦτον**
	3.	(τῑμαέτων)	**τῑμάτων**	(φιλεέτων)	**φιλείτων**	(δηλοέτων)	**δηλούτων**
P.	2.	(τῑμάετε)	**τῑμᾶτε**	(φιλέετε)	**φιλεῖτε**	(δηλόετε)	**δηλοῦτε**
	3.	(τῑμαόντων)	**τῑμώντων**	(φιλεόντων)	**φιλούντων**	(δηλοόντων)	**δηλούντων**
		or	or	or	or	or	or
		(τῑμαέτωσαν)	**τῑμάτωσαν**	(φιλεέτωσαν)	**φιλείτωσαν**	(δηλοέτωσαν)	**δηλούτωσαν**

Present Infinitive.

(τῑμάειν)	**τῑμᾶν**	(φιλέειν)	**φιλεῖν**	(δηλόειν)	**δηλοῦν**

Present Participle (see 340).

(τῑμάων)	**τῑμῶν**	(φιλέων)	**φιλῶν**	(δηλόων)	**δηλῶν**

Imperfect.

S.	1.	(ἐτίμαον)	**ἐτίμων**	(ἐφίλεον)	**ἐφίλουν**	(ἐδήλοον)	**ἐδήλουν**
	2.	(ἐτίμαες)	**ἐτίμᾱς**	(ἐφίλεες)	**ἐφίλεις**	(ἐδήλοες)	**ἐδήλους**
	3.	(ἐτίμαε)	**ἐτίμᾱ**	(ἐφίλεε)	**ἐφίλει**	(ἐδήλοε)	**ἐδήλου**
D.	2.	(ἐτῑμάετον)	**ἐτῑμᾶτον**	(ἐφιλέετον)	**ἐφιλεῖτον**	(ἐδηλόετον)	**ἐδηλοῦτον**
	3.	(ἐτῑμαέτην)	**ἐτῑμάτην**	(ἐφιλεέτην)	**ἐφιλείτην**	(ἐδηλοέτην)	**ἐδηλούτην**
P.	1.	(ἐτῑμάομεν)	**ἐτῑμῶμεν**	(ἐφιλέομεν)	**ἐφιλοῦμεν**	(ἐδηλόομεν)	**ἐδηλοῦμεν**
	2.	(ἐτῑμάετε)	**ἐτῑμᾶτε**	(ἐφιλέετε)	**ἐφιλεῖτε**	(ἐδηλόετε)	**ἐδηλοῦτε**
	3.	(ἐτίμαον)	**ἐτίμων**	(ἐφίλεον)	**ἐφίλουν**	(ἐδήλοον)	**ἐδήλουν**

PASSIVE AND MIDDLE.

Present Indicative.

S.	1.	(τῑμάομαι)	**τῑμῶμαι**	(φιλέομαι)	**φιλοῦμαι**	(δηλόομαι)	**δηλοῦμαι**
	2.	(τῑμάει, τῑμάῃ)	**τῑμᾷ**	(φιλέει, φιλέῃ)	**φιλεῖ, φιλῇ**	(δηλόει, δηλόῃ)	**δηλοῖ**
	3.	(τῑμάεται)	**τῑμᾶται**	(φιλέεται)	**φιλεῖται**	(δηλόεται)	**δηλοῦται**
D.	2.	(τῑμάεσθον)	**τῑμᾶσθον**	(φιλέεσθον)	**φιλεῖσθον**	(δηλόεσθον)	**δηλοῦσθον**
	3.	(τῑμάεσθον)	**τῑμᾶσθον**	(φιλέεσθον)	**φιλεῖσθον**	(δηλόεσθον)	**δηλοῦσθον**
P.	1.	(τῑμαόμεθα)	**τῑμώμεθα**	(φιλεόμεθα)	**φιλούμεθα**	(δηλοόμεθα)	**δηλούμεθα**
	2.	(τῑμάεσθε)	**τῑμᾶσθε**	(φιλέεσθε)	**φιλεῖσθε**	(δηλόεσθε)	**δηλοῦσθε**
	3.	(τῑμάονται)	**τῑμῶνται**	(φιλέονται)	**φιλοῦνται**	(δηλόονται)	**δηλοῦνται**

Present Subjunctive.

S.	1.	(τῑμάωμαι)	**τῑμῶμαι**	(φιλέωμαι)	**φιλῶμαι**	(δηλόωμαι)	**δηλῶμαι**
	2.	(τῑμάῃ)	**τῑμᾷ**	(φιλέῃ)	**φιλῇ**	(δηλόῃ)	**δηλοῖ**
	3.	(τῑμάηται)	**τῑμᾶται**	(φιλέηται)	**φιλῆται**	(δηλόηται)	**δηλῶται**
D.	2.	(τῑμάησθον)	**τῑμᾶσθον**	(φιλέησθον)	**φιλῆσθον**	(δηλόησθον)	**δηλῶσθον**
	3.	(τῑμάησθον)	**τῑμᾶσθον**	(φιλέησθον)	**φιλῆσθον**	(δηλόησθον)	**δηλῶσθον**
P.	1.	(τῑμαώμεθα)	**τῑμώμεθα**	(φιλεώμεθα)	**φιλώμεθα**	(δηλοώμεθα)	**δηλώμεθα**
	2.	(τῑμάησθε)	**τῑμᾶσθε**	(φιλέησθε)	**φιλῆσθε**	(δηλόησθε)	**δηλῶσθε**
	3.	(τῑμάωνται)	**τῑμῶνται**	(φιλέωνται)	**φιλῶνται**	(δηλόωνται)	**δηλῶνται**

Present Optative.

1.	(τῑμαοίμην)	**τῑμῴμην**	(φιλεοίμην)	**φιλοίμην**	(δηλοοίμην)	**δηλοίμην**
2.	(τῑμάοιο)	**τῑμῷο**	(φιλέοιο)	**φιλοῖο**	(δηλόοιο)	**δηλοῖο**
3.	(τῑμάοιτο)	**τῑμῷτο**	(φιλέοιτο)	**φιλοῖτο**	(δηλόοιτο)	**δηλοῖτο**
2.	(τῑμάοισθον)	**τῑμῷσθον**	(φιλέοισθον)	**φιλοῖσθον**	(δηλόοισθον)	**δηλοῖσθον**
3.	(τῑμαοίσθην)	**τῑμῴσθην**	(φιλεοίσθην)	**φιλοίσθην**	(δηλοοίσθην)	**δηλοίσθην**
1.	(τῑμαοίμεθα)	**τῑμῴμεθα**	(φιλεοίμεθα)	**φιλοίμεθα**	(δηλοοίμεθα)	**δηλοίμεθα**
2.	(τῑμάοισθε)	**τῑμῷσθε**	(φιλέοισθε)	**φιλοῖσθε**	(δηλόοισθε)	**δηλοῖσθε**
3.	(τῑμάοιντο)	**τῑμῷντο**	(φιλέοιντο)	**φιλοῖντο**	(δηλόοιντο)	**δηλοῖντο**

Present Imperative.

2.	(τῑμάου)	**τῑμῶ**	(φιλέου)	**φιλοῦ**	(δηλόου)	**δηλοῦ**
3.	(τῑμαέσθω)	**τῑμάσθω**	(φιλεέσθω)	**φιλείσθω**	(δηλοέσθω)	**δηλούσθω**
2.	(τῑμάεσθον)	**τῑμᾶσθον**	(φιλέεσθον)	**φιλεῖσθον**	(δηλόεσθον)	**δηλοῦσθον**
3.	(τῑμαέσθων)	**τῑμάσθων**	(φιλεέσθων)	**φιλείσθων**	(δηλοέσθων)	**δηλούσθων**
2.	(τῑμάεσθε)	**τῑμᾶσθε**	(φιλέεσθε)	**φιλεῖσθε**	(δηλόεσθε)	**δηλοῦσθε**
3.	(τῑμαέσθων)	**τῑμάσθων**	(φιλεέσθων)	**φιλείσθων**	(δηλοέσθων)	**δηλούσθων**
	or	or	or	or	or	or
	(τῑμαέσθωσαν)	**τῑμάσθωσαν**	(φιλεέσθωσαν)	**φιλείσθωσαν**	δηλοέσθωσαν)	**δηλούσθωσαν**

Present Infinitive.

(τῑμάεσθαι)	**τῑμᾶσθαι**	(φιλέεσθαι)	**φιλεῖσθαι**	(δηλόεσθαι)	**δηλοῦσθαι**

Present Participle.

(τῑμαόμενος)	**τῑμώμενος**	(φιλεόμενος)	**φιλούμενος**	(δηλοόμενος)	**δηλούμενος**

Imperfect.

1.	(ἐτῑμαόμην)	**ἐτῑμώμην**	(ἐφιλεόμην)	**ἐφιλούμην**	(ἐδηλοόμην)	**ἐδηλούμην**
2.	(ἐτῑμάου)	**ἐτῑμῶ**	(ἐφιλέου)	**ἐφιλοῦ**	(ἐδηλόου)	**ἐδηλοῦ**
3.	(ἐτῑμάετο)	**ἐτῑμᾶτο**	(ἐφιλέετο)	**ἐφιλεῖτο**	(ἐδηλόετο)	**ἐδηλοῦτο**
2.	(ἐτῑμάεσθον)	**ἐτῑμᾶσθον**	(ἐφιλέεσθον)	**ἐφιλεῖσθον**	(ἐδηλόεσθον)	**ἐδηλοῦσθον**
3.	(ἐτῑμαέσθην)	**ἐτῑμάσθην**	(ἐφιλεέσθην)	**ἐφιλείσθην**	(ἐδηλοέσθην)	**ἐδηλούσθην**
1.	(ἐτῑμαόμεθα)	**ἐτῑμώμεθα**	(ἐφιλεόμεθα)	**ἐφιλούμεθα**	(ἐδηλοόμεθα)	**ἐδηλούμεθα**
2.	(ἐτῑμάεσθε)	**ἐτῑμᾶσθε**	(ἐφιλέεσθε)	**ἐφιλεῖσθε**	(ἐδηλόεσθε)	**ἐδηλοῦσθε**
3.	(ἐτῑμάοντο)	**ἐτῑμῶντο**	(ἐφιλέοντο)	**ἐφιλοῦντο**	(ἐδηλόοντο)	**ἐδηλοῦντο**

493. N. The uncontracted forms of these tenses are not Attic (but see 495, 1). Those of verbs in *αω* sometimes occur in Homer; those of verbs in *εω* are common in Homer and Herodotus; but those of verbs in *οω* are never used. For dialectic forms of these verbs, see 784–786.

494. SYNOPSIS of **τῑμάω, φιλέω, δηλόω,** and **θηράω,** ***hunt,*** in the Indicative of all voices.

ACTIVE.

Pres.	τῑμῶ	φιλῶ	δηλῶ	θηρῶ
Impf.	ἐτίμων	ἐφίλουν	ἐδήλουν	ἐθήρων
Fut.	τῑμήσω	φιλήσω	δηλώσω	θηράσω
Aor.	ἐτίμησα	ἐφίλησα	ἐδήλωσα	ἐθήρᾱσα
Perf.	τετίμηκα	πεφίληκα	δεδήλωκα	τεθήρᾱκα
Plup.	ἐτετῑμήκη	ἐπεφιλήκη	ἐδεδηλώκη	ἐτεθηράκη

MIDDLE.

Pres.	τῑμῶμαι	φιλοῦμαι	δηλοῦμαι	θηρῶμαι
Impf.	ἐτῑμώμην	ἐφιλούμην	ἐδηλούμην	ἐθηρώμην
Fut.	τῑμήσομαι	φιλήσομαι	δηλώσομαι	θηράσομαι
Aor.	ἐτῑμησάμην	ἐφιλησάμην	ἐδηλωσάμην	ἐθηρᾱσάμην
Perf.	τετίμημαι	πεφίλημαι	δεδήλωμαι	τεθήρᾱμαι
Plup.	ἐτετῑμήμην	ἐπεφιλήμην	ἐδεδηλώμην	ἐτεθηράμην

PASSIVE.

Pres. and Imp.: same as Middle.

Fut.	τῑμηθήσομαι	φιληθήσομαι	δηλωθήσομαι	(θηρᾱθήσομαι)
Aor.	ἐτῑμήθην	ἐφιλήθην	ἐδηλώθην	ἐθηράθην

Perf. and Plup.: same as Middle.

Fut. Perf.	τετῑμήσομαι	πεφιλήσομαι	δεδηλώσομαι	(τεθηράσομαι)

495. 1. Dissyllabic verbs in **εω** contract only **εε** and **εει**. Thus πλέω, *sail,* has pres. πλέω, πλεῖς, πλεῖ, πλεῖτον, πλέομεν, πλεῖτε, πλέουσι; imperf. ἔπλεον, ἔπλεις, ἔπλει, etc.; infin. πλεῖν; partic. πλέων.

2. **Δέω,** *bind,* is the only exception, and is contracted in most forms; as δοῦσι, δοῦμαι, δοῦνται, ἔδουν, partic. δῶν, δοῦν. Δέω, *want,* is contracted like πλέω.

496. N. A few verbs in **αω** have **η** for **ᾱ** in the contracted forms; as διψάω, διψῶ, *thirst,* διψῇς, διψῇ, διψῆτε; imperf. ἐδίψων, ἐδίψης, ἐδίψη; infin. διψῆν. So ζάω, *live,* κνάω, *scrape,* πεινάω, *hunger,* σμάω, *smear,* χράω, *give oracles,* with χράομαι, *use,* and ψάω, *rub.*

497. N. Ῥῑγόω, *shiver,* has infinitive ῥῑγῶν (with ῥῑγοῦν), and optative ῥῑγῴην. Ἱδρόω, *sweat,* has ἱδρῶσι, ἱδρῴη, ἱδρῶντι, etc.

Λούω, *wash,* sometimes drops υ, and λόω is then inflected like δηλόω; as ἔλου for ἔλουε, λοῦμαι for λούομαι.

498. N. The third person singular of the imperfect active does not take ν movable in the contracted form; thus ἐφίλεε or ἐφίλεεν gives ἐφίλει (never ἐφίλειν). See 58.

499. For (άειν) ᾶν and (όειν) οῦν in the infinitive, see 39, 5.

CONJUGATION OF VERBS IN MI.

500. The peculiar inflection of verbs in μι affects only the present and second aorist systems, and in a few verbs the second perfect system. Most second aorists and perfects here included do not belong to presents in μι, but are irregular forms of verbs in ω; as ἔβην (second aorist of βαίνω), ἔγνων (γιγνώσκω), ἐπτάμην (πέτομαι), and τέθναμεν, τεθναίην, τεθνάναι (second perfect of θνῄσκω). (See 798 and 799.)

501. Tenses thus inflected are called μι-forms. In other tenses verbs in μι are inflected like verbs in ω (see the synopses, 509). No single verb exhibits all the possible μι-forms, and two of the paradigms, τίθημι and δίδωμι, are irregular and defective in the second aorist active (see 802).

502. There are two classes of verbs in μι: —

(1) Those in ημι (from stems in α or ε) and ωμι (from stems in ο), as ἵ-στη-μι (στα-), *set*, τί-θη-μι (θε-), *place*, δί-δω-μι (δο-), *give*.

(2) Those in νῡμι, which have the μι-form only in the present and imperfect; these add νυ (after a vowel ννυ) to the verb stem in these tenses, as δείκ-νῡ-μι (δεικ-), *show*, ῥώ-ννῡ-μι (ῥω-), *strengthen*. For poetic verbs in νημι (with να added to the stem), see 609 and 797, 2.

503. For a full enumeration of the μι-forms, see 793–804.

---

504. Synopsis of ἵστημι, τίθημι, δίδωμι, and δείκνῡμι in the Present and Second Aorist Systems.

Active.

	Indic.	*Subj.*	*Opt.*	*Imper.*	*Infin.*	*Part.*
Pres. and Impf.	ἵστημι	ἱστῶ	ἱσταίην	ἵστη	ἱστάναι	ἱστάς
	ἵστην					
	τίθημι	τιθῶ	τιθείην	τίθει	τιθέναι	τιθείς
	ἐτίθην					
	δίδωμι	διδῶ	διδοίην	δίδου	διδόναι	διδούς
	ἐδίδουν					
	δείκνῡμι	δεικνύω	δεικνύοιμι	δείκνῡ	δεικνύναι	δεικνύς
	ἐδείκνῡν					

	Indic.	*Subj.*	*Opt.*	*Imper.*	*Infin.*	*Part.*
2 Aor.	ἔστην	στῶ	σταίην	στῆθι	στῆναι	στάς
	ἔθετον dual (506)	θῶ	θείην	θές	θεῖναι	θείς
	ἔδοτον dual (506)	δῶ	δοίην	δός	δοῦναι	δούς
	ἔδῡν (505)	δύω	——	δῦθι	δῦναι	δύς

PASSIVE AND MIDDLE.

Pres. and Impf.	ἵσταμαι ἱστάμην	ἱστῶμαι	ἱσταίμην	ἵστασο	ἵστασθαι	ἱστάμενος
	τίθεμαι ἐτιθέμην	τιθῶμαι	τιθείμην	τίθεσο	τίθεσθαι	τιθέμενος
	δίδομαι ἐδιδόμην	διδῶμαι	διδοίμην	δίδοσο	δίδοσθαι	διδόμενος
	δείκνυμαι ἐδεικνύμην	δεικνύωμαι	δεικνυοίμην	δείκνυσο	δείκνυσθαι	δεικνύμενος
2 Aor. Mid.	ἐπριάμην	πρίωμαι	πριαίμην	πρίω	πρίασθαι	πριάμενος
	ἐθέμην	θῶμαι	θείμην	θοῦ	θέσθαι	θέμενος
	ἐδόμην	δῶμαι	δοίμην	δοῦ	δόσθαι	δόμενος

505. As ἵστημι wants the second aorist middle, ἐπριάμην, *I bought* (from a stem πρια- with no present), is added here and in the inflection. As δείκνῡμι wants the second aorist (502, 2), ἔδῡν, *I entered* (from δύω, formed as if from δῡ-μι), is added. No second aorist middle in υμην occurs, except in scattered poetic forms (see λύω, πνέω, σεύω, and χέω, in the Catalogue).

---

506. INFLECTION of ἵστημι, τίθημι, δίδωμι, and δείκνῡμι in the Present and Second Aorist Systems; with ἔδῡν and ἐπριάμην (505).

ACTIVE.

Present Indicative.

Sing.	1.	ἵστημι	τίθημι	δίδωμι	δείκνῡμι
	2.	ἵστης	τίθης	δίδως	δείκνῡς
	3.	ἵστησι	τίθησι	δίδωσι	δείκνῡσι
Dual	2.	ἵστατον	τίθετον	δίδοτον	δείκνυτον
	3.	ἵστατον	τίθετον	δίδοτον	δείκνυτον
Plur.	1.	ἵσταμεν	τίθεμεν	δίδομεν	δείκνυμεν
	2.	ἵστατε	τίθετε	δίδοτε	δείκνυτε
	3.	ἱστᾶσι	τιθέᾱσι	διδόᾱσι	δεικνύᾱσι

Imperfect.

Sing.	1.	ἵστην	ἐτίθην	ἐδίδουν	ἐδείκνῡν
	2.	ἵστης	ἐτίθεις	ἐδίδους	ἐδείκνῡς
	3.	ἵστη	ἐτίθει	ἐδίδου	ἐδείκνῡ
Dual	2.	ἵστατον	ἐτίθετον	ἐδίδοτον	ἐδείκνυτον
	3.	ἱστάτην	ἐτιθέτην	ἐδιδότην	ἐδεικνύτην
Plur.	1.	ἵσταμεν	ἐτίθεμεν	ἐδίδομεν	ἐδείκνυμεν
	2.	ἵστατε	ἐτίθετε	ἐδίδοτε	ἐδείκνυτε
	3.	ἵστασαν	ἐτίθεσαν	ἐδίδοσαν	ἐδείκνυσαν

Present Subjunctive.

Sing.	1.	ἱστῶ	τιθῶ	διδῶ	δεικνύω
	2.	ἱστῇς	τιθῇς	διδῷς	δεικνύῃς
	3.	ἱστῇ	τιθῇ	διδῷ	δεικνύῃ
Dual	2.	ἱστῆτον	τιθῆτον	διδῶτον	δεικνύητον
	3.	ἱστῆτον	τιθῆτον	διδῶτον	δεικνύητον
Plur.	1.	ἱστῶμεν	τιθῶμεν	διδῶμεν	δεικνύωμεν
	2.	ἱστῆτε	τιθῆτε	διδῶτε	δεικνύητε
	3.	ἱστῶσι	τιθῶσι	διδῶσι	δεικνύωσι

Present Optative.

Sing.	1.	ἱσταίην	τιθείην	διδοίην	δεικνύοιμι
	2.	ἱσταίης	τιθείης	διδοίης	δεικνύοις
	3.	ἱσταίη	τιθείη	διδοίη	δεικνύοι
Dual	2.	ἱσταίητον	τιθείητον	διδοίητον	δεικνύοιτον
	3.	ἱσταιήτην	τιθειήτην	διδοιήτην	δεικνυοίτην
Plur.	1.	ἱσταίημεν	τιθείημεν	διδοίημεν	δεικνύοιμεν
	2.	ἱσταίητε	τιθείητε	διδοίητε	δεικνύοιτε
	3.	ἱσταίησαν	τιθείησαν	διδοίησαν	δεικνύοιεν

Commonly thus contracted: —

Dual	2.	ἱσταῖτον	τιθεῖτον	διδοῖτον
	3.	ἱσταίτην	τιθείτην	διδοίτην
Plur.	1.	ἱσταῖμεν	τιθεῖμεν	διδοῖμεν
	2.	ἱσταῖτε	τιθεῖτε	διδοῖτε
	3.	ἱσταῖεν	τιθεῖεν	διδοῖεν

Present Imperative.

Sing.	2.	ἵστη	τίθει	δίδου	δείκνῡ
	3.	ἱστάτω	τιθέτω	διδότω	δεικνύτω
Dual	2.	ἵστατον	τίθετον	δίδοτον	δείκνυτον
	3.	ἱστάτων	τιθέτων	διδότων	δεικνύτων

Plur.	2.	ἵστατε	τίθετε	δίδοτε	δείκνυτε
	3.	ἱστάντων or ἱστάτωσαν	τιθέντων or τιθέτωσαν	διδόντων or διδότωσαν	δεικνύντων or δεικνύτωσαν

Present Infinitive.

ἱστάναι	τιθέναι	διδόναι	δεικνύναι

Present Participle (335).

ἱστάς	τιθείς	διδούς	δεικνύς

Second Aorist Indicative (802).

Sing.	1.	ἔστην	——	——	ἔδῦν
	2.	ἔστης	——	——	ἔδῦς
	3.	ἔστη	——	——	ἔδῦ
Dual	2.	ἔστητον	ἔθετον	ἔδοτον	ἔδῦτον
	3.	ἐστήτην	ἐθέτην	ἐδότην	ἐδύτην
Plur.	1.	ἔστημεν	ἔθεμεν	ἔδομεν	ἔδῦμεν
	2.	ἔστητε	ἔθετε	ἔδοτε	ἔδῦτε
	3.	ἔστησαν	ἔθεσαν	ἔδοσαν	ἔδῦσαν

Second Aorist Subjunctive.

Sing.	1.	στῶ	θῶ	δῶ	δύω
	2.	στῇς	θῇς	δῷς	δύῃς
	3.	στῇ	θῇ	δῷ	δύῃ
Dual	2.	στῆτον	θῆτον	δῶτον	δύητον
	3.	στῆτον	θῆτον	δῶτον	δύητον
Plur.	1.	στῶμεν	θῶμεν	δῶμεν	δύωμεν
	2.	στῆτε	θῆτε	δῶτε	δύητε
	3.	στῶσι	θῶσι	δῶσι	δύωσι

Second Aorist Optative.

Sing.	1.	σταίην	θείην	δοίην	
	2.	σταίης	θείης	δοίης	
	3.	σταίη	θείη	δοίη	(See 744)
Dual	2.	σταίητον	θείητον	δοίητον	
	3.	σταιήτην	θειήτην	δοιήτην	
Plur.	1.	σταίημεν	θείημεν	δοίημεν	
	2.	σταίητε	θείητε	δοίητε	
	3.	σταίησαν	θείησαν	δοίησαν	

Commonly thus contracted: —

Dual	2.	σταῖτον	θεῖτον	δοῖτον
	3.	σταίτην	θείτην	δοίτην
Plur.	1.	σταῖμεν	θεῖμεν	δοῖμεν
	2.	σταῖτε	θεῖτε	δοῖτε
	3.	σταῖεν	θεῖεν	δοῖεν

Second Aorist Imperative.

Sing.	2.	στῆθι	θές	δός	δῦθι
	3.	στήτω	θέτω	δότω	δύτω
Dual	2.	στῆτον	θέτον	δότον	δῦτον
	3.	στήτων	θέτων	δότων	δύτων
Plur.	2.	στῆτε	θέτε	δότε	δῦτε
	3.	στάντων or στήτωσαν	θέντων or θέτωσαν	δόντων or δότωσαν	δύντων or δύτωσαν

Second Aorist Infinitive.

στῆναι	θεῖναι	δοῦναι	δῦναι

Second Aorist Participle (335).

στάς	θείς	δούς	δύς

PASSIVE AND MIDDLE.

Present Indicative.

Sing.	1.	ἵσταμαι	τίθεμαι	δίδομαι	δείκνυμαι
	2.	ἵστασαι	τίθεσαι	δίδοσαι	δείκνυσαι
	3.	ἵσταται	τίθεται	δίδοται	δείκνυται
Dual	2.	ἵστασθον	τίθεσθον	δίδοσθον	δείκνυσθον
	3.	ἵστασθον	τίθεσθον	δίδοσθον	δείκνυσθον
Plur.	1.	ἱστάμεθα	τιθέμεθα	διδόμεθα	δεικνύμεθα
	2.	ἵστασθε	τίθεσθε	δίδοσθε	δείκνυσθε
	3.	ἵστανται	τίθενται	δίδονται	δείκνυνται

Imperfect.

Sing.	1.	ἱστάμην	ἐτιθέμην	ἐδιδόμην	ἐδεικνύμην
	2.	ἵστασο	ἐτίθεσο	ἐδίδοσο	ἐδείκνυσο
	3.	ἵστατο	ἐτίθετο	ἐδίδοτο	ἐδείκνυτο
Dual	2.	ἵστασθον	ἐτίθεσθον	ἐδίδοσθον	ἐδείκνυσθον
	3.	ἱστάσθην	ἐτιθέσθην	ἐδιδόσθην	ἐδεικνύσθην
Plur.	1.	ἱστάμεθα	ἐτιθέμεθα	ἐδιδόμεθα	ἐδεικνύμεθα
	2.	ἵστασθε	ἐτίθεσθε	ἐδίδοσθε	ἐδείκνυσθε
	3.	ἵσταντο	ἐτίθεντο	ἐδίδοντο	ἐδείκνυντο

Present Subjunctive.

Sing.	1.	ἱστῶμαι	τιθῶμαι	διδῶμαι	δεικνύωμαι
	2.	ἱστῇ	τιθῇ	διδῷ	δεικνύῃ
	3.	ἱστῆται	τιθῆται	διδῶται	δεικνύηται
Dual	2.	ἱστῆσθον	τιθῆσθον	διδῶσθον	δεικνύησθον
	3.	ἱστῆσθον	τιθῆσθον	διδῶσθον	δεικνύησθον
Plur.	1.	ἱστώμεθα	τιθώμεθα	διδώμεθα	δεικνυώμεθα
	2.	ἱστῆσθε	τιθῆσθε	διδῶσθε	δεικνύησθε
	3.	ἱστῶνται	τιθῶνται	διδῶνται	δεικνύωνται

Present Optative.

Sing.	1.	ἱσταίμην	τιθείμην	διδοίμην	δεικνυοίμην
	2.	ἱσταῖο	τιθεῖο	διδοῖο	δεικνύοιο
	3.	ἱσταῖτο	τιθεῖτο	διδοῖτο	δεικνύοιτο
Dual	2.	ἱσταῖσθον	τιθεῖσθον	διδοῖσθον	δεικνύοισθον
	3.	ἱσταίσθην	τιθείσθην	διδοίσθην	δεικνυοίσθην
Plur.	1.	ἱσταίμεθα	τιθείμεθα	διδοίμεθα	δεικνυοίμεθα
	2.	ἱσταῖσθε	τιθεῖσθε	διδοῖσθε	δεικνύοισθε
	3.	ἱσταῖντο	τιθεῖντο	διδοῖντο	δεικνύοιντο

Present Imperative.

Sing.	2.	ἵστασο	τίθεσο	δίδοσο	δείκνυσο
	3.	ἱστάσθω	τιθέσθω	διδόσθω	δεικνύσθω
Dual	2.	ἵστασθον	τίθεσθον	δίδοσθον	δείκνυσθον
	3.	ἱστάσθων	τιθέσθων	διδόσθων	δεικνύσθων
Plur.	2.	ἵστασθε	τίθεσθε	δίδοσθε	δείκνυσθε
	3.	ἱστάσθων or	τιθέσθων or	διδόσθων or	δεικνύσθων or
		ἱστάσθωσαν	τιθέσθωσαν	διδόσθωσαν	δεικνύσθωσαν

Present Infinitive.

ἵστασθαι τίθεσθαι δίδοσθαι δείκνυσθαι

Present Participle (301).

ἱστάμενος τιθέμενος διδόμενος δεικνύμενος

Second Aorist Middle Indicative (505).

Sing.	1.	ἐπριάμην	ἐθέμην	ἐδόμην
	2.	ἐπρίω	ἔθου	ἔδου
	3.	ἐπρίατο	ἔθετο	ἔδοτο
Dual	2.	ἐπρίασθον	ἔθεσθον	ἔδοσθον
	3.	ἐπριάσθην	ἐθέσθην	ἐδόσθην

Plur.	1.	ἐπριάμεθα	ἐθέμεθα	ἐδόμεθα
	2.	ἐπρίασθε	ἔθεσθε	ἔδοσθε
	3.	ἐπρίαντο	ἔθεντο	ἔδοντο

Second Aorist Middle Subjunctive.

Sing.	1.	πρίωμαι	θῶμαι	δῶμαι
	2.	πρίῃ	θῇ	δῷ
	3.	πρίηται	θῆται	δῶται
Dual	2.	πρίησθον	θῆσθον	δῶσθον
	3.	πρίησθον	θῆσθον	δῶσθον
Plur.	1.	πριώμεθα	θώμεθα	δώμεθα
	2.	πρίησθε	θῆσθε	δῶσθε
	3.	πρίωνται	θῶνται	δῶνται

Second Aorist Middle Optative.

Sing.	1.	πριαίμην	θείμην	δοίμην
	2.	πρίαιο	θεῖο	δοῖο
	3.	πρίαιτο	θεῖτο	δοῖτο
Dual	2.	πρίαισθον	θεῖσθον	δοῖσθον
	3.	πριαίσθην	θείσθην	δοίσθην
Plur.	1.	πριαίμεθα	θείμεθα	δοίμεθα
	2.	πρίαισθε	θεῖσθε	δοῖσθε
	3.	πρίαιντο	θεῖντο	δοῖντο

Second Aorist Middle Imperative.

Sing.	2.	πρίω	θοῦ	δοῦ
	3.	πριάσθω	θέσθω	δόσθω
Dual	2.	πρίασθον	θέσθον	δόσθον
	3.	πριάσθων	θέσθων	δόσθων
Plur.	2.	πρίασθε	θέσθε	δόσθε
	3.	πριάσθων or πριάσθωσαν	θέσθων or θέσθωσαν	δόσθων or δόσθωσαν

Second Aorist Middle Infinitive.

πρίασθαι θέσθαι δόσθαι

Second Aorist Middle Participle (301).

πριάμενος θέμενος δόμενος

507. Ἵστημι and a few other verbs have a second perfect and pluperfect of the μι-form. These are never used in the *singular* of the indicative, where the first perfect and pluperfect are the regular forms.

508. These tenses of ἵστημι are thus inflected: —

SECOND PERFECT.

Sing.	1.	———	ἑστῶ	ἑσταίην	
	2.	———	ἑστῇς	ἑσταίης	ἕσταθι
	3.	———	ἑστῇ	ἑσταίη	ἑστάτω
Dual	2.	ἕστατον	ἑστῆτον	ἑσταίητον or -αῖτον	ἕστατον
	3.	ἕστατον	ἑστῆτον	ἑσταιήτην or -αίτην	ἑστάτων
Plur.	1.	ἕσταμεν	ἑστῶμεν	ἑσταίημεν or -αῖμεν	
	2.	ἕστατε	ἑστῆτε	ἑσταίητε or -αῖτε	ἕστατε
	3.	ἑστᾶσι	ἑστῶσι	ἑσταίησαν or -αῖεν	ἑστάντων or ἑστάτωσαν

Infinitive. ἑστάναι Participle. ἑστώς (342)

SECOND PLUPERFECT.

Dual. ἕστατον, ἑστάτην

Plur. ἕσταμεν, ἕστατε, ἕστασαν

For an enumeration of these forms, see 804.

---

509. FULL SYNOPSIS of the Indicative of ἵστημι, τίθημι, δίδωμι, and δείκνῡμι, in all the voices.

ACTIVE.

Pres.	ἵστημι, *set*	τίθημι, *place*	δίδωμι, *give*	δείκνῡμι, *show*
Imperf.	ἵστην	ἐτίθην	ἐδίδουν	ἐδείκνῡν
Fut.	στήσω	θήσω	δώσω	δείξω
1 Aor.	ἔστησα, *set*	ἔθηκα	ἔδωκα	ἔδειξα
2 Aor.	ἔστην, *stood*	ἔθετον etc. in dual and plur.	ἔδοτον etc. in dual and plur.	

1 Perf.	**ἕστηκα**	**τέθηκα**	**δέδωκα**	
2 Perf.	**ἕστατον** etc. in dual and plur., *stand* (508)			**δέδειχα**
1 Plupf.	**εἱστήκη** or **ἑστήκη**	**ἐτεθήκη**	**ἐδεδώκη**	
2 Plupf.	**ἕστατον** etc. in dual and plur., *stood* (508)			**ἐδεδείχη**
Fut. Perf.	**ἑστήξω**, *shall stand* (705)			

MIDDLE.

Pres.	**ἵσταμαι**, *stand*	**τίθεμαι** (trans.)	**δίδομαι** (simple only in pass.)	**δείκνυμαι** (trans.)
Impf.	**ἱστάμην**	**ἐτιθέμην**	**ἐδιδόμην**	**ἐδεικνύμην**
Fut.	**στήσομαι**	**θήσομαι**	**-δώσομαι**	**-δείξομαι**
1 Aor.	**ἐστησάμην** (trans.)	**ἐθηκάμην** (not Attic)		**ἐδειξάμην**
2 Aor.		**ἐθέμην**	**-ἐδόμην**	
Perf.	**ἕσταμαι** (pass.)	**τέθειμαι**	**δέδομαι**	**δέδειγμαι**
Plupf.	(?)	(?)	**ἐδεδόμην**	**ἐδεδείγμην**

PASSIVE.

Present, Imperfect, Perfect, Pluperfect: as in Middle.

Aor.	**ἐστάθην**	**ἐτέθην**	**ἐδόθην**	**ἐδείχθην**
Fut.	**σταθήσομαι**	**τεθήσομαι**	**δοθήσομαι**	**δειχθήσομαι**
Fut. Perf.	**ἑστήξομαι**, *shall stand*	——	——	(**δεδείξομαι**, late)

AUGMENT.

510. In the secondary tenses of the indicative, the verb receives an *augment* (i.e. *increase*) at the beginning, which marks these as *past* tenses.

511. Augment is of two kinds: —

1. *Syllabic* augment, which prefixes **ε** to verbs beginning with a consonant; as **λῡ́ω**, imperfect **ἔ-λῡον**; **λείπω**, second aorist **ἔ-λιπον**.

2. *Temporal* augment, which lengthens the first syllable of verbs beginning with a vowel or diphthong; as **ἄγω**, *lead*, imperf. **ἦγον**; **οἰκέω**, **οἰκῶ**, *dwell*, aor. **ᾤκησα**.

512. The augment is confined strictly to the indicative, never appearing in the other moods or the participle, even when any of these denote past time.

IMPERFECT AND AORIST INDICATIVE.

513. The imperfect and aorist indicative of verbs beginning with a consonant have the syllabic augment ε. *E.g.*

Λύω, ἔλῡον, ἔλῡσα, ἐλῡόμην, ἐλῡσάμην, ἐλύθην; γράφω, *write*, ἔγραφον, ἔγραψα, ἐγράφην; ῥίπτω, *throw*, ἔρρῑπτον, ἐρρίφην.

For ρ doubled after the syllabic augment, see 69.

514. In Homer any liquid (especially λ) may be doubled after the augment ε; as ἔλλαχον for ἔλαχον, ἔμμαθε for ἔμαθε. So sometimes σ; as ἐσσείοντο from σείω.

515. The imperfect and aorist indicative of verbs beginning with a short vowel have the temporal augment, which lengthens the initial vowel; ᾰ and ε becoming η, and ῐ, ο, ῠ becoming ῑ, ω, ῡ. *E.g.*

Ἄγω, *lead*, ἦγον, ἤχθην; ἐλαύνω, *drive*, ἤλαυνον; ἱκετεύω, *implore*, ἱκέτευον, ἱκέτευσα; ὀνειδίζω, *reproach*, ὠνείδιζον; ὑβρίζω, *insult*, ὑβρίσθην; ἀκολουθέω, *accompany*, ἠκολούθησα; ὀρθόω, *erect*, ὤρθωσα.

516. A long initial vowel is not changed, except that ᾱ generally becomes η; as ἀθλέω, *struggle*, ἤθλησα. But both ᾱ and η are found in ἀνᾱλίσκω and ἀνᾱλόω, and ἀΐω (poetic), *hear*, has ἄϊον.

517. Βούλομαι, *wish*, δύναμαι, *be able*, and μέλλω, *intend*, often have η for ε in the augment, especially in later Attic; as ἐβουλόμην or ἠβουλόμην, ἐβουλήθην or ἠβουλήθην; ἐδυνάμην or ἠδυνάμην, ἐδυνήθην or ἠδυνήθην; ἔμελλον or ἤμελλον.

518. A diphthong takes the temporal augment on its first vowel, αι or ᾳ becoming ῃ. *E.g.*

Αἰτέω, *ask*, ᾔτησα; εἰκάζω, *guess*, ᾔκασα; οἰκέω, *dwell*, ᾤκησα; αὐξάνω, *increase*, ηὔξησα, ηὐξήθην; ᾄδω, *sing*, ᾖδον.

519. Ου is never augmented. Ει and ευ are often without augment, especially in later Attic; but MSS. and editors differ in regard to many forms, as εἴκασα or ᾔκασα (from εἰκάζω, *liken*), εὗδον or ηὗδον (from εὕδω, *sleep*), εὑρέθην or ηὑρέθην (from εὑρίσκω, *find*), εὐξάμην or ηὐξάμην (from εὔχομαι, *pray*). Editions vary also in the augment of αὐαίνω, *dry*, and of some verbs beginning with οι, as οἰᾱκοστροφέω, *steer*.

REDUPLICATION.

520. The perfect, pluperfect, and future perfect, in all the moods and in the participle, have a *reduplication*, which is the mark of *completed* action.

Perfect and Future Perfect.

521. Verbs beginning with a single consonant (except ρ) are reduplicated in the perfect and future perfect by prefixing that consonant followed by ε. *E.g.*

Λύω, λέ-λυκα, λέ-λυμαι, λε-λυκέναι, λε-λυκώς, λε-λυμένος, λε-λύσομαι; λείπω, λέλοιπα, λέλειμμαι, λελείψομαι. So θύω, *sacrifice*, τέ-θυκα; φαίνω (φαν), *show*, πέ-φασμαι, πε-φάνθαι; χαίνω, *gape*, κέ-χηνα.

For the pluperfect, see 527.

522. N. (*a*) Five verbs have ει in the perfect instead of the reduplication: —

λαγχάνω (λαχ-), *obtain by lot*, εἴληχα, εἴληγμαι;

λαμβάνω (λαβ-), *take*, εἴληφα, εἴλημμαι (poet. λέλημμαι);

λέγω, *collect*, in composition, -εἴλοχα, -είλεγμαι with -λέλεγμαι; διαλέγομαι, *discuss*, has δι-είλεγμαι;

μείρομαι (μερ-), *obtain part*, εἵμαρται, *it is fated*;

from stem (ῥε-) εἴρηκα, *have said*, εἴρημαι, fut. pf. εἰρήσομαι (see εἶπον).

(*b*) An irregular reduplication appears in Homeric δείδοικα and δείδια, from δείδω, *fear*, and δείδεγμαι (for δέδεγμαι), *greet*, from a stem δεκ- (see δείκνυμι).

523. In verbs beginning with *two* consonants (except a mute and a liquid), with a double consonant (ζ, ξ, ψ), or with ρ, the reduplication is represented by a simple ε, having the same form as the syllabic augment. *E.g.*

Στέλλω, *send*, ἔσταλκα; ζητέω, *seek*, ἐζήτηκα; ψεύδω, *cheat*, ἔψευσμαι, ἐψευσμένος; ῥίπτω, *throw*, ἔρριμμαι, ἐρρῖφθαι (69).

524. 1. Most verbs beginning with a mute and a liquid have the full reduplication; as γράφω, *write*, γέγραφα, γέγραμμαι, γεγράφθαι, γεγραμμένος.

2. But those beginning with γν, and occasionally a few in βλ or γλ, have ε; as γνωρίζω, *recognize*, perf. ἐγνώρικα; γιγνώσκω (γνο-), *know*, ἔγνωκα. See βλαστάνω and γλύφω.

525. N. Μιμνήσκω (μνα-), *remind*, has μέμνημαι (*memini*), *remember*, and κτάομαι, *acquire*, has both κέκτημαι and ἔκτημαι, *possess*. See also Homeric perfect passive of ῥίπτω and ῥυπόω.

526. Verbs beginning with a short vowel lengthen the vowel, and those beginning with a diphthong lengthen its first vowel, in all forms of the perfect and future perfect, the reduplication thus having the form of the temporal augment. *E.g.*

Ἄγω, *lead*, ἦχα, ἦγμαι, ἠγμένος; ἀκολουθέω, *follow*, ἠκολούθηκα, ἠκολουθηκέναι; ὀρθόω, *erect*, ὤρθωμαι; ὁρίζω, *bound*, ὥρικα, ὥρισμαι; ἀτῑμόω, *dishonor*, ἠτίμωκα, ἠτίμωμαι, fut. pf. ἠτῑμώσομαι. Αἱρέω, *take*, ᾕρηκα, ᾕρημαι, ᾑρήσομαι; εἰκάζω, *liken*, ᾔκασμαι; εὑρίσκω, *find*, ηὕρηκα, ηὕρημαι (or εὕρηκα, εὕρημαι, 519).

Long α may become η (see 516); as in ἀνᾱλίσκω, pf. ἀνήλωκα or ἀνᾱλωκα.

PLUPERFECT.

527. When the reduplicated perfect begins with a consonant, the pluperfect prefixes the syllabic augment ε to the reduplication. In other cases the pluperfect keeps the reduplication of the perfect without change. *E.g.*

Λύω, λέλυκα, ἐ-λελύκη, λέλυμαι, ἐ-λελύμην; στέλλω, ἔσταλκα, ἐστάλκη, ἔσταλμαι, ἐστάλμην; λαμβάνω, εἴληφα, εἰλήφη; ἀγγέλλω, ἤγγελκα, ἠγγέλκη, ἤγγελμαι, ἠγγέλμην; αἱρέω, ᾕρηκα, ᾑρήκη; εὑρίσκω, ηὕρηκα, ηὑρήκη, ηὑρήμην, (or εὑρ-).

528. N. From ἵστημι (στα-), *set*, we have both εἱστήκη (older form) and ἑστήκη (through perf. ἕστηκα); and from perf. ἔοικα, *resemble*, ἐῴκη.

ATTIC REDUPLICATION.

529. Some verbs beginning with α, ε, or ο, followed by a single consonant, reduplicate the perfect and pluperfect by prefixing their first two letters, and lengthening the following vowel as in the temporal augment. This is called *Attic reduplication*. *E.g.*

Ἀρόω, *plough*, ἀρ-ήρομαι; ἐμέω, *vomit*, ἐμήμεκα; ἐλέγχω, *prove*, ἐλήλεγμαι; ἐλαύνω (ἐλα-), *drive*, ἐλήλακα, ἐλήλαμαι; ἀκούω, *hear*, ἀκήκοα. For the pluperfect, see 533.

530. N. The *Attic* reduplication (so called by the Greek grammarians) is not peculiarly Attic, and is found in Homer.

531. N. Other verbs which have the Attic reduplication are ἀγείρω, ἀλείφω, ἀλέω, ἐγείρω, ἐρείδω, ἔρχομαι, ἐσθίω, ὄλλῡμι, ὄμνῡμι, ὀρύσσω, φέρω. See also, for Ionic or poetic forms, αἱρέω, ἀλάομαι, ἀλυκτέω, ἀραρίσκω, ἐρείπω, ἔχω, ἠμύω, (ὀδυ-) ὀδώδυσμαι, ὄζω, ὁράω (ὄπωπα), ὀρέγω, ὄρνῡμι (ὀρ-).

532. N. Ἐγείρω (ἐγερ-), *rouse*, has 2 perf. ἐγρ-ήγορα (for ἐγ-ηγορ-α, 643), but perf. mid. ἐγ-ήγερμαι.

533. By strict Attic usage, the pluperfect takes a temporal augment in addition to the Attic reduplication. Thus, ἀκούω, *hear*, ἀκήκοα, plup. ἠκηκόη; so ἀπ-ωλώλει (of ἀπ-όλλῡμι, ἀπ-όλωλα), ὠμωμόκει (of ὄμνῡμι, ὀμώμοκα), and δι-ωρώρυκτο (of δι-ορύσσω, δι-ορώρυγμαι) occur in Attic prose. See also Homeric pluperfects of ἐλαύνω and ἐρείδω.

But the MSS. and the editions of Attic authors often omit the additional augment, as in ἐλ-ηλέγμην (487, 2).

Reduplicated Aorists.

534. N. The second aorist active and middle in all the moods and the participle sometimes has a reduplication in Homer; as πέφραδον from φράζω, *tell;* πέπιθον from πείθω (πιθ-), *persuade;* τεταρπόμην (646) from τέρπω, *delight;* κεκλόμην and κεκλόμενος (650) from κέλομαι, *command;* ἤραρον from ἀραρίσκω (ἀρ-), *join* (531); ὤρορον from ὄρνῡμι (ὀρ-), *rouse;* πεπαλών (partic.) from πάλλω (παλ-), *shake;* κεκάμω (subj.) from κάμνω (καμ-), so λελάχω from λαγχάνω; πεφιδέσθαι, inf. from φείδομαι (φιδ-), *spare*, so λε-λαθέσθαι, λε-λαβέσθαι. In the indicative a syllabic augment may be prefixed to the reduplication; as ἐκεκλόμην, ἔπεφνον (from φεν-), ἐπέφραδον.

535. N. The second aorist of ἄγω, *lead*, has a kind of Attic reduplication (529), which adds the temporal augment in the indicative. Thus ἤγ-αγ-ον (ἀγ-αγ-), subj. ἀγάγω, opt. ἀγάγοιμι, inf. ἀγαγεῖν, part. ἀγαγών; mid. ἠγαγόμην, ἀγάγωμαι, etc., — all in Attic prose. See also the aorists ἤνεγκα and ἤνεγκον (from stem ἐνεκ-, ἐν-ενεκ-, ἐνεγκ-) of φέρω, the Homeric ἄλαλκον (for ἀλ-αλεκ-ον) of ἀλέξω, *ward off*, and ἐνένῑπον or ἠνίπ-απ-ον of ἐνίπτω (ἐνιπ-), *chide*. See also ἐρύκω, ἠρύκ-ακ-ον.

Reduplicated Presents.

536. A few verbs reduplicate the present by prefixing the initial consonant with ι; as γι-γνώσκω (γνο-), *know*, τί-θημι (θε-), *put*, γί-γνομαι (for γι-γεν-ομαι), *become*.

For these see 651 and 652, with 794, 2.

Ε as Augment or Reduplication before a Vowel.

537. 1. Some verbs beginning with a vowel take the syllabic augment, as if they began with a consonant. These verbs also have a simple ε for the reduplication. When another ε follows, εε is contracted into ει. *E.g.*

Ὠθέω (ὠθ-), *push*, ἔωσα, ἔωσμαι, ἐώσθην; ἁλίσκομαι, *be captured*, ἑάλωκα, 2 aor. ἑάλων (or ἥλων); ἄγνυμι (ἀγ-), *break*, ἔαξα, 2 pf. ἔᾱγα; ἔρδω, *do*, Ionic, 2 pf. ἔοργα; ὠνέομαι, *buy*, ἐωνούμην, etc.; ἐθίζω, *accustom*, εἴθισα, εἴθικα (from ἐεθ-); ἐάω, *permit*, εἴᾱσα, εἴᾱκα; ἔχω, *have*, εἶχον (from ἐ-εχον).

2. These verbs are, further, ἑλίσσω, ἕλκω, ἕπω, ἐργάζομαι, ἕρπω or ἑρπύζω, ἑστιάω, ἵημι (ἑ-), with the aorists εἶδον and εἷλον (αἱρέω); the perfects εἴωθα (with irregular ει), Ionic ἔωθα (ἠθ-), and ἔοικα (ἰκ-, εἰκ-), and plpf. εἱστήκη (for ἐ-ἑστ-) of ἵστημι. See also Ionic and poetic forms under ἁνδάνω, ἅπτω, εἴδομαι, εἴλω, εἶπον, εἴρω, ἔλπω, ἕννῡμι, ἵζω, and ἕζομαι.

538. N. Ὁράω, *see*, and ἀν-οίγω, *open*, generally take the temporal augment after ε; as ἑώρων, ἑώρᾱκα (or ἑόρᾱκα), ἑώρᾱμαι (with the aspirate retained); ἀν-έῳγον, ἀν-έῳξα (rarely ἤνοιγον, ἤνοιξα, 544). Homer has ἑήνδανον from ἁνδάνω, *please*; ἐῳνοχόει imp. of οἰνοχοέω, *pour wine*; and 2 plpf. ἐώλπει and ἐώργει from ἔλπω and ἔρδω. Ἑορτάζω, *keep holiday* (Hdt. ὁρτάζω), has Attic imp. ἑώρταζον.

539. N. This form is explained on the supposition that these verbs originally began with the consonant ϝ or σ, which was afterwards dropped. Thus εἶδον, *saw*, is for ἐϝιδον (cf. Latin *vid-i*); ἔοργα is for ϝεϝοργα, from stem ϝεργ-, cf. Eng. *work* (German *Werk*). So ἕρπω, *creep*, is for σ-ερπω (cf. Latin *serpo*), with imperf. ἐ-σερπον, ἐ-ἑρπον, εἷρπον (see 86); and ἔχω, *have*, is for σεχω, whence imp. ἐ-σεχον, ἐ-εχον, εἶχον.

AUGMENT AND REDUPLICATION OF COMPOUND VERBS.

540. In compound verbs (882, 1) the augment or reduplication follows the preposition. Prepositions (except περί and πρό) here drop a final vowel before ε. *E.g.*

Προσ-γράφω, προσ-έγραφον, προσ-γέγραφα; εἰσ-άγω, εἰσ-ῆγον (133, 1); ἐκ-βάλλω, ἐξ-έβαλλον (63); συλ-λέγω, συν-έλεγον; συμ-πλέκω, συν-έπλεκον (78, 1); συγ-χέω, συν-έχεον, συγ-κέχυκα; συ-σκευάζω, συν-εσκεύαζον (81); ἀπο-βάλλω, ἀπ-έβαλλον; ἀνα-βαίνω, ἀν-έβη; — but περι-έβαλλον and προ-έλεγον.

541. N. Πρό may be contracted with the augment; as προὔλεγον and προὔβαινον, for προέλεγον and προέβαινον.

542. N. Ἐκ in composition becomes ἐξ before ε; and ἐν and σύν resume their proper forms if they have been changed. See examples in 540.

543. N. Some denominative verbs (861), derived from nouns or adjectives compounded with prepositions, are augmented or reduplicated after the preposition, like compound verbs; as ὑποπτεύω (from ὕποπτος), *suspect*, ὑπώπτευον, as if the verb were from ὑπό and ὀπτεύω; ἀπολογέομαι, *defend one's self*, ἀπ-ελογησάμην; see also ἐκκλησιάζω. Παρανομέω, *transgress law*, παρηνόμουν, etc., is very irregular. Κατηγορέω (from κατήγορος), *accuse*, has κατηγόρουν (not ἐκατηγόρουν). See διαιτάω and διᾱκονέω in the Catalogue of Verbs.

Such verbs are called *indirect* compounds (882, 2).

544. N. A few verbs take the augment before the preposition, and others have both augments; as καθέζομαι, *sit*, ἐκαθέζετο; καθίζω, ἐκάθιζον; καθεύδω, *sleep*, ἐκάθευδον and καθηῦδον (epic καθεῦδον); ἀνέχω, ἠνειχόμην, ἠνεσχόμην (or ἠνσχόμην); ἀφίημι, ἀφίην or ἠφίην. See also ἀμφιέννῡμι, ἀμφιγνοέω, ἀμπίσχομαι, ἐνοχλέω, and ἀμφισβητέω, *dispute*, impf. ἠμφισβήτουν and ἠμφεσβήτουν (as if the last part were -σβητεω).

545. 1. Indirect compounds of δυσ-, *ill*, and occasionally those of εὖ, *well*, are augmented or reduplicated after the adverb, if the following part begins with a short vowel. *E.g.*

Δυσαρεστέω, *be displeased*, δυσηρέστουν; εὐεργετέω, *do good*, εὐηργέτουν or εὐεργέτουν.

2. In other cases, compounds of δυσ- have the augment or reduplication at the beginning, as δυστυχέω (from δυσ-τυχής, *unfortunate*), ἐδυστύχουν, δεδυστύχηκα; and those of εὖ generally omit the augment.

546. Other indirect compounds are augmented or reduplicated at the beginning; as οἰκοδομέω, *build* (from οἰκοδόμος, *house-builder*), ᾠκοδόμουν, ᾠκοδόμησα, ᾠκοδόμηται. See, however, ὁδοποιέω.

OMISSION OF AUGMENT AND REDUPLICATION.

547. Homer and the lyric poets often omit both the syllabic and the temporal augment; as ὁμίλεον, ἔχον, δῶκε (for ὡμίλουν, εἶχον, ἔδωκε).

548. Herodotus often omits the temporal augment of the imperfect and aorist, and the syllabic augment of the pluperfect. He never adds the temporal augment to the Attic reduplication in the pluperfect (533). He always omits the augment in the iterative forms in σκον and σκομην; as λάβεσκον, ἔχεσκον (778).

549. The Attic tragedians sometimes omit the augment in (lyric) choral passages, seldom in the dialogue.

550. The reduplication is very rarely omitted. But Homer has δέχαται, from δέχομαι, for δεδέχαται, *receive*, and a few other cases. Herodotus occasionally fails to lengthen the initial vowel in the perfect; as in καταρρώδηκας (for κατ-ηρρ-).

ENDINGS.

551. The verb is inflected by adding certain *endings* to the different tense stems. Those which mark the persons in the finite moods are called *personal* endings. There is one class of endings for the active voice, and another for the middle and passive; but the passive aorists have the active endings.

There is also one set of endings in each class for primary tenses, and one for secondary tenses.

552. The personal endings of the indicative, subjunctive, and optative, which are most distinctly preserved in verbs in μι and other primitive forms, are as follows: —

		Active.		Middle and Passive.	
		Primary Tenses.	*Secondary Tenses.*	*Primary Tenses.*	*Secondary Tenses.*
Sing.	1.	μι	ν	μαι	μην
	2.	ς (σι), (θα)	ς	σαι	σο
	3.	σι (τι)	—	ται	το
Dual	2.	τον	τον	σθον (θον)	σθον (θον)
	3.	τον	την	σθον (θον)	σθην (θην)
Plur.	1.	μεν (μες)	μεν (μες)	μεθα	μεθα
	2.	τε	τε	σθε (θε)	σθε (θε)
	3.	νσι (ντι), ᾱσι	ν, σαν	νται	ντο

553. The personal endings of the imperative are as follows: —

	Active.			Middle and Passive.		
	Sing.	*Dual.*	*Plur.*	*Sing.*	*Dual.*	*Plur.*
2.	θι	τον	τε	σο	σθον (θον)	σθε (θε)
3.	τω	των	ντων or τωσαν	σθω (θω)	σθων (θων)	σθων (θων) or σθωσαν (θωσαν)

554. The endings of the infinitive are as follows: —

Active: ειν (contracted with preceding ε to ειν), ναι, sometimes εναι (probably for Fεναι).

Middle and Passive: σθαι (primitive θαι).

555. For the formation of the participles and the verbals in τος and τεος, see 770–776.

Remarks on the Endings.

556. 1. Only verbs in μι have the primary endings μι and σι in the indicative active. For μι in the optative, see 731. The original σι of the second person singular is found only in the epic ἐσ-σί, *thou art* (807, 1). Θα (originally perfect ending) appears in οἶσθα (for οἶδ-θα) from οἶδα (820) and in ἦσ-θα from εἰμί (806); whence (σ)θα in many Homeric forms (780, 4; 787, 4), and rarely in Attic (as ἔφησθα). In the third person singular τι is Doric, as in τίθη-τι for τίθη-σι; and it is preserved in Attic in ἐσ-τί, *is*.

2. A first person dual in μεθον is found three times in poetry: περιδώμεθον, subj. of περιδίδωμι, *Il.* 23, 485; λελείμμεθον, from λείπω, S. *El.* 950; ὁρμώμεθον, from ὁρμάω, S. *Ph.* 1079. Generally the first person plural is used also for the dual.

3. In Homer τον and σθον are sometimes used for την and σθην in the third person dual of past tenses. This occurs rarely in the Attic poets, who sometimes have την for τον in the second person. The latter is found occasionally even in prose.

4. In the first person plural μες is Doric. The poets often have μεσθα for μεθα (777, 1).

5. In the third person plural νσι always drops ν (78, 3) and the preceding vowel is lengthened; as in λῡουσι for λῡο-νσι. The more primitive ντι is Doric; as φέρο-ντι (Latin *ferunt*) for φέρουσι.[1]

[1] A comparison of the various forms of the present indicative of the primitive verb *be* (whose original stem is *as*-, in Greek and Latin *es*-), as it appears in Sanskrit, the older Greek, Latin, Old Slavic, and Lithuanian (the most primitive modern language, *still spoken* on the Baltic), will illustrate the Greek verbal endings.

	Sanskrit.	*Older Greek.*	*Latin.*	*Old Slavic.*	*Lithuanian.*
		SINGULAR.			
1.	as-mi	ἐμ-μί (for ἐσ-μι)	[e]s-um	yes-m'	es-mi
2.	asi	ἐσ-σί	es	yesi	esi
3.	as-ti	ἐσ-τί	es-t	yes-t'	es-ti
		PLURAL.			
1.	s-mas	ἐσ-μέν (Dor. εἰμές)	[e]s-u-mus	yes-mi	es-me
2.	s-tha	ἐσ-τέ	es-tis	yes-te	es-te
3.	s-a-nti	ἐ-ντί (Doric)	[e]s-u-nt	s-u-t'	es-ti

6. Θι seldom appears in the imperative, except in the second aorist active of μι-forms (755), and in the aorist passive, which has the active forms (551).

In the third person plural of the imperative the endings **ντων** and *σθων* (*θων*) are used in the older and better Attic.

7. The primitive middle forms **θον, θην, θε, θαι,** etc. appear in the perfect and pluperfect after consonants; as *τέτρῖφ-θε* (*τρίβ-ω*). See 489.

TENSE STEMS AND FORMS OF INFLECTION.

SIMPLE AND COMPLEX TENSE STEMS.

557. Tense stems are of two classes, *simple* and *complex*. A simple tense stem is the verb stem (often in a modified form), to which the endings are applied *directly*. A complex tense stem is composed of the verb stem (with its modifications) prolonged by a tense suffix (561, 5), to which the endings are applied. See 458.

558. (*Simple Tense Stems.*) Simple tense stems are found

(*a*) in the present and imperfect, the second aorist active and middle, and the second perfect and pluperfect, of the conjugation in *μι* (500), except in the subjunctive;

(*b*) in the perfect and pluperfect middle of all verbs. *E.g.*

(*a*) From *φημί* (stem *φα-*), *say*, come *φα-μέν, φα-τέ, φά-ναι, ἔ-φα-τε*, etc. From *τίθημι* (stem *θε-*), *put*, come 2 aor. *ἔ-θε-τε, ἔ-θε-το, θέ-σθω, θέ-σθαι, θέ-μενος*, etc.; and from the reduplicated *τι-θε-* (536) come *τίθε-μεν, τίθε-τε, τίθε-σαι, τίθε-ται, ἐ-τίθε-ντο, ἐ-τίθε-σθε, τίθε-σο, τίθε-σθαι*, etc.

(*b*) From *λε-λυ-* (reduplicated stem of *λύ-ω*) with the middle endings (552) come *λέλυ-μαι, λέλυ-σαι, λέλυ-σθε, λελύ-σθαι, λελυ-μένος; ἐ-λελύ-μην, ἐ-λέλυ-σο, ἐ-λέλυ-σθε, ἐ-λέλυ-ντο.*

559. (*Complex Tense Stems.*) Complex tense stems are found in all other forms of the verb. *E.g.*

Λύω (stem *λῡ-*), has (pres.) *λύο-μεν, λύε-τε, λύο-μεθα, λύε-σθε, λύο-νται*, etc.; (fut.) *λύσο-μεν, λύσε-τε, λύσε-σθαι*, etc.; (aor.) *ἐ-λύσα-μεν, ἐ-λύσα-τε, ἐ-λύσα-σθε, λύσα-σθαι*, etc.; (1 aor. pass.) *ἐ-λύθη-ν, ἐ-λύθη-μεν, ἐ-λύθη-τε*, etc.

560. This distinction will be seen by a comparison of the present indicative middle of *τίθημι* (*τιθε-*) with that of **φιλέω** (*φιλε-*) in its uncontracted (Homeric) form:—

τίθε-μαι	**φιλέ-ο-μαι**	**τιθέ-μεθα**	**φιλε-ό-μεθα**
τίθε-σαι	**φιλέ-ε-(σ)αι**	**τίθε-σθε**	**φιλέ-ε-σθε**
τίθε-ται	**φιλέ-ε-ται**	**τίθε-νται**	**φιλέ-ο-νται**

561. (*Tense Suffixes.*) 1. In the present, imperfect, and second aorist active and middle of the conjugation in *ω*, in all futures, and in the future perfect, the tense stem ends in a variable vowel, called the ***thematic vowel***, which is *ο* before *μ* and *ν* and in the optative, and is elsewhere *ε*. This is written ο/ε-; as *λῡο/ε-*, present stem of *λύ-ω*; *λιπο/ε-*, second aorist stem of *λείπ-ω*. In the futures and the future perfect the thematic vowel is preceded by *σ*. To these prolonged tense stems the endings are added. *E.g.*

Λύο-μεν, λύε-τε, λύουσι for *λῡο-νσι* (78, 3); *ἔ-λιπο-ν, ἔ-λιπε-ς, ἐ-λίπο-μεν, ἐ-λίπε-τε*; *ἐ-λίπε-σθε, ἐ-λίπο-ντο*; *λύσο-μεν, λύσε-τε, λύσο-νται*. For the terminations *ω, εις, ει* in the singular, see 623.

2. The subjunctive has a long thematic vowel ω/η-, which appears in both conjugations; as *λέγω-μεν, λέγη-τε, λέγω-σι* for *λεγω-νσι* (78, 3); *θῶμεν* for *θέ-ω-μεν, θῆτε* for *θέ-η-τε*.

3. The first aorist stem has a suffix *σα-*, the first perfect *κα-*, and the second perfect *α-*.

4. The first aorist passive has a suffix *θε-* (or *θη-*), and the second aorist passive *ε-* (or *η-*); as *λείπ-ω, ἐλείφ-θη-ν, λειφ-θῆ-ναι*, (*λειφ-θέ-ω*) *λειφθῶ*; *φαίνω* (*φαν-*), *ἐφάν-η-ν, φαν-ῆ-ναι, φαν-έ-ντος*; *ἐλύ-θη-ν, ἐλύ-θη-ς, ἐλύ-θη-μεν, λυ-θέ-ντων, λυ-θέ-ντες*.

The first and second passive futures have *θησο/ε-* and *ησο/ε-*; as *λειφ-θήσο-μαι, λυ-θήσε-σθε, φαν-ήσο-μαι, φαν-ήσε-ται*.

5. The thematic vowels, and *σο/ε-, σα-, κα-* (*α-*), *θε-* (*θη-*) or *ε-* (*η-*), *θησο/ε-* or *ησο/ε-*, (1–4), are called *tense suffixes*.

562. (*Optative Suffix.*) The optative inserts a *mood suffix ι-* or *ιη-* (*ιε-*) between both the simple and the complex tense stem and the personal endings. (See 730.)

For the subjunctive, see 718; 561, 2.

TWO FORMS OF INFLECTION.

563. To the two classes of tense stems correspond generally two forms of inflection,—the *simple form* and the *common form*.

I. The Simple Form of Inflection.

564. To this form (sometimes called the μι-form) belong all tenses which have simple tense stems (558) and also both passive aorists, — always excepting the subjunctives (561, 2.). It has these peculiarities of inflection: —

1. The first and third persons singular of the present indicative active have the endings μι and σι (552); as φη-μί, φη-σί; τίθη-μι, τίθη-σι.

2. The second aorist imperative active generally retains the ending θι (553); as βῆ-θι, *go*. So rarely the present; as φα-θί, *say*. (See 752; 755.)

3. The third person plural has the active endings ᾱσι and σαν (552).

4. The infinitive active has the ending ναι or εναι (554); as τιθέ-ναι, ἱέ-ναι (ἵημι), ἰ-έναι (εἶμι).

5. Participles with stems in οντ have nominatives in ους; as διδούς, διδό-ντ-ος (see 565, 5).

6. In all forms of this class except the second aorist and the optative, the middle endings σαι and σο regularly retain σ; as τίθε-σαι, ἐ-τίθε-σο; λέλυ-σαι, ἐ-λέλυ-σο. But 2 aorist ἔθου (for ἔθε-σο); optative ἱσταῖο (for ἱστα-ι-σο).

7. The passive aorists, which belong here although they do not have simple stems (558), have the inflection of the second aorist active of the μι-form; λύω, ἐλύ-θη-ν; φαίνω (φαν-), ἐφάν-η-ν, φανῶ, φανείην, φάνη-θι, φανῆ-ναι, φανείς (for φαν-ε-ντς), inflected like ἔστην, στῶ, θείην, στῆ-θι, στῆ-ναι, θείς (506).

II. The Common Form of Inflection.

565. To this form belong all parts of the verb in ω, except the perfect and pluperfect middle and the passive aorists, and also all subjunctives. It has the following peculiarities of inflection.

1. It has the thematic vowel and the other tense suffixes mentioned in 561, 1–3. For the inflection of the present and imperfect indicative, see 623 and 624.

2. The imperfect and second aorist have the ending ν in the third person plural; the pluperfect has σαν.

3. The imperative active has no ending in the second person singular. For ον in the first aorist, see 747.

4. The infinitive active has ειν (for ε-εν) in the present, future, and second aorist; ε-ναι in the perfect; and σ-αι (or αι) in the first aorist. See 759–764.

5. Participles with stems in οντ have nominatives in ων (564, 5).

6. The middle endings σαι and σο in the second person singular drop σ and are contracted with the thematic vowel; as λύεσαι, λύεαι, λύῃ or λύει; ἐλύεσο, ἐλύεο, ἐλύου (88, 2). For Ionic uncontracted forms, see 777, 2; 785, 2.

FORMATION AND INFLECTION OF TENSE SYSTEMS.

566. To understand the inflection of the verb, we must know the relation of each tense stem to the verb stem, and also certain internal modifications which the verb stem undergoes in some of the tense systems.

FORMATION OF THE PRESENT STEM FROM THE VERB STEM. — EIGHT CLASSES OF VERBS.

567. When the verb stem does not appear unchanged in the present stem, as it does in λύ-ω and λέγ-ω (459), it generally appears in a strengthened form; as in κόπτ-ω (κοπ-), *cut*, μανθάν-ω (μαθ-), *learn*, ἀρέσκ-ω (ἀρε-), *please*. In a few very irregular verbs no connection is to be seen between the present stem and the stem or stems of other tenses; as in φέρω (φερ-), *bear*, fut. οἴσω, aor. ἤνεγκα.

568. Verbs are divided into eight classes with reference to the relation of the present stem to the verb stem.

569. First Class. (*Verb Stem unchanged in Present.*) Here the present stem is formed by adding the thematic vowel ℅- (565, 1) to the verb stem. *E.g.*

Λέγω (λεγ-), *say*, present stem λεγ℅-, giving λέγο-μεν, λέγε-τε, λέγο-μαι, λέγε-ται, λέγο-νται, ἔ-λεγο-ν, ἔ-λεγε-ς, ἐ-λέγε-τε, ἐ-λέγε-σθε, ἐ-λέγο-ντο, etc. in the present and imperfect. For ω, εις, ει in the present active, see 623.

570. N. Some verbs of this class have the stem variable in quantity in different tenses; as δύω, φύω, θλίβω, πνίγω, τρίβω, τύφω, ψύχω. See these in the Catalogue of Verbs. For λύω, see 471.

571. N. The pure verbs of the first class which irregularly retain a short vowel in certain tenses are given in 639; those which insert σ in certain tenses, in 640. The verbs (of all classes) which add ε to the stem in some or all tenses not of the present system (as βούλομαι) are given in 657 and 658. Reduplicated presents of all classes are given in 651 and 652. These and others which are peculiar in their inflection are found in the Catalogue of Verbs. For special peculiarities, see γίγνομαι, ἔθω, ἕπω, ἔχω, πίπτω, τίκτω.

572. Second Class. (*Stems with Strong Forms.*) This class includes verbs with mute stems which have strong forms with ει (οι), ευ, or η (31) in all tenses except in the second aorist and second passive systems, in which they have the weak forms in ι, υ, and ᾰ. The present stem adds %- to the strong form of the stem. *E.g.*

Λείπ-ω, *leave*, 2 aor. ἔ-λιπ-ον, 2 perf. λέ-λοιπ-α; φεύγ-ω, *flee*, 2 aor. ἔ-φυγ-ον; τήκ-ω, *melt*, 2 aor. pass. ἐ-τάκ-ην; with present stems λειπ%-, φευγ%-, τηκ%-.

573. To this class belong ἀλείφ-ω, ἐρείπ-ω, λείπ-ω, πείθ-ω, στείβ-ω, στείχ-ω, φείδ-ομαι; κεύθ-ω, πεύθ-ομαι, τεύχ-ω, φεύγ-ω; κήδ-ω, λήθ-ω, σήπ-ω, τήκ-ω; with Ionic or poetic ἐρείκ-ω, ἐρεύγ-ομαι, τμήγ-ω; — all with weak stems in ι, υ, or ᾰ. See also θαπ- or ταφ-, stem of τέθηπα and ἔταφον, and εἴκω (ἔοικα). Τρώγ-ω, *gnaw*, 2 aor. ἔ-τραγ-ον, irregularly has ω in the present. For ῥήγ-νῡμι and εἴωθα (ἠθ-), see 689.

For exceptions in a few of these verbs, see 642, 2. See 611.

574. Six verbs in εω with weak stems in υ belong by formation to this class. These originally had the strong form in ευ, which became εϝ (90, 2) before a vowel, and finally dropped ϝ, leaving ε; as πλέ-ω, *sail* (weak stem πλυ-), strong stem πλευ-, πλεϝ-, πλε-, present stem πλε%-.

These verbs are θέ-ω (weak stem θυ-), *run*, νέ-ω (νυ-), *swim*, πλέ-ω (πλυ-), *sail*, πνέ-ω (πνυ-), *breathe*, ῥέ-ω (ῥυ-), *flow*, χέ-ω (χυ-), *pour*. The poetic σεύω (συ-), *urge*, has this formation, with ευ retained. (See 601.)

575. As verbs of the second class have the strong stem in almost all forms, this stem is here called the verb stem.

576. Third Class. (*Verbs in* πτω, *or* T *Class.*) Some labial (π, β, φ) verb stems add τ%-, and thus form the present in πτω; as κόπτ-ω (κοπ-), *cut* (present stem κοπτ%-), βλάπτ-ω (βλαβ-), *hurt*, ῥίπτ-ω (ῥῑφ-, ῥῐφ-), *throw* (71).

577. N. Here the exact form of the verb stem cannot be determined from the present. Thus, in the examples above given, the stem is to be found in the second aorists ἐκόπην, ἐβλάβην, and ἐρρίφην; and in καλύπτω (καλυβ-), *cover*, it is seen in καλύβ-η, *hut*.

578. The verbs of this class are ἅπτ-ω (ἁφ-), βάπτ-ω (βαφ-), βλάπτ-ω (βλαβ-), θάπτ-ω (ταφ-), θρύπτ-ω (τρυφ-), καλύπτ-ω (καλυβ-), κάμπτ-ω (καμπ-), κλέπτ-ω (κλεπ-), κόπτ-ω (κοπ-), κρύπτ-ω (κρυβ- or κρυφ-), κύπτ-ω (κῡφ-), ῥάπτ-ω (ῥαφ-), ῥίπτ-ω (ῥῑφ-, ῥῐφ-), σκάπτ-ω (σκαφ-), σκέπτομαι (σκεπ-), σκήπτω (σκηπ-), σκώπτω (σκωπ-), τύπτω (τυπ-), with Homeric and poetic γνάμπτω (γναμπ-), ἐνίπτω (ἐνιπ-), and μάρπτω (μαρπ-).

579. Fourth Class. (*Iota Class.*) In this class the present stem is formed by adding ι%- to the verb stem and making the euphonic changes which this occasions. (See 84.) There are four divisions.

580. I. (*Verbs in* σσω *or* ττω.) Most presents in σσω (ττω) come from palatal stems, κ or χ and generally γ with ι becoming σσ (ττ). These have futures in ξω; as πράσσω (πρᾱγ-), *do*, present stem πρᾱσσ%- (for πρᾱγι%-), fut. πράξω; μαλάσσω (μαλακ-, seen in μαλακός), *soften*, fut. μαλάξω; ταράσσω (ταραχ-, seen in ταραχή), *confuse*, fut. ταράξω; κηρύσσω (κηρῡκ-), *proclaim*, fut. κηρύξω. (See 84, 1.)

581. So also ᾄσσω (ᾱ̓ϊκ-), ἀλλάσσω (ἀλλαγ-), ἀράσσω (ἀραγ-), βήσσω (βηχ-), δράσσω (δραγ-), ἑλίσσω (ἑλικ-), θράσσω (θραχ-?), μάσσω (μαγ-), μύσσω (μυκ-), ὀρύσσω (ὀρυχ-), πλήσσω (πληγ-, πλαγ-), πτήσσω (πτηκ-), πτύσσω (πτυγ-), σάττω (σαγ-), τάσσω (ταγ-), φράσσω (φραγ-), φρίσσω (φρῑκ-), φυλάσσω (φυλακ-). See also epic δειδίσσομαι, Ionic and poetic ἀμύσσω and πτοΐσσομαι, and poetic ἀφύσσω and νύσσω.[1]

582. Some presents in σσω (ττω) are formed from lingual stems, which have futures in σω or aorists in σα; as ἐρέσσω, *row* (from stem ἐρετ-, seen in ἐρέτης, *rower*), aor. ἤρεσα. So also ἁρμόττω (fut. ἁρμόσω), βλίττω (μελιτ-, 66), λίσσομαι (λιτ-), πάσσω, πλάσσω, πτίσσω, with ἀφάσσω (Hdt.), and poetic ἱμάσσω, κορύσσω (κορυθ-).

Many presents of this kind are formed on the analogy of verbs with real lingual stems (see 587).

583. N. Πέσσω, *cook*, comes from an old stem πεκ-; while the tenses πέψω, ἔπεψα, etc. belong to the stem πεπ-, seen in later πέπτω and Ionic πέπτομαι of Class III.

584. II. (*Verbs in* ζω.) Presents in ζω may be formed in two ways:—

585. (1) From stems in δ, with futures in σω; as κομίζω (κομιδ-, seen in κομιδ-ή), *carry*, fut. κομίσω; φράζω (φραδ-), *say*, fut. φράσω. (See 84, 3.)

[1] The lists of verbs of the fourth class are not complete, while those of the other classes which are given contain all the verbs in common use.

586. So ἁρμόζω (ἁρμοδ-), ἁρπάζω, ἐλπίζω (ἐλπιδ-), ἐρίζω (ἐριδ-), θαυμάζω, ἵζω (ἱδ-) with ἕζομαι (ἑδ-), κτίζω, νομίζω, ὄζω (ὀδ-), πελάζω, σχάζω, σχίζω (σχιδ-), σῴζω.

587. N. Many verbs in ζω, especially most in αζω, with futures in σω, were formed on the analogy of those with actual stems in δ. (See Meyer, *Gr. Gram.* §§ 521, 522.)

588. (2) From stems in γ (or γγ), with futures in ξω; as σφάζω (σφαγ-), *slay* (σφάττω in prose), fut. σφάξω; ῥέζω (ῥεγ-), *do* (poetic and Ionic), fut. ῥέξω; κλάζω (κλαγγ-), *scream* (cf. *clango*), fut. κλάγξω. (See 84, 3.)

589. So κράζω (κραγ-), σαλπίζω (σαλπιγγ-), στίζω (στιγ-); with poetic ἀλαλάζω, βάζω, βρίζω, γρύζω, ἐλελίζω, κρίζω, μύζω, *grumble*, στάζω.

590. N. Some verbs in ζω have stems both in δ and γ; as παίζω (παιδ-, παιγ-), *play*, fut. παιξοῦμαι (666), aor. ἔπαισα. See also poetic forms of ἁρπάζω and νάσσω. (See 587.)

591. N. Νίζω, *wash*, fut. νίψω, forms its tenses from a stem νιβ-, seen in Homeric νίπτομαι and later νίπτω.

592. III. (*Enlarged Liquid Stems in Present.*) Of these there are three divisions: —

593. (1) Presents in λλω are formed from verb stems in λ with ι%- added, λι becoming λλ; as στέλλω, *send*, for στελ-ι-ω; ἀγγέλλω, *announce*, for ἀγγελ-ι-ω; σφάλλω, *trip up*, for σφαλ-ι-ω; present stems στελλ%-, etc. (See 84, 4.)

See ἅλλομαι (ἁλ-), βάλλω (βαλ-), θάλλω (θαλ-), ὀκέλλω (ὀκελ-), πάλλω (παλ-), τέλλω (τελ-), with poetic δαιδάλλω, ἰάλλω, σκέλλω, τίλλω.

594. (2) Presents in αινω and αιρω are formed from verb stems in ᾰν- and ᾰρ- with ι%- added.

Here the ι is transposed and then contracted with α to αι; as φαίνω (φαν-), *show*, for φαν-ι-ω (present stem φαιν%-), future φανῶ; χαίρω (χαρ-), *rejoice*, for χαρ-ι-ω. (See 84, 5.)

595. So εὐφραίνω (εὐφραν-), κερδαίνω (κερδαν-), μαίνομαι (μαν-), μιαίνω (μιαν-), ξαίνω (ξαν-), ξηραίνω (ξηραν-), ποιμαίνω (ποιμαν-), ῥαίνω (ῥαν-), σαίνω (σαν-), σημαίνω (σημαν-), τετραίνω (τετραν-), ὑφαίνω (ὑφαν-), χραίνω (χραν-); with poetic κραίνω (κραν-), πιπταίνω (παπταν-), πιαίνω (πιαν-). Αἴρω (ἀρ-), καθαίρω (καθαρ-), τεκμαίρομαι (τεκμαρ-), with poetic ἐναίρω (ἐναρ-), ἐχθαίρω (ἐχθαρ-), σαίρω (σαρ-).

596. (3) Presents in *ειvω, ειρω, ῑνω, ῑρω, ῡνω*, and *ῡρω* come from stems in *εν, ερ, ῐν, ῐρ, ῠν*, and *ῠρ*, with *ι%-* added.

Here the added *ι* disappears and the preceding *ε, ι*, or *υ* is lengthened to *ει, ῑ*, or *ῡ*; as *τείνω* (*τεν-*), *stretch*, for *τεν-ι-ω*; *κείρω* (*κερ-*), *shear*, for *κερ-ι-ω*; *κρίνω* (*κριν-*), *judge*, for *κριν-ι-ω*; *ἀμύνω* (*ἀμυν-*), *ward off*, for *ἀμυν-ι-ω*; *σύρω* (*συρ-*), *draw*, for *συρ-ι-ω*.

597. So *γείνομαι* (*γεν-*), *κτείνω* (*κτεν-*), and poetic *θείνω* (*θεν-*); *ἀγείρω* (*ἀγερ-*), *δείρω* (*δερ-*), *ἐγείρω* (*ἐγερ-*), *ἱμείρω* (*ἱμερ-*), *μείρομαι* (*μερ-*), *φθείρω* (*φθερ-*), *σπείρω* (*σπερ-*), with poetic *πείρω* (*περ-*). Κλίνω (*κλιν-*), *σίνομαι* (*σιν-*), *αἰσχύνω* (*αἰσχυν-*), *θαρσύνω* (*θαρσυν-*), *ὀξύνω* (*ὀξυν-*), *πλύνω* (*πλυν-*), *μαρτύρομαι* (*μαρτυρ-*), *ὀλοφύρομαι* (*ὀλοφυρ-*). Οἰκτίρω (*οἰκτιρ-*), *pity* (commonly written *οἰκτείρω*), is the only verb in *ῑρω*.

598. N. Ὀφείλω (*ὀφελ-*), *be obliged, owe*, follows the analogy of stems in *εν*, to avoid confusion with *ὀφέλλω* (*ὀφελ-*), *increase;* but in Homer it has the regular present *ὀφέλλω*. Homer has *εἴλομαι*, *press*, from stem *ἑλ-*.

599. N. Verbs of this division (III.) regularly have futures and aorists active and middle of the *liquid* form (663). For exceptions (in poetry), see 668.

600. N. Many verbs with liquid stems do not belong to this class; as *δέμω* and *δέρω* in Class I. For *βαίνω* etc. in Class V., see 610.

601. IV. (*Stems in αυ.*) Here belong *καίω*, *burn*, and *κλαίω*, *weep* (Attic also *κάω* and *κλάω*). The stems *καυ-* and *κλαυ-* (seen in *καύσω* and *κλαύσομαι*) became *καϝι-* and *κλαϝι-*, whence *και-* and *κλαι-* (90, 2). (See 574.)

602. N. The poets form some other presents in this way; as *δαίω* (*δαϝ-*), *burn*, *ναίω* (*ναϝ-*), *swim*. So, from stems in *ασ-*, *μαίομαι* (*μασ-*, *μασι-*, *μαι-*), *seek*, *δαίομαι* (*δασ-*), *divide*. Ὀπυίω, *marry*, has stem *ὀπυ-*, whence fut. *ὀπύσω*.

603. Fifth Class. (N *Class.*) (1) Some verb stems are strengthened in the present by adding *ν* before the thematic vowel %-; as *φθάν-ω* (*φθα-*), *anticipate* (present stem *φθαν%-*); *φθίν-ω* (*φθι-*), *waste; δάκν-ω* (*δακ-*), *bite; κάμν-ω* (*καμ-*), *be weary; τέμν-ω* (*τεμ-*), *cut.*

604. So *βαίνω* (*βα-*, *βαν-*, 610), *πίνω* (*πι-*, see also 621), *τίνω* (*τι-*), *δύνω* (with *δύω*), Hom. *θύνω* (with *θύω*), *rush:* for *ἐλαύνω* (*ἐλα-*), see 612.

605. (2) (*a*) Some consonant stems add αν; ἁμαρτάν-ω (ἁμαρτ-), *err* (present stem ἁμαρταν%ε-); αἰσθάν-ομαι (αἰσθ-), *perceive;* βλαστάν-ω (βλαστ-), *sprout.*

(*b*) Here, if the last vowel of the stem is short, another nasal (μ before a labial, ν before a lingual, γ before a palatal) is inserted after this vowel; as λανθάν-ω (λαθ-, λανθ-), *escape notice* (λανθαν%ε-); λαμβάν-ω (λαβ-, λαμβ-), *take;* θιγγάνω (θιγ-, θιγγ-), *touch.*

606. So αὐξάν-ω (with αὔξ-ω), δαρθάν-ω (δαρθ-), ἀπ-εχθάν-ομαι (ἐχθ-), ἱζάν-ω (with ἵζ-ω), οἰδάν-ω (οἰδ-), ὀλισθάν-ω (ὀλισθ-), ὀφλισκάν-ω (ὀφλ-, ὀφλισκ-, 614); with poetic ἀλιταίν-ομαι (ἀλιτ-, 610), ἀλφάν-ω (ἀλφ-), ἐριδαίν-ω (ἐριδ-). With inserted ν, γ, or μ, ἁνδάν-ω (ἁδ-), κιγχάνω, epic κιχάνω (κιχ-), λαγχάν-ω (λαχ-), μανθάν-ω (μαθ-), πυνθάν-ομαι (πυθ-), τυγχάν-ω (τυχ-), with poetic χανδάν-ω (χαδ-), ἐρυγγάν-ω (ἐρυγ-).

607. (3) A few stems add νε: βῡνέ-ω (with βύ-ω), *stop up,* ἱκνέ-ομαι (with ἵκ-ω), *come,* κυνέ-ω (κυ-), *kiss;* also ἀμπ-ισχνέ-ομαι, *have on,* and ὑπ-ισχνέ-ομαι, *promise,* from ἴσχ-ω.

608. (4) Some stems add νυ or (after a vowel) ννυ. These form the second class (in νῡμι) of verbs in μι, as δείκνῡ-μι (δεικ-), *show,* κεράννῡ-μι (κερα-), *mix,* and are enumerated in 797, 1. Some of these have also presents in νυω. (See 502, 2.)

609. (5) A few poetic (chiefly epic) verbs add να to the stem, forming presents in νημι (or deponents in ναμαι): most of these have presents in ναω; as δάμνημι (δαμ-να-), also δαμνάω, *subdue.* These form a third class of verbs in μι, and are enumerated in 797, 2.

610. N. Βαίνω (βα-, βαν-), *go,* and ὀσφραίνομαι (ὀσφρ-, ὀσφραν-), *smell,* not only add ν or αν, but lengthen αν to αιν on the principle of Class IV. (594). They belong here, however, because they do not have the inflection of liquid verbs (599). See also κερδαίνω, ῥαίνω, τετραίνω, with Homeric ἀλιταίνομαι (ἀλιτ-, ἀλιταν-).

611. N. Some stems of this class lengthen a short vowel (on the principle of Class II.) in other tenses than the present; as λαμβάνω (λαβ-), fut. λήψομαι (ληβ-): so δάκνω, λαγχάνω, λανθάνω, τυγχάνω. See also ἐρυγγάνω, ἔρχομαι, and πυνθάνομαι.

Three verbs in νῡμι (608), ζεύγνῡμι, πήγνῡμι, ῥήγνῡμι, belong equally to Class II. and Class V.

612. N. Ἐλαύνω (ἐλα-), *drive,* is irregular in the present stem (probably for ἐλα-νυ-ω). Ὄλ-λῡ-μι (ὀλ-), *destroy,* adds λυ (by assimilation) instead of νυ to the stem ὀλ-.

613. Sixth Class. (*Verbs in σκω.*) These add σκ%- or ισκ%- to the verb stem to form the present stem; as γηρά-σκω (γηρα-), *grow old* (present stem γηρασκ%-); εὑρ-ίσκω (εὑρ-), *find* (εὑρισκ%-); ἀρέ-σκω (ἀρε-), *please*, στερ-ίσκω (στερ-), *deprive*.

614. These verbs are, further, ἀλ-ίσκομαι, ἀμβλ-ίσκω, ἀμπλακ-ίσκω (poetic), ἀνᾱλ-ίσκω, ἀπαφ-ίσκω (poet.), ἀραρ-ίσκω (poet.), βά-σκω (poet.), βι-βρώ-σκω (βρο-), ἀναβιώ-σκομαι (βιο-), βλώ-σκω (μολ-, βλο-), γεγων-ίσκω, γι-γνώ-σκω (γνο-), δι-δρᾱ́-σκω (δρα-), ἐπαυρ-ίσκω (poet.), ἡβά-σκω, θνῄ-σκω (θαν-, θνα-), θρώ-σκω (θορ-, θρο-), ἱλά-σκομαι, μεθύ-σκω, κικλῄ-σκω (κλη-) (poet.), κυ-ίσκομαι (κυ-), μι-μνῄ-σκω (μνα-), πι-πί-σκω (Ion. and Pind.), πι-πρᾱ́-σκω, πιφαύ-σκω (φαυ-), *declare* (Hom.), τι-τρώ-σκω (τρο-), φά-σκω, χά-σκω. See also the verbs in 617. Ὀφλ-ισκάνω (ὀφλ-) takes ισκ and then adds αν (606).

615. N. Many presents of this classs are reduplicated (536); as γι-γνώσκω (γνο-). See 652, 1. Ἀρ-αρ-ίσκω has a form of Attic reduplication (529).

616. N. Final ο of the verb stem becomes ω, and final ᾰ sometimes becomes ᾱ or η; as in γιγνώσκω (γνο-), διδρᾱ́σκω (δρα-); θνῄσκω (θαν-, θνα-), Doric θνᾱ́σκω (for θνᾱ-ισκω).

617. N. Three verbs, ἀλύ-σκω (ἀλυκ-), *avoid*, διδά-σκω (διδαχ-), *teach*, and λά-σκω (λακ-), *speak*, omit κ or χ before σκω. So Homeric εἴσκω or ἴσκω (εἰκ- or ἰκ-), *liken*, and τιτύσκομαι (τυχ-, τυκ-), for τι-τυκ-σκομαι, *prepare*. See also μίσγω (for μιγ-σκω) and πάσχω (for παθ-σκω).

618. N. These verbs, from their ending σκω, are called *inceptive*, though few have any inceptive meaning.

619. Seventh Class. (*Presents in μι with simple stems.*) Here the verb stem, sometimes reduplicated (652), without the thematic vowel, appears as the present stem. *E.g.*

Φημί (φα-), *say*, φα-μέν, φα-τέ; τίθημι (θε-), *put*, τίθε-μεν, τίθε-τε, τίθε-μαι, τιθέ-μεθα, ἐ-τίθε-σθε, ἐ-τίθε-ντο; δίδωμι (δο-), δί-δο-μεν.

For the strong form of these stems in the singular of the active, see 627.

620. All verbs in μι, except those in νῡμι under 608, and the epic forms in νημι (or ναμαι) with να added to the stem (609), are of this class. They are enumerated in 794. (See 502, 1.)

621. Eighth Class. (*Mixed Class.*) This includes the few irregular verbs which have any of the tense stems so essentially different from others, or are otherwise so peculiar in formation, that they cannot be brought under any of the preceding classes. They are the following: —

αἱρέω (αἱρε-, ἑλ-), *take*, fut. αἱρήσω, 2 aor. εἷλον.

εἶδον (ϝιδ-, ἰδ-), *saw*, *vidi*, 2 aorist (no present act.); 2 pf. οἶδα, *know* (820). Mid. εἴδομαι (poet.). Εἶδον is used as 2 aor. of ὁράω (see below).

εἶπον (εἰπ-, ἐρ-, ῥε-), *spoke*, 2 aor. (no pres.); fut. (ἐρέω) ἐρῶ, pf. εἴ-ρη-κα. The stem ἐρ- (ῥε-) is for ϝερ- (ϝρε-), seen in Lat. *ver-bum* (649). So ἐν-έπω.

ἔρχομαι (ἐρχ-, ἐλευθ-, ἐλυθ-, ἐλθ-), *go*, fut. ἐλεύσομαι (poet.), 2 perf. ἐλήλυθα, 2 aor. ἦλθον. The Attic future is εἶμι, *shall go* (808).

ἐσθίω (ἐσθ-, ἐδ-, φαγ-), *eat*, fut. ἔδομαι, 2 aor. ἔφαγον.

ὁράω (ὁρα-, ὀπ-, ϝιδ-), *see*, fut. ὄψομαι, pf. ἑόρακα, 2 aor. εἶδον (see above).

πάσχω (παθ-, πενθ-), *suffer*, fut. πείσομαι, 2 pf. πέπονθα, 2 aor. ἔπαθον. (See 617.)

πίνω (πι-, πο-), *drink*, fut. πίομαι, pf. πέπωκα, 2 aor. ἔπιον. (See 604.)

τρέχω (τρεχ-, δραμ-), *run*, fut. δραμοῦμαι, pf. δεδράμηκα (657), 2 aor. ἔδραμον.

φέρω (φερ-, οἰ-, ἐνεκ-, by reduplication and syncope ἐν-ενεκ, ἐνεγκ-), *bear*, *fero*; fut. οἴσω, aor. ἤνεγκα, 2 p. ἐν-ήνοχ-α (643; 692), ἐν-ήνεγ-μαι, aor. p. ἠνέχθην.

For full forms of these verbs, see the Catalogue. See also the irregular verbs in μι (805–820).

622. N. Occasional Homeric or poetic irregular forms appear even in some verbs of the first seven classes. See ἀκαχίζω, ἀλέξω, γίγνομαι, and χανδάνω in the Catalogue.

Inflection of the Present and Imperfect Indicative.

623. (*Common Form.*) The present indicative adds the primary endings (552) to the present tense stem in ο/ε-, except in the singular of the active, where it has the terminations ω, εις, ει, the origin of which is uncertain. The first person in ω is independent of that in μι, and both the forms in ω and in μι were probably inherited by the Greek from the parent language. For the third person in ουσι (for οντι), see 556, 5.

624. Of the two forms of the second person singular middle in ῃ and ει (565, 6), that in ει is the true Attic form, which was used in prose and in comedy. But the tragedians seem to have preferred the form in η,[1] which is the regular form in the other dialects, except Ionic, and in the later common dialect. This applies to the future middle and passive and to the future perfect, as well as to the present.

625. Βούλομαι, *wish*, and οἴομαι, *think*, have only βούλει and οἴει, with no forms in η. So ὄψομαι, future of ὁράω, *see*, has only ὄψει.

626. The imperfect adds the secondary endings to the tense stem in ⁰/ₑ-. See the paradigm of λύω.

627. (Μι-*form*.) Here the final vowel of the stem is long (with η, ω, ῡ) in the *singular* of both present and imperfect indicative active, but short (with ᾰ or ε, ο, ῠ) in the dual and plural, and also in most other forms derived from the present stem. This change from the strong stem in the indicative singular to the weak stem in other forms is one of the most important distinctions between the μι-form and that in ω. The endings here include μι, ς, σι in the singular of the present, and σαν in the third person plural of the imperfect. (See 506.)

628. The third person plural of the present active has the ending ᾱσι (552), which is always contracted with α (but never with ε, ο, or υ) of the stem; as ἱστᾶσι (for ἱστα-ᾱσι), but τιθέ-ᾱσι, διδό-ᾱσι, δεικνύ-ᾱσι.

629. The only verbs in μι with consonant stems are the irregular εἰμί (ἐσ-), *be*, and ἧμαι (ἡσ-), *sit*. (See 806 and 814.)

630. Some verbs in ημι and ωμι have forms which follow the inflection of verbs in εω and οω. Thus the imperfect forms ἐτίθεις and ἐτίθει (as if from τιθέω), and ἐδίδουν, ἐδίδους, ἐδίδου (as if from διδόω), are much more common than the regular forms in ης, η and ων, ως, ω. So τιθεῖς for τίθης in the present. (See also 741.)

631. Some verbs in ῡμι have also presents in υω; as δεικνύω for δείκνῡμι.

632. Δύναμαι, *can*, and ἐπίσταμαι, *know*, often have ἐδύνω (or ἠδύνω) and ἠπίστω for ἐδύνασο and ἠπίστασο in the imperfect, and occasionally δύνᾳ and ἐπίστᾳ for δύνασαι and ἐπίστασαι in the present.

633. For the present (with the other tenses) in the dependent moods and the participle, see the account of these (718–775).

[1] Kirchhoff and Wecklein in Aeschylus, and Bergk in Sophocles, give only the form in η.

MODIFICATION OF THE VERB STEM IN CERTAIN TENSE SYSTEMS.

634. Before discussing the other tense systems (II.–IX.), we must mention some modifications which the verb stem regularly undergoes in certain forms. Mere irregularities, such as are found only in verbs of the eighth class (621), are not noticed here.

635. (*Lengthening of Vowels.*) Most stems ending in a short vowel lengthen this vowel before the tense suffix (561, 5) in all tenses formed from them, except the present and imperfect. A and ε become η, and ο becomes ω; but ᾰ after ε, ι, or ρ becomes ᾱ (29). *E.g.*

Τιμάω (τῑμα-), *honor*, τῑμή-σω, ἐτίμη-σα, τετίμη-κα, τετίμη-μαι, ἐτῑμή-θην; φιλέω (φιλε-), *love*, φιλήσω, ἐφίλησα, πεφίληκα, πεφίλημαι, ἐφιλήθην; δηλόω (δηλο-), *show*, δηλώσω, ἐδήλωσα, δεδήλωκα, δακρύω, δακρῡσω. But ἐάω, ἐάσω; ἰάομαι, ἰάσομαι; δράω, δρᾱσω, ἔδρᾱσα, δέδρᾱκα.

636. This applies also to stems which *become* vowel stems by metathesis (649); as βάλλω (βαλ-, βλα-), *throw*, pf. βέβλη-κα; κάμνω (καμ-, κμα-), *labor*, κέκμη-κα; or by adding ε (657); as βούλομαι (βουλ-, βουλε-), *wish*, βουλή-σομαι, βεβούλη-μαι, ἐβουλή-θην.

637. For the long stem vowel in the singular of the present and imperfect indicative of verbs in μι, see 627.

638. N. Ἀκροάομαι, *hear*, has ἀκροάσομαι etc.; χράω, *give oracles*, lengthens ᾰ to η; as χρήσω etc. So τρήσω and ἔτρησα from stem τρᾰ-; see τετραίνω, *bore*.

639. Some vowel stems retain the short vowel, contrary to the general rule (635); as γελάω, *laugh*, γελᾰσομαι, ἐγέλᾰσα; ἀρκέω, *suffice*, ἀρκέσω, ἤρκεσα; μάχομαι (μαχε-), *fight*, μαχέσομαι (Ion.), ἐμαχεσάμην.

(*a*) This occurs in the following verbs: (pure verbs) ἄγαμαι, αἰδέομαι, ἀκέομαι, ἀλέω, ἀνύω, ἀρκέω, ἀρόω, ἀρύω, γελάω, ἑλκύω (see ἕλκω), ἐμέω, ἐράω, ζέω, θλάω, κλάω, *break*, ξέω, πτύω, σπάω, τελέω, τρέω, φλάω, χαλάω; and epic ἀκηδέω, κοτέω, λοέω, νεικέω, and the stems (ἀα-) and (ἀε-);—(other verbs with vowel stems) ἀρέσκω (ἀρε-), ἄχθομαι (ἀχθε-), ἐλαύνω (ἐλα-), ἱλάσκομαι (ἱλα-), μεθύσκω (μεθυ-); also all verbs in αννῡμι and εννῡμι, with stems in α and ε (given in 797, 1), with ὄλλῡμι (ὀλε-) and ὄμνῡμι (ὀμο-).

(*b*) The final vowel of the stem is variable in quantity in different tenses in the following verbs: (pure verbs) αἰνέω, αἱρέω, δέω, *bind*, δύω (see δύνω), ἐρύω (epic), θύω, *sacrifice*, καλέω, λύω, μύω, ποθέω, πονέω; — (other verbs) βαίνω (βα-), εὑρίσκω (εὑρ-, εὑρε-), μάχομαι (μαχε-), πίνω (πι-, πο-), φθάνω (φθα-), φθίνω (φθι-).

640. (*Insertion of σ.*) Vowel stems which retain the short vowel (639) and some others add σ to the final vowel before all endings *not beginning with* σ in the perfect and pluperfect middle. The same verbs have σ before θε or θη in the first passive tense system. *E.g.*

Τελέω, *finish*, τετέλε-σ-μαι, ἐτετελέσμην, ἐτελέσθην, τελεσθήσομαι; γελάω, *laugh*, ἐγελά-σ-θην, γελασθῆναι; χράω, *give oracles*, χρήσω, κέχρη-σ-μαι, ἐχρήσθην.

641. This occurs in all the verbs of 639 (*a*), except ἀρόω, so far as they form these tenses; and in the following: ἀκούω, δράω, θραύω, κελεύω, κλείω (κλῄω), κνάω, κναίω, κρούω, κυλίω (or κυλίνδω), λεύω, νέω, *heap*, ξύω, παίω, παλαίω, παύω, πλέω, πρίω, σείω, τίνω, ὕω, χόω, χράω, χρίω, and poetic ῥαίω. Some, however, have forms both with and without σ. See the Catalogue.

642. (*Strong Form of Stem in Second Class.*) 1. Verbs of the second class have the strong form of the stem (572), as λειπ- or λοιπ- in λείπω, τηκ- in τήκω, νευ- in (νεϝω) νέω, in all tenses except in the second aorist and second passive tense systems; as φεύγω, φεύξομαι, πέφευγα, ἔφυγον; λείπω, λείψω, λέλοιπα, ἔλιπον; τήκω, τήξω, τέτηκα, ἐτάκην; ῥέω (for ῥεϝω), ῥεύσομαι, ἐρρύην.

2. Exceptions are the perfect and aorist passive of τεύχω (τυχ-), which are regular in Ionic, and most tenses of χέω (χυ-) and σεύω (συ-). After the Attic reduplication (529) the weak form appears; as in ἀλείφω (ἀλιφ-), ἀλ-ήλιφα: see also ἐρείκω and ἐρείπω. The perfects ἐρρύηκα (ῥέω) and ἐστίβημαι are from stems in ε- (658, 2).

643. (E *changed to* ο *in Second Perfect.*) In the second perfect system, ε of the verb stem is changed to ο. *E.g.*

Στέργω, *love*, ἔστοργα; πέμπω, *send*, πέπομφα; κλέπτω, *steal*, κέκλοφα (576; 692); τρέφω, *nourish*, τέτροφα; τίκτω (τεκ-), *bring forth*, τέτοκα; γίγνομαι (γεν-), *become*, γέγονα, ἐγεγόνη, γεγονέναι, γεγονώς.

So ἐγείρω (ἐγερ-), ἐγρήγορα (532); κτείνω (κτεν-), ἔκτονα (in compos.); λέγω, *collect*, εἴλοχα; πάσχω (παθ-, πενθ-), πέπονθα; πέρδομαι, πέπορδα; τρέπω, τέτροφα; φέρω (ἐνεκ-), ἐνήνοχα; φθείρω (φθερ-), ἔφθορα; χέζω (χεδ-), κέχοδα.

For λείπ-ω, λέ-λοιπ-α, and πείθ-ω, πέ-ποιθ-α, see 31; 642, 1.

644. (A *lengthened to η or ᾱ in Second Perfect.*) In some verbs ᾰ of the stem is lengthened to η or ᾱ in the second perfect.

These are ἄγνῡμι (ἀγ-), ἔᾱγα (Ionic ἔηγα); θάλλω (θαλ-), τέθηλα; κράζω (κραγ-), κέκρᾱγα; λάσκω (λακ-), λέλᾱκα; μαίνομαι (μαν-), μέμηνα; σαίρω (σαρ-), σέσηρα; φαίνω (φαν-), πέφηνα.

645. (E *changed to* ᾰ.) In monosyllabic liquid stems, ε is generally changed to ᾰ in the first perfect, perfect middle, and second passive tense systems. *E.g.*

Στέλλω (στελ-), *send*, ἔσταλκα, ἔσταλμαι, ἐστάλην, σταλήσομαι; κείρω (κερ-), *shear*, κέκαρμαι, ἐκάρην (Ion.); σπείρω (σπερ-), *sow*, ἔσπαρμαι, ἐσπάρην. So in δέρω, κτείνω, μείρομαι, τείνω, τέλλω, and φθείρω.

646. N. The same change of ε to α (after ρ) occurs in στρέφω, *turn*, ἔστραμμαι, ἐστράφην, στραφήσομαι (but 1 aor. ἐστρέφθην, rare); τρέπω, *turn*, τέτραμμαι, ἐτράπην (but ἐτρέφθην, Ion. ἐτράφθην); τρέφω, *nourish*, τέθραμμαι, ἐτράφην (but ἐθρέφθην); also in the second aorist passive of κλέπτω, *steal*, πλέκω, *weave*, and τέρπω, *delight*, ἐκλάπην, ἐπλάκην, and (epic) ἐτάρπην (1 aor. ἐκλέφθην, ἐπλέχθην, ἐτέρφθην, rarely epic ἐτάρφθην). It occurs, further, in the second aorist (active or middle) of κτείνω, *kill*, τέμνω, *cut*, τρέπω, and τέρπω; viz., in ἔκτανον (poet.), ἔταμον, ἐταμόμην, ἔτραπον, ἐτραπόμην, τεταρπόμην (Hom.); also in several Homeric and poetic forms (see δέρκομαι, πέρθω, and πτήσσω). For τείνω, ἐτάθην, see 711.

647. (N *of stem dropped.*) Four verbs in νω drop ν of the stem in the perfect and first passive systems, and thus have vowel stems in these forms: —

κρίνω (κριν-), *separate*, κέκρικα, κέκριμαι, ἐκρίθην; κλίνω (κλιν-), *incline*, κέκλικα, κέκλιμαι, ἐκλίθην; πλῡνω (πλυν-), *wash*, πέπλυμαι, ἐπλύθην; τείνω (τεν-), *stretch*, τέτακα (645), τέταμαι, ἐτάθην, ἐκταθήσομαι. So κτείνω in some poetic forms; as ἐκτά-θην, ἐκτά-μην. See also epic stem φεν-, φα-. For the regular Homeric ἐκλίνθην and ἐκρίνθην, see 709.

648. When final ν of a stem is not thus dropped, it becomes nasal γ before κα (78, 1), and is generally replaced by σ before μαι (83); as φαίνω (φαν-), πέφαγκα, πέφασμαι, ἐφάνθην. (See 700.)

649. (*Metathesis.*) The stem sometimes suffers *metathesis* (64):

(1) in the present, as θνῄσκω (θαν-, θνα-), *die*, (616);

(2) in other tenses, as βάλλω (βαλ-, βλα-), *throw*, βέβληκα, βέβλημαι, ἐβλήθην; and (poetic) δέρκομαι (δερκ-), *see*, 2 aor. ἔδρακον (δρακ-, 646).

650. (*Syncope.*) Sometimes *syncope* (65):

(1) in the present, as *γίγνομαι* (*γεν-*), *become*, for *γι-γεν-ομαι*;

(2) in the second aorist, as *ἐπτόμην* for *ἐ-πετ-ομην*;

(3) in the perfect, as *πετάννῡμι* (*πετα-*), *expand*, *πέπταμαι* for *πε-πετα-μαι*. See *φέρω* in 621.

651. (*Reduplication.*) Sometimes *reduplication*, besides the regular reduplication of the perfect stem (520):

(1) in the present, as *γι-γνώσκω*, *know*, *γί-γνομαι*, *τί-θημι*.

(2) in the second aorist, as *πείθω* (*πιθ-*), *persuade*, *πέ-πιθον* (epic); so *ἄγω*, *ἤγαγον* (Attic).

652. 1. The following are reduplicated in the present:—

(*a*) In Class I., *γί-γνομαι* (for *γι-γεν-ομαι*); *ἴσχω* (for *σι-σεχ-ω*); *μίμνω* (for *μι-μενω*), poetic for *μένω*; *πίπτω* (for *πι-πετ-ω*); *τίκτω* (for *τι-τεκ-ω*).

(*b*) In Class VI., *βι-βρώσκω* (*βρο-*), *γι-γνώσκω* (*γνο-*), *δι-δρᾱ́σκω* (*δρα-*), *μι-μνῄσκω* (*μνα-*), *πι-πρᾱ́σκω* (*πρα-*), *τι-τρώσκω* (*τρο-*), with poetic *πι-πίσκω* and *πι-φαύσκω*, and *ἀραρίσκω* with peculiar Attic reduplication (615).

(*c*) In Class VII., the verbs in *μι* which are enumerated in 794, 2.

2. For reduplicated second aorists, see 534 and 535.

653. (E *added to Stem.*) New stems are often formed by adding *ε* to the verb stem.

654. (1) From this new stem in *ε* some verbs form the present stem (by adding %-), sometimes also other tense stems. *E.g.*

Δοκέ-ω (*δοκ-*), *seem*, pres. stem (*δοκε*%-, fut. *δόξω*; *γαμέ-ω* (*γαμ-*), *marry*, fut. *γαμῶ*, pf. *γεγάμηκα*; *ὠθέω* (*ὠθ-*), *push*, fut. *ὤσω* (poet. *ὠθήσω*).

655. These verbs are, further, *γεγωνέω*, *γηθέω*, *κτυπέω*, *κυρέω*, *μαρτυρέω* (also *μαρτῡ́ρομαι*), *ῥῑπτέω* (also *ῥίπτω*), *φιλέω* (see epic forms); and poetic *δουπέω*, *εἰλέω*, *ἐπαυρέω*, *κελαδέω*, *κεντέω*, *πατέομαι*, *ῥῑγέω*, *στυγέω*, *τορέω*, and *χραισμέω*. See also *πεκτέω* (*πεκ-*, *πεκτ-*).

Most verbs in *εω* have their regular stems in *ε-*, as *ποιέω* (*ποιε-*), *make*, fut. *ποιήσω*.

656. N. A few chiefly poetic verbs add *α* in the same way to the verb stem. See *βρῡχάομαι*, *γοάω*, *δηριάω*, *μηκάομαι*, *μητιάω*, *μῡκάομαι*.

657. (2) Generally the new stem in *ε* does not appear in the present. But in some verbs it forms special tenses; in others it forms all the tenses except the present, imperfect, second perfect, and the second aorists. *E.g.*

Βούλομαι (βουλ-), *wish*, βουλήσομαι (βουλε-, 636); αἰσθάνομαι (αἰσθ-), *perceive*, αἰσθήσομαι (αἰσθε-), ᾔσθημαι; μένω (μεν-), *remain*, μεμένηκα (μενε-); μάχομαι (μαχ-), *fight*, fut. (μαχέ-ομαι) μαχοῦμαι, ἐμαχεσάμην, μεμάχημαι.

658. 1. The following have the stem in ε in all tenses except those mentioned (657): αἰσθάνομαι (αἰσθ-), ἀλέξω, ἄλθομαι (Ion.), ἁμαρτάνω (ἁμαρτ-), ἁνδάνω (ἁδ-), ἀπ-εχθάνομαι (-εχθ-), αὐξάνω (αὐξ-), ἄχθομαι, βλαστάνω (βλαστ-), βούλομαι, βόσκω, δέω, *want*, ἐθέλω and θέλω, ἔρομαι and εἴρομαι (Ion.), ἔρρω, εὕδω, εὑρίσκω, ἕψω, κέλομαι (poet.), κιχάνω (κιχ-), λάσκω (λακ-), μανθάνω (μαθ-), μάχομαι, μέδομαι, μέλλω, μέλω, μύζω, οἴομαι, οἴχομαι, ὀλισθάνω (ὀλισθ-), ὄλλῡμι, ὀφλισκάνω (ὀφλ-), πέτομαι, στόρνῡμι: see poetic ἀμπλακίσκω and ἀπαφίσκω, and the stem δα-. See also κερδαίνω.

2. The following have the stem in ε in special tenses formed from the verb stem or the weak stem (31): δαρθάνω (δαρθ-), μένω, νέμω, ὀσφραίνομαι (ὀσφρ-), παίω, πέτομαι, πείθω (πιθ-), ῥέω (ῥυ-), στείβω (στιβ-), τυγχάνω (τυχ-), χάζω (χαδ-); with γίγνομαι, ἔχω, τρέχω.

3. The following form certain tenses from a stem made by adding ε to the present stem without the thematic vowel: διδάσκω, καθίζω, κήδω, κλαίω, ὄζω, ὀφείλω, τύπτω, χαίρω.

659. N. In ὄμνῡμι, *swear*, the stem ὀμ- is enlarged to ὀμο- in some tenses, as in ὤμο-σα; in ἁλίσκομαι, *be captured*, ἁλ- is enlarged to ἁλο-, as in ἁλώσομαι. So τρῡ́χω (τρῡχ-), *exhaust*, τρῡχώσω. So probably οἴχομαι, *be gone*, has stem οἰχο- for οἰχε- in the perfect οἴχω-κα (cf. Ion. οἴχη-μαι).

FORMATION OF TENSE STEMS AND INFLECTION OF TENSE SYSTEMS IN THE INDICATIVE.

I. Present System.

660. The formation of the present stem and the inflection of the present and imperfect indicative have been explained in 568–622 and 623–632.

661. The eight remaining tense stems (II.–IX.) are formed from the verb stem. This is the simplest form of the stem in all classes of verbs except the Second, where it is the *strong* form (575; 642).

For special modifications of certain tense stems, see 634–659.

For the inflection of the subjunctive, optative, and imperative in all tenses, see 718–758; for the formation of the infinitive, see 759–769; and for that of the participles and verbals in -τος and -τεος, see 770–776.

II. Future System.

662. (*Future Active and Middle.*) Vowel and mute stems (460) add σ°/ε- to form the stem of the future active and middle. The indicative active thus ends in σω, and the middle in σομαι. They are inflected like the present (see 480). *E.g.*

Τῑμάω, *honor*, τῑμήσω (τῑμησ°/ε-); δράω, *do*, δρᾱ́σω (635); κόπτω (κοπ-), *cut*, κόψω; βλάπτω (βλαβ-), *hurt*, βλάψω, βλάψομαι (74); γράφω, *write*, γράψω, γράψομαι; πλέκω, *twist*, πλέξω; πρᾱ́σσω (πρᾱγ-), *do*, πρᾱ́ξω, πρᾱ́ξομαι; ταράσσω (ταραχ-), *confuse*, ταράξω, ταράξομαι; φράζω (φραδ-), *tell*, φράσω (for φραδ-σω); πείθω, *persuade*, πείσω (for πειθ-σω); λείπω, *leave*, λείψω, λείψομαι (642). So σπένδω, *pour*, σπείσω (for σπενδ-σω, 79), τρέφω, *nourish*, θρέψω, θρέψομαι (95, 5).

663. (*Liquid Futures.*) Liquid stems (460) add ε°/ε- to form the future stem, making forms in έω and έομαι, contracted to ῶ and οῦμαι, and inflected like φιλῶ and φιλοῦμαι (492). See 482. *E.g.*

Φαίνω (φαν-), *show*, fut. (φανέ-ω) φανῶ, (φανέ-ομαι) φανοῦμαι; στέλλω (στελ-), *send*, (στελέ-ω) στελῶ, (στελέ-ομαι) στελοῦμαι; νέμω, *divide*, (νεμέ-ω) νεμῶ; κρίνω (κριν-), *judge*, (κρινέ-ω) κρινῶ.

664. N. Here ε°/ε- is for an original εσ°/ε-, the σ being dropped between two vowels (88).

665. (*Attic Future.*) 1. The futures of καλέω, *call*, and τελέω, *finish*, καλέσω and τελέσω (639), drop σ of the future stem, and contract καλε- and τελε- with ω and ομαι, making καλῶ, καλοῦμαι, τελῶ and (poetic) τελοῦμαι. These futures have thus the same forms as the presents.

So ὄλλῡμι (ὀλ-, ὀλε-), *destroy*, has future ὀλέσω (Hom.), ὀλέω (Hdt.), ὀλῶ (Attic). So μαχέσομαι, Homeric future of μάχομαι (μαχε-), *fight*, becomes μαχοῦμαι in Attic. Καθέζομαι (ἑδ-), *sit*, has καθεδοῦμαι.

2. In like manner, futures in ασω from verbs in αννῡμι, some in εσω from verbs in εννῡμι, and some in ασω from verbs in αζω, drop σ and contract αω and εω to ῶ. Thus σκεδάννῡμι (σκεδα-), *scatter*, fut. σκεδάσω, (σκεδάω) σκεδῶ; στορέννῡμι (στορε-), *spread*, στορέσω, (στορέω) στορῶ; βιβάζω, *cause to go*, βιβάσω, (βιβάω) βιβῶ. So

ἐλαύνω (**ἐλα-**), *drive* (612), future **ἐλάσω**, (**ἐλάω**) **ἐλῶ**. For future **ἐλόω**, **ἐλόωσι**, etc. in Homer, see 784, 2 (*c*).

3. Futures in **ισω** and **ισομαι** from verbs in **ιζω** of more than two syllables regularly drop *σ* and insert **ε**; then **ιέω** and **ιέομαι** are contracted to **ιῶ** and **ιοῦμαι**; as **κομίζω**, *carry*, **κομίσω**, (**κομιέω**) **κομιῶ**, **κομίσομαι**, (**κομιέομαι**) **κομιοῦμαι**, inflected like **φιλῶ**, **φιλοῦμαι** (492). See 785, 1 (end).

4. These forms of future (665, 1–3) are called *Attic*, because the purer Attic seldom uses any others in these tenses; but they are found also in other dialects and even in Homer.

666. (*Doric Future.*) 1. These verbs form the stem of the future middle in **σε%ε-**, and contract **σέομαι** to **σοῦμαι**: **πλέω**, *sail*, **πλευσοῦμαι** (574); **πνέω**, *breathe*, **πνευσοῦμαι**; **νέω**, *swim*, **νευσοῦμαι**; **κλαίω**, *weep*, **κλαυσοῦμαι** (601); **φεύγω**, *flee*, **φευξοῦμαι**; **πίπτω**, *fall*, **πεσοῦμαι**. See also **παίζω** (590) and **πυνθάνομαι**.

The Attic has these, with the regular futures **πλεύσομαι**, **πνεύσομαι**, **κλαύσομαι**, **φεύξομαι** (but never **πέσομαι**).

2. These are called *Doric* futures, because the Doric forms futures in **σέω**, **σῶ**, and **σέομαι**, **σοῦμαι**.

667. N. A few irregular futures drop *σ* of the stem, which thus has the appearance of a present stem. Such are **χέω** and **χέομαι**, fut. of **χέω**, *pour*; **ἔδομαι**, from **ἐσθίω** (**ἐδ-**), *eat*; **πίομαι**, from **πίνω** (**πι-**), *drink* (621).

668. N. A few poetic liquid stems add *σ* like mute stems; **κέλλω** (**κελ-**), *land*, **κέλσω**; **κύρω**, *meet*, **κύρσω**; **ὄρνυμι** (**ὀρ-**), *rouse*, **ὄρσω**. So **θέρομαι**, *be warmed*, Hom. fut. **θέρσομαι**; **φθείρω** (**φθερ-**), *destroy*, Hom. fut. **φθέρσω**. For the corresponding aorists, see 674 (*b*).

III. First Aorist System.

669. (*First Aorist Active and Middle.*) 1. Vowel and mute stems (460) add **σα** to form the stem of the first aorist active and middle. The indicative active thus ends in **σα**, which becomes **σε** in the third person singular; and the middle ends in **σαμην**. *E.g.*

Τιμάω, **ἐτίμησα**, **ἐτῑμησάμην** (635); **δράω**, **ἔδρᾱσα**; **κόπτω**, **ἔκοψα**, **ἐκοψάμην**; **βλάπτω**, **ἔβλαψα**; **γράφω**, **ἔγραψα**, **ἐγραψάμην**; **πλέκω**, **ἔπλεξα**, **ἐπλεξάμην**; **πρᾱ́σσω**, **ἔπρᾱξα**, **ἐπρᾱξάμην**; **ταράσσω**, **ἐτάραξα**; **φράζω**, **ἔφρασα** (for **ἐφραδ-σα**); **πείθω**, **ἔπεισα** (74); **σπένδω**, **ἔσπεισα** (for **ἐσπενδ-σα**); **τρέφω**, **ἔθρεψα**, **ἐθρεψάμην** (95, 5); **τήκω**, *melt*, **ἔτηξα**; **πλέω**, *sail*, **ἔπλευσα** (574).

For the inflection, see 480.

670. Three verbs in *μι*, *δίδωμι* (*δο-*), *give*, *ἵημι* (*ἑ-*), *send*, and *τίθημι* (*θε-*), *put*, have *κα* for *σα* in the first aorist active, giving *ἔδωκα*, *ἧκα*, and *ἔθηκα*. These forms are seldom used except in the indicative, and are most common in the singular, where the second aorists are not in use. (See 802.) Even the middle forms *ἡκάμην* and *ἐθηκάμην* occur, the latter not in Attic Greek (810).

671. N. *Χέω*, *pour*, has aorists *ἔχεα* (Hom. *ἔχευα*) and *ἐχεάμην*, corresponding to the futures *χέω* and *χέομαι* (667). *Εἶπον*, *said*, has also first aorist *εἶπα*; and *φέρω*, *bear*, has *ἤνεγκ-α* (from stem *ἐνεγκ-*).

For Homeric aorists like *ἐβήσετο*, *ἐδύσετο*, *ἷξον*, etc., see 777, 8.

672. (*Liquid Aorists.*) Liquid stems (460) drop *σ* in *σα*, leaving *α*, and lengthen their last vowel, *ᾰ* to *η* (after *ι* or *ρ* to *ᾱ*) and *ε* to *ει* (89). See 482. *E.g.*

Φαίνω (*φαν-*), *ἔφην-α* (for *ἐφανσα*); *στέλλω* (*στελ-*), *ἔστειλ-α* (for *ἐστελ-σα*) *ἐστειλ-άμην*; *ἀγγέλλω* (*ἀγγελ-*), *announce*, *ἤγγειλα*, *ἠγγειλάμην*; *περαίνω* (*περαν-*), *finish*, *ἐπέρᾱνα*; *μιαίνω* (*μιαν-*), *stain*, *ἐμίᾱνα*; *νέμω*, *divide*, *ἔνειμα*, *ἐνειμάμην*; *κρίνω*, *judge*, *ἔκρῑνα*; *ἀμύνω*, *keep off*, *ἤμῡνα*, *ἠμῡνάμην*; *φθείρω* (*φθερ-*), *destroy*, *ἔφθειρα*. Compare the futures in 663, and see 664.

673. N. A few liquid stems lengthen *αν* to *ᾱν* irregularly; as *κερδαίνω* (*κερδαν-*), *gain*, *ἐκέρδᾱνα*. A few lengthen *ραν* to *ρην*; as *τετραίνω* (*τετραν-*), *bore*, *ἐτέτρηνα*.

674. N. (*a*) *Αἴρω* (*ἀρ-*), *raise*, has *ἦρα*, *ἠράμην* (augmented); but *ᾱ* in other forms, as *ἄρω*, *ἆρον*, *ἄρᾱς*, *ἄρωμαι*, *ἀραίμην*, *ἀράμενος*

(*b*) The poetic *κέλλω*, *κύρω*, and *ὄρνῡμι* have aorists *ἔκελσα*, *ἔκυρσα*, and *ὦρσα*. See the corresponding futures (668). But *ὀκέλλω* (in prose) has *ὤκειλα* (see 89).

IV. Second Aorist System.

675. (*Second Aorist Active and Middle.*) The stem of the second aorist active and middle of the common form (565) is the verb stem (in the second class, the *weak* stem) with %- affixed. These tenses are inflected in the indicative like the imperfect (see 626). *E.g.*

Λείπω (572), *ἔλιπον*, *ἐλιπόμην* (2 aor. stem *λιπ*%-); *λαμβάνω* (*λαβ-*), *take*, *ἔλαβον*, *ἐλαβόμην* (2 aor. stem *λαβ*%-). See 481.

676. N. A few second aorist stems change *ε* to *ᾰ*; as *τέμνω* (*τεμ-*), *cut*, Ionic and poetic *ἔταμον*, *ἐταμόμην*. See 646.

677. N. A few stems are syncopated (650); as *πέτομαι* (*πετ-*), *fly*, 2 aor. m. *ἐπτόμην* for *ἐπετ-ομην*; *ἐγείρω* (*ἐγερ-*), *rouse*, *ἠγρόμην* for ἠγερ-ομην; ἦλθον, *went*, from stem ἐλυθ-, for ἤλυθον (Hom.); ἕπομαι (σεπ-), *follow*, ἑσπόμην, for ἐσεπ-ομην; ἔχω (σεχ-), *have*, ἔσχον for ἐ-σεχ-ον. So the Homeric ἐκεκλόμην, for ἐ-κε-κελ-ομην, or κεκλόμην, from κέλομαι, *command;* ἄλαλκον, for ἀλ-αλεκ-ον, from ἀλέξω (ἀλεκ-), *ward off:* for these and other reduplicated second aorists, see 534; 535. For ἤγαγον, 2 aor. of ἄγω, see 535.

678. (Μι-*form.*) The stem of the second aorist of the μι-form is the simple verb stem with no suffix. The stem vowel is regularly long (η, ω, or ῡ) throughout the indicative active, and the third person has the ending σαν. (For the long vowel in the imperative and infinitive, see 755; 766, 2.) *E.g.*

Ἵστημι (στα-), 2 aor. ἔστην, ἔστης, ἔστη, ἔστησαν, etc. For the inflection, see 506. For δίδωμι, ἵημι, and τίθημι, see 802.

For the great variety of forms in these second aorists, see the complete enumeration (798; 799).

679. The second aorist middle of the μι-form regularly drops σ in σο in the second person singular (564, 6) after a short vowel, and then contracts that vowel with ο; as ἔθου for ἐ-θε-σο (ἔθεο); ἔδου for ἐ-δο-σο (ἔδοο).

680. Verbs in ῡμι form no Attic second aorists from the stem in υ (797, 1).

681. For second aorists middle in ημην, ιμην, and υμην, and some from consonant stems, see 800.

V. First Perfect System.

682. (*First Perfect and Pluperfect Active.*) The stem of the first perfect active is formed by adding κα- to the reduplicated verb stem. It has κα, κας, κε, in the indicative singular, and κᾱσι (for κα-νσι), rarely κᾰσι in poetry, in the third person plural. For the inflection, see 480. *E.g.*

Λύω, (λελυκ-) λέλυκα; πείθω, *persuade*, πέπεικα (for πε-πειθ-κα); κομίζω (κομιδ-), *carry*, κεκόμικα (for κε-κομιδ-κα, 73).

683. 1. The pluperfect changes final α- of the perfect stem to ε-, to which are added aoristic terminations α, ας, ε (669) in the singular, εα, εας, εε(ν) being contracted to η, ης, ει(ν) in Attic. The dual and plural add the regular secondary endings (552) to the stem in ε-, with σαν in the third person plural. *E.g.*

Ἐλελύκη, ἐλελύκης, ἐλελύκει(ν), ἐλελύκε-τον, ἐλελύκε-μεν, ἐλελύκε-τε, ἐλελύκε-σαν; στέλλω, ἔσταλκα, ἐστάλκη, ἐστάλκης, ἐστάλκει(ν), ἐστάλκε-μεν, ἐστάλκε-σαν. For ει(ν), see 58.

2. In the singular, Herodotus has the original εα, εας, εε, and Homer has εα, ης, ει(ν); later Attic writers, and sometimes the orators, have ειν, εις, ει. In the dual and plural ει for ε is not classic.

684. The stem may be modified before κ in both perfect and pluperfect, by lengthening its final vowel (635), by changing ε to ᾰ in monosyllabic liquid stems (645), by dropping ν in a few verbs (647), or by metathesis (649); as φιλέω, *love*, πεφίληκα; φθείρω (φθερ-), *destroy*, ἔφθαρκα; κρίνω (κριν-), *judge*, κέκρικα; βάλλω (βαλ-), *throw*, βέβληκα (636).

685. N. Ει of the stem becomes οι in (δείδω) δέδοικα (31).

686. N. The first perfect (or perfect in κα) belongs especially to vowel stems, and in Homer it is found only with these. It was afterwards formed from many liquid stems, and from some lingual stems, τ, δ, or θ being dropped before κα.

VI. Second Perfect System.

687. (*Second Perfect Active.*) The stem of the second perfect of the common form is the reduplicated verb stem with α affixed; as γράφ-ω, *write*, γέγραφα (stem γεγραφα-); φεύγω, *flee*, πέφευγα (642).

688. 1. For the change of ε to ο in the stem, see 643. For λέλοιπα and πέποιθα, see 642, 1, and 31.

2. For the lengthening of ᾰ to η or ᾱ in some verbs, see 644.

3. For the lengthening of the stem vowel in λαγχάνω (λαχ-), λαμβάνω (λαβ-), λανθάνω (λαθ-), τυγχάνω (τυχ-), and some other verbs, see 611.

689. N. Ἔρρωγα from ῥήγνῡμι (ῥηγ-) and εἴωθα (537, 2) from ἔθω (ἠθ-) change η of the stem to ω (31).

690. N. Vowel stems do not form second perfects; ἀκήκο-α, from ἀκού-ω, *hear* (stem ἀκου-, ἀκοϝ-), is only an apparent exception.

691. N. Homer has many second perfects not found in Attic; as προ-βέβουλα from βούλομαι, *wish*; μέμηλα from μέλω, *concern*; ἔολπα from ἔλπω, *hope*; δέδουπα from δουπέω (δουπ-), *resound*.

692. (*Aspirated Second Perfects.*) Most stems ending in π or β change these to φ, and most ending in κ or γ change these to χ, in the second perfect, *if a short vowel precedes.* Those in φ and χ make no change. *E.g.*

Βλάπτω (βλαβ-), βέβλαφα; κόπτω (κοπ-), κέκοφα; ἀλλάσσω (ἀλλαγ-), ἤλλαχα; φυλάσσω (φυλακ-), πεφύλαχα.

But πλήσσω, πέπληγα; φεύγω, πέφευγα; στέργω, ἔστοργα; λάμπω, λέλαμπα. In ἄγω (ἀγ-), ἦχα, η is lengthened by reduplication.

693. The following verbs form aspirated second perfects: ἄγω, ἀλλάσσω, ἀνοίγω, βλάπτω, δείκνῡμι, κηρύσσω, κλέπτω, κόπτω, λαμβάνω, λάπτω, λέγω (*collect*), μάσσω, πέμπω, πρᾱ́σσω, πτήσσω, τάσσω, τρέπω, τρίβω, φέρω, φυλάσσω. Of these δείκνῡμι, κηρύσσω, λαμβάνω, πέμπω, and πτήσσω are exceptions to 692. Ἀνοίγω has both ἀνέῳγα and ἀνέῳχα, and πρᾱ́σσω has both πέπρᾱχα, *have done*, and πέπρᾱγα, *fare* (*well* or *ill*).

694. N. The aspirated perfect is not found in Homer: only τέτροφα (τρέπω) occurs in tragedy, and only πέπομφα in Herodotus and Thucydides. It is common in comedy and in the subsequent prose.

695. The inflection of the second perfect of the common form is the same as that of the first perfect (see 682).

696. (*Second Pluperfect Active.*) The stem of the second pluperfect changes final α- of the second perfect stem to ε-. It has the same inflection as the first pluperfect (683). *E.g.*

Ἐπεφήνη, ἐπεφήνης, ἐπεφήνει(ν), ἐπεφήνεμεν, ἐπεφήνεσαν, etc.

697. (*Μι-forms.*) A few verbs have second perfects and pluperfects of the simple μι-form, which affix the endings directly to the verb stem. They are never found in the singular of the indicative. *E.g.*

Θνήσκω (θνα-, θαν-), *die*, 2 perf. τέθνα-τον, τέθνα-μεν, τεθνᾶσι; 2 plpf. ἐτέθνασαν. (See 508.)

These μι-forms are enumerated in 804.

VII. Perfect Middle System.

698. (*Perfect and Pluperfect Middle.*) The stem of the perfect and pluperfect middle is the reduplicated verb stem, to which the endings are directly affixed. *E.g.*

Λύω, λέλυ-μαι, λέλυ-σαι, λέλυ-ται, λέλυ-σθε, λέλυ-νται; ἐ-λελύ-μην, ἐ-λελύ-μεθα, ἐ-λέλυ-ντο; λείπω (λειπ-), λέλειμ-μαι (75), λέλειψαι, λέλειπ-ται.

For the inflection, see 480.

699. The stem may be modified (in general as in the first perfect active), by lengthening its final vowel (635), by changing ε to α in monosyllabic liquid stems (645), by dropping ν in a few verbs (647), or by metathesis (649); as φιλέ-ω, πεφίλη-μαι, ἐ-πεφιλή-μην; φθείρω (φθερ-), ἔφθαρ-μαι, ἐφθάρ-μην; κρίνω (κριν-), κέκρι-μαι, ἐ-κεκρί-μην; βάλλω (βαλ-, βλα-), βέβλη-μαι, ἐ-βεβλή-μην. (See 684.)

700. When ν is not dropped before μαι (647), it is generally replaced by σ (83), and it sometimes becomes μ (78, 2); as φαίνω (φαν-), πέφασ-μαι, ἐ-πεφάσ-μην; ὀξύνω (ὀξυν-), *sharpen*, ὤξυμ-μαι. Before endings not beginning with μ, the original ν reappears; as πέφαν-ται, πέφαν-θε; but forms in ν-σαι and ν-σο (like πέφαν-σαι, ἐ-πέφαν-σο) seem not to occur.

701. In the third person plural of the perfect and pluperfect middle, consonant stems are compelled to use the perfect participle with εἰσί and ἦσαν (486, 2).

Here, however, the Ionic endings αται and ατο for νται and ντο (777, 3) are occasionally used even in Attic prose; as τετάχ-αται and ἐτετάχ-ατο (Thucyd.) for τεταγμένοι εἰσί and ἦσαν.

702. 1. For perfects in αμμαι of στρέφω, τρέπω, τρέφω, see 646.

2. For the addition of σ to certain vowel stems before endings not beginning with σ, as τετέλεσμαι, see 640.

703. (*Future Perfect.*) The stem of the future perfect is formed by adding σ%- to the stem of the perfect middle. It ends in σομαι, and has the inflection of the future middle (662). A short final vowel is always lengthened before σομαι. *E.g.*

Λύω, λε-λῠ-, λελῡ́-σομαι; γράφ-ω, γε-γραφ-, γεγράψομαι (74); λείπω, λελειπ-, λελείψομαι; δέω, *bind*, δέδεμαι (639), δεδή-σομαι; πράσσω (πρᾱγ-), πεπρᾱγ-, πεπρᾱ́ξομαι.

704. The future perfect is generally passive in sense. But it has a middle meaning in μεμνήσομαι, *shall remember*, and πεπαύσομαι, *shall have ceased*; and it is active in κεκτήσομαι, *shall possess*. It is found in only a small number of verbs.

705. N. Two verbs have a special form in Attic Greek for the future perfect active; θνῄσκω, *die*, has τεθνήξω, *shall be dead*, formed from the perfect stem τεθνηκ-; and ἵστημι, *set*, has ἑστήξω, *shall stand*, from ἑστηκ-, stem of perfect ἕστηκα, *stand*. In Homer, we have also κεχαρήσω and κεχαρήσομαι, from χαίρω (χαρ-), *rejoice*; and κεκαδήσω (irreg.), from χάζω (χαδ-), *yield*.

706. N. In most verbs the future perfect active is expressed by the perfect participle and ἔσομαι (future of εἰμί, *be*); as ἐγνωκότες ἐσόμεθα, *we shall have learnt*. The future perfect passive may also be expressed in this way; as ἀπηλλαγμένοι ἐσόμεθα, *we shall have been freed*.

VIII. First Passive System.

707. (*First Aorist Passive.*) The stem of the first aorist passive is formed by adding θε to the stem as it appears in the perfect middle (omitting the reduplication). In the indicative and infinitive, and in the imperative except before *ντ*, *θε* becomes *θη*. It has the secondary active endings (552), and is inflected (in general) like the second aorist active in *ην* of the *μι*-form (678). *E.g.*

Λύω, λέλυ-μαι, ἐλύθην (λυθη-); λείπω, λέλειμ-μαι, ἐλείφθην (λειπ-θη-, 71); πράσσω (πρᾱγ-), πέπρᾱγμαι, ἐπρᾱ́χθην (πρᾱγ-θη-); πείθω, πέπεισ-μαι, ἐπείσ-θην; φιλέω, πεφίλη-μαι, ἐφιλήθην; πλέω (πλυ-), πέπλευσ-μαι, ἐπλεύσθην (641); τείνω (τεν-), τέτα-μαι, ἐτάθην (647); βάλλω (βαλ-, βλα-), βέβλημαι, ἐβλήθην; τελέω, τετέλεσ-μαι (640), ἐτελέσθην; ἀκούω, ἤκουσμαι, ἠκούσθην. See 480.

708. N. Τρέπω has τέτραμμαι (646), but ἐτρέφθην (Ion. ἐτράφθην); τρέφω has τέθραμμαι, ἐθρέφθην; and στρέφω has ἔστραμμαι, with (rare) ἐστρέφθην (Ion. and Dor. ἐστράφθην). Φαίνω has πέφασμαι (700), but ἐφάνθην.

709. N. Ν is added in Homer to some vowel stems before θ of the aorist passive; as ἱδρύω, *erect*, ἵδρῡμαι, ἱδρύν-θην, as if from a stem in υν (Attic ἱδρύθην). So Hom. ἐκλίνθην and ἐκρίνθην (647), from original stems in ν.

For ἐτέθην from τίθημι (θε-), and ἐτύθην from θύω, *sacrifice*, see 95, 3. For ἐθρέφθην from τρέφω, *nourish*, and other forms with interchangeable aspirates, see 95, 5.

710. (*First Future Passive.*) The stem of the first future passive adds σ%ε- to the prolonged stem (in θη) of the first aorist passive. It ends in *θησομαι*, and is inflected like the future middle (662). *E.g.*

Λύω, ἐλύθην, λυθήσομαι (stem λυθησ%ε-); λείπω, ἐλείφθην, λειφθήσομαι; πρᾱ́σσω (πρᾱγ-), ἐπρᾱ́χθην, πρᾱχθήσομαι; πείθω, ἐπείσθην, πεισθήσομαι; τείνω, ἐτάθην, ταθήσομαι; πλέκω, ἐπλέχθην, πλεχθήσομαι; τῑμάω, ἐτῑμήθην, τῑμηθήσομαι; τελέω, ἐτελέσθην, τελεσθήσομαι; κλίνω, ἐκλίθην, κλιθήσομαι.

711. The first passive system rarely appears in verbs with monosyllabic liquid stems (645). But τείνω (τεν-), *stretch* (647), has ἐτάθην and ταθήσομαι.

IX. Second Passive System.

712. (*Second Aorist Passive.*) The stem of the second aorist passive is formed by adding *ε* to the verb stem (in the second class, to the *weak* stem, 31). In the indicative, infinitive, and imperative, except before *ντ* (707), *ε* becomes *η*. The only regular modification of the stem is the change of *ε* to *α* (645). For the inflection, see 482. *E.g.*

Βλάπτω (βλαβ-), *hurt*, ἐβλάβην; γράφω (γραφ-), *write*, ἐγράφην; ῥίπτω (ῥιφ-), *throw*, ἐρρίφην; φαίνω (φαν-), ἐφάνην; στρέφω, *turn*, ἐστράφην (646); τέρπω, *amuse*, ἐτάρπην; στέλλω (στελ-), *send*, ἐστάλην.

713. N. Πλήσσω (πληγ-), *strike*, has 2 aor. pass. ἐπλήγην, but in composition ἐξ-επλάγην and κατ-επλάγην (from stem πλαγ-).

714. N. Some verbs have both passive aorists; as βλάπτω (βλαβ-), *hurt*, ἐβλάφθην and ἐβλάβην; στρέφω, *turn*, ἐστρέφθην (rare) and ἐστράφην (646). Τρέπω, *turn*, has all the six aorists: ἔτρεψα, ἐτρεψάμην, ἔτραπον (epic and lyric), ἐτραπόμην, ἐτρέφθην, ἐτράπην.

715. (*Second Future Passive.*) The stem of the second future passive adds σ°/ε- to the prolonged stem (in η) of the second aorist passive. It ends in ησομαι and is inflected like the first future (710). *E.g.*

Βλάπτω (βλαβ-), ἐβλάβην, βλαβή-σομαι; γράφω, ἐγράφην, γραφή-σομαι; φαίνω (φαν-), ἐφάνην, φανή-σομαι; στέλλω (στελ-), ἐστάλην, σταλή-σομαι; στρέφω, ἐστράφην, στραφή-σομαι.

716. N. The weak stem of verbs of the second class, which seldom appears in other tenses than the second aorists (642), is seen especially in the second passive system; as σήπω (σαπ-), *corrupt*, ἐσάπην, σαπήσομαι; τήκω (τακ-), *melt*, ἐτάκην; ῥέω (ῥυ-), *flow*, ἐρρύην, ῥυήσομαι; ἐρείπω (ἐριπ-), *throw down*, ἠρίπην (poetic), but 1 aor. ἠρείφθην (ἐρειπ-).

717. The following table shows the nine tense stems (so far as they exist) of λύω, λείπω, πράσσω (πρᾱγ-), φαίνω (φαν-), and στέλλω (στελ-), with their sub-divisions.

Tense System.						
Present.		λῡ°/ε-	λειπ°/ε-	πρᾱσσ°/ε-	φαιν°/ε-	στελλ°/ε-
Future.		λῡσ°/ε-	λειψ°/ε-	πρᾱξ°/ε-	φανε°/ε-	στελε°/ε-
1 *Aorist.*		λῡσα-		πρᾱξα-	φηνα-	στειλα-
2 *Aorist.*			λιπ°/ε-			
1 *Perfect.*		λελυκα-			πεφαγκα-	ἐσταλκα-
2 *Perfect.*			λελοιπα-	πεπρᾱγα- / πεπρᾱχα-	πεφηνα-	
Perf. Mid.	Perf.	λελυ-	λελειπ-	πεπρᾱγ-	πεφαν-	ἐσταλ-
	Fut. P.	λελῡσ°/ε-	λελειψ°/ε-	πεπρᾱξ°/ε-		
1 *Pass.*	Aor.	λυθε(η)-	λειφθε(η)-	πρᾱχθε(η)-	φανθε(η)-	
	Fut.	λυθησ°/ε-	λειφθησ°/ε-	πρᾱχθησ°/ε-	φανθησ°/ε-	
2 *Pass.*	Aor.				φανε(η)-	σταλε(η)-
	Fut.				φανησ°/ε-	σταλησ°/ε-

FORMATION OF THE DEPENDENT MOODS AND THE PARTICIPLE.

SUBJUNCTIVE.

718. The subjunctive has the primary endings (552) in all its tenses. In all forms (even in verbs in μι) it has a long thematic vowel ω/η (561, 2).

719. (*Common Form.*) In the common form of inflection, the present and second aorist tense stems change ο/ε to ω/η, and the first aorist tense stem changes final α to ω/η. All have ω, ῃς, ῃ in the singular, and ωσι for ωνσι (78, 3) in the third person plural, of the active. *E.g.*

Λείπω, pres. subj. λείπω, λείπωμαι, 2 aor. λίπω, λίπωμαι; λύω, 1 aor. λύσω, λύσωμαι.

720. A perfect subjunctive active is rarely formed, on the analogy of the present, by changing final α of the tense stem to ω/η; as λέλυκα, λελύκω; εἴληφα, εἰλήφω. (See 731.) But the more common form of the tense is the perfect active participle with ὦ (subjunctive of εἰμί, *be*); as λελυκὼς ὦ, εἰληφὼς ὦ.

721. The perfect subjunctive middle is almost always expressed by the perfect middle participle and ὦ; as λελυμένος ὦ, ᾖς, ᾖ, etc.

722. A few verbs with vowel stems form a perfect subjunctive middle directly, by adding ω/η to the tense stem; as κτά-ομαι, *acquire*, pf. κέκτημαι, *possess*, subj. κεκτῶμαι (for κε-κτη-ωμαι), κεκτῇ, κεκτῆται; so μιμνῄσκω, *remind*, μέμνημαι, *remember* (*memini*), subj. μεμνῶμαι, μεμνώμεθα (Hdt. μεμνεώμεθα). These follow the analogy of ἱστῶμαι, -ῇ, -ῆται, etc. (724). (For a similar optative, see 734.)

723. (Μι-*form.*) In all μι-forms, including both passive aorists (564), the final vowel of the stem is contracted with the thematic vowel (ω or η), so that the subjunctive ends in ῶ or ῶμαι.

724. 1. Verbs in ημι (with stems in ε- and α-) have ῶ, ῇς, ῇ, ῶμαι, ῇ, ῆται, etc., in the subjunctive, as if all had stems in ε. Thus ἵστημι (στα-) has ἱστῇς, ἱστῇ, ἱστῆται, στῇς, στῇ, etc., as if the uncontracted form were ἱστε-ω, not ἱστα-ω. These verbs have Ionic stems in ε- (see 788, 1).

2. The inflection is that of the subjunctives φιλῶ and φιλῶμαι (492).

725. For the inflection of the aorist passive subjunctive, with ε of the tense stem contracted with ω or η, as λυθῶ (for λυθέ-ω), λυθῶμεν (for λυθέ-ωμεν), etc., φανῶ (for φανέ-ω), etc., see 480, 3.

726. For a few subjunctives of the simple perfect of the μι-form, as ἑστῶ (for ἑστα-ω), βεβῶσι (for βεβα-ωσι), see 508.

727. Verbs in ωμι (with stem in ο) have by contraction ῶ, ῷς, ῷ, etc., ῶμαι, ῷ, ῶται, etc. (for ο-ω, ο-ῃς, ο-ῃ, ο-ωμαι, etc.); as δίδωμι, subj. διδῶ, διδῷς, διδῷ; διδῶμαι, διδῷ, διδῶται, etc.

728. Verbs in νῡμι form the subjunctive (as the optative, 743) like verbs in ω; as δείκνῡμι, subj. δεικνύ-ω, δεικνύ-ωμαι.

729. N. Δύναμαι, *can*, ἐπίσταμαι, *understand*, κρέμαμαι, *hang*, and the second aorist ἐπριάμην, *bought*, accent the subjunctive (as the optative, 742) as if there were no contraction; thus δύνωμαι, ἐπίστωμαι, κρέμωμαι, πρίωμαι (compare τιθῶμαι).

OPTATIVE.

730. 1. The optative adds the secondary endings (552) to the tense stem, preceded by the mood suffix (562) ι or ιη (ιε); as λύοιτε (for λῡο-ι-τε), ἱσταίην (for ἱστα-ιη-ν), λυθεῖεν (for λυθε-ιε-ν). For the ending μι, see 731.

2. The form ιη appears only before active endings. It is always used in the *singular* of μι-forms with these endings (including the aorist passive, 564, 7) and of contracted presents in οιην and ῳην of verbs in αω, εω, and οω. After ιη the first person singular always has the ending ν. See examples in 737 and 739.

3. Before the ending ν of the third person plural ιε is always used; as λύοιεν (for λῡο-ιε-ν).

4. In the second person singular middle, σο drops σ (564, 6); as ἱσταῖο (for ἱστα-ι-σο, ἱστα-ι-ο).

731. (*Verbs in* ω.) Verbs in ω have the ending μι (for ν) in the first person singular in all tenses of the active voice. In the present, future, and second aorist systems, the thematic vowel (always ο) is contracted with ι to οι, giving οιμι, οις, οι, etc., οιμην, οιο, οιτο, etc. In the first aorist system, final α of the tense stem is contracted with ι, giving αιμι, αις, αι, etc. (but see 732), αιμην, αιο, αιτο, etc. The rare perfect active (like the subjunctive, 720) follows the analogy of the present. *E.g.*

Λέγοιμι (for λεγο-ι-μι), λέγοις (for λεγο-ι-ς), λέγοι (for λεγο-ι), λέγοιτε (for λεγο-ι-τε), λέγοιεν (for λεγο-ιε-ν). Λείπω, 2 aor. λίποιμι (for λιπο-ι-μι), λίποιεν (for λιπο-ιε-ν). Λῡ́σαιμι (for λῡσα-ι-μι), λῡ́σαιμεν (for λῡσα-ι-μεν), λῡσαίμην (for λῡσα-ι-μην), λῡ́σαισθε (for λῡσα-ι-σθε). Perf. εἴληφα, opt. εἰλήφοιμι, etc.

732. The Attic generally uses the so-called Aeolic terminations ειας, ειε, and ειαν, for αις, αι, αιεν, in the aorist active; as λῡ́σειας, λῡ́σειε, λῡ́σειαν. See λῡ́ω and φαίνω in 480, 1 and 482.

733. The perfect middle is almost always expressed by the perfect middle participle and εἴην; as λελυμένος εἴην (see 480, 2). The perfect active is more frequently expressed by the perfect active participle and εἴην than by the form in οιμι given in the paradigms; as λελυκὼς εἴην. (See 720; 721.)

734. 1. A few verbs with vowel stems form a perfect optative middle (like the subjunctive, 722) directly, by adding ι-μην or ο-ι-μην to the tense stem; as κτάομαι, pf. κέκτη-μαι, opt. κεκτῄμην, κεκτῇο, κεκτῇτο (for κεκτη-ι-μην, κεκτη-ι-ο, κεκτη-ι-το), etc.; also κεκτῴμην, κεκτῷο, κεκτῷτο (for κεκτη-ο-ι-μην, etc.); so μιμνῄσκω, μέμνημαι, opt. μεμνῄμην or μεμνῴμην; καλέω, κέκλημαι, opt. κεκλῄμην, κεκλῇο, κεκλῄμεθα; and βάλλω, βέβλημαι, opt. δια-βεβλῇσθε. So Hom. λελῦτο or λελῦντο (for λελυ-ι-το or λελυ-ι-ντο), perf. opt. of λῡ́ω. Compare δαινῦτο, pres. opt. of δαίνῡμι.

2. The forms in ῳμην belong to the common form of inflection (with the thematic vowel); those in ῃμην, etc. and ῦτο have the μι-form (740).

735. A few verbs have οιην (737) in the second perfect optative; as ἐκπέφευγα, ἐκπεφευγοίην.

The second aorist optative of ἔχω, *have*, is σχοίην, but the regular σχοῖμι is used in composition.

736. A very few relics remain of an older active optative with ν for μι in the first person singular; as τρέφοι-ν for τρέφοι-μι, ἁμάρτοι-ν for ἁμάρτοι-μι (from ἁμαρτάνω).

737. (*Contract Verbs.*) In the present active of contract verbs, forms in ιη-ν, ιη-ς, ιη, etc., contracted with the thematic vowel ο to οιην, οιης, οιη, etc., are much more common in the *singular* than the regular forms in οιμι, οις, οι, but they seldom occur in the dual and plural. Both the forms in οιην and those in οιμι are again contracted with an α of the verb stem to ῳην and ῳμι, and with an ε or ο to οιην and οιμι. *E.g.*

Τῑμα-ο-ιη-ν, τῑμα-οίην, τῑμῴην; φιλε-ο-ιη-ν, φιλε-οίην, φιλοίην; δηλο-ο-ιη-ν, δηλο-οίην, δηλοίην; τῑμα-ο-ι-μι, τῑμά-οιμι, τῑμῷμι; φιλε-ο-ι-μι, φιλέ-οιμι, φιλοῖμι; δηλο-ο-ι-μι, δηλο-οιμι, δηλοῖμι. (See the inflection in 492.)

It is only the second contraction which makes these *contract* forms.

738. For the optative ῥῑγῴην, from ῥῑγόω, *shiver*, see 497.

739. (Μι-*form.*) 1. The present and second aorist active of the μι-form, and both aorists passive in all verbs, have the suffix ιη, and in the first person singular the ending ν. Here α, ε, or ο of the stem is contracted with ιη to αιη, ειη, or οιη; as ἱστα-ιη-ν, ἱσταίην; στα-ιη-μεν, σταίημεν; λυθε-ιη-ν, λυθείην; δο-ιη-ν, δοίην.

2, In the dual and plural, forms with ι for ιη, and ιε-ν for ιη-σαν in the third person plural, are much more common than the longer forms with ιη; as σταῖμεν, σταῖτε, σταῖεν (better than σταίημεν, σταίητε, σταίησαν). See 506.

740. In the present and second aorist middle of verbs in ημι and ωμι, final α, ε, or ο of the stem is contracted with ι into αι, ει, or οι, to which the simple endings μην, etc., are added. *E.g.*

Ἱσταίμην (for ἱστα-ι-μην), ἱσταῖο, ἱσταῖτο; θείμην (θε-ι-μην), θεῖο (θε-ι-σο, θε-ι-ο), θεῖτο; δοίμην (δο-ι-μην). See the inflection in 506; and 730, 4. See also the cases of perfect optative middle in ῃμην and ῡτο in 734.

741. N. The optatives τιθοίμην, τιθοῖο, τιθοῖτο, etc. (also accented τίθοιο, τίθοιτο, etc.) and (in composition) θοίμην, θοῖο, θοῖτο, etc. (also accented σύν-θοιτο, πρόσ-θοισθε, etc.), as if formed from τιθέω (or τιθω), are found, as well as the regular τιθείμην θείμην, etc. See also πρόοιτο and other forms of ἵημι (810, 2).

742. N. Δύναμαι, ἐπίσταμαι, κρέμαμαι, and the second aorists ἐπριάμην (505) and ὠνήμην (from ὀνίνημι), accent the optative as if there were no contraction; δυναίμην, δύναιο, δύναιτο; ἐπίσταιτο, ἐπίσταισθε, κρέμαιο, πρίαιο, πρίαιντο, ὄναισθε. For the similar subjunctives, see 729.

743. Verbs in νῡμι form the optative (as the subjunctive, 728) like verbs in ω; as δείκνῡμι, opt. δεικνύοιμι, δεικνυοίμην (inflected like λύοιμι, λῡοίμην).

744. N. Second aorists from stems in υ of the μι-form (as ἔδυν) have no optative in Attic (see 506). But Homer has a few forms like δύη, δῦμεν (for δυ-ιη, δυ-ι-μεν), from ἔδυν.

745. A few second perfect optatives of the μι-form are made by adding ιη-ν to stems in α-; as τεθναίην (for τεθνα-ιη-ν), ἑσταίην (508). See the enumeration of μι-forms, 804.

IMPERATIVE.

746. (*Common Form.*) The present and the second aorist active and middle of the common form have the thematic vowel ε (ο before ντων), to which the imperative endings (553) are affixed. But the second person singular in the active has no ending; in the middle it drops σ in σο and contracts ε-ο to ου. *E.g.*

Λεῖπε, λειπέ-τω, λείπε-τον, λειπέ-των, λείπε-τε, λειπό-ντων; λείπου, λειπέ-σθω, λείπε-σθον, λειπέ-σθων, λείπε-σθε, λειπέ-σθων. So λίπε and λιποῦ.

747. The first aorist active and middle are also irregular in the second person singular, where the active has a termination ον and the middle αι for final α of the stem. In other persons they add the regular endings to the stem in σα- (or α-). *E.g.*

Λῦσον, λυσά-τω, λύσα-τον, λυσά-των, λύσα-τε, λυσά-ντων; λῦσαι, λυσά-σθω, λύσα-σθε, λυσά-σθων. Φῆνον, φηνά-τω, etc.; φῆναι, φηνά-σθω, φήνα-σθε, φηνά-σθων.

748. The perfect active is very rare, except in a few cases of the μι-form (508) with a present meaning. But Aristophanes has κεκράγετε, *screech*, from κράζω (κραγ-), and κεχήνετε, *gape*, from χάσκω (χαν-).

749. The third person singular of the perfect passive is the only form of perfect imperative in common use; for this see 1274.

750. N. The second person singular of the middle occasionally occurs as an emphatic form; as πέπαυσο, *stop!*

751. N. The perfect imperative in all voices can be expressed by the perfect participle and ἴσθι, ἔστω, etc. (imperative of εἰμί, *be*); as εἰρημένον ἔστω, for εἰρήσθω, *let it have been said* (i.e. *let what has been said stand*), πεπεισμένοι ἔστων, *suppose them to have been persuaded.*

752. (*Mι-form.*) The present imperative of the μι-form retains θι in the second person singular active only in a few primitive verbs; as in φα-θί from φημί (φα-), *say*, ἴ-θι from εἶμι (ἰ-), *go*, ἴσ-θι from εἰμί, *be*, and from οἶδα, *know*. (See 806; 808; 812; 820.)

For Homeric forms in θι, see 790.

753. The present active commonly omits θι in the second person, and lengthens the preceding vowel of the stem (α, ε, ο, or υ) to η, ει, ου, or ῡ; as ἵστη, τίθει, δίδου, and δείκνῡ. The other persons add the regular endings (553) to the short stem; as ἱστά-τω, ἵστα-τε, ἱστά-ντων; τιθέ-τω; δίδο-τε; δεικνύ-ντων.

754. The present middle of verbs in ημι and ωμι has the regular form in σο, and also poetic forms in ω (for ασο) and ου (for εσο and οσο), in the second person singular; as ἵστασο or ἵστω, τίθεσο or τίθου, δίδοσο or δίδου. But verbs in ῡμι always retain υσο; as δείκνῡμι, δείκνυσο. In the other persons the inflection is regular: see the paradigms (506).

755. 1. In the second aorist active the stem vowel is regularly long (η, ω, ῡ), except before ντων (553), and θι is retained in the second person singular. *E.g.*

Στῆ-θι (στα-), στή-τω, στῆ-τε, στά-ντων; βῆ-θι (βα-), βή-τω, βῆ-τε, βά-ντων; γνῶ-θι, γνώ-τω, γνῶ-τε, γνό-ντων; δῦ-θι, δύ-τω, δῦ-τε, δύ-ντων. (See 678 and 766, 2.)

2. But we have ς for θι in θές (from τί-θημι), δός (from δίδωμι), ἕς (from ἵημι), and σχές (from ἔσχον, 2 aor. of ἔχω). These verbs have the short vowel in all persons; as θές, θέ-τω, θέ-τε, θέ-ντων; δός, δό-τω, δό-τε, δό-ντων.

3. Στῆθι and βῆθι have poetic forms στᾰ and βᾰ, used only in composition; as κατά-βᾱ, *come down*, παρά-στᾱ, *stand near*.

756. 1. In the second aorist middle, σο drops σ in the second person singular after a short vowel, and contracts that vowel with ο. *E.g.*

Ἐπριάμην, πρίασο (poet.), πρίω (for πρια-ο), ἐθέμην, θοῦ (for θε-σο, θε-ο); ἐδόμην, δοῦ (for δο-σο, δο-ο). But epic δέξο (δεχ-σο), λέξο (λεχ-σο).

2. The other persons have the regular endings (553); as πριά-σθω; θέ-σθω, θέ-σθων; δό-σθω, δό-σθε, δό-σθων.

757. 1. The first aorist passive adds the ordinary active endings (θι, τω, etc.) directly to θε- (θη-) of the tense stem (707) after which θι becomes τι (95, 2); as λύθη-τι, λυθή-τω, etc.

2. The second aorist passive adds the same terminations

to ε- (η-) of the tense stem (712), θι being retained; as φάνη-θι, φανή-τω; στάλη-θι, σταλή-τω, etc.

3. Both aorists have ε-ντων in the third person plural; as λυθέ-ντων, φανέ-ντων, σταλέ-ντων.

758. N. A few second perfects of the μι-form have imperatives in θι: see θνήσκω, τέθναθι, and δείδω, δέδιθι, in 804.

INFINITIVE.

759. (*Common Form.*) The present, second aorist, and future active add εν to the tense stem, the thematic vowel (here always ε-) being contracted with εν to ειν; as λέγειν (for λεγ-ε-εν), ἰδεῖν (for ἰδ-έ-εν), λέξειν (for λεξ-ε-εν).

760. N. The ending εν (without preceding ε) appears in Doric; as γᾱρύ-εν in Pindar (Attic γηρύειν).

761. N. For contract presents in ᾶν (not ᾷν) for άειν, and οῦν for όειν, see 39, 5.

762. N. The second aorist in εῖν is probably contracted from έ-εν, not from έ-ειν (759).

763. The first aorist active substitutes αι (of uncertain origin) for final α of the tense stem (669); as λῦσαι, φῆναι.

764. The perfect active substitutes ε-ναι for final α of the tense stem; as λελυκ-έ-ναι, γεγραφ-έ-ναι, πεφην-έ-ναι, λελοιπ-έ-ναι.

765. 1. The infinitive middle adds σθαι to the tense stem in the present, future, and first and second aorists. *E.g.*

Λέγε-σθαι, λέξε-σθαι, φαίνε-σθαι, φανεῖ-σθαι (for φανέε-σθαι), φήνα-σθαι, λῡσα-σθαι, λιπέ-σθαι.

2. Both passive futures likewise add σθαι. *E.g.*

Λυθήσε-σθαι, λειφθήσε-σθαι, φανήσε-σθαι, σταλήσε-σθαι.

3. For the perfect middle and the passive aorists, see 766, 1; 768.

766. (Μι-*forms.*) 1. The present, second aorist, and second perfect active of the μι-form, and both passive aorists, add ναι to the tense stem in the infinitive. *E.g.*

Ἱστά-ναι, τιθέ-ναι, διδό-ναι, δεικνύ-ναι, στῆ-ναι, γνῶ-ναι, δῦ-ναι, τεθνά-ναι, λυθῆ-ναι (707), φανῆ-ναι (712).

2. In the second aorist active the final vowel of the stem is regularly long (678; 755, 1); as ἵστημι (στα-), στῆ-ναι; ἔβην (βα-), βῆ-ναι.

767. Some μι-forms have the more primitive ending εναι (for ϝεναι) in the infinitive active. Such are δοῦναι (from old δο-ϝεναι, δο-εναι); θεῖναι (for θε-ϝεναι); εἶναι, 2 aor. of ἵημι (for ἑ-ϝεναι); 2 perf. δεδιέναι (for δε-δϝι-ϝεναι).

768. In all the simple forms of the middle voice (the present and second aorist of the μι-form, and all perfects), vowel stems add σθαι directly to the tense stem. *E.g.*

Ἵστα-σθαι, τίθε-σθαι, δίδο-σθαι, θέ-σθαι, δό-σθαι, ἕ-σθαι (from ἵημι); λελύ-σθαι, τετῑμῆ-σθαι, δεδηλῶ-σθαι, δεδό-σθαι, πτά-σθαι (from πέτο-μαι, πτα-).

769. Consonant stems here (768) add the more primitive ending θαι (554). *E.g.*

Ἐστάλ-θαι, λελεῖφ-θαι (71), πεπλέχ-θαι, τετρῖφ-θαι, πεφάν-θαι. So ἧσ-θαι, pres. inf. of ἧμαι (ἡσ-), *sit*.

PARTICIPLES AND VERBALS IN τος AND τεος.

770. All active tenses (except the perfect) and both aorists passive add ντ to their tense stem to form the stem of the participle. Stems in οντ of the common form have nominatives in ων; those of the μι-form have nominatives in ους. *E.g.*

Λέγω: pres. λεγο-ντ-, nom. λέγων; fut. λεξο-ντ-, nom. λέξων; 1 aor. λεξα-ντ-, nom. λέξᾱς. Φαίνω: aor. φηνα-ντ-, nom. φήνᾱς. Λείπω: 2 aor. λιπο-ντ-, nom. λιπών; 1 aor. pass. λειφθε-ντ-, nom. λειφθείς (79). Στέλλω (σταλ-): 2 aor. pass. σταλε-ντ-, nom. σταλείς. Ἵστημι: pres. ἱστα-ντ-, nom. ἱστάς, 2 aor. στα-ντ-, nom. στάς. Τίθημι: pres. τιθε-ντ-, nom. τιθείς; 2 aor. θε-ντ-, nom. θείς. Δίδωμι: pres. διδο-ντ-, nom. διδούς; 2 aor. δο-ντ-, nom. δούς. Δείκνῡμι: δεικνυ-ντ-, nom. δεικνύς. Δύνω: 2 aor. δυ-ντ-, nom. δύς.

771. For the inflection of these participles and the formation of the feminines, see 335–337.

772. The perfect active participle changes final α of the tense stem to οτ in the stem of the participle. *E.g.*

Λελυκα-, λελυκοτ-, nom. λελυκώς; πεφηνα-, πεφηνοτ-, nom. πεφηνώς.

For the inflection, and for the irregular feminine in υια, see 335; 337, 2.

773. N. Homer has many varieties of the second perfect participle of the μι-form; in αώς, gen. αῶτος (sometimes αότος), fem. αυῖα, as γεγαώς, βεβαώς; in ηώς, gen. ηῶτος or ηότος, fem. ηυῖα, as τεθνηώς, τεθνηῶτος or -ότος, τεθνηυῖα (804). Herodotus has εώς, εῶσα, εός, gen. εῶτος, εώσης, as ἑστεώς, etc., some forms of which (*e.g.* ἑστεῶτα, τεθνεῶτι) occur in Homer. The Attic contracts αώς, αῶσα, αός, to ώς, ῶσα, ός (or ώς) (342), gen. ῶτος, ώσης, etc., but leaves τεθνεώς (2 perfect of θνήσκω) uncontracted.

774. N. The stem of the feminine of the second perfect participle in Homer often has a short vowel when the other genders have a long one; as ἀρηρώς, ἀρᾰρυῖα; τεθηλώς, τεθᾰλυῖα.

775. All tenses of the middle voice add μενο to the tense stem to form the stem of the participle. *E.g.*

Λῡόμενος (λῡό-μενο-), λῡσόμενος (λῡσο-μενο-), λῡσάμενος (λῡσα-μενο-), ἱστάμενος (ἱστα-μενο-), θέμενος (θε-μενο-), πριάμενος (πρια-μενο-), λιπόμενος (λιπο-μενο-), λελυμένος (λελυ-μενο-).

For the inflection of participles in μενος, see 301.

776. 1. The stem of the verbals in τος and τεος is formed by adding το or τεο to the verb stem, which generally has the same form as in the first aorist passive (with the change of φ and χ to π and κ, 71); as λυτός, λυτέος (stems λυ-το-, λυ-τεο-), aor. pass. ἐλύθην; τρῑπτός, πειστέος (stems τρῑπ-το-, πεισ-τεο-), aor. pass. ἐτρίφθην, ἐπείσθην; τακτός, τακτέος, from τάσσω (stem ταγ-), aor. pass. ἐτάχ-θην; θρεπτός from τρέφω (95, 5).

2. The verbal in τος is sometimes equivalent to a perfect passive participle, as κριτός, *decided*, τακτός, *ordered*; but oftener it expresses *capability*, as λυτός, *capable of being loosed*, ἀκουστός, *audible*; πρᾱκτός, *that may be done.*

3. The verbal in τεος is equivalent to a future passive participle (the Latin participle in *dus*); as λυτέος, *that must be loosed, solvendus*; τῑμητέος, *to be honored, honorandus.* (See 1594.)

For the impersonal use of the neuter in τεον in the sense of δεῖ and the infinitive active, see 1597.

DIALECTIC AND POETIC FORMS OF VERBS IN Ω.

777. 1. The Doric has the personal endings τι for σι, μες for μεν, τᾱν for την, σθᾱν for σθην, μᾱν for μην, ντι for νσι. The poets have μεσθα for μεθα.

2. When σ is dropped in σαι and σο of the second person (565, 6), Homer often keeps the uncontracted forms εαι, ηαι, αο, εο. Herodotus has εαι and αο (indic.), but generally ῃ for ηαι (subj.). In Hdt. and sometimes in Homer, εο may become ευ. In Homer σαι and σο sometimes drop σ even in the perf. and pluperf.; as

μέμνῃαι for μέμνησαι, ἔσσυο for ἔσσυσο. A lingual sometimes becomes σ before σαι; as in κέκασσαι for κεκαδ-σαι (κέκασμαι).

For Ionic contract forms, see 785, 2.

3. The Ionic has αται and ατο for νται and ντο in the third person plural of the perfect and pluperfect, and ατο for ντο in the optative. Before these endings π, β, κ, and γ are aspirated (φ, χ); as κρύπτω (κρυβ-), κεκρύφ-αται; λέγω, λελέχ-αται, λελέχ-ατο. Hdt. shortens η to ε before αται and ατο; as οἰκέ-αται (pf. of οἰκέω), Att. ᾤκη-νται; ἐτετῑμέ-ατο (plpf. of τῑμάω), Att. ἐτετίμη-ντο. Hom. rarely inserts δ between the vowel of a stem and αται or ατο; as ἐληλέ-δατο (ἐλαύνω); see also ῥαίνω.

The forms αται and ατο sometimes occur in Attic (701). Herodotus has them also in the present and imperfect of verbs in μι.

4. Herodotus has εα, εας, εε(ν) in the pluperfect active, as ἐτεθήπεα; whence comes the older and better Attic η, ης, ει(ν). Homer has εα, ης, ει(ν), with εε in ᾔδεε (821, 2), and rarely ον, ες, ε.

5. Homer and Herodotus generally have the uncontracted forms of the future (in εω and εομαι) of liquid stems; as μενέω, Attic μενῶ. When they are contracted, they follow the analogy of verbs in εω.

6. The Doric has σέω, σέομαι (contracted σῶ, σοῦμαι or σεῦμαι) for σω, σομαι in the future. The Attic has σοῦμαι in the future middle of a few verbs (666).

7. In Homer σ is sometimes doubled after a short vowel in the future and aorist; as τελέω, τελέσσω; καλέω, ἐκάλεσσα. In κομίζω, Hom. ἐκόμισσα, ἐκομισσάμην, the stem ends in δ (see 777, 2).

8. In Homer aorists with σ sometimes have the inflection of second aorists; as ἷξον, ἷξες, from ἱκνέομαι, *come*; ἐβήσετο (more common than ἐβήσατο), from βαίνω, *go*. These are called *mixed* aorists.

9. In the poets ησαν of the aorist passive indicative often becomes εν; as ὥρμηθεν for ὡρμήθησαν, from ὁρμάω, *urge*. So ἄν or εν for ησαν or εσαν in the active of verbs in μι (787, 4).

778. Homer and Herodotus have *iterative* forms in σκον and σκομην in the imperfect and second aorist active and middle. Homer has them also in the first aorist. These are added to the tense stem; as ἔχω, impf. ἔχε-σκον; ἐρύω, 1 aor. ἐρύσα-σκε; φεύγω, 2 aor. (φυγ-) φύγε-σκον; ἵστημι (στα-), στά-σκε; δίδωμι (δο-), δό-σκε. Verbs in εω have εε-σκον or ε-σκον in the imperfect; as καλέε-σκον; πωλέ-σκετο (dropping one ε). Verbs in αω have αασκον or ασκον; as γοάα-σκε, νικά-σκομεν. Rarely other verbs have ασκον in the imperfect; as κρύπτασκον from κρύπτω.

These forms are inflected like imperfects, and are confined to the indicative, and denote *repetition;* as πωλέσκετο, *he went* (regularly). They generally (in Hdt. always) omit the augment.

For μι-forms with these endings see 787, 5.

779. Some verbs have poetic stems, made by adding θ%ε- to the present or the second aorist tense stem, in which α or ε (rarely υ) takes the place of the thematic vowel; as ἀμῡναθ%ε-, διωκαθ%ε-, φλεγεθ%ε-, from ἀμύνω, *ward off,* διώκω, *pursue,* φλέγω, *burn.* From these special forms are derived, — sometimes presents, as φλεγέθω; sometimes imperfects, as ἐδιώκαθον; sometimes second aorists, as ἔσχεθον (σχεθ%ε-); also subjunctives and optatives, as εἰκάθω, εἰκάθοιμι, ἀμυνάθοιτο; imperatives, as ἀμυνάθατε, ἀμυνάθου; infinitives, as ἀμυνάθειν, διωκάθειν, εἰκάθειν, σχεθεῖν; and participles, as εἰκάθων, σχεθών. As few of these stems form a present indicative, many scholars consider ἐδιώκαθον, ἔργαθον, etc., with the subjunctives, etc., second aorists, and accent the infinitives and participles διωκαθεῖν, ἀμυναθεῖν, εἰκαθεῖν, εἰκαθών, etc., although the traditional accent is on the penult.

See in the Lexicon ἀλκάθειν, ἀμυνάθω, διωκάθω, εἰκάθειν, ἐργάθειν, ἠερέθομαι, ἠγερέθομαι, μετακιάθω, σχέθω, φθινύθω, φλεγέθω.

780. (*Subjunctive.*) 1. In Homer the subjunctive (especially in the first aor. act. and mid.) often has the short thematic vowels ε and ο (Attic η and ω), yet never in the singular of the active voice nor in the third person plural; as ἐρύσσομεν, ἀλγήσετε, μυθήσομαι, εὔξεαι, δηλήσεται, ἀμείψεται, ἐγείρομεν, ἱμείρεται. So sometimes in Pindar.

2. In both aorist passive subjunctives Herodotus generally has the uncontracted forms in εω, εωμεν, εωσι, but contracts εη and εῃ to η and ῃ; as ἀφαιρεθέω (Att. -θῶ), φανέωσι (Att. -ῶσι), but φανῇ and φανῆτε (as in Attic).

3. In the second aorist passive subjunctive of some verbs, Homer has forms in ειω, ῃης, ῃῃ, ειομεν, ηετε (780, 1), as they are commonly written; as δαμείω (from ἐδάμην, 2 aor. pass. of δαμνάω, *subdue*), δαμήῃς, δαμήῃ, δαμήετε; τραπείομεν (from ἐτάρπην, of τέρπω, *amuse*). It is highly probable that η should be written for ει in all persons. This is more fully developed in the second aorist active of the μι-form (see 788, 2).

4. In the subjunctive active Homer often has ωμι, ῃσθα, ῃσι; as ἐθέλωμι, ἐθέλῃσθα, ἐθέλῃσι.

781. (*Optative.*) 1. The so-called Aeolic forms of the first aorist optative active in ειας, ειε, ειαν are the common forms in all dialects.

2. Homer sometimes has *οισθα* (556, 1) in the second person for *οις*; as *κλαίοισθα*. For *ατο* (for *ντο*) see 777, 3.

782. (*Infinitive.*) 1. Homer often has *μεναι* and *μεν* for *εν* (759) in the infinitive active; as *ἀμῡνέμεναι, ἀμῡνέμεν* (Attic *ἀμῡ́νειν*); *ἐλθέμεναι, ἐλθέμεν* (*ἐλθεῖν*); *ἀξέμεναι, ἀξέμεν* (*ἄξειν*). For the perfect (only of the *μι*-form), see 791: the perf. in *έναι* does not occur in Homer. So Hom. *μεναι*, Dor. *μεν* for *ναι* in the aorist passive; as *ὁμοιωθή-μεναι* (*ὁμοιωθῆ-ναι*), *δαή-μεναι* (also *δαῆ-ναι*), Hom.; *αἰσχυνθῆ-μεν* (*αἰσχυνθῆ-ναι*), Pind. (See 784, 5.)

2. The Doric has *εν* (760) and the Aeolic *ην* for *ειν* in the infin.; thus *ἀεῖδεν* and *γᾱρύεν* (Dor.) for *ἀείδειν* and *γηρύειν*; *φέρην* and *ἔχην* (Aeol.) for *φέρειν* and *ἔχειν*; *εἴπην* (Aeol.) for *εἰπεῖν*.

783. (*Participle.*) The Aeolic has *οισα* for *ουσα*, and *αις*, *αισα* for *ᾱς*, *ᾱσα*, in the participle; as *ἔχοισα, θρέψαις, θρέψαισα*.

SPECIAL DIALECTIC FORMS OF CONTRACT VERBS.

784. (*Verbs in αω.*) 1. In Homer verbs in *αω* are often contracted as in Attic. In a few cases they remain uncontracted; sometimes without change, as *ναιετάουσι, ναιετάων*, from *ναιετάω*, *dwell*; sometimes with *ᾱ*, as in *πεινάω*, *hunger*, *διψάω*, *thirst*; sometimes with *εον* for *ᾰον* in the imperfect, as *μενοίνεον* from *μενοινάω*, *long for*.

2. (*a*) The Mss. of Homer often give peculiar forms of verbs in *αω*, by which the two vowels (or the vowel and diphthong) which elsewhere are contracted are *assimilated*, so as to give a double A or a double O sound.[1] The second syllable, if it is short by nature or has a diphthong with a short initial vowel, is generally prolonged; sometimes the former syllable; rarely both. We thus have *αᾱ* (sometimes *ᾱα*) for *αε* or *αη* (*αᾳ* for *αει* or *αῃ*), and *οω* (sometimes *ωο* or *ωω*) for *αο* or *αω* (*οῳ* for *αοι*):

ὁράᾳς	for	ὁράεις	ὁρόω	for	ὁράω
ὁράᾳ	"	ὁράει or ὁράῃ	ὁρόωσι	"	ὁράουσι (*i.e.* ὁραονσι)
ὁράασθε	"	ὁράεσθε	ὁρόωσα	"	ὁράουσα (*i.e.* ὁραοντ-ια)
ὁράασθαι	"	ὁράεσθαι	ὁρόῳεν	"	ὁράοιεν
μνάασθαι	"	μνάεσθαι	ὁρόωνται	"	ὁράονται
ὁράᾱν	"	ὁράειν (Dor. ὁράεν)	αἰτιόῳο	"	αἰτιάοιο

(*b*) The lengthening of the *former* vowel occurs only when the word could not otherwise stand in the Homeric verse; as in

[1] Although these forms are found in all editions of Homer, yet most Homeric scholars are agreed that they are not genuine, but are early substitutes for the regular forms in *αω* etc. which they represent. See Monro, *Homeric Grammar* (2 ed.), pp. 50–54.

ἡβώοντες for ἡβάοντες, ἡβώοιμι for ἡβάοιμι, μνάασθαι for μνάεσθαι, μνώοντο for (ἐ)μνάοντο. In this case the second vowel or diphthong is not lengthened. But it may be long in a final syllable, as in μενοινάᾳ (for -άει); or when ωσα or ωσι comes from οντια or οντι, as in ἡβώωσα, δρώωσι, for ἡβα-οντια, δρα-οντι. The assimilation never occurs unless the second vowel is long either by nature or by position; thus ὁράομεν, ὁράετε, ὁραέτω cannot become ὁρόωμεν, ὁραατε, ὁρααατο.

(*c*) These forms extend also to the so-called Attic futures in άσω, άω, ῶ (665, 2); as ἐλόω, ἐλόωσι, κρεμόω, δαμάᾳ, δαμόωσι, for ἐλάσω (ἐλάω), etc.

3. The Doric contracts αε and αη to η; as ὁρῆτε for ὁράετε, ὁρῇ for ὁράει and ὁράῃ. A peculiar form (of contraction?) occurs in the dual of a few imperfects in Homer, as προσαυδήτην (from προσαυδάω), φοιτήτην (φοιτάω), συλήτην (συλάω). So Hom. ὅρηαι (or ὁρῆαι) for ὁράεαι (Attic ὁρᾷ) in the pres. ind. middle of ὁράω. (See 785, 4.)

4. Herodotus sometimes changes αω, αο, and αου to εω, εο, and εου, especially in ὁράω, εἰρωτάω, and φοιτάω; as ὁρέω, ὁρέοντες, ὁρέουσι, εἰρώτεον, ἐφοίτεον. These forms are generally uncontracted. In other cases Herodotus contracts verbs in αω regularly.

5. Homer sometimes forms the present infinitive active of verbs in άω and έω in ήμεναι; as γοήμεναι (γοάω), πεινήμεναι (πεινάω), φιλήμεναι (φιλέω). (See 785, 4.)

785. (*Verbs in* εω.) 1. Verbs in εω generally remain uncontracted in both Homer and Herodotus. But Homer sometimes contracts εε or εει to ει, as τάρβει (τάρβεε). Hdt. has generally δεῖ, *must*, and δεῖν, but impf. ἔδεε. Both Homer and Herodotus sometimes have ευ as a contract form for εο; as ἀγνοεῦντες, διανοεῦντο: so in the Attic futures in ιέω, ιέομαι (665, 3), as κομιεύμεθα (Hdt.). Forms in ευ for εου, like οἰχνεῦσι, ποιεῦσι, are of very doubtful authority.

2. Homer sometimes drops ε in εαι and εο (for ἔσαι, ἔσο, 777, 2) after ε, thus changing έεαι and έεο to έαι and έο, as μυθέαι for μυθέεαι (from μυθέομαι), ἀποαιρέο (for ἀποαιρέεο); and he also contracts έεαι and έεο to εῖαι and εῖο, as μυθεῖαι, αἰδεῖο (for αἰδέεο). Herodotus sometimes drops the second ε in έεο; as φοβέο, αἰτέο, ἐξηγέο.

3. Homer sometimes has a form in ειω for that in εω; as νεικείω (νεικέω). So in ἐτελείετο from τελείω (τελέω).

4. For Homeric infinitives in ήμεναι, see 784, 5. Φορέω, *carry*, has φορήμεναι and φορῆναι. Homer has a few dual imperfects like ὁμαρτήτην (ὁμαρτέω) and ἀπειλήτην (ἀπειλέω). (See 784, 3.)

786. (*Verbs in οω.*) 1. Verbs in οω are always contracted in Herodotus, and his Mss. sometimes have ευ (for ου) from οο or οου, especially in δικαιόω, *think just.*

2. They are always contracted in Homer, except in the few cases in which they have forms in οω or οῳ resembling those of verbs in αω (784, 2); as ἀρόωσι (from ἀρόω, *plough*); δηιόῳεν and (impf.) δηιόωντο (from δηιόω).

DIALECTIC FORMS OF VERBS IN MI.

787. 1. Homer and Herodotus have many forms (some doubtful) in which verbs in ημι (with stems in ε) and ωμι have the inflection of verbs in εω and οω; as τιθεῖ, διδοῖς, διδοῖ. So in compounds of ἵημι, as ἀνιεῖς (or ἀνίεις), μεθιεῖ (or -ίει) in pres., and προΐειν, προΐεις, ἀνίει, in impf. Hom. has imperat. καθ-ίστᾱ (Attic -η). Hdt. has ἱστᾷ (for ἵστησι), ὑπερ-ετίθεα in impf., and προσθέοιτο (for -θεῖτο), etc. in opt. For ἐδίδουν, etc. and ἐτίθεις, ἐτίθει (also Attic), see 630.

2. In the Aeolic dialect most verbs in αω, εω, and οω take the form in μι; as φίλημι (with φίλεισθα, φίλει) in Sappho, for φιλέω, etc.; ὄρημι (for ὁράω), κάλημι, αἴνημι.

3. A few verbs in Hom. and Hdt. drop σ in σαι and σο of the second person after a vowel; as imperat. παρίσταο (for -ασο) and impf. ἐμάρναο (Hom.); ἐξεπίστεαι (for -ασαι) with change of α to ε (Hdt.). So θέο, imperat. for θεσο (Att. θοῦ) and ἔνθεο (Hom.).

4. The Doric has τι, ντι for σι, νσι. Homer sometimes has σθα (556, 1) for σ in 2 pers. sing., as δίδωσθα (δίδοισθα or διδοῖσθα), τίθησθα. The poets have ν for σαν (with preceding vowel short) in 3 pers. plur., as ἔσταν (for ἔστησαν), ἴεν (for ἵεσαν), πρότιθεν (for προετίθεσαν); see 777, 9.

5. Herodotus sometimes has αται, ατο for νται, ντο in the present and imperfect of verbs in μι, with preceding α changed to ε; as προτιθέαται (for -ενται), ἐδυνέατο (for -αντο). For the iterative endings σκον, σκομην, see 778; these are added directly to the stem of verbs in μι, as ἵστα-σκον, δό-σκον, ζωννύ-σκετο, ἔ-σκον (εἰμί, *be*).

6. For poetic (chiefly Homeric) second aorists in ημην, ιμην, υμην, and from consonant stems, see 800.

788. 1. Herodotus sometimes leaves εω uncontracted in the subjunctive of verbs in ημι; as θέωμεν (Att. θῶμεν), διαθέωνται (-θῶνται), ἀπ-ιέωσι (Att. ἀφ-ιῶσι, from ἀφ-ίημι). He forms the subj. with εω in the plural also from stems in α; as ἀπο-στέ-ωσι (-στῶσι), ἐπιστέ-ωνται (for ἐπιστα-ονται, Att. ἐπίστωνται). Homer sometimes has these forms with εω; as θέωμεν, στέωμεν (724, 1).

2. Generally, when the second aorist subjunctive active is uncontracted in Homer, the final vowel of the stem is lengthened, ε (or α) to η or ει, ο to ω, while the short thematic vowels ε and ο are used in the dual and plural, except before σι (for νσι). Thus we find in Homer: —

(Stems in α.)
βείω (Attic **βῶ**)
στήῃς
στήῃ, βήῃ, βέῃ, φθήῃ
στήετον
στήομεν, στείομεν, στέωμεν
στήωσι, στείωσι, φθέωσι

(Stems in ε.)
θείω, ἐφ-είω
θήῃς
θήῃ, ἀν-ήῃ
θείομεν

(Stems in ο.)
γνώω
γνώῃς
γνώῃ, δώῃ, δώῃσιν
γνώομεν, δώομεν
γνώωσι, δώωσι

The editions of Homer retain ει of the Mss. before ο and ω; but probably η is the correct form in all persons (see 780, 3).

3. A few cases of the middle inflected as in 2 occur in Homer; as *βλή-εται* (*βάλλω*), *ἄλ-εται* (*ἄλλομαι*), *ἀπο-θείομαι*, *κατα-θείομαι*; so *κατα-θῆαι* (Hesiod) for *καταθέ-ηαι* (Att. *καταθῇ*).

789. For Homeric optatives of *δαίνῡμι*, *δύω*, *λύω*, and *φθίνω*, — *δαινῦτο*, *δύη* and *δῦμεν*, *λελῦτο* or *λελῦντο*, *φθίμην* (for *φθι-ιμην*), — see these verbs in the Catalogue, with 734, 1; 744.

790. Homer sometimes retains **θι** in the present imperative, as **δίδωθι**, *ὄμνυθι* (752). Pindar often has **δίδοι**.

791. Homer has **μεναι** or **μεν** (the latter only after a short vowel) for **ναι** in the infinitive. The final vowel of the stem is seldom long in the present; as **ἱστά-μεναι**, **ἱέ-μεναι**, **μεθιέ-μεν**, *ὀρνύ-μεναι*, *ὀρνύ-μεν*, **τιθέ-μεν**, but **τιθή-μεναι**. In the second aorist active the vowel is regularly long (766, 2), as **στή-μεναι**, **γνώ-μεναι**; but **τίθημι**, **δίδωμι**, and *ἵημι* have **θέμεναι** and **θέμεν**, *δόμεναι* and **δόμεν**, and (**ἕμεν**) **μεθ-έμεν**. (See 802.) In the perfect of the **μι**-form we have **ἑστά-μεναι**, **ἑστά-μεν**, **τεθνά-μεναι**, **τεθνά-μεν**.

792. Homer rarely has **ημενος** for **εμενος** in the participle. For second-perfect participles in **ως** (**αως**, **εως**, **ηως**), see 773.

ENUMERATION OF THE MI-FORMS.

The forms with this inflection are as follows: —

793. I. *Presents in μι.* These belong to the Seventh and the Fifth Class of verbs (see 619 and 608).

794. Those of the Seventh Class are

1. **Verbs in μι with the simple stem in the present.** These are the irregular εἰμί, *be*, εἶμι, *go*, φημί, *say*, ἧμαι, *sit*, and κεῖμαι, *lie*, which are inflected in 806–818; with ἠμί, *say*, and the deponents ἄγαμαι, δύναμαι, ἐπίσταμαι, ἔραμαι, κρέμαμαι.

See these last in the Catalogue, and also Ionic or poetic (chiefly Homeric) forms under ἄημι, δέαμαι, δίεμαι (stem διε-), δίζημαι, ἔδω, ἵλημι, κιχάνω, ὄνομαι, ῥύομαι and ἐρύομαι, σεύω, στεῦμαι, φέρω.

For δάμνημι and other verbs in νημι, see 797, 2.

2. Verbs in μι with reduplicated present stems (651). These are ἵστημι, τίθημι, and δίδωμι, inflected in 506, ἵημι, inflected in 810, δίδημι (rare for δέω), *bind*, κίχρημι (χρα-), *lend*, ὀνίνημι (ὀνα-), *benefit*, πίμπλημι (πλα-), *fill*, πίμπρημι (πρα-), *burn*. (For the last five, see the Catalogue.)

See also ἵπταμαι (late), and Hom. βιβάς, *striding*, present participle of rare βίβημι.

795. N. Πίμπλημι and πίμπρημι insert μ before π; but the μ generally disappears after μ (for ν) in ἐμ-πίπλημι and ἐμ-πίπρημι; but not after ν itself, as in ἐν-επίμπλασαν.

796. N. Ὀνίνημι (of uncertain formation) is perhaps for ὀν-ονη-μι, by reduplication from stem ὀνα-.

797. Those of the Fifth Class are

1. Verbs in νυμι, which add νυ (after a vowel, ννυ) to the verb stem in the present (608). **These are all inflected like δείκνυμι (506), and, except σβέννυμι, *quench* (803, 1), they have no Attic μι-forms except in the present and imperfect. The following belong to this class:—**

(Stems in α), κερά-ννυμι, κρεμά-ννυμι, πετά-ννυμι, σκεδά-ννυμι;—(stems in ε for εσ), ἕ-ννυμι, κορέ-ννυμι, σβέ-ννυμι;—(stems in ω), ζώ-ννυμι, ῥώ-ννυμι, στρώ-ννυμι;—(consonant stems), ἄγ-νυμι, ἄρ-νυμαι, δείκ-νυμι, εἴργ-νυμι, ζεύγ-νυμι, ἀπο-κτίν-νυμι (κτείνω), μίγ-νυμι, οἴγ-νυμι (in compos.), ὄλ-λυμι, ὄμ-νυμι, ὀμόργ-νυμι, ὄρ-νυμι, πήγ-νυμι (παγ-), πτάρ-νυμαι, ῥήγ-νυμι (ῥηγ-), στόρ-νυμι, φράγ-νυμι. See these in the Catalogue, and also Ionic or poetic (chiefly Homeric) forms under αἴνυμαι, ἄχνυμαι, γάνυμαι, δαίνυμι, καίνυμαι, κίνυμαι, ὀρέγ-νυμι, τάνυμαι (see τείνω), τίνυμαι (see τίνω).

2. Verbs in νημι (chiefly epic), which add νά to the verb stem in the present (609). These are δάμνημι, κίρνημι, κρήμνημι, μάρναμαι, πέρνημι, πίλναμαι, πίτνημι, σκίδνημι or κίδνημι. Many of these have also forms in ναω. (See the Catalogue.)

798. II. *Second Aorists of the μι-Form.* The only second aorists formed from verbs in μι are those of ἵημι (810), of ἵστημι, τίθημι, and δίδωμι (506), of σβέννῡμι (803, 1); with ἐπριάμην (505); also the irregular ὠνήμην (later ὠνάμην), of ὀνίνημι, and ἐπλήμην (poetic) of πίμπλημι.

See also Homeric aorist middle forms of μίγνῡμι, ὄρνῡμι, and πήγνῡμι, in the Catalogue.

799. The second aorists of this form belonging to verbs in ω are the following: —

Ἁλίσκομαι (ἁλ-), *be taken:* ἑάλων or ἥλων, *was taken*, ἁλῶ, ἁλοίην, ἁλῶναι, ἁλούς. (See 803, 2.)

Βαίνω (βα-), *go:* ἔβην, βῶ, βαίην, βῆθι (also βᾱ in comp.), βῆναι, βάς. Hom. βάτην for ἐβήτην.

Βιόω (βιο-), *live:* ἐβίων, βιῶ, βιῴην (irregular), βιῶναι, βιούς. (Hom. imper. βιώτω.)

Γηράσκω (γηρα-), *grow old*, 2 aor. inf. γηράναι (poet.), Hom. part. γηράς.

Γιγνώσκω (γνο-), *know:* ἔγνων, γνῶ, γνοίην, γνῶθι, γνῶναι, γνούς.

Διδράσκω (δρα-), *run:* ἔδρᾱν, ἔδρᾱς, ἔδρᾱ, etc., subj. δρῶ, δρᾷς, δρᾷ, etc., opt. δραίην, δρᾶναι, δράς. Hdt. ἔδρην, δρῆναι, δράς. Only in composition. (See 801.)

Δύω (δυ-), *enter:* ἔδῡν, *entered* (506), δύω, (for opt. see 744), δῦθι, δῦναι, δύς.

Κτείνω (κτεν-, κτα-), *kill:* act. (poetic) ἔκτᾰν, ἔκτᾰς, ἔκτᾰ, ἔκτᾰμεν (3 pl. ἔκτᾰν, subj. κτέωμεν, inf. κτάμεναι, κτάμεν, Hom.), κτάς. Mid. (Hom.) ἐκτάμην, *was killed*, κτάσθαι, κτάμενος.

Πέτομαι (πτα-, πτε-), *fly:* act. (poetic) ἔπτην, (πτῶ, late), πταίην (πτῆθι, πτῆναι, late), πτάς. Mid. ἐπτάμην, πτάσθαι, πτάμενος.

[Τλάω] (τλα-), *endure:* ἔτλην, τλῶ, τλαίην, τλῆθι, τλῆναι, τλάς.

Φθάνω (φθα-), *anticipate:* ἔφθην, φθῶ, φθαίην, φθῆναι, φθάς.

Φύω (φυ-), *produce:* ἔφῡν, *was produced, am*, φύω, φῦναι, φύς (like ἔδῡν).

Add to these the single forms, ἀπο-σκλῆναι, of ἀποσκέλλω, *dry up*, σχές, imperat. of ἔχω, *have*, πῖθι, imperat. of πίνω, *drink*, and epic forms of ξυμβάλλω (800, 1) and of κιγχάνω (κιχάνω).

800. 1. Some poetic (chiefly Homeric) second aorists of the μι-form in ημην, ιμην, and υμην are formed from stems in α, ι, and υ belonging to verbs in ω. *E.g.*

Βάλλω (βαλ-, βλα-), *throw*, 2 aor. act. (ἔβλην) ξυμ-βλήτην (dual); mid. (ἐβλήμην) ἔβλητο; φθίνω (φθι-), *waste*, 2 a. m. ἐφθίμην; σεύω (συ-), *urge*, ἐσσύμην (in Attic poets ἔσυτο, σύμενος); χέω (χυ-), *pour*, ἐχύμην, χύμενος.

See these verbs in the Catalogue. For other Homeric aorists see ἄω, ἀπαυράω, βιβρώσκω, κλύω, κτίζω, λύω, οὐτάω, πελάζω, πλώω, πνέω, πτήσσω.

2. Some are formed from consonant stems, with the simple ending *μην*. *E.g.*

Ἅλλομαι (ἁλ-), *leap*, 2 a. m. (ἁλ-μην) ἆλσο, ἆλτο; δέχομαι (δεχ-), *receive*, (ἐδέγ-μην) δέκτο; (ἐλέγ-μην) ἔλεκτο, *laid himself to rest* (see stem λεχ-).

Besides these, see ἀραρίσκω, γέντο, *grasped*, πάλλω, πέρθω.

3. For the inflection, see 803, 3.

801. N. Second aorists in ην or αμην from stems in α are inflected like ἔστην or ἐπριάμην; but ἔδρᾶν substitutes ᾱ (after ρ) for η, and ἔκτᾰν is irregular.

802. 1. The second aorists active of τίθημι, ἵημι, and δίδωμι have the short vowel (ε or ο) of the stem (678; 755) in the indicative (dual and plural) and imperative (εἶτον, εἶμεν, etc., being augmented): in the infinitive they have θεῖναι, εἶναι, and δοῦναι, and in the second person of the imperative θές, ἕς, and δός.

2. As these tenses have no forms for the indicative singular, this is supplied by the irregular first aorists ἔθηκα, ἧκα, and ἔδωκα (670); so that the actual aorist indicative active is as follows:—

ἔθηκα, ἔθηκας, ἔθηκε, ἔθετον, ἐθέτην, ἔθεμεν, ἔθετε, ἔθεσαν.

ἧκα, ἧκας, ἧκε, εἶτον, εἵτην, εἶμεν, εἶτε, εἶσαν.

ἔδωκα, ἔδωκας, ἔδωκε, ἔδοτον, ἐδότην, ἔδομεν, ἔδοτε, ἔδοσαν.

803. 1. The two other second aorists active from stems in ε are ἔσβην, *went out* (σβέννῡμι, *quench*), inflected like ἔστην, and ἀποσκλῆναι, *dry up* (σκέλλω). See 797, 1; 799.

2. The other second aorists, from stem in ο, are inflected like ἔγνων, as follows:—

Indic. ἔγνων, ἔγνως, ἔγνω, ἔγνωτον, ἐγνώτην, ἔγνωμεν, ἔγνωτε, ἔγνωσαν. *Subj.* γνῶ (like δῶ). *Opt.* γνοίην (like δοίην). *Imper.* γνῶθι, γνώτω, γνῶτον, γνώτων, γνῶτε, γνόντων (755). *Infin.* γνῶναι. *Partic.* γνούς (like δούς).

3. The second aorists ὠνήμην and ἐπλήμην (798), and the poetic aorists in ημην, ιμην, and υμην (800, 1) or in μην from consonant stems (800, 2), are inflected like the pluperfect middle (698).

804. III. *Second Perfects and Pluperfects of the μι-Form.* The following verbs have forms of this class in Attic Greek, most of them even in prose:—

Ἵστημι (στα-); see 508 (paradigm). For Ionic forms of the participle, see 773.

Βαίνω (βα-), *go;* poetic 2 pf. **βεβᾶσι** (Hom. **βεβάᾱσι**), subj. **βεβῶσι**, inf. **βεβάναι** (Hom. **βεβάμεν**), part. **βεβώς** (Hom. **βεβαώς**, **βεβαυῖα**); 2 plup. (Hom. **βέβασαν**).

Γίγνομαι (γεν-, γα-), *become*, 2 pf. **γέγονα**, *am;* (Hom. 2 pf. **γεγάᾱσι**, 2 plup. dual **γεγάτην**, inf. **γεγάμεν**, part. **γεγαώς**, **γεγαυῖα**), Att. **γεγώς**, **γεγῶσα** (poetic).

Θνήσκω (θαν-, θνα-), *die;* 2 pf. **τέθνατον**, **τέθναμεν**, **τεθνᾶσι**, opt. **τεθναίην**, imper. **τέθναθι**, **τεθνάτω**, inf. **τεθνάναι** (Hom. **τεθνάμεναι** or **τεθνάμεν**), part. **τεθνεώς** (773), **τεθνεῶσα** (Hom. **τεθνηώς**, with **τεθνηυίης**), 2 plup. **ἐτέθνασαν**.

Δείδω (δει-, δι-), epic in pres., *fear*, Attic 2 pf. **δέδια**, **δέδιας**, **δέδιε**, plur. **δέδιμεν**, **δέδιτε**, **δεδίᾱσι**; 2 plup. **ἐδεδίειν**, **ἐδέδισαν**; subj. **δεδίῃ**, **δεδίωσι**, opt. **δεδιείη**, imper. **δέδιθι**, inf. **δεδιέναι**, part. **δεδιώς**. (Hom. 2 pf. **δείδια**, **δείδιας**, **δείδιε**, pl. **δείδιμεν**, imper. **δείδιθι**, **δείδιτε**, inf. **δειδίμεν**, part. **δειδιώς**; plup. **ἐδείδιμεν**, **ἐδείδισαν**, rarely **δείδιε** (777, 4).

[Εἴκω] (εἰκ-, ἰκ-), 2 pf. **ἔοικα**, *seem;* also 2 pf. **ἔοιγμεν**, **εἴξᾱσι** (for **ἐοίκᾱσι**), inf. **εἰκέναι**, part. **εἰκώς** (Hom. 2 pf. **ἔικτον**, 2 plup. **ἐίκτην**), used with the regular forms of **ἔοικα**, **ἐῴκη** (see Catalogue).

Οἶδα (ἰδ-), *know;* see 820 (paradigm).

See also poetic, chiefly Homeric, forms under the following verbs in the Catalogue: **ἀνώγω**, **βιβρώσκω**, **ἐγείρω**, **ἔρχομαι**, **κράζω**, **μαίομαι**, **πάσχω**, **πείθω**, **πίπτω**, **[τλάω]**, **φύω**, and stem (δα-).

IRREGULAR VERBS OF THE MI-FORM.

805. The verbs **εἰμί**, *be*, **εἶμι**, *go*, **ἵημι**, *send*, **φημί**, *say*, **ἧμαι**, *sit*, **κεῖμαι**, *lie*, and the second perfect **οἶδα**, *know*, are thus inflected.

806. 1. εἰμί (stem ἐσ-, Latin *es-se*), *be*.

PRESENT.

		Indicative.	*Subjunctive.*	*Optative.*	*Imperative.*
Sing.	1.	εἰμί	ὦ	εἴην	
	2.	εἶ	ᾖς	εἴης	ἴσθι
	3.	ἐστί	ᾖ	εἴη	ἔστω
Dual	2.	ἐστόν	ἦτον	εἶτον or εἴητον	ἔστον
	3.	ἐστόν	ἦτον	εἴτην or εἰήτην	ἔστων
Plur.	1.	ἐσμέν	ὦμεν	εἶμεν or εἴημεν	
	2.	ἐστέ	ἦτε	εἶτε or εἴητε	ἔστε
	3.	εἰσί	ὦσι	εἶεν or εἴησαν	ἔστων, ἔστωσαν, ὄντων

Infin. **εἶναι**. *Partic.* **ὤν**, **οὖσα**, **ὄν**, gen. **ὄντος**, **οὔσης**, etc.
Verbal Adjective, **ἐστέος** (συν-εστέον).

		Imperfect.	Future.		
		Indicative.	*Indicative.*	*Optative.*	*Infinitive.*
Sing.	1.	ἦ or ἦν	ἔσομαι	ἐσοίμην	ἔσεσθαι
	2.	ἦσθα	ἔσει, ἔσῃ	ἔσοιο	
	3.	ἦν	ἔσται	ἔσοιτο	
Dual	2.	ἦστον or ἦτον	ἔσεσθον	ἔσοισθον	*Partic.*
	3.	ἤστην or ἤτην	ἔσεσθον	ἐσοίσθην	ἐσόμενος
Plur.	1.	ἦμεν	ἐσόμεθα	ἐσοίμεθα	
	2.	ἦτε or ἦστε	ἔσεσθε	ἔσοισθε	
	3.	ἦσαν	ἔσονται	ἔσοιντο	

2. Εἰμί is for ἐσ-μι (footnote on 556, 5), εἶ for ἐσ-σί (ἐσι), for ἐστί see 556, 1; ὦ is for ἔω (ἐσ-ω), εἴην for ἐσ-ιη-ν), εἶναι for ἐσ-ναι, ὤν for ἐών (ἐσ-ων). 3. For the accent, see 141, 3 and 144, 5. The participle ὤν keeps its accent in composition, as παρών, παροῦσα, παρόντος, etc.; so ἔσται (for ἔσεται), as παρέσται.

807. Dialects. 1. *Present Indic.* Aeolic ἔμμι, the most primitive form, nearest to ἐσ-μι (806, 2). Hom. ἐσσί and εἶς (for εἶ), εἰμέν (for ἐσμέν), ἔᾱσι. Hdt. εἶς and εἰμέν. Doric ἠμί, ἐσσί, εἰμέν and εἰμές (older ἠμέν), ἐντί (for εἰσί).

2. *Imperfect.* Hom. ἦα, ἔα, ἔον; ἔησθα, ἦεν, ἔην, ἤην; ἔσαν (for ἦσαν). Hdt. ἔα, ἔας, ἔατε. Ionic (iterative) ἔσκον. Later ἦς for ἦσθα. Doric 3 sing. ἦς, 1 pl. ἦμες. 3. *Future.* Hom. ἔσσομαι, etc., with ἐσσεῖται and ἔσεται; Dor. ἐσσῇ, ἐσσεῖται, ἐσσοῦνται.

4. *Subj.* Ionic ἔω, ἔῃς, ἔῃ (ἔῃσι, ᾖσι), etc., ἔωσι; Hom. also εἴω. 5. *Opt.* Ionic ἔοις, ἔοι. 6. *Imper.* Hom. ἔσ-σο (a regular middle form). 7. *Infin.* Hom. ἔμμεναι, ἔμεναι, ἔμεν, ἔμμεν; Dor. ἦμεν or εἶμεν; lyric ἔμμεν. 8. *Partic.* Ionic and Doric ἐών.

808. 1. εἶμι (stem ἰ-, Latin *i-re*), *go*.

Present.

		Indicative.	*Subjunctive.*	*Optative.*	*Imperative.*
Sing.	1.	εἶμι	ἴω	ἴοιμι or ἰοίην	
	2.	εἶ	ἴῃς	ἴοις	ἴθι
	3.	εἶσι	ἴῃ	ἴοι	ἴτω
Dual	2.	ἴτον	ἴητον	ἴοιτον	ἴτον
	3.	ἴτον	ἴητον	ἰοίτην	ἴτων
Plur.	1.	ἴμεν	ἴωμεν	ἴοιμεν	
	2.	ἴτε	ἴητε	ἴοιτε	ἴτε
	3.	ἴᾱσι	ἴωσι	ἴοιεν	ἰόντων, ἴτων, or ἴτωσαν

Infin. ἰέναι. *Partic.* ἰών, ἰοῦσα, ἰόν, gen. ἰόντος, ἰούσης, etc.
Verbal Adjectives, ἰτός, ἰτέος, ἰτητέος.

IMPERFECT.

	Sing.	*Dual.*	*Plural.*
1.	**ᾖα** or **ᾔειν**		**ᾖμεν**
2.	**ᾔεις** or **ᾔεισθα**	**ᾖτον**	**ᾖτε**
3.	**ᾔει** or **ᾔειν**	**ᾔτην**	**ᾖσαν** or **ᾔεσαν**

Imperfect forms **ᾔειμεν** and **ᾔειτε** are rare and doubted.

2. In compounds the participle *ἰών* keeps the accent of the simple form; as **παριών, πάριοῦσα, παριόντος, παριοῦσι.** (See 806, 3.)

3. The present **εἶμι** generally (always in Attic) has a future sense, ***shall go***, taking the place of a future of *ἔρχομαι*, whose future **ἐλεύσομαι** is rarely (or never) used in Attic prose.

809. DIALECTS. 1. *Present Indic.* Hom. *εἶσθα* for *εἶ*. 2. *Imperf.* Hom. 1 p. *ἤϊα, ἤϊον*, 3 p. *ἤϊε, ᾖε, ἴε*; dual *ἴτην*; pl. 1 p. *ᾔομεν*, 3 p. *ἤϊον, ἤϊσαν (ᾖσαν), ἴσαν*. Hdt. *ἤϊα, ἤϊε, ἤϊσαν*. 3. *Subj.* Hom. *ἴῃσθα, ἴῃσι*. 4. *Opt.* Hom. **ἰείη** (for **ἴοι**). 5. ***Infin.*** Hom. *ἴ-μεναι*, or **ἴ-μεν** (for *ἰ-έναι*), rarely **ἴμμεναι.**

6. ***Future***, Hom. **εἴσομαι**; ***Aorist***, Hom. **εἰσάμην** or **ἐεισάμην.**

810. 1. *ἵημι* (stem *ἑ-*), *send.*

ACTIVE.

PRESENT.

		Indicative.	*Subjunctive.*	*Optative.*	*Imperative.*	
Sing.	1.	**ἵημι**	**ἱῶ**	**ἱείην**		
	2.	**ἵης**	**ἱῇς**	**ἱείης**	**ἵει**	*Infin.*
	3.	**ἵησι**	**ἱῇ**	**ἱείη**	**ἱέτω**	**ἱέναι**
Dual	2.	**ἵετον**	**ἱῆτον**	**ἱεῖτον** or **ἱείητον**	**ἵετον**	
	3.	**ἵετον**	**ἱῆτον**	**ἱείτην** or **ἱειήτην**	**ἱέτων**	*Partic.*
Plur.	1.	**ἵεμεν**	**ἱῶμεν**	**ἱεῖμεν** or **ἱείημεν**		**ἱείς**
	2.	**ἵετε**	**ἱῆτε**	**ἱεῖτε** or **ἱείητε**	**ἵετε**	**ἱεῖσα, ἱέν**
	3.	**ἱᾶσι**	**ἱῶσι**	**ἱεῖεν** or **ἱείησαν**	**ἱέντων** or **ἱέτωσαν**	

IMPERFECT.

Sing.	1.	**ἵην**
	2.	**ἵεις**
	3.	**ἵει**
Dual	2.	**ἵετον**
	3.	**ἱέτην**
Plur.	1.	**ἵεμεν**
	2.	**ἵετε**
	3.	**ἵεσαν**

Future, **ἥσω**, etc., regular.

First Aorist, **ἧκα, ἧκας, ἧκε**, only in indic. (802).

Perfect (in composition), **εἷκα**, etc., regular.

Second Aorist (generally in composition).

		Indicative.	*Subjunctive.*	*Optative.*	*Imperative.*	
Sing.	1.	——(802)	ὧ	εἵην		*Infin.*
	2.	——	ᾗς	εἵης	ἕς	εἷναι
	3.	——	ᾗ	εἵη	ἕτω	
Dual	2.	εἷτον	ἧτον	εἷτον or εἵητον	ἕτον	*Partic.*
	3.	εἵτην	ἧτον	εἵτην or εἱήτην	ἕτων	εἷς, εἷσα, ἕν
Plur.	1.	εἷμεν	ὧμεν	εἷμεν or εἵημεν		
	2.	εἷτε	ἧτε	εἷτε or εἵητε	ἕτε	
	3.	εἷσαν	ὧσι	εἷεν or εἵησαν	ἕντων or ἕτωσαν	

MIDDLE.

Present.

		Indicative.	*Subjunctive.*	*Optative.*	*Imperative.*	
Sing.	1.	ἵεμαι	ἱῶμαι	ἱείμην		*Infin.*
	2.	ἵεσαι	ἱῇ	ἱεῖο	ἵεσο	ἵεσθαι
	3.	ἵεται	ἱῆται	ἱεῖτο	ἱέσθω	
Dual	2.	ἵεσθον	ἱῆσθον	ἱεῖσθον	ἵεσθον	
	3.	ἵεσθον	ἱῆσθον	ἱείσθην	ἱέσθων	*Partic.*
Plur.	1.	ἱέμεθα	ἱώμεθα	ἱείμεθα		ἱέμενος
	2.	ἵεσθε	ἱῆσθε	ἱεῖσθε	ἵεσθε	
	3.	ἵενται	ἱῶνται	ἱεῖντο	ἱέσθων or ἱέσθωσαν	

Imperfect.

Sing.	1.	ἱέμην
	2.	ἵεσο
	3.	ἵετο
Dual	2.	ἵεσθον
	3.	ἱέσθην
Plur.	1.	ἱέμεθα
	2.	ἵεσθε
	3.	ἵεντο

Future (in composition), ἥσομαι, etc., regular.

First Aorist (in composition), ἡκάμην (only in indic.), 670.

Perfect (in composition), εἷμαι. *Imper.* εἵσθω. *Infin.* εἷσθαι. *Partic.* εἱμένος.

Second Aorist (generally in composition).

		Indicative.	Subjunctive.	Optative.	Imperative.	
Sing.	1.	εἵμην	ὧμαι	εἵμην		
	2.	εἷσο	ᾗ	εἷο	οὗ	*Infin.*
	3.	εἷτο	ἧται	εἷτο	ἕσθω	ἕσθαι
Dual	2.	εἷσθον	ἧσθον	εἷσθον	ἕσθον	
	3.	εἵσθην	ἧσθον	εἵσθην	ἕσθων	*Partic.*
Plur.	1.	εἵμεθα	ὥμεθα	εἵμεθα		ἕμενος
	2.	εἷσθε	ἧσθε	εἷσθε	ἕσθε	
	3.	εἷντο	ὧνται	εἷντο	ἕσθων or ἕσθωσαν	

Aorist Passive (in composition), εἵθην. *Subj.* ἑθῶ. *Partic.* ἑθείς.
Future Passive (in composition), ἑθήσομαι.
Verbal Adjectives (in composition), ἑτός, ἑτέος.

2. The imperfect active of ἀφίημι is ἀφίην or ἠφίην (544). The optatives ἀφίοιτε and ἀφίοιεν, for ἀφιεῖτε and ἀφιεῖεν, and πρόοιτο, πρόοισθε, and πρόοιντο (also accented προοῖτο, etc.), for προεῖτο, προεῖσθε, and προεῖντο, sometimes occur. For similar forms of τίθημι, see 741.

811. Dialects. 1. Hom. ἵημι (with initial ῐ); imp. ἵειν for ἵην; 1 aor. ἕηκα for ἧκα; 2 aor. ἕσαν, ἕμην, ἕντο, by omission of augment, for εἷσαν, εἵμην, εἷντο; infin. ἕμεν for εἶναι. In ἀνίημι, Hom. fut. ἀνέσω, aor. ἄνεσα.

2. Hdt. perf. mid. ἀν-έωνται for ἀν-εῖνται, and perf. pass. partic. με-μετ-ι-μένος, for μεθ-ειμένος, *summoned.*

812. φημί (stem φα-), *say.*

Pres.	Imperf.	
φημί	ἔφην	*Subj.* φῶ, φῇς, φῇ, etc.
φῄς or φής	ἔφησθα or ἔφης	*Opt.* φαίην, φαίης, etc.
φησί	ἔφη	*Imper.* φαθί or φάθι, φάτω, etc.
φατόν	ἔφατον	
φατόν	ἐφάτην	*Infin.* φάναι.
φαμέν	ἔφαμεν	*Partic.* φάς, φᾶσα, φάν,—in Attic prose φάσκων is used.
φατέ	ἔφατε	
φᾱσί	ἔφασαν	

Future, φήσω, φήσειν, φήσων.
Aorist, ἔφησα, φήσω, φήσαιμι, φῆσαι, φήσᾱς.
Verbal Adjectives, φατός, φατέος.

A perfect passive imperative (3 pers.) πεφάσθω occurs.

813. Dialects. 1. *Present. Ind.* Doric **φᾶμί, φᾱτί, φαντί**; Hom. **φῆσθα** for **φῄς**. *Infin.* poet. **φάμεν**.

Imperfect. Hom. **φῆν, φῆς** or **φῆσθα, φῆ** (Doric **ἔφᾱ** and **φᾶ**), **ἔφαν** and **φάν** (for **ἔφασαν** and **φάσαν**).

Aorist. Doric **φᾶσε** for **ἔφησε**.

2. Homer has some middle forms of **φημί**; *pres. imper.* **φάο, φάσθω, φάσθε**; *infin.* **φάσθαι**; *partic.* **φάμενος**; *imperf.* **ἐφάμην** or **φάμην, ἔφατο** or **φάτο, ἔφαντο** and **φάντο**. Doric *fut.* **φάσομαι**. These all have an active sense.

814. ἧμαι (stem ἡσ-), *sit.*

(Chiefly poetic in simple form: in Attic prose **κάθ-ημαι** is generally used.)

Present. Indic. **ἧμαι, ἧσαι, ἧσται; ἧσθον; ἥμεθα, ἧσθε, ἧνται.** *Imper.* **ἧσο, ἥσθω**, etc. *Infin.* **ἧσθαι.** *Partic.* **ἥμενος.**

Imperfect. **ἥμην, ἧσο, ἧστο; ἧσθον, ἥσθην; ἥμεθα, ἧσθε, ἧντο.**

815. **Κάθημαι** is thus inflected: —

Present. Indic. **κάθημαι, κάθησαι, κάθηται; κάθησθον; καθήμεθα, κάθησθε, κάθηνται.** *Subj.* **καθῶμαι, καθῇ, καθῆται**, etc. *Opt.* **καθοίμην, καθοῖο, καθοῖτο**, etc. *Imper.* **κάθησο** (in comedy, **κάθου**), **καθήσθω**, etc. *Infin.* **καθῆσθαι.** *Partic.* **καθήμενος.**

Imperfect. **ἐκαθήμην, ἐκάθησο, ἐκάθητο**, etc., also **καθήμην, καθῆσο, καθῆστο** and **καθῆτο**, etc.

816. N. The σ of the stem is dropped except before **ται** and **το**, and in **κάθη-ται** and (**ἐ**)**κάθη-το** even there. The middle endings added directly to a consonant stem or to a long vowel or diphthong (as in **κεῖμαι**) give the present and imperfect the appearance of a perfect and pluperfect (803, 3).

817. Dialects. Homer has **εἵαται**, rarely **ἕαται**, for **ἧνται**; and **εἵατο**, rarely **ἕατο**, for **ἧντο**. Hdt. has **κατέαται** and **κατέατο**.

818. κεῖμαι (stem κει-, κε-), *lie.*

Present. Indic. **κεῖμαι, κεῖσαι, κεῖται; κεῖσθον; κείμεθα, κεῖσθε, κεῖνται.** *Subj.* and *Opt.* These forms occur: **κέηται, δια-κέησθε, κέοιτο, προσ-κέοιντο.** *Imper.* **κεῖσο, κείσθω**, etc. *Infin.* **κεῖσθαι.** *Partic.* **κείμενος.**

Imperfect. **ἐκείμην, ἔκεισο, ἔκειτο; ἔκεισθον, ἐκείσθην; ἐκείμεθα, ἔκεισθε, ἔκειντο.**

Future. **κείσομαι**, regular.

819. Dialects. Homer has κέαται, κείαται, and κέονται, for κεῖνται; κέσκετο (iterative) for ἔκειτο; κέατο and κείατο for ἔκειντο; subj. κῆται. Hdt. has κέεται, κεέσθω, κέεσθαι, and ἐκέετο, for κεῖται, etc.; and always κέαται and ἐκέατο for κεῖνται and ἔκειντο.

820. *οἶδα* (stem *ἰδ-*), *know.*

(Οἶδα is a second perfect of the stem ἰδ-: see εἶδον in the Catalogue, and 804.)

Second Perfect.

		Indicative.	*Subjunctive.*	*Optative.*	*Imperative.*
Sing.	1.	οἶδα	εἰδῶ	εἰδείην	
	2.	οἶσθα	εἰδῇς	εἰδείης	ἴσθι
	3.	οἶδε	εἰδῇ	εἰδείη	ἴστω
Dual	2.	ἴστον	etc.	etc.	ἴστον
	3.	ἴστον	regular	regular	ἴστων
Plur.	1.	ἴσμεν			
	2.	ἴστε			ἴστε
	3.	ἴσᾱσι			ἴστων or ἴστωσαν

Infin. εἰδέναι. *Partic.* εἰδώς, εἰδυῖα, εἰδός, gen. εἰδότος, εἰδυίας (335).

Second Pluperfect.

	Sing.	*Dual.*	*Plur.*
1.	ᾔδη or ᾔδειν		ᾖσμεν
2.	ᾔδησθα or ᾔδεισθα	ᾖστον	ᾖστε
3.	ᾔδει(ν)	ᾔστην	ᾖσαν or ᾔδεσαν

Future, εἴσομαι etc., regular. *Verbal Adjective,* ἰστέος.

821. Dialects. 1. The Ionic occasionally has the regular forms οἶδας, οἴδαμεν, οἴδᾱσι; and very often ἴδμεν for ἴσμεν. Ionic fut. εἰδήσω (rare and doubtful in Attic).

2. Ionic ᾔδεα, ᾔδεε, ᾐδέατε, Hom. ᾐείδης and ᾔδης, ᾐείδη, ἴσαν, in pluperfect. The Attic poets rarely have ᾔδεμεν and ᾔδετε (like ᾔδεσαν).

3. Hom. εἴδομεν etc., for εἰδῶμεν in subj.; ἴδμεναι and ἴδμεν in infin.; ἰδυῖα for εἰδυῖα in the participle.

4. Aeolic Boeotian ἴττω for ἴστω in imperative.

5. For Doric ἴσᾱμι (= οἶδα), see Catalogue.

PART III.

FORMATION OF WORDS.

822. (*Simple and Compound Words.*) A *simple* word is formed from a single stem; as λόγος (stem λεγ-), *speech*, γράφω (γραφ-), *write*. A *compound* word is formed by combining two or more stems; as λογο-γράφος (λογο-, γραφ-), *speech-writer*; ἀκρό-πολις, *citadel* (*upper city*).

FORMATION OF SIMPLE WORDS.

823. (*Primitives and Denominatives.*) (*a*) Nouns or adjectives formed directly from a root (153) or from a verb stem are called *primitives*; as ἀρχή (stem ἀρχᾱ-), *beginning*, from ἀρχ-, stem of ἄρχω; γραφεύς (γραφευ-), *writer*, γραφίς (γραφιδ-), *style* (for writing), γραμμή (γραμμᾱ- for γραφ-μᾱ-), *line* (828), γράμμα (γραμματ-), *written document*, γραφικός (γραφικο-), *able to write*, all from γραφ-, stem of γράφω, *write*; ποιη-τής, *poet* (*maker*), ποίη-σις, *poesy* (*making*), ποίη-μα, *poem*, ποιη-τικός, *able to make*, from ποιε-, stem of ποιέω, *make*. So δίκη (δικᾱ-), *justice*, from the root δικ-; κακός, *bad*, from κακ-.

824. Nouns, adjectives, and verbs formed from the stems of nouns or adjectives, are called *denominatives*; as βασιλείᾱ, *kingdom*, from βασιλε(υ)- (263); ἀρχαῖος, *ancient*, from ἀρχᾱ- (stem of ἀρχή); δικαιοσύνη, *justice*, from δικαιο-; τῑμά-ω, *honor*, from τῑμᾱ-, stem of the noun τῑμή.

825. N. (1) The name *verbal* is often applied to primitive words, because generally their root or stem actually occurs as a verb stem. This, however, does not show that the noun or adjective is *derived from the verb*, but merely that both have the same root or stem. Thus the root γραφ- contains only the general idea *write*, not as yet developed into a noun, adjective, or verb. By adding ᾱ it becomes γραφᾱ-, the stem of *γραφή, a writing*, which stem generally appears as *γραφᾰ-* in the plural, and is modified by case-endings to *γραφᾰ-ί, γραφά-ς*, etc. (See 168; 170.) By adding the thematic vowel %/ε (561, 1), *γράφ-* is developed into *γραφ*%/ε-, the present stem of the verb *γράφω, write*, which is modified by personal endings to *γράφο-μεν, we write, γράφε-τε, you write*, etc.

(2) Even a noun or adjective derived from the stem of a denominative verb is called primitive; as *αὐλητής, flute-player*, from *αὐλε-*, the stem of *αὐλέω, play the flute;* the latter, however, is formed from the stem of *αὐλό-ς, flute* (829).

826. (*Suffixes.*) Roots or stems are developed into new stems by the addition of syllables (not themselves stems) called *suffixes*. Thus, in the examples in 823, final *α-* in *ἀρχᾱ-*, *ευ-* in *γραφευ-*, *ιδ-* in *γραφιδ-*, *μα-* in *γραμμα-*, *ματ-* in *γραμματ-*, *ικο-* in *γραφικο-*, etc. are suffixes.

827. N. Rarely a noun stem has no suffix, and is identical with the verb stem; as in *φύλαξ, guard*, from stem *φυλακ-*, seen also in *φυλάσσω, I guard* (580); *φλόξ* (*φλογ-*), *flame*, from same stem as *φλέγ-ω* (831).

828. N. The final consonant of a stem is subject to the same euphonic changes before a suffix as before an ending; as in *γράμ-μα* for *γραφ-μα*, *λέξις* for *λεγ-σις*, *δικασ-τής* for *δικαδ-της*. (See 71; 74; 75.)

829. N. A final vowel of the stem may be contracted with a vowel of the suffix; as in *ἀρχαῖος, ancient*, from *ἀρχα-* and *ιο-ς* (850). But such a vowel is sometimes dropped; as in *οὐράν-ιος, heavenly*, from *οὐρανο-* and *ιο-ς*, *βασιλ-ικός, kingly*, from *βασιλε(υ)-* and *ικο-ς*; *εὔνο-ια, good-will*, from *εὐνοο-* and *ια* (842).

A final stem vowel is sometimes changed; especially from *ο* to *ε* in denominatives, as in *οἰκέ-ω, dwell* (*οἶκο-ς, house*), *οἰκέ-της, house-servant*, and *οἰκεῖος* (*οἰκε-ιος*), *domestic*; — sometimes from *ᾱ* to *ω*, as in *στρατιώ-της, soldier* (*στρατιᾱ-*), *Σικελιώ-της, Sicilian Greek* (*Σικελιᾱ-*); — sometimes from *ᾱ* to *η*, as in *ὑλή-εις, woody*, from *ὕλη* (*ὑλᾱ-*).

830. N. (1) Many vowel stems (especially verb stems) lengthen their final vowel before a consonant of the suffix, as in verbs (635); as *ποίη-μα, ποίη-σις, ποιη-τικός, ποιη-τής*, from *ποιε-*.

(2) Many add *σ* before *μ* and *τ* of a suffix, as in the perfect and aorist passive (640); as *κελευ-σ-τής, commander, κέλευ-σ-μα, command*, from *κελευ-* (*κελεύω*), *κεκέλευ-σ-μαι*.

(3) Others add *θ*, as *σταθ-μός, station*, from *στα-* (*ἵστημι*).

(4) Others drop a final consonant, as *σωφρο-σύνη, temperance*, from *σωφρον-*.

831. N. In many nouns and adjectives, especially those in *ος* and *η*, the interior vowel of the stem is lengthened or otherwise modified, as in the second perfect (643; 644). A change of *ε* to *ο* (*ει* and *ευ* to *οι* and *ου*) is especially common (31). Thus *λήθη, forgetfulness*, from *λαθ-* (cf. *λέληθα*); *γόνος, offspring*, from *γεν-* (cf. *γέγονα*); *λοιπός, remaining*, from *λειπ-* (cf. *λέλοιπα*); *στοργή, affection*, from *στεργ-* (cf. *ἔστοργα*); *πομπή, sending*, from *πεμπ-* (cf. *πέπομφα*); *τρόπος, turn*, from *τρεπ-*; *φλόξ, flame*, gen. *φλογός*, from *φλεγ-*; *σπουδή, haste*, from *σπευ-*. So also in adverbs; see *συλ-λήβ-δην* (*λαβ-*): see 860, 2.

I. FORMATION OF NOUNS.

PRIMITIVE NOUNS.

832. The simplest and most common suffixes in nouns are **ο-** (nom. ος or ον) and **ᾱ-** (nom. α or η). Nouns thus formed have a great variety of meanings. The change of ε to ο (831) is here regular. *E.g.*

Λόγο-ς (λογ-ο-), *speech*, from λεγ-, stem of λέγω (831); **τρόπος**, *turn*, from **τρεπ-** (stem of **τρέπω**, *turn*); **στόλος**, *expedition*, and **στολή**, *equipment*, from **στελ-** (stem of **στέλλω**, *send*); **μάχ-η (μαχ-α-)**, *battle*, from **μαχ-** (stem of **μάχομαι**, *fight*).

833. (*Agent.*) 1. The following suffixes denote the *agent*:—

ευ- (nom. **εύς**): **γραφ-εύ-ς**, *writer*, from **γραφ-** (**γράφω**); **γον-εύ-ς**, *parent*, from **γεν-**.

τηρ- (nom. τήρ): **σωτήρ**, *saviour*, from **σω-** (**σώω**, **σῴζω**, *save*).

τορ- (nom. **τωρ**): **ῥήτωρ**, *orator*, from **ῥε-** (**ἐρέω**, **ἐρῶ**, *shall say*).

τα- (nom. **της**): **ποιητής**, *poet* (*maker*), from **ποιε-** (**ποιέω**); **ὀρχη-σ-τής**, *dancer*, from **ὀρχε-** (**ὀρχέομαι**, *dance*). (See 830, 1, 2.)

2. To these correspond the following feminine forms:—

τειρᾰ- (nom. **τειρᾰ**): **σώτειρα**, fem. of **σωτήρ**.

τριᾰ- (nom. **τριᾰ**): **ποιήτρια**, *poetess*; **ὀρχήστρια**, *dancing-girl*.

τριδ- (nom. **τρίς**): **ὀρχηστρίς**, *dancing-girl*, gen. **-ίδος**.

τιδ- (nom. **τις**): **προφῆτις**, *prophetess*; **οἰκέτις**, *female servant*.

3. Verbals in **τηρ** and **τρις** are oxytone: those in **τωρ**, **τρια**, and **τειρα** have recessive accent (110, 4).

834. (*Action.*) These suffixes denote *action*:—

τι- (nom. **τις**, fem.): **πίσ-τις**, *belief*, from **πιθ-** (**πείθω**, *believe*).

σι- (nom. **σις**, fem.): **λύ-σις**, *loosing*, from **λυ-** (**λῡω**).

σιᾱ- (nom. **σιᾱ**, fem.): **δοκιμα-σίᾱ**, *testing* (**δοκιμάζω**, *test*).

μο- (nom. **μός**, masc.): **ὀδυρμός**, *wailing* (**ὀδύρ-ομαι**, *wail*); **σπασ-μός**, *spasm* (**σπά-ω**, *draw*); **ῥυθμός** (830, 3), *rhythm* (**ῥέω**, *flow*, stem **ῥυ-**). (See 574.)

835. N. The suffix **μᾱ-** (nom **μη**, fem.) has the same force as simple **ᾱ-**(832); as **γνώμη**, *knowledge* (**γνο-**); **ὀδμή**, *odor* (**ὄζω**, **ὀδ-**).

836. N. From stems in **ευ** (**εϝ**) of verbs in **ευω** come nouns in **ειᾱ** denoting action; as **βασιλειᾱ**, *kingly power*, *kingdom*, **παιδειᾱ**, *education*. For feminines in **ειᾰ** of nouns in **ευς**, see 841.

837. (*Result.*) These suffixes denote the *result* of an action:—

ματ- (nom. **μα**, neut.): **πρᾶγ-μα**, *thing*, *act*, from **πρᾱγ-** (**πρᾱ́σσω**, *do*); **ῥῆμα**, *saying* (*thing said*), from **ῥε-** (fut. **ἐρῶ**); **τμῆ-μα**, *section*, gen. **τμήματος**, from **τμε-**, **τεμ-** (**τέμνω**, *cut*).

εσ- (nom. **ος**, neut.): **λάχος** (**λαχεσ-**), *lot*, from **λαχ-** (**λαγχάνω**, *gain by lot*); **ἔθος** (**ἐθεσ-**), *custom*, from **ἐθ-** (**εἴωθα**, *am accustomed*); **γένος** (**γενεσ-**), *race*, from **γεν-** (**γέ-γον-α**, 831).

In some primitives this suffix **εσ-** denotes *quality*; as **βάθος** (**βαθεσ-**), *depth* (from root **βαθ-**); **βάρος** (**βαρεσ-**), *weight* (from root **βαρ-**); **θάλπος** (**θαλπεσ-**), *heat* (**θάλπ-ω**, *warm*).

838. (*Means* or *Instrument*.) This is denoted by

τρο- (nom. **τρον**, Latin *trum*): **ἄρο-τρον**, *plough*, *aratrum*, from **ἀρο-** (**ἀρόω**, *plough*); **λύ-τρον**, *ransom*, from **λυ-** (**λύω**); **λοῦ-τρον**, *bath*, from **λου-** (**λούω**, *wash*).

839. N. The feminine in **τρᾱ** sometimes denotes an *instrument*, as **χύτρᾱ**, *earthen pot*, from **χυ-** (**χέω**, *pour*); **ξύ-σ-τρᾱ**, *scraper* (**ξύ-ω**, *scrape*); sometimes other relations, e.g. *place*, as **παλαί-σ-τρᾱ**, *place for wrestling*, from **παλαι-** (**παλαίω**, wrestle, 640).

840. Some primitives are formed from stems in

ανο-, as **στέφ-ανο-ς**, *crown* (**στέφ-ω**, *crown*);

ονᾱ-, as **ἡδ-ονή**, *pleasure* (**ἥδ-ομαι**, *be pleased*);

ον- or **ων-**, as **εἰκ-ών**, *image*, from **εἰκ-** (**ἔοικα**, *resemble*), **κλύδ-ων**, *wave*, from **κλυδ-** (**κλύζω**, *dash*).

DENOMINATIVE NOUNS.

841. (*Person Concerned*.) A person concerned with anything may be denoted by the following suffixes: —

ευ-, masc. (nom. **εύς**), sometimes **ειᾰ-** (for **εϝ-ια**), fem. (nom. **ειᾰ**): **ἱερ-εύς**, *priest*, from **ἱερό-ς**, *sacred* (829), fem. **ἱέρ-εια**, *priestess*; **βασιλ-εύς**, *king* (derivation uncertain), fem. **βασίλ-εια**, *queen*; **πορθμ-εύς**, *ferryman*, from **πορθμό-ς**, *ferry*.

τᾱ-, masc. (nom. **της**), **τιδ-**, fem. (nom. **τις**): **πολί-της**, *citizen*, from **πόλι-ς**, *city*, fem. **πολῖ-τις**, *female citizen*; **οἰκέ-της**, *house-servant*, from **οἶκο-ς**, *house*, fem. **οἰκέ-τις**, *housemaid*; **στρατιώ-της**, *soldier*, from **στρατιά**, *army* (829).

842. (*Quality*.) Nouns denoting *quality* are formed from adjective stems by these suffixes: —

τητ- (nom. **της**, fem.): **νεό-της** (**νεοτητ-**), *youth*, from **νέο-ς** *young*; **ἰσό-της** (**ἰσοτητ-**), *equality*, from **ἴσο-ς**, *equal* (cf. Latin *vēritas*, gen. *vēri-tātis*, and *virtūs*, gen. *vir-tūtis*).

συνᾱ- (nom. **σύνη**, fem.): **δικαιο-σύνη**, *justice*, from **δίκαιο-ς**, *just*; **σωφρο-σύνη**, *temperance*, from **σώφρων** (**σωφρον-**), *temperate*.

ιᾱ- (nom. **ιᾱ** or **ιᾰ**, fem.): **σοφ-ίᾱ** *wisdom* (**σοφό-ς**), **κακίᾱ**, *vice* (**κακό-ς**), **ἀλήθεια**, *truth*, for **ἀληθεσ-ια** (**ἀληθής**, *true*), **εὔνοια**, *kindness*, for **εὐνο-ια** (**εὔνοο-ς**, **εὔνους**, *kind*).

843. (*Place.*) This is denoted by these suffixes: —

1. **ιο-** (nom. **ιον**, neut.) with the termination **τηρ-ιον**: **δικαστήρ-ιον**, *court-house*, **ἀκροᾱ-τήρ-ιον**, *place of hearing* (*auditorium*). These are probably from old stems in **τηρ-** (Babrius has **δικαστήρων**, from **δικαστήρ**, for **δικαστῶν**, *of judges*). So **σημαν-τήρ-ιον**, *seal* (*place of sealing*), from **σημαντήρ**.

ειο- for **ε-ιο-**: **κουρεῖον**, *barber's shop*, from **κουρεύ-ς**, *barber;* so **λογ-εῖον** (**λόγο-ς**), *speaking-place*, **Μουσ-εῖον** (**Μοῦσα**), *haunt of the Muses.*

2. **ων-** (nom. **ών**, masc.): **ἀνδρών**, *men's apartment*, from **ἀνήρ**, gen. **ἀνδρ-ός**, *man;* **ἀμπελών**, *vineyard*, from **ἄμπελο-ς**, *vine.*

844. (*Diminutives.*) These are formed from noun stems by the following suffixes: —

ιο- (nom. **ιον**, neut.): **παιδ-ίον**, *little child*, from **παιδ-** (**παῖς**, *child*); **κηπ-ίον**, *little garden* (**κῆπος**). Sometimes also **ιδιο-**, **αριο-**, **υδριο-**, **υλλιο-** (all with nom. in **ιον**); **οἰκ-ίδιον**, *little house* (**οἶκος**); **παιδ-άριον**, *little child;* **μελ-ύδριον**, *little song* (**μέλος**); **ἐπ-ύλλιον**, *little verse, versicle*, Latin *versiculus* (**ἔπος**). Here final **εσ-** of the stem is dropped.

ισκο- (nom. **ίσκος**, masc.) and **ισκᾱ-** (nom. **ίσκη**, fem.): **παιδ-ίσκος**, *young boy*, **παιδ-ίσκη**, *young girl;* so **νεᾱνίσκος**, **νεᾱνίσκη**, from stem **νεᾱν-** (nom. **νεάν**, *youth*).

845. N. Diminutives sometimes express *endearment*, and sometimes *contempt;* as **πατρίδιον**, *papa* (**πατήρ**, *father*), **Σωκρατίδιον**, **Εὐρῑπίδιον**.

846. (*Patronymics.*) These denote *descent* from a parent or ancestor (generally a father), and are formed from proper names by the suffixes **δᾱ-** (nom. **δης**, masc. parox.) and **δ-** (nom. **ς** for **δς**, fem. oxytone); after a consonant **ιδᾱ-** and **ιδ-** (nom. **ίδης** and **ίς**).

1. Stems (in **ᾱ-**) of the first declension shorten **α** and add **δᾱ-** and **δ-**; as **Βορεά-δης**, *son of Boreas*, and **Βορεά-ς**, gen. **Βορεά-δος**, *daughter of Boreas*, from **Βορέᾱς**, *Boreas.*

2. Stems of the second declension drop the final **ο** and add **ιδᾱ-** and **ιδ-**; as **Πριαμ-ίδης**, *son of Priam*, **Πριαμ-ίς**, gen. **Πριαμίδος**, *daughter of Priam*, from **Πρίαμο-ς**. Except those in **ιο-**, which change **ο** to **α**, making nominatives in **ιάδης** and **ιάς** (as in 1); as **Θεστιάδης** and **Θεστιάς**, *son* and *daughter of Thestius* (**Θέστιο-ς**).

3. Stems of the third declension add **ιδᾱ-** and **ιδ-**, those in **ευ** dropping **υ** before **ι**; as **Κεκροπ-ίδης**, *son* (or *descendant*) *of Cecrops*, **Κεκροπ-ίς**, gen. **ίδος**, *daughter of Cecrops*, from **Κέκροψ**, gen. **Κέκροπ-ος**; **Ἀτρείδης** (Hom. **Ἀτρεΐδης**), *son of Atreus*, from **Ἀτρεύ-ς**, gen. **Ἀτρέ-ως**; **Πηλείδης** (Hom. **Πηλεΐδης**), *son of Peleus*,

from Πηλεύ-ς, gen. Πηλέ-ως, Hom. also Πηληιάδης (as if from a form Πηλήιος).

847. N. Occasionally patronymics are formed by the suffix **ιον-** or **ιων-** (nom. **ιων**); as **Κρονίων**, gen. **Κρονίωνος** or **Κρονίονος** (to suit the metre), *son of Cronos* (**Κρόνο-ς**).

848. (*Gentiles.*) 1. These designate a person as belonging to some *country* or *town*, and are formed by the following suffixes:—

ευ- (nom. **εύς**, masc.): **Ἐρετρι-εύς**, *Eretrian* (**Ἐρετρίᾱ**); **Μεγαρ-εύς**, *Megarian* (**Μέγαρα**, pl.); **Κολωνεύς**, *of Colonos* (**Κολωνό-ς**).

τᾱ- (nom. **της**, masc. parox.): **Τεγεά-της**, *of Tegea* (**Τεγέᾱ**), **Ἠπειρώ-της**, *of Epirus* (**Ἤπειρος**), **Σικελιώ-της**, *Sicilian Greek* (**Σικελίᾱ**). (See 829.)

2. Feminine stems in **ιδ-** (nom. ις, gen. ιδος) correspond to masculines in ευ-; as **Μεγαρίς**, *Megarian woman*; and feminines in **τιδ-** (nom. **τις**, gen. τιδος), to masculines in τᾱ-, as Σικελιῶ-τις, *Sicilian woman.*

ADJECTIVES.

849. 1. The simplest suffixes by which primitive adjectives (like nouns) are formed from roots or stems are **ο-** and **ᾱ-** (nom. masc. **ος**; fem. **η**, **ᾱ**, or **ος**; neut. **ον**): **σοφ-ός**, **σοφή**, **σοφόν**, *wise*; **κακ-ός**, *bad*; **λοιπ-ός**, *remaining* (**λειπ-**, **λοιπ-**, 831).

2. Some have **υ-** (nom. **ύς**, **εῖα**, **ύ**), added only to roots: **ἡδ-ύς**, *sweet*, from **ἡδ-** (**ἥδομαι**, *be pleased*); **βαρ-ύς**, *heavy* (root **βαρ-**, cf. **βάρ-ος**, *weight*); **ταχ-ύς**, *swift* (root **ταχ-**, cf. **τάχος**, *swiftness*).

3. Some have **εσ-** (nom. **ης**, **ες**): **ψευδής** (**ψευδεσ-**), *false* (**ψεύδ-ομαι**, *lie*); **σαφ-ής** (**σαφεσ-**), *plain* (root **σαφ-**).

Most adjectives in **ης** are compounds (881).

4. Some expressing *inclination* or *tendency* have **μον-** (nom. **μων**, **μον**): **μνή-μων**, *mindful*, from **μνα-** (**μέ-μνη-μαι**); **τλή-μων**, *suffering*, from **τλα-** (see **τλάω**); **ἐπι-λήσ-μων**, *forgetful*, from **λαθ-** (**λανθάνω**).

850. Adjectives signifying *belonging* or *related* in any way *to* a person or thing are formed from noun stems by the suffix **ιο-** (nom. **ιος**): **οὐράν-ιος**, *heavenly* (**οὐρανό-ς**), **οἰκεῖος**, *domestic* (**οἶκο-ς**, see 829); **δίκαιος**, *just* (**δικᾱ-**), **Ἀθηναῖος**, *Athenian* (**Ἀθῆναι**, stem **Ἀθηνᾱ-**).

851. 1. Denominatives formed by **ικο-** (nom. **ικός**) denote *relation*, like adjectives in **ιος** (850), sometimes *fitness* or *ability*. Stems in **ι** drop **ι** before **ικο-**. *E.g.*

Ἀρχ-ικός, *fit for rule* (**ἀρχή**, *rule*); **πολεμ-ικός**, *warlike, of war* (**πόλεμο-ς**); **φυσ-ικός**, *natural* (**φυσι-**); **βασιλ-ικός**, *kingly* (**βασιλ-εύς**); **γραφ-ικός**, *capable of writing* or *drawing* (**γραφή**).

2. Similar adjectives are formed directly from verb stems by

τικο- (nom. **τικος**): **πρᾱκ-τικός**, *fit for action, practical*, from **πρᾱγ-** (πράσσω); αἰσθη-τικός, *capable of feeling*.

852. Adjectives denoting *material* are formed by

ινο- (nom. **ινος**, proparoxytone), as **λίθ-ινος**, *of stone* (**λίθος**);

εο- (nom. **εος**, contr. **οῦς**), as **χρύσεος**, **χρῡσοῦς**, *golden* (**χρῡσός**).

853. N. Adjectives in **ινός** (oxytone) denote time, as **ἐαρ-ινός**, *vernal* (**ἔαρ**, *spring*), **νυκτερ-ινός**, *by night* (**νύξ**, *night*, **νύκτερος**, *by night*).

854. Those denoting *fulness* (chiefly poetic) are formed by **εντ-** (nom. **εις**, **εσσα**, **εν**); **χαρίεις**, *graceful* (**χάρι-ς**), gen. **χαρί-εντος**; **ὑλή-εις** (872), *woody*; cf. 829. Latin *grātiōsus*, *silvōsus*.

855. Other adjectives with various meanings are formed by various suffixes besides the simple **ο-**; as **νο-**, **λο-**, **ρο-**, **ιμο-**, **μο-**, or **σιμο-**, **τηριο-**, all with nom. in **ος**: **δει-νός** (**δει-**), *terrible*, **δει-λός**, *timid*, **φθονε-ρός**, *envious* (**φθονός**, *envy*), **μάχ-ιμος**, *warlike*, **χρή-σιμος**, *useful*, **ἱππά-σιμος**, *fit for riding* (or *for cavalry*) (from **ἱππά-ζομαι**), **πεισ-τήριος**, *persuasive* (**πείθ-ω**). Verbals in **λός** are active, those in **νός** are passive; those in **ρός** are generally active but sometimes passive, as **φοβε-ρός**, both *frightful* and *afraid*.

856. N. Most adjectives in **νος**, **λος**, and **ρος** are oxytone.

857. All participles are primitive (verbal) adjectives: so the verbals in **τος** and **τεος**.

858. Comparatives and superlatives in **τερος** and **τατος** are denominatives; but those in **ῑων** and **ιστος** are primitives, adding these terminations directly to the root (357, 2).

ADVERBS.

859. Most adverbs are formed from adjectives (see 365–367).

860. Adverbs may be formed also from the stems of nouns or verbs by the following suffixes: —

1. **δόν** (or **δά**), **ηδόν**: **ἀνα-φαν-δόν**, *openly* (**ἀνα-φαίνω**, **φαν-**), poet. also **ἀναφανδά**; **κυν-ηδόν**, *like a dog* (**κύων**, gen. **κυν-ός**).

2. **δην** or **άδην**: **κρύβ-δην**, *secretly* (**κρύπτω**, *conceal*); **συλλήβ-δην**, *collectively* (**συλλαμβάνω**, **λαβ-**, 611); **σπορ-άδην**, *scatteredly* (**σπείρω**, *sow, scatter*, stem **σπερ-**); **ἀνέ-δην**, *profusely* (**ἀν-ίημι**, *let out*, stem **ἑ-**).

3. **τί**: **ὀνομασ-τί**, *by name* (**ὀνομάζω**); **ἑλληνισ-τί**, *in Greek* (**ἑλληνίζω**).

4. See also the local endings **θι**, **θεν**, **δε**, etc. (292–296).

DENOMINATIVE VERBS.

861. A verb whose stem is derived from the stem of a noun or adjective is called a *denominative* (824). The following are the principal terminations of such verbs in the present indicative active: —

1. **αω** (stem in *α*-): *τῑμάω*, *honor*, from noun *τῑμή* (*τῑμᾱ*-), *honor*.
2. **εω** (*ε*-): *ἀριθμέω*, *count*, from *ἀριθμό-ς*, *number* (829).
3. **οω** (*ο*-): *μισθόω*, *let for hire*, from *μισθό-ς*, *pay*.
4. **ευω** (*ευ*-): *βασιλεύω*, *be king*, from *βασιλεύ-ς*, *king* (see 863).
5. **αζω** (*αδ*-): *δικάζω*, *judge*, from *δίκη* (*δικᾱ*-), *justice* (862).
6. **ιζω** (*ιδ*-): *ἐλπίζω*, *hope*, from *ἐλπίς* (*ἐλπιδ*-), *hope* (862).
7. **αινω** (*αν*-): *σημαίνω*, *signify*, from *σῆμα* (*σηματ*-), *sign* (865).
8. **ῡνω** (*υν*-): *ἡδύνω*, *sweeten*, from *ἡδύ-ς*, *sweet* (865).

862. Verbs in *αζω*, *ιζω*, *αινω*, and *ῡνω* are of the fourth class: for their formation, see 579–596. Some denominatives of this class end in *λλω*, *αιρω*, *ειρω*, and *ῡρω*; as *ἀγγέλλω* (*ἄγγελο-ς*), *announce*, *καθαίρω* (*καθαρό-ς*), *purify*, *ἱμείρω* (*ἵμερο-ς*), *long for*, *μαρτύρομαι* (*μαρτύς*, stem *μαρτυρ*-), *call to witness*.

863. Many verbs in *ευω* are formed merely by the analogy of those (like *βασιλεύ-ω*) with stems in *ευ*: thus *βουλεύω*, *take counsel*, from *βουλή*; *ἀληθεύω*, *be truthful*, from *ἀληθής*.

864. Likewise many in *ιζω* and most in *αζω* merely follow the analogy of those like *ἐλπίζω* (*ἐλπιδ*-) and *φράζω* (*φραδ*-), which have actual stems in *δ* (see 587).

865. The stems in *αν* and *υν* of verbs in *αινω* and *ῡνω* come from nominal stems without *ν*: see the examples above.

866. Some verbs in *εω* come from adjectives in *ης* by dropping *εσ*- of the stem; as *εὐτυχέω*, *be fortunate*, from *εὐτυχής* (*εὐτυχεσ*-).

867. N. Verbs formed from the same noun stem with different endings sometimes have different meanings; as *πολεμέω* and (poetic) *πολεμίζω*, *make war*, *πολεμόω*, *make hostile*, both from *πόλεμο-ς*, *war*; *δουλόω*, *enslave*, *δουλεύω*, *be a slave*, from *δοῦλο-ς*, *slave*.

868. (*Desideratives.*) 1. Verbs expressing a *desire* to do anything are sometimes formed from other verbs and from nouns by the ending *σειω* (stem in *σει*-), sometimes *αω* or *ιαω* (*α*- or *ια*-); as *δρᾱ-σείω*, *desire to do* (*δρά-ω*); *γελα-σείω*, *desire to laugh* (*γελά-ω*); *φον-άω*, *be blood-thirsty* (*φόνος*); *κλαυ-σ-ιάω*, *desire to weep* (*κλαίω*, stem *κλαυ*-).

2. Some verbs in *ιαω* denote a bodily condition; as *ὀφθαλμιάω*, *have diseased eyes* (ophthalmia), *ὠχριάω*, *be pale*, *ἐρυθριάω*, *blush*.

COMPOUND WORDS.

869. In a compound word we have to consider (1) the first part of the compound, (2) the last part, and (3) the meaning of the whole.

870. N. The modifications which are necessary when a compound consists of more than two parts will suggest themselves at once.

I. FIRST PART OF A COMPOUND WORD.

871. 1. When the first part of a compound is a noun or adjective, only its stem appears in the compound.

2. Before a consonant, stems of the first declension generally change final ᾱ to ο; those of the second declension retain ο; and those of the third add ο. Before a vowel, stems of the first and second declensions drop ᾱ or ο. *E.g.*

Θαλασσο-κράτωρ (θαλασσᾱ-), *ruler of the sea*, χορο-διδάσκαλος (χορο-), *chorus-teacher*, παιδο-τρίβης (παιδ-), *trainer of boys*, κεφαλ-αλγής (κεφαλᾱ-), *causing headache*, χορ-ηγός (χορο-), (orig.) *chorus-director;* so ἰχθυο-φάγος (ἰχθυ-), *fish-eater*, φυσιο-λόγος, *enquiring into nature*. The analogy of the second (or ο-) declension prevails throughout.

872. N. There are many exceptions. Sometimes η takes the place of ο; as χοη-φόροι (χοή, *libation*), *bringer of libations*, ἐλαφη-βόλος (ἔλαφο-ς), *deer-slayer*. Stems in εσ (226) often change εσ to ο; as τειχο-μαχία (τειχεσ-), *wall-fighting*. The stems of ναῦς, *ship*, and βοῦς, *ox*, generally appear without change (ναυ- and βου); as ναυ-μαχία, *sea-fight*, βου-κόλος, *herdsman*. Sometimes a noun appears in one of its cases, as if it were a distinct word; as νεώσ-οικος, *ship-house*, ναυσί-πορος, *traversed by ships*.

873. Compounds of which the first part is the stem of a verb are chiefly poetic.

1. Here the verbal stem sometimes appears without change before a vowel, and with ε, ι, or ο added before a consonant. *E.g.*

Πείθ-αρχος, *obedient to authority;* μεν-ε-πτόλεμος, *steadfast in battle;* ἀρχ-ι-τέκτων, *master-builder;* λιπ-ό-γαμος, *marriage-leaving (adulterous)*.

2. Sometimes σι (before a vowel σ) is added to the verb stem. *E.g.*

Λῡ-σί-πονος, *toil-relieving;* στρεψί-δικος (στρεφ-), *justice-twisting;* τερψί-νοος (τερπ-), *soul-delighting;* πλήξ-ιππος (πληγ-), *horse-lashing*.

874. 1. A preposition or an adverb may be the first part of a compound word; as in προ-βάλλω, *throw before* (882, 1), ἀει-λογίᾱ, *continual talking*, εὐ-γενής, *well-born*.

2. Here no change of form occurs, except when a final vowel is elided, or when πρό contracts ο with a following ε or ο into ου, as in προὔχω (πρό, ἔχω), *hold before;* προὔργου (πρό, ἔργου), *forward;* φροῦδος (πρὸ, ὁδοῦ), *gone* (93).

3. Euphonic changes occur here as usual; as in ἐγχώριος (ἐν and χώρα): see 78.

875. The following *inseparable* prefixes are never used alone: —

1. **αν-** (α- before a consonant), called *alpha privative*, with a negative force, like English *un-*, Latin *in-*. It is prefixed to noun, adjective, and verb stems, to form adjectives; as ἀν-ελεύθερος, *unfree*, ἀν-αιδής, *shameless*, ἀν-όμοιος, *unlike*, ἄ-παις, *childless*, ἄ-γραφος, *unwritten*, ἄ-θεος, *godless*, ἄ-(ϝ)οινος, *wineless*.

2. **δυσ-**, *ill* (opposed to εὖ, *well*), denoting *difficulty* or *trouble;* as δύσ-πορος, *hard to pass* (opposed to εὔ-πορος); δυσ-τυχής, *unfortunate* (opposed to εὐ-τυχής).

3. **νη-** (Latin *ne*), a poetic *negative* prefix; as νή-ποινος, *unavenged; νη-μερτής*, *unerring* (for νη-αμερτής).

4. **ἡμι-** (Latin *semi-*), *half;* as ἡμί-θεος, *demigod*.

876. N. A few intensive prefixes are found in poetry, — ἀρι-, ἐρι-, δα-, ζα-, as ἀρί-γνωτος, *well-known;* δα-φοινός, *bloody*.

877. N. The prefix α- is sometimes *copulative* (denoting *union*); as in ἄ-λοχος, *bedfellow* (from λέχος).

II. LAST PART OF A COMPOUND WORD.

878. At the beginning of the last part of a compound noun or adjective, α, ε, or ο (unless it is long by position) is very often lengthened to η or ω. *E.g.*

Στρατ-ηγός (στρατό-ς, ἄγω), *general; ὑπ-ήκοος* (ὑπό, ἀκούω), *obedient; κατ-ηρεφής* (κατά, ἐρέφω), *covered; ἐπ-ώνυμος* (ἐπί, ὄνομα), *naming* or *named for; κατ-ήγορος* (κατά, ἀγορά), *accuser;* but ἄν-ολβος, *unblest*.

879. The last part of a compound noun or adjective is often changed in form before the suffix. This takes place especially in compound adjectives, and when an abstract noun forms the last part of a compound noun. *E.g.*

Φιλό-τῑμος (τῑμή), *honor-loving; εὔ-φρων* (φρήν), *joyous; πολυ-πράγμων* (πρᾶγμα), *meddlesome; λιθο-βολίᾱ* (λίθος, βολή), *stone-throwing, ναυ-μαχίᾱ* (ναῦς, μάχη), *sea-fight; εὐ-πρᾱξίᾱ* (πρᾶξις), *success (doing well)*.

880. N. An abstract noun compounded with a preposition may retain its form; as προ-βουλή, *forethought*.

881. Compound adjectives in ης (849, 3) are especially frequent.

1. The last part may be a noun, generally a neuter in ος (stem

in εσ-); as εὐ-γενής (γένος), *well born*, δεκα-ετής (ἔτος), *of ten years;* εὐ-τυχής (τύχη), *fortunate.*

2. The last part may be formed from a verb stem; as ἀ-φαν-ής (φαν), *unseen*, ἡμι-θανής (θαν-), *half-dead.*

882. 1. A compound verb can be formed *directly* only by prefixing a preposition to a verb; as προσ-άγω, *bring to.*

2. Indirect compounds (denominatives) are formed from compound nouns or adjectives. *E.g.*

Λιθοβολέω, *throw stones*, denom. from λιθο-βόλος, *stone-thrower;* νομοθετέω, *make laws*, from νομο-θέτης, *law-maker;* ἀπειθέω, *disobey*, from ἀπειθής, *disobedient;* κατηγορέω, *accuse*, from κατ-ήγορος (878), *accuser.* See 543.

III. MEANING OF COMPOUNDS.

883. Compound nouns and adjectives are of three classes, distinguished by the relation of the parts of the compound to each other and to the whole.

884. (1) *Objective* compounds are those composed of a noun and a verb, adjective, or preposition, in which the noun (as first or second part) stands to the other part in some relation (commonly that of object) which could be expressed by an oblique case of the noun. *E.g.*

Λογο-γράφος, *speech-writer* (λόγους γράφων); μισ-άνθρωπος, *man-hating* (μισῶν ἀνθρώπους); λῡσί-πονος, *toil-relieving;* στρατ-ηγός, *general* (*army-leading*, στρατὸν ἄγων); ἀξιό-λογος, *worthy of mention* (ἄξιος λόγου); ἁμαρτ-ί-νοος (873, 1), *erring in mind* (ἁμαρτὼν νοῦ); ἰσό-θεος, *godlike* (ἴσος θεῷ); τερπ-ι-κέραυνος (873, 1), *delighting in thunder* (τερπόμενος κεραυνῷ); διο-τρεφής, *reared by Zeus* (cf. δι-πετής, *fallen* or *sent from Zeus*, and Δι-τρεφής, a proper name). So with a preposition: ἐγ-χώριος, *native* (ἐν χώρᾳ); ἐφ-ίππιος, *belonging on a horse* (ἐφ' ἵππῳ); ἐφ-έστιος, *on the hearth* (ἐφ' ἑστίᾳ).

885. N. When the last part of an objective compound is a *transitive* verbal in ος formed by the suffix ο- (832), it generally accents the penult if this is *short*, otherwise the last syllable. But if the last part is intransitive or passive (in sense), the accent is recessive. Thus λογο-γράφος, *speech-writer;* λιθο-βόλος, *thrower of stones*, but λιθό-βολος, *pelted with stones;* μητρο-κτόνος, *matricide, matricidal;* but στρατ-ηγός, *general;* λογο-ποιός, *story-maker.*

886. (2) *Determinative* compounds are nouns or adjectives in which the first part, generally as adjective or adverb, qualifies (or *determines*) the second part. *E.g.*

Ἀκρό-πολις, *citadel* (ἄκρᾱ πόλις); μεσ-ημβρίᾱ (μεσῃ ἡμέρᾳ, 66), *mid-day; ψευδό-μαντις, false prophet;* ὁμό-δουλος, *fellow-slave* (ὁμοῦ δουλεύων); δυσ-μαθής, *learning with difficulty;* ὠκυ-πέτης, *swift-flying;* προ-βουλή, *forethought;* ἀμφι-θέατρον, *amphitheatre* (*theatre extending all round*); ἄ-γραφος, *unwritten*. Here belong adjectives like μελι-ηδής (ἡδύς), *honey-sweet*, Ἀρηΐ-θοος, *swift as Ares* (*Ares-swift*).

887. N. Here belong a few compounds sometimes called *copulative*, made of two nouns or two adjectives, and signifying a combination of the two things or qualities. Strictly, the first part limits the last, like an adjective or adverb. Such are ἰατρό-μαντις, *physician-prophet* (a *prophet* who is also a *physician*); ξιφο-μάχαιρα, *sword-sabre;* ἀνδρό-παις, *man-child;* γλυκύ-πικρος, *sweetly bitter;* θεό-ταυρος, *god-bull* (of Zeus changed to a bull).

888. (3) *Possessive* or *attributive* compounds are adjectives in which the first part qualifies the second (as in determinatives), and the whole denotes a quality or attribute belonging to some person or thing. *E.g.*

Ἀργυρό-τοξος, *with silver-bow* (ἀργυροῦν τόξον ἔχων); κακο-δαίμων, *ill-fated* (κακὸν δαίμονα ἔχων); πικρό-γαμος, *wretchedly married* (πικρὸν γάμον ἔχων); ὁμό-νομος, *having the same laws;* ἑκατογ-κέφαλος, *hundred-headed;* δεκα-ετής, *of ten years* (duration); ἀγαθο-ειδής, *having the appearance* (εἶδος) *of good;* ἔν-θεος, *inspired* (*having God within*); ὠκύ-πους, *swift-footed* (ὠκεῖς πόδας ἔχων), — but ποδ-ώκης (πόδας ὠκύς), *foot-swift*, is a determinative.

889. N. In compound verbs, the original verb remains the fundamental part, modified more or less in meaning by the preposition prefixed. Other compounds than those here mentioned present no difficulties in respect to meaning.

PART IV.

SYNTAX.

DEFINITIONS.

890. (*Subject and Predicate.*) Every sentence must contain two parts, a *subject* and a *predicate*. The subject is that of which something is stated. The predicate is that which is stated of the subject. Thus in the sentence Δαρεῖος βασιλεύει τῶν Περσῶν, *Darius is king of the Persians*, Δαρεῖος is the subject and βασιλεύει τῶν Περσῶν is the predicate.

891. 1. When any part of *εἰμί*, *be*, connects the subject with a following noun or adjective, the verb is called the *copula* (i.e. *means of coupling*), and what follows is called the predicate; as *Δαρεῖός ἐστι βασιλεύς*, *Darius is king*, *Σόλων ἐστὶ σοφός*, *Solon is wise*, where *ἐστί* is the copula. The copulas *ἐστί* and *εἰσί* are often omitted, especially in proverbial sayings, as *χαλεπὰ τὰ καλά*, *fine things are hard*, P. *Rp.* 435[c], with nouns like *ἀνάγκη*, *necessity*, *ὥρα*, *time*, and with the impersonal verbal in *-τέον*. For copulative verbs, see 908.

2. *Εἰμί*, however, can form a complete predicate, as in *εἰσὶ θεοί*, *Gods exist.*

892. (*Object.*) That upon which the action of a verb is exerted is called the *object*. The object may be either *direct* or *indirect:* thus, in ἔδωκε τὰ χρήματα τῷ ἀνδρί, *he gave the money to the man*, *χρήματα* is the direct object and *ἀνδρί* is the indirect (or remote) object.

893. Verbs which can have a direct object are called *transitive;* those which cannot are called *intransitive.*

SUBJECT AND PREDICATE.

SUBJECT.

894. The subject of a finite verb (446) is in the nominative; as ὁ ἀνὴρ ἦλθεν, *the man came.*

895. 1. The subject of the infinitive is in the accusative; as φησὶ τοὺς ἄνδρας ἀπελθεῖν, *he says that the men went away.*

2. But the subject of the infinitive is generally omitted when it is the same as the subject or the object (direct or indirect) of the leading verb; as βούλεται ἀπελθεῖν, *he wishes to go away;* φησὶ γράφειν, *he says that he is writing;* παραινοῦμέν σοι μένειν, *we advise you to remain.*

3. So when it is the same with any important adjunct of the leading verb; as κακούργου ἐστὶ κριθέντ' ἀποθανεῖν, *it is like a malefactor to die by sentence of the law* (928, 2), D. 4, 47.

896. The subject nominative of the first or second person is omitted, except when special emphasis is required.

897. The nominative of the third person is omitted:—

1. When it is expressed or implied in the context; as ὁ Κῦρος πράσσει ἃ βούλεται, *Cyrus does what he* (Cyrus) *pleases;*

2. When it is a general word for *persons;* as λέγουσι, *they say, it is said;*

3. When it is indefinite; as in ὀψὲ ἦν, *it was late;* καλῶς ἔχει, *it is well;* δηλοῖ, *it is evident* (*the case shows*): so in the impersonal construction with the verbal in τέον, as in πειστέον (ἐστὶ) τῷ νόμῳ, *we must obey the law* (1597).

4. When the verb implies its own subject, as κηρύσσει, *the herald* (κῆρυξ) *proclaims,* ἐσάλπιγξε, *the trumpeter sounded the trumpet,* κωλύει, *a hindrance occurs.* In passive expressions like παρεσκεύασταί μοι, *preparation has been made by me* (*I am prepared*), the subject is really the idea of *preparation* etc. contained in the verb. See 1240.

5. With verbs like ὕει, *it rains,* ἀστράπτει, *it lightens,* σείει, *there is an earthquake* (*it shakes*), where, however, some subject like Ζεύς or θεός was originally supplied.

898. Many verbs in the third person singular have an infinitive or a sentence as their subject. These are called *impersonal* verbs. Such are πρέπει and προσήκει, *it is proper*, ἔνεστι and ἔξεστι, *it is possible*, δοκεῖ, *it seems good*, συμβαίνει, *it happens*, and the like; as ἔξεστιν ὑμῖν τοῦτο ποιεῖν, *it is in your power to do this* (*to do this is possible for you*). So also δεῖ and χρή, *it is required*, *we ought*; as δεῖ ἡμᾶς ἀπελθεῖν, *we must go away*.

The name *impersonal* is applied with greater propriety (though less frequently) to the verbs of 897, 3 and 4.

SUBJECT NOMINATIVE AND VERB.

899. 1. A verb agrees with its subject nominative in number and person; as (ἐγὼ) λέγω, *I say*, οὗτος λέγει, *this man says*, οἱ ἄνδρες λέγουσιν, *the men say*.

2. But a nominative in the *neuter plural* regularly takes a singular verb; as ταῦτα ἐγένετο, *these things happened*, τὰ οἰκήματα ἔπεσεν, *the buildings fell*. So ἀδύνατά ἐστι (or ἀδύνατόν ἐστι), *it is impossible*.

Exceptions sometimes occur, especially with nouns denoting persons. Several are found in Xenophon; as in *A*. 1, 7[17].

900. A singular collective noun denoting persons *may* take a plural verb; as τὸ πλῆθος ἐψηφίσαντο πολεμεῖν, *the majority voted for war*, T. 1, 125.

901. N. When several subjects are connected by *and*, they generally have a plural verb. But the verb may agree with one of the subjects (generally the nearest), and be understood with the rest. The latter generally happens when they are connected by *or* or *nor*. *E.g.*

Σοφοὶ ἐγώ τε καὶ σὺ ἦμεν, *you and I were wise*, P. *Th.* 154[d]; μαχούμεθα κοινῇ ἐγώ τε καὶ σύ, *you and I will fight together*, P. *Rp.* 335[e]; οὐ σὺ μόνος οὐδὲ οἱ σοὶ φίλοι πρῶτον ταύτην δόξαν ἔσχετε, *it was not you alone nor your friends who first took up this notion*, P. *Lg.* 888[b]. Ἐμὲ οὔτε καιρὸς οὔτ' ἐλπὶς οὔτε φόβος οὔτ' ἄλλο οὐδὲν ἐπῆρεν, *neither opportunity nor hope nor fear nor anything else incited me*, D. 18, 298.

902. N. If the subjects are of different persons, the verb is in the first person rather than the second or third, and in the second rather than the third. (See examples under 901.)

903. N. A verb in the dual may follow two subjects in the singular, or even a plural subject denoting two persons or things. But even a subject in the dual may have a verb in the plural. (See *Il.* 4, 453; 5, 10, 275; 16, 218.)

904. N. Sometimes a verb agrees with the predicate nominative; as *αἱ δὲ εἰσφοραὶ καὶ χορηγίαι εὐδαιμονίας ἱκανὸν σημεῖόν ἐστιν, his taxes and payments for choruses are a sufficient sign of prosperity*, Ant. 2, γ. 8.

905. N. Rarely a singular verb has a masculine or feminine subject in the plural; as *ἔστι δὲ ἑπτὰ στάδιοι ἐξ Ἀβύδου ἐς τὴν ἀπαντίον, and there is a distance of seven stades from Abydos to the opposite coast*, Hd. 7, 34. In such cases the plural form often seems to have arisen from an afterthought, especially when the subject follows the verb.

See also the phrases *ἔστιν οἵ* etc., 1029.

906. N. A preposition with a numeral may represent the subject of a verb; as *ἀπέθανον αὐτῶν περὶ τριακοσίους, about three hundred of them perished*, X. *H.* 4, 6^{11}.

PREDICATE NOUN AND ADJECTIVE.

907. With verbs signifying *to be, to become, to appear, to be named, chosen, made, thought* or *regarded*, and the like, a noun or adjective in the predicate is in the same case as the subject. *E.g.*

Οὗτός ἐστι βασιλεύς, this man is king; Ἀλέξανδρος θεὸς ὠνομάζετο, Alexander was named a God; ᾑρέθη στρατηγός, he was chosen general; ἡ πόλις φρούριον κατέστη, the city became a fortress, T. 7, 28; *οὗτός ἐστιν εὐδαίμων, this man is happy; ἡ πόλις μεγάλη ἐγένετο, the city became great; ηὔξηται μέγας, he has grown (to be) great; νομίζεται σοφός, he is thought wise.*

908. The verbs which are here included with the copula *εἰμί* (891, 1) are called *copulative* verbs. The predicate nominative with the passive verbs of this class represents the predicate accusative of the active construction (1077).

909. The predicate *adjective* with these verbs agrees with the subject in gender and number, as well as in case. (See 919.)

910. The predicate of an infinitive with its subject accusative expressed (895, 1) is in the accusative; as *βούλεται τὸν υἱὸν εἶναι σοφόν, he wishes his son to be wise.* So when the participle is used like the infinitive in indirect discourse (1494); as *ᾔδεσαν τὸν Κῦρον βασιλέα γενόμενον, they knew that Cyrus had become king.*

For such a predicate with the subject omitted, see 927 and 928.

APPOSITION.

911. A noun annexed to another noun to describe it, and denoting the same person or thing, agrees with it in case. This is called *apposition*, and the noun thus used is called an *appositive*. *E.g.*

Δαρεῖος ὁ βασιλεύς, *Darius the king.* Ἀθῆναι, μεγάλη πόλις, *Athens, a great city.* Ὑμᾶς τοὺς σοφούς, *you, the wise ones.* Ἡμῶν τῶν Ἀθηναίων, *of us, the Athenians.* Θεμιστοκλῆς ἥκω (sc. ἐγὼ) παρὰ σέ, *I, Themistocles, am come to you,* T. 1, 137. Φιλήσιος καὶ Λύκων οἱ Ἀχαιοί, *Philesius and Lycon, the Achaeans,* X. *A.* 5, 6[27].

912. N. A noun in apposition with two or more nouns is generally plural (or dual); as ὕπνος πόνος τε, κύριοι ξυνωμόται, *sleep and toil, lordly conspirators,* A. *Eu.* 127; θάρρος καὶ φόβον, ἄφρονε ξυμβούλω, *daring and fear, two senseless counsellors,* P. *Ti.* 69[d].

913. N. An adjective may have a genitive in apposition with a genitive which it implies; as Ἀθηναῖος ὤν, πόλεως τῆς μεγίστης, *being (a citizen) of Athens, the greatest city,* P. *Ap.* 29[d].

For a genitive in apposition with the genitive implied in a possessive pronoun, see 1001.

914. N. A noun which might stand in the *partitive* genitive (1088) sometimes takes the case of the words denoting its parts, especially when the latter include the *whole* of the former; as οἰκίαι αἱ μὲν πολλαὶ πεπτώκεσαν, ὀλίγαι δὲ περιῆσαν, *most of the houses had fallen, but a few remained* (where we might have τῶν οἰκιῶν), T. 1, 89. So οὗτοι ἄλλος ἄλλα λέγει, *these men all say different things,* X. *A.* 2, 1[15]. This is called *partitive* apposition.

915. N. A noun may be in apposition with a whole sentence, being in the nominative when it is closely connected in thought with the subject of the sentence, elsewhere in the accusative; as κεῖνται πεσόντες, πίστις οὐ σμικρὰ πόλει, *they lie prostrate,—no small (cause of) confidence to the city,* E. *Rh.* 415. Ἑλένην κτάνωμεν, Μενέλεῳ λύπην πικράν, *let us kill Helen, (which will be) a bitter grief to Menelaus,* E. *Or.* 1105.

916. N. A noun may be in apposition with the subject or the object of a sentence, where we use *as* or a like word; as ἵπποι ἤγοντο θῦμα τῷ Ἡλίῳ, *horses were brought as an offering to the Sun* (in active, ἵππους ἄγειν θῦμα, *to bring horses as an offering*), X. *C.* 8, 3[12]; ἔξεστιν ὑμῖν ἡμᾶς λαβεῖν ξυμμάχους, *you can gain us as allies,* X. *A.* 5, 4[6]. So τυχεῖν τινος φίλου, *to gain some one as a friend;* χρῶμαι τούτῳ φίλῳ, *I treat him as a friend.* So τίνος διδάσκαλοι ἥκετε; *as teachers of what are you come?* P. *Eu.* 287[a]. See 1080.

917. N. Homer often adds an appositive denoting a *part* to a noun or pronoun denoting a person; as Δηιοπίτην οὔτασεν ὦμον, *he wounded D. in the shoulder*, *Il.* 11, 420; ἀλλ' οὐκ Ἀτρεΐδῃ Ἀγαμέμνονι ἥνδανε θυμῷ, *but he was not pleasing to the heart of Agamemnon, son of Atreus* (lit. to *A., his heart*), *Il.* 1, 24.

For ὁ δέ in Homer followed by a noun in apposition, see 937, 1.

AGREEMENT OF ADJECTIVES.

918. Adjectives agree with their nouns in gender, number, and case. This applies also to the article and to adjective pronouns and participles. *E.g.*

Ὁ σοφὸς ἀνήρ, *the wise man*; τοῦ σοφοῦ ἀνδρός, τῷ σοφῷ ἀνδρί, τὸν σοφὸν ἄνδρα, τῶν σοφῶν ἀνδρῶν, etc. Οὗτος ὁ ἀνήρ, *this man*; τούτου τοῦ ἀνδρός, τούτων τῶν ἀνδρῶν. Αἱ πρὸ τοῦ στόματος νῆες ναυμαχοῦσαι, *the ships engaged in battle before the mouth* (*of the harbor*), T. 7, 23.

This includes predicate adjectives with copulative verbs, the *case* of which has already been considered (907); as αἱ ἄρισται δοκοῦσαι εἶναι φύσεις, *the natures which seem to be best*, X. *M.* 4, 1[3].

919. The adjective may be either *attributive* or *predicate*. An attributive adjective simply qualifies the noun, without the intervention of any verbal form (like all the adjectives in 918, except ἄρισται). The predicate adjective may be connected with its noun by the copula (891) or by a copulative verb (908); as ὁ ἀνὴρ ἀγαθός ἐστιν, *the man is good*; καλεῖται ἀγαθός, *he is called good*. It may stand to its noun in any relation which implies some part of εἰμί; as πτηνὰς διώκεις τὰς ἐλπίδας, *you are pursuing hopes which are winged* (i.e. *hopes being winged*), E. frag. 273; ἀθάνατον τὴν μνήμην καταλείψουσιν, *immortal is the memory they will leave behind them* (i.e. τὴν μνήμην οὖσαν ἀθάνατον), I. 9, 3; ποιεῖ τοὺς Μήδους ἀσθενεῖς, *he makes the Medes* (*to be*) *weak*. Every adjective which is not attributive is classed as a predicate.

A predicate adjective is often known by its position with respect to the article; see 971, and the examples.

920. N. A collective noun in the singular denoting persons may take a plural *participle*; as Τροίαν ἑλόντες Ἀργείων στόλος, *the Argives' army having taken Troy*, A. *Ag.* 577.

921. N. An adjective may conform to the *real* rather than the *grammatical* gender of a noun denoting a person; as φίλε τέκνον, *dear child!* *Il.* 22, 84.

922. N. Δύο, *two*, is often used with a plural noun; as εὖρος δύο πλέθρων (1085, 5), *of two plethra in breadth*, X. *A.* 1, 2[23].

923. N. An *attributive* adjective belonging to several nouns generally agrees with the nearest or the most prominent one, and is understood with the rest; as τὸν καλὸν κἀγαθὸν ἄνδρα καὶ γυναῖκα, *the honorable man and woman*, P. *G.* 470[e]; παντὶ καὶ λόγῳ καὶ μηχανῇ, *by every word and device.*

924. N. (*a*) A *predicate* adjective (like a verb, 901) is regularly plural if it belongs to several singular nouns, or dual if it belongs to two. If the nouns are of different genders, the adjective is commonly masculine if one of the nouns denotes a male *person*, and commonly neuter if all denote things. Thus, εἶδε πατέρα τε καὶ μητέρα καὶ ἀδελφοὺς καὶ τὴν ἑαυτοῦ γυναῖκα αἰχμαλώτους γεγενημένους, *he saw that both his father and his mother, his brothers, and his own wife had been made captives*, X. *C.* 3, 1[7]; δόξα δὴ καὶ ἐπιμέλεια καὶ νοῦς καὶ τέχνη καὶ νόμος σκληρῶν καὶ μαλακῶν πρότερα ἂν εἴη, P. *Lg.* 892[b].

(*b*) But it sometimes follows both the gender and number of the nearest or most prominent noun; as πρόρριζος αὐτὸς, ἡ γυνὴ, τὰ παιδία, κάκιστ' ἀπολοίμην, *may I perish most wretchedly root and branch, myself, my wife, my children*, Ar. *R.* 587.

925. N. A masculine or feminine noun in the singular, denoting a class rather than an individual, may have a neuter predicate adjective, which is used as a noun; as καλὸν ἡ ἀλήθεια, *a beautiful thing is truth*, P. *Lg.* 663[e]; ἀθάνατον ἄρα ἡ ψυχή; *is the soul then immortal (an immortal thing)?* P. *Ph.* 105[e].

926. N. A predicate adjective is sometimes used where we should use an adverb or adverbial phrase; as ἑκόντες ἦλθον, *they came willingly;* ὅρκιος δέ σοι λέγω, *I say it to you on my oath*, S. *An.* 305; πρῶτος δ' ἐξερέεινε Νέστωρ, *and first, Nestor inquired*, *Il.* 10, 543. There is often, however, a great distinction between the adjective and the adverb; as πρῶτος αὐτοὺς εἶδον, *I was the first to see them;* πρώτους αὐτοὺς εἶδον, *they were the first whom I saw;* πρῶτον (adv.) αὐτοὺς εἶδον, *first* (of all that I did) *I saw them.*

ADJECTIVES BELONGING TO THE OMITTED SUBJECT OF AN INFINITIVE.

927. When the subject of an infinitive is omitted because it is the same as the subject nominative of the leading verb (895, 2), adjective words and nouns which would agree with the omitted subject are assimilated to the preceding nominative. *E.g.*

Βούλεται σοφὸς εἶναι, *he wishes to be wise;* Πέρσης ἔφη εἶναι, *he said he was a Persian*, X.*A*.4,4[17]. Οὐχ ὁμολογήσω ἄκλητος ἥκειν, *I shall not admit that I am come unbidden*, P.*Sy*.174[4]; οὐκ ἔφη αὐτὸς ἀλλ' ἐκεῖνον στρατηγεῖν, *he* (Cleon) *said that not* (*he*) *himself, but he* (Nicias) *was general;* he said οὐκ (ἐγὼ) αὐτὸς (στρατηγῶ) ἀλλ' ἐκεῖνος στρατηγεῖ, αὐτός being adjective (989, 1) and ἐκεῖνος substantive; T.4,28. Such adjective words or nouns may be in the predicate with copulative verbs (907) or in other constructions. The assimilating nominative may be either expressed or understood.

928. But when the subject of an infinitive is omitted because it is the same as the object or other adjunct (895, 3) of the leading verb, —

1. If this adjunct is a dative, adjective words and nouns may either be assimilated to the dative, or stand in the accusative in agreement with the omitted subject of the infinitive. *E.g.*

Πρέπει σοι εἶναι προθύμῳ (or πρόθυμον), *it becomes you to be zealous;* νῦν σοι ἔξεστιν ἀνδρὶ γενέσθαι, *now it is in your power to show yourself a man*, X.*A*.7,1[21]; παντὶ προσήκει ἄρχοντι φρονίμῳ εἶναι, *it becomes every ruler to be prudent*, X.*Hip*.7,1; συμφέρει αὐτοῖς φίλους εἶναι, *it is for their interest to be friends*, X.*Oe*.11,23. Ἔδοξεν αὐτοῖς συσκευασαμένοις ἃ εἶχον καὶ ἐξοπλισαμένοις προϊέναι, *they decided to pack up what they had and arm themselves completely, and to advance*, X.*A*.2,1[2]; but ἔδοξεν αὐτοῖς προφυλακὰς καταστήσαντας συγκαλεῖν τοὺς στρατιώτας, *they decided to station pickets and to assemble the soldiers* (*ib*.3,2[1]); in 1,2[1], we find two datives and an accusative.

2. If the adjunct is a genitive, *predicate* adjectives are generally assimilated to it; but other adjective words and all nouns stand in the accusative. *E.g.*

Κύρου ἐδέοντο ὡς προθυμοτάτου γενέσθαι, *they asked Cyrus to be as devoted to them as possible*, X.*H*.1,5[2]; but (with a noun) Ἀθηναίων ἐδεήθησαν σφίσι βοηθοὺς γενέσθαι, *they asked the Athenians to become their helpers*, Hd.6,100; κακούργου ἐστὶ κριθέντ' ἀποθανεῖν, στρατηγοῦ δὲ μαχόμενον τοῖς πολεμίοις, *it is like a malefactor to die by the sentence of a court, but like a general* (*to die*) *fighting the enemy*, D.4,47; δέομαι ὑμῶν μεμνημένους τῶν εἰρημένων τὰ δίκαια ψηφίσασθαι, *I beg of you to remember what has been said, and to vote what is just*, I.19,51.

929. Words in the construction of 928 which refer to a preceding accusative are of course in the accusative; as ἄλλους πέπεικα συμμαθητάς μοι φοιτᾶν, *I have induced others to go as my fellow-pupils*, P. *Eu.* 272ᵉ.

930. N. The principles of 927 and 928 apply also to a predicate with ὤν or with the participle of a copulative verb; as ᾔδεσαν σοφοὶ ὄντες, *they knew that they were wise* (but ᾔδεσαν τούτους σοφοὺς ὄντας, *they knew that these men were wise*).

931. N. When an infinitive depends on a participle which supplies its omitted subject, predicate words take the case of the participle; as ἦλθον ἐπί τινα τῶν δοκούντων εἶναι σοφῶν, *I went to one of those who seemed to be wise*, P. *Ap.* 21ᵇ; τῶν προσποιουμένων εἶναι σοφιστῶν τινας, *some of those who profess to be sophists*, I. 15, 221. So τοῖς δοκοῦσιν εἶναι σοφοῖς, *to those who seem to be wise.*

ADJECTIVE USED AS A NOUN.

932. 1. An adjective or participle, generally with the article, may be used as a noun. *E.g.*

Ὁ δίκαιος, *the just man*; ὁ ἐχθρός, *the enemy*; φίλος, *a friend*; κακή, *a base woman*; τὸ μέσον or μέσον, *the middle*; οἱ κακοί, *the bad*; τοῖς ἀγαθοῖς, *to the good*; τῶν κρατούντων, *of those in power*; κακά, *evils*; τὰ θνητά, *mortal things*: οἱ γραψάμενοι Σωκράτην, *the accusers of Socrates.*

2. In some cases, a noun is distinctly implied; as τῇ ὑστεραίᾳ (*sc.* ἡμέρᾳ), *on the next day*; ἡ δεξιά (*sc.* χείρ), *the right hand*; ἡ εὐθεῖα (*sc.* ὁδός), *the straight road*; ὁ ἄκρατος (*sc.* οἶνος), *unmixed wine*; ἐς τὴν ἑαυτῶν (*sc.* γῆν), *into their own land.*

933. The neuter singular of an adjective with the article is often used as an abstract noun; as τὸ καλόν, *beauty* (= κάλλος), τὸ δίκαιον, *justice* (= δικαιοσύνη).

934. N. The participle, which is a verbal adjective, is occasionally thus used for the infinitive, which is a verbal noun; as τὸ δεδιός, *fear* (= τὸ δεδιέναι), T. 1, 36; ἐν τῷ μὴ μελετῶντι, *in the want of practice* (*in the not practising*) (= ἐν τῷ μὴ μελετᾶν), T. 1, 142. So in Latin, opus est maturato, *there is need of haste.*

THE ARTICLE.

HOMERIC USE OF THE ARTICLE.

935. In Homer the article appears generally as a demonstrative or personal pronoun; sometimes (in the forms beginning with τ) as a relative. *E.g.*

Τὴν δ' ἐγὼ οὐ λύσω, *but I will not free her*, *Il.* 1, 29; τοῦ δὲ κλύε Φοῖβος Ἀπόλλων, *and Phoebus Apollo heard him*, *Il.* 1, 43; ὁ γὰρ ἦλθε θοὰς ἐπὶ νῆας Ἀχαιῶν, *for he came to the swift ships of the Achaeans*, *Il.* 1, 12. As relative, πυρὰ πολλὰ τὰ καίετο, *many fires which were burning*, *Il.* 10, 12; δῶρα τά οἱ ξεῖνος δῶκε, *gifts which a stranger gave him*, *Od.* 21, 13.

936. N. Even in Homer, adjectives and participles used as nouns (932, 1) have the article, as in Attic Greek; as οἱ γὰρ ἄριστοι ἐν νηυσὶν κέαται, *for the bravest sit by the ships*, *Il.* 11, 658; οἱ ἄλλοι, *the others*; τά τ' ἐόντα τά τ' ἐσσόμενα, *both things that are and things that are to be*, *Il.* 1, 70.

937. 1. When the article is used with nouns in Homer, it is generally a pronoun (especially ὁ δέ), with which the noun is in apposition; as ὁ δ' ἔβραχε χάλκεος Ἄρης, *and he, brazen Ares, roared*, *Il.* 5, 859; ἡ δ' ἀέκουσ' ἅμα τοῖσι γυνὴ κίεν, *and she, the woman, went with them unwilling*, *Il.* 1, 348.

2. Nearer the Attic use of the article are examples like these: αὐτὰρ ὁ τοῖσι γέρων ὁδὸν ἡγεμόνευεν, *but he, the old man, showed them the way*, *Od.* 24, 225; τὸν δ' οἶον πατέρ' εὗρον, *and they found him, the father, alone*, *ib.* 226.

3. Hardly, if at all, to be distinguished from the Attic article is that found in examples like these: ὅτε δὴ τὴν νῆσον ἀφικόμεθ', *when now we came to the island*, *Od.* 9, 543; τό τε σθένος Ὠρίωνος, *and the might of Orion*, *Il.* 18, 486; αἱ δὲ γυναῖκες ἱστάμεναι θαύμαζον, *and the women stood and wondered*, *Il.* 18, 495.

4. It is, therefore, often difficult to decide the exact force of an article in early Greek. The above examples show a gradual transition, even in Homer, from the original pronoun to the true definite article.

938. N. The examples in 937, 3, are exceptional; and in such cases the nouns usually stand without the article in Homer, as in Latin. Thus δεινὴ δὲ κλαγγὴ γένετ' ἀργυρέοιο βιοῖο, *and terrible came the clang from the silver bow*, *Il.* 1, 49, would in Attic Greek require ἡ κλαγγὴ and τοῦ βιοῦ.

939. Herodotus generally uses the forms of the article beginning with τ in the place of the ordinary relative, — of which he uses only the forms ὅς, ἥ, οἵ, and αἵ, except after prepositions. Thus ἄλλος ὄρνις ἱρὸς, τῷ οὔνομα Φοῖνιξ, *another sacred bird, whose name is Phoenix*, 2, 73. In other respects, he uses the article as it is used in Attic prose.

940. N. The lyric poets follow the Homeric usage with respect to the article more closely than Herodotus; and the tragic poets, especially in the lyric chorus, admit the Homeric use of the article as a relative or a personal pronoun.

ATTIC USE OF THE ARTICLE.

941. In Attic Greek the article generally corresponds to our article *the;* as ὁ ἀνήρ, *the man;* τῶν πόλεων, *of the cities;* τοῖς Ἕλλησιν, *to the Greeks;* τὰ δέκα ἔτη, *the* (well known) *ten years* (at Troy), T. 1, 11.

942. The Greek may use the article in certain cases in which the English omits it. Such are the following (943–951): —

943. Proper names may take the article; as ὁ Σωκράτης or Σωκράτης, *Socrates.*

944. Abstract nouns often take the article; as ἡ ἀρετή, *virtue,* ἡ δικαιοσύνη, *justice;* ἡ εὐλάβεια, *caution.* But ἀρετή etc. are also used in the same sense.

945. 1. Nouns qualified by a demonstrative pronoun regularly take the article; as οὗτος ὁ ἀνήρ, *this man;* ἐν ταῖσδε ταῖς πόλεσιν, *in these cities.* (For the position, see 974.)

2. But the article may be omitted with proper names, as οὗτος Νεοπτόλεμος, *this Neoptolemus,* D. 18, 114; also where the demonstrative is equivalent to *here* or *there,* as ὁρῶμεν ὀλίγους τούτους ἀνθρώπους, *we see few men here,* X. A. 4, 7[5]; so οὑτοσὶ ἀνήρ, *this man here,* and οὗτος ἀνήρ used contemptuously; see also νῆες ἐκεῖναι ἐπιπλέουσι, *ships are sailing up yonder,* T. 1, 51.

3. The tragedians often omit this article with demonstratives.

946. 1. Nouns with a possessive pronoun take the article when they refer to definite individuals, but not otherwise; as ὁ ἐμὸς πατήρ, *my father,* ὁ σὸς κοινωνός, *your partner,* D. 18, 21; but σὸς κοινωνός would mean *a partner of yours.* (For predicates, see 956.)

2. So also with nouns on which a possessive genitive of a personal, demonstrative, or reflexive pronoun depends; as ὁ πατήρ μου, *my father;* ὁ ἐμαυτοῦ πατήρ, *my own father;* ὁ τούτων πατήρ, *their father;* ἡ ἑαυτῶν γῆ, *their own land.* But παῖς ἑαυτοῦ, *a child of his own.*

947. Τοιοῦτος, τοσοῦτος, τοιόσδε, τοσόσδε, and τηλικοῦτος may take the article; as τὸν τοιοῦτον ἄνδρα, *such a man.* It is always used with δεῖνα, *such a one* (420).

948. A numeral may have the article, (*a*) to distinguish a part of a number; (*b*) to express a round number, especially with ἀμφί, περί, ὑπέρ, or εἰς; (*c*) to express merely a number in the abstract. Thus, τῶν πέντε τὰς δύο μοίρας νέμονται, *they hold two of the five parts*, T. 1, 10; ἔμειναν ἡμέρας ἀμφὶ τὰς τριάκοντα, *they remained about thirty days*, X. *A.* 4, 8[22]; ὅπως μὴ ἐρεῖς ὅτι ἐστὶ τὰ δώδεκα δὶς ἕξ, *don't say that twelve is twice six*, P. *Rp.* 337[b].

949. The article is often used, where we use a possessive pronoun, to mark something as belonging to a person or thing mentioned in the sentence; as ἔρχεται αὐτή τε ἡ Μανδάνη πρὸς τὸν πατέρα καὶ τὸν Κῦρον τὸν υἱὸν ἔχουσα, *Mandane comes to her father* (lit. *to the father*) *herself, and with her son Cyrus*, X. *C.* 1, 3[1].

950. The article may have a generic force, marking an object as the representative of a class; as ὁ ἄνθρωπος, *man* (in general); οἱ γέροντες, *the aged* (as a class).

951. The article sometimes has a distributive force, where we should use *each* or *a*; as ὑπισχνεῖται δώσειν τρία ἡμιδαρεικὰ τοῦ μηνὸς τῷ στρατιώτῃ, *he promises to give three half-darics a month to each soldier*, X. *A.* 1, 3[21].

952. 1. An adverb, a preposition with its case, or any similar expression, may be used with the article to qualify a noun, like an attributive adjective; as οἱ τότε ἄνθρωποι, *the men of that time*; τοῦ πάλαι Κάδμου, *of ancient Cadmus*, S. *O. T.* 1; οἱ ἐν ἄστει Ἀθηναῖοι, *the Athenians in the city.*

2. Here a noun denoting *men* or *things* is often omitted; as οἱ ἐν ἄστει, *those in the city*; τοῖς τότε, *to those of that time*; οἱ ἀμφὶ Πλάτωνα, *those about Plato* (generally *Plato and his school*, or simply *Plato*).

953. The nouns γῆ, *land*, πράγματα, *things* or *affairs*, υἱός, *son*, and sometimes other nouns which are readily suggested by the context, may be omitted after the article, when a qualifying adjective or genitive is added; as εἰς τὴν ἑαυτῶν (sc. γῆν), *to their own land*; ἐκ τῆς περιοικίδος, *from the neighboring country*; τὰ τῆς πόλεως, *the affairs of the state*; τὰ τῶν πολεμίων, *what belongs to the enemy*; Περικλῆς ὁ Ξανθίππου (*sc.* υἱός), *Pericles, the son of Xanthippus*; τὴν ταχίστην (sc. ὁδόν), *the quickest way.* Expressions like τὰ (or τὸ) τῆς Τύχης, τὰ τῆς ὀργῆς, with no definite nouns understood, sometimes do not differ from Τύχη, *Fortune*, and ὀργή, *wrath.*

954. Instead of repeating a noun with new adjuncts in the same sentence, it may be sufficient to repeat its article; as οἱ τῶν πολιτῶν παῖδες καὶ οἱ τῶν ἄλλων, *the children of the citizens and those of the others.*

955. 1. The infinitive, as a verbal noun (1516), may take a neuter article; as τὸ εἰδέναι, *the knowing;* σοὶ τὸ μὴ σιγῆσαι λοιπὸν ἦν, *it remained for you not to be silent,* D. 18, 23.

2. In like manner, a neuter article may precede a whole clause considered as a noun; as τὸ γνῶθι σαυτὸν πανταχοῦ 'στι χρήσιμον, *the saying "know thyself" is everywhere useful.*

956. A predicate noun or adjective seldom has the article; as νὺξ ἡ ἡμέρη ἐγένετο, *the day became night,* Hd. 1, 103; καλεῖται ἡ ἀκρόπολις ἔτι ὑπ' Ἀθηναίων πόλις, *the citadel is still called "city" by the Athenians,* T. 2, 15. So when it has a possessive pronoun; as οὗτος ἐμὸς ἑταῖρος ἦν, *he was my companion,* P. *Ap.* 21ᵃ.

But when the predicate refers definitely to distinct persons or things, it may have the article; as εἰσὶ δ' οὗτοι οἱ εἰδότες τἀληθές; *and are these those* (whom I mean) *who know the truth?* P. *H. M.* 284ᵉ.

957. N. Βασιλεύς is generally used without the article to designate the king of Persia; as τούτους ἀποπέμπει βασιλεῖ, *he sends these to the King,* T. 1, 128. But the article is sometimes found: compare I. 4, 166 and 179. So sometimes μέγας βασιλεύς; as μεγάλου βασιλέως βασίλεια, *a palace of the Great King,* X. *A.* 1, 2⁸.

958. N. The article is often omitted in some familiar expressions of time and place, which are probably older than the Attic use of the article; as ἅμα ἕῳ, *at daybreak;* νυκτός, *by night;* ἅμα ἦρι, *at the opening of spring;* ἐν ἀγορᾷ, *in the market-place;* κατ' ἄγρον, *in the country;* κατὰ γῆν, *by land;* κατὰ θάλασσαν, *by sea;* ἐκ δεξιᾶς, *from the right;* etc.

POSITION OF THE ARTICLE.

959. (*Attributive Position.*) 1. An attributive adjective which qualifies a noun with the article commonly stands between the article and the noun; as ὁ σοφὸς ἀνήρ, *the wise man;* τῶν μεγάλων πόλεων, *of the great cities.*

2. The noun with the article may be followed by the adjective with the article repeated. The first article is sometimes omitted. In these cases the noun has greater emphasis than in the preceding form (1). *E.g.*

Ὁ ἀνὴρ ὁ σοφός, sometimes ἀνὴρ ὁ σοφός, *the wise man* (but *not* ὁ ἀνὴρ σοφός, see 971); αἱ πόλεις αἱ δημοκρατούμεναι, *the states which are under democracies;* ἄνθρωποι οἱ ἀδικώτατοι, *men who are the most unjust;* πῶς ἡ ἄκρατος δικαιοσύνη πρὸς ἀδικίαν τὴν ἄκρατον ἔχει, (the question) *how pure justice is related to pure injustice,* P. *Rp.* 545ᵃ.

960. This applies to possessive pronouns and all expressions which have the force of attributive adjectives, when they are preceded by the article (952, 1), and to dependent genitives (except *partitives* and the genitive of the *personal* pronoun); as ὁ ἐμὸς πατήρ, *my father;* ἡ σὴ μήτηρ, *thy mother;* ὁ ἐμαυτοῦ πατήρ, *my own father* (but ὁ πατήρ μου, *my father*, see 977); οἱ ἐν ἄστει ἄνθρωποι or οἱ ἄνθρωποι οἱ ἐν ἄστει, *the men in the city;* οὐδεὶς τῶν τότε Ἑλλήνων, *none of the Greeks of that time*, τὸ τῷ ὄντι ψεῦδος, *the real falsehood;* εἰς τὴν ἐκείνων πόλιν, *into their city;* οἱ τῶν Θηβαίων στρατηγοί, *the generals of the Thebans*, ἐν τῇ ἀναβάσει τῇ μετὰ Κύρου, *in the upward march with Cyrus*, X. *A.* 5, 1[1]. For participles, see 969.

961. N. Two or even three articles may thus stand together; as τὰ γὰρ τῆς τῶν πολλῶν ψυχῆς ὄμματα, *the eyes of the soul of the multitude*, P. *So.* 254[a].

962. An adjective in either of these positions with reference to the article (959) is said to be in the *attributive* position, as opposed to the *predicate* position (see 971).

963. N. Of the three attributive positions, the first (*e.g.* ὁ σοφὸς ἀνήρ) is the most common and the most simple and natural; the second (ὁ ἀνὴρ ὁ σοφός) is the most formal; the third (ἀνὴρ ὁ σοφός) is the least common.

964. N. The article at the beginning of a clause may be separated from its noun by μέν, δέ, τέ, γέ, γάρ, δή, οὖν, and by τὶς in Herodotus.

965. The *partitive* genitive (1088) rarely stands in either of the attributive positions (962), but either precedes or follows the governing noun and its article; as οἱ κακοὶ τῶν πολιτῶν, or τῶν πολιτῶν οἱ κακοί, *the bad among the citizens* (rarely οἱ τῶν πολιτῶν κακοί).

Even the other forms of the adnominal genitive occasionally have this position, as διὰ τὸν ὄλεθρον τῶν συστρατιωτῶν ὀργιζόμενοι, *angered by the death of their fellow soldiers*, X. *A.* 1, 2[26].

966. 1. Ὁ ἄλλος in the singular generally means *the rest*, seldom *the other;* οἱ ἄλλοι means *the others:* as ἡ ἄλλη πόλις, *the rest of the state* (but ἄλλη πόλις, *another state*); οἱ ἄλλοι Ἕλληνες, *the other Greeks.*

2. Both ὁ ἄλλος and ἄλλος (rarely ἕτερος) may have the meaning of *besides;* as εὐδαιμονιζόμενος ὑπὸ τῶν πολιτῶν καὶ τῶν ἄλλων ξένων, *congratulated by the citizens and the foreigners besides*, P. *G.* 473[c]; οὐ γὰρ ἦν χορτὸς οὐδὲ ἄλλο οὐδὲν δένδρον, *for there was no grass, neither any tree* (lit. *nor any other tree*), X. *A.* 1, 5[5].

967. N. Πολύς with the article generally (though not always) means the *greater part*, especially in οἱ πολλοί, *the multitude, the majority*, and τὸ πολύ, *the greater part*. So οἱ πλείονες, *the majority*, τὸ πλεῖον, *the greater part*, οἱ πλεῖστοι and τὸ πλεῖστον, *the greatest number* or *part*.

968. N. When a noun has two or more qualifying words, each of them may take an article and stand in either attributive position (959), or all may stand between one article and its noun; as κατὰ τὴν Ἀττικὴν τὴν παλαιὰν φωνήν, *according to the old Attic dialect*, P. *Crat.* 398^d; τὰ τείχη τὰ ἑαυτῶν τὰ μακρά, *their own long walls*, T. 1, 108; πέμποντες εἰς τὰς ἄλλας Ἀρκαδικὰς πόλεις, *sending to the other Arcadian cities*, X. *H.* 7, 4^38; τὴν ὑπ' Ἀρετῆς Ἡρακλέους παίδευσιν, *the instruction of Hercules by Virtue*, X. *M.* 2, 1^34. Occasionally one stands between the article and the noun, while another follows the noun without an article; as οἱ ἀπὸ τῶν ἐν τῇ Ἀσίᾳ πόλεων Ἑλληνίδων, *those (coming) from the Greek cities in Asia*, X. *H.* 4, 3^15.

969. N. When an attributive participle (919) with dependent words qualifies a noun with the article, either the participle or the dependent words may follow the noun; as τὸν ῥέοντα ποταμὸν διὰ τῆς πόλεως, *the river which runs through the city*, X. *H.* 5, 2^4; τὸν ἐφεστηκότα κίνδυνον τῇ πόλει, *the danger impending over the city*, D. 18, 176; ἡ ἐν τῷ Ἰσθμῷ ἐπιμονὴ γενομένη, *the delay which occurred at the Isthmus*, T. 2, 18. But such expressions may also take either of the attributive positions (959, 1 or 2).

970. N. The Greeks commonly said *the Euphrates river*, τὸν Εὐφράτην ποταμόν, etc., rather than *the river Euphrates*. So sometimes with names of mountains (rarely with those of cities or islands).

971. (*Predicate Position.*) When an adjective either precedes the article, or follows the noun without taking an article, it is always a predicate adjective (see 919). *E.g.*

Ὁ ἀνὴρ σοφός or σοφὸς ὁ ἀνήρ (sc. ἐστίν), *the man is wise*, or *wise is the man*; πολλοὶ οἱ πανοῦργοι, *many are the evil-doers*; ἐφημέρους γε τὰς τύχας κεκτήμεθα, *we possess our fortunes for a day* (sc. οὔσας), Gnom.

972. N. The predicate force of such adjectives must often be expressed by a periphrasis; as πτηνὰς διώκεις τὰς ἐλπίδας, *the hopes you are pursuing are winged*, lit. *you are pursuing hopes (being) winged*, E. frag. 273; ἡγούμενοι αὐτονόμων τῶν ξυμμάχων, *being leaders of allies who were independent*, T. 1, 97; ψιλὴν ἔχων τὴν κεφαλήν, *having his head bare*, X. *A.* 1, 8^6. So πόσον ἄγει τὸ στράτευμα; *how great is the army he is bringing?*

973. The position of such an adjective (971) with reference to the article is called the *predicate* position.

974. When a demonstrative pronoun agrees with a noun, it takes the article, and stands in the predicate position (971). *E.g.*

Οὗτος ὁ ἀνήρ, *this man*, or ὁ ἀνὴρ οὗτος (never ὁ οὗτος ἀνήρ). Περὶ τούτων τῶν πόλεων, *about these cities*. (See 945, 1–3.)

975. N. But if an adjective or other qualifying word is added, the demonstrative may stand between this and its noun; as ἡ στενὴ αὕτη ὁδός, *this narrow road*, X. *A*. 4, 2[a]; τῷ ἀφικομένῳ τούτῳ ξένῳ, *to this stranger who has come*, P. *Pr*. 313[b]. (See 977, 2.)

976. N. Ἕκαστος, ἑκάτερος, ἄμφω, and ἀμφότερος have the predicate position like a demonstrative, as ἑκάστη ἡ ἡμέρα, *each day;* but with ἕκαστος the article may be omitted. Τοιοῦτος, τοσοῦτος, τοιόσδε, τοσόσδε and τηλικοῦτος, when they take the article, have the first attributive position (959, 1).

977. 1. A dependent genitive of the *personal* pronoun (whether partitive or not) has the predicate position (971), while that of other pronouns (unless it is partitive) has the first attributive position (959, 1); as ἡ μ ῶ ν ἡ πόλις or ἡ πόλις ἡ μ ῶ ν, *our city* (not ἡ ἡ μ ῶ ν πόλις); ἡ τούτων πόλις, *these men's city* (not ἡ πόλις τούτων); μετεπέμψατο Ἀστυάγης τὴν ἑ α υ τ ο ῦ θυγατέρα καὶ τὸν παῖδα α ὐ τ ῆ ς, *Astyages sent for his own daughter and her son*, X. *C*. 1, 3[1].

2. But if a qualifying word is added, the personal pronoun may stand between this and the noun; as ἡ δοκοῦσα ἡ μ ῶ ν πρότερον σωφροσύνη, *what previously seemed to be our modesty*, T. 1, 32. (See 975.)

978. 1. The adjectives ἄκρος, μέσος, and ἔσχατος, when they are in the predicate position (971), mean *the top* (or *extremity*), *the middle, the last*, of the thing which their nouns denote; as ἡ ἀγορὰ μέση or μέση ἡ ἀγορά, *the middle of the market* (while ἡ μέση ἀγορά would mean *the middle market*); ἄκρα ἡ χείρ, *the extremity of the hand*.

2. When no article is used, as in the older poetry, the context must decide the meaning. Compare *summus, medius, extremus*, and *ultimus* in Latin.

979. Πᾶς and σύμπας, *all*, and ὅλος, *whole*, generally have the predicate position; as πάντες οἱ ἄνδρες or οἱ ἄνδρες πάντες, *all the men;* ὅλη ἡ πόλις or ἡ πόλις ὅλη, *all the city*. But they can also be used like attributive adjectives, preceded by the article; as ἡ πᾶσα Σικελία, *the whole of Sicily*, τὸ ὅλον γένος, *the entire race*.

The distinction here was probably no greater than that between *all the city* and *the whole city* in English. We find even οἱ πάντες ἄνθρωποι, *all mankind*, X. *A*. 5, 6[7].

980. Αὐτός as an intensive pronoun, *ipse* (989, 1), has the predicate position; as αὐτὸς ὁ ἀνήρ, *the man himself*. But ὁ αὐτὸς ἀνήρ, *the same man* (989, 2).

PRONOMINAL ARTICLE IN ATTIC GREEK.

981. In Attic prose the article retains its original demonstrative force chiefly in the expression ὁ μέν . . . ὁ δέ, *the one . . . the other.*[1] *E.g.*

Οἱ μὲν αὐτῶν ἐτόξευον, οἱ δ' ἐσφενδόνων, *some of them shot with bows, and others used slings*, X. *A*. 3, 3[7]. Δεῖ τοὺς μὲν εἶναι δυστυχεῖς, τοὺς δ' εὐτυχεῖς, *some must be unfortunate, and others fortunate*, E. frag. 207. Τῶν πόλεων αἱ μὲν τυραννοῦνται, αἱ δὲ δημοκρατοῦνται, αἱ δὲ ἀριστοκρατοῦνται, *some states are governed by tyrants, others by democracies, and others by aristocracies*, P. *Rp*. 338[d].

982. N. The neuter τὸ μέν . . . τὸ δέ may be used adverbially, *partly . . . partly*. For τοῦτο μέν . . . τοῦτο δέ in this sense, see 1010.

983. N. (*a*) Ὁ δέ etc. sometimes mean *and he, but he*, etc., even when no ὁ μέν precedes; as Ἰνάρως Ἀθηναίους ἐπηγάγετο· οἱ δὲ ἦλθον, *Inaros called in Athenians; and they came*, T. 1, 104.

(*b*) With prepositions these expressions are generally inverted; as πολλὰ μὲν . . . ἐν δὲ τοῖς, P. *Eu*. 303[c]; παρὰ μὲν τοῦ ξύλα, παρὰ δὲ τοῦ σίδηρος, X. *Rp. A*. 2, 11.

984. A few other relics of the demonstrative meaning of the article are found in Attic, chiefly the following: —

Τὸν καὶ τόν, *this man and that;* τὸ καὶ τό, *this and that;* τὰ καὶ τά, *these and those;* as ἔδει γὰρ τὸ καὶ τὸ ποιῆσαι, καὶ τὸ μὴ ποιῆσαι, *for we ought to have done this thing and that, and not to have done the other*, D. 9, 68.

Πρὸ τοῦ (or προτοῦ), *before this, formerly.*

Καὶ τόν or καὶ τήν, before an infinitive; as καὶ τὸν κελεῦσαι δοῦναι (sc. λέγεται), *and* (*it is said*) *he commanded him to give it*, X. *C*. 1, 3[9].

So occasionally τῷ, *therefore*, which is common in Homer.

[1] In this use, and in other pronominal uses of the article (as in Homer), the forms ὁ, ἡ, οἱ, and αἱ were probably oxytone (ὅ, ἥ, οἵ, αἵ). They are printed here without accents in conformity with the prevailing usage in school editions of Greek authors. See 139.

PRONOUNS.

PERSONAL AND INTENSIVE PRONOUNS.

985. The nominatives of the personal pronouns are seldom used, except for emphasis. (See 896.)

986. The forms ἐμοῦ, ἐμοί, and ἐμέ are more emphatic than the enclitics μοῦ, μοί, μέ. The latter seldom occur after prepositions, except in πρός με.

987. Of the personal pronouns of the third person, οὗ, οἷ, etc. (389), only οἷ and the plural forms in σφ- are used in Attic prose. There they are generally *indirect reflexives*, that is, in a dependent clause (or joined with an infinitive or participle in the leading clause) referring to the subject of the leading verb. *E.g.*

Ἔλεξαν ὅτι πέμψειε σφᾶς ὁ Ἰνδῶν βασιλεύς, *they said that the king of the Indians had sent them*, X. *C.* 2, 4[7]. Ἐπρεσβεύοντο ἐγκλήματα ποιούμενοι, ὅπως σφίσιν ὅτι μεγίστη πρόφασις εἴη τοῦ πολεμεῖν, *they sent embassies, making charges, that they might have the strongest possible ground for war*, T. 1, 126. Ἐνταῦθα λέγεται Ἀπόλλων ἐκδεῖραι Μαρσύαν νικήσας ἐρίζοντά οἱ περὶ σοφίας, *here Apollo is said to have flayed Marsyas, having beaten him in a contest (with himself,* οἷ*) in skill*, X. *A.* 1, 2[8].

For the restricted use of these pronouns in Attic Greek, see also 392.

988. In Homer and Herodotus, and when they occur in the Attic poets, all these pronouns are generally personal pronouns, though sometimes (direct or indirect) reflexives. *E.g.*

Ἐκ γάρ σφεων φρένας εἵλετο Παλλὰς Ἀθήνη, *for Pallas Athena bereft them of their senses*, *Il.* 18, 311; τὸν κριὸν ἀπὸ ἕο (144, 4) πέμπε θύραζε, *he sent the ram forth from himself through the door*, *Od.* 9, 461. Αὐτίκα δέ οἱ εὕδοντι ἐπέστη ὄνειρος, *and soon a dream came to him in his sleep*, Hd. 1, 34; οὐδαμοῖσι τῶν νῦν σφεας περιοικεόντων εἰσὶ ὁμόγλωσσοι, *they have the same speech with none of their present neighbors*, Hd. 1, 57. Τίνι τρόπῳ θανεῖν σφε φῄς; *in what manner do you say she died?* S. *Tr.* 878.

989. Αὐτός has three uses: —

1. In all its cases it may be an intensive adjective pronoun, *himself, herself, itself, themselves* (like *ipse*). *E.g.*

Αὐτὸς ὁ στρατηγός, *the general himself;* ἐπ' αὐτοῖς τοῖς αἰγιαλοῖς, *on the very coasts*, T. 1, 7; ἐπιστήμη αὐτή, *knowledge itself.*

2. Αὐτός in all its cases, when preceded by the article, means *the same* (*idem*). *E.g.*

Ὁ αὐτὸς ἀνήρ, *the same man;* τὸν αὐτὸν πόλεμον, *the same war;* ταὐτά, *the same things* (42).

3. The *oblique cases* of αὐτός are the ordinary personal pronouns of the third person, *him, her, it, them. E.g.*

Στρατηγὸν αὐτὸν ἀπέδειξε, *he designated him as general.* See four other examples in X. *A.* 1, 1, 2 & 3.

It will be noticed that the *nominative* of αὐτός is never a personal pronoun.

For σφέ, σφίν, νίν, and μίν, see 394 and 395.

990. N. A pronoun with which αὐτός intensive agrees is often omitted; as ταῦτα ἐποιεῖτε αὐτοί (*sc.* ὑμεῖς), *you did this yourselves;* πλευστέον εἰς ταύτας αὐτοῖς ἐμβᾶσιν (sc. ὑμῖν), *you must sail, embarking on these yourselves* (*in person*), D. 4, 16. So αὐτὸς ἔφη (ipse dixit), *himself* (*the master*) *said it.*

991. N. Αὐτός with an ordinal numeral (372) may designate a person as the chief of a given number; as ᾑρέθη πρεσβευτὴς δέκατος αὐτός, *he was chosen ambassador as the chief of ten* (*himself the tenth*), X. *H.* 2, 2[17].

992. N. The oblique cases of αὐτός are often used where the indirect reflexives (987) might stand, and sometimes even where the direct reflexives (993) would be allowed; as ἁπλῶς τὴν ἑαυτοῦ γνώμην ἀπεφαίνετο Σωκράτης πρὸς τοὺς ὁμιλοῦντας αὐτῷ, *Socrates used to declare his own opinion plainly to those who conversed with him,* X. *M.* 4, 7[1], where οἷ might have been used; but in 1, 2[8], we have ἐλπίζειν ἐποίει τοὺς συνδιατρίβοντας ἑαυτῷ. The union of an intensive and a personal pronoun in αὐτός explains this freedom of usage.

REFLEXIVE PRONOUNS.

993. The reflexive pronouns (401) refer to the subject of the clause in which they stand. Sometimes in a dependent clause they refer to the subject of the leading verb, — that is, they are *indirect* reflexives (987). *E.g.*

Γνῶθι σαυτόν, *know thyself;* ἐπέσφαξεν ἑαυτόν, *he slew himself.* Δίδωμί σοι ἐμαυτὸν δοῦλον, *I give myself to you as a slave,* X. *C.* 4, 6[2]. Οἱ ἡττώμενοι ἑαυτούς τε καὶ τὰ ἑαυτῶν πάντα ἀποβάλλουσιν, *the vanquished lose both themselves and all that belongs to them*, X. *C*. 3, 3[45]. Ἔπεισεν Ἀθηναίους ἑαυτὸν κατάγειν, *he persuaded the Athenians to restore him* (*from exile*), T. 1, 111.

994. N. Occasionally a reflexive refers to some emphatic word which is neither the leading nor a dependent subject; as ἀπὸ σαυτοῦ 'γώ σε διδάξω, *I will teach you from your own case* (*from yourself*), Ar. *N*. 385. In fact, these pronouns correspond almost exactly in their use to the English reflexives, *myself, thyself, himself*, etc.

995. N. The third person of the reflexive is sometimes used for the first or second; as δεῖ ἡμᾶς ἐρέσθαι ἑαυτούς, *we must ask ourselves*, P. *Ph*. 78[b].

996. N. The reflexive is sometimes used for the reciprocal (404); ἡμῖν αὐτοῖς διαλεξόμεθα, *we will discourse with one another* (i.e. *among ourselves*), D. 48, 6.

997. N. A reflexive may be strengthened by a preceding αὐτός; as οἷός τε αὐτὸς αὑτῷ βοηθεῖν, *able* (*himself*) *to help himself*, P. *G*. 483[b]. Τὸ γιγνώσκειν αὐτὸν ἑαυτόν, *for one* (*himself*) *to know himself*, P. *Ch*. 165[b].

For the personal pronouns οὗ, οἷ, etc. as direct and indirect reflexives, see 987 and 988.

POSSESSIVE PRONOUNS.

998. 1. The possessive pronouns (406) are generally equivalent to the *possessive* genitive (1085, 1) of the personal pronouns. Thus ὁ σὸς πατήρ = ὁ πατήρ σου, *your father*.

For the article with possessives, see 946, 1.

2. For ἐμός and σός here the enclitic forms μοῦ (not ἐμοῦ) and σοῦ may be used; ἡμῶν and ὑμῶν for ἡμέτερος and ὑμέτερος are less frequent. These genitives have the predicate position as regards the article (971).

999. The possessive is occasionally equivalent to the *objective* genitive of the personal pronoun; as ἡ ἐμὴ εὔνοια, which commonly means *my good-will* (*towards others*), rarely means *good-will* (*shown*) *to me*; as εὐνοίᾳ γὰρ ἐρῶ τῇ σῇ, *for I shall speak out of good-will to you*, P. *G*. 486[a] (See 1085, 3.)

1000. N. Σφέτερος, *their*, and (poetic) ὅς, *his, her, its*, are regularly (directly or indirectly) reflexive.

1001. N. An adjective or an appositive in the genitive may refer to the genitive implied in a possessive; as τἀμὰ δυστήνου *κακά, the woes of me, unhappy one,* S. *O. C.* 344; τὴν ὑμετέραν τῶν σοφιστῶν τέχνην, *the art of you Sophists,* P. *H. M.* 281[d]. See 913.

1002. N. By the possessive pronouns and the possessive genitive, the words *my father* can be expressed in Greek in five forms: ὁ ἐμὸς πατήρ, ὁ πατὴρ ὁ ἐμός, πατὴρ ὁ ἐμός, ὁ πατήρ μου, and (after another word) μου ὁ πατήρ (as ἔφη μου ὁ πατήρ). So ὁ σὸς πατήρ, etc.

1003. N. (*a*) *Our own, your own* (plural), and *their own* are generally expressed by ἡμέτερος, ὑμέτερος, and σφέτερος, with αὐτῶν (989, 1) strengthening the ἡμῶν, ὑμῶν, or σφῶν implied in the possessive; as τὸν ἡμέτερον αὐτῶν πατέρα, *our own father;* τῇ ὑμετέρᾳ αὐτῶν μητρί, *to your own mother;* τοὺς σφετέρους αὐτῶν παῖδας, *their own children.* For the third person plural ἑαυτῶν can be used; as τοὺς ἑαυτῶν παῖδας (also σφῶν αὐτῶν παῖδας, without the article); but we seldom find ἡμῶν (or ὑμῶν) αὐτῶν.

(*b*) Expressions like τὸν ἐμὸν αὐτοῦ πατέρα for τὸν ἐμαυτοῦ πατέρα, etc., with singular possessives, are poetic. In prose the genitive of the reflexive (ἐμαυτοῦ, σεαυτοῦ, or ἑαυτοῦ), in the attributive position (959), is the regular form; as μετεπέμψατο τὴν ἑαυτοῦ θυγατέρα, *he sent for his (own) daughter,* X. *C.* 1, 3[1].

DEMONSTRATIVE PRONOUNS.

1004. Οὗτος and ὅδε, *this,* generally refer to what is near in place, time, or thought; ἐκεῖνος, *that,* refers to what is more remote.

1005. N. The distinction between οὗτος and ὅδε, both of which correspond to our *this,* must be learned by practice. In the historians, οὗτος (with τοιοῦτος, τοσοῦτος, and οὕτως) frequently refers to a speech just made, while ὅδε (with τοιόσδε, τοσόσδε, and ὧδε) refers to one about to be made; as τάδε εἶπεν, *he spoke as follows,* but ταῦτα εἶπεν, *thus he spoke* (said after the speech): see T. 1, 72 and 79, 85, and 87. But elsewhere οὗτος (especially in the neuter) often refers to something that follows; as ῥᾷον γὰρ τούτων προειρημένων μαθήσει, *for you will more easily understand it when this* (the following) *is premised,* P. *Rp.* 510[b].

1006. N. Οὗτος is sometimes exclamatory, as οὗτος, τί ποιεῖς; *You there! what are you doing?* A. *R.* 198.

1007. N. The Greek has no word exactly corresponding to the unemphatic demonstrative which is often used in English as the antecedent of a relative, as *I saw those who were present.* Here a participle with the article is generally used; as εἶδον τοὺς παρόντας;

if a demonstrative is used (*εἶδον τούτους οἳ παρῆσαν, I saw these men who were present*), it has special emphasis (1030). A relative with omitted antecedent sometimes expresses the sense required; as *εἶδον οὓς ἔλαβεν, I saw (those) whom he took* (1026).

1008. N. The demonstratives, especially ὅδε, may call attention to the presence or approach of an object, in the sense of *here* or *there; ὅδε γὰρ δὴ βασιλεὺς χώρας, for here now is the king of the land*, S. *An.* 155; for νῆες ἐκεῖναι (T. 1, 51) see 945, 2.

1009. N. Οὗτος sometimes repeats a preceding description for emphasis in a single word; as ὁ γὰρ τὸ σπέρμα παρασχών, οὗτος τῶν φύντων αἴτιος, *for he who supplied the seed — that man is responsible for the harvest*, D. 18, 159.

1010. N. Τοῦτο μέν . . . τοῦτο δέ, *first . . . secondly, partly . . . partly*, is used nearly in the sense of τὸ μέν . . . τὸ δέ (982), especially by Herodotus.

For οὑτοσί, ὁδί, ἐκεινοσί, οὑτωσί, ὡδί, etc., see 412.

INTERROGATIVE PRONOUN.

1011. The interrogative τίς; *who? what?* may be either substantive or adjective; as τίνας εἶδον; *whom did I see?* or τίνας ἄνδρας εἶδον; *what men did I see?*

1012. Τίς may be used both in direct and in indirect questions; as τί βούλεται; *what does he want?* ἐρωτᾷ τί βούλεσθε, *he asks what you want.*

1013. N. In indirect questions, however, the relative ὅστις is more common; as ἐρωτᾷ ὅ τι βούλεσθε (1600).

1014. N. The same principles apply to the pronominal adjectives πόσος, ποῖος, etc. (429).

INDEFINITE PRONOUN.

1015. 1. The indefinite τὶς (enclitic) generally means *some, any*, and may be either substantive or adjective; as τοῦτο λέγει τις, *some one says this;* ἄνθρωπός τις, *some man.*

2. It is sometimes nearly equivalent to the English *a* or *an;* as εἶδον ἄνθρωπόν τινα, *I saw a certain man*, or *I saw a man.*

1016. N. Τὶς sometimes implies that the word to which it is joined is not to be taken in its strict meaning; as κλέπτης τις ἀναπέφανται, *he has been shown up as a sort of thief*, P. *Rp.* 334[a]; μέγας τις, *rather large;* τριάκοντά τινας ἀπέκτειναν, *they killed some thirty*, T. 8, 73.

So with the adverbial τὶ (1060); as σχέδον τι, *very nearly*, T. 3, 68.

1017. N. Occasionally τὶς means *every one*, like πᾶς τις; as εὖ μέν τις δόρυ θηξάσθω, *let every one sharpen well his spear*, *Il.* 2, 382.

1018. N. The neuter τὶ may mean *something important;* as οἴονταί τι εἶναι, ὄντες οὐδενὸς ἄξιοι, *they think they are something, when they are worth nothing*, P. *Ap.* 41[e].

RELATIVE PRONOUNS.

1019. A relative agrees with its antecedent in gender and number; but its case depends on the construction of the clause in which it stands. *E.g.*

Εἶδον τοὺς ἄνδρας οἳ ἦλθον, *I saw the men who came;* οἱ ἄνδρες οὓς εἶδες ἀπῆλθον, *the men whom you saw went away.*

1020. N. The relative follows the person of the antecedent; as ὑμεῖς οἳ τοῦτο ποιεῖτε, *you who do this;* ἐγὼ ὃς τοῦτο ἐποίησα, *I who did this.*

1021. N. (*a*) A relative referring to several antecedents follows the rule given for predicate adjectives (924); as περὶ πολέμου καὶ εἰρήνης, ἃ μεγίστην ἔχει δύναμιν ἐν τῷ βίῳ τῶν ἀνθρώπων, *about war and peace, which have the greatest power in the life of men*, I. 8, 2; ἀπαλλαγέντες πολέμων καὶ κινδύνων καὶ ταραχῆς, εἰς ἣν νῦν πρὸς ἀλλήλους καθέσταμεν, *freed from wars, dangers, and confusion, in which we are now involved with one another*, I. 8, 20.

(*b*) The relative may be plural if it refers to a collective noun (900); as πλήθει οἵπερ δικάσουσιν, *to the multitude who are to judge*, P. *Phdr.* 260[a].

(*c*) On the other hand, ὅστις, *whoever*, may have a plural antecedent; as πάντα ὅ τι βούλονται, *everything, whatsoever they want.*

1022. N. A neuter relative may refer to a masculine or feminine antecedent denoting a thing; as διὰ τὴν πλεονεξίαν, ὃ πᾶσα φύσις διώκειν πέφυκεν, *for gain, which every nature naturally follows*, P. *Rp.* 359[c]. (See 925.)

1023. 1. In Homer the forms of the relative are sometimes used as demonstrative pronouns, like the article (935); as ὃς γὰρ δεύτατος ἦλθεν, *for he came second*, *Od.* 1, 286; ὃ γὰρ γέρας ἐστὶ θανόντων, *for this is the right of the dead*, *Il.* 23, 9.

2. A few similar expressions occur in Attic prose, especially the Platonic ἦ δ' ὅς, *said he* (where ἦ is imperfect of ἠμί, *say*). So καὶ ὅς, *and he*, καὶ οἵ, *and they*, and (in Hdt.) ὃς καὶ ὅς, *this man and that.* (Compare τὸν καὶ τόν, 984.) So also ὃς μέν . . . ὃς δέ, in the oblique cases, are occasionally used for ὁ μέν . . . ὁ δέ; as πόλεις Ἑλληνίδας, ἃς μὲν ἀναιρῶν, εἰς ἃς δὲ τοὺς φυγάδας κατάγων, *destroying some Greek cities, and restoring their exiles to others*, D. 18, 71.

1024. N. (*a*) In the epic and lyric poets τέ is often appended to relative words without affecting their meaning; as οὐκ ἀΐεις ἅ τέ φησι θεά; *dost thou not hear what the Goddess says?* *Il.* 15, 130. Sometimes it seems to make the relative more indefinite, like τις in ὅστις, *whoever, quicumque.*

(*b*) But οἷός τε in Attic Greek means *able, capable*, like δυνατός, being originally elliptical for τοιοῦτος οἷος, *such as*, τέ having no apparent force.

1025. (*Preposition omitted.*) When the relative and its antecedent would properly have the same preposition, it is usually expressed only with the antecedent; as ἀπὸ τῆς αὐτῆς ἀγνοίας ἧσπερ πολλὰ προΐεσθε τῶν κοινῶν, *by the same want of sense by which* (for ἀφ' ἧσπερ) *you sacrifice many of your public interests*, D. 18, 134.

Omission of the Antecedent.

1026. The antecedent of a relative may be omitted when it can easily be supplied from the context, especially if it is indefinite (1426). *E.g.*

Ἔλαβεν ἃ ἐβούλετο, *he took what he wanted;* ἔπειθεν ὁπόσους ἐδύνατο, *he persuaded as many as he could.* Ἃ μὴ οἶδα οὐδὲ οἴομαι εἰδέναι, *what I do not know I do not even think I know*, P. *Ap.* 21[d]. Ἐγὼ καὶ ὧν ἐγὼ κρατῶ μενοῦμεν παρὰ σοί, *I and those whom I command will remain with you*, X. *C.* 5, 1[26].

1027. N. In such cases it is a mistake to say that ταῦτα, ἐκεῖνοι, etc., are *understood;* see 1030. The relative clause here really becomes a substantive, and contains its antecedent within itself. Such a relative clause, as a substantive, may even have the article; as ἔχουσα τὴν ἐπωνυμίαν τὴν τοῦ ὃ ἔστιν, *having the name of the absolutely existent* (*of the "what is"*), P. *Ph.* 92[d]; ἐκείνου ὀρέγεται τοῦ ὃ ἔστιν ἴσον, *they aim at that absolute equality* (*at the "what is equal"*), *ibid.* 75[b]; τῷ σμικρῷ μέρει, τῷ ὃ ἦρχε ἐν αὐτῷ, *through the small part, which was shown to be the ruling power within him* (*the "what ruled"*), P. *Rp.* 442[c]. Here it must not be thought that τοῦ and τῷ are antecedents, or pronouns at all.

1028. N. Most relative adverbs regularly omit the antecedent; as *ἦλθεν ὅτε τοῦτο εἶδεν, he came when he saw this* (for *then, when*).

1029. N. The following expressions belong here:—*ἔστιν οἵ* (*ὧν, οἷς, οὕς*), *some* (905), more common than the regular *εἰσὶν οἵ*, sunt qui, *there are* (*those*) *who; ἔστιν οἵτινες* (especially in questions); *ἔνιοι* (from *ἔνι*, = *ἔνεστι* or *ἔνεισι*, and *οἵ*), *some; ἐνίοτε* (*ἔνι* and *ὅτε*), *sometimes; ἔστιν οὗ, somewhere; ἔστιν ᾗ, in some way; ἔστιν ὅπως, somehow.*

1030. N. When a clause containing a relative with omitted antecedent precedes the leading clause, the latter often contains a demonstrative referring back with emphasis to the omitted antecedent; as *ἃ ἐβούλετο ταῦτα ἔλαβεν, what he wanted, that he took*, entirely different from *ταῦτα ἃ ἐβούλετο ἔλαβεν, he took these* (definite) *things, which he wanted; ἃ ποιεῖν αἰσχρὸν, ταῦτα νόμιζε μηδὲ λέγειν εἶναι καλόν, what it is base to do, this believe that it is not good even to say*, I. 1, 15 (here *ταῦτα* is not the *antecedent* of *ἅ*, which is indefinite and is not expressed). See 1007.

ASSIMILATION AND ATTRACTION.

1031. When a relative would naturally be in the accusative as the object of a verb, it is generally *assimilated* to the case of its antecedent if this is a genitive or dative. *E.g.*

Ἐκ τῶν πόλεων ὧν ἔχει, from the cities which he holds (for *ἃς ἔχει*); *τοῖς ἀγαθοῖς οἷς ἔχομεν, with the good things which we have* (for *ἃ ἔχομεν*). *Ἄξιοι τῆς ἐλευθερίας ἧς κέκτησθε, worthy of the freedom which you have*, X. *A.* 1, 7^{3}; *εἰ τῷ ἡγεμόνι πιστεύσομεν ᾧ ἂν Κῦρος διδῷ, if we shall trust the guide whom Cyrus may give us*, X. *A.* 1, 3^{16}. This assimilation is also called *attraction.*

1032. N. When an antecedent is omitted which (if expressed) would have been a genitive or dative, the assimilation still takes place; and a preposition which would have belonged to the antecedent passes over to the relative; as *ἐδήλωσε τοῦτο οἷς ἔπραττε, he showed this by what he did* (like *ἐκείνοις ἅ*); *σὺν οἷς μάλιστα φιλεῖς, with those whom you most love* (*σὺν ἐκείνοις οὕς*), X. *A.* 1, 9^{25}; *ἀμελήσας ὧν με δεῖ πράττειν, having neglected what* (*ἐκείνων ἅ*) *I ought to do*, X. *C.* 5, 1^{8}; *οἷς εὐτυχήκεσαν ἐν Λεύκτροις οὐ μετρίως κέχρηντο, they had not used moderately the successes which they had gained at Leuctra* (*τοῖς εὐτυχήμασιν ἃ εὐτυχήκεσαν*, see 1054), D. 18, 18.

1033. N. A relative is seldom assimilated *from* any other construction than that of the object accusative, or *into* any other case than the genitive or dative. Yet exceptions occur; as παρ' ὧν βοηθεῖς οὐκ ἀπολήψει χάριν, *you will get no thanks from those whom* (παρ' ἐκείνων οἷς) *you help*, Aesch. 2, 117. Even the nominative may be assimilated; as βλάπτεσθαι ἀφ' ὧν ἡμῖν παρεσκεύασται, *to be injured by what has been prepared by us* (like ἀπ' ἐκείνων ἅ), T. 7, 67.

1034. N. A like assimilation takes place in relative adverbs; as διεκομίζοντο εὐθὺς ὅθεν ὑπεξέθεντο παῖδας καὶ γυναῖκας, *they immediately brought over their children and women from the places in which they had placed them for safety* (where ὅθεν, *from which*, stands for ἐκεῖθεν οἷ, *from the places whither*), T. 1, 89.

1035. N. The antecedent occasionally is assimilated to the case of the relative, when this immediately follows; as ἔλεγον ὅτι πάντων ὧν δέονται πεπραγότες εἶεν, *they said that they had done all things which* (πάντα ὧν) *they needed*, X. *H.* 1, 4². Τὴν οὐσίαν ἣν κατέλιπε οὐ πλείονος ἀξία ἐστὶν ἢ τεττάρων καὶ δέκα ταλάντων, *the estate which he left is not worth more than fourteen talents*, L. 19, 47. Compare *urbem quam* statuo vestra est, Verg. *Aen.* 1, 573. Such expressions involve an *anacoluthon*.

This *inverted assimilation* takes place in οὐδεὶς ὅστις οὐ, *everybody*, in which οὐδείς follows the case of the relative; as οὐδενὶ ὅτῳ οὐκ ἀποκρινόμενος (for οὐδείς ἐστιν ὅτῳ), *replying to everybody*, P. *Men.* 70ᶜ.

1036. N. A peculiar assimilation occurs in certain expressions with οἷος; as χαριζόμενον οἵῳ σοι ἀνδρί, *pleasing a man like you* (for τοιούτῳ οἷος σύ), X. *M.* 2, 9³; πρὸς ἄνδρας τολμηροὺς οἵους καὶ Ἀθηναίους, *against bold men like the Athenians*, T. 7, 21.

1037. The antecedent is often *attracted* into the relative clause, and agrees with the relative. *E.g.*

Μὴ ἀφέλησθε ὑμῶν αὐτῶν ἣν διὰ παντὸς ἀεὶ τοῦ χρόνου δόξαν κέκτησθε καλήν, *do not take from yourselves the good reputation which* (*what good reputation*) *you have always had through all time* (for τὴν καλὴν δόξαν ἣν κέκτησθε), D. 20, 142: notice the omission of the article, which regularly occurs.

The subject of a verb is rarely thus attracted; as οἴχεται φεύγων ὃν εἶχες μάρτυρα, *the witness whom you had* (for ὁ μάρτυς ὃν εἶχες) *has run away*, Ar. *Pl.* 933.

1038. N. This *attraction* may be joined with assimilation (1031); as ἀμαθέστατοί ἐστε ὧν ἐγὼ οἶδα Ἑλλήνων, *you are the most* *ignorant of the Greeks whom I know* (for τῶν Ἑλλήνων οὓς οἶδα), T. 6, 40; ἐξ ἧς τὸ πρῶτον ἔσχε γυναικός, *from the wife which he took first*, D. 57, 37; ἐπορεύετο σὺν ᾗ εἶχε δυνάμει, *he marched with the force which he had* (for σὺν τῇ δυνάμει ἣν εἶχεν), X. *H.* 4, 1[23].

RELATIVE IN EXCLAMATIONS.

1039. Οἷος, ὅσος, and ὡς are used in exclamations; as ὅσα πράγματα ἔχεις, *how much trouble you have!* X. *C.* 1, 3[4]; ὡς ἀστεῖος, *how witty!*

RELATIVE NOT REPEATED.

1040. A relative is seldom repeated *in a new case* in the same sentence, but a personal or demonstrative pronoun commonly takes its place. *E.g.*

Ἐκεῖνοι τοίνυν, οἷς οὐκ ἐχαρίζονθ' οἱ λέγοντες οὐδ' ἐφίλουν αὐτοὺς ὥσπερ ὑμᾶς οὗτοι νῦν, *those men, then, whom the orators did not try to gratify, and whom they did not love as these now love you* (lit. *nor did they love them as* etc.), D. 3, 24. Here αὐτούς is used to avoid repeating the relative in a new case, οὕς.

1041. N. Sometimes, however, a new case of the relative is understood in the latter part of a sentence; as Ἀριαῖος δέ, ὃν ἡμεῖς ἠθέλομεν βασιλέα καθιστάναι, καὶ ἐδώκαμεν καὶ ἐλάβομεν πιστά, *and Ariaeus, whom we wished to make king, and (to whom) we gave and (from whom) we received pledges*, etc., X. *A.* 3, 2[5].

THE CASES.

1042. The Greek is descended from a language which had *eight* cases, — an *ablative*, a *locative*, and an *instrumental*, besides the five found in Greek. The functions of the ablative were absorbed chiefly by the genitive, partly by the dative; those of the instrumental and locative chiefly by the dative.

NOMINATIVE AND VOCATIVE.

1043. The nominative is used chiefly as the subject of a finite verb (894), or in the predicate after verbs signifying *to be*, etc. (907).

1044. The vocative, with or without ὦ, is used in addressing a person or thing; as ὦ ἄνδρες Ἀθηναῖοι, *men of Athens!* ἀκούεις, Αἰσχίνη; *dost thou hear, Aeschines?*

1045. N. The nominative is sometimes used in exclamations, and even in other expressions, where the vocative is more common; as ὤμοι ἐγὼ δειλός, *O wretched me!* So ἡ Πρόκνη ἔκβαινε, *Procne, come out!* Ar. *Av.* 665.

ACCUSATIVE.

1046. The primary purpose of the accusative is to denote the nearer or *direct* object of a verb, as opposed to the remoter or *indirect* object denoted by the dative (892). It thus bears the same relation to a verb which the objective genitive (1085, 3) bears to a noun. The object denoted by the accusative may be the external object of the action of a transitive verb, or the internal (cognate) object which is often implied in the meaning of even an intransitive verb. But the accusative has also assumed other functions, as will be seen, which cannot be brought under this or any other single category.

ACCUSATIVE OF DIRECT (EXTERNAL) OBJECT.

1047. The direct object of the action of a transitive verb is put in the accusative; as τοῦτο σῴζει ἡμᾶς, *this preserves us;* ταῦτα ποιοῦμεν, *we do these things.*

1048. N. Many verbs which are transitive in English, and govern the objective case, take either a genitive or a dative in Greek. (See 1099; 1160; 1183.)

1049. N. Many verbs which are transitive in Greek are intransitive in English; as ὀμοῦμαι τοὺς θεούς, *I will swear by the Gods;* πάντας ἔλαθεν, *he escaped the notice of all;* αἰσχύνεται τὸν πατέρα, *he feels shame before his father;* σιγᾷ (or σιωπᾷ) τι, *he keeps silent about something.*

1050. N. Verbal adjectives and even verbal nouns occasionally take an object accusative instead of the regular objective genitive (1142; 1085, 3), as ἐπιστήμονες ἦσαν τὰ προσήκοντα, *they were acquainted with what was proper,* X. *C.* 3, 3⁹. So τὰ μετέωρα φροντιστής, *one who ponders on the things above* (like φροντίζων), P. *Ap.* 18ᵇ.

COGNATE ACCUSATIVE (INTERNAL OBJECT).

1051. Any verb whose meaning permits it may take an accusative of kindred signification. This accusative repeats the idea *already contained* in the verb, and may follow intransitive as well as transitive verbs. *E.g.*

Πάσας ἡδονὰς ἥδεσθαι, *to enjoy all pleasures*, P. *Phil.* 63[a]. Εὐτύχησαν τοῦτο τὸ εὐτύχημα, *they enjoyed this good fortune*, X. *A.* 6, 3[6]. So πεσεῖν πτώματα, *to suffer (to fall) falls*, A. *Pr.* 919. Νόσον νοσεῖν or νόσον ἀσθενεῖν or νόσον κάμνειν, *to suffer under a disease*; ἁμάρτημα ἁμαρτάνειν, *to commit an error* (*to sin a sin*); δουλείαν δουλεύειν, *to be subject to slavery*; ἀρχὴν ἄρχειν, *to hold an office*; ἀγῶνα ἀγωνίζεσθαι, *to undergo a contest*; γραφὴν γράφεσθαι, *to bring an indictment*; γραφὴν διώκειν, *to prosecute an indictment*; δίκην ὀφλεῖν, *to lose a lawsuit*; νίκην νικᾶν, *to gain a victory*; μάχην νικᾶν, *to gain a battle*; πομπὴν πέμπειν, *to form* or *conduct a procession*; πληγὴν τύπτειν, *to strike a blow*; ἐξῆλθον ἐξόδους, *they went out on expeditions*, X. *H.* 1, 2[17].

1052. N. It will be seen that this construction is far more extensive in Greek than in English. It includes not only accusatives of kindred formation and meaning, as νίκην νικᾶν, *to gain a victory*; but also those of merely kindred meaning, as μάχην νικᾶν, *to gain a battle*. The accusative may also limit the meaning of the verb to one of many applications; as Ὀλύμπια νικᾶν, *to gain an Olympic victory*, T. 1, 126; ἑστιᾶν γάμους, *to give a wedding feast*, Ar. *Av.* 132; ψήφισμα νικᾷ, *he carries a decree* (*gains a victory with a decree*), Aesch. 3, 68; βοηδρόμια πέμπειν, *to celebrate the Boedromia by a procession*, D. 3, 31. So also (in poetry) βαίνειν (or ἐλθεῖν) πόδα, *to step* (*the foot*): see E. *Al.* 1153.

For the cognate accusative becoming the subject of a passive verb, see 1240.

1053. The cognate accusative may follow adjectives or even nouns. *E.g.*

Κακοὶ πᾶσαν κακίαν, *bad with all badness*, P. *Rp.* 490[d]; δοῦλος τὰς μεγίστας δουλείας, *a slave to the direst slavery*, *ibid.* 579[d].

1054. A neuter adjective sometimes represents a cognate accusative, its noun being implied in the verb. *E.g.*

Μεγάλα ἁμαρτάνειν (sc. ἁμαρτήματα), *to commit great faults*; ταὐτὰ λυπεῖσθαι καὶ ταὐτὰ χαίρειν, *to have the same griefs and the same joys*, D. 18, 292. So τί χρήσομαι τούτῳ; (= τίνα χρείαν χρήσομαι;), *what use shall I make of this?* and οὐδὲν χρήσομαι τούτῳ, *I shall make no use of this* (1183). So χρήσιμος οὐδέν, *good for nothing* (1053). See 1060.

1055. 1. Here belongs the accusative of *effect*, which

expresses a result beyond the action of the verb, which is effected by that action. *E.g.*

Πρεσβεύειν τὴν εἰρήνην, *to negotiate a peace* (as ambassadors, πρέσβεις), D. 19, 134; but πρεσβεύειν πρεσβείαν, *to go on an embassy.* Compare the English *breaking a hole*, as opposed to *breaking a stick.*

2. So after verbs of *looking* (in poetry); as Ἄρη δεδορκέναι, *to look war* (*Ares*) (see A. *Se.* 53); ἡ βουλὴ ἔβλεψε νᾶπυ, *the Senate looked mustard*, Ar. *Eq.* 631.

1056. N. For verbs which take a cognate accusative and an ordinary object accusative at the same time, see 1076.

1057. N. Connected with the cognate accusative is that which follows verbs of motion to express the *ground over which* the motion passes; as ὁδὸν ἰέναι (ἐλθεῖν, πορεύεσθαι, etc.), *to go (over) a road;* πλεῖν θάλασσαν, *to sail the sea;* ὄρος καταβαίνειν, *to descend a mountain;* etc. These verbs thus acquire a transitive meaning.

ACCUSATIVE OF SPECIFICATION. — ADVERBIAL ACCUSATIVE.

1058. The accusative of *specification* may be joined with a verb, adjective, noun, or even a whole sentence, to denote a *part*, *character*, or *quality* to which the expression refers. *E.g.*

Τυφλὸς τὰ ὄμματ' εἶ, *you are blind in your eyes*, S. *O.T.* 371; καλὸς τὸ εἶδος, *beautiful in form;* ἄπειροι τὸ πλῆθος, *infinite in number;* δίκαιος τὸν τρόπον, *just in his character;* δεινοὶ μάχην, *mighty in battle;* κάμνω τὴν κεφαλήν, *I have a pain in my head;* τὰς φρένας ὑγιαίνειν, *to be sound in their minds;* διαφέρει τὴν φύσιν, *he differs in nature.* Ποταμὸς, Κύδνος ὄνομα, εὖρος δύο πλέθρων, *a river, Cydnus by name, of two plethra in breadth* (922), X. *A.* 1, 2[23]. Ἕλληνές εἰσι τὸ γένος, *they are Greeks by race.* Γένεσθε τὴν διάνοιαν μὴ ἐν τῷ δικαστηρίῳ, ἀλλ' ἐν τῷ θεάτρῳ, *imagine yourselves (become in thought) not in court, but in the theatre*, Aesch. 3, 153. Ἐπίστασθέ (με) οὐ μόνον τὰ μεγάλα ἀλλὰ καὶ τὰ μικρὰ πειρώμενον ἀεὶ ἀπὸ θεῶν ὁρμᾶσθαι, *you know that, not only in great but even in small things, I try to begin with the Gods*, X. *C.* 1, 5[14].

1059. N. This is sometimes called the accusative by *synecdoche*, or the *limiting* accusative. It most frequently denotes a *part;* but it may refer to any circumstance to which the meaning of the expression is restricted. This construction sometimes resembles that of 1239, with which it must not be confounded.

1060. An accusative in certain expressions has the force of an adverb. *E.g.*

Τοῦτον τὸν τρόπον, in this way, thus; τὴν ταχίστην (sc. ὁδόν), *in the quickest way; (τὴν) ἀρχήν, at first* (with negative, *not at all*); *τέλος, finally; προῖκα, as a gift*, gratis; *χάριν, for the sake of; δίκην, in the manner of; τὸ πρῶτον* or *πρῶτον, at first; τὸ λοιπόν, for the rest; πάντα, in all things; τἆλλα, in other respects; οὐδέν, in nothing, not at all; τί; in what, why? τὶ, in any respect, at all; ταῦτα, in respect to this, therefore.* So τοῦτο μέν . . . τοῦτο δέ (1010).

1061. N. Several of these (1060) are to be explained by 1058, as τἆλλα, τί; *why?* ταῦτα, τοῦτο (with μέν and δέ), and sometimes οὐδέν and τὶ. Some are to be explained as cognate accusatives (see 1053 and 1054), and some are of doubtful origin.

ACCUSATIVE OF EXTENT.

1062. The accusative may denote *extent* of time or space. *E.g.*

Αἱ σπονδαὶ ἐνιαυτὸν ἔσονται, *the truce is to be for a year*, T. 4, 118. Ἔμεινεν ἡμέρας πέντε, *he remained five days.* Ἀπέχει ἡ Πλάταια τῶν Θηβῶν σταδίους ἑβδομήκοντα, *Plataea is seventy stades distant from Thebes*, T. 2, 5. Ἀπέχοντα Συρακουσῶν οὔτε πλοῦν πολὺν οὔτε ὁδόν, (Megara) *not a long sail or land-journey distant from Syracuse*, T. 6, 49.

1063. N. This accusative with an *ordinal* number denotes *how long since* (including the date of the event); as ἑβδόμην ἡμέραν τῆς θυγατρὸς αὐτῷ τετελευτηκυίας, *when his daughter had died six days before* (i.e. *this being the seventh day*), Aesch. 3, 77.

1064. N. A peculiar idiom is found in expressions like τρίτον ἔτος τουτί (*this the third year*), i.e. *two years ago;* as ἀπηγγέλθη Φίλιππος τρίτον ἢ τέταρτον ἔτος τουτὶ Ἡραῖον τεῖχος πολιορκῶν, *two or three years ago Philip was reported to be besieging Heraion Teichos*, D. 3, 4.

TERMINAL ACCUSATIVE (POETIC).

1065. In poetry, the accusative without a preposition may denote the place or object *towards which* motion is directed. *E.g.*

Μνηστῆρας ἀφίκετο, *she came to the suitors*, *Od.* 1, 332. Ἀνέβη μέγαν οὐρανὸν Οὔλυμπόν τε, *she ascended to great heaven and*

Olympus, Il. 1, 497. Τὸ κοῖλον Ἄργος βὰς φυγάς, *going as an exile to the hollow Argos,* S. *O.C.* 378.

In prose a preposition would be used here.

ACCUSATIVE IN OATHS WITH νή AND μά.

1066. The accusative follows the adverbs of swearing νή and μά, *by*.

1067. An oath introduced by νή is affirmative; one introduced by μά (unless ναί, *yes*, precedes) is negative; as νὴ τὸν Δία, *yes, by Zeus;* μὰ τὸν Δία, *no, by Zeus;* but ναί, μὰ Δία, *yes, by Zeus.*

1068. N. Μά is sometimes omitted when a negative precedes; as οὔ, τόνδ' Ὄλυμπον, *no, by this Olympus,* S. *An.* 758.

TWO ACCUSATIVES WITH ONE VERB.

1069. Verbs signifying *to ask, to demand, to teach, to remind, to clothe* or *unclothe, to conceal, to deprive,* and *to take away,* may take two object accusatives. *E.g.*

Οὐ τοῦτ' ἐρωτῶ σε, *I am not asking you this,* Ar. *N.* 641; οὐδένα τῆς συνουσίας ἀργύριον πράττει, *you demand no fee for your teaching from any one,* X. *M.* 1, 6[11]; πόθεν ἤρξατό σε διδάσκειν τὴν στρατηγίαν; *with what did he begin to teach you strategy? ibid.* 3, 1[5]; τὴν ξυμμαχίαν ἀναμιμνήσκοντες τοὺς Ἀθηναίους, *reminding the Athenians of the alliance,* T. 6, 6; τὸν μὲν ἑαυτοῦ (χιτῶνα) ἐκεῖνον ἠμφίεσε, *he put his own (tunic) on the other boy,* X. *Cy.* 1, 3[17]; ἐκδύων ἐμὲ χρηστηρίαν ἐσθῆτα, *stripping me of my oracular garb,* A. *Ag.* 1269; τὴν θυγατέρα ἔκρυπτε τὸν θάνατον τοῦ ἀνδρός, *he concealed from his daughter her husband's death,* L. 32, 7; τούτων τὴν τιμὴν ἀποστερεῖ με, *he cheats me out of the price of these,* D. 28, 13; τὸν πάντα δ' ὄλβον ἦμαρ ἕν μ' ἀφείλετο, *but one day deprived me of all my happiness,* E. *Hec.* 285.

1070. N. In poetry some other verbs have this construction; thus χρόα νίζετο ἅλμην, *he washed the dried spray from his skin, Od.* 6, 224; so τιμωρεῖσθαί τινα αἷμα, *to punish one for blood (shed),* see E. *Al.* 733.

1071. N. Verbs of this class sometimes have other constructions. For verbs of *depriving* and *taking away,* see 1118. For the accusative and genitive with verbs of *reminding,* see 1106.

1072. N. The accusative of a thing with some of these verbs is really a cognate accusative (1076).

1073. Verbs signifying *to do anything to* or *to say anything of* a person or thing take two accusatives. *E.g.*

Ταυτί με ποιοῦσιν, *they do these things to me;* τί μ' εἰργάσω; *what didst thou do to me?* Κακὰ πολλὰ ἔοργεν Τρῶας, *he has done many evils to the Trojans, Il.* 16, 424. Ἐκεῖνόν τε καὶ τοὺς Κορινθίους πολλά τε καὶ κακὰ ἔλεγε, *of him and the Corinthians he said much that was bad,* Hd. 8, 61; οὐ φροντιστέον τί ἐροῦσιν οἱ πολλοὶ ἡμᾶς, *we must not consider what the multitude will say of us,* P. *Cr.* 48[a].

1074. These verbs often take εὖ or καλῶς, *well,* or κακῶς, *ill,* instead of the accusative of a thing; τούτους εὖ ποιεῖ, *he does them good;* ὑμᾶς κακῶς ποιεῖ, *he does you harm;* κακῶς ἡμᾶς λέγει, *he speaks ill of us.*

For εὖ πάσχειν, εὖ ἀκούειν, etc., as passives of these expressions, see 1241.

1075. N. Πράσσω, *do,* very seldom takes two accusatives in this construction, ποιέω being generally used. Εὖ πράσσω and κακῶς πράσσω are intransitive, meaning *to be well off, to be badly off.*

1076. A transitive verb may have a cognate accusative (1051) and an ordinary object accusative at the same time. *E.g.*

Μέλητός με ἐγράψατο τὴν γραφὴν ταύτην, *Meletus brought this indictment against me,* P. *Ap.* 19[b]; Μιλτιάδης ὁ τὴν ἐν Μαραθῶνι μάχην τοὺς βαρβάρους νικήσας, *Miltiades, who gained the battle at Marathon over the barbarians,* Aesch. 3, 181; ὥρκωσαν πάντας τοὺς στρατιώτας τοὺς μεγίστους ὅρκους, *they made all the soldiers swear the strongest oaths,* T. 8, 75.

On this principle (1076) verbs of *dividing* may take two accusatives; as τὸ στράτευμα κατένειμε δώδεκα μέρη, *he made twelve divisions of the army,* X. *C.* 7, 5[13].

1077. Verbs signifying *to name, to choose* or *appoint, to make, to think* or *regard,* and the like, may take a predicate accusative besides the object accusative. *E.g.*

Τί τὴν πόλιν προσαγορεύεις; *what do you call the state?* Τὴν τοιαύτην δύναμιν ἀνδρείαν ἔγωγε καλῶ, *such a power I call courage,* P. *Rp.* 430[b]. Στρατηγὸν αὐτὸν ἀπέδειξε, *he appointed him general,* X. *A.* 1, 1[2]; εὐεργέτην τὸν Φίλιππον ἡγοῦντο, *they thought Philip a benefactor,* D. 18, 43; πάντων δεσπότην ἑαυτὸν πεποίηκεν, *he has made himself master of all,* X. *C.* 1, 3[18].

1078. This is the active construction corresponding to the passive with copulative verbs (908), in which the object accusative becomes the subject nominative (1234) and the predicate accusative becomes a predicate nominative (907). Like the latter, it includes also predicate adjectives; as τοὺς συμμάχους προθύμους ποιεῖσθαι, *to make the allies eager*; τὰς ἁμαρτίας μεγάλας ἦγεν, *he thought the faults great.*

1079. N. With verbs of *naming* the infinitive εἶναι may connect the two accusatives; as σοφιστὴν ὀνομάζουσι τὸν ἄνδρα εἶναι, *they name the man (to be) a sophist*, P. *Pr.* 311[e].

1080. N. Many other transitive verbs may take a predicate accusative in apposition with the object accusative; as ἔλαβε τοῦτο δῶρον, *he took this as a gift*; ἵππους ἄγειν θῦμα τῷ Ἡλίῳ, *to bring horses as an offering to the Sun*, X. *C.* 8, 3[12] (see 916). Especially an interrogative pronoun may be so used; as τίνας τούτους ὁρῶ; *who are these whom I see?* lit. *I see these, being whom?* (See 919; 972.)

1081. N. A predicate accusative may denote the *effect* of the action of the verb upon its direct object; as παιδεύειν τινὰ σοφόν (or κακόν), *to train one (to be) wise* (or *bad*); τοὺς υἱεῖς ἱππότας ἐδίδαξεν, *he taught his sons to be horsemen.* See 1055.

1082. N. For one of two accusatives retained with the passive, see 1239.

For the accusative absolute, see 1569.

GENITIVE.

1083. As the chief use of the accusative is to limit the meaning of a verb, so the chief use of the genitive is to limit the meaning of a noun. When the genitive is used as the object of a verb, it seems to depend on the nominal idea which belongs to the verb: thus ἐπιθυμῶ involves ἐπιθυμίαν (as we can say ἐπιθυμῶ ἐπιθυμίαν, 1051); and in ἐπιθυμῶ τούτου, *I have a desire for this*, the nominal idea preponderates over the verbal. So βασιλεύει τῆς χώρας (1109) involves the idea βασιλεύς ἐστι τῆς χώρας, *he is king of the country.* The Greek is somewhat arbitrary in deciding when it will allow either idea to preponderate in the construction, and after some verbs it allows both the accusative and the genitive (1108). In the same general sense the genitive follows verbal adjectives. It has also uses which originally belonged to the ablative; for example, with verbs of *separation* and to express *source.* (See 1042.)

GENITIVE AFTER NOUNS (ATTRIBUTIVE GENITIVE).

1084. A noun in the genitive may limit the meaning of another noun, to express various relations, most of which are denoted by *of* or by the possessive case in English.

1085. The genitive thus depending on a noun is called *attributive* (see 919). Its most important relations are the following: —

1. Possession or other close relation: as *ἡ τοῦ πατρὸς οἰκία, the father's house; ἡμῶν ἡ πατρίς, our country; τὸ τῶν ἀνδρῶν γένος, the lineage of the men.* So *ἡ τοῦ Διός, the daughter of Zeus; τὰ τῶν θεῶν, the things of the Gods* (953). **The Possessive Genitive.**

2. The Subject of an action or feeling: as *ἡ τοῦ δήμου εὔνοια, the good-will of the people* (i.e. *which the people feel*). **The Subjective Genitive.**

3. The Object of an action or feeling: as *διὰ τὸ Παυσανίου μῖσος, owing to the hatred of* (i.e. *felt against*) *Pausanias,* T. 1, 96; *πρὸς τὰς τοῦ χειμῶνος καρτερήσεις, as regards his endurance of the winter,* P. *Sy.* 220[a]. So *οἱ θεῶν ὅρκοι, the oaths* (*sworn*) *in the name of the Gods* (as we say *θεοὺς ὀμνύναι,* 1049), X. *A.* 2, 5[7]. **The Objective Genitive.**

4. Material or Contents, including that of which anything consists: as *βοῶν ἀγέλη, a herd of cattle; ἄλσος ἡμέρων δένδρων, a grove of cultivated trees,* X. *A.* 5, 3[12]; *κρήνη ἡδέος ὕδατος, a spring of fresh water,* X. *A.* 6, 4[4]; *δύο χοίνικες ἀλφίτων, two quarts of meal.* **Genitive of Material.**

5. Measure, of space, time, or value: as *τριῶν ἡμερῶν ὁδός, a journey of three days; ὀκτὼ σταδίων τεῖχος, a wall of eight stades* (*in length*); *τριάκοντα ταλάντων οὐσία, an estate of thirty talents; μισθὸς τεττάρων μηνῶν, pay for four months; πράγματα πολλῶν ταλάντων, affairs of* (i.e. *involving*) *many talents,* Ar. *N.* 472. **Genitive of Measure.**

6. Cause or Origin: *μεγάλων ἀδικημάτων ὀργή, anger at great offences; γραφὴ ἀσεβείας, an indictment for impiety.* **The Causal Genitive.**

7. The Whole, after nouns denoting a part: as *πολλοὶ τῶν ῥητόρων, many of the orators; ἀνὴρ τῶν ἐλευθέρων, a man* (i.e. *one*) *of the freemen.* **The Partitive Genitive.** (See also 1088.)

These seven classes are not exhaustive: but they will give a general idea of these relations, many of which it is difficult to classify.

1086. N. Examples like πόλις Ἄργους, *the city of Argos*, Ar. *Eq.* 813, Τροίης πτολίεθρον, *the city of Troy*, *Od.* 1, 2, in which the genitive is used instead of apposition, are poetic.

1087. Two genitives denoting different relations may depend on one noun; as ἵππου δρόμον ἡμέρας, *within a day's run for a horse*, D. 19, 273; διὰ τὴν τοῦ ἀνέμου ἄπωσιν αὐτῶν ἐς τὸ πέλαγος, *by the wind's driving them (the wrecks) out into the sea*, T. 7, 34.

1088. (*Partitive Genitive.*) The partitive genitive (1085, 7) may follow all nouns, pronouns, adjectives (especially superlatives), participles with the article, and adverbs, which denote a part. *E.g.*

Οἱ ἀγαθοὶ τῶν ἀνθρώπων, *the good among the men*; ὁ ἥμισυς τοῦ ἀριθμοῦ, *the half of the number*; ἄνδρα οἶδα τοῦ δήμου, *I know a man of the people*; τοῖς θρανίταις τῶν ναυτῶν, *to the upper benches of the sailors*, T. 6, 31; οὐδεὶς τῶν παίδων, *no one of the children*; πάντων τῶν ῥητόρων δεινότατος, *the most eloquent of all the orators*, ὁ βουλόμενος καὶ ἀστῶν καὶ ξένων, *any one who pleases of both citizens and strangers*, T. 2, 34; δῖα γυναικῶν, *divine among women*, *Od.* 4, 305; ποῦ τῆς γῆς; ubi terrarum? *where on the earth?* τίς τῶν πολιτῶν; *who of the citizens?* δὶς τῆς ἡμέρας, *twice a day*; εἰς τοῦτο ἀνοίας, *to this pitch of folly*; ἐπὶ μέγα δυνάμεως, *to a great degree of power*, T. 1, 118; ἐν τούτῳ παρασκευῆς, *in this state of preparation*. Ἃ μὲν διώκει τοῦ ψηφίσματος ταῦτ' ἐστίν, *the parts of the decree which he prosecutes are these* (lit. *what parts of the decree he prosecutes*, etc.), D. 18, 56. Εὐφημότατ' ἀνθρώπων, *in the most plausible way possible* (*most plausibly of men*), D. 19, 50. Ὅτε δεινότατος σαυτοῦ ταῦτα ἦσθα, *when you were at the height of your power in these matters*, X. *M.* 1, 2[46]. (See 965.)

1089. The partitive genitive has the predicate position as regards the article (971), while other attributive genitives (except *personal* pronouns, 977) have the attributive position (959).

1090. N. An adjective or participle generally agrees in gender with a dependent partitive genitive. But sometimes, especially when it is singular, it is neuter, agreeing with μέρος, *part*, understood; as τῶν πολεμίων τὸ πολύ (for οἱ πολλοί), *the greater part of the enemy*.

1091. N. A partitive genitive sometimes depends on τὶς or μέρος understood; as ἔφασαν ἐπιμιγνύναι σφῶν τε πρὸς ἐκείνους καὶ ἐκείνων πρὸς ἑαυτούς, *they said that some of their own men had mixed with them, and some of them with their own men* (τινάς being understood with σφῶν and ἐκείνων), X. *A.* 3, 5[16].

1092. N. Similar to such phrases as ποῦ γῆς; εἰς τοῦτο ἀνοίας, etc., is the use of ἔχω and an adverb with the genitive; as πῶς ἔχεις δόξης; *in what state of opinion are you?* P. *Rp.* 456[d]; εὖ σώματος ἔχειν, *to be in a good condition of body, ibid.* 404[d]; ὡς εἶχε τάχους, *as fast as he could* (lit. *in the condition of speed in which he was*), T. 2, 90; so ὡς ποδῶν εἶχον, Hd. 6, 116; εὖ ἔχειν φρενῶν, *to be right in his mind* (see E. *Hip.* 462).

GENITIVE AFTER VERBS.

Predicate Genitive.

1093. As the attributive genitive (1084) stands in the relation of an attributive adjective to its leading substantive, so a genitive may stand in the relation of a predicate adjective (907) to a verb.

1094. Verbs signifying *to be* or *to become* and other copulative verbs may have a predicate genitive expressing any of the relations of the attributive genitive (1085). *E.g.*

1. (*Possessive.*) Ὁ νόμος ἐστὶν οὗτος Δράκοντος, *this law is Draco's*, D. 23, 51. Πενίαν φέρειν οὐ παντός, ἀλλ' ἀνδρὸς σοφοῦ, *to bear poverty is not in the power of every one, but in that of a wise man*, Men. *Mon.* 463. Τοῦ θεῶν νομίζεται (ὁ χῶρος); *to what God is the place held sacred?* S. *O. C.* 38.

2. (*Subjective.*) Οἶμαι αὐτὸ (τὸ ῥῆμα) Περιάνδρου εἶναι, *I think it (the saying) is Periander's*, P. *Rp.* 336[a].

3. (*Objective.*) Οὐ τῶν κακούργων οἶκτος, ἀλλὰ τῆς δίκης, *pity is not for evil doers, but for justice*, E. frag. 272.

4. (*Material.*) Ἕρυμα λίθων πεποιημένον, *a wall built of stones*, T. 4, 31. Οἱ θεμέλιοι παντοίων λίθων ὑπόκεινται, *the foundations are laid (consisting) of all kinds of stones*, T. 1, 93.

5. (*Measure.*) (Τὰ τείχη) σταδίων ἦν ὀκτώ, *the walls were eight stades (in length)*, T. 4, 66. Ἐπειδὰν ἐτῶν ᾖ τις τριάκοντα, *when one is thirty years old*, P. *Lg.* 721[a].

6. (*Origin.*) Τοιούτων ἐστὲ προγόνων, *from such ancestors are you sprung*, X. *A.* 3, 2[14].

7. (*Partitive.*) Τούτων γενοῦ μοι, *become one of these for my sake*, Ar. *N.* 107. Σόλων τῶν ἑπτὰ σοφιστῶν ἐκλήθη, *Solon was called one of the Seven Wise Men*, I. 15, 235.

1095. Verbs signifying *to name*, *to choose* or *appoint*, *to make*, *to think* or *regard*, and the like, which generally take two accusatives (1077), may take a genitive in place of the predicate accusative. *E.g.*

Τὴν Ἀσίαν ἑαυτῶν ποιοῦνται, *they make Asia their own*, X. *Ag.* 1, 33. Ἐμὲ θὲς τῶν πεπεισμένων, *put me down as (one) of those who are persuaded*, P. *Rp.* 424ᵉ. (Τοῦτο) τῆς ἡμετέρας ἀμελείας ἂν τις θείη δικαίως, *any one might justly regard this as belonging to our neglect*, D. 1, 10.

1096. These verbs (1095) in the passive are among the copulative verbs of 907, and they still retain the genitive. See the last example under 1094, 7.

GENITIVE EXPRESSING A PART.

1097. 1. Any verb may take a genitive if its action affects the object *only in part*. *E.g.*

Πέμπει τῶν Λυδῶν, *he sends some of the Lydians* (but πέμπει τοὺς Λυδούς, *he sends the Lydians*). Πίνει τοῦ οἴνου, *he drinks of the wine*. Τῆς γῆς ἔτεμον, *they ravaged (some) of the land*, T. 1, 30.

2. This principle applies especially to verbs signifying *to share* (i.e. *to give* or *take a part*) or *to enjoy*. *E.g.*

Μετεῖχον τῆς λείας, *they shared in the booty*; so often μεταποιεῖσθαί τινος, *to claim a share of anything* (cf. 1099); ἀπολαύομεν τῶν ἀγαθῶν, *we enjoy the blessings* (i.e. *our share of them*); οὕτως ὄναισθε τούτων, *thus may you enjoy these*, D. 28, 20. So οὐ προσήκει μοι τῆς ἀρχῆς, *I have no concern in the government*; μέτεστί μοι τούτου, *I have a share in this* (1161).

1098. N. Many of these verbs also take an accusative, when they refer to the whole object. Thus ἔλαχε τούτου means *he obtained a share of this by lot*, but ἔλαχε τοῦτο, *he obtained this by lot*. Μετέχω and similar verbs may regularly take an accusative like μέρος, *part*; as τῶν κινδύνων πλεῖστον μέρος μεθέξουσιν, *they will have the greatest share of the dangers*, I. 6, 3 (where μέρους would mean that they have only *a part of a share*). This use of μέρος shows the nature of the genitive after these verbs.

In συντρίβειν τῆς κεφαλῆς, *to bruise his head*, and κατεαγέναι τῆς κεφαλῆς, *to have his head broken*, the genitive is probably partitive. See Ar. *Ach.* 1180, *Pa.* 71; I. 18, 52. These verbs take also the accusative.

GENITIVE WITH VARIOUS VERBS.

1099. The genitive follows verbs signifying *to take*

hold of, to touch, to claim, to aim at, to hit, to attain, to miss, to make trial of, to begin. *E.g.*

Ἐλάβετο τῆς χειρὸς αὐτοῦ, *he took his hand*, X. *H.* 4, 1[38]; πυρὸς ἔστι θιγόντα μὴ εὐθὺς καίεσθαι, *it is possible to touch fire and not be burned immediately*, X. *C.* 5, 1[16]; τῆς ξυνέσεως μεταποιεῖσθαι, *to lay claim to sagacity*, T. 1, 140; ἥκιστα τῶν ἀλλοτρίων ὀρέγονται, *they are least eager for what is another's*, X. *Sy.* 4, 42; οὐδὲ μὴν ἄλλου στοχαζόμενος ἔτυχε τούτου, *nor did he aim at another man and hit this one*, Ant. 2 α, 4; τῆς ἀρετῆς ἐφικέσθαι, *to attain to virtue*, I. 1, 5; ὁδοῦ εὐπόρου τυχεῖν, *to find a passable road*, X. *H.* 6, 5[52]; πολλῶν καὶ χαλεπῶν χωρίων ἐπελάβοντο, *they took possession of many rough places, ibid.*; ταύτης ἀποσφαλέντα τῆς ἐλπίδος, *disappointed in this hope*, Hd. 6, 5; σφαλεὶς τῆς ἀληθείας, *having missed the truth*, P. *Rp.* 451[a]; τὸ ἐψεῦσθαι τῆς ἀληθείας, *to be cheated out of the truth, ibid.* 413[a]; πειράσαντες τοῦ χωρίου, *having made an attempt on the place*, T. 1, 61; εἰκὸς ἄρχειν με λόγου, *it is proper that I should speak first*, X. *C.* 6, 1[6].

1100. N. Verbs of *taking hold* may have an object accusative, with a genitive of the part taken hold of; as ἔλαβον τῆς ζώνης τὸν Ὀρόνταν, *they seized Orontas by his girdle*, X. *A.* 1, 6[10].

1101. 1. The poets extend the construction of verbs of *taking hold* to those of *pulling, dragging, leading*, and the like; as ἄλλον μὲν χλαίνης ἐρύων ἄλλον δὲ χιτῶνος, *pulling one by the cloak, another by the tunic*, *Il.* 22, 493; βοῦν ἀγέτην κεράων, *the two led the heifer by the horns*, *Od.* 3, 439.

2. So even in prose: τὰ νήπια παιδία δέουσι τοῦ ποδὸς σπάρτῳ, *they tie the infants by the foot with a cord*, Hd. 5, 16; μήποτε ἄγειν τῆς ἡνίας τὸν ἵππον, *never to lead the horse by the bridle*, X. *Eq.* 6, 9.

3. Under this head is usually placed the poetic genitive with verbs of *imploring*, denoting the part grasped by the suppliant; as ἐμὲ λισσέσκετο γούνων, *she implored me by* (i.e. *clasping*) *my knees*, *Il.* 9, 451. The explanation is less simple in λίσσομαι Ζηνὸς Ὀλυμπίου, *I implore by Olympian Zeus*, *Od.* 2, 68: compare νῦν δέ σε πρὸς πατρὸς γουνάζομαι, *and now I implore thee by thy father*, *Od.* 13, 324.

1102. The genitive follows verbs signifying *to taste, to smell, to hear, to perceive, to comprehend, to remember, to forget, to desire, to care for, to spare, to neglect, to wonder at, to admire, to despise.* *E.g.*

Ἐλευθερίης γευσάμενοι, *having tasted of freedom*, Hd. 6, 5; κρομμύων ὀσφραίνομαι, *I smell onions*, Ar. *R.* 654; φωνῆς ἀκούειν μοι δοκῶ, *methinks I hear a voice*, Ar. *Pa.* 61; αἰσθάνεσθαι, μεμνῆσθαι, or ἐπιλανθάνεσθαι τούτων, *to perceive, remember*, or *forget these*; ὅσοι ἀλλήλων ξυνίεσαν, *all who comprehended each other's speech*, T. 1, 3 (1104); τούτων τῶν μαθημάτων ἐπιθυμῶ, *I long for this learning*, X. *M.* 2, 6[30]; χρημάτων φείδεσθαι, *to be sparing of money*, *ibid.* 1, 2[22]; τῆς ἀρετῆς ἀμελεῖν, *to neglect virtue*, I. 1, 48; εἰ ἄγασαι τοῦ πατρός, *if you admire your father*, X. *C.* 3, 1[15]. Μηδενὸς οὖν ὀλιγωρεῖτε μηδὲ καταφρονεῖτε τῶν προστεταγμένων, *do not then neglect or despise any of my injunctions*, I. 3, 48. Τῶν κατηγόρων θαυμάζω, *I am astonished at my accusers*, L. 25, 1. (For a causal genitive with verbs like θαυμάζω, see 1126.)

1103. N. Verbs of *hearing, learning*, etc. may take an accusative of the thing heard etc. and a genitive of the person heard from; as τούτων τοιούτους ἀκούω λόγους, *I hear such sayings from these men*; πυθέσθαι τοῦτο ὑμῶν, *to learn this from you*. The genitive here belongs under 1130. A sentence may take the place of the accusative; as τούτων ἄκουε τί λέγουσιν, *hear from these what they say*. See also ἀποδέχομαι, *accept (a statement) from*, in the Lexicon.

1104. N. Verbs of *understanding*, as ἐπίσταμαι, have the accusative. Συνίημι, quoted above with the genitive (1102), usually takes the accusative of a thing.

1105. The impersonals μέλει and μεταμέλει take the genitive of a thing with the dative of a person (1161); as μέλει μοι τούτου, *I care for this*; μεταμέλει σοι τούτου, *thou repentest of this*. Προσήκει, *it concerns*, has the same construction, but the genitive belongs under 1097, 2.

1106. Causative verbs of this class take the accusative of a person and the genitive of a thing; as μή μ' ἀναμνήσῃς κακῶν, *do not remind me of evils* (i.e. *cause me to remember them*), E. *Al.* 1045; τοὺς παῖδας γευστέον αἵματος, *we must make the children taste blood*, P. *Rp.* 537[a].

But verbs of *reminding* also take two accusatives (1069).

1107. N. Ὄζω, *emit smell (smell of)*, has a genitive (perhaps by an ellipsis of ὀσμήν, *odor*); as ὄζουσ' ἀμβροσίας καὶ νέκταρος, *they smell of ambrosia and nectar*, Ar. *Ach.* 196. A second genitive may be added to designate the source of the odor; as εἰ τῆς κεφαλῆς ὄζω μύρου, *if my head smells of perfume*, Ar. *Eccl.* 524.

1108. N. Many of the verbs of 1099 and 1102 may take also the accusative. See the Lexicon.

1109. The genitive follows verbs signifying *to rule*, *to lead*, or *to direct*. *E.g.*

Ἔρως τῶν θεῶν βασιλεύει, *Love is king of the Gods*, P. *Sy.* 195[e]; Πολυκράτης Σάμου τυραννῶν, *Polycrates, while he was tyrant of Samos*, T. 1, 13; Μίνως τῆς νῦν Ἑλληνικῆς θαλάσσης ἐκράτησε καὶ τῶν Κυκλάδων νήσων ἦρξε, *Minos became master of what is now the Greek sea, and ruler of the Cyclades*, T. 1, 4; ἡδονῶν ἐκράτει, *he was master of pleasures*, X. *M.* 1, 5[6]; ἡγούμενοι αὐτονόμων τῶν ξυμμάχων, *leading their allies (who were) independent* (972), T. 1, 97.

1110. N. This construction is sometimes connected with that of 1120. But the genitive here depends on the idea of *king* or *ruler* implied in the verb, while there it depends on the idea of *comparison* (see 1083).

1111. N. For other cases after many of these verbs, see the Lexicon. For the dative in poetry after ἡγέομαι and ἀνάσσω, see 1164.

1112. Verbs signifying *fulness* and *want* take the genitive of material (1085, 4). *E.g.*

Χρημάτων εὐπόρει, *he had abundance of money*, D. 18, 235; σεσαγμένος πλούτου τὴν ψυχὴν ἔσομαι, *I shall have my soul loaded with wealth*, X. *Sy.* 4, 64. Οὐκ ἂν ἀποροῖ παραδειγμάτων, *he would be at no loss for examples*, P. *Rp.* 557[d]; οὐδὲν δεήσει πολλῶν γραμμάτων, *there will be no need of many writings*, I. 4, 78.

1113. Verbs signifying *to fill* take the accusative of the thing filled and the genitive of material. *E.g.*

Δακρύων ἔπλησεν ἐμέ, *he filled me with tears*, E. *Or.* 368.

1114. N. Δέομαι, *I want*, besides the ordinary genitive (as τούτων ἐδέοντο, *they were in want of these*), may take a cognate accusative of the thing; as δεήσομαι ὑμῶν μετρίαν δέησιν, *I will make of you a moderate request*, Aesch. 3, 61. (See 1076.)

1115. N. Δεῖ may take a dative (sometimes in poetry an accusative) of the person besides the genitive; as δεῖ μοι τούτου, *I need this*; αὐτὸν γάρ σε δεῖ Προμηθέως, *for thou thyself needest a Prometheus*, A. *Pr.* 86 (cf. οὐ δεῖ με ἐλθεῖν).

1116. N. (*a*) Besides the common phrases πολλοῦ δεῖ, *it is far from it*, ὀλίγου δεῖ, *it wants little of it*, we have in Demosthenes οὐδὲ πολλοῦ δεῖ (like παντὸς δεῖ), *it wants everything of it* (lit. *it does not even want much*).

(*b*) By an ellipsis of δεῖν (1534), ὀλίγου and μικροῦ come to mean *almost*; as ὀλίγου πάντες, *almost all*, P. *Rp.* 552[d].

GENITIVE OF SEPARATION AND COMPARISON.

1117. The genitive (as ablative) may denote that from which anything is *separated* or *distinguished*. On this principle the genitive follows verbs denoting *to remove, to restrain, to release, to cease, to fail, to differ, to give up*, and the like. *E.g.*

Ἡ νῆσος οὐ πολὺ διέχει τῆς ἠπείρου, *the island is not far distant from the main-land.* Ἐπιστήμη χωριζομένη δικαιοσύνης, *knowledge separated from justice*, P. *Menex.* 246[e]; λῦσόν με δεσμῶν, *release me from chains;* ἐπέσχον τῆς τειχήσεως, *they ceased from building the wall;* τούτους οὐ παύσω τῆς ἀρχῆς, *I will not depose these from their authority*, X. *C.* 8, 6[3]; οὐ παύεσθε τῆς μοχθηρίας, *you do not cease from your rascality;* οὐκ ἐψεύσθη τῆς ἐλπίδος, *he was not disappointed in his hope*, X. *H.* 7, 5[24]; οὐδὲν διοίσεις Χαιρεφῶντος, *you will not differ from Chaerephon*, Ar. *N.* 503; τῆς ἐλευθερίας παραχωρῆσαι Φιλίππῳ, *to surrender freedom to Philip*, D. 18, 68. So εἶπον (αὐτῷ) τοῦ κήρυκος μὴ λείπεσθαι, *they told him not to be left behind the herald* (i.e. *to follow close upon him*), T. 1, 131; ἡ ἐπιστολὴ ἣν οὗτος ἔγραψεν ἀπολειφθεὶς ἡμῶν, *the letter which this man wrote without our knowledge* (lit. *separated from us*), D. 19, 36.

Transitive verbs of this class may take also an accusative.

1118. Verbs of *depriving* may take a genitive in place of the accusative of a thing, and those of *taking away* a genitive in place of the accusative of a person (1069; 1071); as ἐμὲ τῶν πατρῴων ἀπεστέρηκε, *he has deprived me of my paternal property*, D. 29, 3; τῶν ἄλλων ἀφαιρούμενοι χρήματα, *taking away property from the others*, X. *M.* 1, 5[3]; πόσων ἀπεστέρησθε, *of how much have you been bereft!* D. 8, 63.

1119. N. The poets use this genitive with verbs of *motion;* as Οὐλύμποιο κατήλθομεν, *we descended from Olympus*, *Il.* 20, 125; Πυθῶνος ἔβας, *thou didst come from Pytho*, S. *O. T.* 152. Here a preposition would be used in prose.

1120. The genitive follows verbs signifying *to surpass, to be inferior*, and all others which imply comparison. *E.g.*

(Ἄνθρωπος) ξυνέσει ὑπερέχει τῶν ἄλλων, *man surpasses the others in sagacity*, P. *Menex.* 237[d]; ἐπιδείξαντες τὴν ἀρετὴν τοῦ πλήθους περιγιγνομένην, *showing that bravery proves superior to numbers*, I. 4, 91; ὁρῶν ὑστερίζουσαν τὴν πόλιν τῶν καιρῶν, *seeing the city too late for its opportunities*, D. 18, 102; ἐμπειρίᾳ πολὺ προέχετε τῶν *ἄλλων, in experience you far excel the others,* X. *H.*7,1[4]; *οὐδὲν πλήθει γε ἡμῶν λειφθέντες, when they were not at all inferior to (left behind by) us in numbers,* X. *A.*7,7[31]. So *τῶν ἐχθρῶν νικᾶσθαι* (or *ἡσσᾶσθαι*), *to be overcome by one's enemies;* but these two verbs take also the genitive with *ὑπό* (1234). So *τῶν ἐχθρῶν κρατεῖν, to prevail over one's enemies,* and *τῆς θαλάσσης κρατεῖν, to be master of the sea.* Compare the examples under 1109, and see 1110.

GENITIVE WITH VERBS OF ACCUSING ETC.

1121. Verbs signifying *to accuse, to prosecute, to convict, to acquit,* and *to condemn* take a genitive denoting the *crime,* with an accusative of the person. *E.g.*

Αἰτιῶμαι αὐτὸν τοῦ φόνου, *I accuse him of the murder;* ἐγράψατο αὐτὸν παρανόμων, *he indicted him for an illegal proposition;* διώκει με δώρων, *he prosecutes me for bribery (for gifts).* Κλέωνα δώρων ἑλόντες καὶ κλοπῆς, *having convicted Cleon of bribery and theft,* Ar. *N.*591. Ἔφευγε προδοσίας, *he was brought to trial for treachery,* but ἀπέφυγε προδοσίας, *he was acquitted of treachery.* Ψευδομαρτυριῶν ἁλώσεσθαι προσδοκῶν, *expecting to be convicted of false-witness,* D.39,18.

1122. Ὀφλισκάνω, *lose a suit,* has the construction of a passive of this class (1239); as ὦφλε κλοπῆς, *he was convicted of theft.* It may also have a cognate accusative; as ὦφλε κλοπῆς δίκην, *he was convicted of theft* (1051). For other accusatives with ὀφλισκάνω, as μωρίαν, *folly,* αἰσχύνην, *shame,* χρήματα, *money (fine),* see the Lexicon.

1123. Compounds of κατά of this class, including κατηγορῶ (882, 2), commonly take a genitive of the *person,* which depends on the κατά. They may take also an object accusative denoting the crime or punishment. *E.g.*

Οὐδεὶς αὐτὸς αὑτοῦ κατηγόρησε πώποτε, *no man ever himself accused himself,* D.38,26; κατεβόων τῶν Ἀθηναίων, *they decried the Athenians,* T.1,67; θάνατον κατέγνωσαν αὐτοῦ, *they condemned him to death,* T.6,61; ὑμῶν δέομαι μὴ καταγνῶναι δωροδοκίαν ἐμοῦ, *I beg you not to declare me guilty of taking bribes,* L.21,21; τὰ πλεῖστα κατεψεύσατό μου, *he told the most lies against me,* D.18,9; λέγω πρὸς τοὺς ἐμοῦ καταψηφισαμένους θάνατον, *I speak to those who voted to condemn me to death,* P. *Ap.* 38[d].

1124. N. Verbs of *condemning* which are compounds of κατά may take three cases; as πολλῶν οἱ πατέρες ἡμῶν μηδισμοῦ θάνατον κατέγνωσαν, *our fathers condemned many to death for Medism,* I.4,157.

For a genitive (of *value*) denoting the penalty, see 1133.

1125. N. The verbs of 1121 often take a cognate accusative (1051) on which the genitive depends; as γραφὴν γράφεσθαι ὕβρεως, *to bring an indictment for outrage;* γραφὴν (or δίκην) ὑπέχειν, φεύγειν, ἀποφεύγειν, ὀφλεῖν, ἁλῶναι, etc. The force of this accusative seems to be felt in the construction of 1121.

GENITIVE OF CAUSE AND SOURCE.

1126. The genitive often denotes a *cause*, especially with verbs expressing emotions, as *admiration*, *wonder*, *affection*, *hatred*, *pity*, *anger*, *envy*, or *revenge*. *E.g.*

(Τούτους) τῆς μὲν τόλμης οὐ θαυμάζω, τῆς δὲ ἀξυνεσίας, *I wonder not at their boldness, but at their folly*, T. 6, 36; πολλάκις σε εὐδαιμόνισα τοῦ τρόπου, *I often counted you happy for your character*, P. *Cr.* 43[b]; ζηλῶ σε τοῦ νοῦ, τῆς δὲ δειλίας στυγῶ, *I envy you for your mind, but loathe you for your cowardice*, S. *El.* 1027; μή μοι φθονήσῃς τοῦ μαθήματος, *don't grudge me the knowledge*, P. *Eu.* 297[b]; συγγιγνώσκειν αὐτοῖς χρὴ τῆς ἐπιθυμίας, *we must forgive them for their desire*, *ibid.* 306[c]; καί σφεας τιμωρήσομαι τῆς ἐνθάδε ἀπίξιος, *and I shall punish them for coming hither*, Hd. 3, 145. Τούτους οἰκτίρω τῆς νόσου, *I pity these for their disease*, X. *Sy.* 4[37]; τῶν ἀδικημάτων ὀργίζεσθαι, *to be angry at the offences*, L. 31, 11.

Most of these verbs may take also an accusative or dative of the person.

1127. N. The genitive sometimes denotes a *purpose* or *motive* (where ἕνεκα is generally expressed); as τῆς τῶν Ἑλλήνων ἐλευθερίας, *for the liberty of the Greeks*, D. 18, 100; so 19, 76. (See 1548.)

1128. N. Verbs of *disputing* take a causal genitive; as οὐ βασιλεῖ ἀντιποιούμεθα τῆς ἀρχῆς, *we do not dispute with the King about his dominion*, X. *A.* 2, 3[23]; Εὔμολπος ἠμφισβήτησεν Ἐρεχθεῖ τῆς πόλεως, *Eumolpus disputed with Erechtheus for the city* (i.e. *disputed its possession with him*), I. 12, 193.

1129. The genitive is sometimes used in *exclamations*, to give the cause of the astonishment. *E.g.*

Ὦ Πόσειδον, τῆς τέχνης, *O Poseidon, what a trade!* Ar. *Eq.* 144. Ὦ Ζεῦ βασιλεῦ, τῆς λεπτότητος τῶν φρενῶν! *O King Zeus! what subtlety of intellect!* Ar. *N.* 153.

1130. 1. The genitive sometimes denotes the *source*. *E.g.*

Τοῦτο ἔτυχόν σου, *I obtained this from you.* Μάθε μου τάδε, *learn this from me*, X. *C.* 1, 6[44]. Add the examples under 1103.

2. So with γίγνομαι, in the sense *to be born;* as Δαρείου καὶ Παρυσάτιδος γίγνονται παῖδες δύο, *of Darius and Parysatis are born two sons*, X. *A.* 1, 1[1].

1131. In *poetry*, the genitive occasionally denotes the *agent* after a passive verb, or is used like the *instrumental* dative (1181). *E.g.*

Ἐν Ἅιδᾳ δὴ κεῖσαι, σᾶς ἀλόχου σφαγεὶς Αἰγίσθου τε, *thou liest now in Hades, slain by thy wife and Aegisthus*, E. *El.* 122. Πρῆσαι πυρὸς δηΐοιο θύρετρα, *to burn the gates with destructive fire*, *Il.* 2, 415.

These constructions would not be allowed in prose.

GENITIVE AFTER COMPOUND VERBS.

1132. The genitive often depends on a preposition included in a compound verb. *E.g.*

Πρόκειται τῆς χώρας ἡμῶν ὄρη μεγάλα, *high mountains lie in front of our land*, X. *M.* 3, 5[25]; ὑπερεφάνησαν τοῦ λόφου, *they appeared above the hill*, T. 4, 93; οὕτως ὑμῶν ὑπεραλγῶ, *I grieve so for you*, Ar. *Av.* 466; ἀποτρέπει με τούτου, *it turns me from this*, P. *Ap.* 31[d]; τῷ ἐπιβάντι πρώτῳ τοῦ τείχους, *to him who should first mount the wall*, T. 4, 116; οὐκ ἀνθρώπων ὑπερεφρόνει, *he did not despise men*, X. *Ag.* 11, 2.

For the genitive after verbs of *accusing* and *condemning*, compounds of κατά, see 1123.

GENITIVE OF PRICE OR VALUE.

1133. The genitive may denote the *price* or *value* of a thing. *E.g.*

Τεύχε' ἄμειβεν, χρύσεα χαλκείων, ἑκατόμβοι' ἐννεαβοίων, *he gave gold armor for bronze, armor worth a hundred oxen for that worth nine oxen*, *Il.* 6, 235. Δόξα χρημάτων οὐκ ὠνητή (sc. ἐστίν), *glory is not to be bought with money*, I. 2, 32. Πόσου διδάσκει; πέντε μνῶν. *For what price does he teach? For five minae.* P. *Ap.* 20[b]. Οὐκ ἂν ἀπεδόμην πολλοῦ τὰς ἐλπίδας, *I would not have sold my hopes for a great deal*, P. *Ph.* 98[b]; μείζονος αὐτὰ τιμῶνται, *they value them more*, X. *C.* 2, 1[13]. (But with verbs of *valuing* περί with the genitive is more common.)

In judicial language, τιμᾶν τινί τινος is said of the court's judgment in estimating the penalty, τιμᾶσθαί τινί τινος of either party to the suit in proposing a penalty; as ἀλλὰ δὴ φυγῆς τιμήσωμαι; ἴσως γὰρ ἄν μοι τούτου τιμήσαιτε, *but now shall I propose exile as my punishment?—you* (the court) *might perhaps fix my penalty at this*, P. *Ap.* 37[c]. So τιμᾶται δ' οὖν μοι ὁ ἀνὴρ θανάτου, *so the man estimates my punishment at death* (i.e. *proposes death as my punish-*

ment), P. *Ap.* 36b. So also Σφοδρίαν ὑπῆγον θανάτου, *they impeached Sphodrias on a capital charge* (cf. 1124), X. *H.* 5, 4[24].

1134. The thing bought sometimes stands in the genitive, either by analogy to the genitive of price, or in a causal sense (1126); as τοῦ δώδεκα μνᾶς Πασίᾳ (sc. ὀφείλω); *for what (do I owe) twelve minae to Pasias?* Ar. *N.* 22; οὐδένα τῆς συνουσίας ἀργύριον πράττει, *you ask no money of anybody for your teaching*, X. *M.* 1, 6[11].

1135. The genitive depending on ἄξιος, *worth, worthy*, and its compounds, or on ἀξιόω, *think worthy*, is the genitive of *price* or *value*; as ἄξιός ἐστι θανάτου, *he is worthy of death*; οὐ Θεμιστοκλέα τῶν μεγίστων δωρεῶν ἠξίωσαν; *did they not think Themistocles worthy of the highest gifts?* I. 4, 154. So sometimes ἄτιμος and ἀτιμάζω take the genitive. (See 1140.)

GENITIVE OF TIME AND PLACE.

1136. The genitive may denote the *time within which* anything takes place. *E.g.*

Ποίου χρόνου δὲ καὶ πεπόρθηται πόλις; *well, how long since (within what time) was the city really taken?* A. *Ag.* 278. Τοῦ ἐπιγιγνομένου χειμῶνος, *during the following winter*, T. 8, 29. Ταῦτα τῆς ἡμέρας ἐγένετο, *this happened during the day*, X. *A.* 7, 4[14] (τὴν ἡμέραν would mean *through the whole day*, 1062). Δέκα ἐτῶν οὐχ ἥξουσι, *they will not come within ten years*, P. *Lg.* 642e. So δραχμὴν ἐλάμβανε τῆς ἡμέρας, *he received a drachma a day* (951).

1137. A similar genitive of the place *within which* or *at which* is found in poetry. *E.g.*

Ἦ οὐκ Ἄργεος ἦεν Ἀχαιικοῦ; *was he not in Achaean Argos?* *Od.* 3, 251; Οἵη νῦν οὐκ ἔστι γυνὴ κατ' Ἀχαιΐδα γαῖαν, οὔτε Πύλου ἱερῆς οὔτ' Ἄργεος οὔτε Μυκήνης, *a woman whose like there is not in the Achaean land, not at sacred Pylos, nor at Argos, nor at Mycenae*, *Od.* 21, 107. So in the Homeric πεδίοιο θέειν, *to run on the plain* (i.e. *within its limits*), *Il.* 22, 23, λούεσθαι ποταμοῖο, *to bathe in the river*, *Il.* 6, 508, and similar expressions. So ἀριστερῆς χειρός, *on the left hand*, even in Hdt. (5, 77).

1138. N. A genitive denoting *place* occurs in Attic prose in a few such expressions as ἰέναι τοῦ πρόσω, *to go forward*, X. *A.* 1, 3[1], and ἐπετάχυνον τῆς ὁδοῦ τοὺς σχολαίτερον προσιόντας, *they hurried over the road those who came up more slowly*, T. 4, 47. These genitives are variously explained.

GENITIVE WITH ADJECTIVES.

1139. The *objective* genitive follows many verbal adjectives.

1140. These adjectives are chiefly kindred (in meaning or derivation) to verbs which take the genitive. *E.g.*

Μέτοχος σοφίας, *partaking of wisdom*, P. *Lg.* 689[d]; ἰσόμοιροι τῶν πατρῴων, *sharing equally their father's estate*, Isae. 6, 25. (1097, 2.)

Ἐπιστήμης ἐπήβολοι, *having attained knowledge*, P. *Eu.* 289[b]; θαλάσσης ἐμπειρότατοι, *most experienced in the sea (in navigation)*, T. 1, 80. (1099.)

Ὑπήκοος τῶν γονέων, *obedient (hearkening) to his parents*, P. *Rp.* 463[d]; ἀμνήμων τῶν κινδύνων, *unmindful of the dangers*, Ant. 2 *a*, 7; ἄγευστος κακῶν, *without a taste of evils*, S. *An.* 582; ἐπιμελὴς ἀγαθῶν, ἀμελὴς κακῶν, *caring for the good, neglectful of the bad; φειδωλοὶ χρημάτων, sparing of money*, P. *Rp.* 548[b]. (1102.)

Τῶν ἡδονῶν πασῶν ἐγκρατέστατος, *most perfect master of all pleasures*, X. *M.* 1, 2[14]; νεὼς ἀρχικός, *fit to command a ship*, P. *Rp.* 488[d]; ἑαυτοῦ ὢν ἀκράτωρ, *not being master of himself, ibid.* 579[c]. (1109.)

Μεστὸς κακῶν, *full of evils*; ἐπιστήμης κενός, *void of knowledge*, P. *Rp.* 486[c]; λήθης ὢν πλέως, *being full of forgetfulness, ibid.*; πλείστων ἐνδεέστατος, *most wanting in most things, ibid.* 579[e]; ἡ ψυχὴ γυμνὴ τοῦ σώματος, *the soul stript of the body*, P. *Crat.* 403[b]; καθαρὰ πάντων τῶν περὶ τὸ σῶμα κακῶν, *free (pure) from all the evils that belong to the body, ibid.* 403[e]; τοιούτων ἀνδρῶν ὀρφανή, *bereft of such men*, L. 2, 60; ἐπιστήμη ἐπιστήμης διάφορος, *knowledge distinct from knowledge*, P. *Phil.* 61[d]; ἕτερον τὸ ἡδὺ τοῦ ἀγαθοῦ, *the pleasant (is) distinct from the good*, P. *G.* 500[d]. (1112; 1117.)

Ἔνοχος δειλίας, *chargeable with cowardice*, L. 14, 5; τούτων αἴτιος, *responsible for this*, P. *G.* 447[a]. (1121.)

Ἄξιος πολλῶν, *worth much*, genitive of *value* (1135).

1141. Compounds of *alpha privative* (875, 1) sometimes take a genitive of kindred meaning, which depends on the idea of *separation* implied in them; as ἄπαις ἀρρένων παίδων, *destitute (childless) of male children*, X. *C.* 4, 6[2]; τιμῆς ἄτιμος πάσης, *destitute of all honor*, P. *Lg.* 774[b]; χρημάτων ἀδωρότατος, *most free from taking bribes*, T. 2, 65; ἀπήνεμον πάντων χειμώνων, *free from the blasts of all storms*, S. *O. C.* 677; ἀψόφητος ὀξέων κωκυμάτων, *without the sound of shrill wailings*, S. *Aj.* 321.

1142. Some of these adjectives (1139) are kindred to verbs which take the accusative. *E.g.*

Ἐπιστήμων τῆς τέχνης, *understanding the art*, P. *G.* 448[b] (1104);

ἐπιτήδευμα πόλεως ἀνατρεπτικόν, a practice subversive of a state, P. *Rp.* 389[d]; *κακοῦργος τῶν ἄλλων, ἑαυτοῦ δὲ πολὺ κακουργότερος, doing evil to the others, but far greater evil to himself,* X. *M.* 1, 5[a]; *συγγνώμων τῶν ἀνθρωπίνων ἁμαρτημάτων, considerate of human faults,* X. *C.* 6, 1[37]; *σύμψηφός σοί εἰμι τούτου τοῦ νόμου, I vote with you for this law,* P. *Rp.* 380[c].

1143. The possessive genitive sometimes follows adjectives denoting *possession*. *E.g.*

Οἱ κίνδυνοι τῶν ἐφεστηκότων ἴδιοι, the dangers belong to the commanders, D. 2, 28; *ἱερὸς ὁ χῶρος τῆς Ἀρτέμιδος, the place is sacred to Artemis,* X. *A.* 5, 3[13]; *κοινὸν πάντων, common to all,* P. *Sy.* 205[a].

For the dative with such adjectives, see 1174.

1144. 1. Such a genitive sometimes denotes mere *connection;* as *συγγενὴς αὐτοῦ, a relative of his,* X. *C.* 4, 1[22]; *Σωκράτους ὁμώνυμος, a namesake of Socrates,* P. *So.* 218[b].

The adjective is here really used as a substantive. Such adjectives naturally take the dative (1175).

2. Here probably belongs *ἐναγὴς τοῦ Ἀπόλλωνος, accursed (one) of Apollo,* Aesch. 3, 110; also *ἐναγεῖς καὶ ἀλιτήριοι τῆς θεοῦ, accursed of the Goddess,* T. 1, 126, and *ἐκ τῶν ἀλιτηρίων τῶν τῆς θεοῦ,* Ar. *Eq.* 445; — *ἐναγής* etc. being really substantives.

1145. After some adjectives the genitive can be best explained as depending on the substantive implied in them; as *τῆς ἀρχῆς ὑπεύθυνος, responsible for the office,* i.e. *liable to εὔθυναι for it,* D. 18, 117 (see *δέδωκά γε εὐθύνας ἐκείνων,* in the same section); *παρθένοι γάμων ὡραῖαι, maidens ripe for marriage,* i.e. *having reached the age (ὥρα) for marriage,* Hd. 1, 196 (see *ἐς γάμου ὥρην ἀπικομένην,* Hd. 6, 61); *φόρου ὑποτελεῖς, subject to the payment (τέλος) of tribute,* T. 1, 19.

1146. N. Some adjectives of place, like *ἐναντίος, opposite,* may take the genitive instead of the regular dative (1174), but chiefly in poetry; as *ἐναντίοι ἔσταν Ἀχαιῶν, they stood opposite the Achaeans, Il.* 17, 343.

See also *τοῦ Πόντου ἐπικάρσιαι, at an angle with the Pontus,* Hd. 7, 36.

GENITIVE WITH ADVERBS.

1147. The genitive follows adverbs derived from adjectives which take the genitive. *E.g.*

Οἱ ἐμπείρως αὐτοῦ ἔχοντες, those who are acquainted with him, ἀναξίως τῆς πόλεως, in a manner unworthy of the state. *Τῶν ἄλλων*

Ἀθηναίων ἁπάντων διαφερόντως, *beyond all the other Athenians*, P. *Cr.* 52[b]. Ἐμάχοντο ἀξίως λόγου, *they* (the Athenians at Marathon) *fought in a manner worthy of note*, Hd. 6, 112. So ἐναντίον (1146).

1148. The genitive follows many adverbs of place. *E.g.*

Εἴσω τοῦ ἐρύματος, *within the fortress*; ἔξω τοῦ τείχους, *outside of the wall*; ἐκτὸς τῶν ὅρων, *without the boundaries*; χωρὶς τοῦ σώματος, *apart from the body*; πέραν τοῦ ποταμοῦ, *beyond the river*, T. 6, 101; πρόσθεν τοῦ στρατοπέδου, *in front of the camp*, X. *H.* 4, 1[22]; ἀμφοτέρωθεν τῆς ὁδοῦ, *on both sides of the road*, *ibid.* 5, 2[6]; εὐθὺ τῆς Φασήλιδος, *straight towards Phaselis*, T. 8, 88.

1149. N. Such adverbs, besides those given above, are chiefly ἐντός, *within*; δίχα, *apart from*; ἐγγύς, ἄγχι, πέλας, and πλησίον, *near*; πόρρω (πρόσω), *far from*; ὄπισθεν and κατόπιν, *behind*; and a few others of similar meaning. The genitive after most of them can be explained as a *partitive* genitive or as a genitive of *separation*; that after εὐθύ resembles that after verbs of *aiming at* (1099).

1150. N. Λάθρᾳ (Ionic λάθρῃ) and κρύφα, *without the knowledge of*, sometimes take the genitive; as λάθρῃ Λαομέδοντος, *without the knowledge of Laomedon*, *Il.* 5, 269; κρύφα τῶν Ἀθηναίων, T. 1, 101.

1151. N. Ἄνευ and ἄτερ, *without*, ἄχρι and μέχρι, *until*, ἕνεκα (οὕνεκα), *on account of*, μεταξύ, *between*, and πλήν, *except*, take the genitive like prepositions. See 1220.

GENITIVE ABSOLUTE.

1152. A noun and a participle not grammatically connected with the main construction of the sentence may stand by themselves in the genitive. This is called the *genitive absolute*. *E.g.*

Ταῦτ' ἐπράχθη Κόνωνος στρατηγοῦντος, *this was done when Conon was general*, I. 9, 56. Οὐδὲν τῶν δεόντων ποιούντων ὑμῶν κακῶς τὰ πράγματα ἔχει, *affairs are in a bad state while you do nothing which you ought to do*, D. 4, 2. Θεῶν διδόντων οὐκ ἂν ἐκφύγοι κακά, *if the Gods should grant* (it to be so), *he could not escape evils*, A. *Se.* 719. Ὄντος γε ψεύδους ἔστιν ἀπάτη, *when there is falsehood, there is deceit*, P. *So.* 260[c].

See 1568 and 1563.

GENITIVE WITH COMPARATIVES.

1153. Adjectives and adverbs of the comparative degree take the genitive (without ἤ, *than*). *E.g.*

Κρείττων ἐστὶ τούτων, *he is better than these.* Νέοις τὸ σιγᾶν κρεῖττόν ἐστι τοῦ λαλεῖν, *for youth silence is better than prating,* Men. *Mon.* 387. (Πονηρία) θᾶττον θανάτου θεῖ, *wickedness runs faster than death,* P. *Ap.* 39ª.

1154. N. All adjectives and adverbs which *imply* a comparison may take a genitive: as ἕτεροι τούτων, *others than these;* ὕστεροι τῆς μάχης, *too late for* (*later than*) *the battle;* τῇ ὑστεραίᾳ τῆς μάχης, *on the day after the battle.* So τριπλάσιον ἡμῶν, *thrice as much as we.*

1155. N. The genitive is less common than ἤ when, if ἤ were used, it would be followed by any other case than the nominative or the accusative without a preposition. Thus for ἔξεστι δ' ἡμῖν μᾶλλον ἑτέρων, *and we can* (*do this*) *better than others* (T. 1, 85), μᾶλλον ἢ ἑτέροις would be more common.

1156. N. After πλέον (πλεῖν), *more,* or ἔλασσον (μεῖον), *less,* ἤ is occasionally omitted before a numeral without affecting the case; as πέμψω ὄρνις ἐπ' αὐτόν, πλεῖν ἑξακοσίους τὸν ἀριθμόν, *I will send birds against him, more than six hundred in number,* Ar. *Av.* 1251.

DATIVE.

1157. The primary use of the *dative* case is to denote that *to* or *for* which anything is or is done: this includes the dative of the remote or indirect object, and the dative of *advantage* or *disadvantage.* It also denotes that *by* which or *with* which, and the time (sometimes the place) *in* which, anything takes place, — *i.e.* it is not merely a *dative,* but also an *instrumental* and a *locative* case. (See 1042.) The object of motion after *to* is not regularly expressed by the Greek dative, but by the accusative with a preposition. (See 1065.)

DATIVE EXPRESSING *TO* OR *FOR.*

Dative of the Indirect Object.

1158. The *indirect object* of the action of a transitive verb is put in the dative. This object is generally introduced in English by *to.* *E.g.*

Δίδωσι μισθὸν τῷ στρατεύματι, *he gives pay to the army;* ὑπισχνεῖταί σοι δέκα τάλαντα, *he promises ten talents to you* (or *he promises you ten talents*); βοήθειαν πέμψομεν τοῖς συμμάχοις, *we will send aid to our allies;* ἔλεγον τῷ βασιλεῖ τὰ γεγενημένα, *they told the king what had happened.*

1159. Certain intransitive verbs take the dative, many

of which in English may have a direct object without *to*. *E.g.*

Τοῖς θεοῖς εὔχομαι, *I pray (to) the Gods*, D. 18, 1; λυσιτελοῦν τῷ ἔχοντι, *advantageous to the one having it*, P. *Rp.* 392e; εἴκουσ' ἀνάγκῃ τῇδε, *yielding to this necessity*, A. *Ag.* 1071; τοῖς νόμοις πείθονται, *they are obedient to the laws (they obey the laws)*, X. *M.* 4, 4[15]; βοηθεῖν δικαιοσύνῃ, *to assist justice*, P. *Rp.* 427e. Εἰ τοῖς πλέοσιν ἀρέσκοντές ἐσμεν, τοῖσδ' ἂν μόνοις οὐκ ὀρθῶς ἀπαρέσκοιμεν, *if we are pleasing to the majority, it cannot be right that we should be displeasing to these alone*, T. 1, 38. Ἐπίστευον αὐτῷ αἱ πόλεις, *the cities trusted him*, X. *A.* 1, 9[8]. Τοῖς Ἀθηναίοις παρῄνει, *he used to advise the Athenians*, T. 1, 93. Τὸν μάλιστα ἐπιτιμῶντα τοῖς πεπραγμένοις ἡδέως ἂν ἐροίμην, *I should like to ask the man who censures most severely what has been done*, D. 18, 64. Τί ἐγκαλῶν ἡμῖν ἐπιχειρεῖς ἡμᾶς ἀπολλύναι; *what fault do you find with us that you try to destroy us?* P. *Cr.* 50d. Τούτοις μέμφει τι; *have you anything to blame these for?* *ibid.* Ἐπηρεάζουσιν ἀλλήλοις καὶ φθονοῦσιν ἑαυτοῖς μᾶλλον ἢ τοῖς ἄλλοις ἀνθρώποις, *they revile one another, and are more malicious to themselves than to other men*, X. *M.* 3, 5[16]. Ἐχαλέπαινον τοῖς στρατηγοῖς, *they were angry with the generals*, X. *A.* 1, 4[12]; ἐμοὶ ὀργίζονται, *they are angry with me*, P. *Ap.* 23c. So πρέπει μοι λέγειν, *it is becoming (to) me to speak*; προσήκει μοι, *it belongs to me*; δοκεῖ μοι, *it seems to me*; δοκῶ μοι, *methinks*.

1160. The verbs of this class which are not translated with *to* in English are chiefly those signifying *to benefit, serve, obey, defend, assist, please, trust, satisfy, advise, exhort*, or any of their opposites; also those expressing *friendliness, hostility, blame, abuse, reproach, envy, anger, threats*.

1161. N. The impersonals δεῖ, μέτεστι, μέλει, μεταμέλει, and προσήκει take the dative of a *person* with the genitive of a *thing*; as δεῖ μοι τούτου, *I have need of this*; μέτεστί μοι τούτου, *I have a share in this*; μέλει μοι τούτου, *I am interested in this*; προσήκει μοι τούτου, *I am concerned in this*. (For the genitive, see 1097, 2; 1105; 1115.) Ἔξεστι, *it is possible*, takes the dative alone.

1162. N. Δεῖ and χρή take the accusative when an infinitive follows. For δεῖ (in poetry) with the accusative and the genitive, see 1115.

1163. N. Some verbs of this class (1160) may take the accusative; as οὐδεὶς αὐτοὺς ἐμέμφετο, *no one blamed them*, X. *A.* 2, 6[30]. Others, whose meaning would place them here (as μισέω, *hate*), take only the accusative. Λοιδορέω, *revile*, has the accusative, but λοιδορέομαι (middle) has the dative. Ὀνειδίζω, *reproach*, and ἐπιτιμῶ, *censure*, have the accusative as well as the dative; we have also ὀνειδίζειν (ἐπιτιμᾶν) τί τινι, *to cast any reproach* (or *censure*) *on any one*. Τιμωρεῖν τινι means regularly *to avenge some one* (*to take vengeance for him*); τιμωρεῖσθαι (rarely τιμωρεῖν) τινα, *to punish some one* (*to avenge oneself on him*): see X. *C*.4,6[8], τιμωρήσειν σοι τοῦ παιδὸς τὸν φονέα ὑπισχνοῦμαι, *I promise to avenge you on the murderer of your son* (or *for your son*, 1126).

1164. 1. Verbs of *ruling* (as ἀνάσσω), which take the genitive in prose (1109), have the dative in poetry, especially in Homer; as πολλῇσιν νήσοισι καὶ Ἄργεϊ παντὶ ἀνάσσειν, *to rule over many islands and all Argos*, *Il*. 2, 108; δαρὸν οὐκ ἄρξει θεοῖς, *he will not rule the Gods long*, A. *Pr*. 940. Κελεύω, *to command*, which in Attic Greek has only the accusative (generally with the infinitive), has the dative in Homer; see *Il*. 2, 50.

2. Ἡγέομαι, in the sense of *guide* or *direct*, takes the dative even in prose; as οὐκέτι ἡμῖν ἡγήσεται, *he will no longer be our guide*, X. *A*. 3, 2[20].

Dative of Advantage or Disadvantage.

1165. The person or thing for whose *advantage* or *disadvantage* anything is or is done is put in the dative (*dativus commodi et incommodi*). This dative is generally introduced in English by *for*. *E.g.*

Πᾶς ἀνὴρ αὑτῷ πονεῖ, *every man labors for himself*, S. *Aj*. 1366. Σόλων Ἀθηναίοις νόμους ἔθηκε, *Solon made laws for the Athenians.* Καιροὶ προεῖνται τῇ πόλει, lit. *opportunities have been sacrificed for the state* (*for its disadvantage*), D. 19, 8. Ἡγεῖτο αὐτῶν ἕκαστος οὐχὶ τῷ πατρὶ καὶ τῇ μητρὶ μόνον γεγενῆσθαι, ἀλλὰ καὶ τῇ πατρίδι, *each of them believed that he was born not merely for his father and mother, but for his country also*, D. 18, 205.

1166. N. A peculiar use of this dative is found in statements of time; as τῷ ἤδη δύο γενεαὶ ἐφθίατο, *two generations had already passed away for him* (i.e. *he had seen them pass away*), *Il*. 1, 250. Ἡμέραι μάλιστα ἦσαν τῇ Μυτιλήνῃ ἑαλωκυίᾳ ἑπτά, *for Mitylene captured* (i.e. *since its capture*) *there had been about seven days*, T. 3, 29. Ἦν ἡμέρα πέμπτη ἐπιπλέουσι τοῖς Ἀθηναίοις, *it was the fifth day for the Athenians sailing out* (i.e. *it was the fifth day since they began to sail out*), X. *H*. 2, 1[27].

1167. N. Here belong such Homeric expressions as τοῖσι δ' ἀνέστη, *and he rose up for them* (i.e. *to address them*), *Il*. 1, 68; τοῖσι μύθων ἦρχεν, *he began to speak before them* (*for them*), *Od*. 1, 28.

1168. N. In Homer, verbs signifying *to ward off* take an accusative of the thing and a dative of the person; as Δαναοῖσι λοιγὸν ἄμυνον, *ward off destruction from the Danai* (lit. *for the Danai*), *Il.* 1, 456. Here the accusative may be omitted, so that Δαναοῖσι ἀμύνειν means *to defend the Danai.* For other constructions of ἀμύνω, see the Lexicon.

1169. N. Δέχομαι, *receive*, takes a dative in Homer by a similar idiom; as δέξατό οἱ σκῆπτρον, *he took his sceptre from him* (lit. *for him*), *Il.* 2, 186.

1170. N. Sometimes this dative has a force which seems to approach that of the possessive genitive; as γλῶσσα δέ οἱ δέδεται, *and his tongue is tied* (lit. *for him*), Theog. 178; οἱ ἵπποι αὐτοῖς δέδενται, *they have their horses tied* (lit. *the horses are tied for them*), X. *A.* 3, 4[35]. The dative here is the *dativus incommodi* (1165).

1171. N. Here belongs the so-called *ethical dative*, in which the personal pronouns have the force of *for my sake* etc., and sometimes cannot easily be translated; as τί σοι μαθήσομαι; *what am I to learn for you?* Ar. *N.* 111; τούτῳ πάνυ μοι προσέχετε τὸν νοῦν, *to this, I beg you, give your close attention*, D. 18, 178.

For a dative with the dative of βουλόμενος etc., see 1584.

Dative of Relation.

1172. 1. The dative may denote a person to whose case a statement is limited, — often belonging to the whole sentence rather than to any special word. *E.g.*

Ἅπαντα τῷ φοβουμένῳ ψοφεῖ, *everything sounds to one who is afraid*, S. frag. 58. Σφῷν μὲν ἐντολὴ Διὸς ἔχει τέλος, *as regards you two, the order of Zeus is fully executed*, A. *Pr.* 12. Ὑπολαμβάνειν δεῖ τῷ τοιούτῳ, ὅτι εὐήθης τις ἄνθρωπος, *with regard to such a one we must suppose that he is a simple person*, P. *Rp.* 598[d]. Τέθνηχ' ὑμῖν πάλαι, *I have long been dead to you*, S. *Ph.* 1030.

2. So in such expressions as these: ἐν δεξιᾷ ἐσπλέοντι, *on the right as you sail in* (*with respect to one sailing in*), T. 1, 24; συνελόντι, or ὡς συνελόντι εἰπεῖν, *concisely*, or *to speak concisely* (lit. *for one having made the matter concise*). So ὡς ἐμοί, *in my opinion.*

Dative of Possession.

1173. The dative with εἰμί, γίγνομαι, and similar verbs may denote the *possessor*. *E.g.*

Εἰσὶν ἐμοὶ ἐκεῖ ξένοι, *I have* (sunt mihi) *friends there*, P. *Cr.* 45[c]; τίς ξύμμαχος γενήσεταί μοι; *what ally shall I find?* Ar. *Eq.* 222; ἄλλοις μὲν χρήματά ἐστι πολλά, ἡμῖν δὲ ξύμμαχοι ἀγαθοί, *others have plenty of money, but we have good allies*, T. 1, 86.

DATIVE WITH ADJECTIVES AND ADVERBS.

1174. The dative follows many adjectives and adverbs and some verbal nouns of kindred meaning with the verbs of 1160 and 1165. *E.g.*

Δυσμενὴς φίλοις, *hostile to friends*, E. *Me.* 1151; ὕποχος τοῖς νόμοις, *subject to the laws*; ἐπικίνδυνον τῇ πόλει, *dangerous to the state*; βλαβερὸν τῷ σώματι, *hurtful to the body*; εὔνους ἑαυτῷ, *kind to himself*; ἐναντίος αὐτῷ, *opposed to him* (cf. 1146); τοῖσδ' ἅπασι κοινόν, *common to all these*, A. *Ag.* 523. Συμφερόντως αὐτῷ, *profitably to himself*; ἐμποδὼν ἐμοί, *in my way*.

(*With Nouns.*) Τὰ παρ' ἡμῶν δῶρα τοῖς θεοῖς, *the gifts (given) by us to the Gods*, P. *Euthyph.* 15ᵃ. So with an objective genitive and a dative; as ἐπὶ καταδουλώσει τῶν Ἑλλήνων Ἀθηναίοις, *for the subjugation of the Greeks to Athenians*, T. 3, 10.

DATIVE OF RESEMBLANCE AND UNION.

1175. The dative is used with all words implying *likeness* or *unlikeness*, *agreement* or *disagreement*, *union* or *approach*. This includes verbs, adjectives, adverbs, and nouns. *E.g.*

Σκιαῖς ἐοικότες, *like shadows*; τὸ ὁμοιοῦν ἑαυτὸν ἄλλῳ, *to make himself like to another*, P. *Rp.* 393ᶜ; τούτοις ὁμοιότατον, *most like these*, P. *G.* 513ᵇ; ὡπλισμένοι τοῖς αὐτοῖς Κύρῳ ὅπλοις, *armed with the same arms as Cyrus*, X. *C.* 7, 1²; ἢ ὁμοίου ὄντος τούτοις ἢ ἀνομοίου, *being either like or unlike these*, P. *Ph.* 74ᶜ; ὁμοίως δίκαιον ἀδίκῳ βλάψειν, *that he will punish a just and an unjust man alike*, P. *Rp.* 364ᶜ; ἰέναι ἀλλήλοις ἀνομοίως, *to move unlike one another*, P. *Ti.* 36ᵈ; τὸν ὁμώνυμον ἐμαυτῷ, *my namesake*, D. 3. 21. Οὔτε ἑαυτοῖς οὔτε ἀλλήλοις ὁμολογοῦσιν, *they agree neither with themselves nor with one another*, P. *Phdr.* 237ᶜ; ἀμφισβητοῦσι οἱ φίλοι τοῖς φιλοῖς, ἐρίζουσι δὲ οἱ ἐχθροὶ ἀλλήλοις, *friends dispute with friends, but enemies quarrel with one another*, P. *Pr.* 337ᵇ; τοῖς πονηροῖς διαφέρεσθαι, *to be at variance with the bad*, X. *M.* 2, 9⁸; ἦν αὐτῷ ὁμογνώμων, *he was of the same mind with him*, T. 8, 92. Κακοῖς ὁμιλῶν, *associating with bad men*, Men. *Mon.* 274; τοῖς φρονιμωτάτοις πλησίαζε, *draw near to the wisest*, I. 2, 13; ψόφοις πλησιάζειν (τὸν ἵππον), *to bring him near to noises*, X. *Eq.* 2, 5; ἄλλοις κοινωνεῖν, *to share with others*, P. *Rp.* 369ᵉ; τὸ ἑαυτοῦ ἔργον ἅπασι κοινὸν κατατιθέναι, *to make his own work common to all*, *ibid.*; δεόμενοι τοὺς φεύγοντας ξυναλλάξαι σφίσι, *asking to bring the exiles to terms with them*, T. 1. 24; βούλομαί σε αὐτῷ διαλέγεσθαι, *I want you to converse with him*, P. *Lys.* 211[c].

(*With Nouns.*) Ἄτοπος ἡ ὁμοιότης τούτων ἐκείνοις, *the likeness of these to those is strange*, P. *Th.* 158[c]; ἔχει κοινωνίαν ἀλλήλοις, *they have something in common with each other*, P. *So.* 257[a]; προσβολὰς ποιούμενοι τῷ τείχει, *making attacks upon the wall*, ἐπιδρομὴν τῷ τειχίσματι, *an assault on the wall*, T. 4, 23; Διὸς βρονταῖσιν εἰς ἔριν, *in rivalry with the thunderings of Zeus*, E. *Cyc.* 328; ἐπανάστασις μέρους τινὸς τῷ ὅλῳ τῆς ψυχῆς, *a rebellion of one part of the soul against the whole*, P. *Rp.* 444[b].

1176. The dative thus depends on adverbs of *place* and *time;* as ἅμα τῇ ἡμέρᾳ, *at daybreak*, X. *A.* 2, 1[2]; ὕδωρ ὁμοῦ τῷ πηλῷ ἡματωμένον, *water stained with blood together with the mud*, T. 7, 84; τὰ τούτοις ἐφεξῆς, *what comes next to this*, P. *Ti.* 30[c]; τοῖσδ' ἐγγύς, *near these*, E. *Her.* 37 (ἐγγύς generally has the genitive, 1149).

1177. To this class belong μάχομαι, πολεμέω, and others signifying *to contend* or *quarrel with;* as μάχεσθαι τοῖς Θηβαίοις, *to fight with the Thebans;* πολεμοῦσιν ἡμῖν, *they are at war with us.* So ἐς χεῖρας ἐλθεῖν τινι, or ἐς λόγους ἐλθεῖν τινι, *to come to a conflict* (or *to words*) *with any one;* also διὰ φιλίας ἰέναι τινί, *to be friendly* (*to go through friendship*) *with one:* see T. 7, 44: 8, 48; X. *A.* 3, 2[8].

1178. N. After adjectives of *likeness* an abridged form of expression may be used; as κόμαι Χαρίτεσσιν ὁμοῖαι, *hair like* (*that of*) *the Graces*, *Il.* 17, 51; τὰς ἴσας πληγὰς ἐμοί, *the same number of blows with me*, Ar. *R.* 636.

DATIVE AFTER COMPOUND VERBS.

1179. The dative follows many verbs compounded with ἐν, σύν, or ἐπί; and some compounded with πρός, παρά, περί, and ὑπό. *E.g.*

Τοῖς ὅρκοις ἐμμένει ὁ δῆμος, *the people abide by the oaths*, X. *H.* 2, 4[43]; αἱ ... ἡδοναὶ ψυχῇ ἐπιστήμην οὐδεμίαν ἐμποιοῦσιν, (*such*) *pleasures produce no knowledge in the soul*, X. *M.* 2, 1[20]; ἐνέκειντο τῷ Περικλεῖ, *they pressed hard on Pericles*, T. 2, 59; ἐμαυτῷ συνῄδη οὐδὲν ἐπισταμένῳ, *I was conscious to myself that I knew nothing* (lit. *with myself*), P. *Ap.* 22[d]; ἤδη ποτέ σοι ἐπῆλθεν; *did it ever occur to you?* X. *M.* 4, 3[3]; προσέβαλλον τῷ τειχίσματι, *they attacked the fortification*, T. 4, 11; ἀδελφὸς ἀνδρὶ παρείη, *let a brother stand by a man* (i.e. *let a man's brother stand by him*), P. *Rp.* 362[d]; τοῖς κακοῖς περιπίπτουσιν, *they are involved in evils*, X. *M.* 4, 2[27]; ὑπόκειται τὸ πεδίον τῷ ἱερῷ, *the plain lies below the temple*, Aesch. 3, 118.

1180. N. This dative sometimes depends strictly on the preposition, and sometimes on the idea of the compound *as a whole*.

CAUSAL AND INSTRUMENTAL DATIVE.

1181. The dative is used to denote *cause*, *manner*, and *means* or *instrument*. *E.g.*

CAUSE: Νόσῳ ἀποθανών, *having died of disease*, T. 8, 84; οὐ γὰρ κακονοίᾳ τοῦτο ποιεῖ, ἀλλ' ἀγνοίᾳ, *for he does not do this from ill-will, but from ignorance*, X. *C.* 3, 1[38]; βιαζόμενοι τοῦ πιεῖν ἐπιθυμίᾳ, *forced by a desire to drink*, T. 7, 84; αἰσχύνομαί τοι ταῖς πρότερον ἁμαρτίαις, *I am ashamed of (because of) my former faults*, Ar. *N.* 1355. MANNER: Δρόμῳ ἵεντο ἐς τοὺς βαρβάρους, *they rushed against the barbarians on the run*, Hd. 6, 112; κραυγῇ πολλῇ ἐπίασιν, *they will advance with a loud shout*, X. *A.* 1, 7[4]. Τῇ ἀληθείᾳ, *in truth*; τῷ ὄντι, *in reality*; βίᾳ, *forcibly*; ταύτῃ, *in this manner, thus*; λόγῳ, *in word*, ἔργῳ, *in deed*; τῇ ἐμῇ γνώμῃ, *in my judgment*; ἰδίᾳ, *privately*; δημοσίᾳ, *publicly*; κοινῇ, *in common*. MEANS OR INSTRUMENT: Ὁρῶμεν τοῖς ὀφθαλμοῖς, *we see with our eyes*; γνωσθέντες τῇ σκευῇ τῶν ὅπλων, *recognized by the fashion of their arms*, T. 1, 8; κακοῖς ἰᾶσθαι κακά, *to cure evils by evils*, S. frag. 75; οὐδεὶς ἔπαινον ἡδοναῖς ἐκτήσατο, *no one gains praise by pleasures*, Stob. 29, 31.

1182. N. The dative of *respect* is a form of the dative of *manner*; as τοῖς σώμασιν ἀδύνατοι, . . . ταῖς ψυχαῖς ἀνόητοι, *incapable in their bodies, . . . senseless in their minds*, X. *M.* 2, 1[31]; ὕστερον ὂν τῇ τάξει, πρότερον τῇ δυνάμει καὶ κρεῖττόν ἐστιν, *although it is later in order, it is prior and superior in power*, D. 3, 15. So πόλις, Θάψακος ὀνόματι, *a city, Thapsacus by name*, X. *A.* 1, 4[11].

This dative often is equivalent to the accusative of specification (1058).

1183. Χράομαι, *to use (to serve one's self by)*, takes the dative of *means*; as χρῶνται ἀργυρίῳ, *they use money*. A neuter pronoun (*e.g.* τί, τὶ, ὅ τι, or τοῦτο) may be added as a cognate accusative (1051); as τί χρήσεταί ποτ' αὐτῷ; *what will he do with him?* (lit. *what use will he make of him?*), Ar. *Ach.* 935. Νομίζω has sometimes the same meaning and construction as χράομαι.

1184. The dative of *manner* is used with comparatives to denote the *degree of difference*. *E.g.*

Πολλῷ κρεῖττόν ἐστιν, *it is much better (better by much)*; ἐὰν τῇ κεφαλῇ μείζονά τινα φῇς εἶναι καὶ ἐλάττω, *if you say that anyone is a head taller or shorter* (lit. *by the head*), P. *Ph.* 101[a]. Πόλει λογίμῳ ἡ Ἑλλὰς γέγονε ἀσθενεστέρη, *Greece has become weaker by one illustrious city*, Hd. 6, 106. Τοσούτῳ ἥδιον ζῶ, *I live so much the more happily*, X. *C.* 8, 3[40]; τέχνη δ' ἀνάγκης ἀσθενεστέρα μακρῷ, *and art is weaker than necessity by far*, A. *Pr.* 514.

1185. So sometimes with superlatives, and even with other expressions which imply comparison; as ὀρθότατα μακρῷ, *most correctly by far*, P. *Lg.* 768[c]; σχεδὸν δέκα ἔτεσι πρὸ τῆς ἐν Σαλαμῖνι ναυμαχίας, *about ten years before the sea-fight at Salamis*, *ibid.* 698[c].

DATIVE OF AGENT.

1186. The dative sometimes denotes the *agent* with the perfect and pluperfect passive, rarely with other passive tenses. *E.g.*

Ἐξετάσαι τί πέπρακται τοῖς ἄλλοις, *to ask what has been done by the others*, D. 2, 27; ἐπειδὴ αὐτοῖς παρεσκεύαστο, *when preparation had been made by them* (*when they had their preparation made*), T. 1, 46; πολλαὶ θεραπεῖαι τοῖς ἰατροῖς εὕρηνται, *many cures have been discovered by physicians*, I. 8, 39.

1187. N. Here there seems to be a reference to the agent's interest in the result of the *completed* action expressed by the perfect and pluperfect. With other tenses, the agent is regularly expressed by ὑπό etc. and the genitive (1234); only rarely by the dative, except in poetry.

1188. With the verbal adjective in -τέος, in its personal construction (1595), the agent is expressed by the dative; in its impersonal construction (1597), by the dative or the accusative.

DATIVE OF ACCOMPANIMENT.

1189. The dative is used to denote that by which any person or thing is *accompanied*. *E.g.*

Ἐλθόντων Περσῶν παμπληθεῖ στόλῳ, *when the Persians came with an army in full force*, X. *A.* 3, 2[11]; ἡμεῖς καὶ ἵπποις τοῖς δυνατωτάτοις καὶ ἀνδράσι πορευώμεθα, *let us march both with the strongest horses and with men*, X. *C.* 5, 3[35]; οἱ Λακεδαιμόνιοι τῷ τε κατὰ γῆν στρατῷ προσέβαλλον τῷ τειχίσματι καὶ ταῖς ναυσίν, *the Lacedaemonians attacked the wall both with their land army and with their ships*, T. 4, 11.

1190. This dative is used chiefly in reference to military forces, and is originally connected with the dative of *means*. The last example might be placed equally well under 1181.

1191. This dative sometimes takes the dative of αὐτός for emphasis; as μίαν (ναῦν) αὐτοῖς ἀνδράσιν εἷλον, *they took one (ship) men and all*, T.2,90. Here no instrumental force is seen, and the dative may refer to any class of persons or things; as χαμαὶ βάλε δένδρεα μακρὰ αὐτῇσιν ῥίζῃσι καὶ αὐτοῖς ἄνθεσι μήλων, *he threw to the ground tall trees, with their very roots and their fruit-blossoms*, *Il.* 9,541.

DATIVE OF TIME.

1192. The dative without a preposition often denotes time *when*. This is confined chiefly to nouns denoting *day*, *night*, *month*, or *year*, and to names of *festivals*. *E.g.*

Τῇ αὐτῇ ἡμέρᾳ ἀπέθανεν, *he died on the same day;* (Ἑρμαῖ) μιᾷ νυκτὶ οἱ πλεῖστοι περιεκόπησαν, *the most of the Hermae were mutilated in one night*, T.6,27; οἱ Σάμιοι ἐξεπολιορκήθησαν ἐνάτῳ μηνί, *the Samians were taken by siege in the ninth month*, T.1,117; δεκάτῳ ἔτει ξυνέβησαν, *they came to terms in the tenth year*, T.1, 103; ὡσπερεὶ Θεσμοφορίοις νηστεύομεν, *we fast as if it were (on) the Thesmophoria*, Ar. *Av.* 1519. So τῇ ὑστεραίᾳ (sc. ἡμέρᾳ), *on the following day*, and δευτέρᾳ, τρίτῃ, *on the second*, *third*, etc., in giving the day of the month.

1193. N. Even the words mentioned, except names of festivals, generally take ἐν when no adjective word is joined with them. Thus ἐν νυκτί, *at night* (rarely, in poetry, νυκτί), but μιᾷ νυκτί, *in one night.*

1194. N. A few expressions occur like ὑστέρῳ χρόνῳ, *in after time;* χειμῶνος ὥρᾳ, *in the winter season;* νουμηνίᾳ (*new-moon day*), *on the first of the month;* and others in poetry.

1195. N. With other datives expressing time ἐν is regularly used; as ἐν τῷ αὐτῷ χειμῶνι, *in the same winter*, T.2,34. But it is occasionally omitted.

DATIVE OF PLACE.

1196. In poetry, the dative without a preposition often denotes the place *where*. *E.g.*

Ἑλλάδι οἰκία ναίων, *inhabiting dwellings in Hellas*, *Il.* 16,595; αἰθέρι ναίων, *dwelling in heaven*, *Il.* 4,166; οὔρεσι, *on the mountains*, *Il.* 13,390; τόξ' ὤμοισιν ἔχων, *having his bow on his shoulders*, *Il.* 1,45; μίμνει ἀγρῷ, *he remains in the country*, *Od.* 11,188. Ἧσθαι δόμοις, *to sit at home*, A. *Ag.* 862. Νῦν ἀγροῖσι τυγχάνει (sc. ὤν), *now he happens to be in the country*, S. *El.* 313.

1197. In prose, the dative of place is chiefly confined to the names of Attic demes; as ἡ Μαραθῶνι μάχη, *the battle at Marathon* (but ἐν Ἀθήναις): see μὰ τοὺς Μαραθῶνι προκινδυνεύσαντας τῶν προγόνων καὶ τοὺς ἐν Πλαταιαῖς παραταξαμένους καὶ τοὺς ἐν Σαλαμῖνι ναυμαχήσαντας, *no, by those of our ancestors who stood in the front of danger at Marathon, and those who arrayed themselves at Plataea, and those who fought the sea-fight at Salamis*, D. 18, 208.

Still some exceptions occur.

1198. N. Some adverbs of place are really *local* datives; as ταύτῃ, τῇδε, *here*; οἴκοι, *at home*. So κύκλῳ, *in a circle, all around*. (See 436.)

PREPOSITIONS.

1199. The prepositions were originally adverbs, and as such they appear in composition with verbs (see 882, 1). They are used also as independent words, to connect nouns with other parts of the sentence.

1200. Besides the prepositions properly so called, there are certain adverbs used in the same way, which cannot be compounded with verbs. These are called *improper* prepositions. For these see 1220.

1201. 1. Four prepositions take the *genitive* only: ἀντί, ἀπό, ἐξ (ἐκ), πρό, — with the improper prepositions ἄνευ, ἄτερ, ἄχρι, μέχρι, μεταξύ, ἕνεκα, πλήν.

2. Two take the *dative* only: ἐν and σύν.

3. Two take the *accusative* only: ἀνά and εἰς or ἐς, — with the improper preposition ὡς. For ἀνά in poetry with the dative, see 1203.

4. Four take the *genitive* and *accusative*: διά, κατά, μετά, and ὑπέρ. For μετά with the dative in Homer, see 1212, 2.

5. Six take the *genitive*, *dative*, and *accusative*: ἀμφί (rare with genitive), ἐπί, παρά, περί, πρός, and ὑπό.

USES OF THE PREPOSITIONS.[1]

1202. ἀμφί (Lat. amb-, compare ἄμφω, *both*), originally *on both sides of*; hence *about*. Chiefly poetic and Ionic. In Attic prose περί is generally used in most senses of ἀμφί.

1. with the GENITIVE (very rare in prose), *about, concerning*: ἀμφὶ γυναικός, *about a woman*, A. *Ag.* 62.

[1] Only a general statement of the various uses of the prepositions is given here. For the details the Lexicon must be consulted.

2. with the DATIVE (only poetic and Ionic), *about*, *concerning*, *on account of*: ἀμφ' ὤμοισι, *about his shoulders*, *Il.* 11, 527; ἀμφὶ τῷ νόμῳ τούτῳ, *concerning this law*, Hd. 1, 140; ἀμφὶ φόβῳ, *through fear*, E. *Or.* 825.

3. with the ACCUSATIVE, *about*, *near*, of place, time, number, etc.: ἀμφ' ἅλα, *by the sea*, *Il.* 1, 409; ἀμφὶ δείλην, *near evening*, X. *C.* 5, 4[16]; ἀμφὶ Πλειάδων δύσιν, *about* (the time of) *the Pleiads' setting*, A. *Ag.* 826. So ἀμφὶ δεῖπνον εἶχεν, *he was at supper*, X. *C.* 5, 5[44]. Οἱ ἀμφί τινα (as οἱ ἀμφὶ Πλάτωνα) means *a man with his followers*.

In COMP.: *about*, *on both sides*.

1203. ἀνά (cf. adv. ἄνω, *above*), originally *up* (opposed to κατά).

1. with the DATIVE (only epic and lyric), *up on*: ἀνὰ σκήπτρῳ, *on a staff*, *Il.* 1, 15.

2. with the ACCUSATIVE, *up along*; and of motion *over*, *through*, *among* (cf. κατά):—

(*a*) of PLACE: ἀνὰ τὸν ποταμόν, *up the river*, Hd. 2, 96; ἀνὰ στρατόν, *through the army*, *Il.* 1, 10; οἰκεῖν ἀνὰ τὰ ὄρη, *to dwell on the tops of the hills*, X. *A.* 3, 5[16].

(*b*) of TIME: ἀνὰ τὸν πόλεμον, *through the war*, Hd. 8, 123; ἀνὰ χρόνον, *in course of time*, Hd. 5, 27.

(*c*) In DISTRIBUTIVE expressions: ἀνὰ ἑκατόν, *by hundreds*, X. *A.* 5, 4[12]; ἀνὰ πᾶσαν ἡμέρην, *every day*, Hd. 2, 37 (so X. *C.* 1, 2[8]).

In COMP.: *up*, *back*, *again*.

1204. ἀντί, with GENITIVE only, *instead of*, *for*: ἀντὶ πολέμου εἰρήνην ἑλώμεθα, *in place of war let us choose peace*, T. 4, 20; ἀνθ' ὧν, *wherefore*, A. *Pr.* 31; ἀντ' ἀδελφοῦ, *for a brother's sake*, S. *El.* 537. Original meaning, *over against*, *against*.

In COMP.: *against*, *in opposition*, *in return*, *instead*.

1205. ἀπό (Lat. ab), with GENITIVE only, *from*, *off from*, *away from*; originally (as opposed to ἐκ) denoting *separation* or *departure* from something:—

(*a*) of PLACE: ἀφ' ἵππων ἆλτο, *he leaped from the car* (horses), *Il.* 16, 733; ἀπὸ θαλάσσης, *at a distance from the sea*, T. 1, 7.

(*b*) of TIME: ἀπὸ τούτου τοῦ χρόνου, *from this time*, X. *A.* 7, 5[8].

(*c*) of CAUSE OR ORIGIN: ἀπὸ τούτου τοῦ τολμήματος ἐπῃνέθη, *for this bold act he was praised*, T. 2, 25; τὸ ζῆν ἀπὸ πολέμου, *to live by war*, Hd. 5, 6; ἀπ' οὗ ἡμεῖς γεγόναμεν, *from whom we are sprung*, Hd. 7, 150; sometimes the *agent* (as source): ἐπράχθη ἀπ' αὐτῶν οὐδέν, *nothing was done by them*, T. 1, 17.

In COMP.: *from*, *away*, *off*, *in return*.

1206. διά, *through* (Lat. di-, dis-).

1. with the GENITIVE;

(*a*) of PLACE: διὰ ἀσπίδος ἦλθε, *it went through the shield*, *Il.* 7, 251.

(*b*) of TIME: διὰ νυκτός, *through the night*, X. *A.* 4, 6[22].

(*c*) of INTERVALS of time or place: διὰ πολλοῦ χρόνου, *after a long time*, Ar. *Pl.* 1045; διὰ τρίτης ἡμέρης, *every other day*, Hd. 2, 37.

(*d*) of MEANS: ἔλεγε δι' ἑρμηνέως, *he spoke through an interpreter*, X. *A.* 2, 3[17].

(*e*) in various phrases like δι' οἴκτου ἔχειν, *to pity*; διὰ φιλίας ἰέναι, *to be in friendship* (*with one*). See 1177.

2. with the ACCUSATIVE:

(*a*) of AGENCY, *on account of, by help of, by reason of*: διὰ τοῦτο, *on this account*; δι' Ἀθήνην, *by help of Athena*, *Od.* 8, 520; οὐ δι' ἐμέ, *not owing to me*, D. 18, 18.

(*b*) of PLACE or TIME, *through, during* (poetic): διὰ δώματα, *through the halls*, *Il.* 1, 600; διὰ νύκτα, *through the night*, *Od.* 19, 66.

In COMP.: *through*, also *apart* (Lat. **di-**, **dis-**).

1207. εἰς or ἐς, with ACCUSATIVE only, *into, to*, originally (as opposed to ἐκ) *to within* (Lat. in with the accusative): εἰς always in Attic prose, except in Thucydides, who has ἐς. Both εἰς and ἐς are for ἐνς; see also ἐν.

(*a*) of PLACE: διέβησαν ἐς Σικελίαν, *they crossed over into Sicily*, T. 6, 2; εἰς Πέρσας ἐπορεύετο, *he departed for Persia* (*the Persians*), X. *C.* 8, 5[20]; τὸ ἐς Παλλήνην τεῖχος, *the wall towards* (*looking to*) *Pallene*, T. 1, 56.

(*b*) of TIME: ἐς ἠῶ, *until dawn*, *Od.* 11, 375; so of a time *looked forward to*: προεῖπε τοῖς ἑαυτοῦ εἰς τρίτην ἡμέραν παρεῖναι, *he gave notice to his men to be present the next day but one*, X. *C.* 3, 1[42]. So ἔτος εἰς ἔτος, *from year to year*, S. *An.* 340. So ἐς ὅ, *until*; εἰς τὸν ἅπαντα χρόνον, *for all time*.

(*c*) of NUMBER and MEASURE: εἰς διακοσίους, (*amounting*) *to two hundred*; εἰς δύναμιν, *up to one's power*.

(*d*) of PURPOSE or REFERENCE: παιδεύειν εἰς τὴν ἀρετήν, *to train for virtue*, P. *G.* 519[e]; εἰς πάντα πρῶτον εἶναι, *to be first for everything*, P. *Ch.* 158[a]; χρήσιμον εἴς τι, *useful for anything*.

In COMP.: *into, in, to*.

1208. ἐν, with DATIVE only, *in* (Hom. ἐνί), equivalent to Lat. in with the ablative:

(*a*) of PLACE: ἐν Σπάρτῃ, *in Sparta*;—with words implying a number of people, *among*: ἐν γυναιξὶ ἄλκιμος, *brave among women*, E. *Or.* 754; ἐν πᾶσι, *in the presence of all*; ἐν δικασταῖς, *before* (coram) *a court*.

(*b*) of TIME: ἐν τούτῳ τῷ ἔτει, *in this year*; ἐν χειμῶνι, *in winter*; ἐν ἔτεσι πεντήκοντα, *within fifty years*, T. 1, 118.

(*c*) of other relations: τὸν Περικλέα ἐν ὀργῇ εἶχον, *they were angry with P.* (*held him in anger*), T. 2, 21; ἐν τῷ θεῷ τὸ τούτου τέλος ἦν, οὐκ ἐν ἐμοί, *the issue of this was with* (*in the power of) God, not with me*, D. 18, 193; ἐν πολλῇ ἀπορίᾳ ἦσαν, *they were in great perplexity*, X. *A.* 3, 1[2].

As ἐν (like εἰς and ἐς) comes from ἐνς (see εἰς), it originally allowed the accusative (like Latin in), and in Aeolic ἐν may be used like εἰς; as ἐν Καλλίσταν, *to Calliste*, Pind. *Py.* 4, 258.

In COMP.: *in, on, at.*

1209. ἐξ or ἐκ, with GENITIVE only (Lat. **ex**, **e**), *from, out of;* originally (as opposed to ἀπό) *from within* (compare εἰς).

(*a*) of PLACE: ἐκ Σπάρτης φεύγει, *he is banished from Sparta.*

(*b*) of TIME: ἐκ παλαιοτάτου, *from the most ancient time*, T. 1, 18.

(*c*) of ORIGIN: ὄναρ ἐκ Διός ἐστιν, *the dream comes from Zeus*, *Il.* 1, 63. So also with *passive* verbs (instead of ὑπό with gen.): ἐκ Φοίβου δαμείς, *destroyed by Phoebus*, S. *Ph.* 335 (the agent viewed as the *source*), seldom in Attic prose. (See 1205.)

(*d*) of GROUND for a judgment: ἐβουλεύοντο ἐκ τῶν παρόντων, *they took counsel with a view to (starting from) the present state of things*, T. 3, 29.

In COMP.: *out, from, away, off.*

1210. ἐπί, *on, upon.*

1. with the GENITIVE:

(*a*) of PLACE: ἐπὶ πύργου ἔστη, *he stood on a tower*, *Il.* 16, 700; sometimes *towards:* πλεύσαντες ἐπὶ Σάμου, *having sailed towards Samos*, T. 1, 116; so ἐπὶ τῆς τοιαύτης γενέσθαι γνώμης, *to adopt (go over to) such an opinion*, D. 4, 6.

(*b*) of TIME: ἐφ' ἡμῶν, *in our time;* ἐπ' εἰρήνης, *in time of peace*, *Il.* 2, 797.

(*c*) of RELATION OF REFERENCE to an object: τοὺς ἐπὶ τῶν πραγμάτων, *those in charge of (public) affairs*, D. 18, 247; ἐπὶ Λιβύης ἔχειν τὸ ὄνομα, *to be named for Libya*, Hd. 4, 45; ἐπὶ τινος λέγων, *speaking with reference to some one*, see P. *Ch.* 155[d]; so ἐπὶ σχολῆς, *at leisure;* ἐπ' ἴσας (sc. μοίρας), *in equal measure*, S. *El.* 1061.

2. with the DATIVE:

(*a*) of PLACE: ἧντ' ἐπὶ πύργῳ, *they sat on a tower*, *Il.* 3, 153; πόλις ἐπὶ τῇ θαλάττῃ οἰκουμένη, *a city situated upon (by) the sea*, X. *A.* 1, 4[1].

(*b*) of TIME (of immediate succession): ἐπὶ τούτοις, *thereupon*, X. *C.* 5, 5[21].

(*c*) of CAUSE, PURPOSE, CONDITIONS, etc.: ἐπὶ παιδεύσει μέγα φρονοῦντες, *proud of their education*, P. *Pr.* 342[d]; ἐπ' ἐξαγωγῇ, *for exportation*, Hd. 7, 156; ἐπὶ τοῖσδε, *on these conditions*, Ar. *Av.* 1602; ἐπὶ τῇ ἴσῃ καὶ ὁμοίᾳ, *on fair and equal terms*, T. 1, 27. So ἐφ' ᾧ and ἐφ' ᾧ τε (1460).

(*d*) Likewise *over, for, at, in addition to, in the power of;* and in many other relations: see the Lexicon.

3. with the ACCUSATIVE:

(*a*) of PLACE: *to, up to, towards, against:* ἀναβὰς ἐπὶ τὸν ἵππον, *mounting his horse*, X. *A.* 1, 8[3]; ἐπὶ δεξιά, *to the right, on the right hand*, X. *A.* 6, 4[1]; ἐπὶ βασιλέα ἰέναι, *to march against the King*, X. *A.* 1, 3[1].

(*b*) of TIME or SPACE, denoting *extension:* ἐπὶ δέκα ἔτη, *for ten years*, T. 3, 68; ἐπ' ἐννέα κεῖτο πέλεθρα, *he covered (lay over) nine plethra*, *Od.* 11, 577; so ἐπὶ πολύ, *widely;* τὸ ἐπὶ πολύ, *for the most part;* ἐκ τοῦ ἐπὶ πλεῖστον, *from the remotest period*, T. 1, 2.

(*c*) of an OBJECT aimed at: κατῆλθον ἐπὶ ποιητήν, *I came down here for a poet*, Ar. *R.* 1418.

In COMP.: *upon, over, after, toward, to, for, at, against, besides.*

1211. κατά (cf. adverb κάτω, *below*), originally *down* (opposed to ἀνά).

1. with the GENITIVE:

(*a*) *down from:* ἀλλόμενοι κατὰ τῆς πέτρας, *leaping down from the rock*, X. *A.* 4, 2[17].

(*b*) *down upon:* μύρον κατὰ τῆς κεφαλῆς καταχέαντες, *pouring perfumes on his head*, P. *Rp.* 398[a].

(*c*) *beneath:* κατὰ χθονὸς ἔκρυψε, *he buried beneath the earth*, S. *An.* 24; οἱ κατὰ χθονὸς θεοί, *the Gods below*, A. *Pe.* 689.

(*d*) *against:* λέγων καθ' ἡμῶν, *saying against me (us)*, S. *Ph.* 65.

2. with the ACCUSATIVE, *down along;* of motion *over, through, among, into, against;* also *according to, concerning.*

(*a*) of PLACE: κατὰ ῥοῦν, *down stream;* κατὰ γῆν καὶ κατὰ θάλατταν, *by land and by sea*, X. *A.* 3, 2[13]; κατὰ Σινώπην πόλιν, *opposite the city Sinope*, Hd. 1, 76.

(*b*) of TIME: κατὰ τὸν πόλεμον, *during (at the time of) the war*, Hd. 7, 137.

(*c*) DISTRIBUTIVELY: κατὰ τρεῖς, *by threes, three by three;* καθ' ἡμέραν, *day by day, daily.*

(*d*) *according to, concerning:* κατὰ τοὺς νόμους, *according to law*, D. 8, 2; τὸ κατ' ἐμέ, *as regards myself*, D. 18, 247; so κατὰ πάντα, *in all respects;* τὰ κατὰ πόλεμον, *military matters.*

In COMP.: *down, against.*

1212. μετά, *with, amid, among.* See σύν.

1. with the GENITIVE:

(*a*) *with, in company with:* μετ' ἄλλων λέξο ἑταίρων, *lie down with the rest of thy companions*, *Od.* 10, 320; μετὰ ζώντων, *among the living*, S. *Ph.* 1312.

(*b*) *in union with, with the coöperation of:* μετὰ Μαντινέων ξυνεπολέμουν, *they fought in alliance with the Mantineans*, T. 6, 105; οἵδε μετ' αὐτοῦ ἦσαν, *these were on his side*, T. 3, 56; Ὑπέρβολον ἀποκτείνουσι μετὰ Χαρμίνου, *they put Hyperbolus to death by the aid of Charminus*, T. 8, 73.

2. with the DATIVE (poetic, chiefly epic), *among:* μετὰ δὲ τριτάτοισιν ἄνασσεν, *and he was reigning in the third generation*, *Il.* 1, 252.

3. with the ACCUSATIVE:

(*a*) *into* (*the midst of*), *after* (*in quest of*), *for* (poetic): μετὰ στρατὸν ἤλασ' Ἀχαιῶν, *he drove into the army of the Achaeans*, *Il.* 5, 589; πλέων μετὰ χαλκόν, *sailing after* (*in quest of*) *copper*, *Od.* 1, 184.

(*b*) generally *after*, *next to*: μετὰ τὸν πόλεμον, *after the war*; μέγιστος μετὰ Ἴστρον, *the largest* (*river*) *next to the Ister*, Hd. 4, 53.

In COMP.: *with* (of sharing), *among*, *after* (*in quest of*): it also denotes *change*, as in μετανοέω, *change one's mind*, *repent*.

1213. παρά (Hom. also παραί), *by*, *near*, *alongside of* (see 1221, 2).

1. with the GENITIVE, *from beside*, *from*: παρὰ νηῶν ἀπονοστήσειν, *to return from the ships*, *Il.* 12. 114; παρ' ἡμῶν ἀπάγγελλε τάδε, *take this message from us*, X. *A.* 2, 1[20].

2. with the DATIVE, *with*, *beside*, *near*: παρὰ Πριάμοιο θύρῃσιν, *at Priam's gates*, *Il.* 7, 346; παρὰ σοὶ κατέλυον, *they lodged with you* (*were your guests*), D. 18, 82.

3. with the ACCUSATIVE, *to* (*a place*) *near*, *to*; also *by the side of*, *beyond* or *beside*, *except*, *along with*, *because of*.

(*a*) of PLACE: τρέψας πὰρ ποταμόν, *turning to the* (*bank of the*) *river*, *Il.* 21, 603; εἰσιόντες παρὰ τοὺς φίλους, *going in to* (*visit*) *their friends*, T. 2, 51.

(*b*) of TIME: παρὰ πάντα τὸν χρόνον, *throughout the whole time*, D. 18, 10.

(*c*) of CAUSE: παρὰ τὴν ἡμετέραν ἀμέλειαν, *on account of our neglect*, D. 4, 11.

(*d*) of COMPARISON: παρὰ τἄλλα ζῷα, *compared with* (*by the side of*) *other animals*, X. *M.* 1, 4[14].

(*e*) with idea of *beyond* or *beside*, and *except*: οὐκ ἔστι παρὰ ταῦτ' ἄλλα, *there are no others besides these*, Ar. *N.* 698; παρὰ τὸν νόμον, *contrary to the law* (properly *beyond* it).

In COMP.: *beside*, *along by*, *hitherward*, *wrongly* (*beside the mark*), *over* (as in *overstep*).

1214. περί, *around* (on all sides), *about* (compare ἀμφί).

1. with the GENITIVE, *about*, *concerning* (Lat. **de**): περὶ πατρὸς ἐρέσθαι, *to inquire about his father*, *Od.* 3, 77; δεδιὼς περὶ αὐτοῦ, *fearing concerning him*, P. *Pr.* 320[a]. Poetic (chiefly epic) *above*, *surpassing*: κρατερὸς περὶ πάντων, *mighty above all*, *Il.* 21, 566.

2. with the DATIVE, *about*, *around*, *concerning*, of PLACE or CAUSE (chiefly poetic): ἔνδυνε περὶ στήθεσσι χιτῶνα, *he put on his tunic about his breast*, *Il.* 10, 21; ἔδδεισεν περὶ Μενελάῳ, *he feared for Menelaus*, *Il.* 10, 240; δείσαντες περὶ τῇ χώρᾳ, *through fear for our land*, T. 1, 74.

3. with the ACCUSATIVE (nearly the same as ἀμφί), *about*, *near*: ἵστάμεναι περὶ τοῖχον, *to stand around the wall*, *Il.* 18, 374; περὶ Ἑλλήσποντον, *about* (*near*) *the Hellespont*, D. 8, 3; περὶ

τούτους τοὺς χρόνους, *about these times*, T. 3, 89; ὢν περὶ ταῦτα, *being about (engaged in) this*, T. 7, 31.

In COMP.: *around, about, exceedingly.*

1215. πρό (Lat. pro), with the GENITIVE only, *before:*

(*a*) of PLACE: πρὸ θυρῶν, *before the door*, S. *El.* 109.

(*b*) of TIME: πρὸ δείπνου, *before supper*, X. *C.* 5, 5[39].

(*c*) of DEFENCE: μάχεσθαι πρὸ παίδων, *to fight for their children*, *Il.* 8, 57; διακινδυνεύειν πρὸ βασιλέως, *to run risk in behalf of the king*, X. *C.* 8, 8[4].

(*d*) of CHOICE OF PREFERENCE: κέρδος αἰνῆσαι πρὸ δίκας, *to approve craft before justice*, Pind. *Py.* 4, 140; πρὸ τούτου τεθνάναι ἂν ἕλοιτο, *before this he would prefer death*, P. *Sy.* 179[a].

In COMP.: *before, in defence of, forward.*

1216. πρός (Hom. also προτί or ποτί), *at* or *by* (in front of).

1. with the GENITIVE:

(*a*) *in front of, looking towards:* κεῖται πρὸς Θρᾴκης, *it lies over against Thrace*, D. 23, 182. In swearing: πρὸς θεῶν, *before (by) the Gods.* Sometimes *pertaining to* (as character): ἦ κάρτα πρὸς γυναικός, *surely it is very like a woman*, A. *Ag.* 592.

(*b*) *from (on the part of):* τιμὴν πρὸς Ζηνὸς ἔχοντες, *having honor from Zeus*, *Od.* 11, 302. Sometimes with passive verbs (like ὑπό), especially Ionic: ἀτιμάζεσθαι πρὸς Πεισιστράτου, *to be dishonored by Pisistratus*, Hd. 1, 61; ἀδοξοῦνται πρὸς τῶν πόλεων, *they are held in contempt by states*, X. *Oec.* 4, 2.

2. with the DATIVE:

(*a*) *at:* ἐπεὶ πρὸς Βαβυλῶνι ἦν ὁ Κῦρος, *when Cyrus was at Babylon*, X. *C.* 7, 5[1].

(*b*) *in addition to:* πρὸς τούτοις, *besides this;* πρὸς τοῖς ἄλλοις, *besides all the rest*, T. 2, 61.

3. with the ACCUSATIVE:

(*a*) *to:* εἶμ' αὐτὴ πρὸς Ὄλυμπον, *I am going myself to Olympus*, *Il.* 1, 420.

(*b*) *towards:* πρὸς Βορρᾶν, *towards the North*, T. 6, 2; (of persons) πρὸς ἀλλήλους ἡσυχίαν εἶχον, *they kept the peace towards one another*, I. 7, 51.

(*c*) *with a view to, according to:* πρὸς τί με ταῦτ' ἐρωτᾷς, (to what end) *for what do you ask me this?* X. *M.* 3, 7[2]; πρὸς τὴν παροῦσαν δύναμιν, *according to their power at the time*, D. 15, 28.

In COMP.: *to, towards, against, besides.*

1217. σύν, older Attic ξύν (Lat. cum), with DATIVE only, *with, in company with*, or *by aid of.* Σύν is chiefly poetic; it seldom occurs in Attic prose except in Xenophon, μετά with the genitive taking its place.

(*a*) *in company with*: ἤλυθε σὺν Μενελάῳ, *he came with Menelaus*, *Il.* 3, 206.

(*b*) *by aid of*: σὺν θεῷ, *with God's help*, *Il.* 9, 49.

(*c*) *in accordance with*: σὺν δίκᾳ, *with justice*, Pind. *Py.* 9, 96.

(*d*) sometimes instrumental (like simple dative): μέγαν πλοῦτον ἐκτήσω ξὺν αἰχμῇ, *thou didst gain great wealth by* (*with*) *thy spear*, *A. Pe.* 755.

In COMP.: *with*, *together*, *altogether*.

1218. ὑπέρ (Hom. also ὑπείρ), *over* (Lat. **super**).

1. with the GENITIVE:

(*a*) of PLACE: στῆ ὑπὲρ κεφαλῆς, *it stood over* (*his*) *head*, *Il.* 2, 20; of motion *over*: ὑπὲρ θαλάσσης καὶ χθονὸς ποτωμένοις (sc. ἡμῖν), *as we flit over sea and land*, A. *Ag.* 576.

(*b*) *for*, *in behalf of* (opposed to κατά): θυόμενα ὑπὲρ τῆς πόλεως, *sacrificed in behalf of the city*, X. *M.* 2, 2[13]; ὑπὲρ πάντων ἀγών, *a struggle for our all*, A. *Pe.* 405. Sometimes with τοῦ and infin., like ἵνα with subj.: ὑπὲρ τοῦ τὰ συνήθη μὴ γίγνεσθαι, *to prevent what is customary from being done*, Aesch. 3, 1.

(*c*) chiefly in the orators, *concerning* (like περί): τὴν ὑπὲρ τοῦ πολέμου γνώμην ἔχοντας, *having such an opinion about the war*, D. 2, 1.

2. with the ACCUSATIVE, *over*, *beyond*, *exceeding*: ὑπὲρ οὐδὸν ἐβήσετο δώματος, *he stepped over the threshold of the house*, *Od.* 7, 135; ὑπεὶρ ἅλα, *over the sea*, *Od.* 3, 73; ὑπὲρ τὸ βέλτιστον, *beyond what is best*, A. *Ag.* 378; ὑπὲρ δύναμιν, *beyond its power*, T. 6, 16.

In COMP.: *over*, *above*, *beyond*, *in defence of*, *for the sake of*.

1219. ὑπό (Hom. also ὑπαί), *under* (Lat. **sub**), *by*.

1. with the GENITIVE:

(*a*) of PLACE: τὰ ὑπὸ γῆς, *things under the earth*, P. *Ap.* 18[b]. Sometimes *from under* (chiefly poetic): οὓς ὑπὸ χθονὸς ἧκε φόωσδε, *whom he sent to light from beneath the earth*, Hes. *Th.* 669.

(*b*) to denote the AGENT with passive verbs: εἴ τις ἐτιμᾶτο ὑπὸ τοῦ δήμου, *if any one was honored by the people*, X. *H.* 2, 3[15].

(*c*) of CAUSE: ὑπὸ δέους, *through fear*; ὑφ' ἡδονῆς, *through pleasure*; ὑπ' ἀπλοίας, *by detention in port*, T. 2, 85.

2. with the DATIVE (especially poetic): τῶν ὑπὸ ποσσί, *beneath their feet*, *Il.* 2, 784; τῶν θανόντων ὑπ' Ἰλίῳ, *of those who fell under* (*the walls of*) *Ilium*, E. *Hec.* 764; ὑπὸ τῇ ἀκροπόλει, *under the acropolis*, Hd. 6, 105; οἱ ὑπὸ βασιλεῖ ὄντες, *those who are under the king*, X. *C.* 8, 1[6].

3. with the ACCUSATIVE:

(*a*) of PLACE, *under*, properly *to* (*a place*) *under*: ὑπὸ σπέος ἤλασε μῆλα, *he drives* (*drove*) *the sheep into* (*under*) *a cave*,

Il. 4, 279; ἤλθετ' ὑπὸ Τροίην, *you came to Troy* (i.e. *to besiege it*), *Od.* 4, 146; τάδε πάντα ὑπὸ σφᾶς ποιεῖσθαι, *to bring all these under their sway*, T. 4, 60.

(*b*) of TIME, *towards* (*entering into*): ὑπὸ νύκτα, *at nightfall* (Lat. sub noctem), T. 1, 115. Sometimes *at the time of, during*: ὑπὸ τὸν σεισμόν, *at the time of the earthquake*, T. 2, 27.

In COMP.: *under* (in place or rank), *underhand, slightly, gradually* (like **sub**).

1220. (*Improper Prepositions.*) These are ἄνευ, ἄτερ, ἄχρι, μέχρι, μεταξύ, ἕνεκα, πλήν, and ὡς (see 1200). All take the genitive except ὡς, which takes the accusative. They are never used in composition.

1. **ἄνευ**, *without, except, apart from*: ἄνευ ἀκολούθου, *without an attendant*, P. *Sy.* 217[a]; ἄνευ τοῦ καλὴν δόξαν ἐνεγκεῖν, *apart from* (*besides*) *bringing good reputation*, D. 18, 89.

2. **ἄτερ**, *without, apart from* (poetic): ἄτερ Ζηνός, *without* (*the help of*) *Zeus*, *Il.* 15, 292.

3. **ἄχρι**, *until, as far as*: ἄχρι τῆς τελευτῆς, *until the end*, D. 18, 179.

4. **μέχρι**, *until, as far as*: μέχρι τῆς πόλεως, *as far as the city*, T. 6, 96.

5. **μεταξύ**, *between*: μεταξὺ σοφίας καὶ ἀμαθίας, *between wisdom and ignorance*, P. *Sy.* 202[a].

6. **ἕνεκα** or **ἕνεκεν** (Ionic εἵνεκα, εἵνεκεν), *on account of, for the sake of* (generally after its noun): ὕβριος εἵνεκα τῆσδε, *on account of this outrage*, *Il.* 1, 214; μηδένα κολακεύειν ἕνεκα μισθοῦ, *to flatter no one for a reward*, X. *H.* 5, 1[17]. Also οὕνεκα (οὗ ἕνεκα) for ἕνεκα, chiefly in the dramatists.

7. **πλήν**, *except*: πλὴν γ' ἐμοῦ καὶ σοῦ, *except myself and you*, S. *El.* 909.

8. **ὡς**, *to*, used with the accusative like εἰς, but only with *personal* objects: ἀφίκετο ὡς Περδίκκαν καὶ ἐς τὴν Χαλκιδικήν, *he came to Perdiccas and into Chalcidice*, T. 4, 79.

1221. 1. In general, the accusative is the case used with prepositions to denote that *towards* which, *over* which, *along* which, or *upon* which *motion* takes place; the genitive, to denote that *from* which anything proceeds; the dative, to denote that *in* which anything takes place.

2. It will be noticed how the peculiar meaning of each case often modifies the expression by which we translate a given preposition: thus παρά means *near, by the side of*; and we have παρὰ τοῦ βασιλέως, *from the neighborhood of the king*; παρὰ τῷ βασιλεῖ, *in the neighborhood of the king*: παρὰ τὸν βασιλέα, *into the neighborhood of the king*.

1222. 1. The original adverbial use of the prepositions sometimes appears when they are used without a noun; this occurs especially in the older Greek, seldom in Attic prose. Thus περί, *round about* or *exceedingly*, in Homer; and πρὸς δέ or καὶ πρός, *and besides; ἐν δέ, and among them; ἐπὶ δέ, and upon this; μετὰ δέ, and next;* in Herodotus.

2. The preposition of a compound verb may also stand separately, in which case its adverbial force plainly appears; as ἐπὶ κνέφας ἦλθεν (κνέφας ἐπῆλθεν), *darkness came on*, *Il.* 1,475; ἡμῖν ἀπὸ λοιγὸν ἀμῦναι (ἀπαμῦναι), *to ward off destruction from us*, *Il.* 1, 67.

This is called *tmesis*, and is found chiefly in Homer and the early poets.

1223. A preposition sometimes follows its case, or a verb to which it belongs; as νεῶν ἄπο, παιδὸς πέρι; ὀλέσας ἄπο (for ἀπολέσας), *Od.* 9, 534. For the change of accent (*anastrophe*), see 116, 1.

1224. N. A few prepositions are used adverbially, with a verb (generally ἐστί) understood; as πάρα for πάρεστι, ἔπι and μέτα (in Homer) for ἔπεστι and μέτεστι. So ἔνι for ἔνεστι, and poetic ἄνα, *up!* for ἀνάστα (ἀνάστηθι). For the accent, see 116, 2.

1225. 1. Sometimes εἰς with the accusative, and ἐκ or ἀπό with the genitive, are used in expressions which themselves imply no motion, with reference to some motion implied or expressed in the context; as αἱ ξύνοδοι ἐς τὸ ἱερὸν ἐγίγνοντο, *the synods were held in the temple* (lit. *into the temple*, involving the idea of going *into* the temple to hold the synods), T. 1, 96; τοῖς ἐκ Πύλου ληφθεῖσι (ἐοικότες), *like those captured* (in Pylos, and brought home) *from Pylos*, i.e. *the captives from Pylos*, Ar. *N.* 186; διήρπαστο καὶ αὐτὰ τὰ ἀπὸ τῶν οἰκιῶν ξύλα, *even the very timbers in the houses* (lit. *from the houses*) *had been stolen*, X. *A.* 2, 2[16].

2. So ἐν with the dative sometimes occurs with verbs of motion, referring to rest which follows the motion; as ἐν τῷ ποταμῷ ἔπεσον, *they fell* (into and remained) *in the river*, X. *Ag.* 1, 32: ἐν γούνασι πίπτε Διώνης, *she fell on Dione's knees*, *Il.* 5, 370: see S. *El.* 1476.

These (1 and 2) are instances of the so-called *constructio praegnans*.

1226. N. Adverbs of place are sometimes interchanged in the same way (1225); as ὅποι καθέσταμεν, *where we are standing*, lit. *whither having come we are standing*, S. *O.C.* 23; τίς ἀγνοεῖ τὸν ἐκεῖθεν πόλεμον δεῦρο ἥξοντα; *who does not know that the war that is there will come hither?* D. 1, 15.

So ἔνθεν καὶ ἔνθεν, *on this side and on that*, like ἐκ δεξιᾶς (a dextra), *on the right*.

1227. A preposition is often followed by its own case when it is part of a compound verb. *E.g.*

Παρεκομίζοντο τὴν Ἰταλίαν, *they sailed along the coast of Italy*, T. 6, 44; ἐσῆλθέ με, *it occurred to me*, Hd. 7, 46; ἐξελθέτω τις δωμάτων, *let some one come forth from the house*, A. *Ch.* 663; ξυνέπρασσον αὐτῷ Ἀμφισσῆς, *Amphisseans assisted him*, T. 3, 101. For other examples of the genitive, see 1132; for those of the dative, see 1179.

ADVERBS.

1228. Adverbs qualify verbs, adjectives, and other adverbs. *E.g.*

Οὕτως εἶπεν, *thus he spoke;* ὡς δύναμαι, *as I am able;* πρῶτον ἀπῆλθε, *he first went away;* τὸ ἀληθῶς κακόν, *that which is truly evil;* αὗταί σ' ὁδηγήσουσι καὶ μάλ' ἀσμένως, *these will guide you even most gladly*, A. *Pr.* 728.

1229. N. For adjectives used as adverbs, see 926. For adverbs preceded by the article, and qualifying a noun like adjectives, see 952. For adverbs with the genitive or dative, see 1088; 1092; 1148; 1174; 1175. For adverbs used as prepositions, see 1220.

THE VERB.

VOICES.

ACTIVE.

1230. In the active voice the subject is represented as acting; as τρέπω τοὺς ὀφθαλμούς, *I turn my eyes;* ὁ πατὴρ φιλεῖ τὸν παῖδα, *the father loves the child;* ὁ ἵππος τρέχει, *the horse runs.*

1231. The form of the active voice includes most intransitive verbs; as τρέχω, *run.* On the other hand, the form of the middle or passive voice includes many deponent verbs which are active and transitive in meaning; as βούλομαι τοῦτο, *I want this.* Some transitive verbs have certain intransitive tenses, which generally have the meaning of the middle voice, as ἕστηκα, *I stand,* ἔστην, *I stood,* from ἵστημι, *place;* others have a passive force, as ἀνέστησαν ὑπ' αὐτοῦ, *they were driven out by him*, T. 1, 8.

1232. The same verb may be both transitive and intransitive;

as ἐλαύνω, *drive* (trans. or intrans.) or *march*; ἔχω, *have*, sometimes *hold* or *stay* (as ἔχε δή, *stay now*, P. *Pr.* 349[d]); with adverbs, *be*, as εὖ ἔχει, *it is well*, bene se habet. So πράττω, *do*, εὖ (or κακῶς) πράττω, *I am well* (or *badly*) *off*, *I do well* (or *badly*). The intransitive use sometimes arose from the omission of a familiar object; as ἐλαύνειν (ἵππον or ἅρμα), *to drive*, τελευτᾶν (τὸν βίον), *to end* (*life*) or *to die*. Compare the English verbs *drive*, *turn*, *move*, *increase*, etc.

PASSIVE.

1233. In the passive voice the subject is represented as *acted upon;* as ὁ παῖς ὑπὸ τοῦ πατρὸς φιλεῖται, *the child is loved by the father.*

1234. The *object* of the active becomes the subject of the passive. The *subject* of the active, the personal agent, is generally expressed by ὑπό with the genitive in the passive construction.

1235. The dative here, as elsewhere, generally expresses the inanimate instrument; as βάλλονται λίθοις, *they are pelted by stones.*

1236. Even a genitive or dative depending on a verb in the active voice can become the subject of the passive; as καταφρονεῖται ὑπ' ἐμοῦ, *he is despised by me* (active, καταφρονῶ αὐτοῦ, 1102); πιστεύεται ὑπὸ τῶν ἀρχομένων, *he is trusted by his subjects* (active, πιστεύουσιν αὐτῷ, 1160); ἄρχονται ὑπὸ βασιλέων, *they are ruled by kings* (active, βασιλεῖς ἄρχουσιν αὐτῶν). Ὑπὸ ἀλλοφύλων μᾶλλον ἐπεβουλεύοντο, *they were more plotted against by men of other races*, T. 1, 2 (active, ἐπεβούλευον αὐτοῖς).

1237. N. Other prepositions than ὑπό with the genitive of the agent, though used in poetry, are not common in Attic prose: such are παρά, πρός, ἐκ, and ἀπό. (See 1209, *c*.)

1238. 1. The perfect and pluperfect passive may have the *dative* of the agent.

2. The personal verbal in -τέος takes the dative (1596), the impersonal in -τέον the dative or accusative, of the agent (1597).

1239. When the active is followed by two accusatives, or by an accusative of a thing and a dative of a person, the case denoting a *person* is generally made the subject of the passive, and the other (an accusative) remains unchanged. *E.g.*

Οὐδὲν ἄλλο διδάσκεται ἄνθρωπος, *a man is taught nothing else* (in the active, οὐδὲν ἄλλο διδάσκουσι ἄνθρωπον), P. *Men.* 87[e]. Ἄλλο τι μεῖζον ἐπιταχθήσεσθε, *you will have some other greater command imposed on you* (active, ἄλλο τι μεῖζον ὑμῖν ἐπιτάξουσιν, *they will impose some other greater command on you*), T. 1, 140. Οἱ ἐπιτετραμμένοι τὴν φυλακήν, *those to whom the guard has been intrusted* (active, ἐπιτρέπειν τὴν φυλακὴν τούτοις), T. 1, 126. Διφθέραν ἐνημμένος, *clad in a leathern jerkin* (active, ἐνάπτειν τί τινι, *to fit a thing on one*), Ar. *N.* 72. So ἐκκόπτεσθαι τὸν ὀφθαλμόν, *to have his eye cut out*, and ἀποτέμνεσθαι τὴν κεφαλήν, *to have his head cut off*, etc., from possible active constructions ἐκκόπτειν τί τινι, and ἀποτέμνειν τί τινι. This construction has nothing to do with that of 1058.

The first two examples are cases of the cognate accusative (1051) of the *thing* retained with the passive, while the accusative or dative of the *person* is made the subject.

1240. 1. A cognate accusative (1051) of the active form, or a neuter pronoun or adjective representing such an accusative, may become the subject of the passive. *E.g.*

Ὁ κίνδυνος κινδυνεύεται, *the risk is run* (active, τὸν κίνδυνον κινδυνεύει, *he runs the risk*): see P. *Lach.* 187[b]. Εἰ οὐδὲν ἡμάρτηταί μοι, *if no fault has been committed by me* (active, οὐδὲν ἡμάρτηκα), And. 1, 33.

2. The passive may also be used impersonally, the cognate subject being implied in the verb itself; as ἐπειδὴ αὐτοῖς παρεσκεύαστο, *when preparation had been made*, T. 1, 46; οὔτε ἠσέβηται οὔτε ὡμολόγηται (sc. ἐμοί), *no sacrilege has been done and no confession has been made (by me)*, And. 1, 71.

3. This occurs chiefly in such neuter participial expressions as τὰ σοὶ κἀμοὶ βεβιωμένα, *the lives passed by you and by me*, D. 18, 265; αἱ τῶν πεπολιτευμένων εὔθυναι, *the accounts of their public acts*, D. 1, 28: so τὰ ἠσεβημένα, *the impious acts which have been done;* τὰ κινδυνευθέντα, *the risks which were run;* τὰ ἡμαρτημένα, *the errors which have been committed*, etc. Even an intransitive verb may thus have a passive voice.

1241. N. Some intransitive active forms are used as passives of other verbs. Thus εὖ ποιεῖν, *to benefit*, εὖ πάσχειν, *to be benefited;* εὖ λέγειν, *to praise*, εὖ ἀκούειν (poet. κλύειν), *to be praised;* αἱρεῖν, *to capture*, ἁλῶναι, *to be captured;* ἀποκτείνειν, *to kill*, ἀποθνῄσκειν, *to be killed;* ἐκβάλλειν, *to cast out*, ἐκπίπτειν, *to be cast out;* διώκειν, *to prosecute*, φεύγειν, *to be prosecuted (to be a defendant);* ἀπολύω, *to acquit*, ἀποφεύγω, *to be acquitted.*

MIDDLE.

1242. In the middle voice the subject is represented as acting upon himself, or in some manner which concerns himself.

1. As acting *on himself.* *E.g.*

Ἐτράποντο πρὸς λῃστείαν, *they turned themselves to piracy*, T. 1, 5. So παύομαι, *cease* (*stop one's self*), πείθεσθαι, *trust* (*persuade one's self*), φαίνομαι, *appear* (*show one's self*). This most natural use of the middle is the least common.

2. As acting *for himself* or *with reference to himself.* *E.g.*

Ὁ δῆμος τίθεται νόμους, *the people make laws for themselves*, whereas τίθησι νόμους would properly be said of a lawgiver; τοῦτον μεταπέμπομαι, *I send for him* (*to come to me*); ἀπεπέμπετο αὐτούς, *he dismissed them;* προβάλλεται τὴν ἀσπίδα, *he holds his shield to protect himself.*

3. As acting on an object *belonging to himself.* *E.g.*

Ἦλθε λυσόμενος θύγατρα, *he came to ransom his* (*own*) *daughter*, *Il.* 1, 13.

1243. N. The last two uses may be united in one verb, as in the last example.

1244. N. Often the middle expresses no more than is *implied* in the active; thus τρόπαιον ἵστασθαι, *to raise a trophy for themselves*, generally adds nothing but the *expression* to what is implied in τρόπαιον ἱστάναι, *to raise a trophy;* and either form can be used. The middle sometimes appears not to differ at all from the active in meaning; as the poetic ἰδέσθαι, *to see*, and ἰδεῖν.

1245. N. The middle sometimes has a *causative* meaning; as ἐδιδαξάμην σε, *I had you taught*, Ar. *N.* 1338; but ἐδιδαξάμην means also *I learned.*

This gives rise to some special uses of the middle; as in δανείζω, *lend*, δανείζομαι, *borrow* (*cause somebody to lend to one's self*); μισθῶ, *let*, μισθοῦμαι, *hire* (*cause to be let to one's self*); *I let myself for pay* is ἐμαυτὸν μισθῶ. So τίνω, *pay a penalty*, τίνομαι, *punish* (*make another pay a penalty*).

1246. N. The middle of certain verbs is peculiar in its meaning. Thus, αἱρῶ, *take*, αἱροῦμαι, *choose;* ἀποδίδωμι, *give back*, ἀποδίδομαι, *sell;* ἅπτω, *fasten*, ἅπτομαι, *cling to* (*fasten myself to*), so ἔχομαι, *hold to*, both with genitive; γαμῶ τινα, *marry* (said of a man), γαμοῦμαι *τινι, marry* (said of a woman); γράφω, *write* or *propose a vote*, γράφομαι, *indict*; τιμωρῶ τινι, *I avenge a person*, τιμωροῦμαί τινα, *I avenge myself on a person* or *I punish a person*; φυλάττω τινά, *I guard some one*, φυλάττομαί τινα, *I am on my guard against some one.*

1247. N. The passive of some of these verbs is used as a passive to both active and middle; thus γραφῆναι can mean either *to be written* or *to be indicted*, αἱρεθῆναι either *to be taken* or *to be chosen.*

1248. N. The future middle of some verbs has a passive sense; as ἀδικῶ, *I wrong*, ἀδικήσομαι, *I shall be wronged.*

TENSES.

1249. The tenses may express two relations. They may designate the time of an action as *present, past,* or *future;* and also its character as *going on*, as simply *taking place*, or as *finished*. The latter relation appears in all the moods and in the infinitive and participle; the former appears always in the indicative, and to a certain extent (hereafter to be explained) in some of the dependent moods and in the participle.

I. TENSES OF THE INDICATIVE.

1250. The tenses of the indicative express action as follows: —

1. Present, action going on in present time: γράφω, *I am writing.*

2. Imperfect, action going on in past time: ἔγραφον, *I was writing.*

3. Perfect, action finished in present time: γέγραφα, *I have written.*

4. Pluperfect, action finished in past time: ἐγεγράφη, *I had written.*

5. Aorist, action simply taking place in past time: ἔγραψα, *I wrote.*

6. Future, future action (either in its *progress* or in its mere *occurrence*): γράψω, *I shall write* or *I shall be writing.*

7. Future Perfect, action to be finished in future time: γεγράψεται, *it will have been written.*

1251. This is shown in the following table:—

	Present Time.	*Past Time.*	*Future Time.*
Action going on	PRESENT	IMPERFECT	FUTURE
Action simply taking place		AORIST	FUTURE
Action finished	PERFECT	PLUPERFECT	FUT. PERFECT

For the present and the aorist expressing a general truth (*gnomic*), see 1292.

1252. In narration, the present is sometimes used vividly for the aorist. *E.g.*

Κελεύει πέμψαι ἄνδρας· ἀποστέλλουσιν οὖν, καὶ περὶ αὐτῶν ὁ Θεμιστοκλῆς κρύφα πέμπει, *he bids them send men: accordingly they dispatch them, and Themistocles sends secretly about them*, T. 1, 91.

This is called the Historic Present.

1253. 1. The present often expresses a customary or repeated action in present time; as οὗτος μὲν ὕδωρ, ἐγὼ δὲ οἶνον πίνω, *he drinks water, and I drink wine*, D. 19, 46. (See 1292.)

2. The imperfect likewise may express customary or repeated past action; as Σωκράτης ὥσπερ ἐγίγνωσκεν οὕτως ἔλεγε, *as Socrates thought, so he used to speak*, X. *M.* 1, 1[4].

1254. The present μέλλω, with the present or future (seldom the aorist) infinitive, forms a periphrastic future, which sometimes denotes intention or expectation; as μέλλει τοῦτο ποιεῖν (or ποιήσειν), *he is about to do this*; εἰ μέλλει ἡ πολιτεία σῴζεσθαι, *if the constitution is to be saved*, P. *Rp.* 412[a].

1255. The present and especially the imperfect often express an *attempted* action; as πείθουσιν ὑμᾶς, *they are trying to persuade you*, Isae. 1, 26; Ἁλόννησον ἐδίδου, *he offered* (*tried to give*) *Halonnesus*, Aesch. 3, 83; ἃ ἐπράσσετο οὐκ ἐγένετο, *what was attempted did not happen*, T. 6, 74.

1256. The presents ἥκω, *I am come*, and οἴχομαι, *I am gone*, have the force of perfects; the imperfects having the force of pluperfects.

1257. The present εἶμι, *I am going*, with its compounds, has a future sense, and is used as a future of ἔρχομαι, ἐλεύσομαι not being in good use in Attic prose. In Homer εἶμι is also present in sense.

1258. The present with πάλαι or any other expression of past time has the force of a present and perfect combined; as πάλαι τοῦτο λέγω, *I have long been telling this* (*which I now tell*).

1259. 1. The *aorist* takes its name (ἀόριστος, *unlimited, unqualified*) from its denoting a simple past *occurrence*, with none of the limitations (ὅροι) as to *completion, continuance, repetition*, etc., which belong to the other past tenses. It corresponds to the ordinary preterite in English, whereas the Greek imperfect corresponds to the forms *I was doing*, etc. Thus, ἐποίει τοῦτο is *he was doing this* or *he did this habitually;* πεποίηκε τοῦτο is *he has already done this;* ἐπεποιήκει τοῦτο is *he had already* (*at some past time*) *done this;* but ἐποίησε τοῦτο is simply *he did this*, without qualification of any kind. The aorist is therefore commonly used in rapid narration, the imperfect in detailed description. The aorist is more common in negative sentences.

2. As it is not always important to distinguish between the progress of an action and its mere occurrence, it is occasionally indifferent whether the imperfect or the aorist is used; compare ἔλεγον in T. 1, 72 (end) with εἶπον, ἔλεξαν, and ἔλεξε in 1, 79. The two tenses show different views (both natural views) of the same act of speaking.

1260. The aorist of verbs which denote a *state* or *condition* may express the *entrance into* that state or condition; as πλουτῶ, *I am rich;* ἐπλούτουν, *I was rich;* ἐπλούτησα, *I became rich.* So ἐβασίλευσε, *he became king;* ἦρξε, *he took office* (also *he held office*).

1261. After ἐπεί and ἐπειδή, *after that*, the aorist is generally to be translated by our pluperfect; as ἐπειδὴ ἀπῆλθον, *after they had departed.* Compare *postquam venit.*

1262. N. The aorist (sometimes the perfect) participle with ἔχω may form a periphrastic perfect, especially in Attic poetry; as θαυμάσας ἔχω τόδε, *I have wondered at this*, S. *Ph.* 1362. In prose, ἔχω with a participle generally has its common force; as τὴν προῖκα ἔχει λαβών, *he has received and has the dowry* (not simply *he has taken it*), D. 27, 17.

1263. N. Some perfects have a present meaning; as θνῄσκειν, *to die*, τεθνηκέναι, *to be dead;* γίγνεσθαι, *to become*, γεγονέναι, *to be;* μιμνῄσκειν, *to remind*, μεμνῆσθαι, *to remember;* καλεῖν, *to call*, κεκλῆσθαι, *to be called.* So οἶδα, *I know*, novi, and many others. This is usually explained by the meaning of the verb.

In such verbs the pluperfect has the force of an imperfect; as ᾔδη, *I knew.*

1264. N. The perfect sometimes refers vividly to the future; as εἴ με αἰσθήσεται, ὄλωλα, *if he shall perceive me, I am ruined* (perii), S. *Ph.* 75. So sometimes the present, as ἀπόλλυμαι, *I perish!* (for *I shall perish*), L. 12, 14; and even the aorist, as ἀπωλόμην εἴ με λείψεις, *I perish if you leave me*, E. *Al.* 386.

1265. N. The second person of the future may express a *permission*, or even a *command;* as πράξεις οἷον ἂν θέλῃς, *you may act as you please*, S. *O. C.* 956; πάντως δὲ τοῦτο δράσεις, *and by all means do this* (*you shall do this*), Ar. *N.* 1352. So in imprecations; as ἀπολεῖσθε, *to destruction with you!* (lit. *you shall perish*).

For the periphrastic future with μέλλω and the infinitive, see 1254.

1266. N. The future perfect is sometimes merely an emphatic future, denoting that a future act will be *immediate* or *decisive;* as φράζε, καὶ πεπράξεται, *speak, and it shall be* (*no sooner said than*) *done*, Ar. *Pl.* 1027. Compare the similar use of the perfect infinitive, 1275.

1267. 1. The division of the tenses of the indicative into *primary* (or *principal*) and *secondary* (or *historical*) is explained in 448.

2. In dependent clauses, when the construction allows both subjunctive and optative, or both indicative and optative, the subjunctive or indicative regularly follows primary tenses, and the optative follows secondary tenses. *E.g.*

Πράττουσιν ἃ ἂν βούλωνται, *they do whatever they please;* ἔπραττον ἃ βούλοιντο, *they did whatever they pleased.* Λέγουσιν ὅτι τοῦτο βούλονται, *they say that they wish for this;* ἔλεξαν ὅτι τοῦτο βούλοιντο, *they said that they wished for this.*

These constructions will be explained hereafter (1431; 1487).

1268. N. The gnomic aorist is a primary tense, as it refers to present time (1292); and the historic present is secondary, as it refers to past time (1252).

1269. The only exception to this principle (1267, 2) occurs in indirect discourse, where the form of the direct discourse can always be retained, even after secondary tenses. (See 1481, 2).

1270. 1. The distinction of primary and secondary tenses extends to the dependent moods only where the tenses there keep the same distinction of time which they have in the indicative, as in the optative and infinitive of indirect discourse (1280).

2. An optative of future time generally assimilates a dependent conditional relative clause or protasis to the optative when it might otherwise be in the subjunctive: thus we should generally have πράττοιεν ἂν ἃ βούλοιντο, *they would do whatever they might please.* See 1439. Such an optative seldom assimilates the subjunctive or indicative of a final or object clause (1362) in prose; but oftener in poetry. It very rarely assimilates an *indicative* of indirect discourse, although it may assimilate an interrogative *subjunctive* (1358).

II. TENSES OF THE DEPENDENT MOODS.

A. Not in Indirect Discourse.

1271. In the subjunctive and imperative, and also in the optative and infinitive when they are *not in indirect discourse* (1279), the tenses chiefly used are the present and aorist.

1272. 1. These tenses here differ only in this, that the present expresses an action in its duration, that is, as *going on* or *repeated*, while the aorist expresses simply its *occurrence*, the time of both being otherwise precisely the same. *E.g.*

Ἐὰν ποιῇ τοῦτο, *if he shall be doing this*, or *if he shall do this (habitually)*, ἐὰν ποιήσῃ τοῦτο, (simply) *if he shall do this;* εἰ ποιοίη τοῦτο, *if he should be doing this*, or *if he should do this (habitually)*, εἰ ποιήσειε τοῦτο, (simply) *if he should do this;* ποίει τοῦτο, *do this (habitually)*, ποίησον τοῦτο, (simply) *do this.* Οὕτω νικήσαιμί τ' ἐγὼ καὶ νομιζοίμην σοφός, *on this condition may I gain the victory* (aor.) *and be thought* (pres.) *wise*, Ar. *N.* 520. Βούλεται τοῦτο ποιεῖν, *he wishes to be doing this* or *to do this (habitually)*, βούλεται τοῦτο ποιῆσαι, (simply) *he wishes to do this.*

2. This is a distinction entirely unknown to the Latin, which has (for example) only one form, *si faciat*, corresponding to εἰ ποιοίη and εἰ ποιήσειεν.

1273. The perfect, which seldom occurs in these constructions, represents an action as *finished* at the time at which the present would represent it as *going on.* *E.g.*

Δέδοικα μὴ λήθην πεποιήκῃ, *I fear lest it may prove to have caused forgetfulness* (μὴ ποιῇ would mean *lest it may cause*), D. 19, 3. Μηδενὶ βοηθεῖν ὃς ἂν μὴ πρότερος βεβοηθηκὼς ὑμῖν ᾖ, *to help no one who shall not previously have helped you* (ὃς ἂν μὴ . . . βοηθῇ would mean *who shall not previously help you*), D. 19, 16. Οὐκ ἂν διὰ *τοῦτό γ' εἶεν οὐκ εὐθὺς δεδωκότες, they would not (on enquiry) prove to have failed to pay immediately on this account* (with *διδοῖεν* this would mean *they would not fail to pay*), D. 30, 10. *Οὐ βουλεύεσθαι ἔτι ὥρα, ἀλλὰ βεβουλεῦσθαι, it is no longer time to be deliberating, but (it is time) to have finished deliberating*, P. *Cr.* 46[a].

1274. N. The perfect *imperative* generally expresses a command that something shall be *decisive* and *permanent;* as *ταῦτα εἰρήσθω, let this have been said* (i.e. *let what has been said be final*), or *let this (which follows) be said once for all; μέχρι τοῦδε ὡρίσθω ὑμῶν ἡ βραδυτής, at this point let the limit of your sluggishness be fixed*, T. 1, 71. This is confined to the third person singular passive; the rare second person singular middle being merely emphatic. The *active* is used only when the perfect has a present meaning (1263).

1275. N. The perfect *infinitive* sometimes expresses *decision* or *permanence* (like the imperative, 1274), and sometimes it is merely more emphatic than the present; as *εἶπον τὴν θύραν κεκλεῖσθαι, they ordered the gate to be shut (and kept so)*, X. *H.* 5, 4[7]. *Ἤλαυνεν ἐπὶ τοὺς Μένωνος, ὥστ' ἐκείνους ἐκπεπλῆχθαι καὶ τρέχειν ἐπὶ τὰ ὅπλα, so that they were (once for all) thoroughly frightened and ran to arms*, X. *A.* 1, 5[13]. The regular meaning of this tense, when it is not in indirect discourse, is that given in 1273.

1276. The future infinitive is regularly used only to represent the future indicative in *indirect discourse* (1280).

1277. It occurs occasionally in other constructions, in place of the regular present or aorist, to make more emphatic a future idea which the infinitive receives from the context. *E.g.*

Ἐδεήθησαν τῶν Μεγαρέων ναυσὶ σφᾶς ξυμπροπέμψειν, they asked the Megarians to escort them with ships, T. 1, 27. *Οὐκ ἀποκωλύσειν δυνατοὶ ὄντες, not being able to prevent*, T. 3, 28. In all such cases the future is strictly exceptional (see 1271).

1278. One regular exception to the principle just stated is found in the periphrastic future (1254).

B. In Indirect Discourse.

1279. The term *indirect discourse* includes all clauses depending on a verb of *saying* or *thinking* which contain the thoughts or words of any person stated *indirectly, i.e.* incorporated into the general structure of the sentence. It includes of course all *indirect* quotations and questions.

1280. When the optative and infinitive stand in indirect discourse, each tense represents the *corresponding tense* of the same verb in the direct discourse. *E.g.*

Ἔλεγεν ὅτι γράφοι, *he said that he was writing* (he said γράφω, *I am writing*); ἔλεγεν ὅτι γράψοι, *he said that he would write* (he said γράψω, *I will write*); ἔλεγεν ὅτι γράψειεν, *he said that he had written* (he said ἔγραψα); ἔλεγεν ὅτι γεγραφὼς εἴη, *he said that he had already written* (he said γέγραφα). Ἤρετο εἴ τις ἐμοῦ εἴη σοφώτερος, *he asked whether any one was wiser than I* (he asked ἔστι τις;), P. *Ap.* 21ᵃ.

Φησὶ γράφειν, *he says that he is writing* (he says γράφω); φησὶ γράψειν, *he says that he will write* (γράψω); φησὶ γράψαι, *he says that he wrote* (ἔγραψα); φησὶ γεγραφέναι, *he says that he has written* (γέγραφα). For the participle, see 1288.

Εἶπεν ὅτι ἄνδρα ἄγοι ὃν εἷρξαι δέοι, *he said that he was bringing a man whom it was necessary to confine* (he said ἄνδρα ἄγω ὃν εἷρξαι δεῖ), X. *H.* 5, 4⁸. Ἐλογίζοντο ὡς, εἰ μὴ μάχοιντο, ἀποστήσοιντο αἱ πόλεις, *they considered that, if they should not fight, the cities would revolt* (they thought ἐὰν μὴ μαχώμεθα, ἀποστήσονται, *if we do not fight, they will revolt*), *ibid.* 6, 4⁶.

1281. N. These constructions are explained in 1487, 1494, and 1497. Here they merely show the force of the *tenses* in indirect discourse. Compare especially the difference between φησὶ γράφειν and φησὶ γράψαι above with that between βούλεται ποιεῖν and βούλεται ποιῆσαι under 1272. Notice also the same distinction in the present and aorist optative.

1282. N. The construction of 1280 is the strictly proper use of the future infinitive (1276; 1277).

1283. N. The future perfect infinitive is occasionally used here, to express future completion; as νομίζετε ἐν τῇδε τῇ ἡμέρᾳ ἐμὲ κατακεκόψεσθαι, *believe that on that day I shall have been already* (i.e. *shall be the same as*) *cut in pieces*, X. *A.* 1, 5¹⁶.

1284. N. The future perfect participle very rarely occurs in a similar sense (see T. 7, 25).

1285. 1. The present infinitive may represent the *imperfect* as well as the present indicative; as τίνας εὐχὰς ὑπολαμβάνετ' εὔχεσθαι τὸν Φίλιππον ὅτ' ἔσπενδεν; *what prayers do you suppose Philip made when he was pouring libations?* (i.e. τίνας ηὔχετο;), D. 19, 130. The perfect infinitive likewise represents both perfect and pluperfect. In such cases the time of the infinitive must always be shown by the context (as above by ὅτ' ἔσπενδεν). See 1289.

2. For the present optative representing the imperfect, see 1488.

1286. Verbs of *hoping, expecting, promising, swearing*, and a few others, form an intermediate class between verbs which take the infinitive in indirect discourse and those which do not (see 1279); and though they regularly have the future infinitive (1280), the present and aorist are allowed. *E.g.*

Ἤλπιζον μάχην ἔσεσθαι, *they expected that there would be a battle*, T. 4, 71; but ἃ οὔποτε ἤλπισεν παθεῖν, *what he never expected to suffer*, E. *H. F.* 746. Xenophon has ὑπέσχετο μηχανὴν παρέξειν, *C.* 6, 1[21], and also ὑπέσχετο βουλεύσασθαι, *A.* 2, 3[20]. Ὀμόσαντες ταύταις ἐμμενεῖν, *having sworn to abide by these*, X. *H.* 5, 3[26]; but ὀμόσαι εἶναι μὲν τὴν ἀρχὴν κοινήν, πάντας δ' ὑμῖν ἀποδοῦναι τὴν χώραν, *to swear that the government should be common, but that all should give up the land to you*, D. 23, 170.

In English we can say *I hope* (*expect* or *promise*) *to do this*, like ποιεῖν or ποιῆσαι; or *I hope I shall do this*, like ποιήσειν.

1287. N. The future optative is never used except as the representative of the future indicative, either in indirect discourse (see 1280), or in the construction of 1372 (which is governed by the principles of indirect discourse). Even in these the future indicative is generally retained. See also 1503.

III. TENSES OF THE PARTICIPLE.

1288. The tenses of the participle generally express the same time as those of the indicative; but they are present, past, or future *relatively* to the time of the verb with which they are connected. *E.g.*

Ἁμαρτάνει τοῦτο ποιῶν, *he errs in doing this*; ἡμάρτανε τοῦτο ποιῶν, *he erred in doing this*; ἁμαρτήσεται τοῦτο ποιῶν, *he will err in doing this*. (Here ποιῶν is first present, then past, then future, absolutely; but always *present* to the verb of the sentence.) So in indirect discourse: οἶδα τοῦτον γράφοντα (γράψαντα, γράψοντα, or γεγραφότα), *I know that he is writing* (*that he wrote, will write*, or *has written*). Οὐ πολλοὶ φαίνονται ἐλθόντες, *not many appear to have gone* (*on the expedition*), T. 1, 10. (For other examples, see 1588.)

Ταῦτα εἰπόντες, ἀπῆλθον, *having said this, they departed*. Ἐπῄνεσαν τοὺς εἰρηκότας, *they praised those who had* (*already*) *spoken*. Τοῦτο ποιήσων ἔρχεται, *he is coming to do this*; τοῦτο ποιήσων ἦλθεν, *he came to do this*. Ἄπελθε ταῦτα λαβών, *take this and be off* (λαβών being past to ἄπελθε, but absolutely future).

1289. The present may here also represent the imperfect; as οἶδα κἀκείνω σωφρονοῦντε, ἔστε Σωκράτει συνήστην, *I know that they both were temperate as long as they associated with Socrates* (i.e. ἐσωφρονείτην), X. *M.* 1,2[18]. (See 1285.)

1290. N. The aorist participle in certain constructions (generally with a verb in the aorist) does not denote time past with reference to the leading verb, but expresses time coincident with that of the verb. See examples in 1563, 8; 1585; 1586. See *Greek Moods*, §§ 144–150.

IV. GNOMIC AND ITERATIVE TENSES.

1291. The present is the tense commonly used in Greek, as in English, to denote a general truth or an habitual action. *E.g.*

Τίκτει τοι κόρος ὕβριν, ὅταν κακῷ ὄλβος ἕπηται, *satiety begets insolence, whenever prosperity follows the wicked*, Theog. 153.

1292. In animated language the aorist is used in this sense. This is called the *gnomic aorist*, and is generally translated by the English present. *E.g.*

Ἤν τις τούτων τι παραβαίνῃ, ζημίαν αὐτοῖς ἐπέθεσαν, i.e. *they impose a penalty on all who transgress*, X. *C.* 1,2[2]. Μί' ἡμέρα τὸν μὲν καθεῖλεν ὑψόθεν, τὸν δ' ἦρ' ἄνω, *one day (often) brings down one man from a height and raises another high*, E. frag. 424.

1293. N. Here one case in past time is vividly used to represent all possible cases. Examples containing such adverbs as πολλάκις, *often*, ἤδη, *already*, οὔπω, *never yet*, illustrate the construction; as ἀθυμοῦντες ἄνδρες οὔπω τρόπαιον ἔστησαν, *disheartened men never yet raised* (i.e. *never raise*) *a trophy*, P. *Critias*, 108[c].

1294. N. An aorist resembling the gnomic is found in Homeric similes; as ἤριπε δ' ὡς ὅτε τις δρῦς ἤριπεν, *and he fell, as when some oak falls* (lit. *as when an oak once fell*), *Il.* 13, 389.

1295. The perfect is sometimes gnomic, like the aorist. *E.g.*

Τὸ δὲ μὴ ἐμποδὼν ἀνανταγωνίστῳ εὐνοίᾳ τετίμηται, *but those who are not before men's eyes are honored with a good will which has no rivalry*, T. 2, 45.

1296. The imperfect and aorist are sometimes used with the adverb ἄν to denote a *customary* action. *E.g.*

Διηρώτων ἂν αὐτοὺς τί λέγοιεν, *I used to ask them* (*I would often ask them*) *what they said*, P. *Ap.* 22[b]. Πολλάκις ἠκούσαμεν ἂν ὑμᾶς, *we used often to hear you*, Ar. *Lys.* 511.

1297. N. This iterative construction must be distinguished from that of the potential indicative with ἄν (1335). It is equivalent to our phrase *he would often do this* for *he used to do this.*

1298. N. The Ionic has iterative forms in -σκον and -σκομην in both imperfect and aorist. (See 778.) Herodotus uses these also with ἄν, as above (1296).

THE PARTICLE ἄΝ.

1299. The adverb ἄν (epic κέ, Doric κά) has two distinct uses.

1. It may be joined to all the secondary tenses of the indicative (in Homer also to the future indicative), and to the optative, infinitive, or participle, to denote that the action of the verb is dependent on some circumstances or condition, expressed or implied. Here it belongs strictly to the verb.

2. It is joined regularly to εἰ, *if*, to all relative and temporal words, and sometimes to the final particles ὡς, ὅπως, and ὄφρα, when these are followed by the subjunctive. Here, although as an adverb it qualifies the verb, it is always closely attached to the particle or relative, with which it often forms one word, as in ἐάν, ὅταν, ἐπειδάν.

1300. N. There is no English word which can translate ἄν. In its first use it is expressed in the *would* or *should* of the verb (βούλοιτο ἄν, *he would wish*; ἑλοίμην ἄν, *I should choose*). In its second use it generally has no force which can be made apparent in English.

1301. N. The following sections (1302–1309) enumerate the various uses of ἄν: when these are explained more fully elsewhere, reference is made to the proper sections.

1302. The present and perfect indicative never take ἄν.

1303. The future indicative sometimes takes ἄν (or κέ) in the early poets, especially Homer; very rarely in Attic Greek. *E.g.*

Καί κέ τις ὧδ' ἐρέει, *and some one will* (or *may*) *thus speak*, *Il.* 4, 176; ἄλλοι οἵ κέ με τιμήσουσι, *others who will (perchance) honor me,*

Il. 1, 174. The future with ἄν seems to be an intermediate form between the simple future, *will honor*, and the optative with ἄν, *would honor*. One of the few examples in Attic prose is in P. *Ap.* 29c.

1304. 1. The past tenses of the indicative (generally the imperfect or aorist) are used with ἄν in a potential sense (1335), or in the apodosis of an unfulfilled condition (1397). *E.g.*

Οὐδὲν ἂν κακὸν ἐποίησαν, *they could* (or *would*) *have done no harm;* ἦλθεν ἂν εἰ ἐκέλευσα, *he would have come if I had commanded him.*

2. The imperfect and aorist indicative with ἄν may also have an iterative sense. (See 1296.)

1305. 1. In Attic Greek the subjunctive is used with ἄν only in the dependent constructions mentioned in 1299, 2, where ἄν is attached to the introductory particle or relative word.

See 1367; 1376; 1382; 1428, 2.

2. In epic poetry, where the independent subjunctive often has the sense of the future indicative (1355), it may take κέ or ἄν, like the future (1303). *E.g.*

Εἰ δέ κε μὴ δώησιν, ἐγὼ δέ κεν αὐτὸς ἕλωμαι, *and if he does not give her up, I will take her myself, Il.* 1, 324.

1306. The optative with ἄν has a potential sense (1327), and it often forms the apodosis of a condition expressed by the optative with εἰ, denoting what *would happen* if the condition should be fulfilled (1408).

1307. N. The *future* optative is never used with ἄν (1287).

1308. 1. The present and aorist (rarely the perfect) infinitive and participle with ἄν represent the indicative or optative with ἄν; each tense being equivalent to the *corresponding tense* of one of these moods with ἄν, — the present representing also the imperfect, and the perfect also the pluperfect (1285; 1289).

2. Thus the present infinitive or participle with ἄν may represent either an imperfect indicative or a present optative with ἄν; the aorist, either an aorist indicative or an

aorist optative with ἄν; the perfect, either a pluperfect indicative or a perfect optative with ἄν. *E.g.*

(*Pres.*) Φησὶν αὐτοὺς ἐλευθέρους ἂν εἶναι, εἰ τοῦτο ἔπραξαν, *he says that they would* (*now*) *be free* (ἦσαν ἄν), *if they had done this;* φησὶν αὐτοὺς ἐλευθέρους ἂν εἶναι, εἰ τοῦτο πράξειαν, *he says that they would* (*hereafter*) *be free* (εἶεν ἄν), *if they should do this.* Οἶδα αὐτοὺς ἐλευθέρους ἂν ὄντας, εἰ τοῦτο ἔπραξαν, *I know that they would* (*now*) *be free* (ἦσαν ἄν), *if they had done this;* οἶδα αὐτοὺς ἐλευθέρους ἂν ὄντας, εἰ ταῦτα πράξειαν, *I know that they would* (*hereafter*) *be free* (εἶεν ἄν), *if they should do this.* Πολλ' ἂν ἔχων ἕτερ' εἰπεῖν, *although I might* (= ἔχοιμι ἄν) *say many other things,* D. 18, 258.

(*Aor.*) Φασὶν αὐτὸν ἐλθεῖν ἂν (or οἶδα αὐτὸν ἐλθόντα ἄν), εἰ τοῦτο ἐγένετο, *they say* (or *I know*) *that he would have come* (ἦλθεν ἄν), *if this had happened;* φασὶν αὐτὸν ἐλθεῖν ἂν (or οἶδα αὐτὸν ἐλθόντα ἄν), εἰ τοῦτο γένοιτο, *they say* (or *I know*) *that he would come* (ἔλθοι ἄν), *if this should happen.* Ῥᾳδίως ἂν ἀφεθείς, προείλετο ἀποθανεῖν, *whereas he might easily have been acquitted* (ἀφείθη ἄν), *he preferred to die,* X. *M.* 4, 4[4].

(*Perf.*) Εἰ μὴ τὰς ἀρετὰς ἐκείνας παρέσχοντο, πάντα ταῦθ' ὑπὸ τῶν βαρβάρων ἂν ἑαλωκέναι (φήσειεν ἄν τις), *had they not exhibited those exploits of valor, we might say that all this would have been captured by the barbarians* (ἑαλώκει ἄν), D. 19, 312. Οὐκ ἂν ἡγοῦμαι αὐτοὺς δίκην ἀξίαν δεδωκέναι, εἰ αὐτῶν καταψηφίσαισθε, *I do not think they would* (*then,* in the future, *prove to*) *have suffered proper punishment* (δεδωκότες ἂν εἶεν), *if you should condemn them,* L. 27, 9.

The context must decide in each case whether we have the equivalent of the indicative or of the optative with ἄν. In the examples given, the form of the protasis generally settles the question.

1309. The infinitive with ἄν is used chiefly in indirect discourse (1494); but the participle with ἄν is more common in other constructions (see examples above).

As the early poets who use the future indicative with ἄν (1303) seldom use this construction, the future infinitive and participle with ἄν are very rare.

1310. When ἄν is used with the subjunctive (as in 1299, 2), it is generally separated from the introductory word only by monosyllabic particles like μέν, δέ, τέ, γάρ, etc.

1311. When ἄν is used with the indicative or optative, or in any other potential construction, it may either be placed next to its verb, or be attached to some other emphatic word (as a nega-

-tive or interrogative, or an important adverb); as τάχιστ' ἄν τε πόλιν οἱ τοιοῦτοι ἑτέρους πείσαντες ἀπολέσειαν, *such men, if they should get others to follow them, would very soon destroy a state*, T. 2, 63.

1312. In a long apodosis ἄν may be used twice or even three times with the same verb. *E.g.*

Οὐκ ἂν ἡγεῖσθ' αὐτὸν κἂν ἐπιδραμεῖν; *do you not think that he would even have rushed thither?* D. 27, 56. In T. 2, 41, ἄν is used three times with παρέχεσθαι.

1313. Ἄν may be used elliptically with a verb understood. *E.g.*

Οἱ οἰκέται ῥέγκουσιν· ἀλλ' οὐκ ἂν πρὸ τοῦ (sc. ἔρρεγκον), *the slaves are snoring; but in old times they wouldn't have done so*, Ar. *N.* 5. So in φοβούμενος ὥσπερ ἂν εἰ παῖς, *fearing like a child* (ὥσπερ ἂν ἐφοβεῖτο εἰ παῖς ἦν), P. *G.* 479ᵃ.

1314. When an apodosis consists of several *co-ordinate* verbs, ἄν generally stands only with the first. *E.g.*

Οὐδὲν ἂν διάφορον τοῦ ἑτέρου ποιοῖ, ἀλλ' ἐπὶ ταὐτὸν ἴοιεν ἀμφότεροι, *he would do nothing different from the other, but both would aim at the same object* (ἄν belongs also to ἴοιεν), P. *Rp.* 360ᶜ.

1315. Ἄν never begins a sentence or a clause.

1316. N. The adverb τάχα, *quickly, soon, readily*, is often prefixed to ἄν, in which case τάχ' ἄν is nearly equivalent to ἴσως, *perhaps*. The ἄν here always belongs in its regular sense (1299, 1) to the verb of the sentence; as τάχ' ἂν ἔλθοι, *perhaps he would come*; τάχ' ἂν ἦλθεν, *perhaps he would* (or *might*) *have come*.

THE MOODS.

1317. The indicative is used in simple, absolute assertions, and in questions which include or concern such assertions; as γράφει, *he writes*; ἔγραψεν, *he wrote*; γράψει, *he will write*; γέγραφεν, *he has written*; τί ἐγράψετε; *what did you write?* ἔγραψε τοῦτο; *did he write this?*

1318. The indicative has a tense to express every variety of time which is recognized by the Greek verb, and thus it can state a supposition as well as make an assertion in the past, present, or future. It also expresses certain other relations which in other languages (as in Latin) are generally expressed by a different mood. The following examples will illustrate these uses: —

Εἰ τοῦτο ἀληθές ἐστι, χαίρω, *if this is true, I rejoice* (1390); εἰ ἔγραψεν, ἦλθον ἄν, *if he had written, I should have come* (1397); εἰ γράψει, γνώσομαι, *if he shall write* (or *if he writes*), *I shall know* (1405). Ἐπιμελεῖται ὅπως τοῦτο γενήσεται, *he takes care that this shall happen* (1372). Λέγει ὅτι τοῦτο ποιεῖ, *he says that he is doing this;* sometimes, εἶπεν ὅτι τοῦτο ποιεῖ, *he said that he was doing this* (he said ποιῶ). (1487.) Εἴθε με ἔκτεινας, ὡς μήποτε τοῦτο ἐποίησα, *O that thou hadst killed me, that I might never have done this!* (1511; 1371). Εἴθε τοῦτο ἀληθὲς ἦν, *O that this were true!* (1511).

1319. N. These constructions are explained in the sections referred to. Their variety shows the impossibility of including all the actual uses even of the indicative under any single fundamental idea.

1320. The various uses of the subjunctive are shown by the following examples: —

Ἴωμεν, *let us go* (1344). Μὴ θαυμάσητε, *do not wonder* (1346). Τί εἴπω; *what shall I say?* (1358). Οὐ μὴ τοῦτο γένηται, *this (surely) will not happen* (1360). Οὐδὲ ἴδωμαι (Homeric), *nor shall I see* (1355).

Ἔρχεται ἵνα τοῦτο ἴδῃ, *he is coming that he may see this* (1365); φοβεῖται μὴ τοῦτο γένηται, *he fears lest this may happen* (1378). Ἐὰν ἔλθῃ, τοῦτο ποιήσω, *if he comes* (or *if he shall come*), *I shall do this* (1403); ἐάν τις ἔλθῃ, τοῦτο ποιῶ, *if any one (ever) comes, I (always) do this* (1393, 1). Ὅταν ἔλθῃ, τοῦτο ποιήσω, *when he comes* (or *when he shall come*), *I shall do this* (1434); ὅταν τις ἔλθῃ, τοῦτο ποιῶ, *when any one comes, I (always) do this* (1431, 1).

1321. N. The subjunctive, in its simplest and apparently most primitive use, expresses simple futurity, like the future indicative; this is seen in the Homeric independent construction, ἴδωμαι, *I shall see;* εἴπῃσί τις, *one will say.* Then, in exhortations and prohibitions it is still future; as ἴωμεν, *let us go;* μὴ ποιήσητε τοῦτο, *do not do this.* In final and object clauses it expresses a future purpose or a future object of fear. In conditional and conditional relative sentences it expresses a future supposition; except in *general* conditions, where it is indefinite (but never strictly present) in its time.

1322. The various uses of the optative are shown by the following examples: —

Εὐτυχοίης, *may you be fortunate*; μὴ γένοιτο, *may it not be done*; εἴθε μὴ ἀπόλοιντο, *O that they may not perish* (1507). Ἔλθοι ἄν, *he may go*, or *he might go* (1327).

Ἦλθεν ἵνα τοῦτο ἴδοι, *he came that he might see this* (1365); ἐφοβεῖτο μὴ τοῦτο γένοιτο, *he feared lest this should happen* (1378). Εἰ ἔλθοι, τοῦτ' ἂν ποιήσαιμι, *if he should come, I should do this* (1408); εἴ τις ἔλθοι, τοῦτ' ἐποίουν, *if any one (ever) came, I (always) did this* (1393, 2). Ὅτε ἔλθοι, τοῦτ' ἂν ποιήσαιμι, *whenever he should come (at any time when he should come), I should do this* (1436); ὅτε τις ἔλθοι, τοῦτ' ἐποίουν, *whenever any one came, I (always) did this* (1431, 2). Ἐπεμελεῖτο ὅπως τοῦτο γενήσοιτο, *he took care that this should happen* (1372). Εἶπεν ὅτι τοῦτο ποιοίη (ποιήσοι or ποιήσειε), *he said that he was doing (would do* or *had done) this* (1487).

1323. N. The optative in many of its uses is a vaguer and less distinct form of expression than the subjunctive, indicative, or imperative, in constructions of the same general character. This appears especially in its independent uses; as in the Homeric Ἑλένην ἄγοιτο, *he may take Helen away*, *Il.* 4, 19 (see γυναῖκα ἀγέσθω, *Il.* 3, 72, referring to the same thing, and καί ποτέ τις εἴπῃσιν, and *sometime one will say*, 1303, above); ἴοιμεν, *may we go* (cf. ἴωμεν, *let us go*); μὴ γένοιτο, *may it not happen* (cf. μὴ γένηται, *let it not happen*); ἕλοιτο ἄν (Hom. sometimes ἕλοιτο alone), *he would take* (cf. Hom. ἕληται sometimes with κέ, *he will take*). So in future conditions; as εἰ γένοιτο, *if it should happen* (cf. ἐὰν γένηται, *if it shall happen*). In other dependent clauses it is generally a correlative of the subjunctive, sometimes of the indicative; here it represents a dependent subjunctive or indicative in its *changed relation* when the verb on which it depends is changed from present or future to past time. The same change in relation is expressed in English by a change from *shall*, *will*, *may*, *do*, *is*, etc. to *should*, *would*, *might*, *did*, *was*, etc. To illustrate these last relations, compare ἔρχεται ἵνα ἴδῃ, φοβεῖται μὴ γένηται, ἐάν τις ἔλθῃ τοῦτο ποιῶ, ἐπιμελεῖται ὅπως τοῦτο γενήσεται, and λέγει ὅτι τοῦτο ποιεῖ, with the corresponding forms after past leading verbs given in 1322.

For a discussion of the whole relation of the optative to the subjunctive and the other moods, and of the original meaning of the subjunctive and optative, see *Moods and Tenses*, pp. 371–389.

1324. The imperative is used to express commands and prohibitions; as τοῦτο ποίει, *do this*; μὴ φεύγετε, *do not fly*.

1325. The infinitive, which is a verbal noun, and the participle and the verbal in -*τέος*, which are verbal adjectives, are closely connected with the moods of the verb in many constructions.

1326. The following sections (1327–1515) treat of all constructions which require any other form of the finite verb than the indicative in simple assertions and questions (1317). The infinitive and participle are included here so far as either of them is used in indirect discourse, in protasis or apodosis, or after *ὥστε* (*ὡς*, *ἐφ' ᾧ* or *ἐφ' ᾧτε*) and *πρίν*. These constructions are divided as follows:—

I. Potential Optative and Indicative with *ἄν*.
II. Imperative and Subjunctive in commands, exhortations, and prohibitions. — Subjunctive and Indicative with *μή* or *μὴ οὐ* in cautious Assertions. — *Ὅπως* and *ὅπως μή* with the independent Future Indicative.
III. Independent Homeric Subjunctive, like Future Indicative. — Interrogative Subjunctive.
IV. *Οὐ μή* with Subjunctive and Future Indicative.
V. Final and Object Clauses with *ἵνα*, *ὡς*, *ὅπως*, *ὄφρα*, and *μή*.
VI. Conditional Sentences.
VII. Relative and Temporal Sentences, including consecutive sentences with *ὥστε* etc.
VIII. Indirect Discourse or *Oratio Obliqua*.
IX. Causal Sentences.
X. Expressions of a Wish.

I. POTENTIAL OPTATIVE AND INDICATIVE WITH ἄν.

POTENTIAL OPTATIVE.

1327. The optative with *ἄν* expresses a future action as dependent on circumstances or conditions. Thus *ἔλθοι ἄν* is *he may go, he might* (*could* or *would*) *go*, or *he would be likely to go*, as opposed to an absolute statement like *he will go*. *E.g.*

Ἔτι γάρ κεν ἀλύξαιμεν κακὸν ἦμαρ, *for* (*perhaps*) *we may still escape the evil day*, Od. 10, 269. *Πᾶν γὰρ ἂν πύθοιό μου*, *for you can learn anything you please from me*, A. *Pr*. 617. Τί τόνδ' ἂν εἴποις ἄλλο; *what else could you say of this man?* S. *An*. 646. Οὐκ ἂν λειφθείην, *I would not be left behind* (*in any case*), Hd. 4, 97. Δὶς ἐς τὸν αὐτὸν ποταμὸν οὐκ ἂν ἐμβαίης, *you cannot* (*could not*) *step twice into the same river*, P. *Crat*. 402ᵃ. Ἡδέως ἂν ἐροίμην Λεπτίνην, *I would gladly ask* (*I should like to ask*) *Leptines*, D. 20, 129. Ποῖ οὖν τραποίμεθ' ἂν ἔτι; *in what other direction can we* (*could we*) *possibly turn?* P. *Eu*. 290ᵃ. So βουλοίμην ἄν, *velim*, *I should like*: cf. ἐβουλόμην ἄν, *vellem* (1339).

1328. The optative thus used is called *potential*, and corresponds generally to the English potential forms with *may*, *can*, *might*, *could*, *would*, etc. It is equivalent to the Latin potential subjunctive, as dicas, credas, cernas, putes, etc., *you may say*, *believe*, *perceive*, *think*, etc. The limiting condition is generally too indefinite to be distinctly present to the mind, and can be expressed only by words like *perhaps*, *possibly*, or *probably*, or by such vague forms as *if he pleased*, *if he should try*, *if he could*, *if there should be an opportunity*, etc. Sometimes a general condition, like *in any possible case*, is felt to be implied, so that the optative with ἄν hardly differs from an absolute future; as in οὐκ ἂν μεθείμην τοῦ θρόνου, *I will not* (*would never*) *give up the throne*, Ar. *R*. 830. See the examples in 1330.

1329. The potential optative can express every degree of potentiality from the almost absolute future of the last example to the apodosis of a future condition expressed by the optative with εἰ (1408), where the form of the condition is assimilated to that of the conclusion. The intermediate steps may be seen in the following examples:—

Οὐκ ἂν δικαίως ἐς κακὸν πέσοιμί τι, *I could not justly fall into any trouble*, S. *An*. 240, where δικαίως points to the condition *if justice should be done*. Οὔτε ἐσθίουσι πλείω ἢ δύνανται φέρειν· διαρραγεῖεν γὰρ ἄν, *nor do they eat more than they can carry*, *for* (*if they did*) *they would burst*, X. *C*. 8, 2²¹, where εἰ ἐσθίοιεν is implied by the former clause.

1330. N. The potential optative of the second person may express a mild command or exhortation; as χωροῖς ἂν εἴσω, *you may go in*, or *go in*, S. *Ph*. 674; κλύοις ἂν ἤδη, *hear me now*, S. *El*. 637. See 1328.

1331. N. The potential optative may express what may hereafter prove to be true or to have been true; as ἡ ἐμὴ (σοφία) φαύλη τις ἂν εἴη, *my wisdom may turn out to be of a mean kind*,

P. *Sy.* 175ᵉ; ποῦ δῆτ' ἂν εἶεν οἱ ξένοι; *where may the strangers be?* (i.e. *where is it likely to prove that they are*)? S. *El.* 1450; εἴησαν δ' ἂν οὗτοι Κρῆτες, *and these would probably prove to be* (or *to have been*) *Cretans*, Hd. 1, 2; αὗται δὲ οὐκ ἂν πολλαὶ εἴησαν, *and these* (the islands) *would not prove to be many*, T. 1, 9.

1332. N. Occasionally ἄν is omitted with the potential optative, chiefly in Homer; as οὔ τι κακώτερον ἄλλο πάθοιμι, *I could suffer nothing else that is worse*, *Il.* 19, 321.

1333. N. The Attic poets sometimes omit ἄν after such indefinite expressions as ἔστιν ὅστις, ἔστιν ὅπως, ἔστιν ὅποι, etc.; as ἔστ' οὖν ὅπως Ἄλκηστις ἐς γῆρας μόλοι; *is it possible then that Alcestis can come to old age?* E. *Al.* 52; so 113, and A. *Pr.* 292.

1334. N. For the potential optative in Homer referring to past time, see 1399.

POTENTIAL INDICATIVE.

1335. The past tenses of the indicative with ἄν express a past action as dependent on past circumstances or conditions. Thus, while ἦλθεν means *he went*, ἦλθεν ἄν means *he would have gone* (*under some past circumstances*).

1336. This is called the potential indicative; and it probably arose as a past form of the potential optative, so that, while ἔλθοι ἄν meant originally *he may go* or *he would be likely to go*, ἦλθεν ἄν meant *he may have gone* or *he would have been likely to go*. It is the equivalent of the Latin forms like diceres, *you would have said*, crederes, *you would have believed*, cerneres, putares, etc., which are past potential forms corresponding to dicas, credas, cernas, putes, etc. (1328). Thus putet and putaret are equivalent to οἴοιτο ἄν, *he would be likely to think*, and ᾤετο ἄν, *he would have been likely to think*.

1337. The potential indicative sometimes expresses (in its original force) what *would have been likely* to happen, i.e. *might have* happened (and perhaps *did* happen) with no reference to any definite condition. *E.g.*

Ὑπό κεν ταλασίφρονά περ δέος εἷλεν, *fear might have seized* (i.e. *would have been likely to seize*) *even a man of stout heart*, *Il.* 4, 421. Ἦλθε τοῦτο τοὔνειδος τάχ' ἂν ὀργῇ βιασθέν, *this disgrace may perhaps have come from violence of wrath*, S. *O. T.* 523. Ἐν ταύτῃ τῇ ἡλικίᾳ λέγοντες πρὸς ὑμᾶς ἐν ᾗ ἂν μάλιστα ἐπιστεύσατε, *talking to you at that age at which you would have been most likely to put trust in them*, P. *Ap.* 18ᶜ.

1338. Generally, however, the potential indicative implies a reference to some circumstances different from the real ones, so that ἦλθεν ἄν commonly means *he would have gone* (*if something had not been as it was*). The unreal past condition here may be as vague and indefinite as the future condition to which the potential optative refers (1328). *E.g.*

Οὐ γάρ κεν δυνάμεσθα (impf.) θυράων ἀπώσασθαι λίθον, *for we could not have moved the stone from the doorway*, Od. 9, 304. Compare οὐδὲν ἂν κακὸν ποιήσειαν, *they could do no harm* (*if they should try*), with οὐδὲν ἂν κακὸν ἐποίησαν, *they could have done no harm* (*if they had tried*). Τούτου τίς ἂν σοι τἀνδρὸς ἀμείνων εὑρέθη; *who could have been found better than this man?* S. *Aj.* 119. Ὀψὲ ἦν, καὶ τὰς χεῖρας οὐκ ἂν καθεώρων, *it was late, and they would not have seen the show of hands*, X. *H.* 1. 7[7]. Ποίων ἂν ἔργων ἀπέστησαν; *from what labors would they have shrunk?* I. 4. 83.

1339. When no definite condition is understood with the potential indicative, the imperfect with ἄν is regularly past, as it always is in Homer (1398). See the examples in 1338.

The imperfect with ἄν referring to present time, which is common in apodosis after Homer (1397), appears seldom in purely potential expression, chiefly in ἐβουλόμην ἄν, vellem, *I should wish, I should like* (which can mean also *I should have wished*); as ἐβουλόμην ἂν αὐτοὺς ἀληθῆ λέγειν, *I should like it if they spoke the truth*, L. 12, 22.

1340. The potential indicative may express every degree of potentiality from that seen in 1337 to that of the apodosis of an unfulfilled condition actually expressed. (Compare the potential optative, 1329.) Here, after Homer, the imperfect with ἄν may express present time (see 1397). The intermediate steps to the complete apodosis may be seen in the following examples:—

Ἤγετε τὴν εἰρήνην ὅμως· οὐ γὰρ ἦν ὅ τι ἂν ἐποιεῖτε, *you still kept the peace; for there was nothing which you could have done* (*if you had not*), D. 18, 43. Πολλοῦ γὰρ ἂν τὰ ὄργανα ἦν ἄξια, *for the tools would be worth much* (*if they had this power*), P. *Rp.* 374[d].

For the full conditional sentences, see 1397.

1341. N. For a peculiar potential expression formed by imperfects denoting *obligation* etc., like ἔδει, χρῆν, etc., with the infinitive, see 1400.

II. IMPERATIVE AND SUBJUNCTIVE IN COMMANDS, EXHORTATIONS, AND PROHIBITIONS. — SUBJUNCTIVE AND INDICATIVE WITH μή OR μὴ οὐ IN CAUTIOUS ASSERTIONS. — Ὅπως AND ὅπως μή WITH FUTURE INDICATIVE IN COMMANDS AND PROHIBITIONS.

1342. The imperative expresses a command, exhortation, or entreaty; as λέγε, *speak thou;* φεῦγε, *begone!* ἐλθέτω, *let him come;* χαιρόντων, *let them rejoice.*

1343. N. A combination of a command and a question is found in such phrases as οἶσθ' ὃ δρᾶσον; *dost thou know what to do?* Ar. *Av.* 54, where the imperative is the verb of the relative clause. So οἶσθα νῦν ἅ μοι γενέσθω; *do you know what must be done for me?* E. *I. T.* 1203.

1344. The *first person* of the subjunctive (generally *plural*) is used in exhortations. Its negative is μή. *E.g.*

Ἴωμεν, *let us go;* ἴδωμεν, *let us see;* μὴ τοῦτο ποιῶμεν, *let us not do this.* This supplies the want of a first person of the imperative.

1345. N. Both subjunctive and imperative may be preceded by ἄγε (ἄγετε), φέρε, or ἴθι, *come!* These words are used without regard to the number or person of the verb which follows; as ἄγε μίμνετε πάντες, *Il.* 2, 331.

1346. In prohibitions, in the second and third persons, the *present imperative* or the *aorist subjunctive* is used with μή and its compounds. *E.g.*

Μὴ ποίει τοῦτο, *do not do this (habitually)*, or *do not go on doing this;* μὴ ποιήσῃς τοῦτο, (simply) *do not do this.* Μὴ κατὰ τοὺς νόμους δικάσητε· μὴ βοηθήσητε τῷ πεπονθότι δεινά· μὴ εὐορκεῖτε, "*do not judge according to the laws; do not help him who has suffered outrages; do not abide by your oaths,*" D. 21, 211.

The two forms here differ merely as *present* and *aorist* (1272).

1347. N. The *third* person of the aorist imperative sometimes occurs in prohibitions; the *second* person very rarely.

1348. In Homer the independent subjunctive with μή (generally in the third person) may express fear or anxiety, with a desire to avert the object of the fear. *E.g.*

Μὴ δὴ νῆας ἕλωσι, *may they not seize the ships (as I fear they may)*, *Il.* 16, 128. Μή τι χολωσάμενος ῥέξῃ κακὸν υἷας Ἀχαιῶν, *may he not (as I fear he may) in his wrath do any harm to the sons of the Achaeans*, *Il.* 2. 195.

1349. N. This usage occurs also in Euripides and Plato. See *Moods and Tenses*, §§ 261–264.

1350. An independent subjunctive with μή may express a cautious assertion, or a suspicion that something *may be* true; and with μὴ οὐ a cautious negation, or a suspicion that something *may not be* true. This is a favorite usage with Plato. *E.g.*

Μὴ ἀγροικότερον ᾖ τὸ ἀληθὲς εἰπεῖν, *I suspect that the truth may be too rude a thing to tell*, P. *G.* 462[e]. Ἀλλὰ μὴ οὐ τοῦτ' ᾖ χαλεπόν *but I rather think that this may not be a difficult thing*, P. *Ap.* 39[a].

1351. The indicative may be thus used (1350) with μή or μὴ οὐ, referring to present or past time. *E.g.*

Ἀλλὰ μὴ τοῦτο οὐ καλῶς ὡμολογήσαμεν, *but perhaps we did not do well in assenting to this*, P. *Men.* 89[c]. (Compare φοβοῦμαι μὴ ἔπαθεν, *I fear that he suffered*, 1380.)

1352. In Attic Greek ὅπως and ὅπως μή are used colloquially with the future indicative in commands and prohibitions. *E.g.*

Νῦν οὖν ὅπως σώσεις με, *so now save me*, Ar. *N.* 1177. Κατάθου τὰ σκεύη, χὤπως ἐρεῖς ἐνταῦθα μηδὲν ψεῦδος, *put down the packs, and tell no lies here*, Ar. *R.* 627. Ὅπως οὖν ἔσεσθε ἄξιοι τῆς ἐλευθερίας, (*see that you*) *prove yourselves worthy of freedom*, X. *A.* 1, 7[3]. Ὅπως μοι μὴ ἐρεῖς ὅτι ἔστι τὰ δώδεκα δὶς ἕξ, *see that you do not tell me that twelve is twice six*, P. *Rp.* 337[b].

1353. N. The construction of 1352 is often explained by an ellipsis of σκόπει or σκοπεῖτε (see 1372).

1354. N. The subjunctive occasionally occurs here with ὅπως μή, but not with ὅπως alone.

III. HOMERIC SUBJUNCTIVE LIKE FUTURE INDICATIVE. —INTERROGATIVE SUBJUNCTIVE.

1355. In Homer, the subjunctive in independent sentences sometimes has the force of a future indicative. *E.g.*

Οὐ γάρ πω τοίους ἴδον ἀνέρας, οὐδὲ ἴδωμαι, *for I never yet saw nor shall I ever see such men*, *Il.* 1, 262. Καί ποτέ τις εἴπῃσιν, *and one will* (or *may*) *some time say*, *Il.* 6, 459.

1356. N. This subjunctive may, like the future indicative, take κέ or ἄν in a potential sense. (See 1305, 2.)

1357. N. The question τί πάθω; *what will become of me?* or *what harm will it do me?* (literally, *what shall I undergo?*) carries this use even into Attic Greek. *E.g.*

Ὢ μοι ἐγώ, τί πάθω; *Od.* 5, 465. Τί πάθω τλήμων; *what will become of me, wretched one?* A. *P.* 912. Τὸ μέλλον, εἰ χρή, πείσομαι· τί γὰρ πάθω; *I shall suffer what is to come, if it must be; for what harm can it do me?* E. *Ph.* 895.

1358. The first person of the subjunctive may be used in questions of appeal, where a person asks himself or another *what he is to do.* The negative is μή. It is often introduced by βούλει or βούλεσθε (in poetry θέλεις or θέλετε). *E.g.*

Εἴπω ταῦτα; *shall I say this?* or βούλει εἴπω ταῦτα; *do you wish that I should say this?* Ποῖ τράπωμαι; ποῖ πορευθῶ; *whither shall I turn? whither shall I go?* E. *Hec.* 1099. Ποῦ δὴ βούλει καθιζόμενοι ἀναγνῶμεν; *where now wilt thou that we sit down and read?* P. *Phdr.* 228[e].

1359. N. The third person is sometimes found in these questions, chiefly when τὶς has the force of *we;* as Τί τις εἶναι τοῦτο φῇ; *what shall we say this is?* D. 19, 88.

IV. Οὐ μή WITH SUBJUNCTIVE AND FUTURE INDICATIVE.

1360. The subjunctive (generally the aorist) and sometimes the future indicative are used with the double negative οὐ μή in the sense of an emphatic future indicative with οὐ. *E.g.*

Οὐ μὴ πίθηται, *he will not obey,* S. *Ph.* 103. Οὔτε γὰρ γίγνεται οὔτε γέγονεν, οὐδὲ οὖν μὴ γένηται, *for there is not, nor has there been, nor will there ever be,* etc., P. *Rp.* 492[e]. Οὔ ποτ' ἐξ ἐμοῦ γε μὴ πάθῃς τόδε, *you never shall suffer this at my hands,* S. *El.* 1029. Οὔ τοι μήποτέ σε . . . ἄκοντά τις ἄξει, *no one shall ever take you against your will,* etc., S. *O. C.* 176.

1361. In the dramatic poets, the second person singular of the future indicative (occasionally of the aorist subjunctive) with οὐ μή may express a strong prohibition. *E.g.*

Οὐ μὴ καταβήσει, *don't come down* (*you shall not come down*), Ar. *V.* 397. Οὐ μὴ τάδε γηρύσει, *do not speak out in this way,* E. *Hip.* 213. Οὐ μὴ σκώψῃς, *do not jeer,* Ar. *N.* 296.

This construction is not interrogative.

V. FINAL AND OBJECT CLAUSES AFTER ἵνα, ὡς, ὅπως, ὄφρα, AND μή.

1362. The final particles are ἵνα, ὡς, ὅπως, and (epic and lyric) ὄφρα, *that, in order that.* To these must be added μή, *lest* or *that*, which became in use a negative final particle. The clauses which are introduced by these particles may be divided into three classes: —

1. Pure *final* clauses, expressing a purpose or motive; as ἔρχεται ἵνα τοῦτο ἴδῃ, *he is coming that he may see this.* Here all the final particles are used (see 1368).

2. *Object* clauses with ὅπως after verbs signifying *to strive for, to care for, to effect;* as σκόπει ὅπως τοῦτο γενήσεται, *see to it that this is done.*

3. Clauses with μή after verbs of *fear* or *caution;* as φοβεῖται μὴ τοῦτο γένηται, *he fears that* (or *lest*) *this may happen.*

1363. The first two classes are to be specially distinguished. The object clauses in 2 are the *direct object* of the leading verb, and can even stand in apposition to an object accusative like τοῦτο; as σκόπει τοῦτο, ὅπως μή σε ὄψεται, *see to this, namely, that he does not see you.* But a final clause could stand in apposition only to τούτου ἕνεκα, *for the sake of this;* or διὰ τοῦτο, *to this end;* as ἔρχεται τούτου ἕνεκα, ἵνα ἡμᾶς ἴδῃ, *he is coming for this purpose, namely, that he may see us.*

For the origin of the clauses in 3, and the development of final clauses, see *Moods and Tenses*, §§ 307–316.

1364. The negative in all these clauses is μή; except after μή, *lest*, where οὐ is used.

I. PURE FINAL CLAUSES.

1365. Final clauses take the subjunctive after primary tenses, and the optative after secondary tenses. *E.g.*

Δοκεῖ μοι κατακαῦσαι τὰς ἁμάξας, ἵνα μὴ τὰ ζεύγη ἡμῶν στρατηγῇ, *I think we should burn our wagons, that our cattle may not be our commanders*, X. *A.* 3, 2[27]. Εἴπω τι δῆτα κἄλλ', ἵν' ὀργίζῃ πλέον; *shall I speak still further, that you may be the more angry?* S. *O. T.* 364. Παρακαλεῖς ἰατρούς, ὅπως μὴ ἀποθάνῃ, *you call in physicians, that he may not die*, X. *M.* 2, 10[2]. Λυσιτελεῖ ἐᾶσαι ἐν τῷ παρόντι, μὴ *καὶ τοῦτον πολέμιον προσθώμεθα, it is expedient to allow it for a time, lest we add him to the number of our enemies*, X. *C.*2,4[12]. Φίλος ἐβούλετο εἶναι τοῖς μέγιστα δυναμένοις, ἵνα ἀδικῶν μὴ διδοίη δίκην, *he wished to be a friend to the most powerful, that he might do wrong and not be punished*, X. *A.*2,6[21]. Τούτου ἕνεκα φίλων ᾤετο δεῖσθαι, ὡς συνέργους ἔχοι, *he thought he needed friends for this purpose, namely, that he might have helpers*, X. *A.*1,9[21]. Ἀφικόμην, ὅπως σοῦ πρὸς δόμους ἐλθόντος εὖ πράξαιμί τι, *I came that I might gain some good by your return home*, S. *O. T.* 1005.

Κεφαλῇ κατανεύσομαι, ὄφρα πεποίθῃς, *I will nod my assent, that you may trust me*, *Il.* 1, 522. Ἔνθα κατέσχετ', ὄφρ' ἕταρον θάπτοι, *he tarried there, that he might bury his companion*, *Od.* 3, 284.

1366. N. The future indicative is rarely found in final clauses after ὅπως, ὄφρα, ὡς, and μή. This is almost entirely confined to poetry. See *Od.* 1, 56, 4, 163; *Il.* 20, 301; Ar. *Eccl.* 495.

1367. N. The adverb ἄν (κέ) is sometimes joined with ὡς, ὅπως, and ὄφρα before the subjunctive in final clauses; as ὡς ἂν μάθῃς, ἀντάκουσον, *hear the other side, that you may learn*, X. *A.*2, 5[16].
For this use, see *Moods and Tenses*, §§ 325–28. The final optative with ἄν is probably always potential (1327).

1368. N. Ὄφρα is the most common final particle in Homer, ὡς in tragedy, and ἵνα in comedy and prose. But ὅπως exceeds ἵνα in Thucydides and Xenophon. Ὡς was never in good use in prose, except in Xenophon.

1369. As final clauses express the purpose or motive of *some person*, they admit the double construction of indirect discourse (1481, 2; 1503). Hence, instead of the optative after past tenses, we can have the mood and tense which would be used when a person conceived the purpose; that is, we can say either ἦλθεν ἵνα ἴδοι, *he came that he might see* (1365), or ἦλθεν ἵνα ἴδῃ, because the person himself would have said ἔρχομαι ἵνα ἴδω, *I come that I may see. E.g.*

Ξυνεβούλευε τοῖς ἄλλοις ἐκπλεῦσαι, ὅπως ἐπὶ πλέον ὁ σῖτος ἀντίσχῃ, *he advised the rest to sail away, that the provisions might hold out longer*, T. 1, 65. Τὰ πλοῖα κατέκαυσεν, ἵνα μὴ Κῦρος διαβῇ, *he burned the vessels, that Cyrus might not pass over*, X. *A.* 1, 4[18].

1370. N. The subjunctive is even more common than the optative after past tenses in certain authors, as Thucydides and Herodotus; but much less so in others, as Homer and Xenophon.

1371. The past tenses of the indicative are used in final clauses with ἵνα, sometimes with ὅπως or ὡς, to denote that the purpose is dependent on some act which does not or did not take place (as on some unfulfilled condition or some unaccomplished wish), and therefore *is not* or *was not attained*. *E.g.*

Τί μ' οὐ λαβὼν ἔκτεινας εὐθύς, ὡς ἔδειξα μήποτε, κ.τ.λ.; *why did you not take me and kill me at once, that I might never have shown (as I have done)*, etc.? S. *O. T.* 1391. Φεῦ, φεῦ, τὸ μὴ τὰ πράγματ' ἀνθρώποις ἔχειν φωνήν, ἵν' ἦσαν μηδὲν οἱ δεινοὶ λόγοι, *Alas! alas! that the facts have no voice for men, so that words of eloquence might be as nothing*, E. frag. 442.

II. OBJECT CLAUSES WITH ὅπως AFTER VERBS OF *STRIVING*, ETC.

1372. Object clauses depending on verbs signifying *to strive for*, *to care for*, *to effect*, regularly take the future indicative with ὅπως or ὅπως μή after both primary and secondary tenses.

The future optative *may* be used after secondary tenses, as the correlative of the future indicative, but commonly the indicative is retained on the principle of 1369. *E.g.*

Φρόντιζ' ὅπως μηδὲν ἀνάξιον τῆς τιμῆς ταύτης πράξεις, *take heed that you do nothing unworthy of this honor*, I. 2, 37. Ἐπεμελεῖτο ὅπως μὴ ἄσιτοί ποτε ἔσοιντο, *he took care that they should never be without food*, X. *C.* 8, 1[43] (here ἔσονται would be more common). Ἔπρασσον ὅπως τις βοήθεια ἥξει, *they were trying to effect (this), that some assistance should come*, T. 3, 4.

For ὅπως and ὅπως μή with the future indicative in commands and prohibitions, often explained by an ellipsis of σκόπει or σκοπεῖτε in this construction, see 1352.

1373. The future indicative with ὅπως sometimes follows verbs of *exhorting*, *entreating*, *commanding*, and *forbidding*, which commonly take an infinitive of the object; as διακελεύονται ὅπως τιμωρήσεται πάντας τοὺς τοιούτους, *they exhort him to take vengeance on all such*, P. *Rp.* 549[e]. (See 1377.)

1374. 1. Sometimes the present or aorist subjunctive and optative is used here, as in final clauses. *E.g.*

Ἄλλου του ἐπιμελήσει ἢ ὅπως ὅ τι βέλτιστοι πολῖται ὦμεν; will you care for anything except that we may be the best possible citizens? P. *G.* 515[b]. Ἐπεμέλετο αὐτῶν, ὅπως ἀεὶ ἀνδράποδα διατελοῖεν, *he took care that they should always remain slaves,* X. *C.* 8, 1[44].

2. Xenophon allows ὡς with the subjunctive or optative here.

1375. N. Μή, *lest,* may be used for ὅπως μή with the subjunctive.

1376. N. Ἄν or κέ can be used here, as in final clauses (1367), with ὅπως or ὡς and the subjunctive.

1377. In Homer the construction of 1372 with ὅπως and the future is not found; but verbs signifying *to plan, consider,* and *try* take ὅπως or ὡς and the subjunctive or optative. *E.g.*

Φραζώμεθ' ὅπως ὄχ' ἄριστα γένηται, *let us consider how the very best may be done, Od.* 13, 365. Φράσσεται ὥς κε νέηται, *he will plan for his return, Od.* 1, 205. Βούλευον ὅπως ὄχ' ἄριστα γένοιτο, *they deliberated that the very best might be done, Od.* 9, 420. So rarely with λίσσομαι, *entreat* (see 1373).

III. CLAUSES WITH μή AFTER VERBS OF *FEARING*, ETC.

1378. After verbs denoting *fear, caution,* or *danger,* μή, *that* or *lest,* takes the subjunctive after primary tenses, and the optative after secondary tenses. The subjunctive may also follow secondary tenses, to retain the mood in which the fear originally occurred to the mind. The negative form is μὴ οὐ (1364). *E.g.*

Φοβοῦμαι μὴ τοῦτο γένηται (vereor *ne* accidat), *I fear that this may happen;* φοβοῦμαι μὴ οὐ τοῦτο γένηται (vereor *ut* accidat), *I fear that this may not happen* (1364). Φροντίζω μὴ κράτιστον ᾖ μοι σιγᾶν, *I am anxious lest it may be best for me to be silent,* X. *M.* 4, 2[39]. Οὐκέτι ἐπετίθεντο, δεδιότες μὴ ἀποτμηθείησαν, *they no longer made attacks, fearing lest they should be cut off,* X. *A.* 3, 4[29]. Ἐφοβοῦντο μή τι πάθῃ, *they feared lest he should suffer anything* (1369), X. *Sy.* 2, 11.

1379. N. The future indicative is very rarely used after μή in this construction. But ὅπως μή is sometimes used here, as in the object clauses of 1372, with both future indicative and subjunctive; as δέδοικα ὅπως μὴ ἀνάγκη γενήσεται, *I fear that there may come a necessity,* D. 9, 75. Ὅπως μή here is the equivalent of μή, *that* or *lest,* in the ordinary construction.

1380. Verbs of *fearing* may refer to objects of fear which are *present* or *past*. Here μή takes the present and past tenses of the indicative. *E.g.*

Δέδοικα μὴ πληγῶν δέει, *I fear that you need blows*, Ar. *N.* 493. Φοβούμεθα μὴ ἀμφοτέρων ἅμα ἡμαρτήκαμεν, *we fear that we have missed both at once*, T. 3, 53. Δείδω μὴ δὴ πάντα θεὰ νημερτέα εἶπεν, *I fear that all which the Goddess said was true*, *Od.* 5, 300. Ὅρα μὴ παίζων ἔλεγεν, *beware lest he was speaking in jest*, P. *Th.* 145[b].

VI. CONDITIONAL SENTENCES.

1381. In conditional sentences the clause containing the condition is called the protasis, and that containing the conclusion is called the apodosis. The protasis is introduced by some form of εἰ, *if*.

Αἰ for εἰ is sometimes used in Homer.

1382. The adverb ἄν (epic κέ or κέν) is regularly joined to εἰ in the *protasis* when the verb is in the subjunctive; εἰ with ἄν forming ἐάν, ἄν, or ἤν. (See 1299, 2.) The simple εἰ is used with the indicative and optative. The same adverb ἄν is used in the *apodosis* with the optative, and also with the past tenses of the indicative when it is implied that the condition is not fulfilled.

1383. 1. The negative adverb of the protasis is regularly μή, that of the apodosis is οὐ.

2. When οὐ stands in a protasis, it generally belongs to some particular word (as in οὐ πολλοί, *few*, οὔ φημι, *I deny*), and not to the protasis as a whole; as ἐάν τε σὺ καὶ Ἄνυτος οὐ φῆτε ἐάν τε φῆτε, *both if you and Anytus deny it and if you admit it*, P. *Ap.* 25[b].

1384. 1. The supposition contained in a protasis may be either *particular* or *general*. A particular supposition refers to a definite act or to several definite acts, supposed to occur at some definite time or times; as *if he (now) has this, he will give it; if he had it, he gave it; if he had had the power, he would have helped me; if he shall receive it* (or *if he receives it*), *he will give it; if he should receive it, he would give it.* A general supposition refers indefinitely to any act or acts of a given class, which may be supposed to occur or to have occurred at any time; as *if ever he receives anything, he (always) gives it; if ever he received anything, he (always) gave it; if (on any occasion) he had had the power, he would (always) have helped me; if ever any one shall* (or *should*) *wish to go, he will* (or *would*) *always be permitted.*

2. Although this distinction is seen in all classes of conditions (as the examples show), it is only in the present and past conditions which do not imply non-fulfilment, *i.e.* in those of class I. (below), that the distinction affects the *construction*. Here, however, we have two classes of conditions which contain only general suppositions.

CLASSIFICATION OF CONDITIONAL SENTENCES.

1385. The classification of conditional sentences is based partly on the time to which the supposition refers, partly on what is implied with regard to the fulfilment of the condition, and partly on the distinction between particular and general suppositions explained in 1384.

1386. Conditional sentences have *four* classes, two (I. and II.) containing present and past suppositions, and two (III. and IV.) containing future suppositions. Class I. has two forms, one (*a*) with chiefly particular suppositions (present and past), the other (*b*) with only general suppositions (1. present, 2. past).

1387. We have thus the following forms: —

I. Present and past suppositions implying nothing as to fulfilment of condition:

(*a*) **Chiefly Particular**: (*protasis*) εἰ with indicative; (*apodosis*) any form of the verb. Εἰ πράσσει τοῦτο, καλῶς ἔχει, *if he is doing this, it is well.* Εἰ ἔπραξε τοῦτο, καλῶς ἔχει, *if he did this, it is well.* (See 1390.) — In Latin: *si hoc facit, bene est.*

(*b*) **General**:

1. (*prot.*) ἐάν with subjunctive; (*apod.*) present indicative. Ἐάν τις κλέπτῃ, κολάζεται, *if any one (ever) steals, he is (always) punished.* (See 1393, 1.)

2. (*prot.*) εἰ with optative; (*apod.*) imperfect indicative. Εἴ τις κλέπτοι, ἐκολάζετο, *if any one ever stole, he was (always) punished.* (See 1393, 2.) — For the Latin, see 1388.

II. Present and past suppositions implying that the condition is not fulfilled:

(*protasis*) εἰ with past tense of indicative; (*apodosis*) past tense of indicative with ἄν. Εἰ ἔπραξε τοῦτο, καλῶς ἂν ἔσχεν, *if he had done this, it would have been well.* Εἰ ἔπρασσε τοῦτο, καλῶς ἂν εἶχεν, *if he were doing this, it would* (*now*) *be well,* or *if he had done this, it would have been well.* (See 1397.)

In Latin: *si hoc faceret, bene esset* (present); *si hoc fecisset, bene fuisset* (past).

III. Future suppositions in more vivid form:

(*prot.*) ἐάν with subjunctive (sometimes εἰ with future indicative); (*apod.*) any future form. Ἐὰν πράσσῃ (or πράξῃ) τοῦτο, καλῶς ἕξει, *if he shall do this* (or *if he does this*), *it will be well* (sometimes also εἰ πράξει τοῦτο, etc.). (See 1403 and 1405.)

In Latin: *si hoc faciet* (or *fecerit*), *bene erit.*

IV. Future suppositions in less vivid form:

(*prot.*) εἰ with optative; (*apod.*) optative with ἄν. Εἰ πράσσοι (or πράξειε) τοῦτο, καλῶς ἂν ἔχοι, *if he should do this, it would be well.* (See 1408.)

In Latin: *si hoc faciat, bene sit.*

1388. N. The Latin commonly agrees with the English in not marking the distinction between the general and the particular present and past conditions by different forms, and uses the indicative in both alike. Occasionally even the Greek does the same (1395).

1389. N. In external form (ἐάν with the subjunctive) the general present condition agrees with the more vivid future condition. But in sense there is a much closer connection between the general and the particular present condition, which in most languages (and sometimes even in Greek) coincide also in form (1388). On the other hand, ἐάν with the subjunctive in a future condition agrees generally in sense with εἰ and the *future* indicative (1405), and is never interchangeable with εἰ and the *present* indicative.

I. PRESENT AND PAST CONDITIONS *WITH NOTHING IMPLIED.*

(*a*) SIMPLE SUPPOSITIONS, CHIEFLY PARTICULAR.

1390. When the protasis *simply states* a present or

past particular supposition, implying nothing as to the fulfilment of the condition, it has the indicative with εἰ. Any form of the verb may stand in the apodosis. *E.g.*

Εἰ ἡσυχίαν Φίλιππος ἄγει, οὐκέτι δεῖ λέγειν, *if Philip is keeping peace (with us), we need talk no longer*, D. 8, 5. Εἰ ἐγὼ Φαῖδρον ἀγνοῶ, καὶ ἐμαυτοῦ ἐπιλέλησμαι· ἀλλὰ γὰρ οὐδέτερα ἐστι τούτων, *if I do not know Phaedrus, I have forgotten myself; but neither of these is so*, P. *Phdr.* 228[a]. Εἰ θεοῦ ἦν, οὐκ ἦν αἰσχροκερδής, *if he was the son of a God, he was not avaricious*, P. *Rp.* 408[c]. Ἀλλ' εἰ δοκεῖ, πλέωμεν, *but if it pleases you, let us sail*, S. *Ph.* 526. Κάκιστ' ἀπολοίμην, Ξανθίαν εἰ μὴ φιλῶ, *may I die most wretchedly, if I do not love Xanthias*, Ar. *R.* 579.

1391. N. Even the future indicative can stand in a protasis of this class if it expresses merely a *present* intention or necessity that something shall hereafter be done; as αἶρε πλῆκτρον, εἰ μαχεῖ, *raise your spur, if you are going to fight*, Ar. *Av.* 759. Here εἰ μέλλεις μάχεσθαι would be the more common expression in prose. It is important to notice that a future of this kind could never be changed to the subjunctive, like the ordinary future in protasis (1405).

1392. N. For present or past conditions containing a potential indicative or optative (with ἄν), see 1421, 3.

(*b*) Present and Past General Suppositions.

1393. In general suppositions, the apodosis expresses a *customary* or *repeated* action or a *general truth* in present or past time, and the protasis refers in a general way to any of a class of acts.

1. Present general suppositions have ἐάν with the subjunctive in the protasis, and the present indicative (or some other present form denoting repetition) in the apodosis. *E.g.*

Ἢν ἐγγὺς ἔλθῃ θάνατος, οὐδεὶς βούλεται θνῄσκειν, *if death comes near, no one is (ever) willing to die*, E. *Al.* 671. Ἅπας λόγος, ἂν ἀπῇ τὰ πράγματα, μάταιόν τι φαίνεται καὶ κενόν, *all speech, if deeds are wanting, appears a vain and empty thing*, D. 2, 12.

2. Past general suppositions have εἰ with the optative in the protasis, and the imperfect indicative (or some other form denoting past repetition) in the apodosis. *E.g.*

Εἴ τινας θορυβουμένους αἴσθοιτο, κατασβεννύναι τὴν ταραχὴν ἐπειρᾶτο, *if he saw any falling into disorder* (or *whenever he saw*, etc.), *he (always) tried to quiet the confusion*, X. *C.* 5, 3[55]. Εἴ τις ἀντείποι, εὐθὺς τεθνήκει, *if any one refused, he was immediately put to death*, T. 8, 66. This construction occurs only once in Homer.

1394. N. The gnomic aorist, which is a primary tense (1268), can always be used here in the apodosis with a dependent subjunctive; as ἤν τις παραβαίνῃ, ζημίαν αὐτοῖς ἐπέθεσαν, *if any one transgresses, they (always) impose a penalty on him*, X. *C.* 1, 2[2].

1395. N. The indicative is occasionally used in the place of the subjunctive or optative in general suppositions; that is, these sentences may follow the construction of ordinary present and past suppositions (1390), as in Latin and English; as εἴ τις δύο ἢ καὶ πλέους τις ἡμέρας λογίζεται, μάταιός ἐστιν, *if any one counts on two or even more days, he is a fool*, S. *Tr.* 944.

1396. N. Here, as in future conditions (1406), εἰ (without ἄν) is sometimes used with the subjunctive in poetry. In Homer this is the more frequent form in *general* conditions.

II. PRESENT AND PAST CONDITIONS *WITH SUPPOSITION CONTRARY TO FACT.*

1397. When the protasis states a present or past supposition, implying that the condition *is not* or *was not fulfilled*, the secondary tenses of the indicative are used in both protasis and apodosis. The apodosis has the adverb ἄν.

The imperfect here refers to present time or to an act as going on or repeated in past time, the aorist to a simple occurrence in past time, and the (rare) pluperfect to an act completed in past or present time. *E.g.*

Ταῦτα οὐκ ἂν ἐδύναντο ποιεῖν, εἰ μὴ διαίτῃ μετρίᾳ ἐχρῶντο, *they would not be able (as they are) to do this, if they did not lead an abstemious life*, X. *C.* 1, 2[16]. Πολὺ ἂν θαυμαστότερον ἦν, εἰ ἐτιμῶντο, *it would be far more wonderful, if they were honored*, P. *Rp.* 489[b]. Εἰ ἦσαν ἄνδρες ἀγαθοί, ὡς σὺ φῄς, οὐκ ἄν ποτε ταῦτα ἔπασχον, *if they had been good men, as you say, they would never have suffered these things* (referring to several cases), P. *G.* 516[e]. Καὶ ἴσως ἂν ἀπέθανον, εἰ μὴ ἡ ἀρχὴ κατελύθη, *and perhaps I should have perished, if the government had not been put down*, P. *Ap.* 32[d]. Εἰ ἀπεκρίνω, ἱκανῶς ἂν ἤδη ἐμεμαθήκη, *if you had answered, I should already have learned enough (which now I have not done)*, P. *Euthyph.* 14^c. Εἰ μὴ ὑμεῖς ἤλθετε, ἐπορευόμεθα ἂν ἐπὶ τὸν βασιλέα, *if you had not come* (aor.), *we should now be on our way* (impf.) *to the King*, X. *A.* 2, 1^4.

1398. N. In Homer the imperfect in this class of sentences is always past (see *Il.* 7, 273; 8, 130); and the present optative is used where the Attic would have the imperfect referring to *present* time; as εἰ μέν τις τὸν ὄνειρον ἄλλος ἔνισπεν, ψεῦδός κεν φαῖμεν καὶ νοσφιζοίμεθα μᾶλλον, *if any other had told this dream* (1397), *we should call it a lie and rather turn away from it*, *Il.* 2, 80: see 24, 222.

1399. N. In Homer the optative with κέ is occasionally past in apodosis; as καί νύ κεν ἔνθ' ἀπόλοιτο Αἰνείας, εἰ μὴ νόησε Ἀφροδίτη, *and now Aeneas would there have perished, had not Aphrodite perceived him*, *Il.* 5, 311. (Here ἀπώλετο would be the regular form in Homer, as in other Greek.)

Homer has also a past potential optative: see *Il.* 5, 85.

1400. 1. The imperfects ἔδει, χρῆν or ἐχρῆν, ἐξῆν, εἰκὸς ἦν, and others denoting *obligation, propriety, possibility*, and the like, are often used with the infinitive to form an apodosis implying the non-fulfilment of a condition. Ἄν is not used here, as these phrases simply express *in other words* what is usually expressed by the indicative with ἄν.

Thus, ἔδει σε τοῦτον φιλεῖν, *you ought to love him (but do not)*, or *you ought to have loved him (but did not)*, is substantially equivalent to *you would love him*, or *would have loved him* (ἐφίλεις ἂν τοῦτον), *if you did your duty* (τὰ δέοντα). So ἐξῆν σοι τοῦτο ποιῆσαι, *you might have done this (but you did not do it)*; εἰκὸς ἦν σε τοῦτο ποιῆσαι, *you would properly* (εἰκότως) *have done this*. The actual apodosis is here always in the infinitive, and the reality of the action of the infinitive is generally denied.

2. When the present infinitive is used, the construction refers to the present or to continued or repeated action in the past; when the aorist is used, it refers to the past. *E.g.*

Τούσδε μὴ ζῆν ἔδει, *these ought not to be living (as they are)*, S. *Ph.* 418. Μένειν γὰρ ἐξῆν, *for he might have stood his ground (but did not)*, D. 3, 17. Θανεῖν σε χρῆν πάρος τέκνων, *you ought to have died before your children*, E. *And.* 1208. Εἰ ἐβούλετο δίκαιος εἶναι, ἐξῆν αὐτῷ μισθῶσαι τὸν οἶκον, *he might have let the house, if he had wished to be just*, L. 32, 23.

1401. N. When the actual apodosis is in the verb of *obligation*, etc., ἔδει ἄν can be used; as εἰ τὰ δέοντα οὗτοι συνεβούλευσαν, οὐδὲν ἂν ὑμᾶς νῦν ἔδει βουλεύεσθαι, *if these men had given you the advice you needed, there would now be no need of your deliberating*, D. 4. 1.

1402. 1. Other imperfects, especially ἐβουλόμην, sometimes take the infinitive without ἄν on the same principle with ἔδει etc.: as ἐβουλόμην οὐκ ἐρίζειν ἐνθάδε, *I would I were not contending here* (*as I am*), or *I would not be contending here*, Ar. *R.* 866.

2. So ὤφελον or ὤφελλον, *ought*, aorist and imperfect of ὀφέλλω, *owe* (epic for ὀφείλω), in Homer; whence comes the use of ὤφελον in wishes (1512); as ὤφελε Κῦρος ζῆν, *would that Cyrus were alive*, X. *A.* 2, 1[4].

3. So ἔμελλον with the infinitive; as φθίσεσθαι ἔμελλον, εἰ μὴ ἔειπες, *I should have perished* (*was about to perish*), *if thou hadst not spoken*, *Od.* 13, 383. So D. 19, 159.

III. FUTURE CONDITIONS, MORE VIVID FORM.

Subjunctive in Protasis with Future Apodosis.

1403. When a supposed future case is stated *distinctly* and *vividly* (as in English, *if I shall go*, or *if I go*), the protasis has the subjunctive with ἐάν (epic εἴ κε), and the apodosis has the future indicative or some other form of future time. *E.g.*

Εἰ μέν κεν Μενέλαον Ἀλέξανδρος καταπέφνῃ, αὐτὸς ἔπειθ' Ἑλένην ἐχέτω καὶ κτήματα πάντα, *if Alexander shall slay Menelaus, then let him have Helen and all the goods himself*, *Il.* 3, 281. Ἄν τις ἀνθιστῆται, πειρασόμεθα χειροῦσθαι, *if any one shall stand opposed to us, we shall try to overcome him*, X. *A.* 7, 3[11]. Ἐὰν οὖν ἴῃς νῦν, πότε ἔσει οἴκοι; *if therefore you go now, when will you be at home?* X. *C.* 5, 3[27].

1404. N. The older English forms *if he shall go* and *if he go* both express the force of the Greek subjunctive and future indicative in protasis; but the ordinary modern English uses *if he goes* even when the time is clearly future.

1405. The future indicative with εἰ is very often used for the subjunctive in future conditions, as a still more vivid form of expression, especially in appeals to the feelings, and in threats and warnings. *E.g.*

Εἰ μὴ καθέξεις γλῶσσαν, ἔσται σοι κακά, *if you do not* (*shall not*) *restrain your tongue, you will have trouble*, E. frag. 5. This common use of the future must not be confounded with that of 1391.

1406. N. In Homer εἰ (without ἄν or κέ) is sometimes used with the subjunctive in future conditions, apparently in the same sense as εἴ κε or ἤν; as εἰ δὲ νῆ' ἐθέλῃ ὀλέσαι, *but if he shall wish to destroy our ship*, *Od.* 12, 348. This is more common in general conditions in Homer (see 1396). The same use of εἰ for ἐάν is found occasionally even in Attic poetry.

1407. N. For the Homeric subjunctive with κέ in the apodosis of a future condition, see 1305, 2.

IV. FUTURE CONDITIONS, LESS VIVID FORM.

Optative in both Protasis and Apodosis.

1408. When a supposed future case is stated in a *less distinct* and *vivid* form (as in English, *if I should go*), the protasis has the optative with εἰ, and the apodosis has the optative with ἄν. *E.g.*

Εἴης φορητὸς οὐκ ἄν, εἰ πράσσοις καλῶς, *you would not be endurable, if you should be in prosperity*, A. *Pr.* 979. Οὐ πολλὴ ἂν ἀλογία εἴη, εἰ φοβοῖτο τὸν θάνατον ὁ τοιοῦτος; *would it not be a great absurdity, if such a man should fear death?* P. *Ph.* 68[b]. Οἶκος δ' αὐτός, εἰ φθογγὴν λάβοι, σαφέστατ' ἂν λέξειεν, *but the house itself, if it should find a voice, would speak most plainly*, A. *Ag.* 37.

1409. The optative with ἄν in apodosis is the potential optative: see 1329.

1410. N. The *future* optative cannot be used in protasis or apodosis, except in indirect discourse representing the future indicative after a past tense (see the second example under 1497, 2).

1411. N. Εἴ κε is sometimes found with the optative in Homer, in place of the simple εἰ (1408); as εἰ δέ κεν Ἄργος ἱκοίμεθ', . . . γαμβρός κέν μοι ἔοι, *and if we should ever come to Argos, he would be my son-in-law*, *Il.* 9, 141.

1412. N. For the Homeric optative used like the past tenses of the indicative in unreal conditions, see 1398 and 1399.

PECULIAR FORMS OF CONDITIONAL SENTENCES.

Ellipsis and Substitution in Protasis or Apodosis.

1413. The protasis sometimes is not expressed in its regular form with εἰ or ἐάν, but is contained in a participle, or implied in an adverb or some other part of the sentence. When a participle represents the protasis, its *tense* is always that in which the verb itself would have stood in the indicative, subjunctive, or optative,—the present (as usual) including the imperfect. *E.g.*

Πῶς δίκης οὔσης ὁ Ζεὺς οὐκ ἀπόλωλεν; *how is it that Zeus has not been destroyed, if Justice exists?* (εἰ δίκη ἐστίν), Ar. *N.* 904. Σὺ δὲ κλύων εἴσει τάχα, *but you will soon know, if you listen* (= ἐὰν κλύῃς), Ar. *Av.* 1390. Ἀπολοῦμαι μὴ τοῦτο μαθών, *I shall be ruined unless I learn this* (ἐὰν μὴ μάθω). Τοιαῦτά τἂν γυναιξὶ συνναίων ἔχοις, *such things would you have to endure if you should dwell among women* (i.e. εἰ συνναίοις), A. *Se.* 195. Ἠπίστησεν ἄν τις ἀκούσας, *any one would have disbelieved (such a thing) if he had heard it* (i.e. εἰ ἤκουσεν), T. 7, 28. Μαμμᾶν δ' ἂν αἰτήσαντος (sc. σοῦ) ἧκόν σοι φέρων ἂν ἄρτον, *and if you (ever) cried for food* (εἰ αἰτήσειας, 1393, 2), *I used to come to you with bread* (1296), Ar. *N.* 1383.

Διά γε ὑμᾶς αὐτοὺς πάλαι ἂν ἀπολώλειτε, *if it had depended on yourselves, you would long ago have been ruined*, D. 18, 49. Οὕτω γὰρ οὐκέτι τοῦ λοιποῦ πάσχοιμεν ἂν κακῶς, *for in that case we should no longer suffer harm* (the protasis being in οὕτω), X. *A.* 1, 1[10]. Οὐδ' ἂν δικαίως ἐς κακὸν πέσοιμί τι, *nor should I justly* (i.e. *if I had justice*) *fall into any trouble*, S. *An.* 240.

1414. 1. There is a (probably unconscious) suppression of the verb of the protasis in several phrases introduced by εἰ μή, *except. E.g.*

Τίς τοι ἄλλος ὁμοῖος, εἰ μὴ Πάτροκλος; *who else is like you, except Patroclus* (i.e. *unless it is P.*)? *Il.* 17, 475. Εἰ μὴ διὰ τὸν πρύτανιν, ἐνέπεσεν ἄν, *had it not been for the Prytanis (except for the P.), he would have been thrown in (to the Pit)*, P. *G.* 516[e].

2. The protasis or the apodosis, or both, may be suppressed with the Homeric ὡς εἰ or ὡς εἴ τε; as τῶν νέες ὠκεῖαι ὡς εἰ πτερὸν ἠὲ νόημα, *their ships are swift as a wing or thought (as they would be if they were*, etc.), *Od.* 7, 36.

For the double ellipsis in ὥσπερ ἂν εἰ, see 1313.

1415. N. In neither of the cases of 1414 is it probable that any definite verb was in the speaker's mind.

1416. N. The apodosis is sometimes entirely suppressed for rhetorical effect; as εἰ μὲν δώσουσι γέρας, *if they shall give me a prize,—very well*, *Il.* 1, 135; cf. 1, 580.

1417. N. Εἰ δὲ μή without a verb often has the meaning *otherwise*, even where the clause would not be negative if completed, or where the verb if supplied would be a subjunctive; as μὴ ποιήσῃς ταῦτα· εἰ δὲ μή, αἰτίαν ἕξεις, *do not do this; otherwise (if you do not do what I say) you will be blamed*, X. *An.* 7, 1[8].

1418. The apodosis may be expressed by an infinitive or participle in indirect discourse, each tense representing its own tenses of the indicative or optative (1280; 1285). If the finite verb in the apodosis would have taken ἄν, this particle is used with the infinitive or participle. *E.g.*

Ἡγοῦμαι, εἰ τοῦτο ποιεῖτε, πάντα καλῶς ἔχειν, *I believe that, if you are doing this, all is well;* ἡγοῦμαι, ἐὰν τοῦτο ποιῆτε, πάντα καλῶς ἕξειν, *I believe that, if you (shall) do this, all will be well;* οἶδα ὑμᾶς, ἐὰν ταῦτα γένηται, εὖ πράξοντας, *I know that you will prosper if this is (shall be) done.* For examples of the infinitive and participle with ἄν, see 1308.

1419. The apodosis may be expressed in an infinitive not in indirect discourse (1271), especially one depending on a verb of *wishing, commanding, advising,* etc., from which the infinitive receives a future meaning. *E.g.*

Βούλεται ἐλθεῖν ἐὰν τοῦτο γένηται, *he wishes to go if this (shall) be done;* κελεύω ὑμᾶς ἐὰν δύνησθε ἀπελθεῖν, *I command you to depart if you can.* For the principle of indirect discourse which appears in the *protasis* here after past tenses, see 1502, 1.

1420. N. Sometimes the apodosis is merely implied in the context, and in such cases εἰ or ἐάν is often to be translated *supposing that, in case that, if perchance,* or *if haply. E.g.*

Ἄκουσον καὶ ἐμοῦ, ἐάν σοι ταὐτὰ δοκῇ, *hear me also, in case the same shall please you* (i.e. *that then you may assent to it*), P. *Rp.* 358[b]. So πρὸς τὴν πόλιν, εἰ ἐπιβοηθοῖεν, ἐχώρουν, *they marched towards the city, in case they (the citizens) should rush out* (i.e. *to meet them if they should rush out*), T. 6, 100. On this principle we must explain αἴ κέν πως βούλεται, *if haply he may wish* (i.e. *in hope that he may wish*), *Il.* 1, 66; αἴ κ' ἐθέλῃσθα, *Od.* 3, 92; and similar passages. For this construction, both in Homer and elsewhere, see *Moods and Tenses,* §§ 486–491.

Mixed Constructions.—Δέ in Apodosis.

1421. The protasis and apodosis sometimes belong to different forms.

1. Especially any tense of the indicative with εἰ in the protasis may be followed by a potential optative with ἄν in the apodosis. *E.g.*

Εἰ κατ' οὐρανοῦ εἰλήλουθας, οὐκ ἂν θεοῖσι μαχοίμην, *if you have come down from heaven, I would not fight against the Gods,* *Il.* 6, 128. Εἰ νῦν γε δυστυχοῦμεν, πῶς τἀναντί' ἂν πράττοντες οὐ σῳζοίμεθ' ἄν; *if we are now unfortunate, how could we help being saved if we should do the opposite?* Ar. *R.* 1449 (here πράττοντες = εἰ πράττοιμεν). Εἰ οὗτοι ὀρθῶς ἀπέστησαν, ὑμεῖς ἂν οὐ χρεὼν ἄρχοιτε, *if these had a right to secede, you cannot (could not) possibly hold your power rightfully,* T. 3, 40.

2. Sometimes a subjunctive or a future indicative in the protasis has a potential optative in the apodosis. *E.g.*

Ἢν ἐφῇς μοι, λέξαιμ' ἄν, *if you (will) permit me, I would fain speak,* S. *El.* 554; οὐδὲ γὰρ ἂν πολλαὶ γέφυραι ὦσιν, ἔχοιμεν ἂν ὅποι φυγόντες σωθῶμεν, *for not even if there shall be many bridges, could we find a place to fly to and be saved,* X. *A.* 2, 4[19]; ἀδικοίημεν ἄν, εἰ μὴ ἀποδώσω, *I should be guilty of wrong, should I (shall I) not restore her,* E. *Hel.* 1010.

3. A potential optative (with ἄν) may express a present condition, and a potential indicative (with ἄν) may express a present or past condition; as εἴπερ ἄλλῳ τῳ πειθοίμην ἄν, καὶ σοὶ πείθομαι, *if there is any man whom I would trust, I trust you,* P. *Pr.* 329[b], εἰ τοῦτο ἰσχυρὸν ἦν ἂν τούτῳ τεκμήριον, κἀμοὶ γενέσθω τεκμήριον, *if this would have been a strong proof for him, so let it be also a proof for me,* D. 49, 58.

1422. The apodosis is sometimes introduced by δέ, ἀλλά, or αὐτάρ, which cannot be translated in English. *E.g.*

Εἰ δέ κε μὴ δώωσιν, ἐγὼ δέ κεν αὐτὸς ἕλωμαι, *but if they do not give her up, then I will take her myself,* *Il.* 1, 137.

Εἰ after Verbs of *Wondering*, etc.

1423. Some verbs expressing *wonder, delight, contentment, disappointment, indignation,* etc. are followed by a protasis with εἰ where a causal sentence would often seem more natural. *E.g.*

Θαυμάζω δ' ἔγωγε εἰ μηδεὶς ὑμῶν μήτ' ἐνθυμεῖται μήτ' ὀργίζεται, *and I wonder that no one of you is either concerned or angry* (lit. *if no one of you is,* etc., *I wonder*), D. 4, 43; ἀγανακτῶ εἰ ἃ νοῶ μὴ οἷός τ' εἰμὶ εἰπεῖν, *I am indignant that* (or *if*) *I am not able to say what I mean,* P. *Lach.* 194[a]. See also 1502, 2, for the principle of indirect discourse applied to these sentences.

1424. N. Such verbs are especially θαυμάζω, αἰσχύνομαι, ἀγαπάω, and ἀγανακτέω, with δεινόν ἐστιν. They sometimes take ὅτι, *because,* and a causal sentence (1505).

VII. RELATIVE AND TEMPORAL SENTENCES.

1425. The principles of construction of relative clauses include all *temporal* clauses. Those introduced by ἕως, πρίν, and other particles meaning *until*, have special peculiarities, and are therefore treated separately (1463–1474).

Relative clauses may be introduced by relative pronouns or adverbs.

1426. The antecedent of a relative is either *definite* or *indefinite*. It is definite when the relative refers to a definite person or thing, or to some definite time, place, or manner; it is indefinite when no such definite person, thing, time, place, or manner is referred to. Both definite and indefinite antecedents may be either expressed or understood. *E.g.*

(*Definite.*) Ταῦτα ἃ ἔχω ὁρᾷς, *you see these things which I have;* or ἃ ἔχω ὁρᾷς. Ὅτε ἐβούλετο ἦλθεν, (*once*) *when he wished, he came.*

(*Indefinite.*) Πάντα ἃ ἂν βούλωνται ἕξουσιν, *they will have everything which they may want;* or ἃ ἂν βούλωνται ἕξουσιν, *they will have whatever they may want.* Ὅταν ἔλθῃ, τοῦτο πράξω, *when he shall come* (or *when he comes*), *I will do this.* Ὅτε βούλοιτο, τοῦτο ἔπρασσεν, *whenever he wished, he* (*always*) *did this.* Ὡς ἂν εἴπω, ποιῶμεν, *as I shall direct, let us act.* Ἃ ἔχει βούλομαι λαβεῖν, *I want to take whatever he has.*

DEFINITE ANTECEDENT.

1427. A relative *as such* has no effect on the mood of the following verb. A relative with a definite antecedent therefore may take the indicative (with οὐ for its negative) or any other construction which could occur in an independent sentence. *E.g.*

Τίς ἔσθ' ὁ χῶρος δῆτ' ἐν ᾧ βεβήκαμεν; *what is the place to which we have come?* S. *O. C.* 52. Ἕως ἐστὶ καιρός, ἀντιλάβεσθε τῶν πραγμάτων, (*now*) *while there is an opportunity, take hold of the business,* D. 1, 20. Τοῦτο οὐκ ἐποίησεν, ἐν ᾧ τὸν δῆμον ἐτίμησεν ἄν, *he did not do this, in which he might have honored the people,* D. 21, 69. So ὃ μὴ γένοιτο, *and may this not happen,* D. 27, 67.

INDEFINITE ANTECEDENT. — CONDITIONAL RELATIVE.

1428. 1. A relative clause with an indefinite antecedent has a conditional force, and is called a conditional relative clause. Its negative is always μή.

2. Relative words, like εἰ, *if*, take ἄν before the subjunctive. (See 1299, 2.) With ὅτε, ὁπότε, ἐπεί, and ἐπειδή, ἄν forms ὅταν, ὁπόταν, ἐπάν or ἐπήν (Ionic ἐπεάν), and ἐπειδάν. Ἅ with ἄν may form ἅν. In Homer we generally find ὅτε κε etc. (like εἴ κε, 1403), or ὅτε etc. alone (1437).

1429. Conditional relative sentences have *four* classes, two (I. II.) containing *present* and *past*, and two (III. IV.) containing *future* conditions, which correspond to those of ordinary protasis (1386). Class I. has two forms, one (*a*) with chiefly particular suppositions, the other (*b*) with only general suppositions.

1430. I. (*a*) Present or past condition *simply stated*, with the indicative, — *chiefly* in particular suppositions (1390). *E.g.*

Ὅ τι βούλεται δώσω, *I will give him whatever he (now) wishes* (like εἴ τι βούλεται, δώσω, *if he now wishes anything, I will give it*). Ἃ μὴ οἶδα, οὐδὲ οἴομαι εἰδέναι, *what I do not know, I do not even think I know* (like εἴ τινα μὴ οἶδα, *if there are any things which I do not know*), P. *Ap.* 21[d]; οὓς μὴ εὕρισκον, κενοτάφιον αὐτοῖς ἐποίησαν, *for any whom they did not find* (= εἴ τινας μὴ εὕρισκον), *they raised a cenotaph*, X. 6, 4[9].

1431. (*b*) 1. Present general condition, depending on a present form denoting repetition, with subjunctive (1393, 1).

2. Past general condition, depending on a past form denoting repetition, with optative (1393, 2). *E.g.*

Ὅ τι ἂν βούληται δίδωμι, *I (always) give him whatever he wants* (like ἐάν τι βούληται, *if he ever wants anything*); ὅ τι βούλοιτο ἐδίδουν, *I (always) gave him whatever he wanted* (like εἴ τι βούλοιτο). Συμμαχεῖν τούτοις ἐθέλουσιν ἅπαντες, οὓς ἂν ὁρῶσι παρεσκευασμένους, *all wish to be allies of those whom they see prepared*, D. 4, 6. Ἡνίκ' ἂν οἴκοι γένωνται, δρῶσιν οὐκ ἀνασχετά, *when they get home, they do things unbearable*, Ar. *Pa.* 1179. Οὓς μὲν ἴδοι εὐτάκτως ἰόντας, τίνες τε εἶεν ἠρώτα, καὶ ἐπεὶ πύθοιτο ἐπῄνει, *he (always) asked those whom he saw (at any time) marching in good order, who they were; and when he learned, he praised them*, X. *C.* 5, 3[55]. Ἐπειδὴ δὲ ἀνοιχθείη, εἰσῄειμεν παρὰ τὸν Σωκράτη, *and (each morning) when the prison was opened, we went in to Socrates*, P. *Ph.* 59[d].

1432. N. The indicative sometimes takes the place of the subjunctive or optative here, as in other general suppositions (1395). This occurs especially with ὅστις, which itself expresses the same idea of indefiniteness which ὅς with the subjunctive or optative usually expresses; as ὅστις μὴ τῶν ἀρίστων ἅπτεται βουλευμάτων, κάκιστος εἶναι δοκεῖ, *whoever does not cling to the best counsels seems to be most base*, S. *An.* 178. (Here ὃς ἂν μὴ ἅπτηται would be the common expression.)

1433. II. Present or past condition stated so as to imply that the condition *is not* or *was not* fulfilled (*supposition contrary to fact*), with the secondary tenses of indicative (1397). *E.g.*

Ἃ μὴ ἐβούλετο δοῦναι, οὐκ ἂν ἔδωκεν, *he would not have given what he had not wished to give* (like εἴ τινα μὴ ἐβούλετο δοῦναι, οὐκ ἂν ἔδωκεν, *if he had not wished to give certain things, he would not have given them*). Οὐκ ἂν ἐπεχειροῦμεν πράττειν ἃ μὴ ἠπιστάμεθα, *we should not (then) be undertaking to do (as we now are) things which we did not understand* (like εἴ τινα μὴ ἠπιστάμεθα, *if there were any things which we did not understand*, the whole belonging to a supposition not realized), P. *Ch.* 171[e]. So ὃν γῆρας ἔτετμεν, *Od.* 1, 218.

This case occurs much less frequently than the others.

1434. III. Future condition in the *more vivid* form, with ἄν and the subjunctive (1403). *E.g.*

Ὅ τι ἂν βούληται, δώσω, *I will give him whatever he may wish* (like ἐάν τι βούληται, δώσω, *if he shall wish anything, I will give it*). Ὅταν μὴ σθένω, πεπαύσομαι, *when I (shall) have no more strength, I shall cease*, S. *An.* 91. Ἀλόχους καὶ νήπια τέκνα ἄξομεν ἐν νήεσσιν, ἐπὴν πτολίεθρον ἕλωμεν, *we will bear off their wives and young children in our ships, when we (shall) have taken the city*, *Il.* 4, 238.

1435. N. The future indicative cannot be substituted for the subjunctive here, as it can in common protasis (1405).

1436. IV. Future condition in the *less vivid* form, with the optative (1408). *E.g.*

Ὅ τι βούλοιτο, δοίην ἄν, *I should give him whatever he might wish* (like εἴ τι βούλοιτο δοίην ἄν, *if he should wish anything, I should give it*). Πεινῶν φάγοι ἂν ὁπότε βούλοιτο, *if he were hungry, he would eat whenever he might wish* (like εἴ ποτε βούλοιτο, *if he should ever wish*), X. *M.* 2, 1[18].

1437. Conditional relative sentences have most of the peculiarities and irregularities of common protasis. Thus, the protasis and apodosis may have different forms (1421); the relative without ἄν or κέ is sometimes found in poetry with the subjunctive (like εἰ for ἐάν or εἴ κε, 1396; 1406), especially in general conditions in Homer; the relative (like εἰ, 1411) in Homer may take κέ or ἄν with the optative; the relative clause may depend on an infinitive, participle, or other construction (1418; 1419); and the conjunction δέ may connect the relative clause to the antecedent clause (1422).

1438. Homeric similes often have the subjunctive with ὡς ὅτε (occasionally ὡς ὅτ' ἄν), sometimes with ὡς or ὥς τε; as ὡς ὅτε κινήσῃ Ζέφυρος βαθὺ λήιον, *as (happens) when the west wind moves a deep grain-field, Il.* 2, 147; ὡς γυνὴ κλαίῃσι . . . ὣς Ὀδυσεὺς δάκρυον εἶβεν, *as a wife weeps*, etc., *so did Ulysses shed tears, Od.* 8, 523.

ASSIMILATION IN CONDITIONAL RELATIVE CLAUSES.

1439. When a conditional relative clause expressing either a future or a general supposition depends on a subjunctive or optative, it regularly takes the same mood by *assimilation*. *E.g.*

Ἐάν τινες οἳ ἂν δύνωνται τοῦτο ποιῶσι, καλῶς ἕξει, *if any who may be able shall do this, it will be well;* εἴ τινες οἳ δύναιντο τοῦτο ποιοῖεν, καλῶς ἂν ἔχοι, *if any who should be* (or *were*) *able should do this, it would be well.* Εἴθε πάντες οἳ δύναιντο τοῦτο ποιοῖεν *O that all who may be* (or *were*) *able would do this.* (Here the optative ποιοῖεν [1507] makes οἳ δύναιντο preferable to οἳ ἂν δύνωνται, which would express the same idea.) Ἐπειδὰν ὧν ἂν πρίηται κύριος γένηται, *when* (in any case) *he becomes master of what he has bought*, D. 18, 47. Ὡς ἀπόλοιτο καὶ ἄλλος, ὅ τις τοιαῦτά γε ῥέζοι, *O that any other might likewise perish who should do the like, Od.* 1, 47. Τεθναίην ὅτε μοι μηκέτι ταῦτα μέλοι, *may I die whenever I shall no longer care for these* (ὅταν μέλῃ would express the same idea), Mimn. 1, 2. So in Latin: Injurias quas ferre *nequeas* defugiendo *relinquas*.

1440. Likewise, when a conditional relative sentence depends on a secondary tense of the indicative implying the non-fulfilment of a condition, it takes by assimilation a similar form. *E.g.*

Εἴ τινες οἳ ἐδύναντο τοῦτο ἔπραξαν, καλῶς ἂν εἶχεν, *if any who had been able had done this, it would have been well.* Εἰ ἐν ἐκείνῃ τῇ φωνῇ τε καὶ τῷ τρόπῳ ἔλεγον ἐν οἷς ἐτεθράμμην, *if I were speaking to you in the dialect and in the manner in which I had been brought up* (all introduced by εἰ ξένος ἐτύγχανον ὤν, *if I happened to be a foreigner*), P. *Ap*. 17[d]. So in Latin: Si solos eos *diceres* miseros quibus moriendum *esset*, neminem tu quidem eorum qui *viverent exciperes*.

1441. N. All clauses which come under this principle of assimilation belong (as conditional forms) equally under 1434, 1436, 1431, or 1433. This principle often decides which form shall be used in future conditions (1270, 2).

RELATIVE CLAUSES EXPRESSING PURPOSE.

1442. The relative with the future indicative may express a *purpose*. *E.g.*

Πρεσβείαν πέμπειν ἥτις ταῦτ' ἐρεῖ καὶ παρέσται τοῖς πράγμασιν, *to send an embassy to say this, and to be present at the transactions*, D. 1, 2. Οὐ γάρ ἐστί μοι χρήματα, ὁπόθεν ἐκτίσω, *for I have no money to pay the fine with*, P. *Ap*. 37[c].

The antecedent here may be definite or indefinite; but the negative particle is always μή, as in final clauses (1364).

1443. N. Homer generally has the subjunctive (with κέ joined to the relative) in this construction after primary tenses, and the optative (without κέ) after secondary tenses. The optative is sometimes found even in Attic prose. The earlier Greek here agrees with the Latin.

1444. N. In this construction the future indicative is very rarely changed to the future optative after past tenses.

RELATIVE CLAUSES EXPRESSING RESULT.

1445. The relative with any tense of the indicative, or with a potential optative, may express a result. The negative is οὐ. *E.g.*

Τίς οὕτω μαίνεται ὅστις οὐ βούλεταί σοι φίλος εἶναι; *who is so mad that he does not wish to be your friend?* X. *A*. 2, 5[12]. (Here ὥστε οὐ βούλεται would have the same meaning.) Οὐδεὶς ἂν γένοιτο οὕτως ἀδαμάντινος, ὃς ἂν μείνειεν ἐν τῇ δικαιοσύνῃ, *no one would ever become so like adamant that he would remain firm in his justice* (= ὥστε μείνειεν ἄν), P. *Rp*. 360[b].

1446. N. This is equivalent to the use of ὥστε with the finite words (1450; 1454). It occurs chiefly after negative leading clauses or interrogatives implying a negative.

1447. The relative with a future (sometimes a present)

indicative may express a result which is *aimed at.* The negative here is μή. *E.g.*

Εὔχετο μηδεμίαν οἱ συντυχίην γενέσθαι, ἥ μιν παύσει καταστρέψασθαι τὴν Εὐρώπην, *he prayed that no such chance might befall him as to prevent him from subjugating Europe* (= ὥστε μιν παῦσαι), Hd. 7,54. Βουληθεὶς τοιοῦτον μνημεῖον καταλιπεῖν ὃ μὴ τῆς ἀνθρωπίνης φύσεώς ἐστιν, *when he wished to leave such a memorial as might be beyond human nature* (= ὥστε μὴ εἶναι), I. 4, 89.

1448. N. This construction (1447) is generally equivalent to that of ὥστε with the infinitive (1450).

CONSECUTIVE CLAUSES WITH THE INFINITIVE AND THE FINITE MOODS.

1449. Ὥστε (sometimes ὡς), *so as, so that,* is used with the infinitive and with the indicative to express a result.

1450. With the infinitive (the negative being μή), the result is stated as one which the action of the leading verb *tends* to produce; with the indicative (the negative being οὐ), as one which that action actually *does* produce. *E.g.*

Πᾶν ποιοῦσιν ὥστε δίκην μὴ διδόναι, *they do everything so as* (i.e. *in such a way as*) *not to be punished,* i.e. *they aim at not being punished,* not implying that they actually escape; P. *G.* 479ᶜ. (But πᾶν ποιοῦσιν ὥστε δίκην οὐ διδόασιν would mean *they do everything so that they are not punished.*) Οὕτως ἀγνωμόνως ἔχετε, ὥστε ἐλπίζετε αὐτὰ χρηστὰ γενήσεσθαι, *are you so senseless that you expect them to become good?* D. 2, 26. (But with ὥστε ἐλπίζειν the meaning would be *so senseless as to expect,* i.e. *senseless enough to expect,* without implying necessarily that you do expect.)

1451. N. These two constructions are essentially distinct in their nature, even when it is indifferent to the general sense which is used in a given case; as in οὕτως ἐστὶ δεινὸς ὥστε δίκην μὴ διδόναι, *he is so skilful as not to be punished,* and οὕτως ἐστὶ δεινὸς ὥστε δίκην οὐ δίδωσιν, *he is so skilful that he is not punished.*

The use of μή with the infinitive and of οὐ with the indicative shows that the distinction was really felt. When the infinitive with ὥστε has οὐ, it generally represents, in indirect discourse, an indicative with οὐ of the direct form (see *Moods and Tenses,* §§ 594–598).

1452. The infinitive with ὥστε may express a purpose like a final clause: see ὥστε δίκην μὴ διδόναι (= ἵνα μὴ διδῶσι), quoted in 1450. It may also be equivalent to an object clause with ὅπως (1372); as in μηχανὰς εὑρήσομεν, ὥστ' ἐς τὸ πᾶν σε τῶνδ' ἀπαλλάξαι πόνων, *we will find devices to wholly free you from these troubles* (= ὅπως σε ἀπαλλάξομεν), A. *Eu.* 82.

1453. The infinitive after ὥστε sometimes expresses a *condition*, like that after ἐφ' ᾧ or ἐφ' ᾧτε (1460). *E.g.*

Ἐξὸν αὐτοῖς τῶν λοιπῶν ἄρχειν Ἑλλήνων, ὥστ' αὐτοὺς ὑπακούειν βασιλεῖ, *it being in their power to rule the rest of the Greeks, on condition that they should themselves obey the King*, D. 6, 11.

1454. As ὥστε with the indicative has no effect on the mood of the verb, it may be used in the same way with any verbal form which can stand in an independent sentence; as ὥστ' οὐκ ἂν αὐτὸν γνωρίσαιμι, *so that I should not know him*, E. *Or.* 379; ὥστε μὴ λίαν στένε, *so do not lament overmuch*, S. *El.* 1172.

1455. N. Ὥς τε (never ὥστε) in Homer has the infinitive only twice; elsewhere it means simply *as*, like ὥσπερ.

1456. Ὡς is sometimes used like ὥστε with the infinitive and the finite moods, but chiefly in Aeschylus, Sophocles, Herodotus, and Xenophon.

1457. N. Verbs, adjectives, and nouns which commonly take the simple infinitive occasionally have the infinitive with ὥστε or ὡς; as ψηφισάμενοι ὥστε ἀμύνειν, *having voted to defend them*, T. 6, 88; πείθουσιν ὥστε ἐπιχειρῆσαι, *they persuade them to make an attempt*, T. 3, 102; φρονιμώτεροι ὥστε μαθεῖν, *wiser in learning*, X. *C.* 4, 3[11]; ὀλίγοι ὡς ἐγκρατεῖς εἶναι, *too few to have the power*, X. *C.* 4, 5[15]; ἀνάγκη ὥστε κινδυνεύειν, *a necessity of incurring risk*, I. 6, 51.

1458. N. In the same way (1457) ὥστε or ὡς with the infinitive may follow the comparative with ἤ (1531); as ἐλάττω ἔχοντα δύναμιν ἢ ὥστε τοὺς φίλους ὠφελεῖν, *having too little power to aid his friends*, X. *H.* 4, 8[23].

1459. N. Ὥστε or ὡς is occasionally followed by a participle; as ὥστε σκέψασθαι δέον, *so that we must consider*, D. 3, 1.

1460. Ἐφ' ᾧ or ἐφ' ᾧτε, *on condition that*, is followed by the infinitive, and occasionally by the future indicative. *E.g.*

Ἀφίεμέν σε, ἐπὶ τούτῳ μέντοι, ἐφ' ᾧτε μηκέτι φιλοσοφεῖν, *we release you, but on this condition, that you shall no longer be a philosopher*, P. *Ap.* 29[c]; ἐπὶ τούτῳ ὑπεξίσταμαι, ἐφ' ᾧτε ὑπ' οὐδενὸς ὑμέων ἄρξομαι, *I withdraw on this condition, that I shall be ruled by none of you*, Hd. 3, 83.

CAUSAL RELATIVE.

1461. A relative clause may express a *cause.* The verb is in the indicative, as in causal sentences (1505), and the negative is generally οὐ. *E.g.*

Θαυμαστὸν ποιεῖς, ὃς ἡμῖν οὐδὲν δίδως, *you do a strange thing in giving us nothing* (like ὅτι σὺ οὐδὲν δίδως), X. *M.* 2,7[13]; δόξας ἀμαθέα εἶναι, ὃς . . . ἐκέλευε, *believing him to be unlearned, because he commanded,* etc., Hd. 1, 33.

Compare causal relative sentences in Latin.

1462. N. When the negative is μή, the sentence is conditional as well as causal; as ταλαίπωρος εἶ, ᾧ μήτε θεοὶ πατρῷοί εἰσι μήθ' ἱερά, *you are wretched, since you have neither ancestral gods nor temples* (implying also *if you really have none*), P. *Eu.* 302[b]. Compare the use of *siquidem* in Latin.

TEMPORAL PARTICLES SIGNIFYING *UNTIL* AND *BEFORE.*

Ἕως, ἔστε, ἄχρι, μέχρι, AND ὄφρα.

1463. When ἕως, ἔστε, ἄχρι, μέχρι, and the epic ὄφρα mean *while, so long as,* they are not distinguished in their use from other relatives. But when they mean *until,* they have many peculiarities. Homer has εἷος or εἵως for ἕως.

1464. When ἕως, ἔστε, ἄχρι, μέχρι, and ὄφρα, *until,* refer to a definite past action they take the indicative, usually the aorist. *E.g.*

Νῆχον πάλιν, εἷος ἐπῆλθον εἰς ποταμόν, *I swam on again, until I came into a river, Od.* 7, 280. Ταῦτα ἐποίουν, μέχρι σκότος ἐγένετο, *this they did until darkness came on,* X. *A.* 4, 2[4].

This is the construction of the relative with a definite antecedent (1427).

1465. These particles follow the construction of conditional relatives in both forms of future conditions, in unfulfilled conditions, and in present and past general suppositions. *E.g.*

Ἐπίσχες, ἔστ' ἂν καὶ τὰ λοιπὰ προσμάθῃς, *wait until you (shall) learn the rest besides* (1434), A. *Pr.* 697. Εἴποιμ' ἂν . . . ἕως παρατείναιμι τοῦτον, *I should tell him,* etc., *until I put him to torture* (1436), X. *C.* 1, 3[11]. Ἡδέως ἂν τούτῳ ἔτι διελεγόμην, ἕως αὐτῷ . . . ἀπέδωκα, *I should (in that case) gladly have continued to talk with him until I had given him back*, etc. (1433), P. *G.* 506. Ἃ δ' ἂν ἀσύντακτα ᾖ, ἀνάγκη ταῦτα ἀεὶ πράγματα παρέχειν, ἕως ἂν χώραν λάβῃ, *whatever things are in disorder, these must always make trouble until they are put in order* (1431, 1), X. *C.* 4, 5[37]. Περιεμένομεν ἑκάστοτε, ἕως ἀνοιχθείη τὸ δεσμωτήριον, *we waited each day until the prison was opened* (1431, 2), P. *Ph.* 59[d].

1466. N. The omission of ἄν after these particles, when the verb is in the subjunctive, is more common than it is after εἰ or ordinary relatives (1406), occurring sometimes in Attic prose; as μέχρι πλοῦς γένηται, *until the ship sails*, T. 1, 137.

1467. Clauses introduced by ἕως etc. frequently imply a *purpose;* see the examples under 1465. When such clauses depend upon a past tense, they admit the double construction of indirect discourse (1502, 3), like final clauses (1369).

1468. N. Homer uses εἰς ὅ κε, *until*, like ἕως κε; and Herodotus uses ἐς ὅ and ἐς οὗ like ἕως.

Πρίν, *before, until.*

1469. Πρίν is followed by the infinitive, and also (like ἕως) by the finite moods.

1470. In Homer πρίν generally has the infinitive without reference to its meaning or to the nature of the leading verb. But in other Greek it has the infinitive chiefly when it means simply *before* and when the leading clause is affirmative; it has the finite moods only when it means *until* (as well as *before*), and chiefly when the leading verb is negative or implies a negative. It has the subjunctive and optative only after negatives.

1471. 1. Examples of πρίν with the infinitive: —

Ναῖε δὲ Πήδαιον πρὶν ἐλθεῖν υἷας Ἀχαιῶν, *and he dwelt in Pedaeum before the coming of the sons of the Achaeans*, *Il.* 13, 172 (here πρὶν ἐλθεῖν = πρὸ τοῦ ἐλθεῖν). Οὐ μ' ἀποτρέψεις πρὶν χαλκῷ μαχέσασθαι, *you shall not turn me away before* (i.e. *until*) *we have fought together*, *Il.* 20, 257 (here the Attic would prefer πρὶν ἂν μαχεσώμεθα). Ἀποπέμπουσιν αὐτὸν πρὶν ἀκοῦσαι, *they send him away before hearing him*, T. 2, 12. Μεσσήνην εἵλομεν πρὶν Πέρσας λαβεῖν τὴν βασιλείαν, *we took Messene before the Persians obtained their kingdom*, I. 6, 26. Πρὶν ὡς Ἄφοβον ἐλθεῖν μίαν ἡμέραν οὐκ ἐχήρευσεν, *she was not a widow a single day before she went to Aphobus*, D. 30, 33 (here the infinitive is required, as πρίν does not mean *until*).

2. Examples of πρίν, *until*, with the indicative (generally after negatives), and with the subjunctive and optative (*always* after negatives), the constructions being the same as those with ἕως (1464–1467) : —

Οὐκ ἦν ἀλέξημ' οὐδὲν, πρίν γ' ἐγώ σφισιν ἔδειξα, etc., *there was no relief, until I showed them*, etc. (1464), A. *Pr.* 479. Οὔ χρή με ἐνθένδε ἀπελθεῖν, πρὶν ἂν δῶ δίκην, *I must not depart hence until I am punished* (1434), X. *An.* 5, 7[5]. Οὐκ ἂν εἰδείης πρὶν πειρηθείης, *you cannot know until you have tried it* (1436), Theog. 125. Ἐχρῆν μὴ πρότερον συμβουλεύειν, πρὶν ἡμᾶς ἐδίδαξαν, etc., *they ought not to have given advice until they had instructed us*, etc. (1433), I. 4, 19. Ὁρῶσι τοὺς πρεσβυτέρους οὐ πρόσθεν ἀπιόντας, πρὶν ἂν ἀφῶσιν οἱ ἄρχοντες, *they see that the elders never go away until the authorities dismiss them* (1431, 1), X. *Cy.* 1, 2[8]. Ἀπηγόρευε μηδένα βάλλειν, πρὶν Κῦρος ἐμπλησθείη θηρῶν, *he forbade any one to shoot until Cyrus should be sated with the hunt* (1467; 1502, 3), X. *C.* 1, 4[14].

1472. N. In Homer πρίν γ' ὅτε (never the simple πρίν) is used with the indicative, and πρίν γ' ὅτ' ἄν (sometimes πρίν, without ἄν) with the subjunctive.

1473. N. Πρίν, like ἕως etc. (1466), sometimes has the subjunctive without ἄν, even in Attic Greek; as μὴ στέναζε πρὶν μάθῃς, *do not lament before you know*, S. *Ph.* 917.

1474. Πρὶν ἤ (a developed form for πρίν) is used by Herodotus (rarely by Homer), and πρότερον ἤ, *sooner than, before*, by Herodotus and Thucydides, in most of the constructions of πρίν. So πάρος, *before*, in Homer with the infinitive. Even ὕστερον ἤ, *later than*, once takes the infinitive by analogy. *E.g.*

Πρὶν γὰρ ἢ ὀπίσω σφέας ἀναπλῶσαι, ἥλω ὁ Κροῖσος, *for before they had sailed back, Croesus was taken*, Hd. 1, 78. Οὐδὲ ᾔδεσαν πρότερον ἤ περ ἐπύθοντο Τρηχινίων, *they did not even know of it until they heard from the Trachinians*, Hd. 7, 175. Μὴ ἀπανίστασθαι ἀπὸ τῆς πόλιος πρότερον ἢ ἐξέλωσι, *not to withdraw from the city until they capture it*, Hd. 9, 86. Πρότερον ἢ αἰσθέσθαι αὐτούς, *before they perceived them*, T. 6, 58. See T. 1, 69; 2, 65. Τέκνα ἐξείλοντο πάρος πετεηνὰ γενέσθαι, *they took away the nestlings before they were fledged*, Od. 16, 218. So also ἔτεσιν ὕστερον ἑκατὸν ἢ αὐτοὺς οἰκῆσαι, *a hundred years after their own settlement*, T. 6, 4.

VIII. INDIRECT DISCOURSE OR ORATIO OBLIQUA.

GENERAL PRINCIPLES.

1475. A *direct* quotation or question gives the exact

words of the original speaker or writer (i.e. of the *oratio recta*). In an *indirect* quotation or question (*oratio obliqua*) the original words conform to the construction of the sentence in which they are quoted.

Thus the words ταῦτα βούλομαι may be quoted either directly, λέγει τις "ταῦτα βούλομαι," or indirectly, λέγει τις ὅτι ταῦτα βούλεται or φησί τις ταῦτα βούλεσθαι, *some one says that he wishes for this*. So ἐρωτᾷ "τί βούλει;" *he asks, "what do you want?"* but indirectly ἐρωτᾷ τί βούλεται, *he asks what he wants*.

1476. Indirect quotations may be introduced by ὅτι or ὡς, *that*, with a finite verb, or by the infinitive (as in the above example); sometimes also by the participle.

1477. N. Ὅτι, *that*, may introduce even a direct quotation; as εἶπον ὅτι ἱκανοί ἐσμεν, *they said, "we are able,"* X. *A*. 5, 4[10].

1478. 1. Ὅπως is sometimes used like ὡς, *that*, especially in poetry; as τοῦτο μή μοι φράζ᾽, ὅπως οὐκ εἶ κακός, S. *O. T.* 548.

2. Homer rarely has ὅ (neuter of ὅς) for ὅτι, *that;* as λεύσσετε γὰρ τό γε πάντες, ὅ μοι γέρας ἔρχεται ἄλλῃ, *for you all see this, that my prize goes another way*, *Il.* 1, 120; so 5, 433.

3. Οὕνεκα and ὁθούνεκα, *that*, sometimes introduce indirect quotations in poetry.

1479. Indirect *questions* follow the same principles as indirect quotations with ὅτι or ὡς, in regard to their moods and tenses.

For the words used to introduce indirect questions, see 1605 and 1606.

1480. The term *indirect discourse* applies to all clauses (even single clauses in sentences of different construction) which indirectly express the words or thought of any person, even those of the speaker himself (see 1502).

1481. Indirect quotations after ὅτι and ὡς and indirect questions follow these general rules: —

1. After primary tenses, each verb retains both the *mood* and the *tense* of the direct discourse.

2. After past tenses, each indicative or subjunctive of the direct discourse may be either changed to the *same tense* of the optative or retained in its original *mood* and *tense*. But all secondary tenses of the indicative in unreal conditions (1397; 1433) and all optatives remain unchanged.

1482. N. The imperfect and pluperfect, having no tenses in the optative, generally remain unchanged in all kinds of sentences (but see 1488). The aorist indicative likewise remains unchanged when it belongs to a *dependent* clause of the direct discourse (1497, 2). (See 1499.)

1483. When the quotation depends on a verb which takes the infinitive or participle, its leading verb is changed to the *corresponding tense* of the infinitive or participle (ἄν being retained when there is one), and its dependent verbs follow the preceding rule (1481).

1484. Ἄν is never omitted with the indicative or optative in indirect discourse, if it was used in the direct form; but when a particle or a relative word has ἄν with the subjunctive in the direct form, as in ἐάν, ὅταν, ὃς ἄν, etc. (1299, 2), the ἄν is dropped when the subjunctive is changed to the optative after a past tense in indirect discourse.

1485. N. Ἄν is never *added* in indirect discourse when it was not used in the direct form.

1486. The negative particle of the direct discourse is regularly retained in the indirect form. (But see 1496.)

SIMPLE SENTENCES IN INDIRECT DISCOURSE.

Indicative and Optative after ὅτι and ὡς, and in Indirect Questions.

1487. After primary tenses an indicative (without ἄν) retains both its mood and its tense in indirect discourse. After past tenses it is either changed to the same tense of the optative or retained in the original mood and tense. *E.g.*

Λέγει ὅτι γράφει, *he says that he is writing;* λέγει ὅτι ἔγραφεν, *he says that he was writing;* λέγει ὅτι ἔγραψεν, *he says that he wrote;* λέξει ὅτι γέγραφεν, *he will say that he has written.* Ἐρωτᾷ τί βούλονται, *he asks what they want;* ἀγνοῶ τί ποιήσουσιν, *I do not know what they will do.*

Εἶπεν ὅτι γράφοι or ὅτι γράφει, *he said that he was writing* (he said γράφω). Εἶπεν ὅτι γράψοι or ὅτι γράψει, *he said that he would write* (he said γράψω). Εἶπεν ὅτι γράψειεν or ὅτι ἔγραψεν, *he said that he had written* (he said ἔγραψα, *I wrote*). Εἶπεν ὅτι γεγραφὼς εἴη or ὅτι γέγραφεν, *he said that he had written* (he said γέγραφα, *I have written*).

(Opt.) Ἐπειρώμην αὐτῷ δεικνύναι, ὅτι οἴοιτο μὲν εἶναι σοφός, εἴη δ' οὔ, *I tried to show him that he believed himself to be wise, but was not so* (i.e. οἴεται μὲν . . . ἔστι δ' οὔ), P. *Ap.* 21[c]. Ὑπειπὼν ὅτι αὐτὸς τἀκεῖ πράξοι, ᾤχετο, *hinting that he would himself attend to things there, he departed* (he said αὐτὸς τἀκεῖ πράξω), T. 1, 90. Ἔλεξαν ὅτι πέμψειε σφᾶς ὁ Ἰνδῶν βασιλεύς, κελεύων ἐρωτᾶν ἐξ ὅτου ὁ πόλεμος εἴη, *they said that the king of the Indians had sent them, commanding them to ask on what account there was war* (they said ἔπεμψεν ἡμᾶς, and the question was ἐκ τίνος ἐστὶν ὁ πόλεμος;), X. *C.* 2. 4[7]. Ἤρετο εἴ τις ἐμοῦ εἴη σοφώτερος, *he asked whether there was any one wiser than I* (i.e. ἔστι τις σοφώτερος;), P. *Ap.* 21[a].

(Indic.) Ἔλεγον ὅτι ἐλπίζουσι σὲ καὶ τὴν πόλιν ἕξειν μοι χάριν, *they said that they hoped you and the state would be grateful to me*, I. 5, 23. Ἧκε δ' ἀγγέλλων τις ὡς Ἐλάτεια κατείληπται, *some one was come with a report that Elatea had been taken* (here the perfect optative might have been used), D. 18, 169. Ἀποκρινάμενοι ὅτι πέμψουσι πρέσβεις, εὐθὺς ἀπήλλαξαν, *having replied that they would send ambassadors, they dismissed them at once*, T. 1, 90. Ἠπόρουν τί ποτε λέγει, *I was uncertain what he meant* (τί ποτε λέγει;), P. *Ap.* 21[b]. Ἐβουλεύοντο τίν' αὐτοῦ καταλείψουσιν, *they were considering (the question) whom they should leave here*, D. 19, 122.

1488. N. Occasionally the present optative represents the imperfect indicative in this construction; as ἀπεκρίναντο ὅτι οὐδεὶς μάρτυς παρείη, *they replied that there had been no witness present* (οὐδεὶς παρῆν), D. 30, 20 (here the context makes it clear that παρείη does not stand for πάρεστι).

1489. 1. In a few cases the Greek changes a present indicative to the imperfect, or a perfect to the pluperfect, in indirect discourse, instead of retaining it or changing it to the optative; as ἐν ἀπορίᾳ ἦσαν, ἐννοούμενοι ὅτι ἐπὶ ταῖς βασιλέως θύραις ἦσαν, προὐδεδώκεσαν δὲ αὐτοὺς οἱ βάρβαροι, *they were in despair, considering that they were at the King's gates, and that the barbarians had betrayed them*, X. *A.* 3. 1[2]. (See the whole passage.) This is also the English usage.

2. In Homer this is the ordinary construction: see *Od.* 3, 166.

Subjunctive or Optative representing the Interrogative Subjunctive.

1490. An interrogative subjunctive (1358), after a primary tense, retains its mood and tense in an indirect question; after a past tense, it may be either changed to the same tense of the optative or retained in the subjunctive. *E.g.*

Βουλεύομαι ὅπως σε ἀποδρῶ, *I am trying to think how I shall escape you* (πῶς σε ἀποδρῶ;), X. *C.*1,4[13]. Οὐκ οἶδ' εἰ Χρυσάντᾳ τούτῳ δῶ, *I do not know whether I shall give* (*them*) *to Chrysantas here, ibid.*8,4[16]. Οὐκ ἔχω τί εἴπω, *I do not know what I shall say* (τί εἴπω;), D.9,54. *Cf.* Non habeo quid dicam. Ἐπήροντο εἰ παραδοῖεν τὴν πόλιν, *they asked whether they should give up the city* (παραδῶμεν τὴν πόλιν; *shall we give up the city?*), T.1,25. Ἠπόρει ὅ τι χρήσαιτο τῷ πράγματι, *he was at a loss how to deal with the matter* (τί χρήσωμαι;), X. *H.*7,4[39]. Ἐβουλεύοντο εἴτε κατακαύσωσιν εἴτε τι ἄλλο χρήσωνται, *they were deliberating whether they should burn them or dispose of them in some other way*, T.2,4.

1491. N. In these questions εἰ (not ἐάν) is used for *whether*, with both subjunctive and optative (see the second example in 1490).

1492. N. An interrogative subjunctive may be changed to the optative when the leading verb is optative, contrary to the general usage of indirect discourse (1270, 2); as οὐκ ἂν ἔχοις ὅ τι χρήσαιο σαυτῷ, *you would not know what to do with yourself*, P. *G.*486[b].

Indicative or Optative with ἄν.

1493. An indicative or optative with ἄν retains its mood and tense (with ἄν) unchanged in indirect discourse after ὅτι or ὡς and in indirect questions. *E.g.*

Λέγει (or ἔλεγεν) ὅτι τοῦτο ἂν ἐγένετο, *he says* (or *said*) *that this would have happened;* ἔλεγεν ὅτι οὗτος δικαίως ἂν ἀποθάνοι, *he said that this man would justly die.* Ἠρώτων εἰ δοῖεν ἂν τὰ πιστά, *they asked whether they would give the pledges* (δοίητε ἄν;), X. *A.*4,8[7].

Infinitive and Participle in Indirect Discourse.

1494. Each tense of the infinitive or participle in indirect discourse represents the tense of the finite verb which would be used in the direct form, the present and perfect including the imperfect and pluperfect. Each tense with ἄν can represent the corresponding tenses of either indicative or optative with ἄν. *E.g.*

Ἀρρωστεῖν προφασίζεται, *he pretends that he is sick*, ἐξώμοσεν ἀρρωστεῖν τουτονί, *he took an oath that this man was sick*, D.19,124. Κατασχεῖν φησι τούτους, *he says that he detained them, ibid.* 39.

Ἔφη χρήμαθ' ἑαυτῷ τοὺς Θηβαίους ἐπικεκηρυχέναι, *he said that the Thebans had offered a reward for him, ibid.* 21. Ἐπαγγέλλεται τὰ δίκαια ποιήσειν, *he promises to do what is right, ibid.* 48.

Ἤγγειλε τούτους ἐρχομένους, *he announced that these were coming* (οὗτοι ἔρχονται); ἀγγέλλει τούτους ἐλθόντας, *he announces that these came* (οὗτοι ἦλθον); ἀγγέλλει τοῦτο γενησόμενον, *he announces that this will be done;* ἤγγειλε τοῦτο γενησόμενον, *he announced that this would be done;* ἤγγειλε τοῦτο γεγενημένον, *he announced that this had been done* (τοῦτο γεγένηται).

See examples of ἄν with infinitive and participle in 1308. For the present infinitive and participle as imperfect, see 1285 and 1289.

1495. The infinitive is said *to stand in indirect discourse*, and its tenses correspond to those of the finite moods, when it depends on a verb implying thought or the expression of thought, and when *also* the thought, *as originally conceived*, would have been expressed by some tense of the indicative (with or without ἄν) or optative (with ἄν), so that it can be transferred without change of tense to the infinitive. Thus in βούλεται ἐλθεῖν, *he wishes to go*, ἐλθεῖν represents no form of either aorist indicative or aorist optative, and is not in indirect discourse. But in φησὶν ἐλθεῖν, *he says that he went*, ἐλθεῖν represents ἦλθον of the direct discourse. (See *Greek Moods and Tenses*, § 684.)

1496. The regular negative of the infinitive and participle in indirect discourse is οὐ, but exceptions occur. Especially the infinitive after verbs of *hoping, promising*, and *swearing* (see 1286) regularly has μή for its negative; as ὤμνυε μηδὲν εἰρηκέναι, *he swore that he had said nothing*, D. 21, 119.

INDIRECT QUOTATION OF COMPLEX SENTENCES.

1497. 1. When a complex sentence is indirectly quoted, its *leading* verb follows the rule for simple sentences (1487–1494).

2. After primary tenses the *dependent* verbs retain the same mood and tense. After past tenses, dependent primary tenses of the indicative and all dependent subjunctives may either be changed to the *same tense* of the optative or retain their original mood and tense. When a subjunctive becomes optative, ἄν is dropped, ἐάν, ὅταν, etc. becoming εἰ, ὅτε, etc. But dependent *secondary* tenses of the indicative remain unchanged. *E.g.*

1. Ἂν ὑμεῖς λέγητε, ποιήσειν (φησὶν) ὃ μήτ' αἰσχύνην μήτ' ἀδοξίαν αὐτῷ φέρει, *if you (shall) say so, he says he will do whatever does not bring shame or discredit to him,* D. 19, 41. Here no change is made, except in ποιήσειν (1494).

2. Ἀπεκρίνατο ὅτι μανθάνοιεν ἃ οὐκ ἐπίσταιντο, *he replied, that they were learning what they did not understand* (he said μανθάνουσιν ἃ οὐκ ἐπίστανται, which might have been retained), P. *Eu.* 276ᵉ. Εἴ τινα φεύγοντα λήψοιτο, προηγόρευεν ὅτι ὡς πολεμίῳ χρήσοιτο, *he announced that, if he should catch any one running away, he should treat him as an enemy* (he said εἴ τινα λήψομαι, χρήσομαι), X. *C.* 3, 1³ (1405). Νομίζων, ὅσα τῆς πόλεως προλάβοι, πάντα ταῦτα βεβαίως ἕξειν, *believing that he should hold all those places securely which he should take from the city beforehand* (ὅσ' ἂν προλάβω, ἕξω), D. 18, 26. Ἐδόκει μοι ταύτῃ πειρᾶσθαι σωθῆναι, ἐνθυμουμένῳ ὅτι, ἐὰν μὲν λάθω, σωθήσομαι, *it seemed best to me to try to gain safety in this way, thinking that, if I should escape notice, I should be saved* (we might have had εἰ λάθοιμι, σωθησοίμην), L. 12, 15. Ἔφασαν τοὺς ἄνδρας ἀποκτενεῖν οὓς ἔχουσι ζῶντας, *they said that they should kill the men whom they had alive* (ἀποκτενοῦμεν οὓς ἔχομεν, which might have been changed to ἀποκτενεῖν οὓς ἔχοιεν), T. 2, 5. Πρόδηλον ἦν (τοῦτο) ἐσόμενον, εἰ μὴ κωλύσετε, *it was plain that this would be so unless you should prevent* (ἔσται, εἰ μὴ κωλύσετε, which might have become εἰ μὴ κωλύσοιτε), Aesch. 3, 90.

Ἤλπιζον τοὺς Σικελοὺς ταύτῃ, οὓς μετεπέμψαντο, ἀπαντήσεσθαι, *they hoped the Sikels whom they had sent for would meet them here,* T. 7, 80.

1498. One verb may be changed to the optative while another is retained; as δηλώσας ὅτι ἕτοιμοί εἰσι μάχεσθαι, εἴ τις ἐξέρχοιτο, *having shown that they were ready to fight if any one should come forth* (ἕτοιμοί ἐσμεν, ἐάν τις ἐξέρχηται), X. *C.* 4, 1¹. This sometimes causes a variety of constructions in the same sentence.

1499. The *aorist* indicative is not changed to the aorist optative in dependent clauses, because in these the aorist optative generally represents the aorist subjunctive.

The present indicative is seldom changed to the present optative in dependent clauses, for a similar reason.

For the imperfect and pluperfect, see 1482.

1500. N. A dependent optative of the direct form of course remains unchanged in all indirect discourse (1481, 2).

1501. N. Occasionally a dependent present or perfect indicative is changed to the imperfect or pluperfect, as in the leading clause (1489).

1502. The principles of 1497 apply also to all dependent clauses after past tenses, which express indirectly the past thought of any person. This applies especially to the following constructions:—

1. Clauses depending on an infinitive after verbs of *wishing, commanding, advising,* and others which imply *thought* but do not take the infinitive in indirect discourse (1495).

2. Clauses containing a protasis with the apodosis implied in the context (1420), or with the apodosis expressed in a verb like θαυμάζω (1423).

3. Temporal clauses expressing a past intention, purpose, or expectation, especially those introduced by ἕως or πρίν.

4. Even ordinary relative sentences, which would regularly take the indicative.

(1) Ἐβούλοντο ἐλθεῖν, εἰ τοῦτο γένοιτο, *they wished to go if this should happen.* (We might have ἐὰν τοῦτο γένηται, expressing the form, *if this shall happen,* in which the wish would be conceived). Here ἐλθεῖν is not in indirect discourse (1495). Ἐκέλευσεν ὅ τι δύναιντο λαβόντας μεταδιώκειν, *he commanded them to take what they could and pursue* (we might have ὅ τι ἂν δύνωνται, representing ὅ τι ἂν δύνησθε), X. *C.*7, 3[7]. Προεῖπον αὐτοῖς μὴ ναυμαχεῖν Κορινθίοις, ἢν μὴ ἐπὶ Κέρκυραν πλέωσι καὶ μέλλωσιν ἀποβαίνειν, *they instructed them not to engage in a sea-fight with Corinthians, unless these should be sailing against Corcyra and should be on the point of landing* (we might have εἰ μὴ πλέοιεν καὶ μέλλοιεν), T. 1, 45.

(2) Φύλακας συμπέμπει, ὅπως φυλάττοιεν αὐτὸν, καὶ εἰ τῶν ἀγρίων τι φανείη θηρίων, *he sends (sent) guards, to guard him and (to be ready) in case any of the savage beasts should appear* (the thought being ἐάν τι φανῇ), X. *C.*1, 4[7]. Τἆλλα, ἢν ἔτι ναυμαχεῖν οἱ Ἀθηναῖοι τολμήσωσι, παρεσκευάζοντο, *they made the other preparations, (to be ready) in case the Athenians should still venture a naval battle,* T. 7, 59. Ὤικτειρον, εἰ ἁλώσοιντο, *they pitied them, if they were to be captured* (the thought being *we pity them if they are to be captured,* εἰ ἁλώσονται, which might be retained), X. *A.*1, 4[7]. Ἔχαιρον ἀγαπῶν εἴ τις ἐάσοι, *I rejoiced, being content if any one would let it pass* (the thought was ἀγαπῶ εἴ τις ἐάσει), P. *Rp.* 450[a]. Ἐθαύμαζεν εἴ τις ἀργύριον πράττοιτο, *he wondered that any one demanded money,* X. *M.*1, 2[7]; but in the same book (1, 1[13]) we find ἐθαύμαζε δ' εἰ μὴ φανερὸν αὐτοῖς ἐστιν, *he wondered that it was not plain.*

(3) Σπονδὰς ἐποιήσαντο ἕως ἀπαγγελθείη τὰ λεχθέντα εἰς Λακεδαίμονα, *they made a truce, (to continue) until what had been said should be reported at Sparta* (their thought was ἕως ἂν ἀπαγγελθῇ), X. *H.* 3, 2[20]. Οὐ γὰρ δή σφεας ἀπίει ὁ θεὸς τῆς ἀποικίης, πρὶν δὴ ἀπίκωνται ἐς αὐτὴν Λιβύην, *for the God did not mean to release them from the colony until they should actually come to Libya* (we might have ἀπίκοιντο), Hd. 4, 157. Μένοντες ἕστασαν ὁππότε πύργος Τρώων ὁρμήσειε, *they stood waiting until* (for the time *when*) *a column should rush upon the Trojans, Il.* 4, 334.

(4) Καὶ ᾔτεε σῆμα ἰδέσθαι, ὅττι ῥά οἱ γαμβροῖο πάρα Προίτοιο φέροιτο, *he asked to see the token, which he was bringing* (as he said) *from Proetus, Il.* 6, 176. Κατηγόρεον τῶν Αἰγινητέων τὰ πεποιήκοιεν προδόντες τὴν Ἑλλάδα, *they accused the Aeginetans for what* (as they said) *they had done in betraying Greece*, Hd. 6, 49.

For the same principle in causal sentences, see 1506.

1503. N. On this principle, clauses introduced by ἵνα, ὅπως, ὡς, ὄφρα, and μή admit the double construction of indirect discourse, and allow the subjunctive or future indicative to stand unchanged after past tenses (see 1369). The same principle extends to all conditional and all conditional relative and temporal sentences depending on clauses with ἵνα, etc., as these too belong to the indirect discourse.

Οὐχ ὅτι, οὐχ ὅπως, μὴ ὅτι, μὴ ὅπως.

1504. These expressions, by the ellipsis of a verb of *saying*, often mean *I do not speak of*, or *not to speak of*. With οὐχ an indicative (*e.g.* λέγω) was originally understood, and with μή an imperative or subjunctive (*e.g.* λέγε or εἴπῃς). *E.g.*

Οὐχ ὅπως τὰ σκεύη ἀπέδοσθε, ἀλλὰ καὶ αἱ θύραι ἀφηρπάσθησαν, *I do not mention your selling the furniture* (i.e. *not only did you sell the furniture*), *but even the doors were carried off*, Lys. 19, 31. Μὴ ὅτι θεὸς, ἀλλὰ καὶ ἄνθρωποὶ . . . οὐ φιλοῦσι τοὺς ἀπιστοῦντας, *not only God (not to speak of God), but also men fail to love those who distrust them*, X. *C.* 7, 2[17]. Πεπαύμεθ' ἡμεῖς, οὐχ ὅπως σε παύσομεν, *we have been stopped ourselves; there is no talk of stopping you*, S. *El.* 796.

When these forms were thus used, the original ellipsis was probably never present to the mind.

IX. CAUSAL SENTENCES.

1505. Causal sentences express a *cause*, and are introduced by ὅτι, ὡς, *because*, ἐπεί, ἐπειδή, ὅτε, ὁπότε, *since*, and by other particles of similar meaning. They have the indicative after both primary and secondary tenses. The negative particle is *οὐ*. *E.g.*

Κήδετο γὰρ Δαναῶν, ὅτι ῥα θνήσκοντας ὁρᾶτο, for she pitied the Danai, because she saw them dying, Il. 1, 56. *Ὅτε τοῦθ' οὕτως ἔχει, προσήκει προθύμως ἐθέλειν ἀκούειν, since this is so, it is becoming that you should be willing to hear eagerly*, D. 1, 1.

A potential optative or indicative may stand in a causal sentence: see D. 18, 49 and 79.

1506. N. On the principle of indirect discourse (1502), a causal sentence after a past tense may have the optative, to imply that the cause is assigned on the authority of some other person than the writer; as *τὸν Περικλέα ἐκάκιζον, ὅτι στρατηγὸς ὢν οὐκ ἐπεξάγοι, they abused Pericles, because (as they said) being general he did not lead them out*, T. 2, 21. (This assigns the *Athenians'* reason for abusing Pericles, but does not show the historian's opinion.)

X. EXPRESSION OF A WISH.

1507. When a wish refers to the future, it is expressed by the optative, either with or without *εἴθε* or *εἰ γάρ* (Homeric also *αἴθε*, *αἲ γάρ*), *O that*, *O if*. The negative is *μή*, which can stand alone with the optative. *E.g.*

Ὑμῖν θεοὶ δοῖεν ἐκπέρσαι Πριάμοιο πόλιν, may the Gods grant to you to destroy Priam's city, Il. 1, 18. *Αἲ γὰρ ἐμοὶ τοσσήνδε θεοὶ δύναμιν περιθεῖεν, O that the Gods would clothe me with so much strength, Od.* 3, 205. *Τὸ μὲν νῦν ταῦτα πρήσσοις τάπερ ἐν χερσὶ ἔχεις, for the present may you continue to do these things which you have now in hand*, Hd. 7, 5. *Εἴθε φίλος ἡμῖν γένοιο, O that you may become our friend*, X. *H.* 4, 1[38]. *Μηκέτι ζῴην ἐγώ, may I no longer live*, Ar. *N.* 1255. *Τεθναίην, ὅτε μοι μηκέτι ταῦτα μέλοι, may I die when I shall no longer care for these things* (1439), Mimn. 1, 2.

The force of the tenses here is the same as in protasis (see 1272).

1508. In poetry *εἰ* alone is sometimes used with the optative in wishes; as *εἴ μοι γένοιτο φθόγγος ἐν βραχίοσιν, O that I might find a voice in my arms*, E. *Hec.* 836.

1509. N. The poets, especially Homer, sometimes prefix *ὡς* (probably exclamatory) to the optative in wishes; as *ὡς ἀπόλοιτο καὶ ἄλλος ὅτις τοιαῦτά γε ῥέζοι, likewise let any other perish who may do the like, Od.* 1, 47.

1510. In poetry, especially in Homer, the optative alone sometimes expresses a *concession* or *permission*, sometimes a *command* or *exhortation;* as αὖτις Ἀργείην Ἑλένην Μενέλαος ἄγοιτο, *Menelaus may take back Argive Helen, Il.* 4, 19. Τεθναίης, ὦ Προῖτ', ἢ κάκτανε Βελλεροφόντην, *either die, or kill Bellerophontes, Il.* 6, 164. Here, and in wishes without εἰ, εἰ γάρ, etc., we probably have an original independent use of the optative; while wishes introduced by any form of εἰ are probably elliptical protases.

(See Appendix I. in *Greek Moods and Tenses*, pp. 371–389.)

1511. When a wish refers to the present or the past, and it is implied that its object *is not* or *was not attained*, it is expressed in Attic Greek by a secondary tense of the indicative with εἴθε or εἰ γάρ, which here cannot be omitted. The negative is μή. The imperfect and aorist are distinguished here as in protasis (1397). *E.g.*

Εἴθε τοῦτο ἐποίει, *O that he were doing this*, or *O that he had done this.* Εἴθε τοῦτο ἐποίησεν, *O that he had done this;* εἰ γὰρ μὴ ἐγένετο τοῦτο, *O that this had not happened.* Εἴθ' εἶχες βελτίους φρένας, *O that thou hadst a better understanding*, E. *El.* 1061. Εἰ γὰρ τοσαύτην δύναμιν εἶχον, *O that I had so great power*, E. *Al.* 1072. Εἴθε σοι τότε συνεγενόμην, *O that I had then met with you*, X. *M.* 1. 2[46].

1512. The aorist ὤφελον, *ought*, of ὀφείλω, *debeo*, *owe*, and in Homer sometimes the imperfect ὤφελλον, are used with the infinitive, chiefly in poetry, to express a present or past unattained wish (1402, 2). *E.g.*

Ὤφελε τοῦτο ποιεῖν, *would that he were doing this* (lit. *he ought to be doing this*), or *would that he had done this* (*habitually*); ὤφελε τοῦτο ποιῆσαι, *would that he had done this.* (For the distinction made by the different tenses of the infinitive, see 1400, 2). Τὴν ὄφελ' ἐν νήεσσι κατακτάμεν Ἄρτεμις, *would that Artemis had slain her at the ships, Il.* 19, 59.

1513. N. Ὤφελον with the infinitive is negatived by μή (not οὐ), and it may even be preceded by εἴθε, εἰ γάρ, or ὡς; as μή ποτ' ὤφελον λιπεῖν τὴν Σκῦρον, *O that I had never left Scyros*, S. *Ph.* 969; εἰ γὰρ ὤφελον οἷοί τε εἶναι, *O that they were able*, P. *Cr.* 44[d]; ὡς ὤφελες ὀλέσθαι, *would that you had perished, Il.* 3, 428.

1514. In Homer the present optative (generally with εἴθε or εἰ γάρ) may express an unattained wish in *present* time; as εἴθ' ὡς *ἡβώοιμι βίη δέ μοι ἔμπεδος εἴη, O that I were again as young and my strength were firm,* Il. 11, 670.

This corresponds to the Homeric use of the optative in unreal conditions and their apodoses (1398). In both constructions the present optative is commonly future in Homer, as in other Greek.

1515. Homer never uses the indicative (1511) in wishes. He always expresses a past wish by the construction with ὤφελον (1512), and a present wish sometimes by ὤφελον and sometimes by the present optative (1514).

THE INFINITIVE.

1516. 1. The infinitive is originally a neuter verbal noun, with many attributes of a verb. Thus, like a verb, it has voices and tenses; it may have a subject or object; and it is qualified by adverbs, not by adjectives.

2. When the definite article came into use with other nouns (see 937, 4), it was used also with the infinitive, which thus became more distinctly a noun with four cases.

For the subject of the infinitive, see 895. For the case of predicate nouns and adjectives when the subject is omitted, see 927 and 928.

INFINITIVE WITHOUT THE ARTICLE.

AS SUBJECT, PREDICATE, OBJECT, OR APPOSITIVE.

1517. The infinitive may be the subject nominative of a finite verb (especially of an impersonal verb, 898, or of ἐστί), or the subject accusative of another infinitive. It may be a predicate nominative (907), and it may stand in apposition to a noun (911). *E.g.*

Συνέβη αὐτῷ ἐλθεῖν, *it happened to him to go;* ἐξῆν μένειν, *it was possible to remain;* ἡδὺ πολλοὺς ἐχθροὺς ἔχειν; *is it pleasant to have many enemies?* Φησὶν ἐξεῖναι τούτοις μένειν, *he says it is possible for these to remain* (μένειν being subject of ἐξεῖναι). Τὸ γνῶναι ἐπιστήμην λαβεῖν ἐστιν, *to learn is to acquire knowledge,* P. Th. 209ᵉ. Τὸ γὰρ θάνατον δεδιέναι οὐδὲν ἄλλο ἐστὶν ἢ δοκεῖν σοφὸν εἶναι μὴ ὄντα, *for to fear death (the fear of death) is nothing else than to seem to be wise without being so,* P. Ap. 29ᵃ. Εἷς οἰωνὸς ἄριστος, ἀμύνεσθαι περὶ πάτρης, *one omen is best, to fight for our country,* Il. 12, 243. For the subject infinitives with the article, see 1542.

1518. The infinitive may be the object of a verb. It generally has the force of an object accusative, sometimes that of an accusative of kindred signification (1051), and sometimes that of an object genitive.

1519. The object infinitive not in indirect discourse (1495) follows verbs whose action naturally implies another action as its object, especially those expressing *wish, command, advice, cause, attempt, intention, prevention, ability, fitness, necessity*, or their opposites. Such verbs are in general the same in Greek as in English, and others will be learned by practice. The negative is μή. *E.g.*

Βούλεται ἐλθεῖν, *he wishes to go;* βούλεται τοὺς πολίτας πολεμικοὺς εἶναι, *he wishes the citizens to be warlike;* παραινοῦμέν σοι μένειν, *we advise you to remain;* προείλετο πολεμῆσαι, *he preferred to make war;* κελεύει σε μὴ ἀπελθεῖν, *he commands you not to depart;* ἀξιοῦσιν ἄρχειν, *they claim the right to rule;* ἀξιοῦται θανεῖν, *he is thought to deserve to die;* δέομαι ὑμῶν συγγνώμην μοι ἔχειν, *I ask you to have consideration for me.* So κωλύει σε βαδίζειν, *he prevents you from marching;* οὐ πέφυκε δουλεύειν, *he is not born to be a slave;* ἀναβάλλεται τοῦτο ποιεῖν, *he postpones doing this;* κινδυνεύει θανεῖν, *he is in danger of death.*

1520. N. The tenses here used are chiefly the present and aorist, and these do not differ in their time (1272). In this construction the infinitive has no more reference to *time* than any other verbal noun would have, but the meaning of the verb generally gives it a reference to the future; as in ἀξιοῦται θανεῖν (above) θανεῖν expresses time only so far as θανάτου would do so in its place.

1521. The infinitive may depend on a noun and a verb (generally ἐστί) which together are equivalent to a verb which takes an object infinitive (1519). *E.g.*

Ἀνάγκη ἐστὶ πάντας ἀπελθεῖν, *there is a necessity that all should withdraw;* κίνδυνος ἦν αὐτῷ παθεῖν τι, *he was in danger of suffering something;* ἐλπίδας ἔχει τοῦτο ποιῆσαι, *he has hopes of doing this.* Ὥρα ἀπιέναι, *it is time to go away,* P. *Ap.* 42[a]. Τοῖς στρατιώταις ὁρμὴ ἐνέπεσε ἐκτειχίσαι τὸ χωρίον, *an impulse to fortify the place fell upon the soldiers,* T. 4, 4.

For the infinitive with τοῦ depending on a noun, see 1547.

1522. 1. The infinitive in indirect discourse (1495) is

generally the object of a verb of *saying* or *thinking* or some equivalent expression. Here each tense of the infinitive corresponds in time to the same tense of some finite mood. See 1494, with the examples.

2. Many verbs of this class (especially the passive of λέγω) allow both a personal and an impersonal construction. Thus we can say λέγεται ὁ Κῦρος ἐλθεῖν, *Cyrus is said to have gone*, or λέγεται τὸν Κῦρον ἐλθεῖν, *it is said that Cyrus went.* Δοκέω, *seem*, is generally used personally; as δοκεῖ εἶναι σοφός, *he seems to be wise.*

1523. 1. Of the three common verbs meaning *to say,* —

(*a*) φημί regularly takes the infinitive in indirect discourse;

(*b*) εἶπον regularly takes ὅτι or ὡς with the indicative or optative;

(*c*) λέγω allows either construction, but in the *active* voice it generally takes ὅτι or ὡς.

Other verbs which regularly take the infinitive in indirect discourse are οἴομαι, ἡγέομαι, νομίζω, and δοκέω, meaning *to believe*, or *to think.*

2. Exceptional cases of εἶπον with the infinitive are more common than those of φημί with ὅτι or ὡς (which are very rare).

For the two constructions allowed after verbs of *hoping, expecting*, etc., see 1286.

1524. N. A relative clause depending on an infinitive in indirect discourse sometimes takes the infinitive by assimilation; as ἐπειδὴ δὲ γενέσθαι ἐπὶ τῇ οἰκίᾳ, (ἔφη) ἀνεῳγμένην καταλαμβάνειν τὴν θύραν, *and when they came to the house, (he said) they found the door open*, P. *Sy.* 174[d]. Herodotus allows this assimilation even after εἰ, *if*, and διότι, *because.*

1525. In narration, the infinitive often seems to stand for the indicative, when it depends on some word like λέγεται, *it is said*, expressed or even implied in what precedes. *E.g.*

Ἀπικομένους δὲ ἐς τὸ Ἄργος, διατίθεσθαι τὸν φόρτον, *and having come to Argos, they were (it is said) setting out their cargo for sale*, Hd. 1, 1. Διατίθεσθαι is an imperfect infinitive (1285, 1): see also Hd. 1, 24, and X. *C.* 1, 3[5].

INFINITIVE WITH ADJECTIVES.

1526. The infinitive may depend on adjectives corresponding in meaning to verbs which take an object infinitive (1519), especially those expressing *ability*, *fitness*, *desert*, *willingness*, and their opposites. *E.g.*

Δυνατὸς ποιεῖν τοῦτο, *able to do this*; δεινὸς λέγειν, *skilled in speaking*; ἄξιος τοῦτο λαβεῖν, *worthy to receive this*; πρόθυμος λέγειν, *eager to speak.* Μαλακοὶ καρτερεῖν, (*too*) *effeminate to endure*, P. *Rp.* 556[b]; ἐπιστήμων λέγειν τε καὶ σιγᾶν, *knowing how both to speak and to be silent*, P. *Phdr.* 276[a].

So τοιοῦτοι οἷοι πονηροῦ τινος ἔργου ἐφίεσθαι, *capable of aiming* (*such as to aim*) *at any vicious act*, X. *C.* 1, 2[3]; also with οἷος alone, οἷος ἀεί ποτε μεταβάλλεσθαι, *one likely to be always changing*, X. *H.* 2, 3[45].

1527. N. Δίκαιος, *just*, and some other adjectives may thus be used *personally* with the infinitive; as δίκαιός ἐστι τοῦτο ποιεῖν, *he has a right to do this* (equivalent to δίκαιόν ἐστιν αὐτὸν τοῦτο ποιεῖν).

LIMITING INFINITIVE WITH ADJECTIVES, ADVERBS, AND NOUNS.

1528. Any adjective or adverb may take an infinitive to limit its meaning to a particular action. *E.g.*

Θέαμα αἰσχρὸν ὁρᾶν, *a sight disgraceful to behold*; λόγοι ὑμῖν χρησιμώτατοι ἀκοῦσαι, *words most useful for you to hear*; τὰ χαλεπώτατα εὑρεῖν, *the things hardest to find.* Πολιτεία ἥκιστα χαλεπὴ συζῆν, *a government least hard to live under*, P. *Pol.* 302[b]. Οἰκία ἡδίστη ἐνδιαιτᾶσθαι, *a house most pleasant to live in*, X. *M.* 3, 8[8]. Κάλλιστα (adv.) ἰδεῖν, *in a manner most delightful to behold*, X. *C.* 8, 3[5].

1529. N. This infinitive (1528) is generally active rather than passive; as πρᾶγμα χαλεπὸν ποιεῖν, *a thing hard to do*, rather than χαλεπὸν ποιεῖσθαι, *hard to be done.*

1530. N. Nouns and even verbs may take the infinitive as a limiting accusative (1058); as θαῦμα ἰδέσθαι, *a wonder to behold*, *Od.* 8, 366. Ἀριστεύεσκε μάχεσθαι, *he was the first in fighting* (like μάχην), *Il.* 6, 460. Δοκεῖς διαφέρειν αὐτοὺς ἰδεῖν; *do you think they differ in appearance* (*to look at*)? P. *Rp.* 495[e].

1531. N. Here belongs the infinitive after a comparative with ἤ, *than*; as νόσημα μεῖζον ἢ φέρειν, *a disease too heavy to bear*, S. *O. T.* 1293.

For ὥστε with this infinitive, see 1458.

Infinitive of Purpose.

1532. 1. The infinitive may express a *purpose*. *E.g.*

Οἱ ἄρχοντες, οὓς εἵλεσθε ἄρχειν μου, *the rulers, whom you chose to rule me*, P. *Ap.* 28[e]. Τὴν πόλιν φυλάττειν αὐτοῖς παρέδωκαν, *they delivered the city to them to guard*, *H.* 4, 4[15]. Θεάσασθαι παρῆν τὰς γυναῖκας πιεῖν φερούσας, *the women were to be seen bringing them (something) to drink*, X. *H.* 7, 2[9].

2. Here, as with adjectives (1529), the infinitive is active rather than passive; as κτανεῖν ἐμοί νιν ἔδοσαν, *they gave her to me to kill (to be killed)*, E. *Tro.* 874.

1533. N. In Homer, where ὥστε only rarely has the sense of *so as* (1455), the simple infinitive may express a *result;* as τίς σφωε ξυνέηκε μάχεσθαι; *who brought them into conflict so as to contend? Il.* 1, 8.

Absolute Infinitive.

1534. The infinitive may stand *absolutely* in parenthetical phrases, generally with ὡς or ὅσον. *E.g.*

The most common of these is ὡς ἔπος εἰπεῖν or ὡς εἰπεῖν, *so to speak.* Others are ὡς συντόμως (or συνελόντι, 1172, 2) εἰπεῖν, *to speak concisely; τὸ ξύμπαν εἰπεῖν, on the whole; ὡς ἀπεικάσαι, to judge* (i.e. *as far as we can judge*); ὅσον γέ μ' εἰδέναι, *as far as I know;* ὡς ἐμοὶ δοκεῖν, or ἐμοὶ δοκεῖν, *as it seems to me;* ὡς οὑτωσὶ ἀκοῦσαι, *at first hearing* (or without ὡς). So ὀλίγου δεῖν and μικροῦ δεῖν, *to want little*, i.e. *almost* (see 1116, *b*).

Herodotus has ὡς λόγῳ εἰπεῖν and οὐ πολλῷ λόγῳ εἰπεῖν, *not to make a long story, in short.*

1535. N. In certain cases εἶναι seems to be superfluous; especially in ἑκὼν εἶναι, *willing* or *willingly*, which generally stands in a *negative* sentence. So in τὸ νῦν εἶναι, *at present;* τὸ τήμερον εἶναι, *to-day;* τὸ ἐπ' ἐκείνοις εἶναι and similar phrases, *as far as depends on them;* τὴν πρώτην εἶναι, *at first*, Hd. 1, 153; κατὰ τοῦτο εἶναι, *so far as concerns this*, P. *Pr.* 317[a]; ὡς πάλαια εἶναι, *considering their age*, T. 1, 21; and some other phrases.

Infinitive in Commands, Wishes, Laws, etc.

1536. The infinitive with a subject nominative is sometimes used like the second person of the imperative, especially in Homer. *E.g.*

Μή ποτε καὶ σὺ γυναικί περ ἤπιος εἶναι, *be thou never indulgent to thy wife*, *Od.* 11, 441. Οἷς μὴ πελάζειν, *do not approach these* (= μὴ πέλαζε), A. *Pr.* 712.

For the third person, with a subject *accusative*, see 1537.

1537. The infinitive with a subject *accusative* sometimes expresses a wish, like the optative (1507); and sometimes a command, like the third person of the imperative. *E.g.*

Ζεῦ πάτερ, ἢ Αἴαντα λαχεῖν ἢ Τυδέος υἱόν, *Father Zeus, may the lot fall either on Ajax or on the son of Tydeus* (=Αἴας λάχοι, etc.), *Il.* 7, 179; θεοὶ πολῖται, μή με δουλείας τυχεῖν, *O ye Gods who hold our city, may slavery not be my lot*, A. *Se.* 253. Τρῶας ἔπειθ' Ἑλένην ἀποδοῦναι, *let the Trojans then surrender Helen* (=ἀποδοῖεν), *Il.* 3, 285.

1538. N. This construction (1537) has been explained by supplying a verb like δός, *grant* (see δὸς τίσασθαι, *grant that I may take vengeance*, *Il.* 3, 351), or γένοιτο, *may it be.*

1539. N. For the infinitive in exclamations, which generally has the article, see 1554.

1540. In *laws*, *treaties*, and *proclamations*, the infinitive often depends on ἔδοξε or δέδοκται, *be it enacted*, or κελεύεται, *it is commanded;* which may be expressed in a previous sentence or understood. *E.g.*

Δικάζειν δὲ τὴν ἐν Ἀρείῳ πάγῳ φόνου, *and (be it enacted) that the Senate on the Areopagus shall have jurisdiction in cases of murder*, D. 23, 22. Ἔτη δὲ εἶναι τὰς σπονδὰς πεντήκοντα, *and that the treaty shall continue fifty years*, T. 5, 18. Ἀκούετε λεῴ· τοὺς ὁπλίτας ἀπιέναι πάλιν οἴκαδε, *hear ye people! let the heavy armed go back again home*, Ar. *Av.* 448.

INFINITIVE WITH THE ARTICLE.

1541. When the infinitive has the article, its character as a neuter noun becomes more distinct, while it loses none of its attributes as a verb. The addition of the article extends its use to many new constructions, especially to those with prepositions; and the article is sometimes allowed even in many of the older constructions in which the infinitive regularly stands alone.

Infinitive with τό as Subject or Object.

1542. The subject infinitive (1517) may take the article to make it more distinctly a noun. *E.g.*

Τὸ γνῶναι ἐπιστήμην λαβεῖν ἐστιν, *to learn is to acquire knowledge*, P. *Th.* 209ᵉ. Τοῦτό ἐστι τὸ ἀδικεῖν, *this is to commit injustice*, P. *G.* 483ᶜ. Τὸ γὰρ θάνατον δεδιέναι οὐδὲν ἄλλο ἐστὶν ἢ δοκεῖν σοφὸν εἶναι μὴ ὄντα, *for to fear death (the fear of death) is nothing else than to seem to be wise without being so*, P. *Ap*. 29ᵉ. The predicate infinitives here omit the article (1517). See 956.

1543. The object infinitive takes the article chiefly after verbs which do not regularly take the simple infinitive (see 1519), or when the relation of the infinitive to the verb is less close than it usually is. *E.g.*

Τὸ τελευτῆσαι πάντων ἡ πεπρωμένη κατέκρινεν, *Fate adjudged death to all* (like θάνατον πάντων κατέκρινεν), I. 1, 43; εἰ τὸ κωλῦσαι τὴν τῶν Ἑλλήνων κοινωνίαν ἐπεπράκειν ἐγὼ Φιλίππῳ, *if I had sold to Philip the prevention of the unity of the Greeks* (i.e. *had prevented this as Philip's hireling*), D. 18, 23. Τὸ ξυνοικεῖν τῇδ᾽ ὁμοῦ τίς ἂν γυνὴ δύναιτο; *to live with her — what woman could do it?* S. *Tr*. 545.

1544. N. Sometimes in poetry the distinction between the object infinitive with and without τό is hardly perceptible; as in τλήσομαι τὸ κατθανεῖν, *I shall endure to die*, A. *Ag*. 1290; τὸ δρᾶν οὐκ ἠθέλησαν, *they were unwilling to act*, S. *O. C*. 442.

Infinitive with τό with Adjectives and Nouns.

1545. N. The infinitive with τό is sometimes used with the adjectives and nouns which regularly take the simple infinitive (1526). *E.g.*

Τὸ βίᾳ πολιτῶν δρᾶν ἔφυν ἀμήχανος, *I am helpless to act in defiance of the citizens*, S. *An*. 79. Τὸ ἐς τὴν γῆν ἡμῶν ἐσβάλλειν . . . ἱκανοί εἰσι, *they have the power to invade our land*, T. 6, 17.

Infinitive with τοῦ, τῷ, or τό in Various Constructions,

1546. The genitive, dative, or accusative of the infinitive with the article may depend on a preposition. *E.g.*

Πρὸ τοῦ τοὺς ὅρκους ἀποδοῦναι, *before taking the oaths*, D. 18, 26; πρὸς τῷ μηδὲν ἐκ τῆς πρεσβείας λαβεῖν, *besides receiving nothing by the embassy*, D. 19, 229; διὰ τὸ ξένος εἶναι οὐκ ἂν οἴει ἀδικηθῆναι; *do you think you would not be wronged on account of your being a stranger?* X. *M*. 2, 1¹⁵. Ὑπὲρ τοῦ τὰ μέτρια μὴ γίγνεσθαι, *that moderate counsels may not prevail* (= ἵνα μὴ γίγνηται), Aesch. 3, 1.

1547. The genitive and dative of the infinitive, with the article, can stand in most of the constructions belonging to those cases; as in that of the attributive genitive, the genitive after a comparative or after verbs and adjectives, the dative of *cause*, *manner*, or *means*, and the dative after verbs and adjectives. *E.g.*

Τοῦ πιεῖν ἐπιθυμία, *a desire to drink*, T.7,84; νεοῖς τὸ σιγᾶν κρεῖττόν ἐστι τοῦ λαλεῖν, *for youth silence is better than prating*, Men. *Mon.* 387; ἐπέσχομεν τοῦ δακρύειν, *we ceased our weeping*, P.*Ph.* 117e; ἀήθεις τοῦ κατακούειν τινός εἰσιν, *they are unused to obeying any one*, D.1,23. Τῷ φανερὸς εἶναι τοιοῦτος ὤν, *by having it evident that he was such a man*, X.*M.*1,2[3]; τῷ κοσμίως ζῆν πιστεύειν, *to trust in an orderly life*, I.15,24; ἴσον τῷ προστένειν, *equal to lamenting beforehand*, A.*Ag.*253.

1548. The infinitive with τοῦ may express a purpose, generally a negative purpose, where with ordinary genitives ἕνεκα is regularly used (see 1127). *E.g.*

Ἐτειχίσθη Ἀταλάντη, τοῦ μὴ λῃστὰς κακουργεῖν τὴν Εὔβοιαν, *Atalante was fortified, that pirates might not ravage Euboea*, T.2,32. Μίνως τὸ λῃστικὸν καθῄρει, τοῦ τὰς προσόδους μᾶλλον ἰέναι αὐτῷ, *Minos put down piracy, that his revenues might come in more abundantly*, T.1,4.

1549. Verbs and expressions denoting *hindrance* or *freedom* from anything allow either the infinitive with τοῦ (1547) or the simple infinitive (1519). As the infinitive after such verbs can take the negative μή without affecting the sense (1615), we have a third and fourth form, still with the same meaning. (See 1551.) *E.g.*

Εἴργει σε τοῦτο ποιεῖν, εἴργει σε τοῦ τοῦτο ποιεῖν, εἴργει σε μὴ τοῦτο ποιεῖν, εἴργει σε τοῦ μὴ τοῦτο ποιεῖν, all meaning *he prevents you from doing this*. Τὸν Φίλιππον παρελθεῖν οὐκ ἐδύναντο κωλῦσαι, *they could not hinder Philip from passing through*, D.5,20. Τοῦ δραπετεύειν ἀπείργουσι; *do they restrain them from running away?* X.*M.*2,1[16]. Ὅπερ ἔσχε μὴ τὴν Πελοπόννησον πορθεῖν, *which prevented (him) from ravaging Peloponnesus*, T.1,73. Δύο ἄνδρας ἕξει τοῦ μὴ καταδῦναι, *it will keep two men from sinking*, X.*A.*3,5[11].

1550. N. When the leading verb is negatived (or is interrogative implying a negative), the double negative μὴ οὐ is generally used with the infinitive rather than the simple μή (1616), so that we can say οὐκ εἴργει σε μὴ οὐ τοῦτο ποιεῖν, *he does not prevent you from doing this*. Τοῦ μὴ οὐ ποιεῖν is rarely (if ever) used.

1551. The infinitive with τὸ μή may be used after expressions denoting *hindrance*, and also after all which even imply *prevention, omission,* or *denial.* This infinitive with τό is less closely connected with the leading verb than are the forms before mentioned (1549), and it may often be considered an accusative of *specification* (1058), and sometimes (as after verbs of *denial*) an object accusative. Sometimes it expresses merely a *result.* *E.g.*

Τὸν ὅμιλον εἶργον τὸ μὴ τὰ ἐγγὺς τῆς πόλεως κακουργεῖν, *they prevented the crowd from injuring the neighboring parts of the city,* T.3,1. Κίμωνα παρὰ τρεῖς ἀφεῖσαν ψήφους τὸ μὴ θανάτῳ ζημιῶσαι, *they allowed Cimon by three votes to escape the punishment of death (they let him off from the punishment of death),* D.23,205. Φόβος ἀνθ᾽ ὕπνου παραστατεῖ, τὸ μὴ βλέφαρα συμβαλεῖν, *fear stands by me instead of sleep, preventing me from closing my eyelids,* A.*Ag.*15.

Thus we have a *fifth* form, εἴργει σε τὸ μὴ τοῦτο ποιεῖν, added to those given in 1549, as equivalents of the English *he prevents you from doing this.*

1552. N. Here, as above (1550), μὴ οὐ is generally used when the leading verb is negatived; as οὐδὲν γὰρ αὐτῷ ταῦτ᾽ ἐπαρκέσει τὸ μὴ οὐ πεσεῖν, *for this will not at all suffice to prevent him from falling,* A.*Pr.*918.

1553. N. The infinitive with τοῦ μή and with τὸ μή may also be used in the ordinary negative sense; as οὐδεμία πρόφασις τοῦ μὴ δρᾶν ταῦτα, *no ground for not doing this,* P.*Ti.*20[c].

1554. 1. The infinitive with τό may be used in exclamations, to express surprise or indignation. *E.g.*

Τῆς μωρίας· τὸ Δία νομίζειν, ὄντα τηλικουτονί, *what folly! to believe in Zeus, now you are so big!* Ar.*N.*819. So in Latin: Mene incepto *desistere* victam!

2. The article here is sometimes omitted; as τοιουτονὶ τρέφειν κύνα, *to keep a dog like that!* Ar.*V.*835.

1555. The infinitive with its subject, object, or other adjuncts (sometimes including dependent clauses) may be preceded by τό, the whole standing as a single noun in any ordinary construction. *E.g.*

Τὸ δὲ μήτε πάλαι τοῦτο πεπονθέναι, πεφηνέναι τέ τινα ἡμῖν συμμαχίαν τούτων ἀντίρροπον, ἂν βουλώμεθα χρῆσθαι, τῆς παρ᾽ ἐκείνων εὐνοίας εὐεργέτημ᾽ ἂν ἔγωγε θείην, *but the fact that we have not suffered this long ago, and that an alliance has appeared to us to balance these, if we (shall) wish to use it, — this I should ascribe as a benefaction to their good-will,* D.1,10. (Here the whole sentence τὸ . . . χρῆσθαι is the object accusative of θείην.)

1556. 1. For the infinitive as well as the finite moods with ὥστε, ὡς, ἐφ' ᾧ and ἐφ' ᾧτε, see 1449–1460.

2. For the infinitive and finite moods with πρίν, see 1469–1474.

3. For the infinitive with ἄν, see 1308.

THE PARTICIPLE.

1557. The participle is a verbal adjective, and has three uses. First, it may express an *attribute*, qualifying a noun like an ordinary adjective (1559–1562); secondly, it may define the *circumstances* under which an action takes place (1563–1577); thirdly, it may be joined to certain verbs to *supplement* their meaning, often having a force resembling that of the infinitive (1578–1593).

1558. N. These distinctions are not always exact, and the same participle may belong to more than one class. Thus, in ὁ μὴ δαρεὶς ἄνθρωπος, *the unflogged man*, δαρείς is both attributive and conditional (1563, 5).

ATTRIBUTIVE PARTICIPLE.

1559. The participle may qualify a noun, like an attributive adjective. Here it may often be translated by a relative and a finite verb, especially when it has the article. *E.g.*

Ὁ παρὼν καιρός, *the present occasion*, D.3,3; θεοὶ αἰὲν ἐόντες, *immortal Gods*, *Il.*21,518; πόλις κάλλει διαφέρουσα, *a city excelling in beauty;* ἀνὴρ καλῶς πεπαιδευμένος, *a man who has been well educated* (or *a well educated man*); οἱ πρέσβεις οἱ ὑπὸ Φιλίππου πεμφθέντες, *the ambassadors who were sent by Philip;* ἄνδρες οἱ τοῦτο ποιήσοντες, *men who are to do this.*

1560. 1. The participle with the article may be used substantively, like any adjective. It is then equivalent to *he who* or *those who* with a finite verb. *E.g.*

Οἱ κρατοῦντες, *the conquerors;* οἱ πεπεισμένοι, *those who have been convinced;* παρὰ τοῖς ἀρίστοις δοκοῦσιν εἶναι, *among those who seem to be best*, X.*M.*4,2[6]; ὁ τὴν γνώμην ταύτην εἰπών, *the one who gave this opinion*, T.8,68; τοῖς Ἀρκάδων σφετέροις οὖσι ξυμμάχοις προεῖπον, *they proclaimed to those who were their allies among the Arcadians*, T.5,64.

2. The article is sometimes omitted; as πολεμούντων πόλις, *a city of belligerents*, X. C.7, 5[78].

1561. N. Sometimes a participle becomes so completely a noun that it takes an object genitive instead of an object accusative; as ὁ ἐκείνου τεκών, *his father* (for ὁ ἐκεῖνον τεκών), E. *El.* 335.

1562. N. The neuter participle with the article is sometimes used as an abstract noun, like the infinitive; as τὸ δεδιός, *fear*, and τὸ θαρσοῦν, *courage*, for τὸ δεδιέναι and τὸ θαρσεῖν, T. 1, 36. Compare τὸ καλόν for τὸ κάλλος, *beauty*. In both cases the adjective is used for the noun.

CIRCUMSTANTIAL PARTICIPLE.

1563. The participle may define the *circumstances* of an action. It may express the following relations:—

1. *Time;* the tenses denoting various points of time, which is relative to that of the verb of the sentence (1288). *E.g.*

Ταῦτα ἔπραττε στρατηγῶν, *he did this while he was general;* ταῦτα πράξει στρατηγῶν, *he will do this while he is general.* Τυραννεύσας δὲ ἔτη τρία Ἱππίας ἐχώρει ἐς Σίγειον, *and when he had been tyrant three years, Hippias withdrew to Sigeum*, T. 6, 59.

2. *Cause. E.g.*

Λέγω δὲ τοῦδ' ἕνεκα, βουλόμενος δόξαι σοι ὅπερ ἐμοί, *and I speak for this reason, because I wish that to seem good to you which seems so to me*, P. *Ph.* 102[d].

3. *Means, manner*, and similar relations, including *manner of employment. E.g.*

Προείλετο μᾶλλον τοῖς νόμοις ἐμμένων ἀποθανεῖν ἢ παρανομῶν ζῆν, *he preferred to die abiding by the laws rather than to live transgressing them*, X. *M.* 4, 4[4]. Τοῦτο ἐποίησε λαθών, *he did this secretly.* Ἀπεδήμει τριηραρχῶν, *he was absent on duty as trierarch.* Ληζόμενοι ζῶσιν, *they live by plunder*, X. *C.* 3, 2[25].

4. *Purpose* or *intention;* generally expressed by the *future* participle. *E.g.*

Ἦλθε λυσόμενος θύγατρα, *he came to ransom his daughter*, *Il.* 1, 13. Πέμπειν πρέσβεις ταῦτα ἐροῦντας καὶ Λύσανδρον αἰτήσοντας, *to send ambassadors to say this and to ask for Lysander*, X. *H.* 2, 1[6].

5. *Condition;* the tenses of the participle representing the corresponding tenses of the indicative, subjunctive, or optative, in all classes of protasis.

See 1413, where examples will be found.

6. *Opposition, limitation,* or *concession;* where the participle is generally to be translated by *although* and a verb. *E.g.*

Ὀλίγα δυνάμενοι προορᾶν πολλὰ ἐπιχειροῦμεν πράττειν, *although we are able to foresee few things, we try to do many things,* X. *C.* 3, 2^{15}.

7. Any *attendant* circumstance, the participle being merely *descriptive.* This is one of the most common relations of this participle. *E.g.*

Ἔρχεται τὸν υἱὸν ἔχουσα, *she comes bringing her son,* X. *C.* 1, 3^1. Παραλαβόντες Βοιωτοὺς ἐστράτευσαν ἐπὶ Φάρσαλον, *they took Boeotians with them and marched against Pharsālus,* T. 1, 111.

The participle here can often be best translated by a verb, as in the last example.

8. That *in which* the action of the verb *consists.* *E.g.*

Τόδ' εἶπε φωνῶν, *thus he spake saying,* A. *Ag.* 205. Εὖ γ' ἐποίησας ἀναμνήσας με, *you did well in reminding me,* P. *Ph.* 60^c.

For the time of the aorist participle here, see 1290.

1564. N. Certain participles of *time* and *manner* have almost the force of adverbs by idiomatic usage. Such are ἀρχόμενος, *at first;* τελευτῶν, *at last, finally;* διαλιπὼν χρόνον, *after a while,* φέρων, *hastily;* φερόμενος, *with a rush;* κατατείνας, *earnestly;* φθάσας, *sooner (anticipating);* λαθών, *secretly;* ἔχων, *continually;* ἀνύσας, *quickly (hastening);* κλαίων, *to one's sorrow;* χαίρων, *to one's joy, with impunity.* *E.g.*

Ἅπερ ἀρχόμενος εἶπον, *as I said at first,* T. 4, 64. Ἐσέπεσον φερόμενοι ἐς τοὺς Ἕλληνας, *they fell upon the Greeks with a rush,* Hd. 7, 210. Τί κυπτάζεις ἔχων; *why do you keep poking about?* Ar. *N.* 509. Κλαίων ἅψει τῶνδε, *you will lay hands on them to your sorrow,* E. *Her.* 270.

1565. N. Ἔχων, φέρων, ἄγων, λαβών, and χρώμενος may often be translated *with.* *E.g.*

Μία ᾤχετο πρέσβεις ἄγουσα, *one* (ship) *was gone with ambassadors,* T. 7, 25. See X. *C.* 1, 3^1, in 1563, 7. Βοῇ χρώμενοι, *with a shout,* T. 2, 84.

1566. N. Τί παθών; *having suffered what?* or *what has happened to him?* and τί μαθών; *what has he taken into his head?* are used in the general sense of *why?* *E.g.*

Τί τοῦτο μαθὼν προσέγραψεν; *with what idea did he add this clause?* D. 20, 127. Τί παθοῦσαι θνηταῖς εἴξασι γυναιξίν; *what makes them look like mortal women?* Ar. *N.* 340.

1567. N. The same participle may sometimes be placed under more than one of these heads (1558).

GENITIVE AND ACCUSATIVE ABSOLUTE.

1568. When a circumstantial participle belongs to a noun which is not grammatically connected with the main construction of the sentence, they stand together in the *genitive absolute*. *E.g.*

Ἀνέβη οὐδενὸς κωλύοντος, *he made the ascent with no one interfering*, X. *A*. 1, 2[22]. See 1152, and the examples there given.

Sometimes a participle stands alone in the genitive absolute, when a subject can easily be supplied from the context, or when some general subject, like ἀνθρώπων or πραγμάτων, is understood; as οἱ πολέμιοι, προσιόντων, τέως μὲν ἡσύχαζον, *but the enemy, as they* (men before mentioned) *came on, kept quiet for a time*, X. *A*. 5, 4[16]. Οὕτω δ' ἐχόντων, εἰκός (ἐστιν), κ.τ.λ., *and this being the case* (sc. πραγμάτων), *it is likely*, etc. X. *A*. 3, 2[10]. So with verbs like ὕει (897, 5); as ὕοντος πολλῷ, *when it was raining heavily* (where originally Διός was understood), X. *H*. 1, 1[16].

1569. The participles of *impersonal* verbs stand in the *accusative absolute*, in the neuter singular, when others would be in the genitive absolute. So passive participles and ὄν, when they are used impersonally. *E.g.*

Τί δή, ὑμᾶς ἐξὸν ἀπολέσαι, οὐκ ἐπὶ τοῦτο ἤλθομεν; *why now, when we might have destroyed you, did we not proceed to do it?* X. *A*. 2, 5[22]. Οἱ δ' οὐ βοηθήσαντες δέον ὑγιεῖς ἀπῆλθον; *and did those who brought no aid when it was needed escape safe and sound?* P. *Alc*. i. 115[b]. So εὖ δὲ παρασχόν, *and when a good opportunity offers*, T. 1, 120; οὐ προσῆκον, *improperly* (*it being not becoming*), T. 4, 95; τυχόν, *by chance* (*it having happened*); προσταχθέν μοι, *when I had been commanded*; εἰρημένον, *when it has been said*; ἀδύνατον ὂν ἐν νυκτὶ σημῆναι, *it being impossible to signal by night*, T. 7, 44.

1570. N. The participles of personal verbs sometimes stand with their nouns in the accusative absolute; but very seldom unless they are preceded by ὡς or ὥσπερ. *E.g.*

Σιωπῇ ἐδείπνουν, ὥσπερ τοῦτο προστεταγμένον αὐτοῖς, *they were supping in silence, as if this had been the command given to them*, X. *Sy*. 1, 11.

1571. N. Ὤν as a circumstantial participle is seldom omitted, except with the adjectives ἑκών, *willing*, and ἄκων, *unwilling*, and after ἅτε, οἷα, ὡς, or καίπερ. See ἐμοῦ οὐχ ἑκόντος, *against my will*, S. *Aj.* 455; Ζεύς, καίπερ αὐθάδης φρενῶν, *Zeus, although stubborn in mind*, A. *Pr.* 907; also ἀπόρρητον πόλει, *when it is forbidden to the state*, S. *An.* 44. See 1612.

ADVERBS WITH CIRCUMSTANTIAL PARTICIPLE.

1572. N. The adverbs ἅμα, μεταξύ, εὐθύς, αὐτίκα, ἄρτι, and ἐξαίφνης are often connected (in position and in sense) with the temporal participle, while grammatically they qualify the leading verb; as ἅμα καταλαβόντες προσεκέατό σφι, *as soon as they overtook them, they pressed hard upon them*, Hd. 9, 57. Νεκὼς μεταξὺ ὀρύσσων ἐπαύσατο, *Necho stopped while digging* (*the canal*), Hd. 2, 158.

1573. N. The participle denoting *opposition* is often strengthened by καί or καίπερ, *even* (Homeric also καί . . . περ), and in negative sentences by οὐδέ or μηδέ; also by καὶ ταῦτα, *and that too;* as ἐποικτίρω νιν, καίπερ ὄντα δυσμενῆ, *I pity him, even though he is an enemy*, S. *Aj.* 122. Οὐκ ἂν προδοίην, οὐδέ περ πράσσων κακῶς, *I would not be faithless, even though I am in a wretched state*, E. *Ph.* 1624.

1574. Circumstantial participles, especially those denoting *cause* or *purpose*, are often preceded by ὡς. This shows that they express the idea or the assertion of the subject of the leading verb or that of some other person prominent in the sentence, *without implying* that it is also the idea of the speaker or writer. *E.g.*

Τὸν Περικλέα ἐν αἰτίᾳ εἶχον ὡς πείσαντα σφᾶς πολεμεῖν, *they found fault with Pericles, on the ground that he had persuaded them to engage in war*, T. 2, 59. Ἀγανακτοῦσιν ὡς μεγάλων τινῶν ἀπεστερημένοι, *they are indignant, because* (*as they say*) *they have been deprived of some great blessings*, P. *Rp.* 329ᵃ.

1575. The causal participle is often emphasized by ἅτε and οἷον or οἷα, *as, inasmuch as;* but these particles have no such force as ὡς (1574); as ἅτε παῖς ὤν, ἥδετο, *inasmuch as he was a child, he was pleased*, X. *C.* 1, 3³.

1576. Ὥσπερ, *as, as it were*, with the participle expresses a comparison between the action of the verb and that of the participle. *E.g.*

Ὠρχοῦντο ὥσπερ ἄλλοις ἐπιδεικνύμενοι, *they danced as if they were showing off to others* (i.e. *they danced, apparently showing off*), X. *A.* 5, 4³⁴. Τί τοῦτο λέγεις, ὥσπερ οὐκ ἐπὶ σοὶ ὂν ὅ τι ἂν βούλῃ λέγειν; *why do you say this, as if it were not in your power to say what you please?* X. *M.* 2, 6[36]. Although we find *as if* a convenient translation, there is really no condition, as appears from the negative οὐ (not μή). See 1612.

1577. N. Ὥσπερ, like other words meaning *as*, may be followed by a protasis; as ὥσπερ εἰ παρεστάτεις, *as* (it would be) *if you had lived near*, A. *Ag.* 1201. For ὥσπερ ἂν εἰ, see 1313.

SUPPLEMENTARY PARTICIPLE.

1578. The supplementary participle completes the idea expressed by the verb, by showing to what its action relates. It may belong to either the subject or the object of the verb, and agree with it in case. *E.g.*

Παύομέν σε λέγοντα, *we stop you from speaking;* παυόμεθα λέγοντες, *we cease speaking.*

1579. This participle has many points of resemblance to the infinitive in similar constructions. In the use of the participle (as in that of the infinitive) we must distinguish between indirect discourse (where each tense preserves its force) and other constructions.

Participle not in Indirect Discourse.

1580. In this sense the participle is used with verbs signifying *to begin, to continue, to endure, to persevere, to cease, to repent, to be weary, to be pleased, displeased,* or *ashamed;* and with the object of verbs signifying *to permit* or *to cause to cease.* *E.g.*

Ἦρχον χαλεπαίνων, *I was the first to be angry, Il.* 2, 378; οὐκ ἀνέξομαι ζῶσα, *I shall not endure my life,* E. *Hip.* 354; ἑπτὰ ἡμέρας μαχόμενοι διετέλεσαν, *they continued fighting seven days,* X. *A.* 4, 3[2]; τιμώμενοι χαίρουσιν, *they delight in being honored,* E. *Hip.* 8; ἐλεγχόμενοι ἤχθοντο, *they were displeased at being tested,* X. *M.* 1, 2[47]; τοῦτο οὐκ αἰσχύνομαι λέγων, *I say this without shame* (see 1581), X. *C.* 5, 1[21]; τὴν φιλοσοφίαν παῦσον ταῦτα λέγουσαν, *make Philosophy stop talking in this style,* P. *G.* 482[a]; παύεται λέγων, *he stops talking.*

1581. Some of these verbs also take the infinitive, but generally with some difference of meaning; thus, αἰσχύνεται τοῦτο λέγειν, *he is ashamed to say this* (and does not say it), — see 1580; ἀποκάμνει τοῦτο ποιεῖν, *he ceases to do this, through weariness* (but ἀποκάμνει τοῦτο ποιῶν, *he is weary of doing this*). So ἄρχεται λέγειν, *he begins to speak* (but ἄρχεται λέγων, *he begins by speaking* or *he is at the beginning of his speech*); παύω σε μάχεσθαι, *I pre-*

vent you from fighting (but παύω σε μαχόμενον, *I stop you while fighting*).

1582. The participle may be used with verbs signifying *to perceive* (in any way), *to find*, or *to represent*, denoting an act or state in which the object is perceived, found, or represented. *E.g.*

Ὁρῶ σε κρύπτοντα χεῖρα, *I see you hiding your hand*, E. *Hec.* 342; ἤκουσά σου λέγοντος, *I heard you speak*; εὗρε Κρονίδην ἄτερ ἥμενον ἄλλων, *he found the son of Cronos sitting apart from the others*, *Il.* 1, 498; βασιλέας πεποίηκε τοὺς ἐν Ἅιδου τιμωρουμένους, *he has represented kings in Hades as suffering punishment*, P. *G.* 525[d].

1583. N. This must not be confounded with indirect discourse, in which ὁρῶ σε κρύπτοντα would mean *I see that you are hiding*; ἀκούω σε λέγοντα, *I hear that you say* (ἀκούω taking the accusative). See 1588.

1584. The participles βουλόμενος, *wishing*, ἡδόμενος, *pleased*, προσδεχόμενος, *expecting*, and some others, may agree in case with a dative which depends on εἰμί, γίγνομαι, or some similar verb. *E.g.*

Τῷ πλήθει οὐ βουλομένῳ ἦν, *it was not pleasing to the majority* (*it was not to them wishing it*), T. 2, 3; προσδεχομένῳ μοι τὰ τῆς ὀργῆς ὑμῶν ἐς ἐμὲ γεγένηται, *I have been expecting the manifestations of your wrath against me*, T. 2, 60.

1585. With verbs signifying *to overlook* or *see*, in the sense of *to allow* or *let happen* (περιορῶ and ἐφορῶ, with περιεῖδον and ἐπεῖδον, sometimes εἶδον), the participle is used in a sense which approaches that of the object infinitive, the present and aorist participles differing merely as the present and aorist infinitives would differ in similar constructions. *E.g.*

Μὴ περιίδωμεν ὑβρισθεῖσαν τὴν Λακεδαίμονα καὶ καταφρονηθεῖσαν, *let us not see Lacedaemon insulted and despised*, I. 6, 108. Μή μ' ἰδεῖν θανόνθ' ὑπ' ἀστῶν, *not to see me killed by citizens*, E. *Or.* 746. Περιιδεῖν τὴν γῆν τμηθεῖσαν, *to let the land be ravaged*, i.e. *to look on and see it ravaged*, T. 2, 18; but in 2, 20 we have περιιδεῖν τὴν γῆν τμηθῆναι, *to permit the land to be ravaged*, referring to the same thing from another point of view, τμηθῆναι being strictly future to περιιδεῖν, while τμηθεῖσαν is coincident with it.

1586. The participle with λανθάνω, *escape the notice of*, τυγχάνω, *happen*, and φθάνω, *anticipate*, contains the leading idea of the expression and is usually translated by a verb.

The aorist participle here coincides in time with the verb (unless this expresses duration) and does not denote past time in itself. (See 1290.) *E.g.*

Φονέα τοῦ παιδὸς ἐλάνθανε βόσκων, *he was unconsciously supporting the slayer of his son*, Hd. 1,44; ἔτυχον καθήμενος ἐνταῦθα, *I happened to be sitting there* (= τύχῃ ἐκαθήμην ἐνταῦθα), P. *Eu.* 272ᵉ; αὐτοὶ φθήσονται τοῦτο δράσαντες, *they will do this themselves first* (= τοῦτο δράσουσι πρότεροι), P. *Rp.* 375ᶜ; τοὺς δ' ἔλαθ' εἰσελθών, *and he entered unnoticed by them* (= εἰσῆλθε λάθρᾳ), *Il.* 24,477; ἔφθησαν πολλῷ τοὺς Πέρσας ἀπικόμενοι, *they arrived long before the Persians*, Hd. 4,136; τοὺς ἀνθρώπους λήσομεν ἐπιπεσόντες, *we shall rush in unnoticed by the men*, X. *A.* 7,3[48].

The perfect participle here has its ordinary force.

1587. N. The participle with διατελέω, *continue* (1580), οἴχομαι, *be gone* (1256), θαμίζω, *be wont* or *be frequent*, and some others, expresses the leading idea; but the aorist participle with these has no peculiar force; as οἴχεται φεύγων, *he has taken flight*, Ar. *Pl.* 933; οὐ θαμίζεις καταβαίνων εἰς τὸν Πειραιᾶ, *you don't come down to the Peiraeus very often*, P. *Rp.* 328ᶜ.

So with the Homeric βῆ and ἔβαν or βάν from βαίνω; as βῆ φεύγων, *he took flight*, *Il.* 2,665; so 2,167.

Participle in Indirect Discourse.

1588. With many verbs the participle stands in indirect discourse, each tense representing the corresponding tense of a finite mood.

Such verbs are chiefly those signifying *to see*, *to hear* or *learn*, *to perceive*, *to know*, *to be ignorant of*, *to remember*, *to forget*, *to show*, *to appear*, *to prove*, *to acknowledge*, and ἀγγέλλω, *announce*. *E.g.*

Ὁρῶ δέ μ' ἔργον δεινὸν ἐξειργασμένην, *but I see that I have done a dreadful deed*, S. *Tr.* 706; ἤκουσε Κῦρον ἐν Κιλικίᾳ ὄντα, *he heard that Cyrus was in Cilicia* (cf. 1583), X. *A.* 1,4[5]; ὅταν κλύῃ ἥξοντ' Ὀρέστην, *when she hears that Orestes will come*, S. *El.* 293. Οἶδα οὐδὲν ἐπιστάμενος, *I know that I understand nothing*; οὐκ ᾔδεσαν αὐτὸν τεθνηκότα, *they did not know that he was dead*, X. *A.* 1,10[16]; ἐπειδὰν γνῶσιν ἀπιστούμενοι, *after they find out that they are distrusted*, X. *C.* 7,2[17]; μέμνημαι ἐλθών, *I remember that I went*; μέμνημαι αὐτὸν ἐλθόντα, *I remember that he went*; δείξω τοῦτον ἐχθρὸν ὄντα, *I shall show that this man is an enemy* (passive οὗτος δειχθήσεται ἐχθρὸς ὤν). Αὐτῷ Κῦρον ἐπιστρατεύοντα πρῶτος ἤγγειλα, *I first announced to him that Cyrus was on his march against him*, X. *A*. 2, 3[19].

See 1494; and 1308 for examples of the participle with ἄν representing both indicative and optative with ἄν.

1589. N. Δῆλός εἰμι and φανερός εἰμι take the participle in indirect discourse, where we use an impersonal construction; as δῆλος ἦν οἰόμενος, *it was evident that he thought* (like δῆλον ἦν ὅτι οἴοιτο).

1590. N. With σύνοιδα or συγγιγνώσκω and a dative of the reflexive, a participle may be in either the nominative or the dative; as σύνοιδα ἐμαυτῷ ἠδικημένῳ (or ἠδικημένος), *I am conscious to myself that I have been wronged.*

1591. Most of the verbs included in 1588 may also take a clause with ὅτι or ὡς in indirect discourse.

1592. 1. Some of these verbs have the infinitive of indirect discourse in nearly or quite the same sense as the participle. Others have the infinitive in a different sense: thus φαίνεται σοφὸς ὤν generally means *he is manifestly wise*, and φαίνεται σοφὸς εἶναι, *he seems to be wise;* but sometimes this distinction is not observed.

2. Others, again, may be used in a peculiar sense, in which they have the infinitive *not* in indirect discourse. Thus οἶδα and ἐπίσταμαι regularly have this infinitive when they mean *know how;* as οἶδα τοῦτο ποιῆσαι, *I know how to do this* (but οἶδα τοῦτο ποιήσας, *I know that I did this*). Μανθάνω, μέμνημαι, and ἐπιλανθάνομαι, in the sense of *learn, remember*, or *forget to do* anything, take the regular object infinitive. See also the uses of γιγνώσκω, δείκνυμι, δηλῶ, φαίνομαι, and εὑρίσκω in the Lexicon.

1593. 1. Ὡς may be used with the participle of indirect discourse in the sense explained in 1574. *E.g.*

Ὡς μηκέτ' ὄντα κεῖνον ἐν φάει νόει, *think of him as no longer living*, S. *Ph*. 415. See 1614.

2. The genitive absolute with ὡς is sometimes found where we should expect the participle to agree with the object of the verb; as ὡς πολέμου ὄντος παρ' ὑμῶν ἀπαγγελῶ; *shall I announce from you that there is war?* (lit. *assuming that there is war, shall I announce it from you?*), X. *A*. 2, 1[21], — where we might have πόλεμον ὄντα with less emphasis and in closer connection with the verb. So ὡς ὧδ' ἐχόντων τῶνδ' ἐπίστασθαί σε χρή, *you must understand that this is so* (lit. *believing this to be so, you must understand it*), S. *Aj*. 281.

VERBAL ADJECTIVES IN -τέος AND -τέον.

1594. The verbal in -*τέος* has both a *personal* and an *impersonal* construction, of which the latter is more common.

1595. In the personal construction it is passive in sense, and expresses *necessity*, like the Latin participle in *-dus*, agreeing with the subject. *E.g.*

Ὠφελητέα σοι ἡ πόλις ἐστίν, *the city must be benefited by you*, X. *M.* 3, 6[3]. Ἄλλας μεταπεμπτέας εἶναι (ἔφη), *he said that other (ships) must be sent for*, T. 6, 25.

1596. N. The noun denoting the agent is here in the dative (1188). This construction is of course confined to transitive verbs.

1597. In the impersonal construction the verbal is in the neuter of the nominative singular (sometimes plural), with ἐστί expressed or understood. The expression is equivalent to δεῖ, (*one*) *must*, with the infinitive. It is practically active in sense, and allows transitive verbals to have an object like their verbs.

The agent is generally expressed by the dative, sometimes by the accusative. *E.g.*

Ταῦτα ἡμῖν (or ἡμᾶς) ποιητέον ἐστίν, *we must do this* (equivalent to ταῦτα ἡμᾶς δεῖ ποιῆσαι). Οἰστέον τάδε, *we must bear these things* (sc. ἡμῖν), E. *Or.* 769. Τί ἂν αὐτῷ ποιητέον εἴη; *what would he be obliged to do?* (= τί δέοι ἂν αὐτὸν ποιῆσαι), X. *M.* 1, 7[2] (1598). Ἐψηφίσαντο πολεμητέα εἶναι, *they voted that they must go to war* (= δεῖν πολεμεῖν), T. 1, 88. Ξύμμαχοι, οὓς οὐ παραδοτέα τοῖς Ἀθηναίοις ἐστίν, *allies, whom we must not abandon to the Athenians*, T. 1, 86.

1598. N. Though the verbal in -*τέον* allows both the dative and the accusative of the agent (1188), the equivalent δεῖ with the infinitive allows only the accusative (1162).

1599. N. The Latin has this construction (1597), but generally only with verbs which do not take an object accusative; as Eundum est tibi (ἰτέον ἐστί σοι),—Moriendum est omnibus. So Bello utendum est nobis (τῷ πολέμῳ χρηστέον ἐστὶν ἡμῖν), *we must go to war*. The earlier Latin occasionally has the exact equivalent of the Greek impersonal construction; as Aeternas poenas timendum est, Lucr. 1, 112. (See Madvig's Latin Grammar, § 421.)

INTERROGATIVE SENTENCES.

1600. All interrogative pronouns, pronominal adjectives, and adverbs can be used in both direct and indirect questions. The relative ὅστις (rarely ὅς) and the relative pronominal adjectives (429) may be used in indirect questions. *E.g.*

Τί λέγει; *what does he say?* Πότε ἦλθεν; *when did he come?* Πόσα εἶδες; *how many did you see?* Ἤροντο τί λέγοι (or ὅ τι λέγοι), *they asked what he said.* Ἤροντο πότε (or ὁπότε) ἦλθεν, *they asked when he came.* Ὁρᾷς ἡμᾶς, ὅσοι ἐσμέν; *do you see how many of us there are?* P. *Rp.* 327ᶜ.

1601. N. The Greek, unlike the English, freely uses two or more interrogatives with the same verb. *E.g.*

Ἡ τίσι τί ἀποδιδοῦσα τέχνη δικαιοσύνη ἂν καλοῖτο; *the art which renders what to what would be called Justice?* P. *Rp.* 332ᵈ. See the five interrogatives (used for comic effect) in D. 4, 36: πρόοιδεν ἕκαστος τίς χορηγός, . . . πότε καὶ παρὰ τοῦ καὶ τί λαβόντα τί δεῖ ποιεῖν, meaning *everybody knows who the* χορηγός *is to be, what he is to get, when and from whom he is to get it, and what he is to do with it.*

1602. N. An interrogative sometimes stands as a predicate with a demonstrative; as τί τοῦτο ἔλεξας; *what is this that you said?* (= ἔλεξας τοῦτο, τί ὄν; lit. *you said this, being what?*); τίνας τούσδ' εἰσορῶ; *who are these that I see?* E. *Or.* 1347.

Such expressions cannot be literally translated.

1603. The principal *direct* interrogative particles are ἆρα and (chiefly poetic) ἦ. These imply nothing as to the answer expected; but ἆρα οὐ implies an *affirmative* and ἆρα μή a *negative* answer. Οὐ and μή are used alone with the same force as with ἆρα. So μῶν (for μὴ οὖν) implies a negative answer, and οὐκοῦν, *therefore* (with no negative force), implies an affirmative answer. *E.g.*

Ἦ σχολὴ ἔσται; *will there be leisure?* Ἆρ' εἰσί τινες ἄξιοι; *are there any deserving ones?* Ἆρ' οὐ βούλεσθε ἐλθεῖν; or οὐ βούλεσθε ἐλθεῖν; *do you not wish to go* (i.e. *you wish, do you not*)? Ἆρα μὴ βούλεσθε ἐλθεῖν; or μὴ (or μῶν) βούλεσθε ἐλθεῖν; *do you wish to go* (*you don't wish to go, do you*)? Οὐκοῦν σοι δοκεῖ σύμφορον εἶναι; *does it not seem to you to be of advantage?* X. *C.* 2, 4¹⁵. This distinction between οὐ and μή does not apply to questions with the interrogative subjunctive (1358), which allow only μή.

1604. Ἆλλο τι ἤ; *is it anything else than?* or (more frequently) ἄλλο τι; *is it not?* is sometimes used as a direct interrogative. *E.g.*

Ἆλλο τι ἢ ὁμολογοῦμεν; *do we not agree?* (*do we do anything else than agree?*), P. *G.* 470[b]. Ἆλλο τι οὖν δύο ταῦτα ἔλεγες; *did you not call these two?* *ibid.* 495[c].

1605. *Indirect* questions may be introduced by εἰ, *whether*; and in Homer by ἤ or εἰ. *E.g.*

Ἠρώτησα εἰ βούλοιτο ἐλθεῖν, *I asked whether he wished to go.* Ὤιχετο πευσόμενος ἤ που ἔτ' εἴης, *he was gone to inquire whether you were still living*, *Od.* 13, 415. Τὰ ἐκπώματα οὐκ οἶδα εἰ τούτῳ δῶ (1490), *I do not know whether I shall give him the cups*, X. *C.* 8, 4[16]. (Here εἰ is used even with the subjunctive: see 1491.)

1606. *Alternative* questions (both direct and indirect) may be introduced by πότερον (πότερα) . . . ἤ, *whether . . . or*. *Indirect* alternative questions can also be introduced by εἰ . . . ἤ or εἴτε . . . εἴτε, *whether . . . or*. Homer has ἦ (ἦε) . . . ἦ (ἦε) in direct, and ἤ (ἠέ) . . . ἤ (ἠε) in indirect, alternatives,—never πότερον. *E.g.*

Πότερον ἐᾷς ἄρχειν ἢ ἄλλον καθίστης; *do you allow him to rule,* or *do you appoint another?* X. *C.* 3, 1[12]. Ἐβουλεύετο εἰ πέμποιέν τινας ἢ πάντες ἴοιεν, *he was deliberating whether they should send some or should all go*, X. *A.* 1, 10[5].

NEGATIVES.

1607. The Greek has two negative adverbs, οὐ and μή. What is said of each of these generally applies to its compounds,—οὐδείς, οὐδέ, οὔτε, etc., and μηδείς, μηδέ, μήτε, etc.

1608. Οὐ is used with the indicative and optative in all *independent* sentences, except *wishes*; also in *indirect discourse* after ὅτι and ὡς, and in *causal* sentences.

1609. N. In indirect *questions*, introduced by εἰ, *whether*, μή can be used as well as οὐ; as βουλόμενος ἐρέσθαι εἰ μαθών τίς τι μεμνημένος μὴ οἶδεν, *wishing to ask whether one who has learnt a thing and remembers it does not know it?* P. *Th.* 163[d]. Also, in the second part of an indirect alternative question (1606), both οὐ and μή are allowed; as σκοπῶμεν εἰ ἡμῖν πρέπει ἢ οὔ, *let us look and see whether it suits us or not*, P. *Rp.* 451[d]; εἰ δὲ ἀληθὲς ἢ μή, πειράσομαι μαθεῖν, *but I will try to learn whether it is true or not*, *ibid.* 339[a].

1610. **Μή** is used with the subjunctive and imperative in all constructions, except with the Homeric subjunctive (1355), which has the force of a future indicative. **Μή** is used in all final and object clauses after **ἵνα, ὅπως**, etc., with the subjunctive, optative, and indicative; except after μή, *lest*, which takes οὐ. It is used in all conditional and conditional relative clauses, and in the corresponding temporal sentences after ἕως, πρίν, etc., in relative sentences expressing a *purpose* (1442), and in all expressions of a wish with both indicative and optative (1507; 1511).

For causal relative clauses with μή (also conditional), see 1462. For εἰ οὐ occasionally used in protasis, see 1383, 2.

1611. Μή is used with the infinitive in all constructions, both with and without the article, except in *indirect discourse.* The infinitive in indirect discourse regularly has οὐ, to retain the negative of the direct discourse; but some exceptions occur (1496).

For ὥστε οὐ with the infinitive, see 1451. For μή with the infinitive after verbs of *hoping, promising, swearing,* etc., see 1496.

1612. When a participle expresses a *condition* (1563, 5), it takes μή; so when it is equivalent to a conditional relative clause; as οἱ μὴ βουλόμενοι, *any who do not wish.* Otherwise it takes οὐ. In indirect discourse it sometimes, like the infinitive, takes μή irregularly (1496).

1613. Adjectives follow the same principle with participles, taking μή only when they do not refer to definite persons or things (i.e. when they can be expressed by a relative clause with an indefinite antecedent); as οἱ μὴ ἀγαθοὶ πολῖται, (*any*) *citizens who are not good,* but οἱ οὐκ ἀγαθοὶ πολῖται means *special citizens who are not good.*

1614. Participles or adjectives connected with a protasis, a command, or an infinitive which would be negatived by μή, generally take μή, even if they would otherwise have οὐ.

1615. When verbs which contain a *negative* idea (as those of *hindering, forbidding, denying, concealing,* and *distrusting*) take the infinitive, μή can be added to the infinitive to strengthen the negation. Such a negative cannot be translated in English, and can always be omitted in Greek. For examples, see 1549–1551.

1616. An infinitive which would regularly be negatived by *μή*, either in the ordinary way (1611) or to strengthen a preceding negation (1615), generally takes the double negative *μὴ οὐ* if the verb on which it depends itself has a negative.

Thus *δίκαιόν ἐστι μὴ τοῦτον ἀφεῖναι*, *it is just not to acquit him*, if we negative the leading verb, generally becomes *οὐ δίκαιόν ἐστι μὴ οὐ τοῦτον ἀφεῖναι*, *it is not just not to acquit him.* So *ὡς οὐχ ὅσιόν σοι ὂν μὴ οὐ βοηθεῖν δικαιοσύνῃ*, *since* (*as you said*) *it was a failure in piety for you not to assist justice*, P. *Rp.* 427[e]. Again, *εἴργει σε μὴ τοῦτο ποιεῖν* (1550), *he prevents you from doing this*, becomes, with *εἴργει* negatived, *οὐκ εἴργει σε μὴ οὐ τοῦτο ποιεῖν*, *he does not prevent you from doing this.*

1617. N. (*a*) Μὴ οὐ is used also when the leading verb is interrogative implying a negative; as *τί ἐμποδὼν μὴ οὐχὶ ὑβριζομένους ἀποθανεῖν; what is there to prevent* (*us*) *from being insulted and perishing?* X. *An.* 3, 1[13].

(*b*) It is sometimes used with participles, or even nouns, to express an *exception* to a negative (or implied negative) statement; as *πόλεις χαλεπαὶ λαβεῖν, μὴ οὐ πολιορκίᾳ*, *cities hard* (i.e. *not easy*) *to capture, except by siege*, D. 19, 123.

1618. When a negative is followed by a *simple* negative (*οὐ* or *μή*) in the same clause, each retains its own force. If they belong to the same word or expression, they make an *affirmative;* but if they belong to different words, each is independent of the other. *E.g.*

Οὐδὲ τὸν Φορμίωνα οὐχ ὁρᾷ, *nor does he not see Phormio* (i.e. *he sees Phormio well enough*), D. 36, 46. *Οὐ δι' ἀπειρίαν γε οὐ φήσεις ἔχειν ὅ τι εἴπῃς*, *it is not surely through inexperience that you will deny that you have anything to say*, D. 19, 120. *Εἰ μὴ Πρόξενον οὐχ ὑπεδέξαντο*, *if they had not refused to receive Proxenus* (*had not not-received him*), D. 19, 74. So *μὴ οὖν . . . διὰ ταῦτα μὴ δότω δίκην*, *do not then on this account let him escape punishment* (*do not let him not be punished*), D. 19, 77.

1619. But when a negative is followed by a *compound* negative (or by several compound negatives) in the same clause, the negation is strengthened. *E.g.*

Οὐδεὶς εἰς οὐδὲν οὐδενὸς ἂν ἡμῶν οὐδέποτε γένοιτο ἄξιος, *no one of us* (in that case) *would ever come to be of any value for anything*, P. *Ph.* 19[b].

For the double negative *οὐ μή*, see 1360 and 1361. For *οὐχ ὅτι, μὴ ὅτι, οὐχ ὅπως, μὴ ὅπως*, see 1504.

PART V.

VERSIFICATION.

RHYTHM AND METRE.

1620. Every verse is composed of definite portions called *feet.* Thus we have four feet in each of these verses: —

Φήσο|μεν πρὸς | τοὺς στρα|τηγούς. |
Fár from | mórtal | cáres re|treáting. |

1621. In each foot there is a certain part on which falls a special stress of voice called *ictus* (*stroke*), and another part on which there is no such stress. The part of the foot on which the *ictus* falls is called the *arsis,* and the rest of the foot is called the *thesis.*[1] The regular alternation of *arsis* and *thesis* in successive feet produces the *rhythm* (*harmonious movement*) of the verse.

1622. In this English verse (as in all English poetry) the rhythm depends entirely on the ordinary *accent* of the words, with which the ictus coincides. In the Greek verse, however, the ictus is entirely independent of the word-accent; and the feet (with the ictus marked by dots) are φ̣ησο, — μ̣εν προς, — τ̣ους στρα, — τ̣ηγους. In Greek poetry a foot consists of a regular combination of syllables of a certain

[1] The term ἄρσις (*raising*) and θέσις (*placing*), as they were used by nearly all the Greek writers on Rhythm, referred to the *raising* and *putting down* of the foot in marching, dancing, or beating time, so that θέσις denoted the part of the foot on which the ictus fell, and ἄρσις the lighter part. Most of the Roman writers, however, inverted this use, and referred *arsis* to the raising of the voice and *thesis* to the lowering of the voice in reading. The prevailing modern use of these terms unfortunately follows that of the Roman writers, and attempts to reverse the settled usage of language are apt to end in confusion.

length; and the place of the ictus here depends on the *quantity* (i.e. the length or shortness) of the syllables which compose the foot, the ictus naturally falling upon a long syllable (1629). The regular alternation of long and short syllables in successive feet makes the verse *metrical*, i.e. *measured* in its time. The rhythm of a Greek verse thus depends closely on its metre, *i.e.* on the *measure* or *quantity* of its syllables.

1623. The fundamental distinction between ancient and most modern poetry is simply this, that in modern poetry the verse consists of a regular combination of *accented* and *unaccented* syllables, while in ancient poetry it consists of a regular combination of *long* and *short* syllables. The *rhythm* is the one essential requisite in the external form of all poetry, ancient and modern; but in ancient poetry, rhythm depends on metre and not on accent; in modern poetry it depends on accent, and the quantity of the syllables (*i.e.* the metre) is generally no more regarded than it is in prose. Both are equally *rhythmical;* but the ancient is also *metrical*, and its metre is the basis of its rhythm. What is called *metre* in English poetry is strictly only rhythm.

1624. The change from metrical to accentual rhythm can best be seen in modern Greek poetry, in which, even when the forms of the ancient language are retained, the rhythm is generally accentual and the metre is no more regarded than it is in English poetry. These are the first two verses in a modern translation of the Odyssey: —

> **Ψάλλε τὸν | ἄνδρα, Θε|ά, τὸν πο|λύτροπον, | ὅστις το|σούτους**
> **Τόπους δι|ῆλθε, πορ|θήσας τῆς | Τροίας τὴν | ἔνδοξον | πόλιν.**

The original verses are: —

> **Ἄνδρα μοι | ἔννεπε, | Μοῦσα, πο|λύτροπον, | ὃς μάλα | πολλὰ**
> **Πλάγχθη, ἐ|πεὶ Τροί|ης ἱε|ρὸν πτολί|εθρον ἔ|περσεν.**

If the former verses set our teeth on edge, it is only through force of *acquired* habit; for these verses have much more of the nature of modern poetry than the Homeric originals, and their rhythm is precisely what we are accustomed to in English verse, where

> **Still stands the | forest pri|meval; but | under the | shade of its | branches**

is dactylic, and

> **And the ol|ive of peace | spreads its branch|es abroad**

is anapaestic.

1625. It is very difficult for us to appreciate the ease with which the Greeks distinguished and reconciled the stress of voice which constituted the ictus and the raising of tone which constituted the word-accent (107, 1). Any combination of the two is now very difficult, and for most persons impossible, because we have only stress of voice to represent both accent and ictus. In reading Greek poetry we usually mark the ictus by our accent, and either neglect the word-accent or make it subordinate to the ictus. Care should always be taken in reading to distinguish the *words*, not the *feet*.

FEET.

1626. 1. The unit of measure in Greek verse is the short syllable (⏑), which has the value of ♪ or an $\frac{1}{8}$ note in music. This is called a *time* or *mora*. The long syllable (–) has generally twice the length of a short one, and has the value of a $\frac{1}{4}$ note or ♩ in music.

2. But a long syllable sometimes has the length of three shorts, and is called a *triseme* (∟), and sometimes that of four shorts, and is called a *tetraseme* (⊔). The triseme has the value of ♩. in music, and the tetraseme that of 𝅗𝅥.

1627. Feet are distinguished according to the number of *times* which they contain. The most common feet are the following: —

1. *Of Three Times (in $\frac{3}{8}$ time).*

Trochee	– ⏑	φαῖνε	♩ ♪
Iambus	⏑ –	ἔφην	♪ ♩
Tribrach	⏑ ⏑ ⏑	λέγετε	♪ ♪ ♪

2. *Of Four Times (in $\frac{2}{4}$ or $\frac{4}{8}$ time).*

Dactyl	– ⏑ ⏑	φαίνετε	♩ ♫
Anapaest	⏑ ⏑ –	σέβομαι	♫ ♩
Spondee	– –	εἰπών	♩ ♩

3. *Of Five Times (in $\frac{5}{8}$ time).*

Cretic	– ⏑ –	φαινέτω	♩ ♪ ♩
Paeon primus	– ⏑ ⏑ ⏑	ἐκτρέπετε	♩ ♪ ♫
Paeon quartus	⏑ ⏑ ⏑ –	καταλέγω	♫ ♪ ♩
Bacchīus	⏑ – –	ἀφεγγής	♪ ♩ ♩
Antibacchīus	– – ⏑	φαίνητε	♩ ♩ ♪

4. *Of Six Times* (*in* $\frac{6}{8}$ *or* $\frac{3}{4}$ *time*).

Ionic *a maiore*	— — ⏑ ⏑	ἐκλείπετε	♩ ♩ ♫
Ionic *a minore*	⏑ ⏑ — —	προσιδέσθαι	♫ ♩ ♩
Choriambus	— ⏑ ⏑ —	ἐκτρέπομαι	♩ ♫ ♩
Molossus (*rare*)	— — —	βουλεύων	♩ ♩ ♩

5. A foot of four shorts (⏑⏑⏑⏑) is called a *proceleusmatic*, and one of two shorts (⏑⏑) a *pyrrhic*.

For the dochmius, ⏑ — — ⏑ —, see 1691. For the epitrite, see 1684.

1628. The feet in $\frac{3}{8}$ time (1), in which the arsis is twice as long as the thesis, form the *double* class (γένος διπλάσιον), as opposed to those in $\frac{2}{4}$ time (2), in which the arsis and thesis are of equal length, and which form the *equal* class (γένος ἴσον). The more complicated relations of arsis and thesis in the feet of five and six *times* are not considered here.

1629. The ictus falls naturally on a long syllable. The first syllable of the trochee and the dactyl, and the last syllable of the iambus and the anapaest, therefore, form the arsis, the remainder of the foot being the thesis; as ⏑́ ⏑, ⏑́ ⏑ ⏑, ⏑ —́, ⏑ ⏑ —́.

1630. When a long syllable in the arsis is resolved into two short syllables (1631), the ictus properly belongs on the two taken together, but in reading it is usually placed on the first. Thus a tribrach used for a trochee (—́ ⏑) is ⏑́ ⏑ ⏑; one used for an iambus (⏑ —́) is ⏑ ⏑́ ⏑. Likewise a spondee used for a dactyl is —́ —; one used for an anapaest is — —́. So a dactyl used for an anapaest (— ⏑ ⏑ for — — for ⏑ ⏑ —) is — ⏑́ ⏑. The only use of the tribrach and the chief use of the spondee are (as above) to represent other feet which have their arsis naturally marked by a long syllable.

RESOLUTION AND CONTRACTION. — IRRATIONAL TIME. — ANACRUSIS. — SYLLABA ANCEPS.

1631. A long syllable, being naturally the metrical equivalent of two short ones (1626), is often resolved into these; as when a tribrach ⏑ ⏑ ⏑ stands for a trochee — ⏑ or an iambus ⏑ —. On the other hand, two short syllables are often contracted into one long syllable; as when a spondee

— — stands for a dactyl — ◡ ◡ or an anapaest ◡ ◡ —. The mark for a long resolved into two shorts is ◡◡ ; that for two shorts contracted into one long is ◡◡.

1632. 1. When a long syllable has the measure of three or four short syllables (1626, 2), it may represent a whole foot: this is called *syncope*. Thus a triseme (∟ = ♩.) may represent a trochee (— ◡), and a *tetraseme* (⊔ = 𝅗𝅥) may represent a dactyl (— ◡ ◡).

2. An apparent trochee (∟ ◡), consisting of a *triseme* (∟) and a short syllable, may be the equivalent of a dactyl or a spondee, that is, a foot of *four* times. This is called a *long* trochee, or a *Doric* trochee (see 1684).

1633. On the other hand, a long syllable may in certain cases be *shortened* so as to take the place of a short syllable. Such a syllable is called *irrational*, and is marked >. The foot in which it occurs is also called *irrational* (πoὺς ἄλογος). Thus, in ἀλλ' ἀπ' ἐχθρῶν (—́ ◡ —́ >), the apparent spondee which takes the place of the second trochee is called an *irrational trochee*; in δοῦναι δίκην (> —́ ◡ —́) that which takes the place of the first iambus is called an *irrational iambus*.

1634. A similar shortening occurs in the so-called *cyclic* dactyl (marked ⏑◡ ◡) and *cyclic* anapaest (marked ◡ ◡⏑), which have the time of only three short syllables instead of four. The cyclic dactyl takes the place of a trochee — ◡, especially in *logaoedic* verses (1679). The cyclic anapaest takes the place of an iambus ◡ —, and is found especially in the iambic trimeter of comedy (1658).

1635. An *anacrusis* (ἀνάκρουσις, *upward beat*) consists of a single syllable (which may be long, short, or irrational) or of two short syllables, prefixed to a verse which begins with an arsis.

1636. The last syllable of every verse is common, and it may be made long or short to suit the metre, without regard to its usual quantity. It is called *syllaba anceps*. But the continuous *systems* described in 1654, 1666, and 1677 allow this only at the end of the system.

RHYTHMICAL SERIES. — VERSE. — CATALEXIS. — PAUSE.

1637. A ***rhythmical series*** is a continuous succession of feet of the same measure. A ***verse*** may consist of one such series, or of several such united.

Thus the verse

πολλὰ τὰ δεινά, κοὐδὲν ἀν‖θρώπου δεινότερον πέλει

consists of a First Glyconic (1682, 4), ⏒⏑ ⏑ | — ⏑ | — ⏑ | ⏗ (at the end of a verse, ⏒⏑ ⏑ | — ⏑ | — ⏑ | — ∧), followed by a Second Glyconic, — ⏓ | ⏒⏑ ⏑ | — ⏑ | — ∧. Each part forms a series, the former ending with the first syllable of **ἀνθρώπου** (see above); and either series might have formed a distinct verse.

1638. The verse must close in such a way as to be distinctly marked off from what follows.

1. It must end with the end of a word.

2. It allows the last syllable (***syllaba anceps***) to be either long or short (1636).

3. It allows ***hiatus*** (34) before a vowel in the next verse.

1639. A verse which has an unfinished foot at the close is called *catalectic* (*καταληκτικός, stopped short*). A complete verse is called *acatalectic*.

1640. 1. If the omitted syllable or syllables in a catalectic verse are the thesis of the foot (as in trochaic and dactylic verses), their place is filled by a *pause*. A pause of one *time*, equivalent to a short syllable (⏑), is marked ∧ (for Λ, the initial of **λεῖμμα**); a pause of two *times* (—) is marked ⊼.

2. But in catalectic iambic and anapaestic verses, the thesis of the last foot is lost, and the place is filled by prolonging the preceding arsis: thus we have ⏑ ⏗́ ⏗́ (not ⏑ —́ ⏑ ∧) as the catalectic form of ⏑ — ⏑ —; and ⏑ ⏑ ⏗́ ⏗́ (not ⏑ ⏑ —́ ⏑ ⏑ ⊼) as that of ⏑ ⏑ — ⏑ ⏑ —. (See 1664 and 1665.)

1641. A verse measured by dipodies (1646) is called ***brachycatalectic*** if it wants a complete foot at the end, and ***hypercatalectic*** if it has a single syllable beyond its last complete dipody.

CAESURA AND DIAERESIS.

1642. 1. *Caesura* (i.e. *cutting*) *of the foot* occurs whenever a word ends before a foot is finished; as in three cases in the following verse:—

πολλὰς | δ' ἰφθί|μους ψῡ|χὰς Ἄϊ|δι προΐ|αψεν.

2. This becomes important only when it coincides with the *caesura of the verse* (as after ἰφθίμους). This caesura is a pause within a foot introduced to make the verse more melodious or to aid in its recital. In some verses, as in the iambic trimeter acatalectic (1658) and the heroic hexameter (1669), it follows definite principles.

1643. When the end of a word coincides with the end of a foot, the double division is called ***diaeresis*** (**διαίρεσις**, ***division***); as after the first foot in the line just quoted. Diaeresis becomes important only when it coincides with a natural pause produced by the ending of a rhythmic series; as in the trochaic tetrameter (1651) and the dactylic pentameter (1670).

1644. The following verse of Aristophanes (*Nub.* 519), in trochaic (3/8) rhythm, shows the irrational long (1633) in the first, second, and sixth feet; the cyclic dactyl (1634) in the third; syncope (1632) in the fourth; and at the end catalexis and pause (1639; 1640), with *syllaba anceps* (1636).

τἀλη|θῆ νὴ | τὸν Διό|νυ‖σον τὸν | ἐκθρέ|ψαντα | με.

– > | – > | –̆ ⏑ ⏑ | ⊔ ‖ – ⏑ | – > | – ⏑ | – ∧

A rhythmical series (1637) ends with the penult of Διόνῡσον. This is a *logaoedic* verse, called *Eupolidēan* (1682, 7).

VERSES.

1645. Verses are called *Trochaic, Iambic, Dactylic,* etc., from their fundamental foot.

1646. In most kinds of verse, a ***monometer*** consists of one foot, a ***dimeter*** of two feet, a ***trimeter, tetrameter, pentameter,*** or ***hexameter*** of three, four, five, or six feet. But in trochaic, iambic, and anapaestic verses, which are measured by ***dipodies*** (i.e. ***pairs of feet***), a monometer consists of one ***dipody*** (or two feet), a dimeter of four feet, a trimeter of six feet, and a tetrameter of eight feet.

1647. When trochaic or iambic verses are measured by single feet, they are called *tripodies, tetrapodies, hexapodies,* etc. (as having three, four, six, etc. feet). Here irrational syllables (1633) seldom occur. (See 1656.)

1648. Rhythms are divided into *rising* and *falling* rhythms. In rising rhythms the arsis follows the thesis, as in the iambus and anapaest; in falling rhythms the thesis follows the arsis, as in the trochee and the dactyl.

1649. In Greek poetry, the same kind of verse may be used *by the line* (κατὰ στίχον), that is, repeated continuously, as in the heroic hexameter and the iambic trimeter of the drama. Secondly, similar verses may be combined into distichs (1670) or into simple systems (1654). Verses of both these classes were composed for recitation or for simple chanting. Thirdly, in lyric poetry, which was composed to be sung to music, verses may be combined into *strophes* of complex rhythmical and metrical structure, with *antistrophes* corresponding to them in form. A strophe and antistrophe may be followed by an epode (*after-song*) in a different metre, as in most of the odes of Pindar.

TROCHAIC RHYTHMS.

1650. Trochaic verses are generally measured by dipodies (1646). The irrational trochee ∠ > (1633) in the form of a spondee can stand in the *second* place of each trochaic dipody except the last, that is, in the *even* feet (second, fourth, etc.), so that the dipody has the form ∠ ⏑ ∠ ⏒. An apparent anapaest (⏑́ ⏑ > for ∠ >) is sometimes used as the equivalent of the irrational trochee. The cyclic dactyl ∠⏑ ⏑ (1634) sometimes stands for the trochee in proper names in both parts of the dipody, except at the end of the verse.

The tribrach (⏑́ ⏑ ⏑) may stand for the trochee (1631) in every foot except the last.

1651. The chief trochaic verse which is used *by the line* (1649) is the TETRAMETER CATALECTIC, consisting of seven feet and a syllable, divided into two rhythmical series (1637) by a diaeresis (1643) after the second dipody. *E.g.*

(1). ὦ σοφώτα | τοι θεαταί, || δεῦρο τὸν νοῦν | πρόσχετε.[1]
⏑́ ⏑ – ⏑ | ⏑́ ⏑ – > || ⏑́ ⏑ – > | ⏑́ ⏑ – ∧

(2) κατὰ σελήνην | ὡς ἄγειν χρὴ || τοῦ βίου τὰς | ἡμέρᾱς.[2]
⏑ ⏑ ⏑ – > | – ⏑ – > || – ⏑ – > | – ⏑ – ∧

(3) ξύγγονόν τ' ἐ | μὴν Πυλάδην τε || τὸν τάδε ξυν | δρῶντά μοι.[3]
– ⏑ – ⏑ | ‿⏑ ⏑ – ⏑ || – ⏑ – > | – ⏑ – ∧

Notice the tribrach in the first place of (2), and the cyclic dactyl in the third place of (3).

This verse is familiar in English poetry, as

Tell me not in mournful numbers, life is but an empty dream.

1652. The *lame* tetrameter (σχάζων), called Hipponactean from Hipponax (see 1663), is the preceding verse with the last syllable but one long. *E.g.*

ἀμφιδέξιος γάρ εἰμι κοὐχ ἁμαρτάνω κόπτων.[4]
– ⏑ – ⏑ | – ⏑ – ⏑ | – ⏑ – ⏑ | – – –

1653. The following are some of the more important lyric trochaic verses: —

1. Tripody acatalectic (the Ithyphallic):

μήποτ' ἐκτακείη.[5] — – ⏑ – ⏑ – ⏑ (1647)

2. Tripody catalectic:

ὅς γε σὰν λιπών.[6] — – ⏑ – ⏑ – ∧

3. Tetrapody or dimeter acatalectic:

τοῦτο τοῦ μὲν ἦρος ἀεὶ — – ⏑ – ⏑ | – ⏑ – ⏑
βλαστάνει καὶ σῡκοφαντεῖ.[7] — – ⏑ – > | – ⏑ – ⏑

4. Tetrapody or dimeter catalectic:

δεινὰ πράγματ' εἴδομεν.[8] — – ⏑ – ⏑ | – ⏑ – ∧
ἀσπίδας φυλλορροεῖ.[9] — – ⏑ – > | – ⏑ – ∧

5. Hexapody or trimeter catalectic:

ἁρπαγαὶ δὲ διαδρομᾶν ὁμαίμονες.[10]
– ⏑ – ⏑ | ⏑ ⏑ ⏑ – ⏑ | – ⏑ – ∧

[1] Ar. *N.* 575.
[2] *ibid.* 626.
[3] E. *Or.* 1535.
[4] Hippon. 83.
[5] A. *Pr.* 535.
[6] S. *Ph.* 1215.
[7] Ar. *Av.* 1478, 1479.
[8] *ibid.* 1472.
[9] *ibid.* 1481.
[10] A. *Se.* 351.

1654. A stanza consisting of a series of dimeters acatalectic (1653, 3), rarely with an occasional monometer (— ∪ — ∪), and ending in a dimeter catalectic (1653, 4), is called a trochaic *system*. *E.g.*

ταῦτα μὲν πρὸς ἀνδρός ἐστι	— ∪ — ∪ | — ∪ — ∪
νοῦν ἔχοντος καὶ φρένας καὶ	— ∪ — > | — ∪ — >
πολλὰ περιπεπλευκότος.[1]	— ∪ ∪ ∪ ∪ | — ∪ — ∧

For iambic and anapaestic systems, formed on the same principle, see 1666 and 1677. See also 1636.

1655. The following contain examples of syncopated trochaic verses (1632, 1):—

νῦν καταστροφαὶ νέων — ∪ — ∪ | — ∪ — ∧
θεσμίων, εἰ κρατήσει δίκᾱ τε καὶ βλάβᾱ
— ∪ ⌞ | — ∪ ⌞ | — ∪ — ∪ | — ∪ — ∧
τοῦδε μητροκτόνου.[2] — ∪ ⌞ | — ∪ — ∧
δωμάτων γὰρ εἱλόμᾱν — ∪ — ∪ | — ∪ — ∧
ἀνατροπάς, ὅταν Ἄρης τιθασὸς ὢν φίλον ἕλῃ.[3]
∪́ ∪ ∪ ⌞ | ∪́ ∪ ∪ ⌞ | ∪́ ∪ ∪ ⌞ | ∪́ ∪ ∪ — ∧

1656. In lyric trochaic and iambic verses, the irrational syllable is found chiefly in comedy, and is avoided in tragedy.

IAMBIC RHYTHMS.

1657. Iambic verses are generally measured by dipodies (1646). The irrational iambus > —́ (1633) in the form of a spondee can stand in the *first* place of each iambic dipody, that is, in the *odd* places (first, third, etc.), so that the dipody has the form ⊽ —́ ∪ —́. An apparent dactyl (> ∪́ ∪ for > —́) is sometimes used as the equivalent of the irrational iambus; and the cyclic anapaest ∪ ∪—́ (1634) is used for the iambus in both parts of the dipody, except in the last foot, especially by the Attic comedians (1658). The tribrach (∪ ∪́ ∪) may stand for the iambus in every foot except the last.

1658. The most common of all iambic verses is the TRIMETER ACATALECTIC, in which most of the dialogue of

[1] Ar. *R.* 534 ff. [2] A. *Eu.* 490 ff. [3] *ibid.* 354 ff.

the Attic drama is composed. It never allows any substitution in the last foot. With this exception it may have the tribrach in any place. The irrational iambus > ⏑́ in the form of a spondee can stand in the first place of every dipody. The *tragedians* allow the (apparent) dactyl > ⏑́ ⏑ only in the first and third places, and the cyclic anapaest only in the first place; but in proper names they allow the anapaest in every place except the last. The *comedians* allow the dactyl > ⏑ ⏑ in all the *odd* places, and the cyclic anapaest in every place except the last (1657). The most common caesura is that after the *thesis* of the third foot.

1659. The following scheme shows the tragic and the comic iambic trimeter compared, — the forms peculiar to comedy being enclosed in [ ].

⏑ ⏑́ ⏑ —	⏑ ⏑́ ⏑ —	⏑ ⏑́ ⏑ —
> —	> —	> —
⏑ ⏑ ⏑ ⏑ ⏑ ⏑	⏑ ⏑ ⏑ ⏑ ⏑ ⏑	⏑ ⏑ ⏑
> ⏑ ⏑	> ⏑ ⏑	[> ⏑ ⏑]
⏑ ⏑— [⏑ ⏑—]	[⏑ ⏑—] [⏑ ⏑—]	[⏑ ⏑—]

1660. When the *tragic* trimeter ends in a word forming a cretic (— ⏑ —), this is regularly preceded by a short syllable or by a monosyllable.[1] In general the tragedians avoid the feet of three syllables, even where they are allowed.

1661. The following are examples of both the tragic and the comic form of the iambic trimeter: —

(Tragic) χθονὸς μὲν εἰς | τηλουρὸν ἥ|κομεν πέδον,
Σκύθην ἐς οἶ|μον, ἄβατον εἰς | ἐρημίᾱν.
Ἥφαιστε, σοὶ | δὲ χρὴ μέλειν | ἐπιστολάς. A. *Pr.* 1–3.
(Comic) ὦ Ζεῦ βασιλεῦ· | τὸ χρῆμα τῶν | νυκτῶν ὅσον
ἀπέραντον· οὐ|δέποθ' ἡμέρᾱ | γενήσεται;
ἀπόλοιο δῆτ', | ὦ πόλεμε, πολ|λῶν οὕνεκα. Ar. *N.* 2, 3, 6.

[1] This is known as "Porson's rule." "Nempe hanc regulam plerumque in senariis observabant Tragici, ut, si voce quae Creticum pedem efficeret terminaretur versus, eamque vocem hypermonosyllabon praecederet, quintus pes iambus vel tribrachys esse deberet." *Suppl. ad Praef. ad Hecubam.*

1662. The Iambic Trimeter appears in English as the Alexandrine, which is seldom used except at the end of a stanza: —

And hópe to mér|it Heáven by mák|ing Eárth a Héll.

1663. The *lame* trimeter (σκάζων), called the *Choliambus* and the Hipponactean (see 1652), is the preceding verse with the last syllable but one long. It is said to have been invented by Hipponax (about 540 B.C.), and it is used in the newly discovered mimes of Herondas. *E.g.*

ἀκούσαθ' Ἱππώνακτος· οὐ γὰρ ἀλλ' ἥκω.[1]
οὕτω τί σοι δοίησαν αἱ φίλαι Μοῦσαι.[2]
⏑ — ⏑ — | ⏑ — ⏑ — | ⏑ — — —

1664. The TETRAMETER CATALECTIC, consisting of seven feet and a syllable, is common in Attic comedy. There is a regular *diaeresis* (1643) after the second dipody, where the first rhythmical series ends (1637).

εἴπερ τὸν ἄνδρ' | ὑπερβαλεῖ, ‖ καὶ μὴ γέλωτ' | ὀφλήσεις.[3]
> ⏑́ ⏑ — | ⏑ ⏑́ ⏑ — ‖ > ⏑́ ⏑ — | ⏑ ⏑́ — (1640, 2)

In English poetry we have

A captain bold | of Halifax, ‖ who lived in coun|try quarters.

1665. The following are some of the more important lyric iambic verses: —

1. Dipody or monometer:

τί δῆθ' ὁρᾷς;[4] ⏑ — ⏑ —

2. Tripody (acatalectic and catalectic):

τί τῶνδ' ἄνευ κακῶν;[5] ⏑ — ⏑ — ⏑ —
ἐπ' ἄλλο πήδᾶ.[6] ⏑ — ⏑ ⊔ —

3. Dimeter (acatalectic and catalectic):

ἰαλτὸς ἐκ δόμων ἔβᾱν.[7] ⏑ ⏑́ ⏑ — | ⏑ ⏑́ ⏑ —
ζηλῶ σε τῆς | εὐβουλίᾱς.[8] > — ⏑ — | > — ⏑ —
καὶ τὸν λόγον | τὸν ἥττω.[9] > — ⏑ — | ⏑ ⊔ — (1640, 2)

[1] Hipp. 47.
[2] Herond. 3, 1.
[3] Ar. *N.* 1035.
[4] *ibid.* 1098.
[5] A. *Ag.* 211.
[6] Ar. *N.* 703.
[7] A. *Ch.* 22.
[8] Ar. *Ach.* 1008.
[9] Ar. *N.* 1452.

4. **Hexapody or trimeter catalectic:**

πρέπει παρῇς φοινίοις ἀμυγμοῖς.[1]
∪ — ∪ — | > — ∪ — | ∪ ⊔ —

1666. Iambic systems are formed on the same principle as trochaic systems (1654), of acatalectic dimeters with an occasional monometer, ending with a catalectic dimeter. *E.g.*

ἠττήμεθ᾽· ὦ βινούμενοι,	> — ∪ — | > — ∪ —
πρὸς τῶν θεῶν δέξασθέ μου	> — ∪ — | > — ∪ —
θοἰμάτιον, ὡς	> ∪ ∪ ∪ —
ἐξαυτομολῶ πρὸς ὑμᾶς.	> — ∪ ∪— | ∪ ⊔ —

These verses end a long iambic system in Ar. *Nub.* 1090–1104: see also *Nub.* 1446–1452, and *Eq.* 911–940.

1667. For the irrational syllable in lyric verse, see 1656.

DACTYLIC RHYTHMS.

1668. The only regular substitute for the dactyl is the spondee, which arises by contraction of the two short syllables of the dactyl (⁄— — from ⁄— ∪ ∪).

1669. The most common of all Greek verses is the HEROIC HEXAMETER, the Homeric verse. It *always* has a spondee in the last place, *often* in the first four places, *seldom* in the fifth (the verse being then called *spondaic*). There is commonly a caesura in the third foot, either after the arsis or (rather more frequently) dividing the thesis. There is sometimes a caesura after the arsis of the fourth foot, and rarely one in the thesis. The caesura after the arsis is called *masculine*, that in the thesis *feminine* or *trochaic*. A diaeresis after the fourth foot, common in bucolic poetry, is called *bucolic*. *E.g.*

ἄνδρα μοι ἔννεπε, Μοῦσα, πολύτροπον, ὃς μάλα πολλὰ
— ∪ ∪ | — ∪ ∪ | — ∪, ∪ | — ∪ ∪ | — ∪ ∪ | — ⏓
πλάγχθη ἐπεὶ Τροίης ἱερὸν πτολίεθρον ἔπερσεν.[2]
— ∪ ∪ | — — | —, ∪ ∪ | — ∪ ∪ | — ∪ ∪ | — ⏓

[1] A. *Ch.* 24. [2] *Od.* 1, 1 and 2.

τίπτ' αὖτ', αἰγιόχοιο Διὸς τέκος, εἰλήλουθας;[1]

— — | — ⏑ ⏑ | — ⏑ ⏑ | — ⏑ ⏑, | — — | — ⏓

εἰπέ μοι, ὦ Κορύδων, τίνος αἱ βόες; ἦρα Φιλώνδα;[2]

— ⏑ ⏑ | — ⏑ ⏑ | — ⏑ ⏑ | — ⏑ ⏑, | — ⏑ ⏑ | — ⏓

1670. The ELEGIAC DISTICH consists of an heroic hexameter followed by the so-called *Elegiac pentameter*. This last verse consists really of two dactylic trimeters with syncope (1632, 1) or catalexis in the last measure; as —

Παλλὰς Ἀ|θηναί|η ‖ χεῖρας ὕ|περθεν ἔ|χει.[3]

— ⏑ ⏑ | — — | ⊔ ‖ — ⏑ ⏑ | — ⏑ ⏑ | — ⊼

At the end of the pentameter verse the pause (⊼) takes the place of syncope (⊔) in the middle. The verse probably arose from a repetition of the first *penthemim* (πενθ-ημι-μερές, *five half-feet*) of the hexameter. But *syllaba anceps* and hiatus are not allowed after the first trimeter, but only at the end of the verse (1638). The last two complete feet are always dactyls. A diaeresis (1643) divides the two parts of the verse. The pentameter is never used by itself.

1671. The following is an Elegiac Distich: —

τίς δὲ βί|ος τί δὲ | τερπνὸν ἄ|νευ χρυ|σέης Ἀφρο|δίτης;

τεθναί|ην ὅτε | μοι ‖ μηκέτι | ταῦτα μέ|λοι.[4]

— ⏑ ⏑ | — ⏑ ⏑ | — ⏑ ⏑ | — — | — ⏑ ⏑ | — —

— — | — ⏑ ⏑ | ⊔ ‖ — ⏑ ⏑ | — ⏑ ⏑ | — ⊼

1672. In the Homeric verse a long vowel or a diphthong in the thesis (not in the arsis) is often shortened at the end of a word when the next word begins with a vowel. This sometimes occurs in the middle of a word. *E.g.*

ὦ πόποι, | ἦ μάλα | δὴ μετε|βούλευ|σαν θεοὶ | ἄλλως.[5]

χρυσέῳ ἀ|νὰ σκή|πτρῳ, καὶ | λίσσετο | πάντας Ἀ|χαιούς (see 47, 1).[6]

βέβληαι, οὐδ' ἅλιον βέλος ἔκφυγεν, ὡς ὄφελόν τοι.[7]

But ἡμετέρῳ ἐνὶ οἴκῳ ἐν Ἄργεϊ, τηλόθι πάτρης.[8]

[1] *Il.* 1, 202.
[2] Theoc. 4, 1.
[3] Solon, 4, 4.
[4] Mimn. 1, 1 and 2.
[5] *Od.* 5, 286.
[6] *Il.* 1, 15.
[7] *Il.* 11, 380.
[8] *Il.* 1, 30.

1673. When a short vowel stands in Homer where a long one is required by the verse, it may be explained in various ways.

1. By supposing λ, μ, ν, ρ, or σ to be doubled at the beginning of certain words; as *πολλὰ λισσομένω* (— — — ⏑ ⏑ —), *Il.* 22, 91 (we have *ἐλλίσσετο* in *Il.* 6, 45).

2. By the original presence of ϝ making position (see 3; 90; 91); as *τοῖόν ϝοι πῦρ* (— — — —), *Il.* 5, 7. So before *δείδω*, *fear*, and other derivatives of the stem *δϝει-*, and before *δήν* (for *δϝην*).

3. By a pause in the verse (1642, 2) prolonging the time; as in

φεύγωμεν· ἔτι γάρ κεν ἀλύξαιμεν κακὸν ἦμαρ.[1]

— — —, ⏑ ⏑ — ⏑ ⏑ — — — ⏑ ⏑ — —

1674. The following are some of the chief lyric dactylic verses: —

1. Dimeter:

μυστοδό|κος δόμος[2] — ⏑ ⏑ | — ⏑ ⏑

μοῖρα δι|ώκει[3] — ⏑ ⏑ | — —

2. Trimeter (acatalectic and catalectic):

παμπρέπτοις ἐν ἕδραισιν.[4] — — | — ⏑ ⏑ | — —

παρθένοι | ὀμβροφό|ροι[5] — ⏑ ⏑ | — ⏑ ⏑ | — ⊼

With anacrusis (1635):

ἐγείνατο μὲν μόρον αὐτῷ ⏑ ⋮ — ⏑ ⏑ — ⏑ ⏑ — —

πατροκτόνον Οἰδιπόδᾱν.[6] ⏑ ⋮ — ⏑ ⏑ — ⏑ ⏑ — ⊼

3. Tetrameter (acatalectic and catalectic):

πέμπει ξὺν δορὶ καὶ χερὶ πράκτορι.[7] — — | — ⏑ ⏑ | — ⏑ ⏑ | — ⏑ ⏑

οὐρανί|οις τε θε|οῖς δω|ρήματα.[8] — ⏑ ⏑ | — ⏑ ⏑ | — — | — ⏑ ⏑

ἔλθετ' ἐ|ποψόμε|ναι δύνα|μιν.[9] — ⏑ ⏑ | — ⏑ ⏑ | — ⏑ ⏑ | — ⊼

ANAPAESTIC RHYTHMS.

1675. Anapaestic verses are generally measured by dipodies (1646). The spondee and the dactyl (— —́ and —́ ⏑ ⏑) may stand for the anapaest.

The long syllable of an anapaest is rarely resolved into two short, making ⏑ ⏑ ⏑́ ⏑ for ⏑ ⏑ —́.

[1] *Od.* 10, 269.
[2] Ar. *N.* 303.
[3] E. *Her.* 612.
[4] A. *Ag.* 117.
[5] Ar. *N.* 299.
[6] A. *Se.* 751, 752.
[7] A. *Ag.* 111.
[8] Ar. *N.* 305.
[9] Ar. *R.* 879.

1676. The following are the most common anapaestic verses:—

1. The monometer:

τρόπον αἰ|γυπιῶν.[1] ⏑ ⏑ — | ⏑ ⏑ —
καὶ θέμις | αἰνεῖν.[2] — ⏑ ⏑ | — —
σύμφω|νος ὁμοῦ.[3] — — | ⏑ ⏑ —

2. The dimeter acatalectic:

μέγαν ἐκ | θυμοῦ | κλάζον|τες Ἄρη.[4] ⏑ ⏑ — | — — | — — | ⏑ ⏑ —
οἵτ' ἐκ|πατίοις | ἄλγεσι | παίδων.[5] — — | ⏑ ⏑ — | — ⏑ ⏑ | — —

And the ó|live of peáce | sends its bránch|es abroád.

3. The dimeter catalectic, or *paroemiac:*

ἦραν | στρατιῶ|τιν ἀρω|γήν.[6] — — | ⏑ ⏑ — | ⏑ ⏑ ⊔ | — (1640, 2)
οὕτω | πλουτή|σετε πάν|τες.[7] — — | — — | ⏑ ⏑ ⊔ | —

The Lórd | is advánc|ing. Prepáre | ye!

4. The TETRAMETER CATALECTIC, consisting of seven feet and a syllable, or of the two preceding verses combined. There is a regular diaeresis after the second dipody. This verse is frequently used *by the line* (1649) in long passages of Aristophanes.

προσχέτε τὸν νοῦν | τοῖς ἀθανάτοις ‖ ἡμῖν, τοῖς αἰ|ὲν ἐοῦσι,
τοῖς αἰθερίοις, | τοῖσιν ἀγήρῳς, ‖ τοῖς ἄφθιτα μη|δομένοισιν.[8]
— ⏖ ⏕ — | — ⏕ ⏖ — ‖ — — ⏕ — | ⏑ ⏑ ⊔ —

1677. An ANAPAESTIC SYSTEM consists of a series of anapaestic dimeters acatalectic, with occasionally a monometer, ending always with the paroemiac (or dimeter catalectic). These are very frequently employed in both tragedy and comedy. *E.g.*

δέκατον μὲν ἔτος τόδ' ἐπεὶ Πριάμου ⏑ ⏑ — ⏑ ⏑ — | ⏑ ⏑ — ⏑ ⏑ —
μέγας ἀντίδικος, ⏑ ⏑ — ⏑ ⏑ —
Μενέλαος ἄναξ ἠδ' Ἀγαμέμνων, ⏑ ⏑ — ⏑ ⏑ — | — ⏑ ⏑ — —
διθρόνου Διόθεν καὶ δισκήπτρου ⏑ ⏑ — ⏑ ⏑ — | — — — —
τιμῆς ὀχυρὸν ζεῦγος Ἀτρειδᾶν, — — ⏑ ⏑ — | — ⏑ ⏑ — —
στόλον Ἀργείων χιλιοναύταν ⏑ ⏑ — — — | — ⏑ ⏑ — —
τῆσδ' ἀπὸ χώρας — ⏑ ⏑ — —
ἦραν, στρατιῶτιν ἀρωγήν.[9] — — ⏑ ⏑ — | ⏑ ⏑ ⊔ —

[1] A. *Ag.* 49. [2] Ar. *Av.* 221. [3] *ibid.* 50. [4] A. *Ag.* 48. [5] *ibid.* 98. [6] *ibid.* 47. [7] Ar. *Av.* 736. [8] *ibid.* 689. [9] A. *Ag.* 40–47.

1678. Anapaestic systems are especially common in march movements in tragedy, where they were probably chanted by the leader of the chorus, as in the πάροδος.

LOGAOEDIC RHYTHMS.

1679. Logaoedic rhythm is a rhythm in $\frac{3}{8}$ time, having the trochee as its foundation, but admitting great freedom of construction. Besides the trochee — ⏑, it admits the irrational trochee — >, the tribrach ⏑ ⏑ ⏑, the cyclic dactyl —⏑ ⏑, and the triseme (1632, 1) or syncopated trochee ⊔. These are all equivalent feet, of three times (= ⏑ ⏑ ⏑).

1680. The first foot of a logaoedic verse allows special freedom. It may be a trochee or an irrational trochee — >, and sometimes a tribrach ⏑ ⏑ ⏑. An apparent iambus (probably with ictus ⏑́ —) sometimes occurs (1682, 7). Great license is here permitted in using different forms in strophe and antistrophe, even in verses which otherwise correspond precisely: see 1682, 7.

When a logaoedic verse has more than one rhythmical series (1637), the first foot of each series has this freedom of form (see 1682, 7).

1681. An anacrusis (1635) may introduce any logaoedic verse.

1682. The following are some of the most important logaoedic verses which have special names: —

1. *Adonic:* σύμμαχος ἔσσο.[1] —⏑ ⏑ | — ⏑ This is the final verse of the Sapphic stanza (6).

2. *First Pherecratic:* ἑπταπύλοισι Θήβαις.[2] —⏑ ⏑ | — ⏑ | — ⏑
   Catal. ἃς τρέμομεν λέγειν.[3] —⏑ ⏑ | — ⏑ | — ∧

3. *Second Pherecratic:* παιδὸς δύσφορον ἄτᾱν.[4] — > | —⏑ ⏑ | — ⏑
   Catal. ἐκ μὲν δὴ πολέμων.[5] — > | —⏑ ⏑ | — ∧

4. *Glyconic:* (Three forms):
   (*a*) ἵππι' ἄναξ Πόσειδον, ᾧ.[6] —⏑ ⏑ | — ⏑ | — ⏑ | — ∧
   (*b*) Θήβᾳ τῶν προτέρων φάος.[7] — > | —⏑ ⏑ | — ⏑ | — ∧
   (*c*) φῶτα βάντα πανσαγίᾳ.[8] — ⏑ | — ⏑ | —⏑ ⏑ | — ∧

[1] Sapph. 1, 28.
[2] Pind. *Py.* 11, 11.
[3] S. *O.C.* 129.
[4] S. *Aj.* 643.
[5] S. *An.* 150.
[6] Ar. *Eq.* 551.
[7] S. *An.* 101.
[8] *ibid.* 107.

5. Three *Alcaics*, which form the Alcaic **stanza** (*a*, *a*, *b*, *c*):

(*a*) ἀσῠνέτημι τῶν ἀνέμων στάσιν·

```
⏒ ⁝ — ⏑ | — ⏑ | ¬⏑ ⏑ | — ⏑ | — ∧
```

(*a*) τὸ μὲν γὰρ ἔνθεν κῦμα κυλίνδεται

```
⏒ ⁝ — ⏑ | — > | ¬⏑ ⏑ | — ⏑ | — ∧
```

(*b*) τὸ δ' ἔνθεν· ἄμμες δ' ἂν τὸ μέσσον

```
⏒ ⁝ — ⏑ | — > | — ⏑ | — ⏑
```

(*c*) νᾶϊ φορήμεθα σὺν μελαίνᾳ.[1]

```
¬⏑ ⏑ | ¬⏑ ⏑ | — ⏑ | — ⏑
```

Compare in Horace (Od. 1, 9):

Vides ut alta stet nive candidum
Soracte, nec iam sustineant onus
Silvae laborantes, geluque
Flumina constiterint acuto.

6. *Sapphic:* ποικι|λόθρον' | ἀθάνατ' | Ἀφρο|δίτᾱ.[2]

```
— ⏑ | — ⏑ | ¬⏑ ⏑ | — ⏑ | — ⏑
    | — > |
```

Three Sapphics and an Adonic (1) form the Sapphic stanza.

7. *Eupolidĕan:* ὦ θε|ώμε|νοι, κατε|ρῶ ‖ πρὸς ὑ|μᾶς ἐ|λευθέ|ρως.[3]

```
— ⏑ | — ⏑ | ¬⏑ ⏑ | ⌞ ‖ — ⏑ | — ⏑ | — ⏑ | — ∧
— > | — > |              — > | — > |
⏑ ⏑ ⏑ |                 ⏑ ⏑ ⏑ |
⏑ — |                   ⏑ — |
```

(See 1644.)

The Eupolidean verse is used by the line in comedy; as in Ar. *Nub.* 518–562.

1683. The first strophe of the first Olympic ode of Pindar is given as an example of the free use of logaoedics in lyric poetry.

ἄριστον μὲν ὕδωρ, ὁ δὲ ‖ χρῡσὸς αἰθόμενον πῦρ

```
⏑ ⁝ ⌞ | ¬⏑ ⏑ | — ⏑ | ⌞ ‖ — ⏑ | ¬⏑ ⏑ | — ⏑
```

ἅτε διαπρέπει ‖ νυκτὶ μεγάνορος ἔξοχα πλούτου·

```
⏑ ⏑ ⏑ | — ⏑ | ⌞ ‖ ¬⏑ ⏑ | ¬⏑ ⏑ | ¬⏑ ⏑ | — ⏑
```

εἰ δ' ἄεθλα γᾱρύεν

```
— ⏑ | — ⏑ | — ⏑ | — ∧
```

[1] Alcae. 18, 1–4. [2] Sapph. 1, 1. [3] Ar. *N.* 518.

ἔλδεαι, φίλον ἦτορ,
— ⏑ | ⌒⏑ ⏑ | — ⏑
μηκέτ' ἀελίου σκόπει
— ⏑ | — ⏑ | — ⏑ | — ∧
ἄλλο θαλπνότερον ἐν ἀμέ‖ρᾳ φάεννον ἄστρον ἐρή‖μᾱς δι' αἰθέρος,
— ⏑ | — ⏑ | ⏑ ⏑ ⏑ ⏑ | — ⏑ ‖ — ⏑ | — ⏑ | ⌒⏑ ⏑ | ⊔ ‖ — ⏑ | — ⏑ | — ∧
μήδ' Ὀλυμπίᾱς ἀγῶνα ‖ φέρτερον αὐδάσομεν·
— ⏑ | — ⏑ | — ⏑ | — ⏑ ‖ ⌒⏑ ⏑ | ⊔ | — ⏑ | — ∧
ὅθεν ὁ πολύφατος ὕμνος ἀμφιβάλλεται
⏑ ⁝ ⏑ ⏑ ⏑ | ⏑ ⏑ ⏑ | — ⏑ | — ⏑ | — ⏑ | — ∧
σοφῶν μητίεσσι, κελαδεῖν
⏑́ ⏕ | — ⏑ | ⊔ | ⏑ ⏑ ⏑ | — ∧
Κρόνου παῖδ', ἐς ἀφνεὰν ἱκομένους
⏑ ⁝ ⊔ | — ⏑ | — ⏑ | ⊔ | ⏑ ⏑ ⏑ | — ∧
μάκαιραν Ἱέρωνος ἑστίᾱν.
⏑ ⁝ ⊔ | ⏑ ⏑ ⏑ | — ⏑ | — ⏑ | — ∧

DACTYLO-EPITRITIC RHYTHMS.

1684. 1. About half of the odes of Pindar are composed in a measure called *dactylo-epitritic*, which consists of dactyls, with their equivalent spondees and syncopated forms (⊔), and epitrites. The epitrite (⊾ ⏑ — —) is composed of a long (or Doric) trochee (⊾ ⏑, see 1632, 2) and a spondee. The dactylic parts of the verse generally have the form —́ ⏑ ⏑ —́ ⏑ ⏑ —́ — or (catalectic) —́ ⏑ ⏑ —́ ⏑ ⏑ —́ ⊼. The epitrite also may be catalectic, ⊾ ⏑ — ⊼. The verse may have an anacrusis.

2. It will be noticed that in this verse the long trochee (⊾ ⏑) has the same length as the dactyl and the dactyl has its full time, while in logaoedic verse the trochee has its ordinary time and the dactyl is cyclic (equivalent in time to the trochee).

1685. The first strophe of Pindar's third Olympic ode is an example of this measure: —

Τυνδαρίδαις τε φιλοξείνοις ἁδεῖν καλ‖λιπλοκάμῳ θ' Ἑλένᾳ
— ⏑ ⏑ | — ⏑ ⏑ | — — | ⊾ ⏑ — — ‖ — ⏑ ⏑ | — ⏑ ⏑ | — ⊼
κλεινὰν Ἀκράγαντα γεραίρων εὔχομαι,
— ⁝ — ⏑ ⏑ | — ⏑ ⏑ | — — | ⊾ ⏑ — ⊼

Θήρωνος Ὀλυμπιονίκᾱν ‖ ὕμνον ὀρθώσαις, ἀκαμαντοπόδων
— ⁝ — ⏑ ⏑ | — ⏑ ⏑ | — — ‖ ∟ ⏑ — — | — ⏑ ⏑̇ | — ⏑ ⏑ | — ⊼
ἵππων ἄωτον. ‖ Μοῖσα δ' οὕτω μοι παρεστᾱ́ ‖ κοι νεοσίγαλον εὑρόντι τρόπον
— ⁝ ∟ ⏑ — — ‖ ∟ ⏑ — — | ∟ ⏑ — — ‖ — ⏑ ⏑ | — ⏑ ⏑ | — — | ∟ ⏑ — ⊼
Δωρίῳ φω ‖ νᾱ̀ν ἐναρμόξαι πεδίλῳ.
∟ ⏑ — — ‖ ∟ ⏑ — — | ∟ ⏑ — —

RHYTHMS WITH FEET OF FIVE OR SIX TIMES.

1686. Some of the more important rhythms with feet of five or six times (1627, 3 and 4) are the following: —

1687. 1. *Choriambic* rhythms, with the choriambus — ⏑ ⏑ — as the fundamental foot: —

> παῖδα μὲν αὐ|τᾶς πόσιν αὐ|τῷ θεμένᾱ.[1]
> — ⏑ ⏑ — | — ⏑ ⏑ — | — ⏑ ⏑ —
> δεινὰ μὲν οὖν, δεινὰ ταράσσει σοφὸς οἰωνοθέτᾱς.[2]
> — ⏑ ⏑ — | — ⏑ ⏑ — | — ⏑ ⏑ — | — ⏑ ⏑ —

2. Choriambic verses of this class are rare. Most verses formerly called choriambic are here explained as logaoedic (1682).

1688. 1. *Ionic* rhythms, with the ionic *a minore* ⏑ ⏑ — — as the fundamental foot, admitting also the equivalent ⏑ ⏑ ⊔ (1626, 2): —

> πεπέρᾱκεν | μὲν ὁ περσέ|πτολις ἤδη
> βασίλειος | στρατὸς εἰς ἀν|τίπορον γεί|τονα χώρᾱν,
> λινοδέσμῳ | σχεδίᾳ πορ|θμὸν ἀμείψᾱς
> Ἀθαμαν|τίδος Ἕλλᾱς.[3]
> ⏑ ⏑ ⊥́ — | ⏑ ⏑ ⊥́ — | ⏑ ⏑ ⊥́ —
> ⏑ ⏑ — — | ⏑ ⏑ — — | ⏑ ⏑ — — | ⏑ ⏑ — —
> ⏑ ⏑ — — | ⏑ ⏑ — — | ⏑ ⏑ — —
> ⏑ ⏑ ⊔ | ⏑ ⏑ — — |

2. A double trochee — ⏑ — ⏑ often takes the place of the two long syllables and the two *following* shorts. This is called *anaclăsis* (ἀνάκλασις, *breaking up*), as it breaks up the feet. *E.g.*

> τίς ὁ κραιπνῷ | ποδὶ πηδή|ματος εὐπε|τοῦς ἀνάσσων;[4]
> ⏑ ⏑ — — | ⏑ ⏑ — — | ⏑ ⏑ — ⏑ | — ⏑ — —

[1] A. *Se.* 929. [2] S. *O. T.* 484. [3] A. *Pe.* 65–70. [4] *ibid.* 95.

1689. *Cretic* rhythms, in which *paeons* occur by resolution of long syllables (— ⏑ ⏑ ⏑ or ⏑ ⏑ ⏑ — for — ⏑ —):—

οὐκ ἀνα|σχήσομαι· | μηδὲ λέγε | μοι σὺ λόγον·
ὡς μεμί|σηκά σε Κλέ|ωνος ἔτι | μᾶλλον, ὃν
κατατεμῶ | τοῖσιν ἱπ|πεῦσι κατ|τύματα.[1]
— ⏑ — | — ⏑ — | — ⏑ ⏑ ⏑ | — ⏑ ⏑ ⏑
— ⏑ — | — ⏑ ⏑ ⏑ | — ⏑ ⏑ ⏑ | — ⏑ —
⏑ ⏑ ⏑ — | — ⏑ — | — ⏑ — | — ⏑ —

1690. *Bacchic* rhythms, with the *bacchīus* ⏑ — — as the fundamental foot:—

τίς ἀχὼ, | τίς ὀδμὰ | προσέπτᾱ | μ' ἀφεγγής;[2]
⏑ — — | ⏑ — — | ⏑ — — | ⏑ — —
στενάζω; | τί ῥέξω; | γένωμαι | δυσοίστᾱ | πολίταις;[3]
⏑ — — | ⏑ — — | ⏑ — — | ⏑ — — | ⏑ — —

DOCHMIACS.

1691. *Dochmiac* verses, which are used chiefly in tragedy to express great excitement, are based upon a foot called the *dochmius*, compounded of an iambus and a cretic (or a bacchius and an iambus) ⏑ — | — ⏑ — (or ⏑ — — | ⏑ —). This peculiar foot appears in nineteen different forms, by resolving the long syllables and admitting irrational longs in place of the two shorts. Its most common forms are ⏑ — | — ⏑ — and ⏑ ⏑ ⏑ | — ⏑ —. As examples may be given

δυσαλγεῖ τύχᾳ.[4] ⏑ — — ⏑ —
πτεροφόρον δέμας.[5] ⏑ ⏑ ⏑ — ⏑ —
μῑσόθεον μὲν οὖν.[6] > ⏑ ⏑ — ⏑ — (for > — — ⏑ —)
μεγάλα μεγάλα καί.[7] ⏑ ⏑ ⏑ ⏑ ⏑ ⏑ — (for ⏑ — — ⏑ —)
μετοικεῖν σκότῳ θανὼν ὁ τλᾱ́μων.[8] ⏑ — — ⏑ — | ⏑ — — > —
μεθεῖται στράτος, στρατόπεδον λιπών.[9] ⏑ — — ⏑ — | ⏑ ⏑ ⏑ — ⏑ —

[1] Ar. *Ach.* 299–301.
[2] A. *Pr.* 115.
[3] A. *Eu.* 788.
[4] A. *Ag.* 1165.
[5] *ibid.* 1147.
[6] *ibid.* 1090.
[7] E. *Ba.* 1198.
[8] E. *Hip.* 837.
[9] A. *Se.* 79.

APPENDIX.

CATALOGUE OF VERBS.

APPENDIX.

1692. CATALOGUE OF VERBS.

NOTE.—This catalogue professes to contain all verbs in ordinary use in classic Greek which have any such peculiarities as to present difficulties to a student. No verb is introduced which does not occur in some form before Aristotle; and no forms are given which are not found in writers earlier than the Alexandrian period, except sometimes the present indicative of a verb which is classic in other tenses, and occasionally a form which is given for completeness and marked as *later*. Tenses which are not used by Attic writers, in either prose or poetry, or which occur only in lyrical parts of the drama, are enclosed in [ ], except occasionally the present indicative of a verb which is Attic in other tenses.

The verb stem, with any other important forms of the stem, is given in ( ) directly after the present indicative, unless the verb belongs to the first class (569). The class of each verb in ω is given by an Arabic numeral in ( ) at the end, unless it is of the first class. Verbs in μι of the Seventh Class (619), enumerated in 794, are marked with (I.); those of the Fifth Class in νῦμι (608), enumerated in 797, 1, with (II.); and the poetic verbs in νημι or ναμαι (609), enumerated in 797, 2, which add να to the stem in the present, with (III.). A few epic peculiarities are sometimes disregarded in the classification.

The modification of the stem made by adding ε in certain tenses (653) is marked by prefixing (ε-) to the first form in which this occurs, unless this is the present. Presents in εω thus formed have a reference to 654. A hyphen prefixed to a form (as -έδρᾶν) indicates that it is found only in composition. This is omitted, however, if the simple form occurs even in later Greek; and it is often omitted when the occurrence of cognate forms, or any other reason, makes it probable that the simple form was in use. It would be extremely difficult to point out an example of every tense of even the best English verbs in a writer of established authority within a fixed period.

The imperfect or pluperfect is generally omitted when the present or perfect is given. Second perfects which are given among the principal parts of a verb (462, 1) are not specially designated (see βλάπτω).

A.

[(ἀα-), *injure*, *infatuate*, stem, with aor. ἄασα (ἀασα), ἆσα; a. p. ἀάσθην; pr. mid. ἀᾶται, aor. ἀασάμην, *erred*. Vb. ἄατος, ἀν-ᾱτος. Epic.]

Ἄγαμαι, *admire*, [epic fut. ἀγάσομαι, rare,] ἠγάσθην, ἠγασάμην. (I.)

Ἀγγέλλω (ἀγγελ-), *announce*, ἀγγελῶ [ἀγγελέω], ἤγγειλα, ἤγγελκα, ἤγγελμαι, ἠγγέλθην, fut. p. ἀγγελθήσομαι; a. m. ἠγγειλάμην. Second aorists with λ are doubtful. (4.)

Ἀγείρω (ἀγερ-), *collect*, a. ἤγειρα; [ep. plpf. p. ἀγηγέρατο; a. p. ἠγέρθην, a. m. (ἠγειράμην) συν-αγείρατο, 2 a. m. ἀγερόμην with part. ἀγρόμενος. See ἠγερέθομαι.] (4.)

Ἄγνυμι (ϝαγ-), in comp. also ἀγνύω, *break*, ἄξω, ἔαξα (537, 1) [rarely epic ἦξα], 2 p. ἔᾱγα [Ion. ἔηγα], 2 a. p. ἐάγην [ep. ἐάγην or ἄγην]. (II.)

Ἄγω, *lead*, ἄξω, ἦξα (rare), ἦχα, ἦγμαι, ἤχθην, ἀχθήσομαι; 2 a. ἤγαγον, ἠγαγόμην; fut. m. ἄξομαι (as pass.), [Hom. a. m. ἀξάμην, 2 a. act. imper. ἄξετε, inf. ἀξέμεναι (777, 8).]

[(ἀδε-), *be sated*, stem with aor. opt. ἀδήσειεν, pf. part. ἀδηκώς. Epic.]

[(ἀε-), *rest*, stem with aor. ἄεσα, ἆσα. Epic.]

Ἄιδω, *sing*, ᾄσομαι (ᾄσω, rare), ᾖσα, ᾔσθην. Ion. and poet. ἀείδω, ἀείσω and ἀείσομαι, ἤεισα.

[**Ἀέξω**: Hom. for αὔξω.]

[**Ἄημι** (ἀε-), *blow*, ἄητον, ἀεισι, inf. ἀῆναι, ἀήμεναι, part. ἀείς; imp. ἄην. Mid. ἄηται and ἄητο, part. ἀήμενος. Poetic, chiefly epic.] (I.)

Αἰδέομαι, poet. αἴδομαι, *respect*, αἰδέσομαι, ᾔδεσμαι, ᾐδέσθην (as mid.), ᾐδεσάμην (chiefly poet.), [Hom. imperat. αἰδεῖο]. 639; 640.

Αἰνέω, *praise*, αἰνέσω [αἰνήσω], ᾔνεσα [ᾔνησα], ᾔνεκα, ᾔνημαι, ᾐνέθην, 639.

[**Αἴνυμαι**, *take*, imp. αἰνύμην. Epic.] (II.)

Αἱρέω (αἱρε-, ἑλ-), *take*, αἱρήσω, ᾕρηκα, ᾕρημαι [Hdt. ἀραίρηκα, ἀραίρημαι], ᾑρέθην, αἱρεθήσομαι; fut. pf. ᾑρήσομαι (rare); 2 a. εἷλον, ἕλω, etc.; εἱλόμην, ἕλωμαι, etc. (8.)

Αἴρω (ἀρ-), *take up*, ἀρῶ, ἦρα (674), ἦρκα, ἦρμαι, ἤρθην, ἀρθήσομαι; ἠράμην (674). Ion. and poet. ἀείρω (ἀερ-), ἤειρα, ἠέρθην, [ἤερμαι (late), Hom. plpf. ἄωρτο for ἤερτο; a. m. ἀειράμην.] Fut. ἀροῦμαι and 2 a. ἠρόμην (with ἄρωμαι (ᾰ) etc.) belong to ἄρνυμαι (ἀρ-). (4.)

Αἰσθάνομαι (αἰσθ-), *perceive*, (ε-) αἰσθήσομαι, ᾔσθημαι; ᾐσθόμην. Pres. αἴσθομαι (rare). (5.)

Ἀΐσσω (ἀϊκ-), *rush*, ἀΐξω, ᾖξα, ᾐχθην, ᾐξάμην. Also ᾄσσω or ᾄττω (also ἄσσω or ἄττω), ᾄξω, ᾖξα. Both rare in prose. (4.)

Αἰσχύνω (αἰσχυν-), *disgrace*, αἰσχυνῶ, ᾔσχῡνα, [p. p. part. ep. ᾐσχυμμένος,] ᾐσχύνθην, *felt ashamed*, αἰσχυνθήσομαι; fut. m. αἰσχυνοῦμαι. (4.)

Ἀΐω, *hear*, imp. ἄϊον, [aor. -ῄϊσα.] Ionic and poetic.

[**Ἀΐω**, *breathe out*, only imp. ἄϊον. Epic. See ἄημι.]

[**Ἀκαχίζω** (ἀχ-, see 587), *afflict*, redupl. pres., with **ἀχέω** and **ἀχεύω**, *be grieved* (only in pr. part. ἀχέων, ἀχεύων), and **ἄχομαι**, *be grieved;* fut. ἀκαχήσω, aor. ἀκάχησα; p. p. ἀκάχημαι (ἀκηχέδαται), ἀκάχησθαι, ἀκαχήμενος or ἀκηχέμενος; 2 aor. ἤκαχον, ἀκαχόμην. See ἄχνυμαι and ἄχομαι. Epic.] (4.)

[**Ἀκαχμένος**, *sharpened*, epic perf. part. with no present in use.]

Ἀκέομαι, *heal*, aor. ἠκεσάμην.

Ἀκηδέω, *neglect*, [aor. ἀκήδεσα epic]. Poetic.

Ἀκούω (ἀκου- for ἀκοϝ-), *hear*, ἀκούσομαι, ἤκουσα [Dor. pf. ἄκουκα], 2 pf. ἀκήκοα (for ἀκ-ηκοϝα, 690), 2 plpf. ἠκηκόη or ἀκηκόη; ἠκούσθην, ἀκουσθήσομαι.

Ἀλαλάζω (ἀλαλαγ-), *raise war-cry*, ἀλαλάξομαι, ἠλάλαξα. (4.)

Ἀλάομαι, *wander*, [pf. ἀλάλημαι (as pres.), w. inf. ἀλάλησθαι, part. ἀλαλήμενος], a. ἀλήθην. Chiefly poetic.

Ἀλδαίνω (ἀλδαν-), *nourish*, [ep. 2 aor. ἤλδανον.] Pres. also ἀλδήσκω. Poetic. (4.)

Ἀλείφω (ἀλειφ-), *anoint*, ἀλείψω, ἤλειψα, ἀλήλιφα, ἀλήλιμμαι, ἠλείφθην, ἀλειφθήσομαι (rare), 2 a. p. ἠλίφην (rare). Mid. f. ἀλείψομαι, a. ἠλειψάμην. 529. (2.)

Ἀλέξω (ἀλεξ-, ἀλεκ-), *ward off*, fut. ἀλέξομαι [ep. (ε-) ἀλεξήσω, Hd. ἀλεξήσομαι]; aor. (ε-) ἠλέξησα (ἤλεξα, rare), ἠλεξάμην; [ep. 2 a. ἄλαλκον for ἀλ-αλεκ-ον.] 657.

[**Ἀλέομαι**, *avoid*, epic; aor. ἠλεάμην.]

Ἀλεύω, *avert*, ἀλεύσω, ἤλευσα. Mid. ἀλεύομαι, *avoid*, aor. ἠλευάμην, with subj. ἐξ-αλεύσωμαι. Poetic.

Ἀλέω, *grind*, ἤλεσα, ἀλήλεσμαι or ἀλήλεμαι. 639; 640.

[**Ἄλθομαι**, *be healed*, (ε-) ἀλθήσομαι.] Ionic and poetic.

Ἁλίσκομαι (ἁλ-, ἁλο-), *be captured*, ἁλώσομαι, ἥλωκα or ἑάλωκα, 2 aor. ἥλων or ἑάλων, ἁλῶ [epic ἁλώω], ἁλοίην, ἁλῶναι, ἁλούς (799); all passive in meaning. 659. No active ἁλίσκω, but see **ἀν-αλίσκω**. (6.)

[**Ἀλιταίνομαι** (ἀλιτ-, ἀλιταν-), with epic pres. act. **ἀλιτραίνω**, *sin;* 2 aor. ἤλιτον, ἀλιτόμην, pf. part. ἀλιτήμενος, *sinning*, ep.]. Poetic, chiefly epic. (4. 5.)

Ἀλλάσσω (ἀλλαγ-), *change*, ἀλλάξω, ἤλλαξα, ἤλλαχα, ἤλλαγμαι, ἠλλάχθην and ἠλλάγην, ἀλλαχθήσομαι and ἀλλαγήσομαι. Mid. fut. ἀλλάξομαι, a. ἠλλαξάμην. (4.)

Ἅλλομαι (ἁλ-), *leap*, ἁλοῦμαι, ἡλάμην; 2 a. ἡλόμην (rare). [Epic 2 a. ἆλσο, ἆλτο, ἄλμενος, by syncope.] 800, 2. (4.)

[**Ἀλυκτάζω** and **ἀλυκτέω**, *be excited*, imp. ἀλύκταζον Hdt. pf. ἀλαλύκτημαι Hom. Ionic.]

'Αλύσκω (ἀλυκ-), *avoid*, **ἀλύξω** [and **ἀλύξομαι**], **ἤλυξα** (rarely -αμην). Poetic. 'Αλύσκω is for ἀλυκ-σκω (617). (6.)

'Αλφάνω (ἀλφ-), *find*, *acquire*, [epic 2 aor. ἦλφον.] (5.)

'Αμαρτάνω (ἁμαρτ-), *err*, (ε-) **ἁμαρτήσομαι**, **ἡμάρτηκα**, **ἡμάρτημαι**, **ἡμαρτήθην**; 2 aor. ἥμαρτον [ep. ἤμβροτον]. (5.)

'Αμβλίσκω (ἀμβλ-), **ἀμβλόω** in compos., *miscarry*, [ἀμβλώσω, late,] ἤμβλωσα, ἤμβλωκα, ἤμβλωμαι, ἠμβλώθην. (6.)

'Αμείρω (ἀμερ-) and **ἀμέρδω**, *deprive*, ἤμερσα, ἠμέρθην. Poetic. (1. 4.)

'Αμπ-έχω and **ἀμπ-ίσχω** (ἀμφί and ἔχω), *wrap about*, *clothe*, **ἀμφέξω**, 2 a. ἤμπι-σχον; [epic impf. ἄμπεχον.] Mid. **ἀμπέχομαι**, **ἀμπίσχομαι**, **ἀμπισχνέομαι**; imp. ἠμπειχόμην; f. **ἀμφέξομαι**; 2 a. **ἠμπι-σχόμην** and **ἠμπ-εσχόμην**, 544. See **ἔχω** and **ἴσχω**.

'Αμπλακίσκω (ἀμπλακ-), *err*, *miss*, ἠμπλάκημαι; 2 a. **ἤμπλακον**, part. ἀμπλακών or **ἀπλακών**. Poetic. (6.)

["**Αμπνυε**, **ἀμπνύνθην**, **ἄμπνῡτο**, all epic: see **ἀναπνέω**.]

'Αμύνω (ἀμυν-), *ward off*; fut. **ἀμυνῶ**, **ἀμυνοῦμαι**; aor. **ἤμῡνα**, **ἠμῡνάμην**. (4.)

'Αμύσσω (ἀμυχ-), *scratch*, [ἀμύξω, ἤμυξα (Theoc.), **ἠμυξάμην**]. Poetic and Ionic. (4.)

'Αμφι-γνοέω, *doubt*, ἠμφιγνόεον and **ἠμφεγνόεον**, **ἠμφεγνόησα**; aor. pass. part. **ἀμφιγνοηθείς**. 544.

'Αμφι-έννῡμι (see ἕννῡμι), *clothe*, fut. [ep. ἀμφιέσω] Att. **ἀμφιῶ**; **ἠμφίεσα**, **ἠμφίεσμαι**; **ἀμφιέσομαι**, **ἀμφιεσάμην** (poet.). 544. (II.)

'Αμφισβητέω, *dispute*, augmented ἠμφισ- and ἠμφεσ- (544); otherwise regular.

'Αναίνομαι (ἀναν-), *refuse*, imp. **ἠναινόμην**, aor. **ἠνηνάμην**, **ἀνήνασθαι**. (4.)

'Ανᾱλίσκω (ἀλ-, ἀλο-, 659), and **ἀνᾱλόω**, *expend*, **ἀνᾱλώσω**, **ἀνάλωσα**, and **ἀνήλωσα** (κατ-ηνάλωσα), **ἀνάλωκα** and **ἀνήλωκα**, **ἀνάλωμαι** and **ἀνήλωμαι** (κατ-ηνάλωμαι), **ἀνᾱλώθην** and **ἀνηλώθην**, **ἀνᾱλωθήσομαι**. See **ἁλίσκομαι**. (6.)

'Αναπνέω, *take breath*; see **πνέω** (πνυ-). [Epic 2 aor. imperat. **ἄμπνυε**, a. p. **ἀμπνύνθην**, 2 a. m. **ἄμπνῡτο** (for **ἀμπνύετο**).]

'Ανδάνω (ϝαδ-, ἁδ-), *please* [impf. Hom. **ἥνδανον** and **ἑήνδανον**, Hdt. **ἥνδανον** and **ἐήνδανον**; fut. (ε-) **ἁδήσω**, Hdt.; 2 pf. **ἕᾱδα**, epic]; 2 aor. **ἅδον** [Ion. **ἕαδον**, epic **εὔαδον** for **ἔϝϝαδον**.] Ionic and poetic. See **ἅσ-μενος**, *pleased*, as adj. (5.)

'Ανέχω, *hold up*; see **ἔχω**, and 544.

[**'Ανήνοθε**, defect. 2 pf., *springs*, *sprung*; in *Il.* 11, 266 as 2 plpf. (777, 4). Epic.]

'Αν-οίγνῡμι and **ἀνοίγω** (see οἴγνῡμι), *open*, imp. **ἀνέῳγον** (**ἤνοιγον**, rare) [epic **ἀνῷγον**]; **ἀνοίξω**, **ἀνέῳξα** (**ἤνοιξα**, rare) [Hdt. **ἄνοιξα**], **ἀνέῳχα**, **ἀνέῳγμαι**, **ἀνεῴχθην** (subj. **ἀνοιχθῶ**, etc.); fut. pf. **ἀνεῴξομαι** (2 pf. **ἀνέῳγα** late, very rare in Attic). (II.)

Ἀν-ορθόω, *set upright*, augment ἀνωρ- and ἠνωρ-. 544.

Ἀνύω, Attic also **ἀνύτω**, *accomplish*; fut. **ἀνύσω** [Hom. ἀνύω], ἀνύσομαι; aor. ἤνυσα, ἠνυσάμην; pf. ἤνυκα, ἤνυσμαι. 639. Poetic also ἄνω.

Ἄνωγα, 2 perf. as pres., *command* [w. 1 pl. ἄνωγμεν, sub. ἀνώγω, opt. ἀνώγοιμι], imper. ἄνωγε (rare), also ἄνωχθι (with ἀνώχθω, ἄνωχθε), [inf. ἀνωγέμεν]; 2 plpf. ἠνώγεα, ἠνώγει (or ἀνώγει), [also ἤνωγον (or ἄνωγον), see 777, 4]. [Present forms ἀνώγει and ἀνώγετον (as if from ἀνώγω) occur; also fut. ἀνώξω, a. ἤνωξα.] Poetic and Ionic.

[**Ἀπ-αυράω**, *take away*, not found in present; imp. ἀπηύρων (as aor.); kindred forms are epic fut. ἀπουρήσω, and aor. part. ἀπούρας, ἀπουράμενος.] Poetic.

[**Ἀπαφίσκω** (ἀπ-αφ-), *deceive*, ἠπάφησα (rare), 2 a. ἤπαφον, m. opt. ἀπαφοίμην]. Poetic. (6.)

Ἀπεχθάνομαι (ἐχθ-), *be hated*, (ε-) ἀπεχθήσομαι, ἀπήχθημαι; 2 a. ἀπηχθόμην. Late pres. ἀπέχθομαι. (5.)

[**Ἀπόερσε**, *swept off*, subj. ἀποέρσῃ, opt. ἀποέρσειε (only in 3 pers.). Epic.]

Ἀποκτίννῡμι and **-ύω**, forms of ἀποκτείνω. See **κτείνω**.

Ἀπόχρη, *it suffices*, impersonal. See **χρή**.

Ἅπτω (ἁφ-), *touch*, fut. ἅψω, ἅψομαι; aor. ἧψα, ἡψάμην; pf. ἧμμαι; a. p. ἥφθην (see ἐάφθη). (3.)

Ἀράομαι, *pray*, ἀρᾱ́σομαι, ἠρᾱσάμην, ἤρᾱμαι. [Ion. ἀρήσομαι, ἠρησάμην. Ep. act. inf. ἀρήμεναι, *to pray*.]

Ἀραρίσκω (ἀρ-), *fit*, ἦρσα, ἤρθην; 2 p. ἄρᾱρα, [Ion. ἄρηρα, plpf. ἀρήρει(ν) and ἠρήρει(ν);] 2 a. ἤραρον; 2 a. m. part. ἄρμενος (as adj.), *fitting*. With form of Attic redupl. in pres. (615). Poetic. (6.)

Ἀράσσω or **ἀράττω** (ἀραγ-), *strike*, ἀράξω, ἤραξα, ἠράχθην. (4.)

Ἀρέσκω (ἀρε-), *please*, ἀρέσω, ἤρεσα, ἠρέσθην; ἀρέσομαι, ἠρεσάμην. 639. (6.)

[**Ἀρημένος**, *oppressed*, perf. pass. part. Epic.]

Ἀρκέω, *assist*, ἀρκέσω, ἤρκεσα. 639.

Ἁρμόττω, poet. **ἁρμόζω** (ἁρμοδ-), *fit*, ἁρμόσω, ἥρμοσα (συνάρμοξα Pind.), ἥρμοκα (Aristot.), ἥρμοσμαι, ἡρμόσθην, fut. p. ἁρμοσθήσομαι; a. m. ἡρμοσάμην. (4.)

Ἄρνυμαι (ἀρ-), *win, secure*, fut. ἀροῦμαι, 2 a. ἠρόμην (ἀρόμην). Chiefly poetic. See αἴρω. (II.)

Ἀρόω, *plough*, ἤροσα, [p. p. Ion. ἀρήρομαι], ἠρόθην. 639.

Ἁρπάζω (ἁρπαγ-), *seize*, ἁρπάσω and ἁρπάσομαι [ep. ἁρπάξω], ἥρπασα [ἥρπαξα], ἥρπακα, ἥρπασμαι (late ἥρπαγμαι), ἡρπάσθην [Hdt. ἡρπάχθην], ἁρπασθήσομαι. For the Attic forms, see 587. (4.)

Ἀρύω and **ἀρύτω**, *draw water*, aor. ἤρυσα, ἠρυσάμην, ἠρύθην [ἠρύσθην, Ion.]. 639.

"Ἄρχω, *begin, rule*, ἄρξω, ἦρξα, (ἦρχα) ἦργμαι (mid.), ἤρχθην, ἀρχθήσομαι (Aristot.), ἄρξομαι, ἠρξάμην.

"Αἴσσω and **ᾄττω**: see ἀΐσσω.

[**Ἀτιτάλλω** (ἀτιταλ-), *tend;* aor. ἀτίτηλα. Epic and lyric.] (4.)

Αὐαίνω (αὐαν-) or **αὑαίνω**; fut. αὐανῶ; aor. ηὔηνα, ηὐάνθην or αὐάνθην, αὐανθήσομαι; fut. m. αὐανοῦμαι (as pass.). Augment ηυ- or αυ- (519). Chiefly poetic and Ionic. (4.)

Αὐξάνω or **αὔξω** (αὐξ-), *increase*, (ε-) αὐξήσω, αὐξήσομαι, ηὔξησα, ηὔξηκα, ηὔξημαι, ηὐξήθην, αὐξηθήσομαι. [Also Ion. pres. ἀέξω, impf. ἄεξον.] (5.)

[**Ἀφάσσω** (see 582 and 587), *feel, handle*, aor. ἤφασα; used by Hdt. for ἁφάω or ἀφάω.] (4.)

Ἀφ-ίημι, *let go*, impf. ἀφίην or ἠφίην (544); fut. ἀφήσω, etc. See the inflection of ἵημι, 810. (I.)

[**Ἀφύσσω** (ἀφυγ-), *draw, pour*, ἀφύξω. Poetic, chiefly epic. See ἀφύω.] (4.)

[**Ἀφύω**, *draw*, ἤφυσα, ἠφυσάμην. Poetic, chiefly epic.]

"Ἄχθομαι, *be displeased*, (ε-) ἀχθέσομαι, ἠχθέσθην, ἀχθεσθήσομαι.

[**"Ἄχνυμαι** (ἀχ-), *be troubled*, impf. ἀχνύμην. Poetic. (II.) Also epic pres. **ἄχομαι**.] See **ἀκαχίζω**.

[**"Ἄω**, *satiate*, ἄσω, ἆσα; 2 aor. subj. ἕωμεν (or ἐῶμεν), pr. inf. ἄμεναι, *to satiate one's self*. Mid. (ἄομαι) ἄαται as fut.; f. ἄσομαι, a. ἀσάμην. Epic.]

B.

Βάζω (βαγ-), *speak, utter*, βάξω, [ep. pf. pass. βέβακται]. Poetic. (4.)

Βαίνω (βα-, βαν-), *go*, βήσομαι, βέβηκα, βέβαμαι, ἐβάθην (rare); 2 a. ἔβην (799); 2 pf., see 804; [a. m. epic ἐβησάμην (rare) and ἐβησόμην, 777, 8.] In active sense, *cause to go*, poet. βήσω, ἔβησα. See 610. The *simple* form is used in Attic prose only in the pres. and perf. active. (5. 4.)

Βάλλω (βαλ-, βλα-), *throw*, f. [βαλέω] βαλῶ, rarely (ε-) βαλλήσω, βέβληκα, βέβλημαι, opt. δια-βεβλῆσθε (734), [epic βεβόλημαι], ἐβλήθην, βληθήσομαι; 2 a. ἔβαλον, ἐβαλόμην; fut. m. βαλοῦμαι; f. p. βεβλήσομαι. [Epic, 2 a. dual ξυμ-βλήτην; 2 a. m. ἐβλήμην, with subj. βλήεται, opt. βλῇο or βλεῖο, inf. βλῆσθαι, pt. βλήμενος; fut. ξυμ-βλήσεαι, pf. p. βέβληαι.] (4.)

Βάπτω (βαφ-), *dip*, βάψω, ἔβαψα, βέβαμμαι, ἐβάφην and (poet.) ἐβάφθην; fut. m. βάψομαι. (3.)

Βάσκω (βα-), poetic form of βαίνω, *go*. (6.)

Βαστάζω (see 587), *carry*, βαστάσω, ἐβάστασα. (Later forms from stem βασταγ-.) Poetic. (4.)

Βήσσω (βηχ-), Att. βήττω, *cough*, βήξω, ἔβηξα. (4.)

[**Βίβημι** (βα-), *go*, pr. part. βιβάς. Epic.] (I.)

Βιβρώσκω (βρο-), *eat*, p. βέβρωκα, βέβρωμαι, [ἐβρώθην; 2 a. ἔβρων; fut. pf. βεβρώσομαι]; 2 p. part. pl. βεβρῶτες (804). [Hom. opt. βεβρώθοις.] (6.)

Βιόω, *live*, βιώσομαι, ἐβίωσα (rare), βεβίωκα, βεβίωμαι; 2 a. ἐβίων (799). (For ἐβιωσάμην, see βιώσκομαι.)

Βιώσκομαι (βιο-), *revive*, ἐβιωσάμην, *restored to life*. (6.)

Βλάπτω (βλαβ-), *injure*, βλάψω, ἔβλαψα, βέβλαφα, βέβλαμμαι, ἐβλάφθην; 2 a. p. ἐβλάβην, 2 f. βλαβήσομαι; fut. m. βλάψομαι; [fut. pf. βεβλάψομαι Ion.]. (3.)

Βλαστάνω (βλαστ-), *sprout*, (ε-) βλαστήσω, βεβλάστηκα and ἐβλάστηκα (524); 2 a. ἔβλαστον. (5.)

Βλέπω, *see*, βλέψομαι [Hdt. ἀνα-βλέψω], ἔβλεψα.

Βλίττω or **βλίσσω** (μελιτ-, βλιτ-, 66), *take honey*, aor. ἔβλισα. (4.)

Βλώσκω (μολ-, μλο-, βλο-, 66), *go*, f. μολοῦμαι, p. μέμβλωκα, 2 a. ἔμολον. Poetic. (6.)

Βοάω, *shout*, βοήσομαι, ἐβόησα. [Ion. (stem βο-), βώσομαι, ἔβωσα, ἐβωσάμην, (βέβωμαι) βεβωμένος, ἐβώσθην.]

Βόσκω, *feed*, (ε-) βοσκήσω.

Βούλομαι, *will*, *wish*, (augm. ἐβουλ- or ἠβουλ-); (ε-) βουλήσομαι, βεβούλημαι, ἐβουλήθην; [2 p. προ-βέβουλα, *prefer*.] [Epic also βόλομαι.] 517.

[(**βραχ-**), stem, with only 2 aor. ἔβραχε and βράχε, *resounded*. Epic.]

Βρίζω (see 587), *be drowsy*, aor. ἔβριξα. Poetic. (4.)

Βρίθω, *be heavy*, βρίσω, ἔβρῖσα, βέβρῖθα. Rare in Attic prose.

[(**βροχ-**), stem, *swallow*, aor. ἔβροξα (opt. -βρόξειε), 2 aor. p. ἀναβροχείς; 2 pf. ἀνα-βέβροχεν, *Il.* 17, 54. Epic.]

Βρῡχάομαι (βρῡχ-, 656), *roar*, 2 p. βέβρῡχα; ἐβρῡχησάμην; βρῡχηθείς.

Βῡνέω or **βύω** (βυ-), *stop up*, βύσω, ἔβῡσα, βέβυσμαι. 607. Chiefly poetic. (5.)

Γ.

Γαμέω (γαμ-), *marry* (said of a man), f. γαμῶ, a. ἔγημα, p. γεγάμηκα; p. p. γεγάμημαι (of a woman). Mid. *marry* (of a woman), f. γαμοῦμαι, a. ἐγημάμην. 654.

Γάνυμαι, *rejoice*, [epic fut. γανύσσομαι.] Chiefly poetic. (II.)

Γέγωνα (γων-), 2 perf. as pres., *shout*, sub. γεγώνω, imper. γέγωνε, [ep. inf. γεγωνέμεν, part. γεγωνώς; 2 plpf. ἐγεγώνει, with ἐγέγωνε and 1 sing. ἐγεγώνευν for -εον (777, 4).] Derived pres. γεγωνέω, w. fut. γεγωνήσω, a. ἐγεγώνησα. Chiefly poetic. Present also γεγωνίσκω. (6.)

Γείνομαι (γεν-), *be born*; a. ἐγεινάμην, *begat*. (4.)

Γελάω, *laugh*, γελάσομαι, ἐγέλασα, ἐγελάσθην. 639.

[**Γέντο**, *seized*, epic 2 aor., *Il.* 18, 476.]

Γηθέω (γηθ-), *rejoice*, [γηθήσω, ἐγήθησα;] 2 p. γέγηθα (as pres.). 654.

Γηράσκω and **γηράω** (γηρα-), *grow old*, γηράσω and γηράσομαι, ἐγήρᾱσα, γεγήρᾱκα (*am old*); 2 a. (799), inf. γηρᾶναι, [Hom. pt. γηράς]. (6.)

Γίγνομαι and **γίνομαι** (γεν-), *become* (651), γενήσομαι, γεγένημαι, [ἐγενήθην Dor. and Ion.], γενηθήσομαι (rare); 2 a. ἐγενόμην [epic γέντο for ἐγένετο]; 2 p. γέγονα, *am* (for γεγάᾱσι, γεγώς, and other μι-forms, see 804).

Γιγνώσκω (γνο-), nosco, *know*, γνώσομαι, [Hdt. ἀν-έγνωσα,] ἔγνωκα, ἔγνωσμαι, ἐγνώσθην; 2 a. ἔγνων, *perceived* (799). Ionic and late Attic γῑνώσκω. (6.)

Γλύφω, *cut*, *grave*, [ἐν-έγλυψα, Hdt., ἐγλυψάμην, Theoc.,] γέγλυμμαι and ἔγλυμμαι (524).

Γνάμπτω (γναμπ-), *bend*, γνάμψω, [ἔγναμψα, ἐγνάμφθην.] Poetic, chiefly epic. (3.)

[**Γοάω** (γο-, 656), *bewail*, 2 a. γόον, only epic in active. Mid. γοάομαι, poetic, epic f. γοήσομαι.]

Γράφω, *write*, γράψω, ἔγραψα, γέγραφα, γέγραμμαι, 2 a. p. ἐγράφην (ἐγράφθην is not classic); 2 f. p. γραφήσομαι; fut. pf. γεγράψομαι, a. m. ἐγραψάμην.

Γρύζω (γρυγ-), *grunt*, γρύξω and γρύξομαι, ἔγρυξα. Chiefly poetic. (4.)

Δ.

[(**δα-**), stem, *teach*, *learn*, no pres., (ε-) δαήσομαι, δεδάηκα, δεδάημαι; 2 a. m. (?) inf. δεδάασθαι; 2 pf. pt. δεδαώς (804); 2 a. ἔδαον or δέδαον, *taught*; 2 a. p. ἐδάην, *learned*. Hom. δήω, *shall find*.] Poetic, chiefly epic.

[**Δαιδάλλω** (δαιδαλ-), *deck out*, *ornament*, epic and lyric. Pindar has pf. p. part. δεδαιδαλμένος, a. pt. δαιδαλθείς; also f. inf. δαιδαλωσέμεν, from stem in ο- (see 659).] (4.)

[**Δαΐζω** (δαϊγ-), *rend*, δαΐξω, ἐδάϊξα, δεδάϊγμαι, ἐδαΐχθην. Epic and lyric.] (4.)

Δαίνῡμι (δαι-), *entertain*, δαίσω, ἔδαισα, (ἐδαίσθην) δαισθείς. [Epic δαίνῡ, impf. and pr. imperat.] Mid. δαίνυμαι, *feast*, δαίσομαι, ἐδαισάμην: [epic pr. opt. δαινῦτο for δαινυι-το, δαινῦατ' for δαινυι-ατο (777, 3): see 734.] (II.)

Δαίομαι (δασ-, δασι-, δαι-, 602), *divide*, [epic f. δάσομαι,] a. ἐδασάμην, pf. p. δέδασμαι [epic δέδαιμαι]. (4.) See also **δατέομαι**.

Δαίω (δαϝ-, δαϝι-, δαι-, 602), *kindle*, [epic 2 p. δέδηα, 2 plpf. 3 pers. δεδήειν; 2 a. (ἐδαόμην) subj. δάηται.] Poetic. (4.)

Δάκνω (δηκ-, δακ-), *bite*, δήξομαι, δέδηγμαι, ἐδήχθην, δηχθήσομαι; 2 a. ἔδακον. (5. 2.)

Δάμνημι (609) and **δαμνάω** (δαμ-, δμα-, δαμα-), also pres. **δαμάζω** (587), *tame*, *subdue*, [fut. δαμάσω, δαμάω, δαμῶ (with Hom. δαμάᾳ, δαμόωσι), a. ἐδάμασα, p. p. δέδμημαι, a. p. ἐδμήθην] and ἐδαμάσθην; [2 a. p. ἐδάμην (with δάμεν); fut. pf. δεδμήσομαι; fut. m. δαμάσομαι,] a. ἐδαμασάμην. In Attic prose only δαμάζω, ἐδαμάσθην, ἐδαμασάμην. 665, 2. (5. 4.)

Δαρθάνω (δαρθ-), *sleep*, 2 a. ἔδαρθον, poet. ἔδραθον; (ε-) p. κατα-δεδαρθηκώς. Only in comp. (usually κατα-δαρθάνω, except 2 aor.). (5.)

Δατέομαι, *divide*, w. irreg. δατέασθαι (?). See δαίομαι.

[**Δέαμαι**, *appear*, only in impf. δέατο, *Od.* 6, 242.]

Δέδια, *fear*: see δέδοικα.

Δέδοικα, perf. as pres. (δϝει-, δϝοι-, δϝι-, 31), [epic δείδοικα,] *fear*. [Epic fut. δείσομαι,] a. ἔδεισα; 2 pf. δέδια [epic δείδια,] for full forms see 804. See 522 (*b*). [From stem δϝι- Homer forms impf. δίον, δίε, *feared, fled.*] [Epic present δείδω, *fear.*] See also δίεμαι. (2.)

Δείκνῡμι (δεικ-), *show*: for synopsis and inflection, see 504, 506, and 509. [Ion. (δεκ-), δέξω, ἔδεξα, δέδεγμαι, ἐδέχθην, ἐδεξάμην.] Epic pf. m. δείδεγμαι (for δέδεγμαι), *greet*, probably comes from another stem δεκ-. (II.)

[**Δέμω** (δεμ-, δμε-), *build*, ἔδειμα, δέδμημαι, ἐδειμάμην.] Chiefly Ionic.

Δέρκομαι, *see*, ἐδέρχθην; 2 a. ἔδρακον, (ἐδράκην) δρακείς (649, 2; 646); 2 p. δέδορκα (643). Poetic.

Δέρω, *flay*, δερῶ, ἔδειρα, δέδαρμαι; 2 a. ἐδάρην. Ionic and poetic also δείρω (δερ-). (4.)

Δέχομαι, *receive*, δέξομαι, δέδεγμαι [Hom. δέχαται for δεδέχαται], ἐδέχθην, ἐδεξάμην; [2 a. m., chiefly epic, ἐδέγμην, δέκτο, imper. δέξο (756, 1), inf. δέχθαι, part. δέγμενος (sometimes as pres.).]

Δέω, *bind*, δήσω, ἔδησα, δέδεκα (rarely δέδηκα), δέδεμαι, ἐδέθην, δεθήσομαι; fut. pf. δεδήσομαι, a. m. ἐδησάμην.

Δέω, *want, need*, (ε-) δεήσω, ἐδέησα [ep. ἔδησα,] δεδέηκα, δεδέημαι, ἐδεήθην. Mid. δέομαι, *ask*, δεήσομαι. From epic stem δευ- (ε-) come [ἐδεύησα, *Od.* 9, 540, and δεύομαι, δευήσομαι.] Impersonal δεῖ, debet, *there is need, (one) ought*, δεήσει, ἐδέησε.

[**Δηριάω**, act. rare (δηρι-, 656), *contend*, aor. ἐδήρῑσα (Theoc.), aor. p. δηρίνθην as middle (Hom.). Mid. δηριάομαι and δηρίομαι, as act., δηρίσομαι (Theoc.), ἐδηρῑσάμην (Hom.).] Epic and lyric.

[**Δήω**, epic present with future meaning, *shall find.*] See (δα-).

Διαιτάω, *arbitrate*, w. double augment in perf. and plpf. and in compounds (543 and 544); διαιτήσω, διῄτησα (ἀπ-εδιῄτησα), δεδιῄτηκα, δεδιῄτημαι, διῃτήθην (ἐξ-εδιῃτήθην, late); διαιτήσομαι, κατ-εδιῃτησάμην.

Διᾱκονέω, *minister*, ἐδιᾱκόνουν; διᾱκονήσω (aor. inf. διᾱκονῆσαι), δεδιᾱκόνημαι, ἐδιᾱκονήθην. Later and doubtful (poetic) earlier forms with augment διη- or δεδιη-. See 543.

Διδάσκω (διδαχ-), for διδαχ-σκω (617), *teach*, διδάξω, ἐδίδαξα [epic ἐδιδάσκησα], **δεδίδαχα, δεδίδαγμαι, ἐδιδάχθην; διδάξομαι, ἐδιδαξάμην.** See stem **δα-**. (**6.**)

Δίδημι, *bind*, chiefly poetic form for **δέω**. (**I.**)

Διδράσκω (δρα-), only in comp., *run away*, -δράσομαι, -δέδρᾱκα; 2 a. -ἔδρᾱν [Ion. -ἔδρην], -δρῶ, -δραίην, -δρᾶναι, -δράς (799). (**6.**)

Δίδωμι (δο-), *give*, δώσω, ἔδωκα, δέδωκα, etc.; see synopsis and inflection in 504, 506, and 509. [Ep. δόμεναι or δόμεν for δοῦναι, fut. διδώσω for δώσω.] (**I.**)

Δίεμαι (διε-), *be frightened, flee* (794, 1), inf. δίεσθαι, *to flee* or *to drive* (*chase*); δίωμαι and διοίμην (cf. δύνωμαι 729, and τιθοίμην 741), *chase*, part. διόμενος, *chasing*. Impf. act. ἐν-δίεσαν, *set on* (of dogs), *Il.* 18, 584. (**I.**)

[**Δίζημαι**, *seek*, with η for ε in present; διζήσομαι, ἐδιζησάμην. Ionic and poetic.] (**I.**)

[(**δικ-**), stem, with 2 aor. ἔδικον, *threw, cast*. In Pindar and the tragedians.]

Διψάω, *thirst*, διψήσω, ἐδίψησα. See 496.

Δοκέω (δοκ-), *seem, think*, δόξω, ἔδοξα, δέδογμαι, ἐδόχθην (rare). Poetic δοκήσω, ἐδόκησα, δεδόκηκα, δεδόκημαι, ἐδοκήθην. Impersonal, **δοκεῖ**, *it seems*, etc. 654.

Δουπέω (δουπ-), *sound heavily*, ἐδούπησα [epic δούπησα and (in tmesis) ἐπι-γδούπησα, 2 pf. δέδουπα, δεδουπώς, *fallen*.] Chiefly poetic. 654.

Δράσσομαι or **δράττομαι** (δραγ-), *grasp*, aor. ἐδραξάμην, pf. δέδραγμαι. (**4.**)

Δράω, *do*, δράσω, ἔδρᾱσα, δέδρᾱκα, δέδρᾱμαι, (rarely δέδρᾱσμαι), (ἐδράσθην) δρᾱσθείς. 640.

Δύναμαι, *be able*, augm. ἐδυν- and ἠδυν- (517); 2 p. sing. pres. (poet.) δύνᾳ [Ion. δύνῃ], impf. ἐδύνασο or ἐδύνω (632); δυνήσομαι, δεδύνημαι, ἐδυνήθην (ἐδυνάσθην, chiefly Ionic), [epic ἐδυνησάμην.] (**I.**)

Δύω, *enter* or *cause to enter*, and **δύνω** (δυ-), *enter*; δύσω, ἔδῡσα, δέδῡκα, δέδυμαι, ἐδύθην, f. p. δυθήσομαι; 2 a. ἔδῡν, inflected 506: see 504 and 799; f. m. δύσομαι, a. m. ἐδῡσάμην [ep. ἐδῡσόμην (777, 8)]. (**5.**)

E.

[**Ἑάφθη** (*Il.* 13, 543; 14, 419), aor. pass. commonly referred to ἅπτω; also to ἕπομαι and to ἰάπτω.]

Ἐάω [epic εἰάω], *permit*, ἐάσω, εἴᾱσα [ep. ἔᾱσα], εἴᾱκα, εἴᾱμαι, εἰάθην; ἐάσομαι (as pass.). For augment, see 537.

Ἐγγυάω, *pledge, betroth*, augm. ἠγγυ- or ἐνεγυ- (ἐγγεγυ-), see 543; 544.

Ἐγείρω (ἐγερ-), *raise, rouse*, ἐγερῶ, ἤγειρα, ἐγήγερμαι, ἠγέρθην; 2 p. ἐγρήγορα, *am awake* [Hom. ἐγρηγόρθᾱσι (for -όρᾱσι), imper. ἐγρήγορθε (for -όρατε), inf. ἐγρήγορθαι or -όρθαι]; 2 a. m. ἠγρόμην [ep. ἐγρόμην]. (**4.**)

Ἔδω, *eat*, (poetic, chiefly epic, present): see **ἐσθίω**.

Ἕζομαι, (ἐδ- for σεδ-; cf. sed-eo), *sit*, [fut. inf. ἐφ-έσσεσθαι (Hom.);] aor. εἱσάμην [epic ἑσσάμην and ἐεσσάμην]. [Active aor. εἷσα and ἕσσα (Hom.).] 86. Chiefly poetic. (4.) See **ἵζω** and **καθέζομαι**.

Ἐθέλω and **θέλω**, *wish*, imp. ἤθελον; (ε-) ἐθελήσω or θελήσω, ἠθέλησα, ἠθέληκα. Ἐθέλω is the more common form except in the tragic trimeter. Impf. always ἤθελον; aor. (probably) always ἠθέλησα, but subj. etc. ἐθελήσω and θελήσω, ἐθελῆσαι and θελῆσαι, etc.

Ἐθίζω (see 587), *accustom*, ἐθίσω, εἴθισα, εἴθικα, εἴθισμαι, εἰθίσθην. The root is σϝεθ- (see 537). (4.)

[**Ἔθων**, Hom pres. part.]: see **εἴωθα**.

Εἶδον (ἰδ-, ϝιδ-), vid-i, 2 aor., *saw*, no present (see 539): ἴδω, ἴδοιμι, ἴδε or ἰδέ, ἰδεῖν, ἰδών. Mid. (chiefly poet.) **εἴδομαι**, *seem*, [ep. εἰσάμην and ἐεισ-;] 2 a. εἰδόμην (in prose rare and only in comp.), *saw*, = εἶδον. **Οἶδα** (2 pf. as pres.), *know*, plp. ᾔδη, *knew*, f. εἴσομαι; see 820. (8.)

Εἰκάζω (see 587), *make like*, εἴκαζον or ᾔκαζον, εἰκάσω, εἴκασα or ᾔκασα, εἴκασμαι or ᾔκασμαι, εἰκάσθην, εἰκασθήσομαι. (4.)

(**Εἴκω**) not used in pres. (εἰκ-, ἰκ-), *resemble*, *appear*, imp. εἶκον, f. εἴξω (rare), 2 p. **ἔοικα** [Ion. οἶκα] (with ἔοιγμεν, [ἔϊκτον,] εἴξᾱσι, εἰκέναι, εἰκώς, chiefly poetic); 2 plp. ἐῴκη [with ἐΐκτην]. Impersonal **ἔοικε**, *it seems*, etc. For ἔοικα, see 537, 2. (2.)

[**Εἰλέω** (ἐλ-, ειλ-), *press*, *roll* (654), aor. ἔλσα, pf. p. ἔελμαι, 2 aor. p. ἐάλην or ἄλην w. inf. ἀλήμεναι. Pres. pass. εἴλομαι. Epic. Hdt. has (in comp.) -είλησα, -είλημαι, -ειλήθην. Pind. has plpf. ἐόλει.] The Attic has εἰλέομαι, and εἴλλω or εἵλλω. 598. See **ἴλλω**. (4.)

Εἰμί, *be*, and **Εἶμι**, *go*. See 806–809.

Εἶπον (εἰπ-), *said*, [epic ἔειπον], 2 aor., no present; εἴπω, εἴποιμι, εἰπέ, εἰπεῖν, εἰπών; 1 aor. εἶπα [poet. ἔειπα,] (opt. εἴπαιμι, imper. εἶπον or εἰπόν, inf. εἶπαι, pt. εἴπᾱς), [Hdt. ἀπ-ειπάμην]. Other tenses are supplied by a stem ἐρ-, ῥε- (for ϝερ-, ϝρε-): [Hom. pres. (rare) εἴρω], f. ἐρέω, ἐρῶ; p. εἴρηκα, εἴρημαι (522); a. p. ἐρρήθην, rarely ἐρρέθην [Ion. εἰρέθην]; fut. pass. ῥηθήσομαι; fut. pf. εἰρήσομαι. See **ἐνέπω**. (8.)

Εἴργνῡμι and **εἰργνύω**, also εἵργω (εἱργ-), *shut in*; εἵρξω, εἷρξα, εἷργμαι, εἵρχθην. Also **ἔργω**, ἔρξω, ἔρξα, [Hom. (ἔργμαι) 3 pl. ἔρχαται w. plpf. ἔρχατο, ἔρχθην]. (II.)

Εἴργω, *shut out*, εἴρξω, εἷρξα, εἷργμαι, εἴρχθην; εἴρξομαι. Also [**ἔργω**, -ερξα, -εργμαι, Ionic]; ἔρξομαι (Soph.). [Epic also ἐέργω.]

[**Εἴρομαι** (Ion.), *ask*, fut. (ε-) εἰρήσομαι. See **ἔρομαι**.]

[**Εἴρω** (ἐρ-), *say*, epic in present.] See **εἶπον**. (4.)

Εἴρω (ἐρ-), sero, *join*, a. -εἶρα [Ion. -ἔρσα], p. -εἶρκα, εἶρμαι [epic ἔερμαι]. Rare except in compos. (4.)

[**Ἐΐσκω** (ἐϊκ-), *liken, compare*, (617); poetic, chiefly epic: pres. also ἴσκω.] 617. Προσ-ῄϊξαι, *art like*, [and epic ῄϊκτο or ἔϊκτο], sometimes referred to εἴκω. See εἴκω. (6.)

Εἴωθα [Ionic ἔωθα] (ἠθ- for σϝηθ-, 537, 2, and 689), 2 perf., *am accustomed*, 2 plpf. εἰώθη. [Hom. has pres. act. part. ἔθων.] (2.)

Ἐκκλησιάζω, *call an assembly*; augm. ἠκκλη- and ἐξεκλη- (543).

Ἐλαύνω, for ἐλα-νυ-ω (612), poetic ἐλάω (ἐλα-), *drive, march*, fut. (ἐλάσω) ἐλῶ (665, 2) [epic ἐλάσσω, ἐλόω;] ἤλασα, ἐλήλακα, ἐλήλαμαι [Ion. and late ἐλήλασμαι, Hom. plup. ἐληλέδατο], ἠλάθην, ἠλασάμην. (5.)

Ἐλέγχω, *confute*, ἐλέγξω, ἤλεγξα, ἐλήλεγμαι (487, 2), ἠλέγχθην, ἐλεγχθήσομαι.

Ἑλίσσω and **εἱλίσσω** (ἑλικ-), *roll*, ἑλίξω and εἱλίξω, εἵλιξα, εἵλιγμαι, εἱλίχθην. [Epic aor. mid. ἑλιξάμην.] (4.)

Ἕλκω (late ἑλκύω), *pull*, ἕλξω (Ion. and late Att. ἑλκύσω), εἵλκυσα, εἵλκυκα, εἵλκυσμαι, εἱλκύσθην. 537.

Ἐλπίζω (ἐλπιδ-), *hope*, aor. ἤλπισα; aor. p. part. ἐλπισθέν. (4.)

[**Ἔλπω**, *cause to hope*, 2 p. ἔολπα, *hope*; 2 plpf. ἐώλπειν (3 pers. sing.). 643. Mid. ἔλπομαι, *hope*, like Attic ἐλπίζω. Epic.]

Ἐμέω, *vomit*, fut. ἐμῶ (rare), ἐμοῦμαι; aor. ἤμεσα. 639.

Ἐναίρω (ἐναρ-), *kill*, 2 a. ἤναρον. [Hom. a. m. ἐνήρατο.] Poetic. (4.)

Ἐνέπω (ἐν and stem σεπ-) or **ἐννέπω**, *say, tell*, [ep. f. ἐνι-σπήσω (σεπ-) and ἐνίψω;] 2 a. ἔνι-σπον, w. imper. ἔνισπε [ep. ἐνίσπες], 2 pl. ἔσπετε (for ἐν-σπετε), inf. ἐνισπεῖν [ep. -έμεν]. Poetic. See εἶπον.

Ἐνίπτω (ἐνιπ-), *chide*, [epic also ἐνίσσω, 2 a. ἐνένιπον and ἠνίπαπον (535). (3.)

Ἕννυμι (ἑ- for ϝεσ-), ves-tio, *clothe*, pres. act. only in comp.; [f. ἕσσω, a. ἕσσα, ἑσσάμην or ἐσσ-; pf. ἕσμαι or εἷμαι,] εἱμένος in trag. In comp. -έσω, -έσα, -εσάμην. Chiefly epic: ἀμφι-έννυμι is the common form in prose. (II.)

Ἐνοχλέω, *harass*, w. double augment (544); ἠνώχλουν, ἐνοχλήσω, ἠνώχλησα, ἠνώχλημαι.

Ἔοικα, *seem*, 2 perfect: see εἴκω.

Ἑορτάζω (see 587), Ion. ὁρτάζω, *keep festival*; impf. ἑώρταζον (538). (4.)

Ἐπ-αυρέω and **ἐπ-αυρίσκω** (αὐρ-), both rare, *enjoy*, [2 a. Dor. and ep. ἐπαῦρον; f. m. ἐπαυρήσομαι,] a. ἐπηυράμην, 2 a. ἐπηυρόμην. Chiefly poetic. 654. (6.)

[**Ἐπ-ενήνοθε**, defect. 2 pf., *sit on, lie on*; also as 2 plpf. (777, 4). Epic.] See ἀνήνοθε.

Ἐπίσταμαι, *understand*, 2 p. sing. (poet.) ἐπίστᾳ [Ion. ἐπίστεαι,] imp. ἠπιστάμην, 2 p. sing. ἠπίστασο or ἠπίστω (632); f. ἐπιστήσομαι, a. ἠπιστήθην. (Not to be confounded with forms of ἐφίστημι.) (I.)

[**Ἕπω** (σεπ-), *be after* or *busy with*, imp. **εἶπον** (poet. **ἕπον**); f. **-έψω**, 2. a. **-έσπον** (for ἐ-σεπ-ον), a. p. **περι-έφθην** (Hdt.): active chiefly Ionic or poetic, and in compos.] Mid. **ἕπομαι** [poet. **ἕσπομαι**], *follow*, f. **ἕψομαι**; 2 a. **ἑσπόμην**, rarely poetic **-εσπόμην**, **σπῶμαι**, etc., w. imp. [σπεῖο (for σπεο),] σποῦ. 86; 537, 2.

Ἐράω, *love*, **ἠράσθην**, **ἐρασθήσομαι**, [ἠρασάμην (epic)]. Poetic pres. **ἔραμαι**, imp. **ἠράμην**. (I.)

Ἐργάζομαι, *work*, *do*, augm. **εἰρ-** (537); **ἐργάσομαι**, **εἴργασμαι**, **εἰργάσθην**, **εἰργασάμην**, **ἐργασθήσομαι**. 587. (4.)

Ἔργω and **ἕργω**: see **εἴργνυμι** (**εἴργω**) and **εἵργω**.

Ἔρδω and **ἕρδω**, *work*, *do*, probably for **ἐρζ-ω** = **ῥέζω** (by metathesis): the stem is ϝεργ- (see 539), whence ϝρεγ-, ῥεγ-; fut. **ἕρξω**, a. **ἕρξα**, [Ion. 2 pf. **ἔοργα**, 2 plpf. **ἐόργεα**.] Ionic and poetic. See **ῥέζω**.

Ἐρείδω, *prop*, **ἐρείσω** (later), **ἤρεισα**, [ἤρεικα, **ἐρήρεισμαι**, with **ἐρηρέδαται** and **-ατο**, 777, 3,] **ἠρείσθην**; **ἐρείσομαι** (Aristot.), **ἠρεισάμην**.

Ἐρείκω (ἐρεικ-, ἐρικ-), *tear*, *burst*, **ἤρειξα**, **ἐρήριγμαι**, 2 a. **ἤρικον**. Ionic and poetic. (2.)

Ἐρείπω (ἐρειπ-, ἐριπ-), *throw down*, **ἐρείψω**, [ἤρειψα, 2 pf. **ἐρήριπα**, *have fallen*, p. p. **ἐρήριμμαι** (plpf. **ἐρέριπτο**, Hom.), 2 a. **ἤριπον**, **ἠρίπην**, a. m. **ἀνηρειψάμην** (Hom.)], a. p. **ἠρείφθην**. (2.)

Ἐρέσσω (ἐρετ-), *strike*, *row*, [ep. aor. **ἤρεσα**.] 582. (4.)

[**Ἐριδαίνω**, *contend*, for **ἐρίζω**; aor. m. inf. **ἐρῑδήσασθαι**. Epic.]

Ἐρίζω (ἐριδ-), *contend*, **ἤρισα**, [ἠρισάμην epic.] (4.)

Ἔρομαι (rare or ?), [Ion. **εἴρομαι**, ep. **ἐρέω** or **ἐρέομαι**], for the Attic **ἐρωτάω**, *ask*, fut. (ε-) **ἐρήσομαι** [Ion. **εἰρήσομαι**], 2 a. **ἠρόμην**. See **εἴρομαι**.

Ἕρπω, *creep*, imp. **εἷρπον**; fut. **ἕρψω**. Poetic. 539.

Ἔρρω, *go to destruction*, (ε-) **ἐρρήσω**, **ἤρρησα**, **εἰσ-ήρρηκα**.

Ἐρυγγάνω (ἐρυγ-), *eruct*, 2 a. **ἤρυγον**. (5.) [Ion. **ἐρεύγομαι**, **ἐρεύξομαι**. (2.)]

Ἐρύκω, *hold back*, [ep. f. **ἐρύξω**] **ἤρῡξα**, [ep. 2 a. **ἠρύκακον**.]

[**Ἐρύω** and **εἰρύω**, *draw*, fut. **ἐρύω**, aor. **εἴρυσα** and **ἔρυσα**, pf. p. **εἴρῡμαι** and **εἴρυσμαι**. Mid. **ἐρύομαι** (ῠ) and **εἰρύομαι**, *take under one's protection*, **ἐρύσομαι** and **εἰρύσομαι**, **ἐρυσάμην** and **εἰρυσάμην**; with Hom. μι-forms of pres. and impf. **εἰρύαται** (3 pl.), **ἔρῡσο**, **ἔρῡτο** and **εἴρῡτο**, **εἴρυντο**, **ἔρυσθαι** and **εἴρυσθαι**. Epic.] 639. See **ῥύομαι**.

Ἔρχομαι (ἐρχ-, ἐλευθ-, ἐλυθ-, ἐλθ-), *go*, *come*, f. **ἐλεύσομαι** (Ion. and poet.), 2 pf. **ἐλήλυθα** [ep. **ἐλήλουθα** and **εἰλήλουθα**], 2 a. **ἦλθον** (poet. **ἤλυθον**): see 31. In Attic *prose*, **εἶμι** is used for **ἐλεύσομαι** (1257). (8.)

Ἐσθίω, also poetic **ἔσθω** and **ἔδω** (ἐσθ-, ἐδ-, φαγ-), edo, *eat*, fut. **ἔδομαι**, p. **ἐδήδοκα**, **ἐδήδεσμαι**, [ep. **ἐδήδομαι**], **ἠδέσθην**; 2 a. **ἔφαγον**; [epic pres. inf. **ἔδμεναι**; 2 perf. part. **ἐδηδώς**.] (8.)

Ἑστιάω, *feast*, augment **εἱστι-** (537).

Εὕδω, *sleep*, impf. εὗδον or ηὗδον (519), (ε-) εὑδήσω, [-εὕδησα]. Commonly in **καθ-εύδω**. 658, 1.

Εὐεργετέω, *do good*, εὐεργετήσω, etc., regular: sometimes augmented εὐηργ- (545, 1).

Εὑρίσκω (εὑρ-), *find*, (ε-) εὑρήσω, ηὕρηκα, ηὕρημαι, ηὑρέθην, εὑρεθήσομαι; 2 a. ηὗρον, ηὑρόμην. 639 (*b*). Often found with augment ευ- (519). (**6**.)

Εὐφραίνω (εὐφραν-), *cheer*, f. εὐφρανῶ; a. ηὔφρᾱνα, [Ion. also εὔφρηνα;] a. p. ηὐφράνθην, f. p. εὐφρανθήσομαι; f. m. εὐφρανοῦμαι. 519. (**4**.)

Ἐχθαίρω (ἐχθαρ-), *hate*, f. ἐχθαροῦμαι, a. ἤχθηρα. (**4**.)

Ἔχω (σεχ-), *have*, imp. εἶχον (539); ἕξω or σχήσω (σχε-), ἔσχηκα, ἔσχημαι, ἐσχέθην (chiefly Ion.); 2 a. ἔσχον (for ἐ-σεχ-ον), σχῶ, σχοίην and -σχοῖμι, σχές, σχεῖν, σχών; poet. ἔσχεθον etc. (779). [Hom. pf. part. συν-οχοκώς for ὀκ-οχ-ως (643; 529), plpf. ἐπ-ώχατο, *were shut*, *Il.* 12, 340.] Mid. **ἔχομαι**, *cling to*, ἕξομαι and σχήσομαι, ἐσχόμην.

Ἕψω, *cook*, (ε-) f. ἕψομαι and ἑψήσομαι, ἑψήσω (rare), a. ἥψησα, [ἥψημαι, ἡψήθην.] 658, 1.

Z.

Ζάω, *live*, w. ζῇς, ζῇ, etc. (496), impf. ἔζων and ἔζην; ζήσω, ζήσομαι, (ἔζησα, ἔζηκα, later). Ion. ζώω.

Ζεύγνῡμι (ζευγ-, ζυγ-, cf. jug-um), *yoke*, ζεύξω, ἔζευξα, ἔζευγμαι, ἐζεύχθην; 2 a. p. ἐζύγην. (**2**. **II**.)

Ζέω, *boil* (poet. **ζείω**), ζέσω, ἔζεσα, [-έζεσμαι Ion.]. 639.

Ζώννῡμι (ζω-), *gird*, ἔζωσα, ἔζωσμαι and ἔζωμαι, ἐζωσάμην. (**II**.)

H.

Ἡβάσκω (ἡβα-), *come to manhood*, with **ἡβάω**, *be at manhood*: ἡβήσω, ἥβησα, ἥβηκα. (**4**.)

Ἠγερέθομαι, *be collected*, poetic passive form of ἀγείρω (ἀγερ-): see 779. Found only in 3 pl. ἠγερέθονται, with the subj., and infin., and ἠγερέθοντο.

Ἥδομαι, *be pleased*; aor. p. ἥσθην, f. p. ἡσθήσομαι, [aor. m. ἥσατο, *Od.* 9, 353.] The act. **ἥδω** w. impf. ἧδον, aor ἧσα, occurs very rarely.

Ἠερέθομαι, *be raised*, poetic passive of ἀείρω (ἀερ-): see 779. Found only in 3 pl. ἠερέθονται (impf. ἠερέθοντο is late).

Ἧμαι, *sit*: see 814.

Ἠμί, *say*, chiefly in imperf. ἦν δ' ἐγώ, *said I*, and ἦ δ' ὅς, *said he* (1023, 2). [Epic ἦ (alone), *he said*.] Ἠμί, *I say*, is colloquial.

Ἠμύω, *bow*, *sink*, aor. ἤμῡσα, [pf. ὑπ-εμν-ήμῡκε (for ἐμ-ημῡκε, 529) Hom.] Poetic, chiefly epic.

Θ.

Θάλλω (θαλ-), *bloom*, [2 perf. τέθηλα (as present)]. (4.)

[**Θάομαι**, *gaze at, admire*, Doric for θεάομαι, Ion. θηέομαι; θάσομαι and θᾱσοῦμαι, ἐθᾱσάμην (Hom. opt. θησαίατ').]

[**Θάομαι**, *milk*, inf. θῆσθαι, aor. ἐθησάμην. Epic.]

θαπ- or **ταφ-**, stem: see θηπ-.

Θάπτω (ταφ- for θαφ-), *bury*, θάψω, ἔθαψα, τέθαμμαι, [Ion. ἐθάφθην, rare;] 2 a. p. ἐτάφην; 2 fut. ταφήσομαι; fut. pf. τεθάψομαι. 95, 5. (3.)

Θαυμάζω (see 587), *wonder*, θαυμάσομαι (θαυμάσω?), ἐθαύμασα, τεθαύμακα, ἐθαυμάσθην, θαυμασθήσομαι. (4.)

Θείνω (θεν-), *smite*, θενῶ, [ἔθεινα Hom.], 2 a. ἔθενον. (4.)

Θέλω, *wish*, (ε-) θελήσω: see **ἐθέλω**.

Θέρομαι, *warm one's self*, [fut. θέρσομαι, 2 a. p. (ἐθέρην) subj. θερέω.] Chiefly epic.

Θέω, (θευ-, θεϝ-, θυ-), *run*, fut. θεύσομαι. 574. (2.)

(**θηπ-**, θαπ-, or ταφ-), *astonish*, stem with [2 perf. τέθηπα, *am astonished*, epic plpf. ἐτεθήπεα; 2 a. ἔταφον, also intransitive]. 31; 95, 5.

Θιγγάνω (θιγ-), *touch*, θίξομαι, 2 a. ἔθιγον. Chiefly poetic. (5.)

[**Θλάω**, *bruise*, ἔθλασα, τέθλασμαι (Theoc.), ἐθλάσθην (Hippoc.). Ionic and poetic. See φλάω.]

Θλίβω (θλῑβ-, θλῐβ-), *squeeze*, θλίψω, ἔθλῖψα, τέθλῖμμαι, ἐθλίφθην; ἐθλίβην; fut. m. θλίψομαι, Hom.

Θνήσκω, earlier form **θνῄσκω** [Doric and Aeolic θνᾱ́σκω] (θαν-, θνα-), *die*, θανοῦμαι, τέθνηκα; fut. pf. τεθνήξω (705), later τεθνήξομαι; 2 a. ἔθανον; 2 perf. see 804 and 773. In Attic prose always ἀπο-θανοῦμαι and ἀπ-έθανον, but τέθνηκα. 616. (6.)

Θράσσω and θράττω (τραχ-, θραχ-), *disturb*, aor. ἔθρᾱξα, ἐθράχθην (rare); [2 pf. τέτρηχα, *be disturbed*, Hom.] See ταράσσω. (4.)

Θραύω, *bruise*, θραύσω, ἔθραυσα, τέθραυσμαι and τέθραυμαι, ἐθραύσθην (641). Chiefly poetic.

Θρύπτω (τρυφ- for θρυφ-), *crush* [ἔθρυψα Hippoc.], τέθρυμμαι, ἐθρύφθην [ep. 2 a. p. ἐτρύφην], θρύψομαι. 95, 5. (3.)

Θρώσκω and **θρῴσκω** (θορ-, θρο-), *leap*, fut. θοροῦμαι, 2 a. ἔθορον. Chiefly poetic. (6.)

Θύω (θυ-), *sacrifice*, imp. ἔθῡον; θύσω, ἔθῡσα, τέθυκα, τέθυμαι, ἐτύθην; θύσομαι, ἐθῡσάμην. 95, 1 and 3.

Θύω or **θύνω**, *rage, rush*. Poetic: classic only in present and imperfect.

I.

Ἰάλλω (ἰαλ-), *send*, fut. -ἰαλῶ, [ep. aor. ἴηλα.] Poetic. (4.)

[**Ἰάχω** and **ἰαχέω**, *shout*, [2 pf. (ἴαχα) ἀμφ-ιαχυῖα]. Poetic, chiefly epic.]

Ἱδρόω, *sweat*, ἱδρώσω, ἵδρωσα: for irregular contraction ἱδρῶσι etc., see 497.

Ἱδρύω, *place*, ἱδρύσω, ἵδρῡσα, ἵδρῡκα, ἵδρῡμαι, ἱδρύθην [or ἱδρύνθην (709), chiefly epic]; ἱδρύσομαι, ἱδρῡσάμην.

Ἵζω (ἱδ-), *seat* or *sit*, mid. ἵζομαι, *sit*; used chiefly in καθ-ίζω, which see. See also **ἧμαι**. (4.) Also **ἱζάνω**. (5.)

Ἵημι (ἑ-), *send*: for inflection see 810. (I.)

Ἱκνέομαι (ἱκ-), poet. ἵκω, *come*, ἵξομαι, ἷγμαι; 2 a. ἱκόμην. In prose usually **ἀφ-ικνέομαι**. From ἵκω, [ep. imp. ἷκον, aor. ἷξον, 777, 8.] Also **ἱκάνω**, epic and tragic. (5.)

Ἱλάσκομαι [epic ἱλάομαι] (ἱλα-), *propitiate*, ἱλάσομαι, ἱλάσθην, ἱλασάμην. (6.)

[**Ἵλημι** (ἱλα-), *be propitious*, pres. only imper. ἵληθι or ἵλᾰθι; pf. subj. and opt. ἱλήκω, ἱλήκοιμι (Hom.). Mid. ἵλαμαι, *propitiate*, epic. Poetic, chiefly epic.] (I.)

Ἴλλω and **ἴλλομαι**, *roll*, for εἴλλω. See **εἰλέω**.

[**Ἱμάσσω** (see 582), *lash*, aor. ἵμασα.] (4.)

Ἱμείρω (ἱμερ-), *long for*, [ἱμειράμην (epic), ἱμέρθην (Ion.)]. Poetic and Ionic. (4.)

Ἵπταμαι (πτα-), *fly*, late present: see **πέτομαι**. (I.)

[**Ἴσᾱμι**, Doric for οἶδα, *know*, with ἴσᾳς, ἴσᾱτι, ἴσαμεν, ἴσαντι.]

[**Ἴσκω**: see ἐΐσκω.]

Ἵστημι (στα-), *set*, *place*: for synopsis and inflection, see 504, 506, 509. (I.)

Ἰσχναίνω (ἰσχναν-), *make lean* or *dry*, fut. ἰσχνανῶ, aor. ἴσχνᾱνα (673) [ἴσχνηνα Ion.], a. p. ἰσχνάνθην; fut. m. ἰσχνανοῦμαι. (4.)

Ἴσχω (for σι-σεχω, σισχω), *have*, *hold*, redupl. for ἔχω (σεχ-ω). 86. See **ἔχω**.

K.

Καθαίρω (καθαρ-), *purify*, καθαρῶ, ἐκάθηρα and ἐκάθᾱρα, κεκάθαρμαι, ἐκαθάρθην; καθαροῦμαι, ἐκαθηράμην. (4.)

Καθ-έζομαι (ἑδ-), *sit down*, imp. ἐκαθεζόμην, f. καθεδοῦμαι. See **ἕζομαι**.

Καθεύδω, *sleep*, imp. ἐκάθευδον and καθηῦδον [epic καθεῦδον], see 544; fut. (ε-) καθευδήσω (658, 1). See **εὕδω**.

Καθίζω, *set*, *sit*, f. καθιῶ (for καθίσω), καθιζήσομαι; a. ἐκάθῑσα or καθῖσα [Hom. καθεῖσα, Hdt. κατεῖσα] ἐκαθισάμην. See **ἵζω**. For inflection of κάθημαι, see 815.

Καίνυμαι, perhaps for καδ-νυμαι (καδ-), *excel*, p. κέκασμαι [Dor. κεκαδμένος]. Poetic. (II.)

Καίνω (καν-), *kill*, f. κανῶ, 2 a. ἔκανον, 2 p. (κέκονα) κατα-κεκονότες (Xen.). Chiefly poetic. (4.)

Καίω (*καυ-, καϝ-, καϝι-, και-*, 601), in Attic prose generally **κάω** (not contracted), *burn*; **καύσω**; **ἔκαυσα**, poet. part. **κέᾱς**, [epic **ἔκηα**]; **κέκαυκα, κέκαυμαι, ἐκαύθην, καυθήσομαι**, [2 a. **ἐκάην**;] fut. mid. **καύσομαι** (rare), [**ἀν-εκαυσάμην**, Hdt.]. (4.)

Καλέω (*καλε-, κλε-*), *call*, fut. **καλῶ** (rare and doubtful in Attic **καλέσω**); **ἐκάλεσα, κέκληκα, κέκλημαι** (opt. **κεκλῇο, κεκλῄμεθα**), **ἐκλήθην, κληθήσομαι**; fut. m. **καλοῦμαι**, a. **ἐκαλεσάμην**; fut. pf. **κεκλήσομαι**. 639 (*b*); 734.

Καλύπτω (*καλυβ-*), *cover*, **καλύψω, ἐκάλυψα, κεκάλυμμαι, ἐκαλύφθην, καλυφθήσομαι**; aor. m. **ἐκαλυψάμην**. In prose chiefly in compounds. (3.)

Κάμνω (*καμ-*), *labor*, **καμοῦμαι, κέκμηκα** [ep. part. **κεκμηώς**]; 2 a. **ἔκαμον**, [ep. **ἐκαμόμην**.] (5.)

Κάμπτω (*καμπ-*), *bend*, **κάμψω, ἔκαμψα, κέκαμμαι** (77), **ἐκάμφθην**. (3.)

Κατηγορέω, *accuse*, regular except in augment, **κατηγόρουν** etc. (543).

[(**καφ-**), *pant*, stem with Hom. perf. part. **κεκαφηώς**; cf. **τεθνηώς**.]

[**Κεδάννῡμι**, epic for **σκεδάννῡμι**, *scatter*, **ἐκέδασσα, ἐκεδάσθην**.] (II.)

Κεῖμαι, *lie*, **κείσομαι**; inflected in 818.

Κείρω (*κερ-*), *shear*, f. **κερῶ**, a. **ἔκειρα** [poet. **ἔκερσα**], **κέκαρμαι**, [(**ἐκέρθην**) **κερθείς**; 2 a. p. **ἐκάρην**;] f. m. **κεροῦμαι**, a. m. **ἐκειράμην** [w. poet. part. **κερσάμενος**.] (4.)

[**Κέκαδον**, 2 aor. *deprived of, caused to leave*, **κεκαδόμην**, *retired*, **κεκαδήσω**, *shall deprive*, reduplicated Hom. forms of **χάζω**.] See **χάζω**.

[**Κελαδέω**, *shout, roar*, fut. **κελαδήσω, κελαδήσομαι**, aor. **ἐκελάδησα**; Hom. pres. part. **κελάδων**. Epic and lyric.]

Κελεύω, *command*, **κελεύσω, ἐκέλευσα, κεκέλευκα, κεκέλευσμαι, ἐκελεύσθην** (641). Mid. (chiefly in compounds) **κελεύσομαι, ἐκελευσάμην**.

Κέλλω (*κελ-*), *land*, **κέλσω, ἔκελσα**. 668; 674 (*b*). Poetic: the prose form is **ὀκέλλω**. (4.)

Κέλομαι, *order*, [epic (*ε-*) **κελήσομαι, ἐκελησάμην**; 2 a. m. **ἐκεκλόμην** (534; 677).] Poetic, chiefly epic.

Κεντέω (*κεντ-, κεντε-*), *prick*, **κεντήσω, ἐκέντησα**, [**κεκέντημαι** Ion., **ἐκεντήθην** later, **συγκεντηθήσομαι** Hdt.]. [Hom. aor. inf. **κένσαι**, from stem **κεντ-**. 654.] Chiefly Ionic and poetic.

Κεράννῡμι (*κερα-, κρα-*), *mix*, **ἐκέρασα** [Ion. **ἔκρησα**], **κέκρᾱμαι** [Ion. **-ημαι**], **ἐκράθην** [Ion. **-ήθην**] and **ἐκεράσθην**; f. pass. **κρᾱθήσομαι**; a. m. **ἐκερασάμην**. (II.)

Κερδαίνω (*κερδ-, κερδαν-*), *gain* (595; 610), f. **κερδανῶ**, a. **ἐκέρδᾱνα** (673), [Ion. **ἐκέρδηνα**]. From stem **κερδ-** (*ε-*) [fut. **κερδήσομαι** and aor. **ἐκέρδησα** (Hdt.)]; pf. **προσ-κεκερδήκᾱσι** (Dem.). (5. 4.)

Κεύθω (*κευθ-, κυθ-*), *hide*, **κεύσω**, [**ἔκευσα**;] 2 p. **κέκευθα** (as pres.); [ep. 2 a. **κύθον**, subj. **κεκύθω**.] Epic and tragic. (2.)

Κήδω (κηδ-, καδ-), *vex*, (ε-) [κηδήσω, -ἐκήδησα; 2 p. κέκηδα]: active only epic. Mid. κήδομαι, *sorrow*, ἐκηδεσάμην, [epic fut. pf. κεκαδήσομαι.] (2.)

Κηρύσσω (κηρυκ-), *proclaim*, κηρύξω, ἐκήρυξα, κεκήρυχα, κεκήρυγμαι, ἐκηρύχθην, κηρυχθήσομαι; κηρύξομαι, ἐκηρυξάμην. (4.)

Κιγχάνω, epic **κιχάνω** (κιχ-), *find*, (ε-) κιχήσομαι, [epic ἐκιχησάμην]; 2 a. ἔκιχον. [Epic forms as if from pres. κίχημι, 2 aor. ἐκίχην: (ἐ)κίχεις, κίχημεν, κιχήτην, κιχείω, κιχείη, κιχῆναι and κιχήμεναι, κιχείς, κιχήμενος.] Poetic. (5.)

[**Κίδνημι** (κιδ-να-), *spread*, Ion. and poetic for **σκεδάννυμι**.] See σκίδνημι. (III.)

[**Κίνυμαι**, *move*, pres. and imp.; as mid. of **κινέω**. Epic.] (II.)

Κίρνημι (III.) and **κιρνάω**: forms (in pres. and impf.) for **κεράννυμι**.

Κίχρημι (χρα-), *lend*, [χρήσω Hdt.], ἔχρησα, κέχρημαι; ἐχρησάμην. (I.)

Κλάζω (κλαγγ-, κλαγ-), *clang*, κλάγξω, ἔκλαγξα; 2 p. κέκλαγγα [epic κέκληγα, part. κεκλήγοντες;] 2 a. ἔκλαγον; fut. pf. κεκλάγξομαι. Chiefly poetic. (4.)

Κλαίω (κλαυ-, κλαϝ-, κλαϝι-, κλαι-, 601), in Attic prose generally **κλάω** (not contracted), *weep*, κλαύσομαι (rarely κλαυσοῦμαι, sometimes κλαιήσω or κλᾱήσω), ἔκλαυσα and ἐκλαυσάμην, κέκλαυμαι; fut. pf. (impers.) κεκλαύσεται. (4.)

Κλάω, *break*, ἔκλασα, κέκλασμαι, ἐκλάσθην; [2 a. pt. κλάς.]

Κλέπτω (κλεπ-), *steal*, κλέψω (rarely κλέψομαι), ἔκλεψα, κέκλοφα (643; 692), κέκλεμμαι, (ἐκλέφθην) κλεφθείς; 2 a. p. ἐκλάπην. (3.)

Κλῄω, later Attic **κλείω**, *shut*, κλῄσω, ἔκλῃσα, κέκλῃκα, κέκλῃμαι, ἐκλῄσθην; κλῃσθήσομαι, κεκλῄσομαι, ἐκλῃσάμην (also later κλείσω, ἔκλεισα, etc.). [Ion. κληΐω, ἐκλήϊσα, κεκλήϊμαι, ἐκληΐσθην.]

Κλίνω (κλιν-), *bend*, *incline*, κλινῶ, ἔκλῑνα, κέκλιμαι, ἐκλίθην [epic ἐκλίνθην, 709], κλιθήσομαι; 2 a. p. ἐκλίνην, 2 f. κλινήσομαι; fut. m. κλινοῦμαι, a. ἐκλινάμην. 647. (4.)

Κλύω, *hear*, imp. ἔκλυον (as aor.); 2 a. imper. κλῦθι, κλῦτε [ep. κέκλυθι, κέκλυτε]. [Part. κλύμενος, *renowned*.] Poetic.

Κναίω, *scrape* (in compos.), -κναίσω, -ἔκναισα, -κέκναικα, -κέκναισμαι, -ἐκναίσθην, -κναισθήσομαι. Also **κνάω**, with αε, αη contracted to η, and αει, αῃ to ῃ (496).

Κομίζω (κομιδ-), *care for*, *carry*, κομιῶ, ἐκόμισα, κεκόμικα, κεκόμισμαι, ἐκομίσθην; κομισθήσομαι; f. m. κομιοῦμαι (665, 3), a. ἐκομισάμην. (4.)

Κόπτω (κοπ-), *cut*, κόψω, ἔκοψα, κέκοφα, 693 [κεκοπώς Hom.], κέκομμαι; 2 aor. p. ἐκόπην, 2 fut. p. κοπήσομαι; fut. pf. κεκόψομαι; aor. m. ἐκοψάμην. (3.)

Κορέννυμι (κορε-), *satiate*, [f. κορέσω (Hdt.), κορέω (Hom.), a. ἐκόρεσα (poet.)], κεκόρεσμαι [Ion. -ημαι], ἐκορέσθην; [epic 2 p. part. κεκορηώς, a. m. ἐκορεσάμην.] (II.)

Κορύσσω (κορυθ-), *arm*, [Hom. a. part. κορυσσάμενος, pf. pt. κεκορυθμένος.] Poetic, chiefly epic. (4.)

[**Κοτέω**, *be angry*, aor. ἐκότεσα, ἐκοτεσάμην, 2 pf. part. κεκοτηώς, *angry*, epic.]

Κράζω (κραγ-), *cry out*, fut. pf. κεκράξομαι (rare); 2 pf. κέκρāγα (imper. κέκραχθι and κεκράγετε, Ar.), 2 plpf. ἐκεκράγετε (Dem.); 2 a. ἔκραγον. (4.)

Κραίνω (κραν-), *accomplish*, κρανῶ, ἔκρāνα [Ion. ἔκρηνα], ἐκράνθην, κρανθήσομαι; p. p. 3 sing. κέκρανται (cf. πέφανται), [f. m. inf. κρανέεσθαι, Hom.]. Ionic and poetic. [Epic **κραιαίνω**, aor. ἐκρήηνα, pf. and plp. κεκράανται and κεκράαντο; ἐκρāάνθην (Theoc.).] (4.)

Κρέμαμαι, *hang*, (intrans.), κρεμήσομαι. See **κρήμνημι** and **κρεμάννῡμι**. (I.)

Κρεμάννῡμι (κρεμα-), *suspend*, κρεμῶ (for κρεμάσω), ἐκρέμασα, ἐκρεμάσθην; [ἐκρεμασάμην.] (II.)

Κρήμνημι, *suspend*, (κρημ-να for κρεμα-να, perhaps through κρημνός), *suspend*; very rare in act., pr. part. κρημνάντων (Pind.). Mid. **κρήμναμαι** = κρέμαμαι. Poetic: used only in pres. and impf. (III.)

Κρίζω (κριγ-), *creak*, *squeak*, [2 a. (ἔκρικον) 3 sing. κρίκε;] 2 p. (κέκρῑγα) κεκρῑγότες, *squeaking* (Ar.). (4.)

Κρίνω (κριν-), *judge*, f. κρινῶ, ἔκρῑνα, κέκρικα, κέκριμαι, ἐκρίθην [ep. ἐκρίνθην], κριθήσομαι; fut. m. κρινοῦμαι, a. m. [epic ἐκρῑνάμην.] 647. (4.)

Κρούω, *beat*, κρούσω, ἔκρουσα, κέκρουκα, κέκρουμαι and κέκρουσμαι, ἐκρούσθην; -κρούσομαι, ἐκρουσάμην.

Κρύπτω (κρυφ-), *conceal*, κρύψω, ἔκρυψα, κέκρυμμαι, ἐκρύφθην; 2. a. p. ἐκρύφην (rare), 2 f. κρυφήσομαι or κρυβήσομαι. (3.)

Κτάομαι, *acquire*, κτήσομαι, ἐκτησάμην, κέκτημαι (rarely ἔκτημαι), *possess* (subj. κεκτῶμαι, opt. κεκτῄμην or κεκτῴμην, 734), ἐκτήθην (as pass.); κεκτήσομαι (rarely ἐκτήσομαι), *shall possess*.

Κτείνω (κτεν-, κτα-), *kill*, f. κτενῶ [Ion. κτενέω, ep. also κτανέω], a. ἔκτεινα, 2 pf. ἀπ-έκτονα, [ep. a. p. ἐκτάθην;] 2 a. ἔκτανον (for poetic ἔκτᾰν and ἐκτάμην, see 799); [ep. fut. m. κτανέομαι.] In Attic prose ἀπο-κτείνω is generally used. 645; 647. (4.)

Κτίζω (see 587), *found*, κτίσω, ἔκτισα, ἔκτισμαι, ἐκτίσθην; [aor. m. ἐκτισάμην (rare)]. (4.)

Κτίννῡμι and **κτιννύω**, in compos., only pres. and impf. See **κτείνω**. (II.)

Κτυπέω (κτυπ-), *sound*, *cause to sound*, ἐκτύπησα, [2 a. ἔκτυπον.] Chiefly poetic. 654.

Κυλίω or **κυλίνδω** and **κυλινδέω**, *roll*, ἐκύλῑσα, κεκύλῑσμαι, ἐκυλίσθην, κυλῑσθήσομαι.

Κυνέω (κυ-), *kiss*, ἔκυσα. Poetic. **Προσ-κυνέω**, *do homage*, f. προσκυνήσω, a. προσεκύνησα (poet. προσέκυσα), is common in prose and poetry. (5.)

Κύπτω (κυφ-), *stoop*, κύψω and κύψομαι, aor. ἔκῡψα, 2 p. κέκῡφα. (3.)

Κύρω (κυρ-), *meet, chance*, κύρσω, ἔκυρσα (668 674 *b*). (4.) **Κυρέω** is regular.

Λ.

Λαγχάνω (λαχ-), *obtain by lot*, f. m. λήξομαι [Ion. λάξομαι], 2 pf. εἴληχα, [Ion. and poet. λέλογχα,] p. m. (εἴληγμαι) εἰληγμένος, a. p. ἐλήχθην; 2 a. ἔλαχον [ep. λελάχω, 534]. (5.)

Λαμβάνω (λαβ-), *take*, λήψομαι, εἴληφα, εἴλημμαι, (poet. λέλημμαι), ἐλήφθην. ληφθήσομαι; 2 a. ἔλαβον, ἐλαβόμην [ep. inf. λελαβέσθαι (534).] [Ion. λάμψομαι, λελάβηκα, λέλαμμαι, ἐλάμφθην; Dor. fut. λᾱψοῦμαι.] (5.)

Λάμπω, *shine*, λάμψω, ἔλαμψα, 2 pf. λέλαμπα; [fut. m. -λάμψομαι Hdt.].

Λανθάνω (λαθ-), *lie hid, escape the notice of* (some one), λήσω, [ἔλησα], 2 p. λέληθα [Dor. λέλᾱθα,] 2 a. ἔλαθον [ep. λέλαθον.] Mid. *forget*, λήσομαι, λέλησμαι [Hom. -ασμαι], fut. pf. λελήσομαι, 2 a. ἐλαθόμην [ep. λελαθόμην.] (5.) Poetic λήθω. (2.)

Λάπτω (λαβ- or λαφ-), *lap, lick*, λάψω, ἔλαψα, 2 pf. λέλαφα (693); f. m. λάψομαι, ἐλαψάμην. (3.)

Λάσκω for λακ-σκω (λακ-), *speak*, (ε-) λακήσομαι, ἐλάκησα, 2 p. λέλᾱκα [ep. λέληκα w. fem. part. λελακυῖα:] 2 a. ἔλακον [λελακόμην]. Poetic. 617. (6.)

[**Λάω**, λῶ, *wish*, λῇς, λῇ, etc.; infin. λῆν. 496. Doric.]

Λέγω, *say*, λέξω, ἔλεξα, λέλεγμαι (δι-είλεγμαι), ἐλέχθην; fut. λεχθήσομαι, λέξομαι, λελέξομαι, all passive. For pf. act. εἴρηκα is used (see εἶπον).

Λέγω, *gather, arrange, count* (Attic only in comp.), λέξω, ἔλεξα, εἴλοχα, εἴλεγμαι or λέλεγμαι, ἐλέχθην (rare); a. m. ἐλεξάμην, 2 a. p. ἐλέγην, f. λεγήσομαι. [Ep. 2 a. m. (ἐλέγμην) λέκτο, *counted*.] See stem **λεχ-**.

Λείπω (λειπ-, λοιπ-, λιπ-), *leave*, λείψω, λέλειμμαι, ἐλείφθην; 2 p. λέλοιπα; 2 a. ἔλιπον, ἐλιπόμην. See synopsis in 476, and inflection of 2 aor., 2 perf., and 2 plpf. in 481. (2.)

[**Λελίημαι**, part. λελιημένος, *eager* (Hom.).]

Λεύω, *stone*, generally κατα-λεύω; -λεύσω, -ἔλευσα, ἐλεύσθην (641), -λευσθήσομαι.

[(**λεχ-**) stem (cf. λέχ-ος), whence 2 a. m. (ἐλέγμην) ἔλεκτο, *laid himself to rest*, with imper. λέξο (also λέξεο), inf. κατα-λέχθαι, pt. κατα-λέγμενος (800, 2). Also ἔλεξα, *laid to rest*, with mid. λέξομαι, *will go to rest*, and ἐλεξάμην, *went to rest*, same forms with tenses of λέγω, *say*, and λέγω, *gather*. Only epic.]

Λήθω, poetic: see **λανθάνω**.

Ληΐζω (ληϊδ-), *plunder*, act. rare, only impf. ἐλήϊζον. Mid. **ληΐζομαι** (as act.), [fut. ληΐσομαι, aor. ἐληϊσάμην, Ion.]. Eurip. has ἐλῃσάμην, and pf. p. λέλῃσμαι. (4.)

Λίσσομαι or (rare) **λίτομαι** (λιτ-), *supplicate* [epic ἐλισάμην, 2 a. ἐλιτόμην.] (4.)

[**Λοέω**, epic for λούω; λοέσσομαι, ἐλόεσσα, ἐλοεσσάμην.]

Λούω or **λόω**, *wash*, regular. In Attic writers and Hdt. the pres. and imperf. generally have contracted forms of λόω, as ἔλου, ἐλοῦμεν, λοῦται, λοῦσθαι, λούμενος (497).

Λύω, *loose*, see synopsis and full inflection in 474 and 480. Hom. also λύω (ῠ) (471). [Epic 2 a. m. ἐλύμην (as pass.), λύτο and λῦτο, λύντο; pf. opt. λελῦτο or λελῦντο (734).]

M.

Μαίνω (μαν-), *madden*, a. ἔμηνα, 2 pf. μέμηνα, *am mad*, 2 a. p. ἐμάνην. Mid. **μαίνομαι**, *be mad* [μανοῦμαι, ἐμηνάμην, μεμάνημαι.] (4.)

Μαίομαι (μασ-, μασι-, μαι-, 602), *desire*, *seek*, [μάσομαι, ἐμασάμην; 2 pf. **μέμονα** (μεν-), *desire eagerly*, in sing., with μι-forms μέματον, μέμαμεν, μέματε, μεμάᾶσι, μεμάτω, μεμαώς, plpf. μέμασαν. Also (μάομαι) Doric contract forms μῶται, μῶνται, μῶσο, μῶσθαι, μώμενος.] Poetic, chiefly epic. (4.)

Μανθάνω (μαθ-), *learn*, (ε-) μαθήσομαι, μεμάθηκα; 2 a. ἔμαθον. (5.)

Μάρναμαι (μαρ-να-), *fight* (subj. μάρνωμαι, imp. μάρναο); a. ἐμαρνάσθην. Poetic. (III.)

Μάρπτω (μαρπ-), *seize*, μάρψω, ἔμαρψα [epic 2 pf. μέμαρπα, 2 aor. μέμαρπον (534), with opt. μεμάποιεν, μαπεῖν.] Poetic. (3.)

Μάσσω (μαγ-), *knead*, μάξω, etc., regular; 2 a. p. ἐμάγην. (4.)

Μάχομαι [Ion. μαχέομαι], *fight*, f. μαχοῦμαι [Hdt. μαχέσομαι, Hom. μαχέομαι or μαχήσομαι], p. μεμάχημαι, a. ἐμαχεσάμην [ep. also ἐμαχησάμην; ep. pres. part. μαχειόμενος or μαχεούμενος].

[**Μέδομαι**, *think of*, *plan*, (ε-) μεδήσομαι (rare). Epic.]

Μεθ-ίημι, *send away*; see ἵημι (810). [Hdt. pf. pt. μεμετιμένος.]

Μεθύσκω (μεθυ-), *make drunk*, ἐμέθυσα. Pass. μεθύσκομαι, *be made drunk*, a. p. ἐμεθύσθην, *became drunk*. See **μεθύω**. (6.)

Μεθύω, *be drunk*, only pres. and impf.

[**Μείρομαι** (μερ-), *obtain*, epic, 2 pf. 3 sing. ἔμμορε;] impers. εἵμαρται, *it is fated*, εἱμαρμένη (as subst.), *Fate*. (4.)

Μέλλω, *intend*, augm. ἐμ- or ἠμ- (517); (ε-) μελλήσω, ἐμέλλησα.

Μέλω, *concern*, *care for*, (ε-) μελήσω [ep. μελήσομαι, 2 p. μέμηλα]; μεμέλημαι [ep. μέμβλεται, μέμβλετο, for μέμλεται, μέμλετο (66, *a*)]; (ἐμελήθην) μεληθείς. Poetic. **Μέλει**, *it concerns*, impers.; μελήσει, ἐμέλησε, μεμέληκε, — used in Attic prose, with ἐπιμέλομαι and ἐπιμελέομαι.

Μέμονα (μεν-), *desire*, 2 perf. with no present. See **μαίομαι**.

Μένω, *remain*, f. μενῶ [Ion. μενέω], ἔμεινα (ε-) μεμένηκα.

Μερμηρίζω (see 587 and 590), *ponder*, [μερμηρίξω, ἐμερμήριξα], ἀπεμερμήρισα (Ar.). Poetic. (**4.**)

Μήδομαι, *devise*, μήσομαι, ἐμησάμην. Poetic.

Μηκάομαι (μηκ-, μακ-, 656), *bleat*, [Hom. 2 a. part. μακών; 2 p. part. μεμηκώς, μεμακυῖα; 2 plp. ἐμέμηκον (777, 4).] Chiefly epic. (**2.**)

[**Μητιάω** (μητι-, 656), *plan*. Mid. **μητιάομαι**, **μητίομαι** (Pind.), μητίσομαι, ἐμητῑσάμην. Epic and lyric.]

Μιαίνω (μιαν-), *stain*, μιανῶ, ἐμίᾱνα [Ion. ἐμίηνα], μεμίασμαι, ἐμιάνθην, μιανθήσομαι. (**4.**)

Μίγνῡμι (μιγ-), Ionic **μίσγω**, *mix*, μίξω, ἔμιξα, μέμῑγμαι, ἐμίχθην, μῑχθήσομαι; 2 a. p. ἐμίγην, [ep. fut. μιγήσομαι; 2 a. m. ἔμικτο and μῖκτο; fut. pf. μεμίξομαι.] (**II.**)

Μιμνήσκω and (older) **μιμνῄσκω** (μνα-), *remind; mid. remember;* μνήσω, ἔμνησα, μέμνημαι, *remember*, ἐμνήσθην (as mid.); μνησθήσομαι, μνήσομαι, μεμνήσομαι; ἐμνησάμην (poet.). **Μέμνημαι** (memini) has subj. μεμνῶμαι, (722), opt. μεμνῴμην or μεμνῄμην (734), imp. μέμνησο [Hdt. μέμνεο], inf. μεμνῆσθαι, pt. μεμνημένος. 616. (**6.**)
[From epic μνάομαι come ἐμνώοντο, μνωόμενος, (?) etc. (784, 2).]

Μίμνω for μι-μενω (652, 1), *remain*, poetic form of μένω.

Μίσγω for μιγ-σκω (617), *mix*, pres. and impf. See **μίγνῡμι**. (**6.**)

Μύζω, *suck*, [Ion. μυζέω, aor. -ἐμύζησα (Hom.)].

Μύζω (μυγ-), *grumble, mutter*, aor. ἔμυξα. Poetic. (**4.**)

Μῡκάομαι (μῡκ-, μῠκ-, 656), *bellow*, [ep. 2 pf. μέμῡκα; 2 a. μύκον;] ἐμυχησάμην. Chiefly poetic. (**2.**)

Μύσσω or **μύττω** (μυκ-), *wipe*, ἀπο-μυξάμενος (Ar.). Generally ἀπομύσσω.

Μύω, *shut (the lips* or *eyes)*, aor. ἔμυσα, pf. μέμῡκα.

N.

Ναίω (ναϝ-, ναϝι-, ναι-, 602), *swim, be full*, impf. ναῖον, *Od.* 9, 222.

Ναίω (νασ-, να-, 602), *dwell*, [ἔνασσα, *caused to dwell*, ἐνασσάμην, *came to dwell*,] ἐνάσθην, *was settled, dwelt*. Poetic. (**4.**)

Νάσσω (ναδ-, ναγ-), *stuff*, [ἔναξα,] νένασμαι or νέναγμαι. 582; 590. (**4.**)

[**Νεικέω** and **νεικείω**, *chide*, νεικέσω, ἐνείκεσα. Ionic, chiefly epic.]

Νέμω, *distribute*, f. νεμῶ, ἔνειμα, (ε-) νενέμηκα, νενέμημαι, ἐνεμήθην; νεμοῦμαι, ἐνειμάμην.

Νέομαι, *go, come*, also in future sense. Chiefly poetic. See **νίσσομαι**.

1. **Νέω** (νευ-, νεϝ-, νυ-), *swim*, ἔνευσα, νένευκα; f. m. (νευσοῦμαι, 666) νευσούμενος. 574. (2.)

2. **Νέω**, *heap up*, ἔνησα, νένημαι or νένησμαι. [Epic and Ion. νηέω, νήησα, ἐνηησάμην.]

3. **Νέω** and **νήθω**, *spin*, νήσω, ἔνησα, ἐνήθην; [ep. a. m. νήσαντο.]

Νίζω, later νίπτω, Hom. νίπτομαι (νιβ-), *wash*, νίψω, ἔνιψα, νένιμμαι, [-ενίφθην;] νίψομαι, ἐνιψάμην. 591. (3. 4.)

Νίσσομαι or **νίσομαι**, *go*, fut. νίσομαι. Νίσομαι, probably the correct form of the present, is, acc. to Meyer (§ 500), for νι-νσ-ι-ομαι, from a stem νεσ- with reduplication. (See pres. νίσεται, Pind. *Ol.* 3, 34.) Poetic. (4.)

Νοέω, *think*, *perceive*, νοήσω, etc., regular in Attic. [Ion. ἔνωσα, νένωκα, νένωμαι, ἐνωσάμην.]

Νομίζω (see 587), *believe*, fut. νομιῶ [νομίσω late], aor. ἐνόμισα, pf. νενόμικα, νενόμισμαι, aor. p. ἐνομίσθην, fut. p. νομισθήσομαι, [f. m. νομιοῦμαι (Hippoc.).] (4.)

Ξ.

Ξέω, *scrape*, [aor. ἔξεσα and ξέσσα, chiefly epic], ἔξεσμαι. 639, 640.

Ξηραίνω (ξηραν-), *dry*, ξηρανῶ, ἐξήρᾱνα [Ion. -ηνα], ἐξήρασμαι and ἐξήραμμαι, ἐξηράνθην. 700. (4.)

Ξύω, *polish*, ἔξῡσα, [ἔξυσμαι,] ἐξύσθην; aor. m. ἐξῡσάμην. 640.

O.

Ὁδοποιέω, *make a way*, regular; but pf. part. ὡδοπεποιημένος occurs. So sometimes with ὁδοιπορέω, *travel*.

(**ὀδυ-**), *be angry*, stem with only [Hom. ὠδυσάμην, ὀδώδυσμαι].

Ὄζω (ὀδ-), *smell*, (ε-) ὀζήσω, ὤζησα [Ion. ὀζέσω, ὤζεσα, late 2 pf. ὄδωδα, Hom. plp. ὀδώδει(ν)]. 658, 3. (4.)

Οἴγω, *open*, poetic οἴξω and ᾦξα [epic also ὤϊξα], a. p. part. οἰχθείς. **Οἴγνῡμι**, simple form late in active, [imp. p. ὠΐγνύμην Hom.], common in composition: see ἀν-οίγνῡμι. (II.)

Οἰδέω, *swell*, ᾤδησα, ᾤδηκα. Also **οἰδάνω**. (5.)

Οἰκτίρω (οἰκτιρ-), commonly written οἰκτείρω, *pity* (597), aor. ᾤκτῑρα (ᾤκτειρα). (4.)

Οἰνοχοέω, *pour wine*, οἰνοχοήσω, [οἰνοχοῆσαι (epic and lyric)]. [Impf. ep. 3 pers. οἰνοχόει, ᾠνοχόει, ἐῳνοχόει.]

Οἴομαι, *think* (625), in prose generally οἶμαι and ᾤμην in 1 per. sing.; (ε-) οἰήσομαι, ᾠήθην. [Ep. act. οἴω (only 1 sing.), often ὀΐω; ὀΐομαι, ὀϊσάμην, ὠΐσθην.]

Οἴχομαι, *be gone*, (ε-) οἰχήσομαι, οἴχωκα or ᾤχωκα (659); [Ion. οἴχημαι or ᾤχημαι, doubtful in Attic].

Ὀκέλλω (ὀκελ-), *run ashore*, aor. ὤκειλα. Prose form of κέλλω. (4.)

Ὀλισθάνω, rarely ὀλισθαίνω (ὀλισθ-), *slip*, [Ion. ὠλίσθησα, ὠλίσθηκα]; 2 a. ὤλισθον (poetic). (5.)

Ὄλλῡμι (probably for ὀλ-νυ-μι, 612), rarely ὀλλύω (ὀλ-), *destroy, lose*, f. ὀλῶ [ὀλέσω, ὀλέω], ὤλεσα, -ὀλώλεκα; 2 p. ὄλωλα, *perish*, 2 plpf. -ὠλώλη (533). Mid. ὄλλυμαι, *perish*, ὀλοῦμαι, 2 a. ὠλόμην [w. ep. part. οὐλόμενος]. In prose ἀπ-όλλῡμι. (II.)

Ὀλοφύρομαι (ὀλοφυρ-), *bewail*, f. ὀλοφυροῦμαι, ὠλοφῡράμην, part. ὀλοφυρθείς (Thuc.). (4.)

Ὄμνῡμι and **ὀμνύω** (ὀμ-, ὀμο-, 659), *swear*, f. ὀμοῦμαι, ὤμοσα, ὀμώμοκα, ὀμώμοσμαι (with ὀμώμοται), ὠμόθην and ὠμόσθην; ὀμοσθήσομαι, a. m. ὠμοσάμην. (II.)

Ὀμόργνῡμι (ὀμοργ-), *wipe*, ὀμόρξομαι, ὤμορξα, ὠμορξάμην; ἀπ-ομορχθείς. Chiefly poetic: only epic in pres. and impf. (II.)

Ὀνίνημι (ὀνα-, 796), *benefit*, ὀνήσω, ὤνησα, ὠνήθην; ὀνήσομαι; 2 a. m. ὠνήμην (late ὠνάμην), ὀναίμην, ὄνασθαι (798; 803, 3), [Hom. imper. ὄνησο, pt. ὀνήμενος]. (I.)

[**Ὄνομαι**, *insult*, inflected like δίδομαι, with opt. ὄνοιτο (Hom.), f. ὀνόσσομαι, a. ὠνοσάμην (ὤνατο, *Il.* 17, 25), a. p. κατ-ονοσθῇς (Hdt.). Ionic and poetic.] (I.)

Ὀξύνω (ὀξυν-), *sharpen*, -οξυνῶ, ὤξῡνα, -ὤξυμμαι, ὠξύνθην, [-ὀξυνθήσομαι, Hippoc.] 700. In Attic prose only in compos. (4.)

Ὀπυίω (ὀπυ-, ὀπυι-, 602), *take to wife*, fut. ὀπύσω (Ar.). (4.)

Ὁράω (ὁρα-, ὀπ-), *see*, imperf. ἑώρων [Ion. ὥρων], ὄψομαι, ἑόρᾱκα or ἑώρᾱκα, ὦμμαι or ἑώρᾱμαι, ὤφθην, ὀφθήσομαι; 2 p. ὄπωπα (Ion. and poet.). For 2 a. εἶδον etc., see **εἶδον**. [Hom. pres. mid. 2 sing. ὅρηαι, 784, 3.] (8.)

Ὀργαίνω (ὀργαν-), *be angry*, aor. ὤργᾱνα, *enraged*. Only in Tragedy. (4.)

Ὀρέγω, *reach*, ὀρέξω, ὤρεξα, [Ion. pf. m. ὤρεγμαι, Hom. 3 plur. ὀρωρέχαται, plp. ὀρωρέχατο,] ὠρέχθην; ὀρέξομαι, ὠρεξάμην. [Epic ὀρέγνῡμι, pr. part. ὀρεγνύς. (II.)]

Ὄρνῡμι (ὀρ-), *raise, rouse*, ὄρσω, ὦρσα, 2 p. ὄρωρα (as mid.); [ep. 2 a. ὤρορον.] Mid. *rise, rush*, [f. ὀροῦμαι, p. ὀρώρεμαι,] 2 a. ὠρόμην [with ὦρτο, imper. ὄρσο, ὄρσεο, ὄρσευ, inf. ὄρθαι, part. ὄρμενος]. Poetic. (II.)

Ὀρύσσω or **ὀρύττω** (ὀρυγ-), *dig*, ὀρύξω, ὤρυξα, ὀρώρυχα (rare), ὀρώρυγμαι (rarely ὤρυγμαι), ὠρύχθην; f. p. κατ-ορυχθήσομαι, 2 f. κατορυχήσομαι; [ὠρυξάμην, *caused to dig*, Hdt.] (4.)

Ὀσφραίνομαι (ὀσφρ-, ὀσφραν-, 610), *smell*, (ε-) ὀσφρήσομαι, ὠσφράνθην (rare), 2 a. m. ὠσφρόμην, [Hdt. ὤσφραντο.] (5. 4.)

Οὐρέω, impf. ἐούρεον, f. οὐρήσομαι, a. ἐούρησα, pf. ἐούρηκα. [Ionic has οὐρ- for Attic ἐουρ-.]

[**Οὐτάζω** (587), *wound*, οὐτάσω, οὔτασα, οὔτασμαι. Chiefly epic.] (4.)

[**Οὐτάω**, *wound*, **οὔτησα**, **οὐτήθην**; 2 a. 3 sing. **οὖτα**, inf. **οὐτάμεναι** and **οὐτάμεν**; 2 a. mid. **οὐτάμενος** as pass. Epic.]

Ὀφείλω (**ὀφελ-**, 598), [epic reg. **ὀφέλλω**], *owe*, (ε-) **ὀφειλήσω**, **ὠφείλησα**, (**ὠφείληκα** ?) a. p. pt. **ὀφειληθείς** (658, 3); 2 a. **ὤφελον**, used in wishes (1512), *O that*. (4.)

Ὀφέλλω (**ὀφελ-**), *increase*, [aor. opt. **ὀφέλλειε** Hom.] Poetic, especially epic. (4.)

Ὀφλισκάνω (**ὀφλ-**, **ὀφλισκ-**), *be guilty*, *incur* (a penalty), (ε-) **ὀφλήσω**, **ὤφλησα** (?), **ὤφληκα**, **ὤφλημαι**; 2 a. **ὦφλον** (**ὄφλειν** and **ὄφλων** are said by grammarians to be Attic forms of inf. and part.). (6. 5.)

Π.

Παίζω (**παιδ-**, **παιγ-**), *sport*, **παιξοῦμαι** (666), **ἔπαισα**, **πέπαικα**, **πέπαισμαι**. 590. (4.)

Παίω, *strike*, **παίσω**, poetic (ε-) **παιήσω**, **ἔπαισα**, **πέπαικα**, **ἐπαίσθην** (640).

Παλαίω, *wrestle*, [**παλαίσω**,] **ἐπάλαισα**, **ἐπαλαίσθην** (640).

Πάλλω (**παλ-**), *brandish*, **ἔπηλα**, **πέπαλμαι**; [Hom. 2 a. **ἀμ-πεπαλών**, as if from **πέπαλον**; 2 a. m. **ἔπαλτο** and **πάλτο**.] (4.)

Παρανομέω, *transgress law*, augm. **παρενόμουν** and **παρηνόμουν**, **παρανενόμηκα** (543).

Παροινέω, *insult* (*as a drunken man*), imp. **ἐπαρῴνουν**; **ἐπαρῴνησα**, **πεπαρῴνηκα**, **παρῳνήθην** (544).

Πάσομαι, fut. *shall acquire* (no pres.), pf. **πέπᾱμαι**, **ἐπᾱσάμην**. Poetic. Not to be confounded with **πάσομαι**, **ἐπασάμην**, etc. (with ᾰ) of **πατέομαι**.

Πάσσω or **πάττω** (582; 587), *sprinkle*, **πάσω**, **ἔπασα**, **ἐπάσθην**. Chiefly poetic. (4.)

Πάσχω (**παθ-**, **πενθ-**), for **παθ-σκω** (617), *suffer*, **πείσομαι** (for **πενθ-σομαι**, 79), 2 pf. **πέπονθα** [Hom. **πέποσθε** for **πεπόνθατε**, and **πεπαθυῖα**]; 2 a. **ἔπαθον**. (8.)

Πατέομαι (**πατ-**), *eat*, f. **πάσονται** (?), **ἐπασάμην**; [ep. plp. **πεπάσμην**.] 655. Ionic and poetic. See **πάσομαι**.

Παύω, *stop*, *cause to cease*, **παύσω**, **ἔπαυσα**, **πέπαυκα**, **πέπαυμαι**, **ἐπαύθην** [**ἐπαύσθην** Hdt.], **παυθήσομαι**, **πεπαύσομαι**. Mid. **παύομαι**, *cease*, **παύσομαι**, **ἐπαυσάμην**.

Πείθω (**πειθ-**, **πιθ-**), *persuade*, **πείσω**, **ἔπεισα**, **πέπεικα**, **πέπεισμαι**, **ἐπείσθην** (71), **πεισθήσομαι**; fut. m. **πείσομαι**; 2 p. **πέποιθα**, *trust*, w. imper. **πέπεισθι** (perhaps for **πέπισθι**), A. *Eu.* 599, [Hom. plp. **ἐπέπιθμεν** for **ἐπεποίθεμεν**;] poet. 2 a. **ἔπιθον** and **ἐπιθόμην**. [Epic (ε-) **πιθήσω**, **πεπιθήσω**, **πιθήσας**.] (2.)

[**Πείκω**, epic pres. = **πεκτέω**, *comb*.]

Πεινάω, *hunger*, regular, except in η for α in contract forms, inf. **πεινῆν** [epic **πεινήμεναι**], etc. See 496.

Πείρω (περ-), *pierce*, epic in pres.; ἔπειρα, πέπαρμαι, [ἐπάρην Hdt.] Ionic and poetic. (4.)

Πεκτέω (πεκ-, πεκτ-, 655), [Dor. f. πεξῶ, a. ἔπεξα (Theoc.), ep. ἐπεξάμην]; a. p. ἐπέχθην. See epic πείκω. Poetic.

Πελάζω (cf. πέλας, *near*; see 587), [poet. πελάω (πελα-, πλα-),] *bring near, approach*, f. πελάσω, Att. πελῶ (665, 2), ἐπέλασα, [πέπλημαι,] ἐπελάσθην and ἐπλάθην; [ἐπελασάμην; 2. a. m. ἐπλήμην, *approached*.] [Also poetic presents πελάθω, πλάθω, πίλναμαι.] (4.)

Πέλω and **πέλομαι**, *be*, imp. ἔπελον, ἐπελόμην [syncop. ἔπλε, ἔπλεο (ἔπλευ), ἔπλετο, for ἔπελε etc.; so ἐπι-πλόμενος and περι-πλόμενος]. Poetic.

Πέμπω, *send*, πέμψω, ἔπεμψα, πέπομφα (643; 693), πέπεμμαι (77; 490, 1), ἐπέμφθην, πεμφθήσομαι; πέμψομαι, ἐπεμψάμην.

Πεπαίνω (πεπαν-), *make soft*, ἐπέπᾱνα (673), ἐπεπάνθην, πεπανθήσομαι. (4.)

[**Πεπαρεῖν**, *show*, 2 aor. inf. in Pind. *Py.* 2, 57.]

Πέπρωται, *it is fated*: see stem (πορ-, προ-).

Πέρδομαι, Lat. *pedo*, 2 fut. (pass.?) παρδήσομαι, 2 p. πέπορδα, 2 a. ἔπαρδον. See 643 and 646.

Πέρθω, *destroy, sack*, πέρσω [πέρσομαι (as pass.) Hom.], ἔπερσα, [ep. 2 a. ἔπραθον (646), m. ἐπραθόμην (as pass.) with inf. πέρθαι for περθ-θαι.] Poetic.

Πέρνημι (περ-να-), *sell*, mid. πέρναμαι: poetic for πιπράσκω. 609. (III.)

Πέσσω or **πέττω**, later πέπτω (πεπ-), *cook*, πέψω, ἔπεψα, πέπεμμαι (75; 490, 1), ἐπέφθην. See 583. (4.)

Πετάννῡμι (πετα-), *expand*, (πετάσω) πετῶ, ἐπέτασα, πέπταμαι, [πεπέτασμαι late], ἐπετάσθην. See πίτνημι. (II.)

Πέτομαι (πετ-, πτ-), *fly* (ε-), πτήσομαι (poet. πετήσομαι); 2 a. m. ἐπτόμην. To **ἵπταμαι** (rare) belong [2 a. ἔπτην (poet.)] and ἐπτάμην (799). The forms πεπότημαι and ἐποτήθην [Dor. -ᾱμαι, -ᾱθην] belong to ποτάομαι.

Πεύθομαι (πυθ-): see **πυνθάνομαι**. (2.)

Πήγνῡμι (πηγ-, παγ-), *fasten*, πήξω, ἔπηξα, ἐπήχθην (rare and poet.); 2 a. p. ἐπάγην, 2 f. p. παγήσομαι; 2 p. πέπηγα, *be fixed*; [ep. 2 a. m. κατ-έπηκτο;] πηγνῦτο (Plat.) pr. opt. for πηγνυ-ι-το (734); [πήξομαι, ἐπηξάμην.] (2. II.)

Πιαίνω (πιαν-), *fatten*, πιανῶ, ἐπίᾱνα, πεπίασμαι, [ἐπιάνθην]. Chiefly poetic and Ionic. (4.)

[**Πίλναμαι** (πιλ-να-), *approach*, only in pres. and impf. 609. Epic.] See **πελάζω**. (III.)

Πίμπλημι (πλα-), *fill*, πλήσω, ἔπλησα, πέπληκα, πέπλησμαι, ἐπλήσθην, πλησθήσομαι; a. m. ἐπλησάμην (trans.); 2 a. m. ἐπλήμην (798), chiefly epic, with ἐν-έπλητο, opt. ἐμ-πλήμην, ἐμ-πλῇτο, imp. ἔμ-πλησο, pt. ἐμ-πλήμενος, in Aristoph. 795. (I.)

Πίμπρημι (πρα-), *burn*, πρήσω, ἔπρησα, πέπρημαι and [πέπρησμαι Hdt.], ἐπρήσθην; [Ion. f. πρήσομαι, fut. pf. πεπρήσομαι.] 795. Cf. πρήθω, *blow*. (I.)

Πινύσκω (πινυ-), *make wise*, [Hom. aor. ἐπίνυσσα]. Poetic. See πνέω. (6.)

Πίνω (πι-, πο-), *drink*, fut. πίομαι (πιοῦμαι rare); πέπωκα, πέπομαι, ἐπόθην, ποθήσομαι; 2 a. ἔπιον. (5. 8.)

[**Πιπίσκω** (πι-), *give to drink*, πίσω, ἔπισα.] Ionic and poetic. See πίνω. (6.)

Πιπράσκω (περα-, πρα-), *sell*, [ep. περάσω, ἐπέρασα,] πέπρᾱκα, πέπρᾱμαι [Hom. πεπερημένος], ἐπράθην [Ion. -ημαι, -ηθην]; fut. pf. πεπράσομαι. The Attic uses ἀποδώσομαι and ἀπεδόμην in fut. and aor. (6.)

Πίπτω (πετ-, πτ-ο-, 659) for πι-πετ-ω, *fall*, f. πεσοῦμαι [Ion. πεσέομαι]; p. πέπτωκα, 2 p. part. πεπτώς [ep. πεπτηώς, or -εώς]; 2 a. ἔπεσον [Dor. ἔπετον, reg.].

[**Πίτνημι** (πιτ-να-), *spread*, pres. and impf. act. and mid. 609. Epic and lyric. See πετάννῡμι.] (III.)

Πίτνω, poetic for πίπτω.

[**Πλάζω** (πλαγγ-), *cause to wander*, ἔπλαγξα. Pass. and mid. πλάζομαι, *wander*, πλάγξομαι, *will wander*, ἐπλάγχθην, *wandered*.] Ionic and poetic. (4.)

Πλάσσω (see 582; 587), *form*, [πλάσω Ion.], ἔπλασα, πέπλασμαι, ἐπλάσθην; ἐπλασάμην. (4.)

Πλέκω, *plait*, *knit*, [πλέξω,] ἔπλεξα, [πέπλεχα or πέπλοχα Ion.], πέπλεγμαι, ἐπλέχθην, πλεχθήσομαι; 2 a. p. ἐπλάκην; a. m. ἐπλεξάμην.

Πλέω (πλευ-, πλεϝ-, πλυ-), *sail*, πλεύσομαι or πλευσοῦμαι, ἔπλευσα, πέπλευκα, πέπλευσμαι, ἐπλεύσθην (later). 574, 641. [Ion. and poet πλώω, πλώσομαι, ἔπλωσα, πέπλωκα, ep. 2 aor. ἔπλων.] (2.)

Πλήσσω or **πλήττω** (πληγ-, πλαγ-, 31), *strike*, πλήξω, ἔπληξα, πέπληγμαι, ἐπλήχθην (rare); 2 p. πέπληγα; 2 a. p. ἐπλήγην, in comp. -επλάγην (713); 2 f. pass. πληγήσομαι and -πλαγήσομαι; fut. pf. πεπλήξομαι; [ep. 2 a. πέπληγον (or ἐπέπλ-), πεπληγόμην; Ion. a. m. ἐπληξάμην.] (2. 4.)

Πλύνω (πλυν-), *wash*, πλυνῶ, ἔπλῡνα, πέπλυμαι, ἐπλύθην; [fut. m. (as pass.) ἐκ-πλυνοῦμαι, a. ἐπλῡνάμην.] 647. (4.)

Πλώω, Ionic and poetic: see πλέω.

Πνέω (πνευ-, πνεϝ-, πνυ-), *breathe*, *blow*, πνεύσομαι and πνευσοῦμαι, ἔπνευσα, πέπνευκα, [epic πέπνῡμαι, *be wise*, pt. πεπνῡμένος, *wise*, plpf. πέπνῡσο; late ἐπνεύσθην, Hom. ἀμ-πνύνθην.] For epic ἄμ-πνυε etc., see ἀνα-πνέω and ἄμ-πνυε. See πινύσκω. (2.)

Πνίγω (πνῑγ-, πνῐγ-), *choke*, πνίξω [later πνίξομαι, Dor. πνιξοῦμαι], ἔπνῑξα, πέπνῑγμαι, ἐπνίγην, πνιγήσομαι.

Ποθέω, *desire*, ποθήσω, ποθήσομαι, ἐπόθησα; and ποθέσομαι, ἐπόθεσα. 639 (*b*).

Πονέω, *labor*, πονήσω etc., regular. [Ionic πονέσω and ἐπόνεσα (Hippoc.).] 639 (*b*).

(**πορ-**, **προ-**), *give, allot*, stem whence 2 a. ἔπορον (poet.), p. p. πέπρωμαι, chiefly impers., πέπρωται, *it is fated* (with πεπρωμένη, *Fate*). See πεπαρεῖν. Compare μείρομαι. Poetic except in perf. part.

Πράσσω or **πράττω** (πρᾱγ-), *do*, πράξω, ἔπρᾱξα, πέπρᾱχα, πέπρᾱγμαι, ἐπράχθην, πρᾱχθήσομαι; fut. pf. πεπράξομαι; 2 p. πέπρᾱγα, *have fared* (*well* or *ill*); mid. f. πράξομαι, a. ἐπρᾱξάμην. [Ionic πρήσσω (πρηγ-), πρήξω, ἔπρηξα, πέπρηχα, πέπρηγμαι, ἐπρήχθην; πέπρηγα; πρήξομαι, ἐπρηξάμην.] (4.)

(**πρια-**), *buy*, stem, with only 2 aor. ἐπριάμην, inflected throughout in 506; see synopsis in 504.

Πρίω, *saw*, ἔπρῑσα, πέπρῑσμαι, ἐπρίσθην. 640.

Προΐσσομαι (προϊκ-), *beg*, once in Archil. (compare προῖκα, *gratis*); fut. only in κατα-προΐξομαι (Ar.) [Ion. κατα-προΐξομαι]. (4.)

Πτάρνυμαι (πταρ-), *sneeze*; [f. πταρῶ;] 2 aor. ἔπταρον, [ἐπταρόμην], (ἐπτάρην) πταρείς. (II.)

Πτήσσω (πτηκ-, πτακ-), *cower*, ἔπτηξα, ἔπτηχα. From stem πτακ-, poet. 2 a. (ἔπτακον) καταπτακών. [From stem πτα-, ep. 2 a. καταπτήτην, dual; 2 pf. pt. πεπτηώς.] Poetic also πτώσσω. (4. 2.)

Πτίσσω, *pound*, [ἔπτισα], ἔπτισμαι, late ἐπτίσθην. (4.)

Πτύσσω (πτυγ-), *fold*, πτύξω, ἔπτυξα, ἔπτυγμαι, ἐπτύχθην; πτύξομαι, ἐπτυξάμην. (4.)

Πτύω, *spit*, [πτύσω, πτύσομαι, ἐπτύσθην, Hippoc.], a. ἔπτυσα.

Πυνθάνομαι (πυθ-), *hear, enquire*, fut. πεύσομαι [Dor. πευσοῦμαι], pf. πέπυσμαι; 2 a. ἐπυθόμην [w. Hom. opt. πεπύθοιτο]. (5.) Poetic also πεύθομαι (πευθ-, πυθ-). (2.)

Ρ.

Ῥαίνω (ῥα-, ῥαν-), *sprinkle*, ῥανῶ, ἔρρᾱνα, (ἐρράνθην) ῥανθείς. [From stem ῥα- (cf. βαίνω), ep. aor. ἔρασσα, pf. p. (ἔρρασμαι) ἔρρανται Aeschyl., ep. ἐρράδαται, plpf. ἐρράδατο, 777, 3.] See 610. Ionic and poetic. (5. 4.)

[**Ῥαίω**, *strike*, ῥαίσω, ἔρραισα,] ἐρραίσθην; [fut. m. (as pass.) ῥαίσομαι.] Poetic, chiefly epic.

Ῥάπτω (ῥαφ-), *stitch*, ῥάψω, ἔρραψα, ἔρραμμαι; 2 a. p. ἐρράφην; a. m. ἐρραψάμην. (3.)

Ῥάσσω (ῥαγ-), = ἀράσσω, *throw down*, ῥάξω, ἔρραξα, ἐρράχθην. See ἀράσσω. (4.)

Ῥέζω (ϝρεγ- for ϝεργ-, 649), *do*, ῥέξω, ἔρεξα; [Ion. a. p. ῥεχθείη, ῥεχθείς.] See ἔρδω. (4.)

Ῥέω (ῥευ-, ῥεϝ-, ῥυ-), *flow*, ῥεύσομαι, ἔρρευσα (rare in Attic), (ε-) ἐρρύηκα; 2 a. p. ἐρρύην, ῥυήσομαι. 574. (2.)

(**ῥε-**), stem of *εἴρηκα*, *εἴρημαι*, *ἐρρήθην* (*ἐρρέθην*), *ῥηθήσομαι*, *εἰρήσομαι*. See **εἶπον**.

Ῥήγνῡμι (*ϝρηγ-*, *ῥαγ-*), *break*; *ῥήξω*, *ἔρρηξα*, [*ἔρρηγμαι* rare, *ἐρρήχθην* rare;] 2 a. p. *ἐρράγην*; *ῥαγήσομαι*; 2 p. *ἔρρωγα*, *be broken* (689); [*ῥήξομαι*,] *ἐρρηξάμην*. (**2. II.**)

Ῥῑγέω (*ῥῑγ-*), *shudder*, [ep. f. *ῥῑγήσω*,] a. *ἐρρίγησα*, [2 p. *ἔρρῑγα* (as pres.)] Poetic, chiefly epic. 655.

Ῥῑγόω, *shiver*, *ῥῑγώσω*, *ἐρρίγωσα*; pres. subj. *ῥῑγῷ* for *ῥῑγοῖ*, opt. *ῥῑγῴην*, inf. *ῥῑγῶν* and *ῥῑγοῦν*: see 497.

Ῥίπτω (*ῥῑφ-*, *ῥῐφ-*), *throw*, *ῥίψω*, *ἔρρῑψα* (poet. *ἔρῑψα*), *ἔρρῑφα*, *ἔρρῑμμαι*, *ἐρρίφθην*, *ῥῑφθήσομαι*; 2 a. p. *ἐρρίφην*. Pres. also **ῥιπτέω** (655). (**3.**)

Ῥύομαι [epic also **ῥῦομαι**], *defend*, *ῥύσομαι*, *ἐρρῡσάμην*. [Epic *μι*-forms: inf. *ῥῦσθαι* for *ῥύεσθαι*; impf. 3 pers. *ἔρρῡτο* and pl. *ῥύατο*.] Chiefly poetic. See **ἐρύω**.

Ῥυπάω, *be foul*, [epic **ῥυπόω**; Ion. pf. pt. *ῥερυπωμένος*].

Ῥώννῡμι (*ῥω-*), *strengthen*, *ἔρρωσα*, *ἔρρωμαι* (imper. *ἔρρωσο*, *farewell*), *ἐρρώσθην*. (**II.**)

Σ.

Σαίνω (*σαν-*), *fawn on*, aor. *ἔσηνα* [Dor. *ἔσᾱνα*]. Poetic. 595. (**4.**)

Σαίρω (*σαρ-*), *sweep*, aor. (*ἔσηρα*) pt. *σήρᾱς*; 2 p. *σέσηρα*, *grin*, esp. in part. *σεσηρώς* [Dor. *σεσᾱρώς*.] (**4.**)

Σαλπίζω (*σαλπιγγ-*), *sound a trumpet*, aor. *ἐσάλπιγξα*. (**4.**)

[**Σαόω**, *save*, pres. rare and poet., *σαώσω*, *σαώσομαι*, *ἐσάωσα*, *ἐσαώθην*; 2 aor. 3 sing. *σάω* (for *ἐσάω*), imperat. *σάω*, as if from Aeol. *σάωμι*. For epic *σάῳς*, *σάῳ*, see **σῴζω**. Epic.]

Σάττω (*σαγ-*), *pack*, *load*, [Ion. *σάσσω*, aor. *ἔσαξα*,] p. p. *σέσαγμαι*. (**4.**)

Σβέννῡμι (*σβε-*), *extinguish*, *σβέσω*, *ἔσβεσα*, *ἔσβηκα*, [*ἔσβεσμαι*,] *ἐσβέσθην*; 2 a. *ἔσβην* (803, 1), *went out*, w. inf. *σβῆναι*, [pt. *ἀπο-σβείς* Hippoc.]; f. m. *σβήσομαι*. (**II.**)

Σέβω, *revere*, aor. p. *ἐσέφθην*, w. part. *σεφθείς*, *awe-struck*.

Σείω, *shake*, *σείσω*, *ἔσεισα*, *σέσεικα*, *σέσεισμαι*, *ἐσείσθην* (640); a. m. *ἐσεισάμην*.

[**Σεύω** (*σευ-*, *συ-*), *move*, *urge*, a. *ἔσσευα*, *ἐσσευάμην*; *ἔσσυμαι*, *ἐσσύθην* (Soph.) or *ἐσύθην*; 2 a. m. *ἐσσύμην* (with *ἔσυτο*, *σύτο*, *σύμενος*).] The Attic poets have [*σεῦται*], *σοῦνται*, *σοῦσθε* (ind. and imper.), *σοῦ*, *σούσθω*. 574. Poetic. (**2.**)

Σημαίνω (*σημαν-*), *show*, *σημανῶ*, *ἐσήμηνα* (sometimes *ἐσήμᾱνα*), *σεσήμασμαι*, *ἐσημάνθην*, *σημανθήσομαι*; mid. *σημανοῦμαι*, *ἐσημηνάμην*. (**4.**)

Σήπω (*σηπ-*, *σαπ-*), *rot*, *σήψω*, 2 p. *σέσηπα* (as pres.); *σέσημμαι* (Aristot.), 2 a. p. *ἐσάπην*, f. *σαπήσομαι*. (**2.**)

Σίνομαι (*σιν-*), *injure*, [aor. *ἐσῑνάμην* Ion.]. 597. (**4.**)

Σκάπτω (*σκαφ-*), *dig*, *σκάψω*, *ἔσκαψα*, *ἔσκαφα*, *ἔσκαμμαι*, *ἐσκάφην*. (**3.**)

Σκεδάννυμι (σκεδα-), *scatter*, f. σκεδῶ [σκεδάσω,] ἐσκέδασα, ἐσκέδασμαι w. part. ἐσκεδασμένος, ἐσκεδάσθην; ἐσκεδασάμην. (**II.**)

Σκέλλω (σκελ-, σκλε-), *dry up*, [Hom. a. ἔσκηλα, Ion. pf. ἔσκληκα]; 2 a. (ἔσκλην) ἀπο-σκλῆναι (799), Ar. (**4.**)

Σκέπτομαι (σκεπ-), *view*, σκέψομαι, ἐσκεψάμην, ἔσκεμμαι, fut. pf. ἐσκέψομαι, [ἐσκέφθην, Ion.]. For pres. and impf. the better Attic writers use σκοπῶ, σκοποῦμαι, etc. (see **σκοπέω**). (**3.**)

Σκήπτω (σκηπ-), *prop*, σκήψω, ἔσκηψα, ἔσκημμαι, ἐσκήφθην; σκήψομαι, ἐσκηψάμην. (**3.**)

Σκίδνημι (σκιδ-να-), mid. σκίδναμαι, *scatter*, also κίδνημι: chiefly poetic for **σκεδάννυμι**. (**III.**)

Σκοπέω, *view*, in better Attic writers only pres. and impf. act. and mid. For the other tenses σκέψομαι, ἐσκεψάμην, and ἔσκεμμαι of σκέπτομαι are used. See **σκέπτομαι**.

Σκώπτω (σκωπ-), *jeer*, σκώψομαι, ἔσκωψα, ἐσκώφθην. (**3.**)

Σμάω, *smear*, with η for ᾱ in contracted forms (496), σμῇ for σμᾷ, etc.; [a. m. ἐσμησάμην Hdt.]. [Ion. σμέω and σμήχω], aor. p. διασμηχθείς (Aristoph.).

Σπάω, *draw*, σπάσω (ᾰ), ἔσπασα, ἔσπακα, ἔσπασμαι, ἐσπάσθην, σπασθήσομαι; σπάσομαι, ἐσπασάμην. 639; 640.

Σπείρω (σπερ-), *sow*, σπερῶ, ἔσπειρα, ἔσπαρμαι; 2 a. p. ἐσπάρην. (**4.**)

Σπένδω, *pour libation*, σπείσω (for σπενδ-σω, 79), ἔσπεισα, ἔσπεισμαι, (see 490, 3); σπείσομαι, ἐσπεισάμην.

Στάζω (σταγ-), *drop*, [στάξω,] ἔσταξα, [ἔσταγμαι, ἐστάχθην.] (**4.**)

Στείβω (στειβ-, στιβ-), *tread*, ἔστειψα, (ε-) ἐστίβημαι (642, 2; 658, 2). Poetic. (**2.**)

Στείχω (στειχ-, στιχ-), *go*, [ἔστειξα, 2 a. ἔστιχον.] Poetic and Ionic. (**2.**)

Στέλλω (στελ-), *send*, στελῶ [στελέω], ἔστειλα, ἔσταλκα, ἔσταλμαι; 2 a. p. ἐστάλην; σταλήσομαι; a. m. ἐστειλάμην. 645. (**4.**)

Στενάζω (στεναγ-), *groan*, στενάξω, ἐστέναξα. (**4.**)

Στέργω, *love*, στέρξω, ἔστερξα; 2 pf. ἔστοργα (643).

Στερέω, *deprive*, στερήσω, ἐστέρησα [epic ἐστέρεσα], ἐστέρηκα, ἐστέρημαι, ἐστερήθην, στερηθήσομαι; 2 aor. p. (ἐστέρην) part. στερείς, 2 fut. (pass. or mid.) στερήσομαι. Also pres. **στερίσκω**. (**6.**) Pres. **στέρομαι**, *be in want*.

[(**Στεῦμαι**), *pledge one's self;* 3 pers. pres. στεῦται, impf. στεῦτο. Poetic, chiefly epic.] (**I.**)

Στίζω (στιγ-), *prick*, στίξω, [ἔστιξα Hdt.], ἔστιγμαι. (**4.**)

Στόρνυμι (στορ-), (ε-) στορῶ (στορέσω), ἐστόρεσα, [ἐστορέσθην], ἐστορεσάμην. (**II.**)

Στρέφω, *turn*, στρέψω, ἔστρεψα, ἔστραμμαι, ἐστρέφθην (rare in prose) [Ion. ἐστράφθην]; 2 pf. ἔστροφα (late); 2 a. p. ἐστράφην, f. στραφήσομαι; mid. στρέψομαι, ἐστρεψάμην. 646.

Στρώννυμι (στρω-), same as **στόρνυμι**; στρώσω, ἔστρωσα, ἔστρωμαι, ἐστρώθην. (II.)

Στυγέω (στυγ-, 654), *dread, hate*, fut. στυγήσομαι (as pass.), a. ἐστύγησα [ep. ἔστυξα, *made terrible*, Ion. pf. ἐστύγηκα], a. p. ἐστυγήθην; [ep. 2 a. ἔστυγον.] Ionic and poetic.

[**Στυφελίζω** (στυφελιγ-), *dash*, aor. ἐστυφέλιξα. Ionic, chiefly epic.] (4.)

Σύρω (συρ-), *draw*, aor. ἔσυρα, ἐσυράμην. (4.)

Σφάζω (σφαγ-), *slay*, Att. prose gen. **σφάττω**; σφάξω, ἔσφαξα, ἔσφαγμαι, [ἐσφάχθην (rare)]; 2 aor. p. ἐσφάγην, fut. σφαγήσομαι; aor. mid. ἐσφαξάμην. (4.)

Σφάλλω (σφαλ-), *trip, deceive*, σφαλῶ, ἔσφηλα, ἔσφαλμαι; 2 a. p. ἐσφάλην, f. p. σφαλήσομαι; fut. m. σφαλοῦμαι (rare). (4.)

Σφάττω: see **σφάζω**.

Σχάζω (see 587), σχάσω, ἔσχασα, ἐσχασάμην; [Ion. ἐσχάσθην.] From pres. σχάω, imp. ἔσχων (Ar.). (4.)

Σῴζω, later **σώζω**, epic usually **σώω** (σω-, σῳδ-), *save*, [ep. pr. subj. σόῃς (σάῳς, σόῳς), σόῃ (σάῳ, σόῳ), σόωσι]; σώσω, ἔσωσα, σέσωκα, σέσωμαι or σέσωσμαι, ἐσώθην, σωθήσομαι; σώσομαι, ἐσωσάμην. See **σαόω**. (4.)

Τ.

(**τα-**), *take*, stem with Hom. imperat. τῆ.

[(**ταγ-**), *seize*, stem with Hom. 2 a. pt. τεταγών.] Cf. Lat. *tango*.

[**Τανύω**, *stretch*, τανύσω (ῠ), ἐτάνυσα, τετάνυσμαι, ἐτανύσθην; aor. m. ἐτανυσσάμην. Pres. pass. (μι-form) τάνυται. Epic form of **τείνω**.]

Ταράσσω (ταραχ-), *disturb*, ταράξω, ἐτάραξα, τετάραγμαι, ἐταράχθην; f. m. ταράξομαι; [ep. 2 p. (τέτρηχα) τετρηχώς, *disturbed*; plp. τετρήχει.] (4.)

Τάσσω (ταγ-), *arrange*, τάξω, ἔταξα, τέταχα, τέταγμαι, ἐτάχθην, ταχθήσομαι; τάξομαι, ἐταξάμην; 2 a. p. ἐτάγην; fut. pf. τετάξομαι. (4.)

(**ταφ-**), stem with 2 aor. ἔταφον: see (**θηπ-**).

Τείνω (τεν-), *stretch*, τενῶ, ἔτεινα, τέτακα, τέταμαι, ἐτάθην, ταθήσομαι; τενοῦμαι, ἐτεινάμην. 645; 647. See **τανύω** and **τιταίνω**. (4.)

Τεκμαίρομαι (τεκμαρ-), *judge, infer*, f. τεκμαροῦμαι, a. ἐτεκμηράμην. Act. **τεκμαίρω**, rare and poetic, a. ἐτέκμηρα. (4.)

Τελέω, *finish*, (τελέσω) τελῶ, ἐτέλεσα, τετέλεκα, τετέλεσμαι, ἐτελέσθην; fut. m. (τελέομαι) τελοῦμαι, a. m. ἐτελεσάμην. 639; 640.

Τέλλω (τελ-), *cause to rise, rise*, aor. ἔτειλα; [plpf. p. ἐτέταλτο.] In compos. ἐν-τέταλμαι, ἐν-ετειλάμην. 645. (4.)

[(**τεμ-**), *find*, stem with Hom. redupl. 2 a. τέτμον or ἔτετμον (534).]

Τέμνω (τεμ-, τμε-) [Ion. and Dor. **τάμνω**, Hom. once τέμω], *cut*, f. τεμῶ, τέτμηκα, τέτμημαι, ἐτμήθην, τμηθήσομαι; 2 a. ἔτεμον, ἐτεμόμην [poet. and Ion. ἔταμον, ἐταμόμην]; fut. m. τεμοῦμαι; fut. pf. τετμήσομαι. See **τμήγω**. (5.)

Τέρπω, *amuse*, τέρψω, ἔτερψα, ἐτέρφθην [ep. ἐτάρφθην, 2 a. p. ἐτάρπην (with subj. τραπείω), 2 a. m. (τ)εταρπόμην], (534); fut. m. τέρψομαι (poet.), [a. ἐτερψάμην epic.] 646.

[**Τέρσομαι**, *become dry*, 2 a. p. ἐτέρσην. Chiefly epic. Fut. act. τέρσω in Theoc.]

Τεταγών, *having seized:* see stem (**ταγ-**).

[**Τετίημαι**, Hom. perf. *am troubled*, in dual τετίησθον and part. τετιημένος; also τετιηώς, *troubled*.]

[**Τέτμον** or **ἔτετμον** (Hom.), *found*, for τε-τεμ-ον (534).] See (**τεμ-**).

Τετραίνω (τετραν-, τρα-), *bore*, late pres. τιτραίνω and τιτράω; [Ion. fut. τετρανέω, aor. ἐτέτρηνα], ἐτετρηνάμην (673). From stem (τρα-), aor. ἔτρησα, pf. p. τέτρημαι. 610. (5. 4.)

Τεύχω (τευχ-, τυχ-), *prepare, make*, τεύξω, ἔτευξα, [ep. τετευχώς as pass.,] τέτυγμαι [ep. τετεύχαται, ἐτετεύχατο], [ἐτύχθην Hom., ἐτεύχθην Hippoc., f. pf. τετεύξομαι Hom.]; f. m. τεύξομαι, [ep. a. ἐτευξάμην, 2 a. (τυκ-) τετυκεῖν, τετυκόμην.] Poetic. (2.)

Τήκω (τηκ-), *melt*, [Dor. τάκω], τήξω, ἔτηξα, ἐτήχθην (rare); 2 a. p. ἐτάκην; 2 p. τέτηκα, *am melted*. (2.)

Τίθημι (θε-), *put;* see synopsis and inflection in 504, 506, and 509. (I.)

Τίκτω (τεκ-), for τι-τεκ-ω (652, 1 *a*), *beget, bring forth*, τέξομαι, poet. also τέξω, [rarely τεκοῦμαι], ἐτέχθην (rare); 2 p. τέτοκα; 2 a. ἔτεκον, ἐτεκόμην.

Τίλλω (τιλ-), *pluck*, τιλῶ, ἔτιλα, τέτιλμαι, ἐτίλθην. Chiefly poetic. (4.)

Τίνω (τι-), Hom. τῑνω, *pay*, τίσω, ἔτῑσα, τέτῑκα, τέτισμαι, ἐτίσθην. Mid. τίνομαι [ep. τίνυμαι], τίσομαι, ἐτῑσάμην. The fut. and aor. are more correctly written τείσω, ἔτεισα, etc., but these forms seldom appear in our editions. See **τίω**. (5.)

[**Τιταίνω** (τιταν-), *stretch*, aor. (ἐτίτηνα) τιτήνας. Epic for τείνω.] (4.)

[**Τιτράω**, *bore*, late present.] See **τετραίνω**.

Τιτρώσκω (τρο-), *wound*, τρώσω, ἔτρωσα, τέτρωμαι, ἐτρώθην, τρωθήσομαι; [fut. m. τρώσομαι Hom.] [Rarely epic τρώω.] (6.)

Τίω, *honor*, [Hom. fut. τίσω, aor. ἔτῑσα, p. p. τέτῑμαι.] After Homer chiefly in pres. and impf. Attic τίσω, ἔτῑσα, etc., belong to τίνω (except προ-τίσᾱς, S. *An.* 22). See **τίνω**.

(**τλα-**, sync. for ταλα-), *endure*, τλήσομαι, τέτληκα, 2 aor. ἔτλην (see 799). [Epic μι-forms of 2 pf. τέτλαμεν, τετλαίην, τέτλαθι, τετλάμεναι and τετλάμεν, τετληώς (804). From (ταλα-), Hom. aor. ἐτάλασσα.] Poetic.

[**Τμήγω** (τμηγ-, τμαγ-), *cut*, poet. for τέμνω; τμήξω (rare), ἔτμηξα, 2 a. ἔτμαγον, ἐτμάγην (τμάγεν for ἐτμάγησαν).] (**2.**)

Τορέω (τορ-), *pierce*, [pres. only in ep. ἀντι-τορεῦντα]; [ep. fut. τορήσω], τετορήσω (Ar.), [ep. a. ἐτόρησα, 2 a. ἔτορον.] 655.

Τρέπω [Ion. τράπω], *turn*, τρέψω, ἔτρεψα, τέτροφα sometimes τέτραφα, τέτραμμαι, ἐτρέφθην [Ion. ἐτράφθην]; f. m. τρέψομαι, a. m. ἐτρεψάμην; 2 a. [ἔτραπον epic and lyric], ἐτράπην, ἐτραπόμην. This verb has all the six aorists (714). 643; 646.

Τρέφω (τρεφ- for θρεφ-, 95, 5), *nourish*, θρέψω, ἔθρεψα, τέτροφα, τέθραμμαι w. inf. τεθράφθαι, ἐθρέφθην w. inf. θρεφθῆναι (rare); 2 a. p. ἐτράφην; [ep. 2 a. ἔτραφον as pass.]; f. m. θρέψομαι, a. m. ἐθρεψάμην. 643; 646.

Τρέχω (τρεχ- for θρεχ-, 95, 5; δραμ-), *run*, f. δραμοῦμαι (-θρέξομαι only in comedy), ἔθρεξα (rare), δεδράμηκα, (ε-) δεδράμημαι; [2 p. δέδρομα (poet.)], 2 a. ἔδραμον. (**8.**)

Τρέω (*tremble*), aor. ἔτρεσα. Chiefly poetic.

Τρίβω (τρῑβ-, τρῐβ-), *rub*, τρίψω, ἔτριψα, τέτριφα, τέτριμμαι (487; 489), ἐτρίφθην; 2 a. p. ἐτρίβην, 2 fut. p. τριβήσομαι; fut. pf. τετρίψομαι; f. m. τρίψομαι, a. m. ἐτριψάμην.

Τρίζω (τρῑγ-), *squeak*, 2 p. τέτρῑγα as present [w. ep. part. τετρῑγῶτας]. Ionic and poetic. (**4.**)

Τρύχω, *exhaust*, fut. [ep. τρύξω] τρῡχώσω (τρῡχο-, 659), a. ἐτρύχωσα, p. part. τετρῡχωμένος, [a. p. ἐτρῡχώθην Ion.].

Τρώγω, (τραγ-, 573), *gnaw*, τρώξομαι [ἔτρωξα,] τέτρωγμαι; 2 a. ἔτραγον. (**2.**)

Τυγχάνω (τευχ-, τυχ-), *hit*, *happen*, τεύξομαι, (ε-) [ep. ἐτύχησα,] pf. τετύχηκα, 2 pf. τέτευχα; 2 a. ἔτυχον. (**5. 2.**)

Τύπτω (τυπ-), *strike*, (ε-) τυπτήσω, ἐτύπτησα (Aristot.), 2 a. p. ἐτύπην, fut. p. τυπτήσομαι or τυπήσομαι. [Ionic and lyric a. ἔτυψα, p.p. τέτυμμαι, 2 a. ἔτυπον; ἀπο-τύψωνται (Hdt.).] 658, 3. (**3.**)

Τύφω (τῡφ- or τῠφ-, for θυφ-), *raise smoke*, *smoke*, τέθυμμαι, 2 a. p. ἐτύφην, 2 f. p. τυφήσομαι (Men.). 95, 5.

Υ.

Ὑπισχνέομαι, Ion. and poet. ὑπίσχομαι (strengthened from ὑπέχομαι), *promise*, ὑποσχήσομαι, ὑπέσχημαι; 2 a. m. ὑπεσχόμην. See ἴσχω and ἔχω. (**5.**)

Ὑφαίνω (ὑφαν-), *weave*, ὑφανῶ, ὕφηνα, ὕφασμαι (648), ὑφάνθην; aor. m. ὑφηνάμην. (**4.**)

Ὕω, *rain*, ὕσω, ὗσα, ὕσμαι, ὕσθην. [Hdt. ὕσομαι as pass.]

Φ.

Φαείνω (φαεν-), *appear*, *shine*, aor. pass. ἐφαάνθην (αα- for αε-), *appeared*. See φαίνω. (**4.**)

Φαίνω (φαν-), *show*, f. φανῶ [φανέω], a. ἔφηνα, πέφαγκα, πέφασμαι (648), ἐφάνθην (rare in prose); 2 a. p. ἐφάνην, 2 f. φανήσομαι; 2 p. πέφηνα; f. m. φανοῦμαι, a. m. ἐφηνάμην (rare and poet.), *showed*, but ἀπεφηνάμην, *declared*; [ep. iter. 2 aor. φάνεσκε, *appeared*.] For full synopsis, see 478; for inflection of certain tenses, see 482. From stem φα- (cf. βαίνω, 610), [Hom. impf. φάε, *appeared*, f. pf. πεφήσεται, *will appear*.] For ἐφαάνθην, see **φαείνω**. (**4**.)

Φάσκω (φα-), *say*, only pres. and impf. See **φημί**. (**6**.)

Φείδομαι (φειδ-, φιδ-), *spare*, φείσομαι, ἐφεισάμην, [Hom. 2 a. m. πεφιδόμην, f. πεφιδήσομαι.] (**2**.)

(**φεν-**, **φα-**), *kill*, stems whence [Hom. πέφαμαι, πεφήσομαι; 2 a. redupl. πέφνον or ἔπεφνον (for πε-φεν-ον) w. part. κατα-πέφνων (or -ών).]

Φέρω (φερ-, οἰ-, ἐνεκ-, ἐνεγκ- for ἐν-ενεκ-), *bear*, f. οἴσω, a. ἤνεγκα, 2 p. ἐνήνοχα, ἐνήνεγμαι, a. p. ἠνέχθην; f. p. ἐνεχθήσομαι and οἰσθήσομαι; 2 a. ἤνεγκον; f. m. οἴσομαι (sometimes as pass.); a. m. ἠνεγκάμην, 2 a. m. imper. ἐνεγκοῦ (So.). 671. [Ion. ἤνεικα and -αμην, ἤνεικον, ἐνήνειγμαι, ἠνείχθην; Hdt. aor. inf. ἀν-οῖσαι (or ἀν-ῷσαι); Hom. aor. imper. οἶσε for οἶσον (777, 8), pres. imper. φέρτε for φέρετε.] (**8**.)

Φεύγω (φευγ-, φυγ-), *flee*, φεύξομαι and φευξοῦμαι (666), 2 p. πέφευγα (642), 2 a. ἔφυγον; [Hom. p. part. πεφυγμένος and πεφυζότες.] (**2**.)

Φημί (φα-), *say*, φήσω, ἔφησα; p. p. imper. πεφάσθω (πεφασμένος belongs to φαίνω). Mid. [Dor. fut. φάσομαι]. For the full inflection, see 812 and 813. (**I**.)

Φθάνω (φθα-), *anticipate*, φθήσομαι (or φθάσω), ἔφθασα; 2 a. act. ἔφθην (like ἔστην), [ep. 2 a. m. φθάμενος.] (**5**.)

Φθείρω (φθερ-), *corrupt*, f. φθερῶ [Ion. φθερέω, ep. φθέρσω], a. ἔφθειρα, p. ἔφθαρκα, ἔφθαρμαι; 2 a. p. ἐφθάρην, 2 f. p. φθαρήσομαι; 2 p. διέφθορα; f. m. φθεροῦμαι. 643; 645. (**4**.)

Φθίνω [epic also φθίω], *waste, decay*, φθίσω, ἔφθισα, ἔφθιμαι, [ep. a. p. ἐφθίθην; fut. m. φθίσομαι;] 2 a. m. ἐφθίμην, *perished*, [subj. φθίωμαι, opt. φθίμην for φθι-ι-μην (734) imper. 3 sing. φθίσθω, inf. φθίσθαι], part. φθίμενος. [Epic φθίνω, φθίσω, ἔφθισα.] Chiefly poetic. Present generally intransitive; future and aorist active transitive. (**5**.)

Φιλέω (φιλ-), *love*, φιλήσω, etc., regular. [Ep. a. m. ἐφιλάμην, inf. pres. φιλήμεναι (784, 5). 655.]

Φλάω, *bruise*, [fut. φλάσω (Dor. φλασσῶ), aor. ἔφλασα, ἔφλασμαι, ἐφλάσθην.] See **θλάω**.

Φράγνῡμι (φραγ-), *fence*, mid. **φράγνυμαι**; only in pres. and impf. See **φράσσω**. (**II**.)

Φράζω (φραδ-), *tell*, φράσω, ἔφρασα, πέφρακα, πέφρασμαι [ep. part. πεφραδμένος,] ἐφράσθην (as mid.); [φράσομαι epic], ἐφρασάμην (chiefly epic). [Ep. 2 a. πέφραδον or ἐπέφραδον.] (**4**.)

Φράσσω (φραγ-), *fence*, ἔφραξα, πέφραγμαι, ἐφράχθην; ἐφραξάμην. See **φράγνῡμι**. (4.)

Φρίσσω or **φρίττω** (φρῑκ-), *shudder*, ἔφρῑξα, πέφρῑκα. (4.)

Φρύγω (φρυγ-), *roast*, φρύξω, ἔφρῡξα, πέφρῡγμαι, [ἐφρύγην].

Φυλάσσω (φυλακ-), *guard*, φυλάξω, ἐφύλαξα, πεφύλαχα, πεφύλαγμαι, ἐφυλάχθην; φυλάξομαι, ἐφυλαξάμην. (4.)

Φύρω, *mix*, [ἔφυρσα,] πέφυρμαι, [ἐφύρθην]; [f. pf. πεφύρσομαι Pind.]. **Φῡράω**, *mix*, is regular, φῡράσω, etc.

Φύω (φυ-), with ῠ in Homer and rarely in Attic, *produce*, φύσω, ἔφῡσα, πέφῡκα, *be* (*by nature*), [with 2 pf. μι-forms, ep. πεφύᾱσι, ἐμ-πεφύῃ, πεφυώς; plpf. ἐπέφῡκον (777, 4)]; 2 a. ἔφῡν, *be*, *be born* (799); 2 a. p. ἐφύην (subj. φυῶ); fut. m. φύσομαι.

X.

Χάζω (χαδ-), *force back*, *yield*, (pres. only in ἀνα-χάζω), [f. χάσομαι, a. -ἔχασσα (Pind.), a. m. ἐχασάμην; from stem καδ- (different from stem of κήδω), 2 a. m. κεκαδόμην; f. pf. κεκαδήσω, *will deprive* (705), 2 a. κέκαδον, *deprived*.] Poetic, chiefly epic; except ἀναχάζοντες and διαχάσασθαι in Xenophon. (4.)

Χαίρω (χαρ-), *rejoice*, (ε-) χαιρήσω (658, 3), κεχάρηκα, κεχάρημαι and κέχαρμαι, 2 a. p. ἐχάρην, [epic a. m. χήρατο, 2 a. m. κεχαρόμην; 2 p. pt. κεχαρηώς; fut. pf. κεχαρήσω, κεχαρήσομαι (705).] (4.)

Χαλάω, *loosen*, [χαλάσω Ion.,] ἐχάλασα [-αξα Pind.], ἐχαλάσθην. 639; 640.

[**Χανδάνω** (χαδ-, χενδ-), *hold*, 2 a. ἔχαδον; fut. χείσομαι (79), 2 pf. κέχανδα (646).] Poetic (chiefly epic) and Ionic. (5.)

Χάσκω, later **χαίνω** (χα-, χαν-), *gape*, f. χανοῦμαι, 2 p. κέχηνα as pres. (644), 2 a. ἔχανον. Ionic and poetic. (6. 4.)

Χέζω (χεδ-), fut. χεσοῦμαι (rarely χέσομαι), ἔχεσα, 2 p. κέχοδα (643), 2 a. ἔχεσον (rare); a. m. only in χέσαιτο, Ar. *Eq.* 1057; p. p. part. κεχεσμένος. (4.)

Χέω (χευ-, χεϝ-, χυ-), epic χείω (785, 3), *pour*, f. χέω [ep. χεύω], a. ἔχεα [ep. ἔχευα], κέχυκα, κέχυμαι, ἐχύθην, χυθήσομαι; a. m. ἐχεάμην [ep. ἐχευάμην], [2 a. m. ἐχύμην (800, 1).] 574. (2.)

[(**χλαδ-**), stem of 2 pf. part. κεχλᾱδώς, *swelling* (Pind.), w. acc. pl. κεχλάδοντας, and inf. κεχλάδειν.]

Χόω, *heap up*, χώσω, ἔχωσα, κέχωκα, κέχωσμαι (641), ἐχώσθην, χωσθήσομαι.

Χραισμέω (χραισμ-), *avert*, *help*, late in present; [Hom. χραισμήσω, ἐχραίσμησα; 2 a. ἔχραισμον]. 654.

Χράομαι, *use*, χρήσομαι, ἐχρησάμην, κέχρημαι, ἐχρήσθην; [fut. pf. κεχρήσομαι Theoc.]. For χρῆται, χρῆσθαι [Hdt. χρᾶται, χρᾶσθαι], etc., see 496.

Χράω, *give oracles*, (Attic χρῇς, χρῇ, etc., 496); χρήσω, ἔχρησα, κέχρηκα, [κέχρησμαι Hdt.], ἐχρήσθην. Mid. *consult an oracle*, [χρήσομαι, ἐχρησάμην.] For χρῇς and χρῇ = χρῄζεις and χρῄζει, see **χρῄζω**.

Χρή (impers.), probably orig. a noun meaning *need* (cf. χρεία), with ἐστί understood, *there is need*, (*one*) *ought*, *must*, subj. χρῇ, opt. χρείη, inf. χρῆναι, (poet. χρῆν); imperf. χρῆν (prob. = χρὴ ἦν) or ἐχρῆν. **Ἀπόχρη**, *it suffices*, inf. ἀποχρῆν, imperf. ἀπέχρη, [Ion. ἀποχρᾷ, ἀποχρᾶν, ἀπέχρα;] ἀποχρήσει, ἀπέχρησε.

Χρῄζω (587), Ion. **χρηΐζω**, *want*, *ask*, χρῄσω [Ion. χρηΐσω], ἔχρῃσα, [Ion. ἐχρήϊσα]. Χρῇς and χρῇ (as if from χράω), occasionally have the meaning of χρῄζεις, χρῄζει. (4.)

Χρίω, *anoint*, *sting*, χρΐσω, ἔχρῖσα, κέχρῖμαι or κέχρισμαι, ἐχρΐσθην; [χρΐσομαι Hom.], ἐχρῖσάμην.

Χρώζω, poet. also **χροΐζω** (587), *color*, *stain*, κέχρωσμαι, ἐχρώσθην. (4.)

Ψ.

Ψάω, *rub*, with η for ᾱ in contracted forms (496), ψῇ, ψῆν, ἔψη, etc.; generally in composition.

Ψεύδω, *deceive*, ψεύσω, ἔψευσα, ἔψευσμαι, ἐψεύσθην, ψευσθήσομαι; ψεύσομαι, ἐψευσάμην. 71; 74.

Ψύχω (ψυχ-), *cool*, ψύξω, ἔψῡξα, ἔψῡγμαι, ἐψύχθην [ψῡχθήσομαι Ion.]; 2 a. p. ἐψύχην or (generally later) ἐψύγην (stem ψυγ-).

Ω.

Ὠθέω (ὠθ-), *push*, impf. gen. ἐώθουν (537, 1); ὤσω [poet. ὠθήσω], ἔωσα [Ion. ὦσα], ἔωσμαι [Ion. ὦσμαι], ἐώσθην; ὠσθήσομαι; f. m. ὤσομαι, a. m. ἐωσάμην [Ion. ὠσάμην]. 654.

Ὠνέομαι, *buy*, imp. ἐωνούμην (537, 1) or ὠνούμην; ὠνήσομαι, ἐώνημαι, ἐωνήθην. Classic writers use ἐπριάμην (504–506) for later ὠνησάμην.

N. B.—In these Indexes the references are made to the SECTIONS of the Grammar, except occasionally to *pages* 3–6 of the Introduction. The verbs which are found in the Catalogue, and the Irregular Nouns of § 291, are generally not included in the Greek Index, except when some special form is mentioned in the text of the Grammar.

GREEK INDEX.

ENGLISH INDEX.

N.B. — See note on p. 408.

CPSIA information can be obtained at www.ICGtesting.com
223901LV00014BA/23/P